Current Issues of Suicidology

Edited by H.-J. Möller,
A. Schmidtke, and R. Welz

With 114 Figures and 160 Tables

Springer-Verlag
Berlin Heidelberg New York
London Paris Tokyo

1988

Prof. Dr. HANS-JÜRGEN MÖLLER
Psychiatrische Klinik und Poliklinik
der Technischen Universität München
Ismaninger Str. 22, D-8000 München 80

Dr. ARMIN SCHMIDTKE
Psychiatrische Klinik und Poliklinik
Universitäts-Nervenklinik
Füchsleinstr. 15, D-8700 Würzburg

Dr. RAINER WELZ
Georg-August-Universität Göttingen
Abteilung Medizinische Psychologie
Humboldtallee 3, D-3400 Göttingen

ISBN 3-540-18806-1 Springer-Verlag Berlin Heidelberg New York
ISBN 0-387-18806-1 Springer-Verlag New York Berlin Heidelberg

Library of Congress Cataloging-in-Publication Data. Current issues of suicidology / edited by H.-J. Möller, A. Schmidtke, R. Welz. p.   cm. Includes contributions from the First European Symposium on Empirical Research into Suicidal Behavior, initiated by Arbeitsgemeinschaft zur Erforschung Suizidalen Verhaltens with Deutsche Gesellschaft für Selbstmordverhütung, and held Mar. 19–22, 1986 in Munich. Includes bibliographies and index. ISBN 0-387-18806-1 (U.S.) 1. Suicide–Congresses. I. Möller, Hans-Jürgen. II. Schmidtke, Armin. III. Welz, Rainer, 1947– . IV. European Symposium on Empirical Research into Suicidal Behavior (1st : 1986 : Munich, Germany) V. Arbeitsgemeinschaft zur Erforschung Suizidalen Verhaltens (Germany) VI. Deutsche Gesellschaft für Selbstmordverhütung. [DNLM: 1 Behavior–congresses. 2. Suicide–congresses. HV 6545 C976 1986] RC569.C867 1988   616.85'8445–dc19   DNLM/DLC   for Library of Congress 88-6418   CIP

© Springer-Verlag Berlin Heidelberg 1988
Printed in Germany

The use of registered names, trademarks, etc. in this publication does not imply, even in the absence of a specific statement, that such names are exempt from the relevant protective laws and regulations and therefore free for general use.

Product liability: The publisher can give no guarantee for information about drug dosage and application thereof contained in this book. In every individual case the respective user must check its accuracy by consulting other pharmaceutical literature.

Typesetting, printing and binding: Konrad Triltsch, D-8700 Würzburg
2125/3130-543210

Preface

This volume resulted from the First European Symposium on Empirical Research into Suicidal Behavior. The symposium was initiated by the Study Group on Suicidal Behavior (Arbeitsgemeinschaft zur Erforschung suizidalen Verhaltens) in collaboration with the German Society for the Prevention of Suicide (Deutsche Gesellschaft für Selbstmordverhütung). The local organization of this symposium, which took place in Munich, was performed by the staff of the Psychiatric Department of the University of Technology, Munich (Head: Prof. H. Lauter).

This volume contains contributions held at the symposium as well as papers especially prepared for this book. It thus fulfills the aim of providing an overview of the current state of research in the field of empirical suicidology with respect to epidemiology, biological and psychological risk factors, follow-up, and treatment evaluation.

We are grateful to all who contributed to this book by submitting papers or making critical comments. We would especially like to thank Mrs. D. Keck for her valuable cooperation.

We have to thank the following pharmaceutical companies for financial support: Organon (München), Ciba Geigy (Frankfurt), Tropon (Köln), Galenus (Mannheim), Wander (Nürnberg).

H.-J. MÖLLER
A. SCHMIDTKE
R. WELZ

Contents

Part III   Biological Factors of Suicidal Behavior

Part IV   Psychosocial Factors of Suicidal Behavior

Part V Treatment Evaluation

List of Contributors

Akil, H., Mental Health Research Institute, University of Michigan, Ann Arbor, MI, USA

Arató, M., National Institute for Nervous and Mental Diseases, OLE, Pf. 1, 1281 Budapest 27, Hungary

Åsberg, M., Department of Psychiatry and Psychology, Karolinska Hospital, Box 60 500, 10401 Stockholm, Sweden

Åsgård, U., Department of Psychiatry, Karolinska Hospital, 10401 Stockholm, Sweden

Banki, C. M., Regional Neuropsychiatric Institute, P.O. Box 37, 4321 Nagykálló, Hungary

Barnas, C., Universitätsklinik für Psychiatrie, Anichstr. 35, 6020 Innsbruck, Austria

Bäuml, J., Psychiatrische Klinik und Poliklinik der Technischen Universität München, Ismaninger Str. 22, 8000 München 80, Federal Republic of Germany

Becker, R., Klinikum Großhadern, Klinik für physikalische Medizin, Marchioninistr. 15, 8000 München 70, Federal Republic of Germany

Bille-Brahe, U., Institute of Psychiatry, Odense University Hospital, J. B. Winsløws Vej 20, 5000 Odense C, Denmark

Bissette, G., Department of Psychiatry, Duke University Medical Center, Durham, NC, USA

Böhme, K., Allgemeines Krankenhaus Ochsenzoll, Langenhorner Chaussee 560, 2000 Hamburg 62, Federal Republic of Germany

Bothge, C., Psychiatrische Klinik und Poliklinik der Technischen Universität München, Ismaninger Str. 22, 8000 München 80, Federal Republic of Germany

Breucha, H. P., Psychiatrische Klinik und Poliklinik der Technischen Universität München, Ismaninger Str. 22, 8000 München 80, Federal Republic of Germany

Bronisch, S., Psychiatrische Klinik und Poliklinik der Technischen Universität München, Ismaninger Str. 22, 8000 München 80, Federal Republic of Germany

Bronisch, T., Max-Planck-Institut für Psychiatrie, Kraepelinstr. 10, 8000 München 40, Federal Republic of Germany

Bürk, F., Psychiatrische Klinik und Poliklinik der Technischen Universität München, Ismaninger Str. 22, 8000 München 80, Federal Republic of Germany

Chambers, D. R., H. M. Coroner's Court St. Pancras, Camley Street, London NW1 OPP, United Kingdom

Christian, M. S., F.R.C.S., Wexham Park Hospital, Slough, Berkshire, United Kingdom

Cremniter, D., Henri Mondor Hospital, 54, Avenue Delattre de Tassigny, 94010 Creteil, France

Crepet, P., Research Unit, National Research Council, Piazza S. Cosimato 40, 00153 Roma, Italy

Demeter, E., Department of Forensic Medicine, Semmelweis Medical University, 1091 Üllöi u. 93, Budapest, Hungary

Demling, J., Psychiatrische Universitätsklinik, Schwabachanlage 6, 8520 Erlangen, Federal Republic of Germany

Diekstra, R. F. W., Division of Mental Health, WHO, 1211 Genève, Switzerland

Dietzfelbinger, T., Psychiatrische Klinik und Poliklinik der Technischen Universität München, Ismaninger Str. 22, 8000 München 80, Federal Republic of Germany

Eisenmenger, W., Institut für Rechtsmedizin der Universität München, Frauenlobstr. 7a, 8000 München 2, Federal Republic of Germany

Ekeberg, Ø., Medical Department 7 and Division of Clinical Pharmacology and Toxocology, Central Laboratory, Ullevaal Hospital, 0407 Oslo, Norway

Falus, A., National Institute for Nervous and Mental Diseases, OLE Pf. 1, 1281 Budapest 27, Hungary

Fehler, I., Psychiatrische Universitätsklinik, Schwabachanlage 6, 8520 Erlangen, Federal Republic of Germany

Fermanian, J., Laboratory of Biostatistics and Computer Applications, Necher Hospitals, 149, Rue de Sevres, 75015 Paris, France

Flaaten, B., Medical Department 7 and Division of Clinical Pharmacology and Toxicology, Central Laboratory, Ullevaal Hospital, 0407 Oslo, Norway

Fleischhacker, W. W., Universitätsklinik für Psychiatrie, Anichstr. 35, 6020 Innsbruck, Austria

Florenzano, F., Research Unit, National Research Council, Piazza S. Cosimato 40, 00153 Rom, Italy

Gast, M., c/o Böhme, K., Allgemeines Krankenhaus Ochsenzoll, Langenhorner Chaussee 560, 2000 Hamburg 62, Federal Republic of Germany

Gilg, T., Institut für Rechtsmedizin der Universität München, Frauenlobstr. 7 a, 8000 München 2, Federal Republic of Germany

Grabisch, R., Bezirkskrankenhaus Erlangen, Am Europakanal 71, 8520 Erlangen, Federal Republic of Germany

Gutscher, H., Psychologisches Institut der Universität Zürich, Abteilung Sozialpsychologie, Nägelistr. 7, 8044 Zürich, Switzerland

Häfner, H., Zentralinstitut für Seelische Gesundheit, J 5, 6800 Mannheim, Federal Republic of Germany

Haring, C., Universitätsklinik für Psychiatrie, Anichstr. 35, 6020 Innsbruck, Austria

Harvey, J. G., Sterling-Winthrop Group Ltd., Onslow Street, Guildford, Surrey GU1 4YS, United Kingdom

Hecht, H., Max-Planck-Institut für Psychiatrie, Kraepelinstr. 2, 8000 München 40, Federal Republic of Germany

Hengeveld, M. W., Department of Psychiatry, University Hospital, B 1-P, P.O. Box 9600, 2300 RC Leiden, The Netherlands

Hole, G., Psychiatrisches Landeskrankenhaus Weissenau, Abteilung Psychiatrie I der Universität Ulm, 7980 Ravensburg- Weissenau, Federal Republic of Germany

Höll, R., Abteilung Psychiatrie der Universität Erlangen-Nürnberg, Schwabachanlage 6, 8520 Erlangen, Federal Republic of Germany

Horn, W., Institut für Medizinische Kybernetik und Artificial Intelligence, Freyung 6, 1010 Wien, Austria

Jacobsen, D., Medical Department 7 and Division of Clinical Pharmacology and Toxicology, Central Laboratory, Ullevaal Hospital, 0407 Oslo, Norway

Kalb, R., Psychiatrische Universitätsklinik, Schwabachanlage 6, 8520 Erlangen, Federal Republic of Germany

Kauert, G., Institut für Rechtsmedizin der Universität München, Frauenlobstr. 7a, 8000 München 2, Federal Republic of Germany

Kerkhof, A. J. F. M., Department of Clinical Psychology, State University, Hooigracht 15, 2312 KM Leiden, The Netherlands

Klein, F., Roßdorfer Str. 44, 6000 Frankfurt/Main 60, Federal Republic of Germany

Kockott, G., Psychiatrische Klinik und Poliklinik der Technischen Universität München, Ismaninger Str. 22, 8000 München 80, Federal Republic of Germany

Korczak, D., GP Forschungsgruppe, Mozartstr. 14, 8000 München 2, Federal Republic of Germany

Kreitman, N., MRC Unit for Epidemiological Studies in Psychiatry, University Department of Psychiatry, Royal Edinburgh Hospital, Morningside Park, Edinburgh EH10 5HF, United Kingdom

Kuda, M., Ärztlich-psychologische Beratungsstelle für Studierende der Universität, Nikolausberger Weg 17, 3400 Göttingen, Federal Republic of Germany

Kulessa, C., Sitzbuchweg 108, 6900 Heidelberg, Federal Republic of Germany

Kurz, A., Psychiatrische Klinik der Technischen Universität München, Klinikum rechts der Isar, Möhlstr. 26, 8000 München 80, Federal Republic of Germany

Langer, K., Forschungsinstitut für experimentelle Ernährung e. V., Langemarckplatz 5, 8520 Erlangen, Federal Republic of Germany

Lauter, H., Psychiatrische Klinik und Poliklinik der Technischen Universität München, Ismaninger Str. 22, 8000 München 80, Federal Republic of Germany

Linder, A., Institute of Psychiatry, University Hospital, J. B. Winsløws Vej 16, 5000 Odense C, Denmark

Mack, A., Medical Department 7 and Division of Clinical Pharmacology and Toxicology, Central Laboratory, Ullevaal Hospital, 0407 Oslo, Norway

Magyar, K., Department of Pharmacodynamics, Semmelweis Medical University, 1091 Üllöi u. 93, Budapest, Hungary

Marazziti, D., Department of Psychiatry, St. Chiara Hospital, Via Roma 67, 56100 Pisa, Italy

Marchner, E., Psychiatrische Klinik und Poliklinik der Technischen Universität München, Ismaninger Str. 22, 8000 München 80, Federal Republic of Germany

Meidinger, A., Laboratory of Biostatistics and Computer Applications, Necker Hospital, 149, Rue de Sevres, 75015 Paris, France

Metzger, R., Psychiatrisches Landeskrankenhaus Bad Schussenried, Bereich Akutpsychiatrie, Klosterhof 1, 7953 Bad Schussenried

Miller, C. H., Universitätsklinik für Psychiatrie, Anichstr. 35, 6020 Innsbruck, Austria

Modestin, J., Psychiatrische Universitätsklinik, Bollingerstr. 111, 3072 Bern, Switzerland

Möller, H.-J., Psychiatrische Klinik und Poliklinik der Technischen Universität München, Ismaninger Str. 22, 8000 München 80, Federal Republic of Germany

Nemeroff, C. B., Department of Psychiatry, Duke University Medical Center, Durham, NC, USA

Nordström, P., Department of Psychiatry and Psychology, Karolinska Hospital, Box 60 500, 10401 Stockholm, Sweden

Ozsváth, K., Medical University of Pecs, Department of Psychology, Szigeti 12, 7624 Pecs, Hungary

Pacifici, G. M., Department of General Pathology, Medical School, University of Pisa, 56100 Pisa, Italy

Pilz, A., Psychiatrische Klinik und Poliklinik der Technischen Universität München, Ismaninger Str. 22, 8000 München 80, Federal Republic of Germany

Platt, S., MRC Unit for Epidemiological Studies in Psychiatry, University Department of Psychiatry, Royal Edinburgh Hospital, Morningside Park, Edinburgh EH10 5HF, United Kingdom

Platzek, M., Psychiatrische Universitätsklinik, Bergische Landstr. 2, 4000 Düsseldorf, Federal Republic of Germany

Poser, W., Zentrum Psychologische Medizin, Universität Göttingen, 3400 Göttingen, Federal Republic of Germany

Rau, E., Allgemeines Krankenhaus Ochsenzoll, Langenhorner Chaussee 560, 2000 Hamburg 62, Federal Republic of Germany

Retterstøl, N., University of Oslo, Gaustad Hospital, P.O. Box 24, Gaustad, 0320 Oslo 3, Norway

Riehl, T., Psychiatrische Klinik und Poliklinik der Technischen Universität München, Klinikum rechts der Isar, Möhlstr. 26, 8000 München 80, Federal Republic of Germany

Rihmer, Z., National Institute for Nervous and Mental Diseases, OLE, Pf. 1, 1281 Budapest 27, Hungary

Schaller, S., Otto-Selz-Institut der Universität Mannheim, Schloß, 6800 Mannheim, Federal Republic of Germany

Schmid-Bode, W., Psychiatrische Klinik und Poliklinik der Technischen Universität München, Ismaninger Str. 22, 8000 München 80, Federal Republic of Germany

Schmidtke, A., Psychiatrische Klinik und Poliklinik der Universität Würzburg, Füchsleinstr. 15, 8700 Würzburg, Federal Republic of Germany

Somogyi, E., Department of Forensic Medicine, Semmelweis Medical University, 1091 Üllöi u. 93, Budapest, Hungary

Sonneck, G., Institut für Medizinische Psychologie der Universität Wien, Severingasse 9, 1090 Wien, Austria

Sótonyi, P., Department of Forensic Medicine, Semmelweis Medical University, 1091 Üllöi u. 93, Budapest, Hungary

Šovljanski, M., Faculty of Medicine, University of Novi Sad, Voj. Misića 11/T., 21000 Novi Sad, Yugoslavia

Šovljanski, R., Faculty of Agriculture, University of Novi Sad, Voj. Misića 11/T., 21000 Novi Sad, Yugoslavia

Stein, W., Abteilung Psychiatrie der Universität Erlangen-Nürnberg, Schwabachanlage 6, 8520 Erlangen, Federal Republic of Germany

Stötzer, A., Klinikum Großhadern, Klinik für physikalische Medizin, Marchioninistr. 15, 8000 München 70, Federal Republic of Germany

Szabó, P., Department of Psychiatry and Psychotherapy, General Hospital, Lenin ltp 7, 7900 Szigetvár, Hungary

Szuchovsky, G., Department of Forensic Medicine, Semmelweis Medical University, 1091 Üllöi u. 93, Budapest, Hungary

Tegeler, J., Psychiatrische Universitätsklinik, Bergische Landstr. 2, 4000 Düsseldorf 12, Federal Republic of Germany

Tekavčič-Grad, O., Center for Mental Health, Poljanski nasip 58, 61000 Ljubljana, Yugoslavia

Temesváry, B., Department of Neurology and Psychiatry, University Medical School, P.O. Box 397, 6701 Szeged, Hungary

Thénault, M., Henri Mondor Hospital, 54, Avenue Delattre de Tassigny, 94010 Creteil, France

Thomssen, C., Psychiatrische Klinik und Poliklinik der Technischen Universität München, Ismaninger Str. 22, 8000 München 80, Federal Republic of Germany

Torhorst, A., Ludwigstr. 10, 8170 Bad Tölz, Federal Republic of Germany

Tóthfalusi, L., Department of Pharamacodynamics, Semmelweis Medical University, 1091 Üllöi u. 93, Budapest, Hungary

Veiel, H. O., Zentralinstitut für Seelische Gesundheit, J 5, 6800 Mannheim, Federal Republic of Germany

Vogel, R., Bezirkskrankenhaus Günzburg, Abteilung Psychiatrie II der Universität Ulm, Ludwig-Heilmeyer-Str. 2, 8870 Günzburg, Federal Republic of Germany

Vogl, A., Psychiatrische Klinik und Poliklinik der Technischen Universität München, Ismaninger Str. 22, 8000 München 80, Federal Republic of Germany

Wächtler, C., Allgemeines Krankenhaus Ochsenzoll, Langenhorner Chaussee 560, 2000 Hamburg 62, Federal Republic of Germany

Wal, J. van der, Department of Clinical Psychology, State University, Hooigracht 15, 2312 KM Leiden, The Netherlands

Wang, A. G., Institute of Psychiatry, University Hospital, J. B. Winsløws Vey 16, 5000 Odense C, Denmark

Watson, S. J., Mental Health Research Institute, University of Michigan, Ann Arbor, MI, USA

Wedler, H., Allgemeines Krankenhaus Ochsenzoll, Medizinische Abteilung, Langenhorner Chaussee 560, 2000 Hamburg 62, Federal Republic of Germany

Welz, R., Abteilung für Medizinische Psychologie der Universität Göttingen, Humboldtallee 3, 3400 Göttingen, Federal Republic of Germany

Winter, I., Psychiatrische Klinik und Poliklinik der Technischen Universität München, Ismaninger Str. 22, 8000 München 80, Federal Republic of Germany

Wolfersdorf, M. G., Psychiatrisches Landeskrankenhaus Weissenau, Bereich Depression, Abteilung Psychiatrie I der Universität Ulm, 7980 Ravensburg-Weissenau, Federal Republic of Germany

Wolk-Wassermann, D., Karolinska Institute, Department of Psychiatry, Huddinge University Hospital, 14186 Huddinge, Sweden

Zavasnik, A., Center for Mental Health, Poljanski nasip 58, 61000 Ljubljana, Yugoslavia

Zucker, T., Insitut für Rechtsmedizin der Universität München, Frauenlobstr. 7a, 8000 München 2, Federal Republic of Germany

Part I   **Epidemiology and Sociodemographic
and Psychiatric Background Variables
of Suicidal Behavior**

Suicide Trends in 24 European Countries, 1972 – 1984

S. PLATT

Introduction

This paper sets out to provide an overview of trends in suicide in 24 European countries over the period 1972 – 1984. All analyses are based on data collected by the various national governments and supplied to the World Health Organisation in Geneva. I am most grateful to W. Gulbinat, Senior Scientist in the Division of Mental Health, for making the suicide data bank available to me.

The use of official suicide statistics has been criticised and defended by innumerable social and medical scientists over the past century. There is probably common agreement that official statistics always underestimate the 'true' frequency of suicide and therefore the 'true' suicide rate. This is not, however, an insuperable problem. As noted by the WHO Working Group on Changing Patterns in Suicidal Behaviour in their 1982 Report (WHO Working Group 1982):

> it is not the ascertainment of absolute rates that is so important, it is whether *relative* differences are due to systematic bias in reporting, or can be taken to mean real differences in the propensity to suicide of the different populations (p. 2)

After assessing findings from a number of empirical studies, the Working Group "expressed confidence in the use of official suicide statistics from European countries for trend analysis . . ." (p. 19). My own view is that while the reliability of official suicide statistics might be adequate for establishing the magnitude and direction of changes over time *within a particular country,* apparent differences *between countries* cannot be treated with a similar degree of confidence. Ascertainment procedures and cultural biases are more likely to invalidate the latter type of comparison. For this reason, the analyses reported here are confined to secular trends and variation by gender and age, separately for each country. I make few comments on differences in the incidence of suicide between pairs or sets of countries, although readers are, of course, free to use the data provided in any way they wish.

Trends in the Suicide Rate, 1972 Onwards

Tables 1 and 2 show the annual suicide rate per 100000 population aged 15 + years for each year since 1972. Among men (Table 1), the trend has been upwards in most countries, with the major exception of Czechoslovakia. In a num-

Table 1.   Crude suicide rate per 100000 males aged 15 + years in 24 European countries, 1972–1984 [a]

Country	1972	1973	1974	1975	1976	1977	1978	1979	1980	1981	1982	1983	1984
Austria	44.9	42.5	45.2	47.4	43.6	45.3	47.2	47.2	47.8	51.3	53.2	50.1	50.1
Belgium	28.2	27.3	28.1	27.4	28.4	32.0	34.8	35.6	36.0	37.0	37.6	37.7	40.7
Bulgaria	20.5	20.7	22.8	23.4	25.5	26.6	24.7	25.7	24.5	24.7	27.9	24.9	31.0
Czechoslovakia	47.1	44.0	44.9	42.6	40.8	43.2	42.4	40.1	39.8	40.6	40.2	39.6	37.7
Denmark	39.4	38.2	44.0	38.8	39.2	39.9	36.0	40.7	52.4	49.0	46.4	46.1	45.3
Finland	51.6	49.4	53.1	52.6	54.7	54.0	53.7	51.7	52.9	49.2	48.5	50.1	51.9
France	30.7	29.9	29.9	30.0	29.8	30.3	32.0	35.0	35.9	36.5	38.9	40.6	41.9
FRG	34.5	35.8	36.2	35.8	37.2	38.3	37.7	36.1	34.9	36.1	36.1	34.8	34.1
Greece	5.3	5.4	6.1	4.6	5.0	6.2	5.5	5.3	6.0	6.1	6.5	6.9	7.4
Hungary	67.6	67.1	74.5	70.7	73.9	71.6	77.5	82.1	83.1	82.3	80.7	86.5	87.3
Iceland	16.7	30.0	21.3	18.3	17.9	22.8	28.7	30.6	16.9	14.3	17.5	36.8	41.0
Ireland	6.3	7.3	8.7	9.7	11.6	8.6	9.2	12.3	11.9	13.2	14.6	16.4	NA
Italy	10.9	10.8	9.8	10.4	10.5	11.7	12.2	12.8	13.1	12.7	NA	NA	NA
Luxembourg	26.2	24.2	23.5	NA	NA	NA	34.7	34.0	24.5	31.4	41.7	40.9	32.5
Netherlands	13.7	13.3	14.8	14.5	15.8	15.2	14.5	15.4	16.6	15.6	16.6	18.4	19.0
Norway	17.2	17.3	21.5	18.6	21.1	22.2	22.7	22.5	23.4	24.6	26.2	26.7	27.6
Poland	27.2	26.1	24.7	25.6	27.1	27.8	30.0	28.8	NA	NA	NA	28.0	31.8
Portugal	18.9	19.1	18.5	18.9	19.6	19.5	20.1	21.2	15.5	15.5	16.4	19.5	19.4
Spain	9.2	8.5	7.9	8.3	8.4	8.4	8.3	8.5	9.2	NA	NA	NA	NA
Sweden	37.3	37.4	36.4	35.2	33.6	35.9	33.1	35.6	34.5	30.7	34.5	33.7	33.8
Switzerland	37.0	35.9	38.1	42.4	41.5	43.7	43.7	43.7	46.0	42.0	43.4	45.1	44.0
UK – England and Wales	12.3	12.5	12.6	12.0	12.8	12.9	13.2	13.8	14.0	14.5	14.6	14.6	14.8
UK – Northern Ireland	5.9	5.8	7.3	6.8	7.9	7.1	7.0	9.9	9.8	NA	10.0	15.3	12.8
UK – Scotland	13.1	13.8	14.1	12.1	13.3	13.1	14.5	15.2	16.8	17.7	18.8	17.6	18.3

NA, not available.
a Source: WHO data bank.

Table 2. Crude suicide rate per 100000 females aged 15 + years in 24 European countries, 1972 – 1984[a]

Country	1972	1973	1974	1975	1976	1977	1978	1979	1980	1981	1982	1983	1984
Austria	18.6	17.5	18.5	17.6	17.0	18.8	17.8	18.2	18.3	18.4	17.5	18.6	17.8
Belgium	13.0	11.9	13.0	14.6	14.4	16.8	17.6	18.6	19.8	18.3	17.1	19.3	18.7
Bulgaria	8.8	8.9	9.7	9.5	10.4	10.2	10.0	11.2	10.3	10.1	11.0	9.2	11.9
Czechoslovakia	17.1	14.8	15.4	15.1	14.5	13.6	14.9	13.1	13.8	12.8	13.3	12.1	12.2
Denmark	22.8	23.8	23.6	23.6	22.6	22.6	23.7	24.9	27.9	26.5	26.1	24.9	25.7
Finland	12.8	13.1	13.3	13.2	12.9	13.3	12.0	12.1	13.2	11.9	13.0	12.1	12.3
France	12.0	11.2	11.3	11.5	11.5	12.6	12.6	13.4	13.9	13.9	14.7	15.3	15.4
FRG	17.8	18.5	18.5	18.2	18.5	19.5	18.4	17.6	16.9	17.2	16.0	16.7	15.4
Greece	2.0	2.5	3.1	2.6	2.3	2.6	2.0	2.4	2.4	2.6	2.6	2.5	2.7
Hungary	26.4	26.5	28.9	27.2	30.2	31.7	33.5	33.4	33.2	36.1	32.9	33.1	32.2
Iceland	8.4	8.3	8.1	10.6	5.2	5.1	3.7	4.9	12.1	4.8	8.2	8.1	7.9
Ireland	2.4	2.7	2.4	4.1	4.8	4.7	4.9	4.1	6.1	5.4	5.2	6.5	NA
Italy	4.7	4.4	4.5	4.4	4.5	4.8	4.8	5.4	5.8	5.1	NA	NA	NA
Luxembourg	12.1	9.8	9.0	NA	NA	NA	11.5	16.6	7.9	10.4	11.6	14.1	14.0
Netherlands	8.7	10.0	9.9	9.3	9.3	9.0	10.7	11.7	9.5	10.0	10.6	11.7	11.9
Norway	6.6	5.5	5.9	7.2	7.3	7.6	7.7	9.1	8.4	8.3	9.4	10.2	8.9
Poland	5.4	5.6	5.4	4.8	5.2	5.2	5.4	5.2	NA	NA	NA	5.6	6.4
Portugal	4.8	5.5	5.8	5.5	5.0	5.9	6.4	6.3	5.0	5.9	6.2	6.6	7.5
Spain	3.1	3.1	3.0	2.7	2.9	2.9	2.9	2.8	2.9	NA	NA	NA	NA
Sweden	14.1	15.1	14.4	13.8	14.1	14.0	14.7	16.0	13.9	13.0	13.7	13.2	14.3
Switzerland	14.4	13.6	15.9	16.4	15.9	17.9	17.8	19.1	18.6	17.6	17.7	16.9	16.8
UK – England and Wales	8.0	8.0	8.2	7.6	7.5	7.9	7.9	8.1	8.3	8.1	7.2	7.0	7.0
UK – Northern Ireland	2.9	6.8	4.1	3.6	4.6	5.6	5.6	3.8	4.6	NA	6.0	8.9	6.1
UK – Scotland	8.9	8.8	8.5	9.6	8.7	8.4	7.8	9.5	9.2	8.2	9.1	7.5	7.3

NA, not available.
[a] Source: WHO data bank.

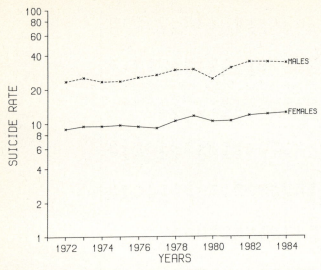

Fig. 1. The median rate is based on 24 countries in 1972−1974, 1978 and 1979; on 23 countries in 1975−1977 and 1980; on 22 countries in 1983; and on 21 countries in 1981, 1982 and 1984

ber of other countries (e.g., Finland, Iceland, Portugal, Sweden), there has been no obvious pattern in the movement of rates over time. Among women also (Table 2), suicide incidence has tended to rise, although once again a number of contrary trends are also visible (e.g., Czechoslovakia, FRG, England and Wales). Figure 1 plots changes in the median suicide rate per 100 000 population aged 15+ years from 1972−1984. The trend for both males and females is clearly upwards. The median male suicide rate rose in all but 4 years of the series (the exceptions being 1974, 1980, 1983 and 1984), from 23.4 in 1972 to 33.8 in 1984 (an increase of 44.4%). The median female rate rose or remained steady in all but 3 years (1976, 1977, 1980), starting at 8.9 in 1972 and reaching 12.2 in 1984 (an increase of 37.1%). Table 3 compares the mean suicide rate in 1983−1984 (or the latest years available) with the mean rate in 1972−1973. Significantly more countries registered an increase in the male suicide rate over the period than a decrease (20 vs 3; $P < 0.001$, two-tailed sign test). Particularly noteworthy is the finding of a more than doubling of the rate in Ireland and Northern Ireland. In addition, Belgium, Iceland, Luxembourg and Norway reported increases of over 40%. Although the female suicide rate increased in more countries (16) than it decreased (8), the trend did not reach statistical significance. Again, there was a marked rise in Ireland (over 100%) and Northern Ireland (over 50%), while a further three countries (Belgium, France and Portugal) registered increases of over 30%.

Table 3.   Changes in the crude suicide rate per 100 000 aged 15 + years in 24 European countries, by gender (mean 1972 – 1973 to mean 1983 – 1984 [a]) [b]

Country	Males			Females		
	Mean 1972 – 73	Mean 1983 – 84 [a]	Change (%)	Mean 1972 – 73	Mean 1983 – 84 [a]	Change (%)
Austria	43.7	50.1	+ 14.6	18.1	18.2	+ 0.6
Belgium	27.8	39.2	+ 41.0	12.6	19.0	+ 50.8
Bulgaria	20.6	28.0	+ 35.9	8.9	10.6	+ 19.1
Czechoslovakia	45.6	38.7	− 15.1	16.0	12.2	− 23.8
Denmark	38.8	45.7	+ 17.8	23.5	25.3	+ 7.7
Finland	50.5	51.0	+ 1.0	13.0	12.2	− 6.2
France	30.3	41.3	+ 36.3	11.6	15.4	+ 32.8
FRG	35.2	34.5	− 2.0	18.2	16.1	− 11.5
Greece	5.4	7.2	+ 33.3	2.3	2.6	+ 13.0
Hungary	67.4	86.9	+ 28.9	26.5	32.7	+ 23.4
Iceland	23.4	38.9	+ 66.2	8.4	8.0	− 4.8
Ireland	6.8	15.5	+ 127.9	2.6	5.9	+ 126.9
Italy	10.9	12.9	+ 18.3	4.6	5.5	+ 19.6
Luxembourg	25.2	36.7	+ 45.6	11.0	14.1	+ 28.2
Netherlands	13.5	18.7	+ 38.5	9.4	11.8	+ 25.5
Norway	17.3	27.2	+ 57.2	6.1	9.6	+ 57.4
Poland	26.7	29.9	+ 12.0	5.5	6.0	+ 9.1
Portugal	19.0	19.5	+ 2.6	5.2	7.1	+ 36.5
Spain	8.9	8.9	−	3.1	2.9	− 6.5
Sweden	37.4	33.8	− 9.6	14.6	13.8	− 5.5
Switzerland	36.6	44.6	+ 21.9	14.0	16.9	+ 20.7
United Kingdom						
− England and Wales	12.4	14.7	+ 18.5	8.0	7.0	− 12.5
− Northern Ireland	5.9	14.0	+ 137.3	4.9	7.5	+ 53.1
− Scotland	13.5	18.0	+ 33.3	8.9	7.4	− 16.9

[a]   Except for the following countries (latest years in parentheses): Ireland (1982 – 1983), Italy (1980 – 1981), Spain (1979 – 1980).
[b]   Source: WHO data bank.

Male: Female Ratio

The ratio of the male:female suicide rate (per 100 000 population aged 15 + years) in 1972 – 1973 and 1983 – 1984 (or the latest years available) is given in Table 4. In 17 countries, the ratio was greater in 1983 – 1984 than in 1972 – 1973 and in only four countries was it smaller. This trend was statistically significant ($P = 0.008$, two-tailed sign test).

Changes in Age-Sex-Specific Rates

Mean age-specific suicide rates in 1983 – 1984 (or the latest years available) are given in Tables 5 and 6. Among men (Table 5), suicide incidence tends to increase with age, with the peak rate found among those aged 75 + years. Only

Table 4. Ratio of male:female suicide rate (per 100000 population aged 15+ years) in 24 European countries, 1972−1973 and 1983−1984 [a,b]

Country	M:F ratio	
	1972−1973	1983−1984 [a]
Austria	2.4	2.8
Belgium	2.2	2.1
Bulgaria	2.3	2.6
Czechoslovakia	2.9	3.2
Denmark	1.7	1.8
Finland	3.9	4.2
France	2.6	2.7
FRG	1.9	2.1
Greece	2.3	2.8
Hungary	2.5	2.7
Iceland	2.8	4.9
Ireland	2.6	2.6
Italy	2.4	2.3
Luxembourg	2.3	2.6
Netherlands	1.4	1.6
Norway	2.8	2.8
Poland	4.9	5.0
Portugal	3.7	2.7
Spain	2.9	3.1
Sweden	2.6	2.4
Switzerland	2.6	2.6
United Kingdom		
− England and Wales	1.6	2.1
− Northern Ireland	1.2	1.9
− Scotland	1.5	2.4

[a] Except for the following countries (latest years in parentheses): Ireland (1982−1983), Italy (1980−1981), Spain (1979−1980).
[b] Source: WHO data bank.

four countries have patterns which are markedly different: Finland and Norway, where no clear age-related trends are visible, and Poland and Scotland, where there is an inverted U-shaped pattern and the peak rate is in the 45−54 age group. It is also worth noting that in several countries with peak rates in the 75+ age group, there is an additional peak in a younger age group, particularly 45−54 years (e.g., Austria, Czechoslovakia, FRG, Hungary, Sweden, England and Wales). Overall, 10 of the 20 countries showed a peak in the 45−54 age group in 1983−1984, compared with only three countries in 1972−1973.

Table 6 presents age-specific rates among women for the latest years available. Again, the suicide rate usually increases with age, but the peak rate is found almost equally in the 65−74 age group (nine countries) and in the 75+ age group (eight countries). In three countries, the overall picture is deviant: Denmark and Finland have an inverted U-shaped pattern, while there is no clear trend in Portugal. In common with the men, the female suicide rate is be-

Table 5. Age-specific suicide rate per 100000 males in 24 European countries, mean 1983–1984[a,b]

Country	Age groups						
	15–24	25–34	35–44	45–54	55–64	65–74	75+
Austria	30.2	37.3	52.6	60.3	52.5	71.4	105.6
Belgium	16.0	36.9	37.1	39.8	44.6	60.8	94.6
Bulgaria	10.2	19.8	22.7	26.0	34.9	53.6	108.0
Czechoslovakia	14.8	31.1	38.3	48.1	43.4	62.6	100.1
Denmark	15.7	36.5	52.0	58.7	63.7	53.0	75.4
Finland	36.3	53.9	53.4	60.4	52.2	53.6	55.8
France	16.4	33.2	36.8	43.4	46.7	64.5	114.6
FRG	19.4	28.3	33.7	40.1	38.1	48.9	73.5
Greece	4.9	7.0	5.1	6.2	9.8	9.3	14.8
Hungary	26.8	60.5	96.3	115.0	102.8	123.8	190.6
Iceland	(37.9)	(20.1)	(35.9)	(46.2)	(41.9)	(94.6)	(34.9)
Ireland	12.4	17.7	15.7	13.6	19.3	19.1	(11.4)
Italy	5.2	8.3	9.0	14.0	16.8	25.7	36.9
Luxembourg	(19.4)	(37.0)	(38.7)	(37.3)	(41.2)	(45.1)	(73.8)
Netherlands	7.3	17.9	17.9	20.6	25.2	27.9	45.7
Norway	23.4	23.8	21.5	33.2	38.4	29.3	25.1
Poland	18.5	34.0	34.2	36.0	30.0	27.3	26.8
Portugal	10.3	14.0	16.6	20.7	29.5	32.7	42.5
Spain	4.2	5.3	6.5	9.8	12.3	17.0	30.5
Sweden	16.3	34.0	34.4	43.4	32.8	39.7	50.7
Switzerland	33.7	39.5	40.2	48.8	51.4	59.6	64.8
United Kingdom							
– England and Wales	7.1	14.0	16.3	17.8	17.5	17.3	22.5
– Northern Ireland	(9.2)	(12.4)	(15.2)	(12.9)	(16.4)	(18.0)	(18.8)
– Scotland	9.7	17.7	20.2	24.5	21.3	20.3	(18.1)

Note: Rate in parentheses based on mean of <20 suicides per annum
[a] Except for the following countries (latest years in parentheses): Ireland (1982–1983), Italy (1980–1981), Spain (1979–1980).
[b] Source: WHO data bank.

ginning to show an early peak in the 45–54 age group. Seven countries showed this pattern in 1983–1984 compared with only one in 1972–1973.

Changes in age-specific suicide rates for men and women over the period under review are given in Tables 7 and 8, respectively. The findings are summarised in Table 9 and Fig. 2. Among men, an increase in the suicide rate was noted in the majority of countries for all age groups. However, this trend reached statistical significance only in the 15–44 age groups. Subdivision of the 15–24 age group showed similar changes among 15–19 and 20–24 year olds. (These data are not presented her for reasons of space.) The greatest increase occurred in the 25–34 age group (+42.5%). Among women, there was an increase in the suicide rate of all age groups, except among 55–64 year olds. However, the only significant trend was found in the 25–34 age group. For all age groups up to 64, the rate of increase was greater for men than for women. Over the age of 64, the female rate of increase was greater.

Table 6. Age-specific suicide rate per 100000 females in 24 European countries, mean 1983−1984[a,b]

Country	Age groups						
	15−24	25−34	35−44	45−54	55−64	65−74	75+
Austria	8.2	9.5	15.0	22.2	21.7	28.2	35.0
Belgium	4.1	12.8	18.5	26.5	27.7	27.9	25.7
Bulgaria	4.6	4.2	5.4	8.3	13.8	24.0	37.3
Czechoslovakia	4.1	7.2	7.6	12.8	16.1	21.9	34.9
Denmark	(4.7)	14.4	26.4	36.7	39.5	37.6	32.5
Finland	5.8	12.4	12.2	17.1	15.3	12.6	11.6
France	4.7	11.2	13.3	16.9	19.7	25.1	(28.8)
FRG	5.8	9.7	14.1	17.3	21.1	25.6	27.8
Greece	(2.1)	(2.2)	(1.4)	3.4	(2.8)	(3.9)	(3.6)
Hungary	8.4	16.6	29.9	33.6	39.4	54.1	81.0
Iceland	(0)	(5.4)	(22.5)	(13.9)	(10.3)	(7.0)	(0)
Ireland	(2.7)	(3.9)	(7.1)	(8.0)	(12.7)	(6.4)	(3.2)
Italy	2.1	3.2	4.3	6.0	8.0	9.9	9.0
Luxembourg	(7.1)	(13.8)	(12.4)	(23.6)	(14.0)	(15.0)	(15.5)
Netherlands	3.5	9.8	10.6	15.6	17.3	20.2	16.4
Norway	(4.3)	(6.2)	10.3	15.1	16.1	11.2	(6.7)
Poland	4.2	5.6	5.8	7.4	7.0	7.2	6.3
Portugal	5.6	4.7	5.8	8.3	6.3	13.3	9.6
Spain	1.2	1.2	2.2	3.4	4.3	5.0	6.2
Sweden	6.2	13.5	14.9	19.6	15.5	16.5	11.8
Switzerland	7.9	12.6	16.6	20.8	22.2	23.7	21.4
United Kingdom							
− England and Wales	1.9	3.6	6.4	9.5	10.7	11.1	10.0
− Northern Ireland	(3.0)	(6.7)	(8.0)	(7.5)	(16.3)	(7.5)	(6.4)
− Scotland	(1.9)	(5.5)	8.5	9.3	11.5	11.1	(7.2)

Note: Rate in parentheses based on mean of < 20 suicides per annum
[a] Except for the following countries (latest years in parentheses): Ireland (1982−1983), Italy (1980−1981), Spain (1979−1980).
[b] Source: WHO data bank.

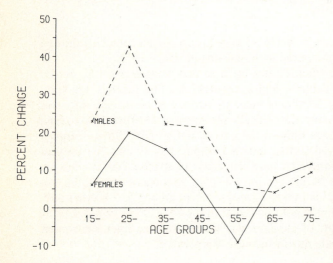

Fig. 2. Median percentage change in suicide rate by age group. Males: The median rate is based on 20 countries (excluding Iceland, Ireland, Luxembourg and Northern Ireland). Females: The median rate is based on 18 countries (excluding Greece, Iceland, Ireland, Luxembourg, Norway and Northern Ireland). Countries are excluded where rates are based on a mean of < 20 suicides per annum in the majority of age groups during either time period

Table 7. Changes in age-specific suicide rate per 100 000 males in 24 European countries, mean 1972 – 1973 to mean 1983 – 1984[a,b]

Country	Age groups						
	15 – 24 (%)	25 – 34 (%)	35 – 44 (%)	45 – 54 (%)	55 – 64 (%)	65 – 74 (%)	75 + (%)
Austria	+ 52.5	+ 27.3	+ 27.1	+ 17.1	− 20.6	+ 11.7	+ 21.9
Belgium	+ 53.8	+ 26.9	+ 91.2	+ 49.6	+ 12.3	+ 0.1	+ 8.4
Bulgaria	+ 8.5	+ 81.7	+ 61.0	+ 43.6	+ 34.7	+ 9.4	+ 9.2
Czechoslovakia	− 48.1	− 10.1	− 20.7	− 8.6	− 15.7	− 5.2	− 2.7
Denmark	+ 25.6	+ 50.2	+ 16.1	+ 8.3	+ 9.3	+ 4.1	+ 23.8
Finland	+ 13.4	+ 18.7	− 2.2	− 5.0	− 23.5	− 11.0	− 16.2
France	+ 113.0	+ 174.4	+ 109.1	+ 74.3	+ 53.1	+ 82.2	+ 185.1
FRG	− 6.3	+ 7.2	− 2.3	− 2.4	− 17.0	− 2.2	+ 15.4
Greece	(+ 96.0)	+ 89.2	(+ 70.0)	+ 19.2	+ 16.7	− 14.7	0
Hungary	+ 4.7	+ 25.5	+ 40.8	+ 33.7	+ 12.7	+ 20.8	+ 16.1
Iceland	(+ 161.4)	(+ 36.7)	(− 17.8)	(+ 139.4)	(− 6.1)	(+ 240.3)	(−)
Ireland	(+ 287.5)	(+ 168.2)	(+ 153.2)	(+ 70.0)	(+ 82.1)	(+ 103.2)	(+ 50.0)
Italy	+ 33.3	+ 40.7	+ 15.4	+ 28.4	− 1.2	+ 3.6	+ 5.1
Luxembourg	(+ 921.1)	(+ 141.8)	(+ 43.3)	(+ 51.6)	(+ 32.9)	(− 26.2)	(+ 1.0)
Netherlands	+ 17.7	+ 126.6	+ 46.7	+ 29.6	+ 16.7	+ 17.2	+ 23.8
Norway	+ 136.4	+ 84.5	+ 32.7	+ 32.3	+ 64.8	+ 42.9	(+ 42.6)
Poland	− 1.6	+ 30.8	+ 11.8	+ 9.4	− 10.2	0	− 3.6
Portugal	+ 134.1	+ 75.0	+ 13.7	− 9.2	− 7.5	− 23.2	− 41.1
Spain	+ 82.6	+ 29.3	− 4.4	− 6.7	− 15.2	− 25.1	+ 7.8
Sweden	− 10.4	+ 8.6	− 18.5	− 7.3	− 29.6	− 5.5	+ 4.3
Switzerland	+ 48.5	+ 52.5	+ 16.9	+ 22.9	+ 1.2	+ 7.8	− 10.2
United Kingdom							
− England and Wales	+ 18.3	+ 44.3	+ 33.6	+ 29.0	+ 10.1	− 8.9	+ 9.2
− N. Ireland	(+ 162.9)	(+ 287.5)	(+ 108.2)	(+ 121.0)	(+ 27.1)	(+ 462.5)	(+ 683.3)
− Scotland	+ 20.0	+ 68.6	+ 44.3	+ 57.1	+ 17.7	+ 10.9	(+ 16.0)

Note: Rate in parentheses based on mean of < 20 suicides per annum in one or both time periods
[a] Except for the following countries (latest years in parentheses): Ireland (1982 – 1983), Italy (1980 – 1981), Spain (1979 – 1980).
[b] Source: WHO data bank.

Discussion

Between the early 1960s and the mid-1970s, significantly more countries reported an increase in both male and female suicide rates than reported a decrease [1]. The same tendency has been noted for the period 1972 – 1984, although the trend reached statistical significance only for men. The doubling of the suicide rate in both the countries of Ireland might warrant closer investigation. Differing trends in the Nordic countries are also of considerable interest. While suicide incidence among both men and women in Norway increased by over 50% during the period under review, rates declined among men and women in Sweden and among women in Finland, while the increase among men in Fin-

Table 8. Changes in age-specific suicide rate per 100 000 females in 24 European countries, mean 1972−1973 to 1983−1984[a,b]

Country	Age groups						
	15−24 (%)	25−34 (%)	35−44 (%)	45−54 (%)	55−64 (%)	65−74 (%)	75+ (%)
Austria	+34.4	+ 3.3	+15.4	− 3.5	−13.2	+ 8.0	+ 6.1
Belgium	+ 5.1	+77.8	+112.6	+94.9	+45.0	+18.7	+27.2
Bulgaria	+17.9	+20.0	+38.5	+ 6.4	−14.3	+20.0	+18.4
Czechoslovakia	−48.8	−20.9	−37.7	−21.5	−19.9	−20.7	−20.1
Denmark	(−24.2)	+110.8	+15.3	+ 3.1	− 0.3	+ 9.9	+67.5
Finland	−31.0	+12.7	−12.2	+ 8.2	−19.9	−10.0	(+24.7)
France	+ 6.8	+67.2	+56.5	+28.0	+15.9	+23.6	(+41.9)
FRG	−13.4	−10.2	− 2.1	−23.8	−20.7	− 1.9	+ 1.1
Greece	(+40.0)	(+100.0)	(−17.6)	(+70.0)	(−17.6)	(− 4.9)	(−21.7)
Hungary	+18.3	+21.2	+51.0	+ 6.7	+11.3	+ 7.3	+20.7
Iceland	(−)	(−64.7)	(+150.0)	(+183.7)	(−44.3)	(−)	(−)
Ireland	(+125.0)	(+85.7)	(+163.0)	(+48.1)	(+353.6)	(+137.0)	(+128.6)
Italy	+ 5.0	+14.3	+22.9	+20.0	+ 8.1	+23.8	+25.0
Luxembourg	(+82.1)	(+115.6)	(+195.2)	(+80.2)	(−38.6)	(−25.4)	(+37.2)
Netherlands	+12.9	+55.6	+17.8	+19.1	+12.3	+37.4	+28.1
Norway	(+13.2)	(+21.6)	(+77.6)	+62.4	(+94.0)	(+75.0)	(+91.4)
Poland	+ 7.7	+24.4	+ 1.8	+ 1.4	0	+ 7.5	+16.7
Portugal	(+124.0)	(+30.6)	+65.7	+43.1	−18.2	+46.2	(−13.5)
Spain	+50.0	−14.3	0	−17.1	−15.7	−18.0	− 6.1
Sweden	−27.1	+19.5	− 5.1	− 1.0	−22.5	+ 7.1	+ 6.3
Switzerland	+27.4	+17.8	+37.2	+ 6.7	+11.0	+42.8	− 4.9
United Kingdom							
− England and Wales	−63.3	−25.0	−12.3	− 9.5	− 5.3	− 2.6	− 5.7
− N. Ireland	(+130.8)	(+148.1)	(+21.2)	(+63.0)	(+79.1)	(−21.9)	(+357.1)
− Scotland	(− 5.0)	(+20.3)	+ 2.4	−15.5	−27.7	+ 5.7	(−28.7)

Note: Rate in parentheses based on mean of <20 suicides per annum in one or both time periods.
[a] Except for the following countries (latest years in parentheses): Ireland (1982−1983), Italy (1980−1981), Spain (1979−1980).
[b] Source: WHO data bank.

land was minimal (1%). As Tables 1 and 2 show, variations in suicide incidence in the three countries are far less marked now than they were a decade ago.

Two major findings from the analysis of age-specific trends are worth further consideration. The first is the emergence of a twin-peak profile. Although suicide rates continue to show a direct relationship with age, more countries are now reporting a peak in a younger age group (45−54 years) than formerly. In future years, there might be a further consolidation of this twin-peak pattern, or else the age profile of suicide might change from a (more or less) linear to an inverted U-shaped pattern. The other finding to which attention should be drawn is the tendency for the 25−34 year age group to suffer the greatest increase in the suicide rate over the period under consideration.

Table 9. Summary of changes in age-specific suicide rates, 1972–1973 to 1983–1984

Age group	Median change	Range of change	Overall change over period			
			Increase (no. of countries)	Decrease (no. of countries)	Same (no. of countries)	Signifi-cance[a]
	(%)	(%)				
Males[b]						
15–24 years	+ 22.8	− 48.1 to + 136.4	16	4	0	P = .012
25–34 years	+ 42.5	− 10.1 to + 174.4	19	1	0	P < .001
35–44 years	+ 22.0	− 20.7 to + 109.1	15	5	0	P = .042
45–54 years	+ 21.1	− 9.2 to + 74.3	14	6	0	NS
55–64 years	+ 5.3	− 29.6 to + 64.8	11	9	0	NS
65–74 years	+ 3.9	− 25.1 to + 82.2	11	8	1	NS
75+ years	+ 9.2	− 41.1 to + 185.1	14	5	1	NS
Females[c]						
15–24 years	+ 6.0	− 63.3 to + 124.0	11	7	0	NS
25–34 years	+ 19.8	− 25.0 to + 77.8	14	4	0	P = .03
35–44 years	+ 15.4	− 37.7 to + 112.6	12	5	1	NS
45–54 years	+ 4.8	− 23.8 to + 94.9	11	7	0	NS
55–64 years	− 9.3	− 27.7 to + 45.0	6	11	1	NS
65–74 years	+ 7.8	− 20.7 to + 46.2	13	5	0	NS
75+ years	+ 11.5	− 28.7 to + 67.5	12	6	0	NS

[a] Sign test, two-tailed.
[b] Based on 20 countries (Iceland, Ireland, Luxembourg and Northern Ireland excluded).
[c] Based on 18 countries (Greece, Iceland, Ireland, Luxembourg, Norway and Northern Ireland excluded).

Given the concern expressed in the United States about a suicide 'epidemic' among teenagers and young adults (i.e., the 15–24 age group) during the last 10–15 years, a similar trend has been expected (and sometimes assumed to have occurred) in Britain and other European countries. This is clearly not the case. The rate of increase in the suicide rate has been marked in *all* age groups between 15 and 54 among men, and in the 25–34 age groups among women. The greater propensity to suicide in all these age groups requires a continuing research effort.

Acknowledgement. This is a revised version of a background paper prepared for the WHO Working Group on Preventive Practices in Suicide and Attempted Suicide, York, September 22–26, 1986, published with permission of the WHO regional office for Europe.

Reference

WHO Working Group (1982) Changing patterns in suicide behavior. Euro reports and studies, no 74. WHO Regional office for Europe, Copenhagen

Frequencies and Trends in Attempted Suicide in the Federal Republic of Germany: A Methodological Study*

A. SCHMIDTKE, H. HÄFNER, H.-J. MÖLLER, H. WEDLER, and K. BÖHME

Problem

The results of several studies on the frequency and trends in attempted suicides in the Federal Republic of Germany differ. On the one hand, a rising trend, particularly in younger age groups, has often been pointed out (Specht 1976; Schmitz 1980; Welz 1978, 1979, 1980, 1984, 1986). On the other hand, it has been stressed that attempted suicides peaked last in the years 1976–1978 and that their frequency has fallen in the last few years (Häfner 1985b). Past research has not shown definitively whether there is a secular trend (Kreitman 1980) in attempted suicides as in suicides: such studies have all been conducted on the basis of service contacts, and, therefore, artifacts resulting from changes in service provision cannot be ruled out. Even the most recent reports on increases refer to data collected several years ago. There is also controversy as to whether certain types of attempted suicides are increasing or decreasing. Radmayr (1980) argues that purely "demonstrative" suicide attempts are decreasing, as there are other types of responses available these days. In Mannheim, Häfner (1985a, b) found indications of the greatest fluctuations occurring in the frequency of less severe parasuicidal acts in which the intention to die was not very serious and was often dominated by other objectives.

Methodology in Studying Frequencies of Attempted Suicides

In studying frequencies of attempted suicides and calculating trends, attention must be paid to various methodological problems, which might be responsible for the differences in the results quoted. First, there is the problem of definition and classification of suicidal behavior. The range of behavior labeled as attempted suicide is often wide, extending from attempts to take one's life that can be regarded as "serious" ("unsuccessful suicides") to acts of self-harm in which a lethal outcome cannot be assumed to have been intended neither in view of the patient himself nor of dying (Häfner and Welz 1980; Schmidtke and Häfner 1986; Häfner and Schmidtke 1987). Particularly in the case of children and adolescents, behavior is often included that cannot be regarded as sui-

* Coordinated at the Central Institute of Mental Health, Mannheim, WHO Collaborating Centre for Research and Training in Mental Health, and the Psychiatric Department of the University of Würzburg.

cidal in a stricter sense (for a critique of such concepts, cf. Berman and Cohen-Sandler 1982). That attempted suicides do not occur among children is also an opinion still held until recently. Poisonings (accidents) among children, however, can in fact be attempted suicides (Krienke and von Mühlendahl 1980; Holinger and Offer 1981). According to an investigation conducted by Moll and al Faraidy (1978) of all the cases of poisoning among children under 14 years of age that received inpatient treatment in a mixed urban/rural region of northwestern Lower Saxony in the period 1964−1974, 3.1% could be classified as attempted suicides.

When official statistics are used, it must also be borne in mind that parasuicidal acts are classified as "self-harm" rather than as attempted suicides if their lethality risk is assessed to be low and the intention to die less serious. Precise criteria of classification do not exist. For attempted suicides, a relationship can therefore be assumed between the assessment of the seriousness of intent of a suicidal act and the probability of being entered in statistics on attempted suicides: the lower the seriousness of intent of an attempted suicide is judged, the lower the probability of entry in official statistics (Schmidtke and Häfner 1985).

As in the case of suicides, the number of unrecorded attempted suicides is influenced by various factors. If, for example, sex-specific differences in methods of attempted suicide − among adolescents and females in particular (Lester 1979; Farmer and Rohde 1980; Neuringer 1982; Neuringer and Lettieri 1982) − are assumed on the basis of the findings of some authors, the data will probably be distorted with respect to sex-specific differences.

In view of their own findings, Stengel (1964) and Kockott et al. (1970) assumed the number of unrecorded cases to be particularly large in higher social classes. In addition, documentation often remains insufficient partly out of ignorance, partly out of the shortsighted intention not to disadvantage certain population groups such as children and adolescents (Schmidtke and Häfner 1985).

For all these reasons, the rates for attempted suicide are assumed to underestimate the actual occurrence by up to 500% (Haim 1970; Jones 1977). Studies of the "true" incidence of attempted suicide based neither on official statistics nor on hospital records exclusively are very rare indeed. Public statistics and studies based on utilization data of psychiatric hospitals can be regarded as yielding conservative estimates, while studies collecting data on all attempted suicides that have received medical treatment in a defined population or studies based on sample interviews provide approximations of the true frequency.

Present Study

Sources of Data

Contrary to other countries (e.g., Great Britain), in the Federal Republic of Germany, attempted suicides are recorded neither by the Federal Bureau of

Statistics nor by the statistics offices of the states. Up to 1965, police authorities are reported to have supplied data on attempted suicides to the Federal Office for Criminal Investigation (*Bundeskriminalamt*), but the practice ceased thereafter. Since 1966, records of attempted suicide have reportedly been kept by the Statistics Offices only in the states of Schleswig-Holstein and Hamburg, and since 1968, in the Saarland too (cf. Dahm and Händel 1970; Ott 1974; Remschmidt and Schwab 1978; Remschmidt 1982).

To estimate the frequency of attempted suicides and calculate trends therein, data were evaluated at four levels within the framework of a WHO project[1]:

1. Utilization data of mental hospitals providing emergency services at a regional general hospital:

a) Data from the Cumulative Case Register of the Central Institute of Mental Health (CIMH) in Mannheim (1985: approximately 302000 inhabitants) for the period 1974–1980. Since the catchment area of the Case Register covered the whole city of Mannheim, the data could be related to the number of inhabitants. In 1980, after the intervention of the Data Protection Commissioner of the state of Baden-Württemberg, the supply of new data to the Case Register had to be stopped. Data back to 1966 were available from earlier research projects (Welz 1979).

b) Data provided by the CIMH research unit "Scientific Documentation" for the period 1978–1985. The catchment area of the CIMH and its emergency services is identical with that of the Case Register (i.e., the city of Mannheim). The Institute runs a 24-h emergency and crisis intervention service and a round-the-clock psychiatric liaison service at the city's largest general hospital, where all the patients admitted with attempted suicides are seen by the staff on duty. Thus, these data could also be related to the size of the population to estimate trends.

For the 3-year period 1978–1980, overlapping with the Case Register data was controlled for and the percentage of contacts by patients with suicide attempts recorded in the CIMH Documentation calculated to take underestimates into account.

c) Data from the Municipal Hospital in Munich-Schwabing (1971–1985) and the University Hospital "rechts der Isar" in Munich (1972–1985). Munich is the second largest city in the Federal Republic of Germany (1985: approximately 1267000 inhabitants). Although the two hospitals care for a large proportion of patients with attempted suicides in Munich, their data do not yield reliable frequency rates. Nevertheless, it was justifiable to relate the data to the population figure in order to estimate trends. For the same purpose, the number of admissions with attempted suicides into the Municipal Hospital in Munich-Schwabing was related to the total number of admissions into that hospital.

d) Data from the Municial Hospital in Darmstadt (a medium-sized city; 1985: approximately 133000 inhabitants) for the period 1969–1984. In this

---

[1] Project carried out in preparation for the WHO meeting "Preventive Practices in Suicide and Attempted Suicide," York, 1986.

case, the population served could not be defined more clearly because the hospital also serves the area around Darmstadt. However, it could be assumed that it had not undergone any essential changes in the period of interest. With these data, trends were therefore calculated on the basis of the absolute figures for attempted suicide and not by relating them to the population figures.

2. Data from the records of the Hamburg police[2]. Hamburg is the largest city in the Federal Republic of Germany (1985: approximately 1 580 000 inhabitants). Data were obtainable for the period 1966 – 1985. The police records cover all attempted suicides that become known to the police. It could be assumed that the method of recording had not changed in the period mentioned. To estimate trends, the data were related to the size of the population. However, the age groups for which figures for attempted suicide were provided are not identical with those used by the Federal Bureau of Statistics (i.e., 14 – 17, 18 – 20, 21 – 44, 45 – 59, 60 and older).

3. To test the reliability of our results, a meta-analysis of earlier studies based mainly on utilization populations was conducted. The data on or estimates of the frequency of attempted suicide were evaluated or the corresponding data calculated from the data reported to determine the absolute frequencies and the ratio of suicides to attempted suicides. A total of 14 studies were included in the analysis.

4. By evaluating the findings of direct retrospective interview studies, we tried to obtain indications of the maximum frequency of attempted suicides.

Results

The CIMH Case Register data showed that the rates for the Mannheim inhabitants who had attempted suicide and received medical treatment kept rising well into the second half of the 1970s. The highest rates were observed for males and females for the years 1976 and 1977 (the exceptions being: male adolescents aged 15 – 19 in 1979; females aged 30 – 34 in 1978). The sizes of the increases depended on the periods compared; since attempted suicides peaked in the various age groups in different years, it would have been misleading to use the same periods. For the 11-year period 1967 – 1977, an increase of some 100% was calculated for the total Mannheim population. The increase was steepest for adolescents, among whom attempted suicides peaked somewhat later. For male adolescents 15 – 19 years of age, an increase of about 340%, and for female adolescents an increase of about 140% (up to the year with the maximum value, i.e., 1977, of around 300%) were observed up to 1979. By contrast, the rates for attempted suicide for males aged 25 – 39 rose by only about 180% and for females by about 65%. The rates for over 65 year olds remained relatively stable. For the overlapping years (1978 – 1980), the CIMH Documentation contained data on almost all the patients aged 15 – 19 recorded in the Case Register. On average, 87% of the males over 20 years of age and 95% of the females

---

[2] We thank the Police Headquarters of Hamburg for making the data available to us.

of the same age groups who had attempted suicide and were recorded in the Case Register were also recorded in the CIMH Documentation. For the various age groups, no essential shortcomings in recording could be observed over the years (20–24: males 82%, females 91%; 30–34: males 92%, females 99%). Thus, the data from the CIMH Documentation provided a reliable basis for the extrapolation of the trend in attempted suicides in Mannheim, when allowance was made for the slight underestimates mentioned above. A time series calculated on the basis of both the Case Register and the Documentation data by controlling for the underestimates in the Documentation data compared with the Case Register data shows that, since 1980, attempted suicides both for males and females have decreased clearly and continuously. In 1985, the rate for attempted suicides for all males 15 years of age or older was 107/100 000 (for comparison, the 1977 peak: 139/100 000; 1976: 131/100 000) and for females of the same age groups 119/100 000 (the 1977 peak: 195/100 000; 1976: 180/100 000). Thus, in 1985, attempted suicides by males decreased to 79% and by females to 63% of the respective maximum rates for 1976/1977. The rates for males and females correlate over time: .78 (Spearman's rank correlation $P < .01$) and .87 (product-moment correlation, $P < .01$).

Especially in younger age groups, the rates for attempted suicide for males and females seem to converge somewhat, even if allowance is made for chance fluctuations. In the period 1983–1985, the rates for attempted suicide for males aged 15–19 were 232, 136, and 164/100 000 (1985: 71% of the figure for 1979) and the corresponding rates for females 306, 261, and 247/100 000 (1985: about 57% of the 1977 and 1979 maximum values). For males aged 20–24, the rates were 183, 153, and 194/100 000 (an average of 61% of the 1977 maximum value) and for females of the same age 235, 193, and 193 (an average of 43% of the 1976 maximum value). The rates for males aged 25–29 amounted to 129, 135, and 77 (1985: 36% of the 1976 maximum value) and for females of the same age to 202, 241, and 213 (1985: 62% of the 1976 maximum value and 65% of the 1977 peak); the corresponding rates for males aged 30–34 were 144, 105, and 113 (1985: 38% of the 1976 maximum value) and for females 228, 178, and 186/100 000 (1985: 59% of the 1978 maximum value). Thus, on average, the 1985 rates in the various age groups amounted to only one-third to two-thirds of the maximum rates in the 1970s.

In Munich, too, the rates for attempted suicide peaked in the years 1976–1978: for males, the highest rates were observed in 1976, the second highest in 1978, and the third highest in 1977. For females, the highest rates were obtained for 1977 and the next highest for 1976 and 1975. After these peaks, the rates for attempted suicide declined continuously. In 1985, the rate for attempted suicides for males 15 years of age and older fell to 56% and that for females to 53% of the maximum rates in the 1970s. The male and female trends were almost identical: rank correlation .91 ($P < .01$; product-moment coefficient of correlation .96, $P < .01$).

In Munich, too, considering the various age groups, the largest decrease occurred in the youngest age groups. In 1985, the rates for males aged 15–19 amounted to 39% and those for females of the same age to 53% of the 1977 and 1978 maximum values. For males aged 20–24, the rates for 1985 decreased to

63% of the 1976 maximum value, for females of the same age to 45% of the 1977 peak, for males aged 25−29 to 44% of the 1978 peak, and for females of the same age to 47% of the 1977 peak. If the reliability of this trend is tested by calculating the percentage of admissions with attempted suicide among total admissions, the same results are obtained: the percentage of admissions with attempted suicide, among the total admissions to the Municipal Hospital in Munich-Schwabing peaked for females in 1976 and for males in 1982 (19%; 1977: 18%).

A similar picture also emerges from the data obtained at another level in a different city, i.e., from the statistics of the Hamburg police. The rates for attempted suicide peaked in the years 1974−1978 (almost identical rates for males in the years 1974 and 1976; the highest rate for females in 1976). Thereafter, the rates have fallen clearly. In 1985, the rate for males aged 14 and over (115/100000) amounted to 47% of the maximum rates (1974: 248/100000; 1976: 244/100000) and for females of the same age (128/100000) to 41% of the maximum value (1976: 309/100000). In the city-state of Hamburg, too, the steepest fall has occurred in the youngest age groups: in 1985, the rate for male adolescents 14−20 years of age amounted to 25% of the 1974 peak and that for females of the same age to 33% of the 1977 and 1976 peaks. For males aged 21−44, the 1985 rate amounted to only 66% of the 1979 peak and for females of the same age group to 52% of the 1976 peak. In Hamburg, too, the trends for both sexes were almost identical: rank correlation .97 ($P<.01$; product-moment coefficient of correlation .93, $P<.01$).

The Darmstadt data yielded similar results, although only absolute numbers for admissions with attempted suicides could be used. The values peaked in 1979 (for males and females). Thereafter, the admission figures show a clear fall. Contrary to the other cities, high admission figures, similar to those for 1979, were observed for earlier years, too (e.g., 1972).

Table 1 depicts the estimated rates for attempted suicide for various age groups in 1985 and the estimated ratios of suicides to attempted suicides calculated on the basis of these rates and the suicide statistics of the Federal Bureau of Statistics. Figure 1 depicts the trends in rates for attempted suicide in the three cities.

The trends for the various age groups in the three cities are fairly similar: the rates for attempted suicide peaked in the years 1975−1979. The only exceptions were male adolescents aged 15−19 and adult males aged 25−29 in Mannheim, who showed further peaks in 1983 and 1982.

If the trends in rates for attempted suicide in the three cities are compared for years for which data for all three cities are available, for Mannheim and Munich a rank correlation coefficient of .52 ($P<.10$; product-moment coefficient of correlation .62, $P<.05$) is obtained for males, the corresponding figures for females being .94 (PM .90; $P<.01$, respectively). The agreement between Mannheim and Munich is .11 (PM .23) for males and .44 (PM .51, $P<.10$) for females. For Hamburg and Munich, a rank correlation coefficient of .58 ($P<.05$; product-moment correlation: .64, $P<.05$) is obtained for males and .57 (PM .69, $P<.05$, respectively) for females. As a whole, for the various time series of the rates of attempted suicide, a mean rank coefficient of .61

Table 1. Ratio of rates for suicide and attempted suicide in 1985: based on data from three sources (with differences in recording)

Age group	Suicide figures FRG	Rates for attempted suicide in			Ratio suicide/attempted suicide		
		Mannheim	Munich	Hamburg	Mannheim	Munich	Hamburg
Males							
15–19	13.65	163.93	64.42	105.68[a]	12.01	4.72	7.74
20–24	25.25	193.90	105.32		7.68	4.17	
25–29	29.36	76.60	50.78		2.61	1.73	
30–34	29.47	113.43	46.33		3.85	1.57	5.58
35–39	26.79	134.31	48.00	163.32[b]	5.01	1.79	
40–44	36.95	120.19	40.03		3.25	1.08	
45–49	40.03	44.60	23.98		1.11	0.60	
50–54	40.73	60.46	22.67	80.57	1.48	0.56	2.07
55–59	35.20	71.79	28.95		2.04	0.82	
60–64	37.61	63.04	26.86		1.68	0.71	
65–69	41.87	49.52	21.99		1.18	0.53	
70–74	57.56	82.10	24.58	51.72	1.43	0.43	0.94
75+	79.34	102.47	37.16		1.29	0.47	
15+	34.80	106.55	44.89	114.54	3.06	1.29	3.29
Females							
15–19	4.21	247.13	197.82	176.78[a]	58.70	46.99	41.99
20–24	6.34	139.38	149.33		21.98	23.55	
25–29	7.98	214.38	116.00		26.86	14.54	
30–34	9.82	187.10	129.36		19.04	13.17	21.02
35–39	10.42	163.70	88.43	199.03[b]	15.71	8.49	
40–44	14.05	166.10	72.71		11.82	5.18	
45–49	14.85	129.88	59.46		8.75	4.00	
50–54	18.57	146.76	68.23	111.47	7.90	3.67	6.58
55–59	17.93	44.03	41.39		2.46	2.31	
60–64	18.70	41.36	42.75		2.21	2.29	
65–69	23.28	53.03	23.53	45.87	2.28	1.01	1.98
70–74	25.86	45.60	45.58		1.76	1.76	
75+	24.53	–	21.52		–	0.88	
15+	14.69	118.86	81.95	127.86	8.09	5.58	8.70

[a] Hamburg: 14–20 years.
[b] Hamburg: 21–44 years.

(PM .65, $P < .05$, respectively) was calculated. The trends for males are less similar (mean rank correlation coefficient .42, not significant; mean product-moment coefficient of correlation .52, $P < .10$) than those for females (mean rank correlation coefficient and product-moment coefficient of correlation .74, $P < .05$).

The meta-analysis of earlier studies, conducted to test the reliability of our results, showed that the lowest rates are obtained on the basis of police statistics (cf. Lungershausen 1966), whereas estimates on the basis of data from sample interviews (Stork 1969, 1972a, b; Schmidtke 1979; Schmidtke and Rimpau 1979; Müller 1978; Döbert and Nunner-Winkler 1984) consistently yield

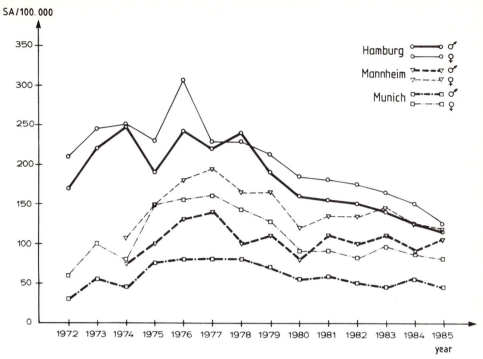

SA/100.000

Fig. 1. Trends in suicide attempts in three German cities. *Bold face*, men; *light print*, women; *circles*, Hamburg; *triangles*, Mannheim; *squares*, Munich

the highest ratios. In estimating rates on the basis of data from sample interviews, the time periods asked about were taken into account whenever possible [e.g., in estimates on the basis of the data from Schmidtke and Rimpau (1979) and Schmidtke (1979)]. Unfortunately, the publications of Stork, Müller, and Döbert and Nunner-Winkler do not contain the corresponding information necessary to convert the figures into rates per time period.

If the data from studies of service utilization and police statistics are taken together and the ratio of suicides to attempted suicides calculated, an average ratio of the frequencies of about 1:12 is obtained for males up to 20 years of age. The range of ratios extends from 1:0.8 to 1:63. The majority of studies have yielded higher relative frequencies of attempted suicide for female adolescents. At about 1:39, the average ratio is three times higher than the equivalent ratio for male adolescents, with the range of ratios extending from 1:4 to 1:165.

The estimated ratios of suicide to attempted suicide for adolescents (in several studies, it remains unclear on which basis these were calculated) reported by various authors vary around 1:10 for males and around 1:30 for females. The overall ratio of suicides to attempted suicides for both sexes has frequently been estimated at 1:7 (e.g., Welz 1980), although this is discrepant from the estimated sex-specific ratios.

A detailed analysis of the data from the CIMH Scientific Documentation showed that the rates can be marred by distortions due to multiple admissions of one and the same person because of repeated suicide attempts during 1 year. In 1978, the case rate, i.e., the percentage of patients vs. the total of treatment episodes for attempted suicide, was about 82.2%; in 1985, it fell to 70.4%. The percentage of patients with two or more treatment episodes for attempted suicide during 1 year rose from 4.9% in 1978 to 9.5% in 1985. This means that the proportion of single suicide attempts and thus presumably also that of less serious suicidal acts is decreasing, whereas the proportion of repeated suicide attempts and thus presumably that of "more severely ill" patients is experiencing a slight relative increase.

Discussion

The evaluation of the data at two levels and the meta-analysis of earlier studies showed that attempted suicides among children are very rare. Contrary to suicides, as demonstrated in several studies, the female sex predominates among suicide attempters over 15 years of age. The proportion of females with suicide attempts is especially high in the age group 14−20, as the majority of authors stress. The ratio of suicides to attempted suicides calculated in the present study shows that the estimate of 1:10 in the report of the Federal Commission on Psychiatry is fairly realistic and that great sex- and age-group-specific differences (males: about 1:3, females: 1:8/9) have to be taken into account. The estimate of the Federal Commission for adolescents is certainly too low, as shown by our calculations and the results of the sample interviews by Stork (1969, 1972a, b), Schmidtke (1979), and Döbert and Nunner-Winkler (1984). In the last two studies, 12% of the adolescents aged 14−22 recalled having attempted suicide in the past (this, however, was reported without any specification of the seriousness of the acts and the time periods concerned). The ratios yielded by utilization and interview studies conducted in other countries are also considerably higher. In the majority of the studies, they range between 1:50 and 1:120 for males and females (in some cases 1:200). These studies also report still higher ratios for attempted suicides for female adolescents (for a review, see Schmidtke 1984). Some authors suppose the actual difference to be even higher, when less severe and thus unrecorded suicide attempts by female adolescents are taken into account. According to the findings of Stork (1971, 1972), it should also be considered that the fewer suicide attempts committed in adolescence that are stated, the more remote the time periods asked about will be from the interview.

Given the sex-specific differences revealed by utilization and interview data and the frequency rates based on more recent documentation data, it should be tested in further studies whether there are true differences in the absolute frequencies of attempted suicides (and in the relative frequencies based on age groups) between female and male adolescents. According to the studies by Stork (1972a, b), Schmidtke (1979), and Schmidtke and Rimpau (1979), the rates for attempted suicide estimated on the basis of interview data for male and female adolescents differ less than those based on utilization data. It was therefore sometimes argued in the past that there are no true sex-specific differences in rates for attempted suicide in childhood and adolescence (e.g., Schneider 1954). The differences calculated on the basis of utilization data might be explainable by differences in help-seeking or referral strategies.

The trend analyses show that in the period 1966–1978 the rates for attempted suicide, especially among young people, increased clearly, and the difference between them and the suicide rates grew. On the basis of the documentation data on all Mannheim inhabitants who had attempted suicide and received medical treatment, an increase of about 100% (cf. also Welz 1979; Häfner 1985b) was calculated for the 11-year period 1967–1977. An age-specific analysis of the data showed that the steepest increase in the rates for attempted suicide occurred among adolescents, whereas the rates for ages 65 and over remained stable. From 1979 onward, the rates declined clearly for all age groups. These trends were confirmed by the Munich and Hamburg data relatively concurrently, although they were obtained from totally different sources. Our findings are also in conformity with the trends recently reported for other countries (Wexler et al. 1978; Bille-Brahe and Juel-Nielsen 1986).

An evaluation of the data specifically with regard to possible changes in the composition of the population of suicide attempters showed that the hypothesis of a relative increase in multiple suicide attempts seems to be tenable (Häfner 1985b). Provided it is not associated with a decrease in nonrepeated and less serious suicide attempts, the finding confirms earlier British studies reporting increases in repeated suicide attempts, particularly among women (Farmer 1979; Kreitman and Schreiber 1979; Kreitman 1980).

To explain the temporal increases in attempted suicides, various hypotheses have been put forward (Schmidtke 1981; Remschmidt 1982; Häfner 1985a, b). A method artifact has been supposed, especially among children and adolescents, in the sense that the reinforced provision of specialist inpatient care and psychological counseling might have led to an apparent increase (e.g., Nissen 1973). This has already been questioned by Ott (1974), who assumed that adolescents might more frequently be spared a referral to psychiatric treatment. Brickenstein (1972) attributed the "steep" increase in attempted suicides in the German Federal Armed Forces to improved recording of such cases and decreased resistance against recording. Now the rates for attempted suicide in the Armed Forces have declined again, simultaneously with those for the general population (Heuser and Scherer 1984). This indicates true changes in the frequency of attempted suicides rather than supporting the plausibility of Brickenstein's assumption.

The fluctuations, especially in younger age groups, might be attributable to a higher susceptibility to contemporary environmental factors. Häfner (1985b) assumes that attempted suicides, particularly those committed with a lower seriousness of intent by younger people, who are more susceptible to behavioral patterns and values determined by the Zeitgeist, might to a greater extent be influenced by short-lived cultural trends in both directions – in the sense of increase and decrease – than more serious suicidal behavior in higher age groups. In this context, it would be interesting to study cohort effects, for example, the question of whether people of certain birth years characterized by an elevated frequency of attempted suicides show a higher frequency of suicides at a higher age.

Acknowledgement. We thank Mrs. A. Komulainen-Tremmel, CIMH, for translating the manuscript.

References

Berman AL, Cohen-Sandler R (1982) Childhood and adolescent suicide research: a critique. Crisis 3:3−15

Bille-Brahe U, Juel-Nielsen N (1986) Trends in attempted suicide in Denmark, 1976−1980. Suicide Life Threat Behav 16:46−55

Brickenstein R (1972) Suicidprävention in der Bundeswehr. Nervenarzt 43:211−216

Dahm K, Händel K (1970) Untersuchungen über Selbstmorde und Selbstmordversuche in einem ländlichen Bevölkerungsgebiet. Mater Med Nordmark 63

Deutscher Bundestag (1975) Bericht über die Lage der Psychiatrie in der Bundesrepublik Deutschland − Zur psychiatrischen und psychotherapeutisch/psychosomatischen Versorgung der Bevölkerung. Drs 7/4200, 7/4201, Bonn

Döbert R, Nunner-Winkler G (1984) Die Bewältigung von Selbstmordimpulsen im Jugendalter. Motiv-Verstehen als Dimension der Ichentwicklung. In: Edelstein W, Habermas J (eds) Soziale Interaktion und soziales Verstehen. Suhrkamp, Frankfurt, pp 348−380

Farmer RTD (1979) The differences between those who repeat and those who do not. In: Farmer RTD, Hirsch SR (eds) The suicide syndrom. Croom Helm, London, pp 187−193

Farmer RTD, Rohde JR (1980) Effect of availability and acceptability of lethal instruments on suicide mortality. Acta Psychiatr Scand 62:436−446

Häfner H (1985a) Sind psychische Erkrankungen häufiger geworden? Nervenarzt 56:120−133

Häfner H (1985b) Are mental disorders increasing over time? Psychopathology 18:66−81

Häfner H, Schmidtke A (1987) Suizid und Suizidversuche. Epidemiologie und Ätiologie. Nervenheilkunde 6:49−63

Häfner H, Welz R (1980) Attempted suicide − a contagious behaviour? Presented at the World Psychiatric Association Regional symposium, 18−21 May, Hong-Kong

Haim A (1970) Adolescent suicide. International University Press, New York

Heuser M, Scherer J (1984) Prävention von Suizid und Suizidalität in der Bundeswehr. In: Rudolf GAE, Tölle R (eds) Prävention in der Psychiatrie. Springer, Berlin Heidelberg, New York, pp 81−83

Holinger PC, Offer D (1981) Perspectives on suicide in adolescence. Res Commun Ment Health 2:139−157

Jones DIR (1977) Self poisoning with drugs: the past 20 years in Sheffield. Br Med J 1:28−29

Kockott G, Heyse H, Feuerlein W (1970) Der Selbstmordversuch durch Intoxikation. Biometrische Untersuchungen an 100 Patienten. Fortschr Neurol Psychiatr 38:441−465

Kreitman N (1980) Die Epidemiologie von Suizid und Parasuizid. Nervenarzt 51:131−138

Kreitman N, Schreiber M (1979) Parasuicide in young Edinburgh women: 1968−1975. In: Farmer R, Hirsch S (eds) The suicide syndrom. Croom Helm, London, pp 54−72

Krienke EG, Mühlendahl KE von (1980) Vergiftungen im Kindesalter. Enke, Stuttgart

Lester D (1979) Sex differences in suicidal behavior. In: Gomberg ES, Franks V (eds) Gender and disordered behavior: Sex differences in psychopathology. Brunner/Mazel, New York, pp 287−300

Lungershausen E (1966) Suizide und Suizidversuche bei Schülern. Z Präventivmed 11:414−433

Moll H, al Faraidy A (1978) Zur Epidemiologie kindlicher Vergiftungen. Öff Gesundheitswes 40:757−762

Müller H (1978) Suizidalität und Suizidprophylaxe bei Kindern und Jugendlichen. Kinderarzt 9:1168−1174

Neuringer C (1982) Suicidal behavior in women. Crisis 3:41−49
Neuringer C, Lettieri D (1982) Suicidal woman. Their thinking and feeling patterns. Gardner, New York
Nissen G (1973) Depressionen und Suizidalität in der Pubertät. Zeitschrift für Allgemeinmedizin 49:435−439
Ott B (1974) Reaktive Selbstmordversuche bei Erwachsenen und Jugendlichen. Med Welt 25:1545−1548
Radmayr E (1980) Zur Suizidproblematik in Vorarlberg. Wien Klin Wochenschr 92:1−6
Remschmidt H (1982) Suizidhandlungen im Kindes- und Jugendalter − Therapie und Prävention. Prax Kinderpsychol Kinderpsychiatr 31:35−40
Remschmidt H, Schwab T (1978) Suizidversuche im Kindes- und Jugendalter. Acta Paedopsychiatr 43:197−208
Schmidtke A (1979) Dimensionierung von Fragebogen zur Erfassung der Suizidalität bei Jugendlichen. Report no 8, Otto-Selz-Institut für Psychologie und Erziehungswissenschaft, Mannheim
Schmidtke A (1981) Entwicklung der Häufigkeit suizidaler Handlungen im Kindes- und Jugendalter in der Bundesrepublik Deutschland. Kinderarzt 12:697−714
Schmidtke A (1984) Zur Entwicklung der Häufigkeit suizidaler Handlungen im Kindes- und Jugendalter in der Bundesrepublik Deutschland 1950−1981. Suizidprophylaxe 11:45−79
Schmidtke A, Häfner H (1985) Suizide und Suizidversuche. Epidemiologie in der Bundesrepublik Deutschland. Münch Med Wochenschr 127:828−832
Schmidtke A, Häfner H (1986) Suizide und Suizidversuche im Kindes- und Jugendalter in der Bundesrepublik Deutschland: Häufigkeiten und Trends. In: Specht F, Schmidtke A (eds) Selbstmordhandlungen bei Kindern und Jugendlichen. Roderer, Regensburg, pp 27−49
Schmidtke A, Rimpau K (1979) Persönlichkeit und Suizidrisiko bei körperbehinderten Jugendlichen. In: Müller-Küppers M, Specht F (eds) Recht, Behörde und Kind. Huber, Bern, pp 297−303
Schmitz G (1980) Selbstmord als Problemlösung. Der praktische Arzt 17:2082−2094
Schneider PB (1954) La tentative de suicide. Delachaux et Niestle, Paris
Specht F (1976) Auswirkungen früherer Beziehungsstörungen in der Adoleszenz. Prax Psychother 21:197−205
Stengel E (1964) Suicide and attempted suicide. Penguin Books, Baltimore
Stork J (1969) Vorläufige Ergebnisse eines Fragebogens über das Suizidverhalten von Adoleszenten. Mater Med Nordmark 21:523−528
Stork J (1971) Suizidverhalten und depressiver Zustand bei Adoleszenten. In: Annell AL (ed) Depressionszustände bei Kindern und Jugendlichen. Almquist and Wiksell, Stockholm, pp 340−348
Stork J (1972a) Suizidtendenz und Suizidversuch. Statistische Analyse des suizidalen Feldes bei Schülern. Z Klin Psychol Psychother 20:123−151
Stork J (1972b) Fragebogentest zur Beurteilung der Suizidgefahr. Müller, Salzburg
Stork J (1977) Das suizidale Feld. Schweiz Arch Neurol Neurochir Psychiatr 120:283−296
Wedler HL (1984) Der Suizidpatient im Allgemeinkrankenhaus. Krisenintervention und psychosoziale Betreuung von Suizidpatienten, vol 29. Enke, Stuttgart
Welz R (1978) Gesellschaftliche Einflußgrößen auf die Selbstmordhandlung. In: Pohlmeier H (eds) Selbstmordverhütung. Anmaßung oder Verpflichtung. Keil, Bonn, pp 51−78
Welz R (1979) Selbstmordversuche in städtischen Lebenswelten. Beltz, Weinheim
Welz R (1980) Selbstmorde und Selbstmordversuche nehmen zu. Betrifft Erziehung 13:26−27
Welz R (1984) Epidemiologie der Suizidalität. Med Welt 35:1163−1168
Welz R (1986) Epidemiologische Aspekte von Suizid und Suizidversuch. Dtsch Krankenpflegeschrift 4:222−225
Wexler L, Weissmann MM, Kasl SV (1978) Suicide attempts 1970−1975: updating a United States study and comparisons with international trends. Br J Psychiatr 132:180−185
Whitehead PC, Johnson FG, Ferrence R (1972) Measuring the incidence of self injury: some methodological and design considerations. In: Litman RE (ed) Proceedings of the 6th international conference for suicide prevention. Edwards, Ann Arbor, pp 274−284

Estimation of Suicidal Behavior in Representative Epidemiologic Studies

D. KORCZAK

Estimation Procedures

There is no single, "true" approach for the estimation of the incidence and prevalence of suicidal behavior. In this respect, empirical suicide research does not differ from other psychosocially related epidemiologic research such as drug, tobacco, alcohol, or psychiatric disease research.

The main empirical information sources for the estimation of suicides, parasuicides, and suicidal attempts in the Federal Republic of Germany are the following:

1. Official statistics
2. Expert ratings
3. Case studies in treatment centers
4. Case registers
5. Socioecological approaches
6. Surveys without probability samples
7. Representative surveys

I will briefly discuss the first five methods and then concentrate on the survey technique.

Official Statistics

The Statistical Office of the Federal Republic of Germany annually publishes suicide figures. In 1983, there were 13075 suicides, i.e., 21.3 per 100000. In the age group of 15−45 years, suicides are the second most frequent cause of death (Statistisches Bundesamt 1985). There is one large advantage of the data from the Federal Statistical Office: they are continuously compiled. Besides this, however, the reliability and validity of these data are under considerable discussion. It is unknown how many people succeed in arranging their suicide as a "normal" death. It has never been analyzed whether the registration facilities and responsibilities in a computerized society have led to a − statistically − higher incidence of suicides, thus explaining the slight increase of the suicide ratio. This and the huge number of unreported and undetected cases make the incidence and prevalence figures of the Federal Statistics Office of questionable value.

Expert Ratings

Expert ratings are mainly used for the estimation of parasuicide and suicide attempts. The ratio of suicides to parasuicides and suicide attempts is also under debate. Up to now, it seems to be appropriate to expect a rate of parasuicides and suicidal attempts ten times higher than suicides. Furthermore, it seems to be accepted that 20% − 25% of all suicide attempts are repeated, and each second or third repetition leads to death. Expert ratings are inherently subjective, but they are always necessary and helpful for evaluation and can provide valuable insights into taboo zones of society.

Case Studies in Treatment Centers

Most of the knowledge about suicides has its origin in case studies. In the Federal Republic of Germany, nearly all treatment institutions and hospital departments which have specific skills for the treatment of suicidal persons publish their findings and experiences. Yet, the reliability and validity of these data are limited because one finds only a selected group of patients in these treatment centers. Again, the parasuicides, the undetected suicides, and the suicide attempters provided with help by friends are not covered by case or event studies. Even if nevertheless the qualitative cognition covers the suicidal problem, it is not possible to estimate reliably the incidence and prevalence for suicidal persons in toto. Hospital and treatment admissions are small in comparison with the overall number of suicides.

Case Registers

Generally speaking, case registers enable the scientist to acquire a better understanding of the suicidal person. This is a result of the data collection process of case registers. Besides their own information, they use numerous additional sources, such as hospital and counseling data, family doctors, or police information.

Still, the limitations are the same as mentioned for case studies. Another limitation that may be pointed out is that case registers depend heavily upon the accuracy and completeness of data reported on individual cases from different sources. Additionally, there is a growing consciousness within the public mind, which is reflected in the legislation regarding data protection in case registers. Due to the implications of data protection, it is nearly impossible to compile case registers in the Federal Republic of Germany.

Socioecological Approach

The socioecological approach follows the tradition of Durkheim (1973; first published in 1897). The general hypothesis is that social disintegration highly correlates with the suicide rate. The empirical subjects of such analysis are city districts. They are compared with each other with regard to their suicide rates. The explanation of different suicide rates is usually based on district-related sociodemographic variables. The categories Welz (1979) found for social disintegration in Mannheim were, e.g., "one-person households", "divorced", "incomplete families", "single women financially responsible for other persons", and "anonymity of living condictions." Braucht (1979) analyzed different neighborhood clusters. He found specifications of suicidal behavior depending on the different neighborhood clusters: "poor minority," "isolated elderly," "destitute male," and "rootless renter." His analysis is another step forward in the socioecological approach because he tried to include individual characteristics. The limited possibilities of taking into consideration all relevant variables when working with aggregate data appears to be the main restriction of the socioecological approach. It is difficult to avoid the error which is known as the ecological logical mistake (Scheuch 1969). That means variables which could be of great importance for the occurrence of suicidal behavior (e.g., continuous noise in the landing path of airplanes) are not covered.

Survey Technique

Epidemiologic field surveys are especially appropriate for the estimation of suicidal behavior and the prevalence of suicidal attempts. The necessary information can be gained by anonymous techniques (e.g., mailed questionnaires), a huge number of variables can be asked about, the analysis of the data can be organized on a strictly anonymous basis using multivariable analysis programs, and the respondents can be selected by a probability sample.

In the following, I present some of the available data acquired by epidemiologic surveys.

Treatment Prevalence of Suicidal Persons

There is only little information about treatment prevalence. Data indicate that between 52% and 75% of suicides have visited a general practitioner before their suicide. Möller and Werner (1979) observed that 34% of the surveyed suicides (pills) looked to physicians as possible helpers. In approximately half of those who went to the doctor because of weariness with life and in just three-quarters who went because of psychosomatic disorders, the doctors did not realize the risk of suicidal attempt. Taking into account the time of the diagnosis, the suicide risk was diagnosed more often 1 week before the suicide attempt, which means during the worsening of the suicidal crisis. Kennedy and Kreitmann (1973) noted that 26% of the suicides were exclusively treated by their family doctors. In a survey with 150 general practitioners and internists that I conducted during the first half of 1980 in Bavaria, 47% of the physicians said that they had treated on average two suicides during this period. A very rough projection of these figures for the Federal Republic of Germany indicates 63000 treated suicides just by general practitioners and internists.

Table 1. Prevalence and average number of suicide attempts

	Prevalence I−IV/1980 (%)	Average number of suicidal attempts per doctor/clinic
Bavarian GPs and internists	47	2
Indoor treatment in hospitals	42	25
Emergency room cases in hospitals	27	10
Pediatricians (1981)	52	2

Similiar percentages can be found for pediatricians. On average, they treated two suicides in 1981. A projection for the pediatricians comes to 4000 suicidal attempts treated in children and youths in 1981.

Including the indoor treatments and emergency-room cases, the projected figure of suicide attempts would reach 115000 per year for the Federal Republic of Germany. This figure does not include the undetected suicide attempts and those who are not treated by the medical professions.

Self-reported Prevalence of Suicidal Thoughts and Suicide Attempts

There are only few representative data about suicidal thoughts and attempts available in the Federal Republic of Germany.

In different representative surveys with youths aged from 12 to 24 years, we found a quite stable percentage of 16% who mentioned suicidal thoughts (lifetime prevalence). This percentage was even stable in the longitudinal perspective.

In another survey with people aged 22−34 years, 0.8% of the males and 1.7% of the females confirmed at least one suicide attempt (lifetime prevalence).

Going to the age of 30−59 years, we found frequencies from 8% to 18% for suicidal thoughts and from 2% to 5% for suicidal attempts in a representative survey.

Two facts suggest the use of simple questions such as a "suicidal thought" concerning representative epidemiologic studies. First, they can be easily included in large-scale studies, they do not demand a lot of time, space, and costs, and the refusal rate of the respondents is low (below 5%). Second, the question about suicidal thoughts obviously has a high correlation with suicidal attempts. However, for the use of a very simple question, it would be necessary to know the correlating different dimensions of suicidal behavior.

Screening Methods for Suicide Risk

Thus, both the high figures for suicidal attempts and the necessity of discovering the different dimensions demonstrate the need for preventive screening methods. This need becomes even more obvious when taking into account that suicide attempts are announced in most cases.

Table 2. Lifetime prevalence and realization of suicidal thoughts (data from representative surveys)

Bavaria 1984	Suicidal thoughts					
	Age				Male	Female
Total 16%	12−14 7%	15−17 17%	18−20 21%	21−24 16%	18−24 14%	18−24 22%

Bavaria 1984	Suicide attempt, within the last 10 years
	Age 22−34 Male: 0.8% Female, 1.7%

FRG 1984	Suicidal thoughts					
	Male			Female		
	30−39 9%	40−49 8%	50−59 8%	30−39 13%	40−49 18%	50−59 10%
	Suicide attempts					
	2%	2%	5%	5%	5%	2%

Therefore, the idea of developing screening scales seemed to suggest itself. For the United States, Brown and Sheran (1972) gave a good synopsis of the most common suicide risk scales as well as of their unsolved reliability − and validity − problems. Resnick and Kendra (1973) proved, e.g., for the suicide risk scale of Tuckman and Youngman (1963), only a very low suitability for the estimation of suicide risk. Pöldinger (1978) could not confirm a correlation between suicidal tendencies and concrete suicide scales within Beck's (1961) depression questionnaire.

Farberow (1950) has developed one of the most ambitious approaches for the determination of suicide risk. He used the Minnesota Multiphasic Personality Inventory (MMPI) test, the Hildreth Feeling and Attitude Scale, the Maslow Self-esteem Scale, and the Rosenzweig Make-a-Picture-Story test. In his own evaluation of the method of scaling, he was able to classify 79% of the suicides 2 years after the suicide (Farberow and Mackinnon 1974). However, there are critics of his evaluation (Rosen et al. 1954; Devries 1966).

Pöldinger's (1968) "risk list for the estimation of suicidal behavior" and Stork's (1972) "questionnaire for the evaluation of suicide risk" have not been validated in such a way that other authors can replicate the results (Schmidtke 1976; Kuda and Kuda-Ebert 1981).

The overall poor validity of all risk lists has stimulated the use of very simple questions. Some authors ask the respondents about suicidal ideas. Besozzi (1971) stated in a survey with Cologne students that 18% of his respondents were thinking seriously of the possibility of suicide. Situations which would finally trigger off the suicidal attempt that were mentioned included incurable disease, extreme living conditions such as war or torture, personal disaster in examinations, job, or partnership, loneliness, loss of a loved person, and despair.

Similar reasons have been listed by suicide attempters in a survey of Schmidtobreick (1980). The most important reason for the suicide attempt for 27% of the cases was: "I couldn't solve the problems with my husband/wife/friend anymore"; 24% mentioned: "I couldn't stand the loneliness/despair/anxiety any longer."

Kuda and Kuda-Ebert (1981) found a high correlation between suicide attempts in the past and suicide ideas. Suicide ideas highly correlated with depressive mood, free-floating anxiety, alcoholism as well as with lack of planning in work, drop in performance, and stress.

In my own epidemiologic work, I looked for additional information about the correlation between suicidal thoughts and suicide attempts. We counted a multiple regression for suicidal thoughts and included 64 different variables covering sociodemographic criteria, family factors, behavior and attitudes, psychosocial, psychosomatic, and personality variables. The two variables with the highest prediction value were "often depressive mood within the last 12 months" and "runaway from home at least once in the past."

We found, more or less, that the clusters of depression, family problems, addictive behavior, and psychosomatic disorders had high correlations with suicidal thoughts. The variable "broken home", which was included in the regression, did not have a predictive value.

Our data from a heterogeneous probability sample indicate that it would be possible and useful to generate simple risk scales for different suicide risk populations. The development of such scales, however, is still in its scientific infancy.

Table 3.   Multiple regression: suicide prediction

64 variables
10 240 cases
Age: 12−25 years
F = 199.7

Variables	Cumulated explained variance (%)	Beta weights
Depressive mood	6	0.13228
Runaway	10.5	0.11675
Problem drinking	12	0.09382
Anxiety	14	0.09400
Different education intended for own children	15	0.07395
Life is regarded as senseless	16	0.07723
Circulatory disorder	17	0.07971
Illegal drug experience	17	0.08319
Insomnia	18	0.07187
Bad relation to father	18	0.06713
Protest behavior	19	0.06068
Loneliness	19	0.05424

References

Beck AT, Ward CH, Mendelsohn M, Erbaught H (1961) An inventory for measuring depression. Arch Gen Psychiatry 4:561−575

Besozzi CH (1971) Soziologische Theorien und soziale Probleme. Eine Untersuchung zum Studenten-Selbstmord. Revue Européenne des Sciences Sociales 25

Braucht GN (1979) Interactional analysis of suicidal behaviour. J Consult Clin Psychol 47:653−669

Brown T, Sheran T (1972) Suicide prediction: A review. Life-Threatening Behaviour 2:67−98

Devries AG (1966) Identification of suicidal behaviour by means of the MMPI. Psychol Rep 19:415−419

Durkheim E (1973) Der Selbstmord. Luchterhand, Berlin

Farberow NL (1950) Personality patterns of suicidal mental hospital patients. Genet Psychol Monogr 42:3−79

Farberow NL, MacKinnon D (1974) A suicide prediction schedule for neuropsychiatric hospital patients. J Nerv Ment Dis 158:408−419

Kennedy P, Kreitman N (1973) An epidemiological survey of parasuicide ('attempted suicide') in general practice. Br J Psychiatry 123

Kuda M, Kuda-Ebert M (1981) Zur Vorhersage der Selbstmordgefährdung bei Studierenden und Drogenabhängigen. Huber, Bern

Lettieri DJ (1978) Drugs and suicide. Sage, Beverly Hills

Möller HJ, Werner V (1979) Betreuung suizidgefährdeter Patienten durch niedergelassene Ärzte. Münch Med Wochenschr 121:213−217

Pöldinger W (1968) Die Abschätzung der Suizidalität. Huber, Bern

Resnick JH, Kendra JM (1973) Predictive value of the 'Scale for assessing suicide risk' with hospitalized psychiatric patients. J Clin Psychol 29:187−190

Ringel R (1953) Der Selbstmord. Abschluß einer krankhaften psychischen Entwicklung. Mandrich, Vienna

Rosen A, Hales WM, Simon W (1954) Classification of suicidal patients. J Consult Clin Psychol 18:359

Scheuch EK (1969) Ökologischer Fehlschluß. In: Bernsdorf W (ed) Wörterbuch der Soziologie. Enke, Stuttgart, pp 757−758

Schmidtke A (1976) Möglichkeiten psychometrischer Verfahren bei der Abschätzung suizidalen Verhaltens Jugendlicher. Suizidprophylaxe 3:108−131

Schmidtke A, Rimpau K (1979) Persönlichkeit und Suizidrisiko bei körperbehinderten Jugendlichen. Research report no 5. of the Otto-Selz-Institut für Psychologie und Erziehungswissenschaft, Mannheim

Schmidtobreick B (1980) Suizidversuche bei Suchtkranken. In: Keup W (ed) Folgen der Sucht. Thieme, Stuttgart, pp 118−126

Statistisches Jahrbuch 1985 (1987) Statistisches Bundesamt, Stuttgart

Stork J (1972) Fragebogentest zur Beurteilung der Suizidgefahr. Müller, Salzburg

Tuckman J, Youngman WF (1963) Suicide risk among persons attempting suicide. Public Health Rep 78:585−587

Welz R (1979) Selbstmordversuche in städtischen Lebensumwelten. Beltz, Weinheim

Birth Cohort Analysis of Suicide Mortality in Sweden *

P. NORDSTRÖM and U. ÅSGÅRD

Introduction

Suicide is a major public health problem. Birth cohort analyses in Canada (Solomon and Hellon 1980), the United States (Murphy and Wetzel 1980), Australia (Goldney and Katsikitis 1983), Austria (Vutuc and Gredler 1984), Sweden (Nordström and Åsgård 1986), the Federal Republic of Germany (Häfner and Schmidtke 1985), and England and Wales (Murphy et al. 1986) have demonstrated an increase in the risk of suicide for young people, particularly for young adult males. The reasons for this shift in the age distribution of suicide mortality remain to be explored.

The purpose of this study was to describe the birth-cohort-specific trends in suicide mortality in Sweden by age for each sex separately.

Material

All deaths by suicide committed by Swedish citizens during 1952−1981 in the age range 15−74 years were extracted from the Causes of Death Register at the National Central Bureau of Statistics and included in the study. In addition, 70% of the open verdicts were added after 1970, since such a large proportion of the uncertain suicides in Sweden are in fact probably suicides (Hörte 1983).

The suicides were grouped according to sex, year of birth, and age at death. The material was subdivided into 12 regions of 26 successive birth cohorts observed during different 5-year aging intervals (Fig. 1).

Method

Cumulative suicide incidence (CSI) (Ahlbohm and Norell 1984) was calculated for each birth cohort as the ratio of the number of suicides during a specified 5-year aging interval to the number of individuals in that birth cohort at the beginning of the observed aging span. Cumulative suicide incidence thus constitutes a statistical estimate of birth-cohort- and age-specific suicide risk.

* Financial support was given by the Swedish Society of Medical Sciences, the Swedish Medical Research Council (5454, 4545), and the Stockholm County Council.

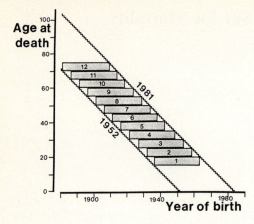

Fig. 1. The birth cohort strategy. Definition of regions

To explore and describe possible trends in suicide risk, i.e., cumulative suicide incidence by consecutive years of birth, an analysis of linear regression was performed for each region, i.e., aging span (Draper and Smith 1966).

A two-tailed t-test was applied to test the hypothesis of a significant linear trend, and relative risk (RR) was calculated as the ratio of the last to the first predicted estimate of suicide risk for each series of birth cohorts. Thereby, the relative risk is constructed as a measure of the relative change in suicide risk.

An attempt was made by means of computerized three-dimensional graphics (DISSPLA 1981) to display a comprehensive, sex-specific picture of the complex age shift in suicide mortality by year of birth.

Results

The linear regression analysis shows a significant increase in cumulative suicide incidence for females in general (Table 1), while the male increase in suicide risk is confined to those 15–49 years old (Table 2). The suicide risk among young adult males increased by a factor of 3.6. Young males are identified as a new high-risk group emerging dramatically fast in Sweden (Fig. 2).

The profound change in the suicide mortality pattern by age and year of birth is visualized for each sex separately in Figs. 3 and 4.

Discussion

This birth cohort approach to the epidemiologic study of suicide risk seems very fruitful and should be further explored in suicide research. The increasing female and young male suicide risk trend in Sweden is alarming. Further research is needed to explain the changing patterns in suicide mortality and to outline what the clinical implications of these findings might be for suicide risk evaluation and attempts to prevent suicide.

Table 1. Female suicide risk trend analysis

Females: Linear regression		Cumulative suicide incidence (/10⁵)				
Year of birth	Aging span	Mean	Slope	t	$P<$	RR
1937 – 1962	15 – 19	25	1.0	4.02	.001	2.9
1932 – 1957	20 – 24	49	1.5	6.43	.001	2.2
1927 – 1952	25 – 29	57	1.5	4.54	.001	2.0
1922 – 1947	30 – 34	67	1.9	5.40	.001	2.1
1917 – 1942	35 – 39	71	2.2	5.64	.001	2.3
1912 – 1937	40 – 44	84	1.7	5.05	.001	1.7
1907 – 1932	45 – 49	94	2.1	5.60	.001	1.8
1902 – 1927	50 – 54	102	2.5	5.45	.001	1.9
1897 – 1922	55 – 59	99	2.3	5.08	.001	1.7
1892 – 1917	60 – 64	91	1.5	3.12	.01	1.5
1887 – 1912	65 – 69	85	1.3	2.98	.01	1.5
1882 – 1907	70 – 74	69	1.3	3.18	.01	1.6

Table 2. Male suicide risk trend analysis

Males: Linear regression		Cumulative suicide incidence (/10⁵)				
Year of birth	Aging span	Mean	Slope	t	$P<$	RR
1937 – 1962	15 – 19	43	1.2	4.17	.001	2.2
1932 – 1957	20 – 24	118	5.3	12.45	.001	3.6
1927 – 1952	25 – 29	146	4.3	9.36	.001	2.2
1922 – 1947	30 – 34	162	3.9	7.74	.001	1.9
1917 – 1942	35 – 39	188	3.4	5.81	.001	1.6
1912 – 1937	40 – 44	218	4.4	5.77	.001	1.7
1907 – 1932	45 – 49	258	2.5	3.99	.001	1.3
1902 – 1927	50 – 54	265	1.0	1.53	NS	
1897 – 1922	55 – 59	260	– 0.6	0.78	NS	
1892 – 1917	60 – 64	239	– 0.3	1.87	NS	
1887 – 1912	65 – 69	227	– 0.8	2.67	NS	
1882 – 1907	70 – 74	224	– 0.5	1.52	NS	

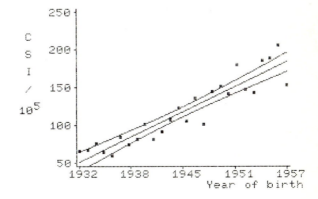

Fig. 2. Linear young adult (20 – 24 years old) male suicide risk trend with 95% confidence limits

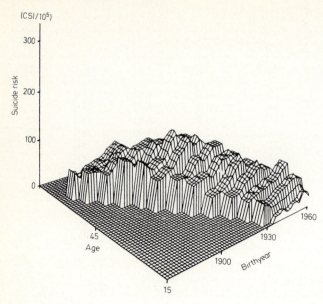

Fig. 3. Female suicide risk by age and year of birth

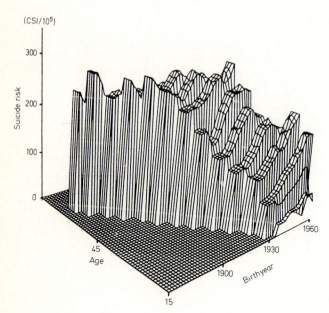

Fig. 4. Male suicide risk by age and year of birth

Acknowledgement. We want to thank Göran Råbäck at the National Central Bureau of Statistics for computerizing and compiling the data and Gunilla Sköllermo at the QZ Stockholm Computer Department for assistance with three-dimensional graphics.

References

Ahlbom A, Norell S (1984) Introduction to modern epidemiology. Epidemiology Resources, Chestnut Hill

DISSPLA (1981) Display Integrated Software System and Plotting Language, version 9.0, ISSCO, San Diego

Draper NR, Smith H (1966) Applied regression analysis. Wiley, New York

Goldney RD, Katsikitis M (1983) Cohort analysis of suicide rates in Australia. Arch Gen Psychiatry 40:71−74

Häfner H, Schmidtke A (1985) Do cohort effects influence suicide rates? Arch Gen Psychiatry 42:926−927

Hörte LG (1983) Ovisshet-ett problem i suicidstatistiken. Hygiea 92:251

Murphy E, Lendesay J, Grundy E (1986) 60 years of suicide in England and Wales. A cohort study. Arch Gen Psychiatry 43:969−976

Murphy GE, Wetzel RD (1980) Suicide risk by birth cohort in the United States 1949 to 1974. Arch Gen Psychiatry 37:519−523

Nordström P, Åsgård U (1986) Suicide risk by age and birth cohort in Sweden. Crisis 7:75−80

Solomon MI, Hellon CP (1980) Suicide and age in Alberta, Canada, 1951 to 1977. Arch Gen Psychiatry 37:511−513

Vutuc C, Gredler B (1984) Entwicklung der Selbstmord-Sterblichkeit in Österreich. Off Gesundheitswes 46:576−577

Epidemiology of Suicide Events in a Hungarian County

K. Ozsváth

National Trends in Suicide Statistics

As may be generally known, Hungary ranks fairly high in suicide rates among the European countries (Diekstra 1982). Figure 1 shows the trends in suicide indexes by sex during the present century. Since the early 1960s, there has been a steady rise in suicides, which reached a peak in 1984 when 4900 people took their own lives.

The geographical distribution of suicide in Hungary is not homogeneous. In Fig. 2, we compare the counties according to suicide rates from 1984 (upper numbers) and 1950 (lower numbers). The lines drawn through the country represent the national average suicide rates of both years. The western and northern parts are characterized by lower indexes; the counties below these lines have always had higher rates than the national average. The suicides have increased in each county, but this distribution has not changed since the beginning of registration.

The last years have witnessed dramatic trends in the incidence of suicide by region and by sex. In 1960–1964, the frequency of suicides was lower in rural districts than in the urban areas. Since 1980, the suicide rates of the villages

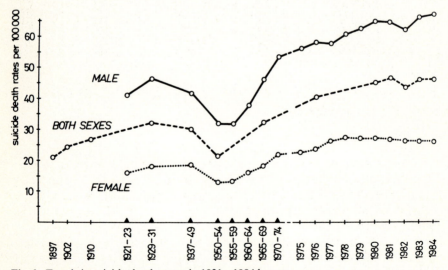

Fig. 1. Trends in suicide deaths rates in 1921–1984 by sex

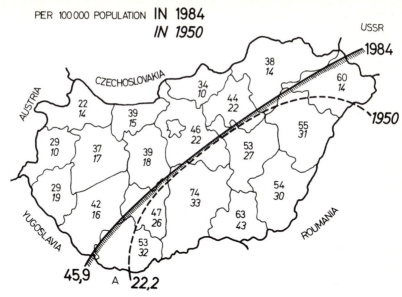

Fig. 2. Counties of Hungary with suicide death rates in 1950 and in 1984. *A,* county of Baranya

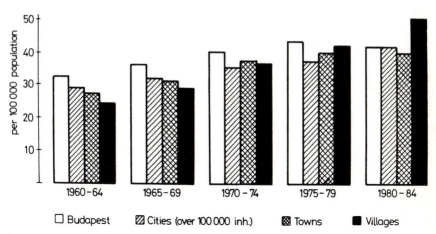

Fig. 3. Suicide death rates by residence between 1960–1984

have exceeded those of the capital and of the towns, as Fig. 3 demonstrates. Figure 4 illustrates the percentual distribution of suicides by sex in rural and urban settlements in 1975 and 1980. Female suicides were fewer in the villages than the national female average, but in the capital more women killed themselves in 1980 than men.

Suicide is the fourth greatest cause of death among adults. The mortality rates of circulatory diseases, tumors, and accidents indicate a similar increasing tendency. In the last 2 decades, a considerable increase has been observed in di-

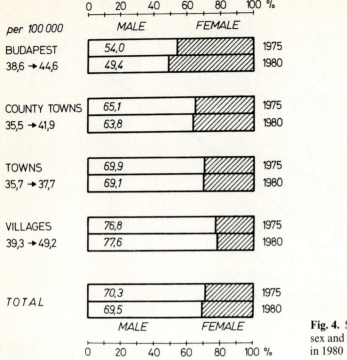

Fig. 4. Suicide death rates by sex and residence in 1975 and in 1980

verse social deviancies (alcoholism, criminality, nonorganic mental disorders). To reveal and analyze the rise in deviant behavioral forms, a multidisciplinary staff worked out the concept and the methods of the medium-term research project: Complex Analysis of Disorders in Social Adjustment in Hungary (Pataki 1986). Within the framework of this project, our study sets out to analyze all suicide events registered in the county of Baranya since 1984. Some aspects of data of the first research year are presented.

Research on Suicide Events in the County of Baranya

Goals

The aims of the study are:

1. To gather knowledge on sociodemographic and psychiatric characteristics of all attempted and committed suicides over a 5-year period to determine factors which are predictive and influence the prognosis.
2. To gather follow-up data on sociogenetic-psychodynamic processes and relationships between environmental and psychological factors which might be significant in prevention, in intervention, and in aftercare with the help of interviews of the survivors and the relatives of suicides.
3. To evaluate the effects of different psychocorrective methods.

Epidemiology

The basic demographic and suicide data of the county are shown in Table 1. The characteristics in the age-gender profile are illustrated in Fig. 5. The general trends correspond to international suicide statistics: males consistently outnumber females in deaths by suicide, and the suicide attempts are more frequent in younger age groups of both sexes, with a slight majority of girls (Kreitman 1980; Stengel 1970; Wedler 1984). The average death/attempt ratio varies from 1:40 (15−19 female age group) to 1:0.7 (male age groups over 70). This ratio between suicide and attempt is 1:4.5 in the villages and 1:6.0 in the urban areas. The percentual sex distribution of the suicide events differs in the several age groups as can bee seen in Table 2. Suicides were more frequent in the middle-aged groups of men, while in the younger and older age groups, the

Table 1. Suicidal events in the county of Baranya in 1984

	In absolute number			In %		Per 100000		
	Total	Male	Female	Male	Female	Total	Male	Female
Population over 10	370660	192448	178312	51.9	48.1			
Suicidal persons	1464[a]	661	803	61.6	38.4	395	342	450
Committed suicides	232	163	69	70.3	29.7	63	91	36
Attempted suicides	1232	498	734	40.4	59.6	332	260	411

[a] Mortality of suicidal events: 15.8%

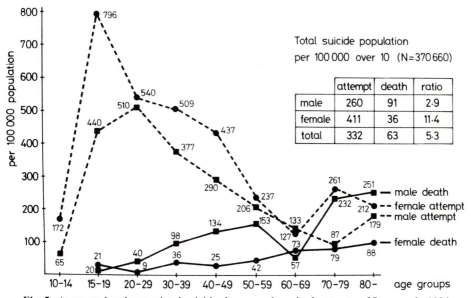

Fig. 5. Attempted and committed suicides by sex and age in the county of Baranya in 1984

Table 2. Percentual distribution of suicide and attempted suicide by sex and age in the county of Baranya in 1984

Age group	Suicide		Attempted suicide	
	Male	Female	Male	Female
10–19	50	50	35	65
20–29	82	18	50	50
30–39	73	23	49	51
40–49	85	15	38	62
50–59	76	24	45	55
60–69	48	62	44	56
70–79	64	36	17	83
80–X	58	42	30	70
10–X	70	30	40	60

male-female percentage was similar. In contrast, the percentual distribution of the attempted suicides was closer in the middle-aged groups. About 50% of suicides and attempted suicides were married, 12% divorced. More single persons attempted suicide than killed themselves: 31% and 11%, respectively. Married men, in absolute numbers, exceeded the other persons, but they had the lowest incidence of suicide per 100 000 population.

Self-destructive behavioral disorders are present in all social groups but the lower ones seem to be more affected. We found that people with a higher education and intellectuals were under-represented in both suicide samples in relation to their distribution in the county population. Except for age and sex, both suicide types were characterized nearly equally by low socioeconomic status and low levels of education.

Pathological Findings

Based on autopsies of the suicides, it is worthwhile emphasizing here that very early arteriosclerosis was found in both sexes and that this alteration was more frequent among the suicides than in a matched sample of people who died in accidents (Harsányi 1986).

Care of Suicidal Patients

The first medical contact with the health system of those people who attempted suicide was in psychiatric wards for 75%, while 25% were treated in intensive care units or general wards (Fig. 6). After somatic treatment, 65% were discharged without any psychotherapeutic intervention; 35% were referred to psychiatric outpatient care, but only 10% of the whole survivor population accepted the help offered.

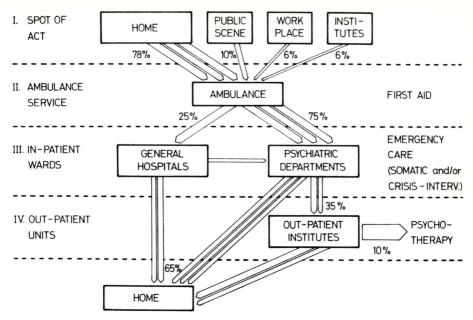

Fig. 6. Phases in suicide care in the county of Baranya in 1984

Evaluation of In-depth Interviews

Endogenous and organic pathology played a small role in the suicidal population, whereas a strong indication existed for pathodynamic personality traits. A great number of suicidal persons were not aware of their self-destructive psychodynamic mechanism.

The common denominator of various forms of suicidal behavior might be a psychic vulnerability, labile self-esteem, and low frustration tolerance. The epidemiologic and psychodynamic figures suggest some overlapping between groups of the survivors and suicides. Suicidal acts have a great deal in common. For us, it seemed to be reasonable to apply the concept of suicidal behavior (Beskow 1983).

In about one-half of the suicidal population, one or more previous suicide attempts came to light during the in-depth interviews with suicides' relatives. Nearly 10% of the suicidal population repeated the attempt in the same year. Immediately prior to their fatal acts, 75% of the actual suicides had been in contact with different medical facilities. The psychocorrective management of suicidal persons has not been accomplished within the framework of the medical care system. The prevalence of suicide attempts can be estimated in the population at about 1%. We found about 20% − 30% mutual overlapping among the different behavior forms.

Discussion

Suicide problems are highly individual in nature. The term "suicide" is not equivalent to that of a mental patient, but they cannot be considered without reserve as psychologically healthy persons. Rather than being a sign of a desire to die, in most cases it is an indication that the person concerned is trying to get rid of some difficult life situation (Achté 1976). Suicide and suicide attempts are not pathognomic of any specific nosologic entity (Mintz 1972). From the psychiatric point of view, suicidal behavior can be considered as a chronic personality development disorder in which the pivotal symptom is the (unconscious) self-destructive tendency; it begins in early childhood and progresses with more or less fatal tendencies. Because suicidal impulses tend to occur under conditions experienced by the person as extremely stressful and because of his internal struggle to resist carrying out these impulses, many patients undergo a regressive reaction at such a time: the mode of thinking may be transformed into a childlike magical one which is drive dominated and supplants normal adult reality (Reimer 1982). For those patients with suicide problems, the narcissistic theory (Kernberg 1979; Henseler and Reimer 1981) seems to be a new and promising approach to suicide care and prevention. All patients with suicidal ideas represent an emergency situation and an urgent therapeutic problem (Lesse 1981), paralleling other types of medical and surgical crises.

It is a fact that, in Hungary, the steady changes since the 1950s in social modernization from an earlier immobile semifeudal social system have had an impact on suicide statistics and on the increasing number of other deviant behavior types. There is also the problem of integration into new cultures, demanding the development of mechanisms for coping with new situations under conditions where the social forces responsible for individual identity have not been effective enough to fortify this personal identity. Indirectly, it might be connected with changes in the female role. Probably the main effect of industrialization is the break-up of the traditional family system: more and more nuclear families came into existence, and more and more women began to work.

Conclusions

On the basis of the first experiences with suicide research in the county of Baranya, the conclusion can be drawn that there is neither a typical suicidal personality nor a life situation in which suicide is the typical reaction. People with unstable self-esteem and with insufficient social relationships respond to the stresses of modern society with self-destructive behavior: one possible form is the suicide act.

References

Achté K (1976) On some psychodynamic mechanism associated with suicide. Psychiatr Fennica [Suppl]: 101 − 109

Beskow J (1983) Longitudinal and transsectional perspectives of suicidal behaviour. Psychiatr Fennica [Suppl]: 55 − 64

Diekstra RFW (1982) Epidemiology of attempted suicide in the EEC. In: Berner P (ed) Bibliotheca psychiatrica, no 162. Karger, Basel, pp 1 − 16

Harsányi L (1986) Research report on suicide in Pécs. In: Kolozsi B, Münnich I (eds) Complex analysis of disorders in social adjustment, Bull VII. Institute of Social Science, Budapest, pp 37 − 52 (in Hungarian)

Henseler H, Reimer C (eds) (1981) Selbstmordgefährdung. Froman-Holzboog, Stuttgart

Kernberg O (1979) Borderline-Störungen und pathologischer Narzißmus. Suhrkamp, Frankfurt/Main

Kreitman N (1980) Die Epidemiologie von Suizid und Parasuizid. Nervenarzt 51: 131 − 142

Lesse S (1981) Principles and techniques in treatment of suicidal patients. Psychiatr Fennica 11: 53 − 68

Mintz RS (1972) Psychotherapy of the suicidal patient. In: Resnik HLP (ed) Suicidal behaviors. Little Brown, Boston, pp 271 − 296

Pataki F (1986) A társadalmi beilleszkedési zavarok Magyarországon (Social maladjustments in Hungary). Kossuth, Budapest

Reimer C (1982) Suizid. Springer, Berlin Heidelberg New York

Stengel E (1970) Suicide and attempted suicide. Penguin, London

Wedler HL (1984) Der Suizidpatient im Allgemeinkrankenhaus. Enke, Stuttgart

Psychiatric Aspects of Suicide in Budapest

E. Demeter, M. Arató, Z. Rihmer, P. Sótonyi, G. Szuchovsky, and E. Somogyi

Introduction

The large differences across nations and changes over time of suicide rates are puzzling phenomena for suicide research. Hungary, with the highest suicide rate in Europe and with an increasing incidence in the last decades, may deserve special attention on this issue. One can hope that exploration of the characteristics of a population of completed suicides can give some clue to this complex problem. The recent literature on suicide research has focused mostly on psychosocial factors in Hungary (Buda 1971; Ozsváth 1986). Since Durkheim's anomic theory, it is well known that social factors may play a substantial role in suicidal behavior; however, the individual occurrence of these social anomalies is less well understood. It can be assumed that individual vulnerability may be related to psychic maladjustment due to various psychiatric diseases. Several studies have shown a strongly positive association between mental illness and completed suicide (Pokorney 1964; Noreik 1975; Tefft et al. 1977; Khuri and Akiskal 1983; Mitterauer 1985).

Subjects and Methods

We investigated 100 consecutive cases of completed suicide using the lifetime version of the Schedule for Affective Disorders and Schizophrenia (SADS) (Spitzer and Endicott 1978). Based on a semistructured standard interview with the closest family member, the suicidal victims were classified according to Research Diagnostic Criteria (RDC) if applicable.

Results

First, as basic background data, all suicides in Budapest in 1985 are briefly described with their demographic features. There were 806 completed suicides in Budapest (Table 1); their age distribution is presented in Fig. 1. The methods most often used are listed in Table 2.

A seasonal variation in suicide is a fairly well-established phenomenon (Lester 1985). The most consistent finding for suicides is a spring peak in the incidence of suicides across different countries and ages. We have found a clear peak in March only in males, as is shown in Fig. 2.

Table 1.   Completed suicides in Budapest in 1985

Males	n = 454	54/100 000
Females	n = 352	36/100 000
Total	n = 806	44/100 000

Table 2.   Most frequent methods of suicides. Cause of death in 806 suicides

	Males	Females
Hanging	41%	9%
Drug OD	29%	62%
Jumping	15%	18%
	(85%)	(89%)

There were 48 males and 52 females in the 100 consecutive cases in which a retrospective psychiatric assessment was carried out based on a standard interview with the closest family member. The age distribution was similar to the data from 1985 (see Fig. 1). The methods for suicide in these 100 cases are shown in Table 3.

The main results of the recent study are presented in Table 4. The number of the cases are given which met the RDC for probable or definite psychiatric disorders. In this latter group, two males and eight females had serious, chronic, mostly incurable, and painful somatic illness (carcinoma, apoplexy, etc.).

Regarding only the "primary" affective disorders (bipolar II, recurrent unipolar, and minor depressive disorders), a previous suicide attempt was found in

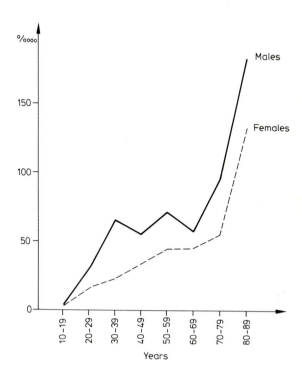

Fig. 1. Age distribution of 806 completed suicides

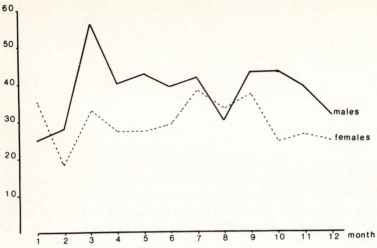

Fig. 2. Monthly numbers of suicides in 1985 ($n = 806$)

Table 3. Methods for suicides. Cause of death in 100 suicides

	Males	Females
Drug OD	19	38
Hanging	15	5
Jumping	10	9
Carbon monoxide poisoning	2	0
Cutting	1	0
Shooting	1	0
	48	52

Table 4. RDC classification of suicides

	Males	Females	Total
Bipolar II depression	14	16	30
Major depressive disorder			
Recurrent unipolar	6	4	10
Situational	2	5	7
Secondary			
Alcoholism	2	0	2
Organic brain syndrome	1	1	2
Minor depressive disorder	6	5	11
Schizophrenia	5	6	11
Schizoaffective disorder	0	1	1
Alcoholism	3	2	5
Drug use disorder	0	1	1
	39	41	80
No RDC diagnosis	9	11	20

48% of cases. A positive family history of completed suicide was reported by family members in 38% of the cases. These findings suggest that a history of suicide attempts and/or suicidal behavior in the family should be considered as a serious risk factor in suicide prediction.

Discussion

Several studies have reported a high rate of psychiatric disorders among completed suicides. The frequency of affective disorders in suicides varied from 30% to 70% in different countries, and the total percentage of psychiatric illness from 93% to 100% (Robins et al. 1959; Dorpat and Ripley 1960; Barraclough et al. 1974; Kraft and Babigian 1976; Mitterauer 1985). Our data are in keeping with the results of these studies and suggest a strong contributory role of mental illness in suicides. From a psychiatric point of view, our study population of completed suicides does not appear different from those of other countries. Our data, therefore, do not give any explanation for the very high Hungarian suicide rate. Nevertheless, these results underline the importance of psychiatric aspects of suicidal behavior and point to the role of mental health care in suicide prevention (Khuri and Akiskal 1983; Achté 1986).

References

Achté K (1986) Depression and suicide depression. Symposium of Psychiatry. University Clinic, Basel

Barraclough B, Bunch J, Nelson B, Sainsbury PA (1974) A hundred cases of suicide. Clinical aspects. Br J Psychiatry 125:355–373

Buda B (1971) Suicide. I. Social factors statistics. II. Hungarian data psychosocial trends. III. Psychological aspects. IV. Prevention (in Hungarian). Orv Hetil 112:1263–1691, 1943–2327

Dorpat TL, Ripley H (1960) A study of suicide in the Seattle area. Compr Psychiatry 1:349–359

Khuri R, Akiskal HS (1983) Suicide prevention. The necessity of treating contributory psychiatric disorders. Psychiatr Clin North Am 6:193–207

Kraft DP, Babigian HM (1976) Suicide by persons with and without psychiatric contacts. Arch Gen Psychiatry 33:209–215

Lester D (1985) Seasonal variation in suicidal death by each method. Psychol Rep 56:650

Mitterauer B (1985) Neuro- and socialpsychiatric aspects of suicide prevention (in German). Wien Med Wochenschr 135:561–568

Noreik K (1975) Attempted suicide and suicide in functional psychoses. Acta Psychiatr Scand 52:81–106

Ozsváth K (1986) Suicidal events in Baranya county in 1984 (in Hungarian). Orv Hetil 127:1179–1182

Pokorny A (1964) Suicide rates in various psychiatric disorders. J Nerv Ment Dis 139:499–506

Robins E, Murphy G, Wilkinson R Jr (1959) Some clinical considerations in the prevention of suicide based on a study of 134 successful suicides. Am J Public Health 49:888–899

Spitzer RL, Endicott J (1978) Schedule for affective disorders and schizophrenia (SADS), 3rd edn. New York State Psychiatric Institute, New York

Tefft BM, Pederson AM, Babigian HM (1977) Patterns of death among suicide attempters a psychiatric population and a general population. Arch Gen Psychiatry 34:1155–1161

Deliberate Overdosage in a Hospital Catchment Area: Preliminary Results of a 7-Year Study

J. G. HARVEY and M. S. CHRISTIAN

Introduction

In 1977, it was estimated that if the current trend in self-poisoning continued, within 10 years in England and Wales, every available emergency medical bed would be occupied by a patient admitted as a result of an overdose (Jones 1977). As it so happened, the timing of this prediction coincided with the reversal of this trend and a progressive decrease in the overall numbers. Figure 1 shows the considerable increase that occurred during the mid-1960s both in fatal and non-fatal self-poisoning. Whereas fatal self-poisoning reached a plateau after 1969, the rise in non-fatal self-poisoning continued for a further 8 years. The ratio of admissions to deaths rose from 10:1 to over 30:1, a factor which was not due to radical improvements in the treatment of overdosed patients. Since 1977, mortality has declined by 25% and admissions have decreased by over 20% according to figures published in the Hospital In-Patient Enquiry

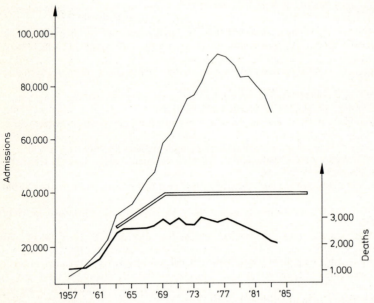

Fig. 1. Admissions to hospital compared with overall mortality after overdose in England and Wales (1957–1983)

for England and Wales. The purpose of this present survey has been to determine the extent of deliberate self-poisoning within a defined area and provide a detailed analysis of the substances taken, persons involved and the overall outcome.

Methods

The study is based on an analysis of the input of patients into an accident and emergency department of a medium-sized general hospital and the outcome within the hospital and its relation to any subsequent incidents. The population in the catchment area is about 350000. During the period of the study from 1979 to the end of 1985, some 3376 patients of 15 years and over who had overdosed presented at or were admitted through this department. In only about 5% was the overdose or ingestion of noxious substances regarded as being accidental. It was also assumed that those seen in hospital would represent the majority of self-poisoning cases in the area, seeing that almost all doctors would refer such patients directly to hospital (Frood 1980). It has been noted that 80% of overdose deaths occur without the opportunity for hospital treatment (Chambers 1976). Therefore, in order to assess overall mortality from overdose and from other forms of self-harm, coroners' records covering the same area were examined.

Incidence of Overdose

Between 1979 and 1982, the yearly totals were constant at about 500 per annum. In 1983, the numbers declined by 10% and have since remained at around 450 per annum. There appears to be no particular weekly or monthly pattern that is readily discernible, although the numbers fluctuate considerably in a range between 2 and 23 per week.

As an indication of the nature of the incident, over 50% required only preliminary treatment in the accident department before discharge, 45% were formally admitted to a medical ward and 4% required treatment in intensive care. In all, about 90% of the patients were discharged within the following 24 h. Mortality of patients admitted for treatment, excluding those who were dead on arrival, amounted to less than 1%.

Types of Person Involved

The ratio of sex and age group is set out in Fig. 2 and confirms the general finding that women are the more frequent attenders with 64% of the total (Alderson 1974). The age groups most frequently seen are the 15−19 age group for women and the 20−24 age group for men. On admission or during subsequent psychiatric assessment, details of past and current treatment, previous attempts and events related to the crisis were obtained. The results are summarised in

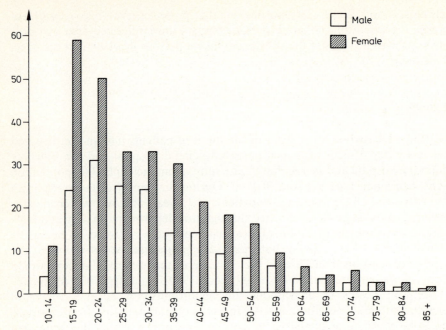

Fig. 2. Input of overdosed patients into hospital by sex and age (average per year, 1981–1985)

Table 1. Background and circumstances related to the admission of overdosed patients (average per year, 1981–1985)

Categories	Patients	Patients in each category	
	(%)	Precipitating factors (%)	Previous overdose (%)
Psychiatric history	19	35	51
Recent visit to doctor	5	61	33
Abusers	8	23	51
No definite psychiatric history	68	78	20
	100		

Table 1 and show that 19% were or had been receiving formal treatment at hospital, a further 5% were known to have recently seen their doctor and 8% had been seen as a result of an incident related to drug or alcohol abuse. The remaining 68% did not appear to have recently seen their doctor or to have had a definite psychiatric history. It is interesting to note that 51% with a psychiatric history had previously overdosed, while only 20% of the non-psychiatric group reported similar activity.

The initial interview with conscious patients at an accident department will emphasise those factors that have directly precipitated the event. In the survey,

such events were noted in 35% of the patients with definite psychiatric symptomology and in 78% of those without such symptomology. In a large proportion of the cases (94%), these factors were related to a disturbance in an in-
ter-personal relationship or a more general disturbance within a family group.
Bereavement was sometimes cited but it must be noted that financial problems
and unemployment were rarely cited (2%) as the prime reason for the incident.

Substances Involved

Information relating to substances ingested can be elicited from conscious patients, their associates, and from evidence produced by the emergency services
either directly or indirectly from the availability and disposition of packs found
at the scene. Apart from the primary history and especially in unconscious patients, blood screening can provide more definite evidence. In the event, the final summary will usually provide a fair appraisal of the entire incident including the type and quantity of substances ingested. Patients being investigated for
symptomatology which later turns out to be undisclosed overdose are fortunately rare. A problem in analysing data and also in treating a patient occurs when
two or more substances have been taken at the same time. Apart from the true
drug cocktail where innumerable undisclosed tablets have been taken it, is usually possible to ascertain the substance most likely to produce the major toxico-
logical risk. A similar problem exists with the concomitant ingestion of alcohol.
In 73% of instances, the ingestion was limited to a single substance, not including alcohol, in 19% to two substances and three or more in 8% of instances. Alcohol was definitely recorded in 37% of overdose admissions.

The types of substance are summarized in Table 2 and show that over half
the admissions were due to psychoactive medicines of which the greater ma-

Table 2. Overall percentage of substances taken by overdosed patients between 1979 and
1985

Group	Percentage of all (%)		Percentage within group (%)	Deaths overall (%)	
1. Barbiturates	3.5			15	
Phenobarbitone			47		
2. Psychoactives	53			49	
Benzodiazepine		37	70		
Antidepressants		10	19		
3. Strong analgesics	8			19	
Narcotics		1.6	21		
4. Mild analgesics	20			10	
Aspirin		8.6			5
Paracetamol		8.3			4
5. Other medicines	11.5			4	
6. Noxious substances	3			4	
With alcohol	37				

jority were benzodiazepines. Strong analgesics accounted for 8% and mild analgesics for 20% during the period. Overdoses solely attributed to aspirin and
paracetamol amounted to 16%, the proportion between the two being equal.
Other medicines were responsible for up to 12% and noxious substances for up
to 3%.

Although barbiturates were responsible for only 3.5% of admissions, they
caused 15% of the deaths that occurred in the area. Strong analgesics were responsible for 19%, aspirin 5% and paracetamol 4% of the deaths overall in the
area.

Conclusions

Comparison with the national figures and other surveys needs to take into consideration how patient input is recorded and the type of catchment area. In the
study, the overall rate of adult overdoses was 16 per 10000, which was similar to another study carried out recently (Adams 1986). Correlations using overall numbers are possible, although in the present instance a relatively small-
stepped decline does not offer much scope. Also ascribing the influence of certain events, including publicity given to incidents of self-harm, to what is essentially a random daily fluctuation, would be hard to justify. From the yearly
averages, there does not seem to be any significant variation in the numbers by
sex or age group nor do there appear to be any differences in the proportions
of psychiatric patients or those with no history.

Any interpretation of results will be determined to a greater extent by the
type of survey carried out. A cross-sectional study will illustrate the total spectrum of overdose patients that are seen at an accident department. The most numerous are those seen for the first time, probably obtaining some cathartic effect from the incident and who rarely reappear. A second group comprises
those who are subject to intermittent crises and respond by episodic overdoses.
A third group are those who continually overdose and in the study made up the
greater part of 6% of patients who repeated within a year. It was also noted that
27% of all patients attending had previously overdosed at some time or other.
To obtain a more accurate picture of outcome, some form of data linkage is essential. This is easier to accomplish in a longitudinal survey but could produce
a distortion when applied to the general situation. For instance, those who continually overdose are commonly those with personality disorders, are prone to
drug and alcohol abuse, are epileptics and are often unemployed, although with
the latter it is not clear whether this is the cause or the result.

The rise in non-fatal overdose seems to be coincident with the increasing
use and availability of psychoactive medicines, in particular the benzodiazepines. The reduction in overdose admissions has been correlated with a
reduction in overall availability of these medicines (Brewer and Farmer 1985).
However, it has also been suggested that these substances have a more causal
role with inappropriate prescribing being held directly responsible (Prescott
and Highley 1985). There does seem to be a blurring in the concept of medical
and social care with medicines being prescribed to ameliorate the effect of what

are virtually social conditions. In the survey, the proportion of psychoactive medicines slightly declined during the period, with an increase in all analgesics, other medicines and noxious substances. About 78% of the poisonings were with prescribed medicines, most of them being the patient's own prescription.

The reasons for the general decline in both fatal and non-fatal overdose are unclear. An area survey can usefully monitor trends and determine the relation of overdose to other forms of self-harm, and gauge the effect of other factors including treatment.

References

Adams RHM (1986) An accident and emergency department view of self-poisoning: a retrospective study from United Norwich Hospitals 1978–1982. Hum Toxicol 5:5–10

Alderson MR (1974) Self-poisoning – What is the future? Lancet 1:1040–1043

Brewer C, Farmer R (1985) Self-poisoning in 1984: a prediction that didn't come true. Br Med J 290:391

Chambers DR (1976) Fatal drug overdosage. J Int Med Res 4 [Suppl 4]:14–24

Frood RAW (1980) Self-poisoning: changing patterns in East Cheshire 1970–5. J R Coll Gen Pract 30:288–291

Hospital in-patient enquiry (England and Wales). Published annually by Department of Health and Social Security/Office of population censuses and surveys. H.M.S.O., London

Jones DIR (1977) Self-poisoning with drugs: the past 20 years in Sheffield. Br Med J 1:28–29

Prescott LF, Highley MS (1985) Drugs prescribed for self-poisoners. Br Med J 290:1633–1636

Self-inflicted Death (1971 – 1985): Preliminary Results of a 15-Year Survey in an Inner City Area on the Incidence and Methods Employed

D. R. CHAMBERS and J. G. HARVEY

Introduction

This survey was based on an analysis of inquest deaths in Inner North London. In this area, over 2000 deaths occurred during this period which were considered to be the result of a self- initiated incident. Of these deaths, only 38% were officially recorded as being suicidal. The study attempted to relate various factors such as sex, age, social considerations and treatment, if any. Detailed pathological evidence was also analysed especially in respect of deaths from overdosage. The overall rate of self-inflicted death has remained fairly constant at about 20 per 100 000. Similarly the sex/age ratio has not shown any marked variation during the period. Methods employed have changed to some extent with a sharp decline in town gas deaths and a steady decline in deaths from overdosage. The fact that the numbers have remained constant is due to an increase in all other methods especially in death from suspension. Reasons for changes in methods are examined, and factors which may be of use in predicting and possibly preventing unnecessary loss of life are discussed.

It is often difficult to determine actual suicidal intent in a fatal incident from reports of a person's actions and motives prior to the event. However, it is easier in most instances to determine whether an incident was entirely accidental. Research in the field of fatal self-destructive behaviour has been hindered by the inability to extract an exact figure for such non-accidental fatal injury from the statistics. Most such figures are compiled from suicide verdicts returned on the basis of moral or legal judgements and reflect only certain aspects of self-destructive behaviour. Efforts to manipulate these figures by adding other verdicts, such as the open verdict, or by reclassifying undetermined as to whether accidental or self-intended do not solve the problem.

From the examination of an extensive direct sample of all violent deaths within a circumscribed area, it should be possible to produce more accurate figures on the extent of non-accidental death which would be irrespective of the verdict given at the inquest. It should also be possible to ascertain any relative change in the type of methods used and the effect on this of social factors and changes in the relative availability or lethality of methods. More accurate information can also be obtained on the types of person, their overall social background and the effects of treatment and other conditions that are relevant (including alcohol and drugs).

Scope of the Survey

A survey has been carried out since 1971 on all inquest deaths in Inner North London. The area consists of the four London Boroughs of Camden, Islington, Hackney and Tower Hamlets with a current population of just under 700 000. Each year there are about 9000 deaths in this area, about 3000 of which are reported to the coroner. Of these, about 600 will be examined in detail under the formal inquest procedure. A post-mortem will be carried out in over 80% of those reported to the coroner and in almost all the inquest cases.

Non-accidental Death

An individual's attitude to self-destructive behaviour will determine the choice of method, that is, if such a choice exists. The verdict given by a coroner is also largely determined by the method selected by the victim.

There are not more than about 12 methods that are employed in fatal self-destructive behaviour. These can be divided into three categories depending on the procedure and effects of the act producing self-harm. They are:

1. *Immediate self-injury / directly inflicted*
   Hanging, firearms, knives, fire, suffocation, traditional poisons, electrocution
2. *Immediate self-injury / indirectly inflicted*
   Fall from height, drowning, rail, road
3. *No immediate self-injury / directly inflicted*
   Overdose of medicines, gassing

In the first group, the differentiation between accident and self-intended harm is usually obvious from the very nature of the incident. With incidents that are indirectly inflicted, the evidence of witnesses and demonstrable motives such as notes and previous behaviour are a valid guide in differentiating those that are less clear-cut. Verdicts of suicide in these instances will only be given when the evidence is absolutely conclusive that a person intended to take his/her life. In the third grouping, the precipitating act does not usually produce external circumstances. In the case of medicine overdosage, although the overdose is almost always deliberate, the actual motive and reason for taking an excess dose is sometimes obscure.

Non-fatal Self-destructive Behaviour

Self-destructive behaviour that does not have a fatal result will also depend largely on the method chosen. For instance, in all except one method, in groups 1 and 2, the behaviour usually results in death. The only exception is the behaviour associated with knives and sharp objects where a gradation of effect is possible. In group 3, especially with overdose of medicines, the position is entirely different. Although the action is directly administered, there is no immediate self-injury and the final outcome is largely out of the patient's control.

Table 1. Fatal self-destructive behaviour in Inner North London, 1971–1985, average per year

	1971–1975	1976–1980	1981–1982	1983–1984	1985
Hanging	11.4	14	11.5	12.5	27
Poisons	3.2	3	0.5	2.5	3
Knives	3	3.6	2.5	1.5	1
Suffocation	2.2	2.8	2	2.5	5
Firearms	0.8	1.8	1	1.5	1
Electricity	1	0.8	3	1	–
Fire	0.2	1.8	3	1.5	1
Fall from height	21.4	23.6	19.5	25.5	27
Drowning	15.4	14.4	20.5	20.5	26
Rail	9.4	10.6	9.5	9	15
Road	0.2	0.6	2.5	3	–
Overdose	84.4	68.4	61.5	66.5	41
Gas	8.6	3	2.5	3.5	2
All	161.2	148.4	139.5	151	149

Table 2. Methods selected in self-inflicted death, ratio between male and female (1981–1985)

Method	Male (% total)	Female (% total)	Total
Overdose	145 (32)	161 (58)	306
Fall from height	69 (15)	47 (17)	116
Drowning	81 (18)	22 (8)	103
Hanging	62 (14)	13 (4.6)	75
Railway	30 (6)	20 (7)	50
Suffocation	8 (1.7)	5	13
Car exhaust	12 (3)	0	12
Road	10 (2)	1	11
Knives	8 (1.7)	1	9
Fire	6	3	9
Electricity	7	1	8
Firearms	5	1	6
Total	450	278	728
% Male/female	62	38	

As a result, the differentiation between suicide, suicide attempt and gradations of self-destructive behaviour is difficult.

Overall Trends (Rates and Methods)

Calculation of rates within a circumscribed area will depend on knowing the exact population of the area and will depend on identifying the deaths of those resident in the area. Over the 15-year period, the population declined by about 15% although in recent years it has stabilised. Taking all these factors into consideration, the rate of non-accidental death (self-initiated) has remained fairly constant.

Although numbers have remained fairly constant, the proportion of methods used has changed to some extent (Table 1). An early reduction in gassing reflected the final changeover to natural gas in the area. Overdose has shown a progressive decline which is matched by that of the national figures and is linked to a progressive decline in barbiturate usage and overdose. However, in 1985, a considerable reduction in overdosage was noted which was replaced mainly by a sharp increase in deaths from suspension.

There is a sex-related difference in choice of method, with a male preference for more direct methods such as hanging, drowning and firearms. Women tended to select indirect methods such as overdose (58% of all modes chosen) (Table 2).

Sex/Age Ratio

The overall sex/age ratio of 62% male to 32% female remained constant throughout the survey. The ratio of male to female was 66% to 34% in the 38% of non-accidental deaths which were recorded as suicide at the inquest.

The proportion by actual numbers (not rates) is set out in Fig. 1. In males, deaths were most numerous between the ages of 20–40, whereas in females, the figures for each age group were more constant with a peak at 25–30 and an increase after 60 years.

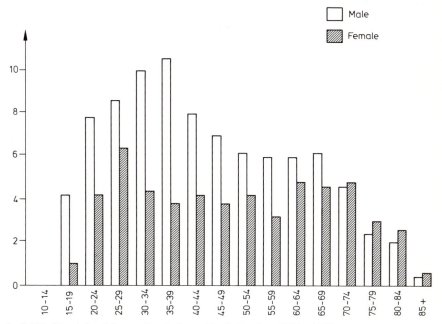

Fig. 1. Self-inflicted death by sex/age in Inner North London, 1981–1985, average per year

It is difficult to plot trends in basic data from a small sample without statistical analysis. However, there does seem to be an increase in the 25−34 age group in both sexes, a decrease in females aged 15−24 and an overall decrease in the 45−54 age group.

Influence of Various Factors, Including Treatment

Although the main purpose of an inquest is to establish the cause of death, it is possible from the enquiry to obtain an insight into factors that led to the fatal incident and elements in past history which indicated predisposition to such activity. Individuals were divided into four groups. Those who were or had been treated in a psychiatric department, those who had seen their general practitioner recently for treatment of psychiatric symptomology and those persons in whom abuse behaviour or alcoholism was the direct contributory factor. In this latter group, only a percentage can be regarded as non-accidental and even in some of these the abuse behaviour was regarded as a part of a more generalised personality disorder. In the remaining individuals, no records of psychiatric referral or diagnosis were noted, nor was there evidence of a recent visit to a doctor for psychiatric symptomology. In some of these individuals, overt symptomology was noted by relatives but in others it was apparently absent or deliberately not reported. Precipitating factors would represent any sudden change or crisis occurring in the patient's life. A brief analysis is set out in Table 3 utilising data from 1981 to 1985.

In 44% no definite psychiatric history was apparent, and in this group, precipitating factors were noted in 55% and concomitant illness in 21%. Of those with known psychiatric history, 41% were known to have made previous attempts.

Table 3. Background and circumstances related to self-inflicted death in Inner North London (1981−1985)

Categories of patient	Patients	Patients in each category			
	(%)	Precipi-tating factors (%)	Previous attempt (%)	Note (%)	Other illness (%)
Psychiatric history	36	20	41	15	1
Recent visit to doctor	11	40	23	20	10
Abusers	8	19	15	15	−
No definite psychiatric history	44	55	12	18	21
	100				

Conclusions

That an incident is regarded as non-accidental must be an arbitrary judgement based on the fact that such an occurrence would be very unlikely in the normal state of affairs (excluding those mediated by alcohol or drugs). Assessment of motive or reason can never be fully understood in the context of an individual's life. However, examination of a person's situation, medical history and events leading up to the incident can help to elucidate this behaviour. How they are interpreted will depend on how these factors are reported and analysed in the overall context. For instance, unemployment can be regarded as a precipitating factor where a change in circumstances has resulted in a crisis, or it can be regarded as a predisposing factor inasmuch as self-harm is disproportionately reported in the unemployed. Unemployment can also be indirectly correlated with self-harm in an aggregate survey. In the present survey, overall rates of self-harm have shown little change over the 15-year period. The ratio between methods has shown some change which has been both predictable and unexplained.

Reducing the overall toll of self-inflicted injury with its consequent personal distress and social waste may not be possible without changing the social climate. However, the most productive results could occur in those groups where improved social and medical care could produce some reduction in the extent and intensity of this type of behaviour. A survey of this type will be instrumental in indicating ways in which this could be achieved.

Suicidal Poisonings Caused by Pesticides in Voivodina (Yugoslavia) During 1960 – 1984

M. Šovljanski and R. Šovljanski

Introduction

Observation of the incidence of suicides and the mode of their realization for a longer period of time in one region, as a rule, reveals definite characteristics. If the region observed still has some specificity, then such observations have even greater significance.

The socialist autonomous province of Voivodina, the province which we deal with in this paper, is a northern part of Yugoslavia and is located in the southern part of the Panonian lowlands, the territory with the highest rate of suicides in the world.

There were 1 854 965 inhabitants living in this territory in 1960; 381 suicides occurred (the rate of suicides was 20.5%), of which 80 were suicidal poisonings, 29 caused by pesticides, accounting for 36.2% of all cases of suicidal poisonings (Šovljanski 1972).

After a quarter of a century (in 1984), the same territory had 2 031 000 inhabitants and 528 cases of suicides yearly (the rate of suicides was 26.0%); 44 cases were suicidal poisonings, with 7 registered as caused by pesticides, accounting for 15.9% of all cases of suicidal poisonings (Šovljanski et al. 1983).

Study

The data in Table 1 show that during the quarter of a century (1960 – 1984) studied, the number of inhabitants in Voivodina increased by 9.1%, the number of suicides increased by 38.6%, and the incidence of suicidal poisonings was practically halved (55.0%).

We compared the number of suicides caused by pesticides in Voivodina with neighboring territories, e.g., Belgrade (Serbia) during 1961 – 1965. Of 74 cases of poisonings, only 7 were caused by pesticides (Bogićević et al. 1968). In Zagreb (Croatia), of 1200 deaths caused by poisonings, there were no cases caused by pesticides (Palmović et al. 1968).

We compared the total consumption of pesticides in the territory of Voivodina with that of the entire republic of Yugoslavia (Table 2). It is evident from Table 2 that Voivodina, based on territorial area and the number of inhabitants, represents less than 10% of the total area of Yugoslavia.

The total consumption of pesticides in Yugoslavia in 1984 was 62 518 t. In 1984, there were 267 pesticide-active ingredients on the market processed in

Table 1. Number and rate of suicides, number and percentage of all poisonings, and poisonings caused by pesticides (1960 – 1984) in Voivodina, Yugoslavia

Years	Suicides		Rate per 100000	Poisonings		Poisonings by pesticides		
	Total	Mean		Number	%	Number	Mean	%
1960 – 1964	1905	381	20.5	400	21.0	145	29.0	36.2
1965 – 1969	2513	503	26.4	384	15.2	110	22.0	38.6
1970 – 1974	2422	484	24.8	387	15.9	88	25.3	22.7
1975 – 1979	2520	504	25.7	275	10.7	44	8.8	16.0
1980 – 1984	2640	528	26.0	220	8.3	35	7.0	15.9
1960 – 1984	12000	480	24.7	1666	14.2	422	16.9	23.9

Table 2. The area of the territory, the number of inhabitants, and the rate of suicides in Voivodina and Yugoslavia

Territory	Area (km²)	Number of inhabitants	Rate of suicides
SFR Yugoslavia	255804	22963000	13.8
SAP Voivodina	21506	2031000	26.0

801 formulations. Zoocides represented 41% of the active substances, fungicides 22%, and herbicides 37%. Classified according to toxicity, active ingredients in group I were used in 15% and those in group IV in 55% of the total number of pesticides.

Among the formulations the number of zoocides represented 39%; classified according to toxicity, the formulations in group I represented only 2.4% and in group IV 71% of the total number of formulated products.

The share in the consumption was: zoocides 40%, fungicides 40%, and herbicides 20%. Let us mention that in 1985 in the Federal Republic of Germany there were 1839 formulated products on the market based on 302 active substances. Zoocides were used in ca. 40%, fungicides in 18.5%, and herbicides in ca. 40% of all pesticides.

The consumption of pesticides in Voivodina was more than 40% of all Yugoslav consumption, and that was one of the reasons why suicides chose these substances as suicide agents.

At the beginning of the period observed, organophosphorus insecticides (especially parathion and malathion) dominated as the suicide agents, and in the last decade, herbicides (2,4-D and paraquat).

The number of suicides caused by drugs remained at a fixed level expressed in absolute numbers, but expressed in relative numbers, it increased.

Discussion

It is evident that the incidence of suicides in Voivodina increased (the rate increased from 20.5% to 26.0%) and the incidence of suicidal poisonings decreased (from 21.0% in 1960−1964 to 7% in 1980−1984). The number of suicidal poisonings caused by pesticides decreased from 36.2% to 15.9% (% of all poisonings) and expressed as a percentage of the number of suicides decreased from 7.6% to 1.32%. For the period of 1960−1964, the share of suicides caused by pesticides was only 3.5% (% of all suicides).

Conclusion

We consider that the better control of pesticides on the market (the reduction in the number of highly toxic pesticides on the market and in their application, e.g., parathion is available only as 5% granules and not as a 20% emulsion concentrate, which was in use especially in the 1960s), quicker and better organization of transport to hospital and medical institutions, and more effective treatment and therapy of poisoned persons contributed to the fact that pesticides used as the agents for the realization of suicides were replaced by more effective and faster-acting means.

References

Bogićević J, Andjelski A, Ćosić V (1968) Stanje, značaj i problemi medicinske toksikologije u našoj zdravstvenoj službi. Odabrana poglavlja iz Toksikologije (State, character and problems of medicinal toxicology in our sanitary service). 1st Yugoslav Symposium of Medical Toxicology, Belgrad, 19th March
Palmović V, Gašparec Z (1968) Vrste trovanja kod umrlih u Zagrebu i okolici (Types of poisonings in dead persons in Zagreb and its neighborhood). 1st Yugoslav Symposium on Medical Toxicology, Belgrad, 19th March
Šovljanski M (1972) Samoubistva u Vojvodini i njihove karakteristike (Suicides in Voivodina and their characteristics). Matica Srpska, Novi Sad, 1−124
Šovljanski M, Simić M, Budakov B (1983) Samoubistva u SAPV za 25 godišnji period (Suicides in SAPV during the period of 25 years). First congress on prevention of suicides, Ohrid, 145−147
Statistički godišnjak SAP Vojvodine (1962−1986) (Statistical yearbook of SAP Voivodina) Novi Sad
Statistički godišnjak Jugoslavije (1962−1986) (Statistical Yearbook of Yugoslavia). Belgrad

Age-Related Differences in Patients Who Attempt Suicide

G. KOCKOTT

Introduction

There is not a great deal of literature on suicidal behavior in the elderly, especially not with respect to patients who have attempted suicide (Batchelor and Napier 1953; Böker 1975; Feuerlein 1977; Kreitman 1976). We were interested to see whether there are age-related differences in patients with self-poisoning. In our opinion, if such differences exist, information about them should be of benefit in the prevention of suicide.

Study

We included in our investigation all patients who had been admitted to a general hospital in Munich following a suicide attempt. There were 4190 patients over a period of 6 years; 32% were men and 68% women. We subdivided the patients into three age groups (Table 1). The patients under the age of 40 (2993) formed the largest group (group I), followed by the patients between the ages of 40 and 64 (group II); the patients aged 65 years and older were the smallest group (group III).

For the three groups we compared sociodemographic data, diagnoses, and the motives for the suicide attempt as given by the patients themselves. Where it was appropriate, we also compared the results with the data of the normal population of Munich.

Table 1. Distribution of the total sample of patients (4190) according to age

Group	Age (years)	Male	Female	Total
I	<40	969	2024	2993
II	40−64	332	685	1017
III	≧65	58	122	180
Total		1359 (= 32%)	2831 (= 68%)	4190 (= 100%)

Results

Sociodemographic Data

Sex Ratio. In comparison with the corresponding age groups of the normal population of Munich, in both younger groups (groups I and II), women were over-represented and men were under-represented.

In our oldest age group (group III), the sex ratio was the same as in the normal population. In other words, whereas women under the age of 65 attempt suicide more often than men, in old age, women make suicide attempts as often as men when compared with the normal population.

Citizenship. In comparison with the distribution in the normal population, foreigners were under-represented in the two younger patient groups but not in the oldest group. Foreigners over the age of 65 attempted suicide as often as nationals. Most of these elderly foreigners who had made a suicide attempt had already lived in Munich for more than 15 years.

Family Status. Being divorced increases the likelihood of a suicide attempt even in old age (Fig. 1). In all three age groups, the percentage of divorced patients was significantly higher than in the normal population, whereas married patients were significantly under-represented in all three age groups. Widowed patients were not over-represented, but it should be borne in mind that we investigated patients who *attempted* suicide; according to the literature (Sainsbury 1975), widowed patients seem to be over-represented in patient groups who *commit* suicide. This seems to me an interesting difference: widowed patients tend to commit suicide due to the loss of the partner, whereas divorced patients tend to *attempt* suicide, maybe to try to appeal to the still-existing partner. The high percentage of single patients in the youngest groups is due to the very low average age of this group.

Diagnoses

Diagnoses were made using the International Classification of Diseases (ICD). In comparison with the younger two groups, the diagnosis of depression (both psychotic and reactive depressions, ICD 296.0; 300.4) was made significantly more often in the oldest age group, whereas other diagnoses such as schizophrenia, character neurosis, and alcoholism occurred less frequently. When, however, we compared these data with data from groups of psychiatric patients corresponding of age who had made no suicide attempts, we found a similar increase in the occurrence of depression with age (Fig. 2).

Motives for the Suicide Attempt

The main motives given by the patients of the oldest group were compared with those given by patients in a previously investigated group with a much lower

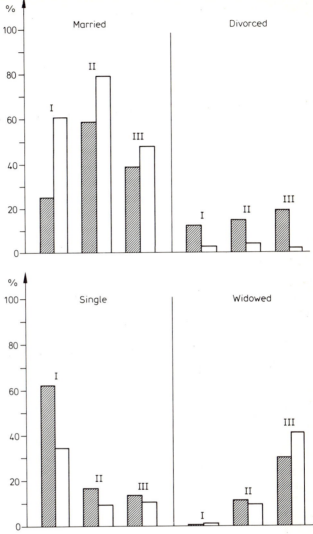

Fig. 1. Percentage comparison of marital status in three age groups (I, ≦40 years; II, 40−64 years; III, ≧65 years) between patients who attempted suicide and the normal population. *Blank columns* stand for the normal population, *hatched columns* for the group who attempted suicide

average age. This comparison can only be made on a descriptive basis. In both groups, but especially in the oldest age group, a certain percentage of patients were not able to define a main motive. These were mainly patients with a psychotic depression. If the motives are put in order of frequency, the similarities are surprising (Table 2). In both groups, conflicts with partners came first, followed by conflicts with close relatives. Social isolation (feeling of loneliness) as a motive for suicide was also mentioned very often in both groups, whereas

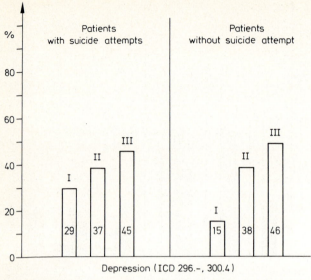

Fig. 2. Percentage comparison of the diagnosis of depression in three age groups (I, ≦40 years; II, 40−64 years; III, ≧65 years) between patients who attempted suicide and psychiatric patients who made no suicide attempts

Table 2. Percentage comparison between main motives for attempting suicide (as given by the patient) of the oldest group (≧65 years) and of a group of previously investigated patients with a much lower average age ($\bar{x}$ = 33.2)

Main motives	A ($\bar{x}$ = 33.2 years) (%)	B (≧65 years) (%)
Conflicts with partner	48	13
Conflicts with close relatives	16	11
Worries about own health	0	10
Social isolation	16	6
Illness phobia	8	4
Fear of a change in living conditions	0	4
Occupational worries	4	1
Other	5	6

worries about their health seemed to be a typical motive for older patients who attempted suicide, as well as the fear of a change in living conditions, such as having to leave their own house and enter a home for the aged.

Conclusions

If generalization is permissible from data taken from an urban population, we can summarize our conclusions as follows:

In old age, suicide attempts occur as often among men as among women, whereas in the younger patient groups men are under-represented. Being a foreigner does not seem to increase the risk that a suicide attempt will be made in old age. The under-representation of foreigners in the younger patient groups may be explained by the very high percentage of foreign workers (*Gastarbeiter*) in these age groups. They usually undergo careful medical screening before they receive permission to come to Germany. Divorce always carries with it a risk that the involved persons will attempt suicide, even in old age, independent of the age at which they were divorced, whereas being married always decreases the risk. The relative increase of suicide attempts in men over the age of 65 corresponds with an increase in the occurrence of depression. As in the younger age groups, in old age, the main motives given by the patients themselves for their suicide attempt are very often conflicts with their partner or with close relatives, whereas worries about their own health and the fear of a change in living conditions seem to be typical motives for suicide attempts in the elderly.

In the light of the literature on patients who commit suicide (Stengel 1969), even in old age there seems to be a difference between patients who attempt suicide and those who commit suicide.

References

Batchelor IRC, Napier MB (1953) Attempted suicide in old age. Br Med J 2:1186–1190
Böcker F (1975) Suicidhandlungen alter Menschen. MMW 117:201–204
Feuerlein W (1977) Ursachen, Motivationen und Tendenzen von Selbstmordhandlungen im Alter. Aktuel Gerontol 7:67–74
Kreitman N (1976) Age and parasuicide ("attempted suicide"). Psychol Med 6:113–121
Sainsbury P (1975) Suicide and attempted suicide. In: Kisker KP, Meyer JE, Müller C, Strömgren E (eds) Psychiatrie der Gegenwart, vol 3, 2nd edn. Springer, Berlin Heidelberg New York, pp 559–606
Stengel E (1969) Selbstmord und Selbstmordversuch. Fischer, Frankfurt

Suicides Among Psychiatric Patients in Funen (Denmark)

A. Linder and A. G. Wang

Introduction

The problem concerning nosocomial suicides is not a new one, as was discussed for example by a Danish author in 1806 when he spoke about "those who in their lunacy terminate their lives in the hospitals".

This problem has attained increasing relevance in the post-war years with the use of more effective pharmacological treatments and other treatments, and hopes were raised that this new era in psychiatry would substantially reduce suicides among psychiatric patients.

This hope has not been fulfilled. On the contrary, Scandinavian studies have shown an increasing tendency to ward suicide among psychotic patients. Danish studies have shown a relative increase in the suicides taking place among inpatients. In Britain, despite a general decline in suicides, this same phenomenon has been observed (Hessø 1977; Retterstøl 1978).

Several hypotheses have been advanced to explain this:

1. Changing patterns with more liberal patient regimens in open wards, day-patient departments, or outpatient treatment for patients who in former times would have been kept in closed wards have increased the temptations and possibilities of suicide.
2. Changing treatment procedures with more aggressive psychotherapy including group treatment enforcing anxiety and psychotic breakdowns.
3. Changing treatment patterns for endogenous depressions from electroconvulsive therapy (ECT) to antidepressants have been less effective against depressive suicidal fantasies (Winokur 1981).
4. Suicides in the hospital environment are often associated with other patient management and administrative problems in the psychiatric service. When the clinician is distracted by organizational or interpersonal strain, the vigilance of the ward personnel is impaired (Anonymous 1977, Kroll 1978).
5. There has been a general increase in suicides in Denmark since the mid-1960s, and during the same period, there has been a weakening in personal social networks (divorces, family disruptions, increased mobility, etc.).

The present study aims to elucidate some aspects of suicides among psychiatric inpatients and freshly discharged patients.

Material and Methods

Denmark has about 5 million inhabitants, and the county of Funen has a population of about 450000. The county has been shown to be representative for Denmark in several demographic and social aspects. The county has therefore become a study area for suicidal behavior in Denmark.

The present study includes all suicides from the county of Funen during 4 years: 1979 – 1982. The suicides were identified by death certificates, and information was supplemented by hospital records, which were identified and studied, and/or summary reports from the department. In Denmark, death certificates are issued by a medical person, and the cause of death is determined by medical probabilities. Furthermore, information from police investigations was used.

Patient status was classified as inpatient, day-patient, outpatient, and discharged without psychiatric treatment. The main status change was used as a description of the change from inpatient status to some other status, indicating that the hospital no longer had total responsibility.

Diagnoses were main diagnoses according to the International Classification of Diseases (ICD 8). "Treatment" refers to pharmacological treatment and ECT on the one hand and therapeutic psychiatric treatment on the other. "Time lapsed since discharge" refers to the time period since the main status change from inpatient status.

Results

The total number of suicides in Funen 1979 – 1982 was 522. Of these, about 40% had at some time been inpatients in psychiatric institutions.

The numbers of inpatients and newly discharged patients (discharged from inpatient status ≦ 12 weeks) are shown in Table 1, which indicates the patient status, and that the majority were inpatients (44) and discharged patients without psychiatric aftercare (40). Most of the wards involved were open wards, and many of the suicides took place when the patient was absent from the ward.

Suicides among inpatients, day-patients, outpatients, and completely discharged former patients comprised about 22%.

Patients included in the above limite comprised 117, and for these, there was complete material about 89 patients.

The motivation for change of status from inpatient to some other more 'liberal' status is shown in Table 2: 90% (80) were discharged according to plan and only 10% (9) on the patient's own insistence (and against psychiatric advice).

Table 1. Suicides (1979 – 1982) in the county of Funen (pop., 450000 in 1975)

Total	Inpatients	Daypatients	Outpatients	Others
522	44	9	24	40

Inpatients and newly discharged (≦ 12 weeks)

117

Table 2. Change of status from inpatient

Planned	80 patients = 90%
On patient's insistence	9 patients = 10%

Table 3. Treatment (main treatment). Inpatients and daypatients ($n = 53$)

Somatic methods	%
Neuroleptics (major tranquilizers)	35
TCA	13
ECT	4
Psychosedatives	26
Lithium	2
Antabuse	2
None	18
Psychotherapeutic methods	
Individual supportive	83
Group treatment	17
Individual psychotherapy (analytical, etc.)	0

Time intervals from change of status as inpatients to other patient status are shown in Fig. 1. In Denmark, treatment as a day-patient or outpatient is used as a follow-up to an inpatient period. Figure 1 shows that 36% of these patients commited suicide in the 1st week after discharge and 7% in the 2nd week; 61% committed suicide in the first 4 weeks. (Nine patients insisted on discharge against advice, of whom four committed suicide in the 1st week and two in the 2nd.)

The diagnostic distribution according to the main diagnosis (ICD 8) for all suicides included in the study is seen in Fig. 2. For inpatients (Fig. 3), there was a concentration of psychoses: schizophrenia (25%), manic-depressive psychoses (25%), and reactive (psychogenic) psychoses (22%). For day-patients and out-patients (Fig. 4), the concentration was for manic-depressives and for other former patients in nonpsychotic conditions.

The main treatment methods employed are shown in Table 3.

Somatic Methods. Neuroleptics (major tranquilizers) were used most (35%), followed by psychosedatives (26%), no somatic treatment (18%), and anti-depressants (tricyclic antidepressants, TCA) (13%). ECT was only used in a very few instances (3%). Hypnotics (sleeping pills) were not included in this study.

Direct cancellation of treatment was only reported in a very few cases (neuroleptics 2% and TCA 3% of the total treated).

Psychotherapeutic Methods. General individual supportive therapy was most frequently used (83%) and group treatment was used in about 17% of the cases. In no cases were more "aggressive" methods used (such as explorative psycho-analysis, gestalt therapy, confrontation group sessions).

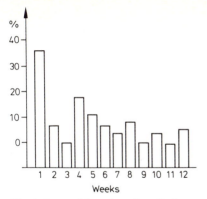

Fig. 1. Interval from inpatient discharge to suicide ($n = 73$ patients)

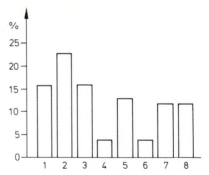

Fig. 2. Diagnoses for inpatients, day-patients, and outpatients ($n = 77$) *1*, schizophrenia; *2*, manic-depressives; *3*, reactive psychoses; *4*, other psychoses; *5*, psychoneuroses; *6*, personality disorders; *7*, alcoholism; *8*, others (affective reactions, etc.)

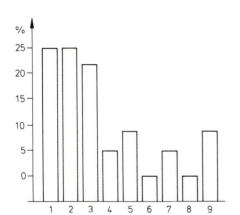

Fig. 3. Diagnoses for inpatients ($n = 44$). *1*, schizophrenia; *2*, manic-depressives; *3*, reactive psychoses; *4*, other psychoses; *5*, psychoneuroses; *6*, personality disorders; *7*, alcoholism; *8*, dementia; *9*, others (affective reactions, etc.)

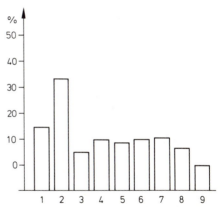

Fig. 4. Diagnoses for day patients and outpatients ($n = 33$). *1*, schizophrenia; *2*, manic-depressives; *3*, reactive psychoses; *4*, other psychoses; *5*, psychoneuroses; *6*, personality disorders; *7*, alcoholism; *8*, dementia; *9*, others (affective reactions, etc.)

Discussion

1. This study shows an accumulation of suicides around hospital admission for psychiatric disorders. Only a handful were in closed wards. The open-ward policy reflects an intentional openness in psychiatry. Many suicides took place when the patient was at home for the weekend, etc.

The study also shows an accumulation around discharge from inpatient status, especially during the first weeks. This could make us question the general policy — both political and ideological — of pressing for short admissions and alternative aftercare. However, we do not really know if suicides could be hindered or only postponed by prolonged hospital care.

The main diagnoses elucidate the spectrum of illnesses. It is rather serious for psychiatry as such that the greatest number are psychotics and especially psychotics with illnesses of an episodic or reactive character. Perhaps we must accept some sort of custodial responsibility here.

The diagnostic distribution for patients discharged without psychiatric aftercare reflects the Danish tradition that so-called minor pschiatry (neuroses, alcoholism, etc.) is to be handled by nonhospital professionals in the aftercare period [general practitioner (GP), alcohol clinics, etc.].

2. For psychotherapy, group treatment is only used occasionally for these patients, and more aggressive therapy not at all. Mainly, some sort of general supportive therapy has been used, but *very unsystematically*. The hypothesis that more aggressive therapy precipitates suicide does not find support. On the contrary, one could assume that *too little* therapeutic contact has been established.

3. The treatment study shows that psychopharmacological treatment is used extensively, and among depressives, *TCA have generally replaced ECT*. Noncompliance *as recorded* in hospital records does not seem to be a major problem.

4, 5. This study shed some light on the first three hypotheses but is not suitable for elucidating the two last hypotheses which are of a more general nature.

We have so far no method with sufficient predictive value to establish individual services for suicide-prone patients. Indications from the present study seem to focus on the liberal open-ward policy, early discharges from inpatient status to alternative forms, and too minimal rather than too intensive therapeutic efforts.

The kind of effort most beneficial for the patients could be a basis for program evaluation studies (Juel-Nielsen 1985).

References

Anonymous (1977) A suicide epidemic in a psychiatric hospital. Dis Nerv Syst 38:328–331
Hessø R (1977) Suicide in Norwegian, Finnish and Swedish psychiatric hospitals. Arch Psychiatr Nervenkr 224:119–127
Juel-Nielsen N (1985) Suicides and functional psychoses. In: Helgason T (ed) The long-term treatment of functional psychoses — needed areas of research. Cambridge University Press, Cambridge
Kroll JL (1978) Self-destructive behavior on an inpatient ward. J Nerv Ment Dis 166:429–434
Retterstøl N (1978) Suicide in psychiatric hospitals in Norway. Psychiatr Fenn 9:89–92
Winokur G (1981) Depression. The facts. Oxford University Press, Oxford

Increasing Suicide Rate in Scandinavian Psychiatric Hospitals

N. RETTERSTØL

Introduction

It is a well-known and accepted fact that the rate of suicide in patients in a psychiatric hospital is far higher than in the general population. Almost all studies show that the majority of those who commit suicide suffer from a psychiatric disorder. Pærregaard (1963), who investigated 1470 suicides in the Copenhagen area, found that 96% of the suicides had a psychiatric diagnosis.

Hospital suicides have interested clinicians for as long as the history of psychiatry. Every psychiatrist has experienced the dramatic effect a hospital suicide has on the staff and relatives, but no less on the responsible psychiatrist him(her)self. Fortunately, years may pass between each such experience. However, in large hospitals there will usually be several suicides every year.

An interesting question, which has occupied many clinicians and researchers, is whether there has been a change in the rate of hospital suicides since the introduction of neuroleptics, which, together with the introduction of new and active milieu-therapeutic principles, opened the way for a marked change in the hospital atmosphere, the treatment facilities, and the circulation of patients.

Most studies on this question are based on investigation of all suicides in a particular hospital over a number of years. The majority of these studies seem to indicate that there has been no great change (Lange 1966; Alsen 1969; Koester 1969; Schwartz 1969; Petri 1970; Ritzel 1974), while some studies seem to indicate the opposite experience (Ravn 1966; Ernst and Kern 1974; Gorence and Bruner 1985; Saugstad and Ødegård 1985).

There are, however, also investigations into conditions within a hospital system (Farberow et al. 1971), within a specific area (Niskanen et al. 1974; Gorence and Bruger 1985), or within all the psychiatric hospitals in a given country (Ødegård 1967; Retterstøl 1978; Hessø 1977; Saugstad and Ødegård 1985).

The suicide rates in all such studies are markedly above the suicide rates for the countries as a whole, as demonstrated by Hessø (1977) for the Nordic countries (Table 1).

Suicide in Norwegian Psychiatric Hospitals

The absolute number of registered suicides in Norwegian psychiatric hospitals in 5-year periods from 1930 to 1984 is shown in Table 2. The suicide rates (per

Table 1. Suicide rates in psychiatric hospitals in Sweden, Finland, and Norway (From Hessø 1977)

	Period	Suicides per 100000 patients per year
Sweden	1955–1959	132
Finland	1965–1969	200
Norway	1970–1974	277

Table 2. Absolute number of registered suicides in Norwegian psychiatric hospitals in 5-year periods from 1930 to 1984

5-year period	Registered suicides in psychiatric hospitals
1930–1934	24
1935–1939	26
1940–1944	19
1945–1949	12
1950–1954	14
1955–1959	35
1960–1964	50
1965–1969	71
1970–1974	108
1975–1979	122
1980–1984	90

Table 3. Suicides per 100000 patients per year in the psychiatric hospitals in Norway indicated in 5-year periods from 1930 to 1984

5-year period	Suicides per 100000 patients
1930–1934	74
1935–1939	76
1940–1944	53
1945–1949	32
1950–1954	35
1955–1959	84
1960–1964	120
1965–1969	169
1970–1974	277
1975–1979	359
1980–1984	373

Table 4. Death by suicide in psychiatric hospitals in Norway 1975–1984

Number of diagnosis	1975	1976	1977	1978	1979	1980	1981	1982	1983	1984
Men										
950.1	1	–	–	1	–	–	3	–	–	–
953.1	1	5	3	5	4	7	8	2	7	3
954.1	–	1	4	2	1	2	3	1	2	4
955.1	–	–	1	–	1	–	–	–	–	–
956.1	1	–	2	–	–	–	1	1	–	–
957.1	2	2	1	1	1	1	1	2	4	2
Absolute number	5	8	11	9	7	10	16	6	13	9
Women										
950.1	–	–	1	1	–	–	–	–	–	1
953.1	3	1	4	4	3	1	–	4	3	1
954.1	3	–	2	5	1	5	1	2	–	1
955.1	–	–	–	–	–	–	–	–	2	–
956.1	1	–	1	–	–	–	–	1	–	–
957.1	–	1	1	1	1	1	–	–	–	1
958.1	–	–	1	–	–	–	–	1	–	–
959.1	–	–	–	1	–	1	–	–	–	–
Absolute number	7	2	10	12	5	8	1	8	5	4

Table 5. Suicides in Norwegian psychiatric hospitals per 100000 first admissions and total admissions, stated in 5-year periods from 1930 to 1984

5-year periods	Suicides per 100000 first admissions	Total admissions
1930–1934	399	265
1935–1939	369	228
1940–1944	261	146
1945–1949	149	81
1950–1954	186	96
1955–1959	394	190
1960–1964	389	170
1965–1969	519	205
1970–1974	647	247
1975–1979	653	244
1980–1984	693	205

100000 per year) in the psychiatric hospitals in Norway indicated in 5-year periods from 1930 to 1984 are shown in Table 3. A survey of death by suicide in psychiatric hospitals in the period 1975 – 1984 is given in Table 4.

The number of admissions to psychiatric hospitals has increased markedly in the period since 1955, and the number of inpatients in hospitals has decreased markedly, due mainly to more active therapeutic methods and to better outpatient facilities and care. This fact may influence the findings. One would expect a higher suicide rate in newly admitted cases. Table 5 clearly demonstrates that if circulation is taken into consideration, the tendency of the reported findings will be moderated. During the last three 5-year periods, suicides per 100000 first admissions and total admissions have remained practically unchanged.

Since 1955, a marked and continuous increase in the suicide rate took place in the psychiatric hospitals and especially among first-time patients until the last three 5-year periods. Saugstad and Ødegård (1985) have recently published a study based on the National Case Register of Serious Mental Disorders for Norway. The investigation of the 10 413 deaths in mental hospitals in Norway 1950 – 1974 revealed a significant rise in unnatural deaths (suicides and accidents) as well as in cardiovascular disease as the cause of death since 1963, despite an overall decline in mortality of 30% – 40% between 1946 and 1950 and 1969 and 1974. The trend in excess mortality from an unnatural death in the period 1950 – 1974 by type of functional psychosis and by sex, all age-adjusted rates per 10000 population, is demonstrated in Table 6, taken from Saugstad and Ødegård (1985).

Suicide in Swedish Psychiatric Hospitals

Similar experiences have been reported in Sweden. The Swedish National Board of Health and Welfare (1985) has published a book on suicides in

Table 6. Trend in excess mortality from unnatural death 1950–1974 by type of functional psychosis and by sex (all ages, age-adjusted rates per 10000 population)

	Males			Females		
	1950–62	1963–68	1969–74	1950–62	1963–68	1969–74
Mort. schizophrenia	98	228	328	67	178	338
General population	82	82	91	23	27	29
Excess mortality	1.2	2.9	3.6	2.6	6.6	11.7
Remaining functional psychosis	225	357	483	96	287	252
General population	82	82	91	23	27	29
Excess mortality	2.8	4.4	5.3	4.0	10.6	7.3

Unnatural deaths 1950–1962 comprised 145 deaths (88 males, 57 females) of which 56% male and 44% female deaths were suicides (incl. probable suicides).

Unnatural deaths 1963–1974 comprised 370 deaths (203 males, 167 females) of which 63% male and 45% female deaths were suicides (incl. probable suicides).

Unnatural deaths 1926–1941 comprised 91 deaths (54 males, 37 females) of which 82% male and 76% female deaths were suicides (incl. probable suicides).

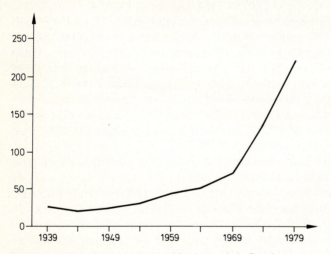

Fig. 1. Number of suicides in psychiatric wards in Sweden

Swedish psychiatric institutions. Figure 1, taken from the publication, demonstrates the increasing number of suicides in psychiatric institutions from 1939 to 1979.

Since January 1, 1983, it is compulsary in Sweden to report suicides during psychiatric care to the National Board of Health and Welfare (an obligation which has for many years been practiced in Norway). In 1983, 149 reports were sent to the National Board regarding suicides during psychiatric care. Examination of these reports will, in the future, create possibilities for identifying situations of risk in psychiatric care so that preventive measures can be taken. Even now it can be noted that many suicides take place during the beginning of the hospital stay or in connection with a change of ward and personnel before the personnel have been able to get to know the patient sufficiently.

Discussion

Several explanations may be given, and some of them may give rise to prophylactic measures.

1. A larger proportion of the psychiatric population is currently admitted for treatment in psychiatric hospitals, which means that a greater part of the population at risk is in a hospital for some time.

2. There has been a considerable shift in the 'clientele' of the psychiatric hospital. In Norway, the number of drug and alcohol dependents has increased markedly, 20-fold, during the period from 1955 until now. This category of patients is at a higher risk for suicide than any other group of patients.

3. A marked change has taken place in the treatment procedures and the attitudes in the psychiatric hospitals during this period. Neuroleptics have been introduced as well as active milieu-therapeutic procedures. These methods may also be provoking for the patients' personalities, giving them a degree of insight into their disease which had not been previously available. Looking in the mirror may not only confront them with the troubles causing or precipitating the symptoms, but also confront them with a condition where they can be classified as neither ill nor well. They may be too healthy to enjoy an institutional life and too ill for a society which has, up to now, not provided sheltered work or housing possibilities for them, nor easy access to jobs or flats.

4. The more liberal attitudes in the psychiatric hospital no doubt play a part. The increase in the suicide rate may be a price we pay for the open-door policy and the more humane and democratic treatment procedures, where emphasis has shifted from security measures to human contact, increased activity, and attractive surroundings.

5. In the new therapeutic wards, the administrative responsibility for the patients has also often been democraticized and transferred from the experienced head physician to less experienced doctors of the ward cooperating with the milieu personnel. Security decisions are, in other words, often made by less experienced and educated groups than before.

6. The increased circulation, which has been mentioned, and the short hospital stay may make the patients anxious and uneasy, give them a feeling that everyone is busy and impatient, and that due time is not given to the individual patient. The "revolving-door policy" has its price.

Prophylactic Measures to Be Taken

The development should not be switched back to the old authoritarian procedures. The door should still be open to a maximal extent, the patients given active treatment procedures, and the hospital stay made as short as possible.

Appropriate services should still be given to those who are in need of it, including drug dependents and alcoholics.

In the psychiatric hospitals, we have not been wise enough in giving specialized service to the suicide-threatened person. This patient should be looked after better, not in the sense of utter control, but in the sense of human contact. A staff person should be attached to him for a time, giving much attention to him as a human being. The depressed suicidal patient should not at once be placed into all activities in an acute ward. He should be given time during which he can act out his feelings and contemplate without all the hurry in acute wards. It is correct that he be in a ward where there is a certain amount of supervision and control. This ward should not be too big. Of greatest importance is that all persons working there know his tendencies, that his behavior be discussed every day, and that information from the one person looking after him reaches all members working on the ward. Often, there is a lack of information exchange between the teams, especially between day and night personnel. Good communication to and from the night personnel is of crucial importance. The best prophylactic measure is probably an alert, well-trained, and well-educated staff, working in good cooperation with each other and with the patients. The closer a positive relationship can be developed between patient and staff, the better will be the chance to obtain information from the patient about suicide plans and to help the patient. The more antagonistic a protest attitude that the suicidal person develops, the less chance we have of obtaining information from him that can enable us to prevent the suicide. It is a well-known fact that suicide and suicide attempts are often a cry for help. For the often lonely suicidal patient, the therapist or the contacts among the staff may be the closest "relatives" and the "important others." A suicide in a hospital may be a "revenge" when the patient feels neglected and not cared for enough. A change in therapist or a leave for holidays by the therapist is often a precipitating factor. These changes should be well prepared. A crucial point is the good cooperation among the staff and between the staff and doctor. The responsibility for leave or discharge should definitely be that of the experienced doctor. The first leave has to be well prepared for with family or friends and the time should be limited. It is good advice that the patient then be together for the whole time with his family who keep an eye on him. However, it is also important that the dignity of the patient is not hurt. Avoiding humiliation of the patient should also belong to the key words in suicidology.

Much consideration should be given to rehabilitation of the patient in his work and family to achieve a situation which is more meaningful than when he was admitted. Discharge of lonely persons without preparation has a great chance of ending in suicide. A network should be built around the patient and made effective. In this network, we should include ourselves and the staff. A member of the team should always be available as helper, and the possibility be made for a telephone contact or consultation when the patient is in trouble. The establishment of social groups for discharged, lonely patients may be considered as an important suicide-prophylactic measure. The quality of the aftercare treatment will be essential to the result, especially during the first 6 – 12 months after discharge. When all the daily problems are there again with which he could not cope, the patient is in need of support. It is not sufficient to tell the patient he can drop in when he is in need. Fixed appointments should be given to the patient, at least during the 1st year after discharge.

Teaching programs in psychiatric hospitals should be established. In my hospital, we have teaching programs on every ward, not least to reach the many new aides and nurses not acquainted with the ward and routine. It is important that these programs are also available to the night personnel who are on duty during the most risky hours. Every half year we run a suicide-prevention program for all the co-workers in the hospital so that suicide can always "live" in the consciousness of the personnel. Finally, whenever there is a suicide, this has to be worked through, not only within the ward where it was committed, but also within the whole hospital. It is the common responsibility for the ward as well as for the hospital to try to find out what went wrong and what can be done better in the future.

National programs should be worked out to prevent suicides in psychiatric hospitals. Such a program has not been worked out for Norway. A national program was established in Sweden, which is also used in Norway, as our wards and treatment facilities and procedures are very similar.

Good suicide-prevention programs for the hospitals will depend on a high level of knowledge of suicidology among doctors and nurses. The higher the level of teaching suicidology can reach in our curricula at the universities and nurses' high schools, the better our chances will be to reduce the increasing suicide rates in our hospitals. It is my conviction that giving an increased level of knowledge of suicidology to the average population is also a preventive measure, making people aware of important signs and signals.

Research in suicidology is of crucial importance also for prophylaxis of hospital suicides. The insight that man's equipment is often insufficient for the destructive world in which he lives, and the necessity to move the perspective from the individual to the different settings in which he lives with all his conflicts, has many consequences both for suicide research and clinical practice. Many prevention measures may be decided and carried out on common levels, whereas other measures may demand analyses on various levels of scientific sophistication. In a doctoral thesis, Wolk-Wasserman (1986) pointed to the fact that the suicide signals are very different for neurotic, psychotic, and drug-dependent people, may easily be overseen, and may also produce countertransference phenomena of a negative character in staff members. The personnel's difficulties in communication with the patients, and the resulting problems, should be discussed.

Finally, it should be mentioned that the *relatives of patients who have committed suicide are badly in need of help.* They often have strong, aggressive feelings toward themselves, toward other close persons, toward the patient, and toward the staff and hospitals. Help and support should be given to them in their situation of grief combined with aggression.

As Beskow (1983) has pointed out, a multiplicity of factors interact before a completed suicide, of which many may be characterized as chance factors. This may ease the often overly heavy burden of remorse felt by relatives as well as mental-care personnel. Much of the preventive work now has to be done on an administrative level. For Sweden, this was done in the publication just referred to and in a ward program of 1985, *Suicide Within the Psychiatric Ward: Information from the National Board of Health and Welfare* (1985).

A ward program, designed for the different types of psychiatric wards, no doubt should be worked out in every country.

References

Alsen V (1969) Selbstmord und Selbstmordversuch in der Klinik. Zentralbl Ges Neurol Psychiatr 196:3

Beskow J (1983) Problemet självmord. Underlag till vårdprogramm (The suicide problem. Basis for a ward program). Socialstyrelsen, Stockholm

Ernst K, Kern R (1974) Suizidstatistik und freiheitliche Klinikbehandlung 1900−1972. Arch Psychiatr Nervenkr 219:255−263

Farberow NL, Genzler S, Cutter F, Reynolds D (1971) An eight year survey of hospital suicides. Suicide Life Threat Behav 1:184−202

Gorenc K, Bruner CA (1985) Suicidal behavior among patients in Bavarian mental hospitals. Acta Psychiatr Scand 71:468−478

Hessø R (1977) Suicides in Norwegian, Finnish and Swedish Psychiatric Hospitals. Arch Psychiatr Nervenkr 224:119−127

Hessø R (1979) Økningen av selvmord blant personer med funksjonell psykose diagnose (The increase of suicides in persons with a diagnosis of functional psychosis). Nord Psykiatr Tidsskrift 33:562−568

Lange E (1966) Die Suicidgefahr beim open-door-system (ODS) in stationären psychiatrischen Einrichtungen. Soc Psychiatry 1:64−72

Koester H (1969) Möglichkeiten und Grenzen der Freizügigkeit in der stationären Behandlung psychisch Kranker. Eine statistische Auswertung über Zwischenfälle im psychiatrischen Krankenhaus. Nervenarzt 40:421−429

Niskanen P, Lönnqvist J, Rinta-Mänty R (1974) Suicides in Helsinki psychiatric hospitals in 1964−1972. Psychiatr Fenn, pp 275−280

Ødegård Ø (1967) Mortality in Norwegian psychiatric hospitals 1950−1962. Acta Genet (Basel) 17:137−153

Pærregaard G (1963) Selvmord og selvmordsforsøg i København (Suicide and suicide attempts in Copenhagen), vols 1−3. Doctoral dissertation

Petri H (1970) Zum Problem des Selbstmordes in psychiatrischen Kliniken. Z Psychother Med Psychol 20:10−19

Ravn J (1966) Antallet af selvmord i en psykiatrisk hospitalsafdeling i løbet af 20 år (Number of suicides in a psychiatric hospital ward during a 20-year period). Nord Psykiatr Tidsskrift 20:196−199

Retterstøl N (1978) Suicide in psychiatric hospitals in Norway. Psychiatr Fenn [Suppl] pp 89−92

Ritzel G (1974) Beitrag zum Suizid in psychiatrischen Kliniken. Fortschr Neurol Psychiatr 42:38−50

Saugstad L, Ødegård Ø (1985) Recent rise in supposedly stress dependent causes of death in psychiatric hospitals in Norway indicating increased "stress" in hospitals? Acta Psychiatr Scand 71:402−409

Schwartz J (1969) Suizid im Krankenhaus. Beitr Gerichtl Med 26:100−103

Swedish National Board on Health and Welfare (1985) Självmord inom den psykiatriska vården (Suicide within the psychiatric ward). Socialstyrelsen, The Swedish National Board on Health and Welfare, Stockholm

Wolk-Wasserman D (1986) Attempted suicide − the patient's family. Social network and therapy. Doctoral thesis, Karolinska Institutet, Stockholm

Suicide in Psychiatric Hospitals: Selected Results of a Study on Suicides Committed During Treatment in Five Psychiatric Hospitals in Southern Germany with Special Regard to Therapy Success and Presuicidal Symptoms

M. G. Wolfersdorf, R. Vogel, and G. Hole

Present State of Research on Clinic Suicide

Reports on suicide in psychiatric institutions have appeared intermittently in the psychological literature ever since the mid-nineteenth century (Wolfersdorf et al. 1986). Since the beginning of the 1950s, there has been a considerable accumulation of studies on the problem of clinic suicide (for general surveys, cf. Grandel 1978; Finzen 1984; Wolfersdorf 1984; Wolfersdorf et al. 1984 etc.). These studies are aimed at:

1. Determining whether suicide rates in psychiatric institutions are rising,
2. Describing the patient group that is most likely to commit suicide during inpatient treatment and after discharge.

Table 1 provides an overall view of suicide rates (primarily of inpatients) in various countries and hospitals. Most of these studies appeared in North America and describe the suicides and suicide rates in a selected number of psychiatric institutions of a single country. These data are supplemented by hospital reports as well as by data from the patient population of a private practitioner. The suicide rates per 100000 patient population, which apply primarily to psychiatric inpatients and to newly admitted patients, range from 34 to 380 and thus for the most part correspond to the rates calculated in other countries. The methodological problems involved in studying clinic suicides will not be treated here in any detail; interested readers should consult the summarizing discussions in Finzen (1983) as well as Wolfersdorf (1984). There does, however, appear to exist agreement in clinics in Scandinavia, Belgium, The Netherlands, Switzerland, and the Federal Republic of Germany that, at least for the European area, clinic suicides during inpatient psychiatric treatment are on the increase, even if the reasons for this postulated increase (if one ignores methodological factors) have remained for the most part in the realm of speculation (Table 2) unless, of course, one accepts the notion that the increase of patient admissions and discharges correlate with increased suicide rates, as depicted in Table 3 using the example of suicides of psychiatric patients at the County Psychiatric Hospital in Weissenau (FRG).

The empirical data which can be gleaned from studies of suicide groups seem to have reached the limits of their informational value. In accordance

Table 1. Suicide rates among psychiatric in- and outpatients: an overview (suicide rate, SR, per 100000 patients, average per year)

No.	Place and source of data	Period covered	Patients	SR
1	Mental Hospital Wash. State (Levy and Southcombe 1953)	1891 – 1949	Inpatients	380
2	New York State Mental Hospitals/USA (Malzberg. In: Dublin 1963)	(April 1957 – March 1959)	Inpatients	34
3	New York State and County Mental Hospitals/USA (Department of Mental Hygiene 1972)	1961 – 1962	Inpatients	36
4	5 State Hospitals, New York/ USA (Gale et al. 1980)	1975 – 1977	In- and outpatients, former patients	190
5	State of California, State and County Mental Hospitals/USA (Department of Mental Hygiene 1972)	1964 – 1966	Inpatients	50
6	27 Psychiatric Hospitals (of 33 public and private), Los Angeles, CA/USA (Schwartz et al. 1975)	1967 – 1972	In- and outpatients, former patients	Not stated (suicide $n=45$)
7	State of Maryland, State and County Mental Hospitals/USA (Department of Mental Hygiene 1972)	1965 – 1967	Inpatients	68
8	Missouri Mental Health Dept. Statistics/USA (Evenson et al. 1982)	1972 – 1974	In- and outpatients, former patients	350
9	5 Missouri State Mental Hospitals/USA (Sletten et al. 1972)	1960 – 1970	In- and outpatients, former patients	90
10	Mental Health Center Southern Arizona/USA (Nathan and Rousch 1984)	1979 – 1981	Inpatients	SR not stated (suicide $n=24$)
11	All VA Neuropsychiatric Hospitals/USA (Farberow et al. 1971)	1959 – 1966	Inpatients	72
12	All VA Neuropsychiatric Hospitals/USA (Farberow and MacKinnon 1975)	1950 – 1972	Inpatients	145
13	VA Neuropsychiatric Hospital, Houston, Texas/USA (Pokorny 1960)	1949 – 1959	Inpatients	250
14	VA Hospital, Kansas/USA (Chapman 1965)	1946 – 1962	In- and outpatients, former patients	78
15	Hillside Division, Long Island Jewish-Hillside Med. Center, Psychiatric Hospital/USA (Rabiner et al. 1982)	1968 – 1980	Inpatients	158

Table 1.   (continued)

No.	Place and source of data	Period covered	Patients	SR
16	Atascadero State Hospital, CA/USA (Haynes and Marques 1984)	1954–1979	Hospitalized ment. disordered offenders (inpatients)	90
17	Psychiatric Hospital/USA (Schwartz and Eisen 1984)	1974–1983	Young psychiatric inpatients, hosp. out-of-state (long-term hosp.)	170
18	Eloise Hospital, Michigan/USA (Lipschutz 1942)	1929–1941	Inpatients	42
19	Psychiatric Emergency Room, Duke University Medical Center/USA (Hillard et al. 1983)	(July 1972– June 1979)	Psychiatric emergency room patients	111
20	Private Practice Population, San Diego, CA/USA (Morrison 1982)	1972–1980	Private practice patients	120
21	Private Psychiatric Centers, San Diego, CA/USA (Morrison 1984)	1972–1980	Private practice patients	139
22	Clarke Institute, Toronto/Canada (Roy 1982)	1968–1979	In- and outpatients, former patients	SR not stated (suicide n=90)
23	Mental Hospital, Perth/Australia (James and Levin 1964)	1955–1961	Not stated	119
24	Glenside Hospital, Adelaide/Australia (Goldney et al. 1985)	1972–1982	In- and outpatients, former patients	222
25	Private Psychiatric Hospital/ New Zealand (and Medlicott 1969)	86 years	In- and outpatients, former patients	SR not stated (suicide n=61)
26	Shalvata Hospital, Hod Hasharon/Israel (Neumann 1971)	14 years since 1957	In- and outpatients, former patients, open hospital	452; SR not stated suicide (n=38)
27	Hadassah University, Psychiatric Hospital/Israel (Lerer and Avni 1976)	1965–1974	Inpatients	456
28	4 Psychiatric Hospitals, Ankara/Turkey (Sayil and Ceyhun 1981)	1965–1980	Inpatients	100 (1965–1970) to 40 (1976–1980)
29	6 Psychiatric Hospitals, Rhineland/FRG (Koester and Engels 1970)	1962–1968	Inpatients	57
30	Psychiatric Hospital, University of Göttingen/FRG (Ritzel 1974)	1955–1970	Inpatients	100
31	Psychiatric Hospital, University of Tübingen/FRG (Grandel 1978)	1965–1974	Inpatients	256

Table 1.   (continued)

No.	Place and source of data	Period covered	Patients	SR
32	Psychiatric Hospital, Med. School, University of Hannover/FRG (Schlosser and Strehle-Jung 1982)	1973 – 1978	Inpatients	426
33	AK Ochsenzoll (Psychiatric Hospital) Hamburg/FRG (Dorr 1984)	1965 – 1979	Inpatients	183
34	10 County Mental Hospitals, Bavaria/FRG (Gorenc-Krause 1980)	1950 – 1959 1967 – 1976	Inpatients Inpatients	50 66
35	County Mental Hospital, Weissenau, Psychiatric Hospital, University of Ulm/FRG (Wolfersdorf et al. 1987)	1970 – 1984	Inpatients	202
36	4 County Mental Hospitals, Baden-Württemberg/FRG (Wolfersdorf et al. 1984)	1970 – 1981	Inpatients	184
37	County Mental Hospital, Hildesheim/Lower Saxony/FRG (Ritzel and Kornek 1983)	1974 – 1981	Inpatients	83
38	County Mental Hospital, Haar-Munich/FRG (Bischof 1983)	1960 – July 1978		614
39	Psychiatric Hospital, University of Mannheim/FRG (Wolpert et al. 1976)	1968 – 1973	Inpatients (special rehabil- itation ward for schizophrenics)	940
40	County Mental Hospital, Weissenau, Psychiatric Hospital, University of Ulm/FRG (Wolfersdorf and Vogel 1984)	1976 – 1983	Inpatients (special ward for depressive inpatients)	669
41	County Mental Hospital, Haar-Munich/FRG (Bischof 1985)	1962 – 1981	Inpatients (forensic inpatient only)	1228
42	County Mental Hospital, Ueckermünde/GDR (Eichhorn et al. 1985)	1981 – 1983	Inpatients	251
43	County Mental Hospital, Müllhausen-Erfurt/GDR (Lange 1966)	1954 – 1963	Inpatients	100
44	Public Asylums, England, Wales, UK (Benham 1903)	1890 – 1902	Inpatients	25
45	Annual Report Mental Hospitals, Scotland, Edinburgh, UK (AZP 45, 1889)	1887	Inpatients	54.4 (based on all pat.) 245.9 (based on admission)
46	Mental Hospitals, England/Wales, UK (Stengel 1958. In: Retterstal 1978)	1920 – 1922 1945 – 1947	Inpatients Inpatients	49 51

Table 1. (continued)

No.	Place and source of data	Period covered	Patients	SR
47	Mental Hospital, West Sussex/UK (Walk 1967)	1954 – 1962	Inpatients	202
48	Psychiatric Hospital, Exe Vale/UK (Langley and Bayatti 1984)	1972 – 1981	Inpatients	SR not stated (suicide n=40)
49	Annual Report Mental Hospitals, Dublin/Ireland (AZP 45, 1889)	1887	Inpatients	49.6 (based on all pat.) 182.1 (based on all admissions)
50	Psychiatric Hospital, University of Zürich/Switzerland (Ernst and Kern 1974)	1900 – 1972	Inpatients	219 (1950 – 1959) 203 (1960 – 1969)
51	Psychiatric Hospital, University of Zürich/Switzerland Ernst 1979)	1900 – 1972	Inpatients	180 (per 100 000 discharged)
52	County Mental Hospital, Beverin/Switzerland (Maier 1981)	1920 – 1979	Inpatients	250 (per 100 000 discharged)
53	Psychiatric Hospital, University of Berne/Switzerland (Modestin 1982)	1961 – 1980	Inpatients	445 (per 100 000 discharged)
54	County Mental Hospital, Münsingen/Switzerland (Modestin 1982)	1961 – 1980	Inpatients	617 (per 100 000 discharged)
55	County Mental Hospital, Wil/Switzerland (Gering 1985)	1950 – 1984	Inpatients	SR not stated (suicide n=59)
56	Psychiatric Hospital, University of Basel/Switzerland (Wiedmer 1982)	1900 – 1979	Inpatients	148 (per 100 000 discharged)
57	County Mental Hospital, Salzburg/Austria (Mitterauer 1981)	1969 – 1979	Inpatients	79
58	21 Mental Hospitals/Sweden (Backlin 1937)	1922 – 1933	Inpatients	220
59	Psychiatric Hospital, University of Umea/Sweden (Perris et al. 1980)	1960 – 1977	Inpatients	SR not stated (suicide n=20)
60	Psych. Hospitals/Sweden Psych. Hospitals/Finland Psych. Hospitals/Norway (Hessö 1977)	1930 – 1959 1950 – 1969 1933 – 1974	Inpatients Inpatients Inpatients	84 169 102
61	Psychiatric Hospitals, Norway (Ödegard 1951)	1926 – 1941	Inpatients	92
62	Psychiatric Hospitals/Norway (Retterstøl 1979)	1930 – 1974	Inpatients	181

Table 1.   (continued)

No.	Place and source of data	Period covered	Patients	SR
63	Hospitals of Mental Health District Helsinki/Finland (Achte et al. 1966)	1952 – 1963	Inpatients	99
64	Hospitals of Mental Health District Helsinki/Finland (Niskanen et al. 1974)	1964 – 1972	Inpatients	140
65	Psychiatric Department, University of Helsinki/Finland (Lönnqvist et al. 1974)	1841 – 1971	Inpatients	134
66	Psychiatric Hospitals/Denmark (Clemmesen 1932)	1922 – 1931	Inpatients	190
67	Psychiatric Hospitals/Denmark (Clausager-Madsen 1943)	1932 – 1941	Inpatients	243
68	Psychiatric Hospital, Dianalund/Denmark (Bille and Dael 1960)	1928 – 1958	Inpatients	121 (per 100 000 discharged)
69	Psychiatric Hospital St. Hans, Roskilde/Denmark (Jensen 1966)	1950 – 1964	Inpatients	254
70	Psychiatric Hospital Departments/Denmark (Barner-Rasmussen 1984)	1971 – 1982	Inpatients	133
71	39 Psychiatric Hospitals, The Netherlands (de Graaf 1979)	1970 – 1974	Inpatients	207
72	Psychiatric Hospitals, The Netherlands (Brook 1985)	1979 – 1981	Inpatients (long-term population only: hospitalization 22 yrs)	482
73	Psychiatric Hospitals, The Netherlands (Speijer 1938)	1882 – 1932	Inpatients	35
74	Psychiatric Hospital, Pruszkow/Poland (Bartoszweski and Moczuliski 1969)	1916 – 1938 1954 – 1967	Inpatients Inpatients	131 57
75	Psychiatric Hospital „Aller Leidtragenden" St. Petersburg (Leningrad)/USSR (Bjeljakow 1894, in AZP 50, 1894)	1884 – 1892	Inpatients	409 (based on all patients)

Table 2. Factors which might have an influence on inpatients' suicides (see also Gorenc and Bruner 1985; here modified and completed)

Hospital organization

    Deficiencies in teaching programs for nurses, physicians, psychologists, social workers, especially in dealing with suicidal persons in the assessment of suicidality
    Deficiencies in supervision of treatment
    Lack of support by the hospital direction (head of hospital management) and lack of guidelines on how to deal with suicidal persons
    Frequent rotation or exchanges of physicians and other important medical personnel, especially frequent changes in the staff of wards of long-term inpatients
    Loss of hospital chief or guidance person
    High turnover rate of the hospitalized population
    Too small or too large wards
    Unexpected hasty and unprepared changes of wards (hospital instability, social changes)

Treatment factors

    Deficient milieu or social support
    Isolation and loneliness especially of long-term hospitalized patients
    Deficient security measures, lack of sufficient personnel-patient contact and control, premature grantings of leave of absence
    Too short treatment times, too short inpatient treatment, forced rehabilitation and discharge
    Frequent changes in treatment strategies, insufficient treatment

Table 3. Suicides and suicide rates 1970 to 1985 among psychiatric inpatients, PLK Weissenau (County Mental Hospital and Psychiatric Hospital, University of Ulm)

Year	Admission (*n*)	Suicides (*n*)	Suicide rate (SR$_A$)	
1970	1230	1	81.3	
1971	1258	2	159.0	
1972	1353	1	73.9	174.4
1973	1613	6	371.9	
1974	1426	2	140.3	
1975	1505	2	132.9	
1976	1901	–	–	
1977	1853	8	431.7	162.2
1978	2281	4	175.4	
1979	2326	2	86.0	
1980	2320	4	172.4	
1981	2345	5	213.2	
1982	2102	6	285.4	208.5
1983	2235	3	134.2	
1984	2511	6	238.9	
1985	2433	10	411.0	

with the present state of knowledge on clinic suicide, it is possible to maintain the following:

1. The mentally ill evince an especially high suicide risk, whereby inpatient psychiatric treatment can represent an additional aggravating factor with regard to the suicide act.

2. In numerical terms, men and women are represented almost evenly in the group of clinic suicides, wherein middle-aged and young people predominate.

3. In terms of diagnostic groups, schizophrenics predominate in absolute numbers, whereas paranoid-hallucinatory and so-called schizophrenic residues are evenly represented. In regard to their share in the population of a psychiatric hospital, depressives predominate in relative terms. Alcoholics, drug abusers, and drug addicts are relatively infrequent among clinic suicides.

4. Long-term patients are represented just as often, if not more so, than short-term ones. Patients who have been hospitalized a number of times are much more frequent clinic suicides than are first-time patients. Especially the second to fifth inpatient admissions are accompanied by clinic suicide, in particular when the time elapsed from the last discharge from inpatient therapy is less than half a year.

5. The long-term mentally ill (in terms of the entire period of illness) are more frequent among clinic suicides than those who have been affected for only a short time.

6. Over half of the suicides take place in the first half year following admission to an inpatient program. Here, suicides of patients diagnosed as having affective mental illnesses and depressive neuroses predominate, whereas patients diagnosed as schizophrenic are distributed evenly.

7. Over half the clinic suicides exhibit suicidal acts in their histories; a small number also attempt suicide during inpatient stay prior to the suicide itself.

8. In the period immediately preceding suicide, a third to almost half of later clinic suicides were adjudged as having apparent suicidal tendencies. More than half were considered inconspicuous with regard to their behavior and psychopathology.

9. The so-called hard methods of committing suicide are preferred (hanging, drowning, being run over by a train, jumping from a high place), whereby the choice of method depends on the possibilities existing in the vicinity of the clinic.

10. Up to two-thirds of the patients were confined to closed wards up until the time of the suicide. Most suicides, however, take place outside the ward, independent of whether it is closed or open. Most suicides occur during ordinary leaves of absence or outings. Escapes from closed wards are rare.

11. Changes in inpatient and/or therapeutic setting as well as in therapeutic personnel in the last 3 weeks prior to suicide were experienced by 30%−40% of suicides. Most patients received psychochemical therapy, psychotherapy, and social therapy (cf. Wolfersdorf 1984).

Results of Our Own Studies

Methodology

The following study, which investigated the 249 clinic suicides that were registered since 1970 within the framework of the clinic suicide study of the working
group "Suicidality and the Psychiatric Hospital," represents a descriptive approach to the problem and hence seeks to replicate the empirical data listed
above. Of the clinic suicide studies that have been carried out in the Federal
Republic of Germany, there are, as of now, only two large-scale studies en-
compassing data on a number of psychiatric hospitals. The first study is our
own; the second is by Gorenc-Krause (1980), which investigated diagnostic
shifts in ten psychiatric hospitals in Bavaria during two time periods
(1950–1959 in comparison with 1967–1976) and the correlation between apparently increasing suicide rates and internal clinic conditions such as number
of doctors, beds, mental-health personnel, and hospital living conditions. In the
following report on the results of our study, we have placed the main emphasis
on describing clinic suicides; the question of whether suicide rates in the psychiatric institutions studied are on the increase has been treated by us elsewhere
(e.g., Wolfersdorf et al. 1984).

Selected Results

Using a standardized questionnaire, we collected data on the clinic suicides that
have occurred in five psychiatric county hospitals since January 1970. This included data on personality and illness, biographical and family anamnestic
data, symptoms at the time of admission, diagnoses and progress of the illness,
suicide and therapy data as well as information on the clinical-therapeutic and
organizational setting. The total group encompassed 249 suicides, of which 60%
($n = 149$) were men and 40% ($n = 100$) were women. In the following discussion, this group will be broken down according to further criteria that appear
relevant for explaining clinic suicide.

Suicides of middle-aged and young people between 21 and 60 years of age
predominated; slightly less than half of the suicides (45%) were between 21 and
40 years of age, another third between 41 and 60 (Table 4). This clearly contradicts the age distribution of suicides in the general population and corresponds
to the age statistics contained in most of the literature on clinic suicide. Half of
the suicides (50%) were single at the time of the suicide, 34% were married. All
in all, 68% were living alone, i.e., were single, divorced, widowed, or estranged.
However, only 34 suicides (14%) lived alone before inpatient treatment.

Most suicides took place during the second to the fifth inpatient stay (52%;
Table 5); only 16% committed suicide during the first inpatient stay. Of the inpatients with two or more clinic stays, 51% had been discharged from the clinic
only a short time before, namely, in a period up to 6 months from the time
of the last discharge. On average, the total length of illness (for $n = 141$
suicides) was 12.2 years; for 56% of the patients, the time of treatment from ad-

Table 4. Hospital suicides (*n*=249) according to age

Age (years)	*n*	%	
20	14	56	
21–30	51	20.5 ⎫ 45.4	
31–40	62	24.9 ⎭	
41–50	50	20.1 ⎫ 36.2	
51–60	40	16.1 ⎭	
61–70	22	8.8	
70	7	2.8	
Not stated	3	1.2	
	249	100.0	

Table 5. Hospital suicides (*n*=249) according to number of admissions (incl. last admission)

Admission	*n*	%	
1	39	15.7 ⎫	
2	42	16.9	
3	39	15.7 ⎬ 67.5	
4	24	9.6	
5	24	9.6 ⎭	
6	13	5.2	
7	11	4.4	
8 and more	55	22.1	
Not stated	2	0.8	
	249	100.0	

mission until suicide ($n = 249$) ranged from 1 day to 6 months, of which 28% committed suicide within the 1st month after admission and a further 28% in the period from the 2nd to the 6th month.

In the diagnoses made in accordance with the International Classification of Diseases (ICD 8) ($n = 211$ suicides), the schizophrenic illnesses predominated with 55%, followed by the affective psychoses with 16%. All in all, the share of depressive illnesses (ICD 8: 296, 298.0, 300.4) was 24.2%. This is clearly higher than the usual proportion of patients with affective mental illnesses in psychiatric county hospitals, a proportion which has been estimated in general terms by the Psychiatry Commission to be 10% and which, based on the statistics compiled by nine state psychiatric hospitals in Baden-Württemberg in 1980, had been estimated at 12%–15% of admissions (Statistisches Landesamt 1980) (Table 6).

In clinical practice, the assessment of suicidality is usually arrived at using the criterion of whether suicide attempts are present in the patient's history. Of the later clinic suicides, 51% had attempted suicide before their last admission to the psychiatric ward; 19% of the group analyzed had attempted suicide during inpatient treatment prior to the suicide (Table 7). For every fifth patient (21%), a suicide attempt was the reason for inpatient treatment, whereby in 31%

Table 6. Hospital suicides according to diagnosis (*n*=211; ICD 8)

ICD 8		*n*	%
295	Schizophrenia	117	55.4
296	Affective psychosis	34	16.1
298.0	Reactive depressive psychosis	5	2.4
300.4	Neurotic depression	12	5.7
303.0/303.1/303.2	Alcoholism	15	7.1
304.0/304.3	Drug addiction	2	1.0
Other diagnosis		26	12.3
Not stated		–	–

Table 7. Hospital suicides according to suicide attempts before last admission and during last treatment

Before admission	*n*	%	During last treatment episode (*n*)	Prior to suicide (%)
Suicide attempts	128	51.4	48	19.3
No suicide attempts	117	47.0	199	70.9
Not stated	4	1.6	2	0.8
	249	100.0	249	100.0

Table 8. Hospital suicides (*n*=249) according to assessment of suicidality in the last 14 days before suicide

Patient denies, physician does not suspect/assume suicidality	150	60.2
Patient denies, physician suspects/assumes suicidality	35	14.1
Patient talks about wishes for calmness, peace, a pause or break in life	1	0.4
Patient says he/she does not want to live anymore	11	4.4
Patient talks about suicide thoughts	24	9.6
Patient reports concrete plans to commit suicide	7	2.8
Other	7	2.8
Not stated	14	5.6
	249	100.0

of the cases, special precautions were taken because of suspected suicidality. These precautions included confinement to closed wards and/or rooms, placing the patient under special observation, sedating the patient, and offering him or her intensive contact and the assistance of guidance personnel.

The data in Table 8 suggest our limited ability to assess suicidality in the period prior to suicide. Sixty per cent of the patients were not considered suicidal 14 days prior to the suicide. On the other hand, a third of the later suicides expressed a desire to commit suicide but could not be prevented from doing so. Fifty-three suicides (21%) had no outings in the last days before the suicide; in 193 cases (78%), an outing was permitted without special arrangement or with the accompaniment of relatives, personnel, or in a group with other patients. Seventy-two patients (29%) committed suicide in the psychiatric ward proper; only 13 suicides (5%) escaped from a closed ward to commit suicide, and 22% did not return from a normal outing or escaped on the way to therapy outside the ward. Most committed suicide during a planned outing, vacation leave, or weekend leave (33%).

Following the pattern established in the literature cited, the most frequently used method of suicide was hanging or strangling (35%), followed by being run over by a train (31%), drowning (10%), jumping from a high place (10%), and taking an overdose of tablets (8%). All other methods (gas, poison, opening of arteries, burning, or shooting) occurred less than 2% of the time.

In regard to the assessment of therapy success (Table 9), for 59% of the patients, a state ranging from unchanged to considerably worsened was noted between the time of admission and suicide. Similarly, 67% were assessed as being continuously ill, as being ill in phases, or as being ill in phases with a tendency toward worsening of the condition and unfavorable prognosis. Only 18% were considered as having a favorable prognosis and showing tendencies toward recovery.

Table 10 records the symptoms appearing in the period 14 days prior to the suicide for those patients who were described as being conspicuous in their behavior or symptoms. This group constitutes 55% of the depressives ($n = 51$ from a total group of 211 suicides) and 54% of the schizophrenics ($n = 117$ from the total population of 211 clinic suicides). If the recorded symptoms are differentiated according to the order of their frequency, the symptoms for the depressives are, as would be expected, the following: depressibility; fear, despair, panic; hopelessness and resignation; inner agitation and restlessness. These comprise the four most frequent symptoms; after that follow hallucinatory symptoms (depressive hallucinations) and, still less frequently, symptoms ranging from withdrawal, autism, and mutism to stupor. Paranoid delusions of being pursued, poisoned, and injured, which are consonant with depression, occurred in 7% of the cases. Imperative voices urging the patient to commit suicide did not occur in the group of suicides diagnosed as depressive; other hallucinations occurred in the case of one suicide. If one observes the group of schizophrenic patients ($n = 117$ from a total population of 211) using the same approach, then the four most frequent symptoms are as follows: depressibility; hopelessness and resignation; inner agitation and restlessness; fear, despair, and panic. The fifth most frequent symptom is withdrawal, autism, and mutism; the

Table 9. Hospital suicides ($n=249$) according to assessment of therapy effect since admission (between last admission and suicide) period

	n	%
No change or deterioration	146	58.6
Amelioration	100	40.2
Not stated	3	1.2

Table 10. Hospital suicides ($n=211$) according to symptoms in the last 14 days before suicide in depressives and schizophrenics

	Depression ($n=51$)		Schizophrenia ($n=117$)	
	no. of assertions	%	no. of assertions	%
No outstanding symptoms in the last 14 days before suicide	22	43	64	55
Not stated	1	2	2	2
Outstanding symptoms, especially:	28	55	51	44
	no. of assertions	% of outstanding pat.	no. of assertions	% of outstanding pat.
Depressed mood	17	61	20	39
Anxiety, despair, panic	14	50	15	29
Hopelessness, resignation	14	50	20	39
Restlessness, agitation	10	36	16	31
Depressive delusion	9	32	5	10
Withdrawal, autism, mutism	4	14	12	24
Inhibition, stupor	4	14	2	4
Delusions of persecution, poisoning	2	7	11	22
Hallucinations	1	4	67	25
Imperative voices (hall.) to commit suicide	–	–	1	2
Aggressive behavior	–	–	9	18
Alcohol and long-term abuse	2	7	3	6
Excitation	–	–	3	6
Hypochondriacal notions	2	7	7	14
Feelings of special mission, megalomania	–	–	2	4
All other symptoms	13	46	23	45

sixth is comprised of illness-specific paranoid delusions. Imperative voices calling for suicide were noted twice in the group of schizophrenic patients, optical and other hallucinations in the case of 36 others.

Discussion and Concluding Remarks

The results of this study tend to confirm the already existing knowledge summarized at the beginning of this paper. Part of the so-called hard data and figures relating to age, gender, diagnosis, regulation of outings and leaves, place of suicide, suicide methods, the assessment of the overall progress of the illness and of therapy success could possibly be of significance in explaining clinic suicide. At least for the relationship between therapist, therapeutic personnel, and patient, the assessment of therapy success and the prognosis assigned to the patient would appear to be of some importance. It is an impressive statistic that 59% and 67% of the patients, respectively, were assessed unfavorably in regard to short-term therapy success and to the overall prognosis of the illness. If one ascribes any significance to the factor of "hopelessness" as has been developed by A. T. Beck in regard to predicting acute suicidality (cf. Beck et al. 1976), then it is permissible to assume a connection between an unfavorable prognosis or resignation on the part of the therapist and hopelessness and resignation on the part of the patient. This is also supported by the frequent mention of hopelessness and resignation as presuicidal symptoms in the time period 14 days prior to suicide, at least for the conspicuous group of later clinic suicides.

It is also appropriate here to point out a further consideration regarding patient symptoms prior to suicide. There most certainly exists a group of patients who are inconspicuous in their behavior and symptoms before the sudden, surprising act of suicide. Possibly this is a group of patients (especially long-term ones) for whom such well-known suicide-related factors as verbal injuries or experiences of loss play an important role, whereby for these patients, general illness-accompanying factors such as feelings of confinement, instability, and a heightened sensibility for disturbed or disrupted emotional relationships are probably more important than a specific set of pathological symptoms. The 55% of the schizophrenics who were assessed as inconspicuous before suicide could provide a clue in this direction, whereas in the case of the 43% of inconspicuous depressives, we are probably dealing with patients who did not evince significant changes in their symptoms and behavior patterns prior to suicide. If, with this in mind, one examines the group that was considered conspicuous at the time of the diagnosis of depression or schizophrenia (55% in the group labeled "depressive," 44% in the group labeled "schizophrenic"), then it is striking that the symptoms named in both diagnostic groups for the most part coincide. This leads to the question of whether a presuicidal syndrome independent of nosologic considerations exists for clinic suicides, whereby for the groups diagnosed as "depressive" and "schizophrenic" nosologic-specific symptoms would become significant only much later on. Similar statements can also be made about the low frequency of imperative voices urging the patient to suicide. Although every clinician knows from his own experience that such hallucinations can be extremely important in individual cases, in relation to the frequency of occurrence, such psychotic events specific to depression and schizophrenia seem to be of much less significance. Similar observations can be found in Wall (1944) and also in Barraclough et al. (1974).

At the present state of research (especially in the German-speaking world), one must recognize that, although statistical depictions of the kind summarized above can be quite helpful, in the future they will provide little in the way of new information. In addition to methodological critiques, retrospective studies of hospital case sheets are also undeniably useful, although the need for such studies seems to have for the most part already been satisfied. For further clinic-suicide research, it would appear expedient to exploit those research approaches that relate to case studies, group comparisons, as well as to the suicide niveau of an entire clinic. In this connection, it is worth mentioning that in all probability (and contrary to what has up to now been assumed) earlier reports on clinic suicides (Wolfersdorf et al. 1988, in press) do not evince significantly lower suicide rates than do today's. By contrast to the customary perspective, which seeks to answer the question of how psychiatric clinics contribute to the number of clinic suicides and to the occurrence of this event in general, the third approach seeks to establish how many suicides were *prevented* by psychiatric intervention in the clinic. The only study in the last 20 years on this topic has been that of Ritzel (1983), who attempted to measure acute and chronic suicidality in the patients of a large psychiatric hospital. In the early clinic-suicide literature of the nineteenth century, this topic was treated by Hagen (1876, cited by Mülberger 1887), who came to the conclusion that "of 100 potential suicides the insane asylums prevent at the very least 90."

References

Achte KA, Stenbäck A, Teräväinen H (1966) On suicides committed during treatment in psychiatric hospitals. Acta Psychiatr Scand 42:272–284

Backlin E (1937) Själrmorden a statens sinnessjukhus in Sverige under aren 1901–1933 (Suicide in the Swedish State Insane Asylum in the years 1901–1933). Hygiea 99:65–100

Barner-Rasmussen P (1984) Suicidier i psykiatriske hospital-safdelinger (Suicide in psychiatric hospitals). Ugeskr Laeger 146:302–303

Barraclough B, Bunch J, Nelson B, Sainsbury P (1974) A hundred cases of suicide: clinical aspects. Br J Psychiatry 125:355–373

Bartoszewski J, Moczuliski W (1969) Samobojstwa chorych psychiczniew szipaln psychiatrycznym. Psychiatr Pol 3:319–326

Beck AT, Weissman A, Kovacs M (1976) Alcoholism, hopelessness and suicidal behavior. J Stud Alcohol 37:60–77

Benham HA (1903) Some remarks on suicide in public asylums. J Ment Sci 49:447–453

Bericht über das Irische Irrenwesen (Annual Report Mental Hospitals) – Dublin 1887 (1889) Allg Z Psychiatrie 45:168

Bericht des „Commissioners in Lunacy" (Annual Report Mental Hospitals) (1889) Allg Z Psychiatrie 45:169

Bille M, Dael M (1960) Nosocomielle suicidier pa et nervesanatorium. Nord Med 64:909–910

Bischof HL (1983) Suizidprophylaxe, ein brennendes Problem moderner Krankenhauspsychiatrie. Psycho 9:138–147

Bischof HL (1985) Todesfälle im Vollzug der Unterbringung im psychiatrischen Krankenhaus (§ 63 StGB). Psychiatr Prax 12:84–89

Bjeljakow SA (1894) Über Selbstmorde und andere Unglücksfälle in den Irrenanstalten St. Petersburg 1893 (Buchbesprechung). AZP 50:280–283

Brook OH (1985) Mortality in the long-stay population of Dutch mental hospitals. Acta Psychiatr Scand 71:626–635

Chapman RF (1965) Suicide during psychiatric hospitalization. Bull Menninger Clin 29:35–44

Claussager-Madsen M (1943) Nosocomiale Suicidier paa Danmarks Sindssygehospitaler 1932–1941 (Suicide in Danish psychiatric hospitals 1932–1941). Nord Med F:8–11

Clemmesen C (1932) Nosocomiale Suicidier paa Danmarks Sindssygehospitaler 1922–1931 (Suicides in Danish psychiatric hospitals 1922–1931). Hospitaltidende 75:1421–1432

Department of Mental Hygiene (1972) Annual reports. In: Kramer M, Pollack ES, Redick RW, Locke BZ (eds) Mental disorder/suicide. Harvard University Press, Cambridge, Mass, p 287

Dorr F (1984) Ein Beitrag zum Suicid im Krankenhaus. Eine Untersuchung von 114 Suiciden, die von 1965–1979 im Allgemeinen Krankenhaus Ochsenzoll in Hamburg stattfanden. Dissertation, University of Heidelberg/FRG

Dublin LJ (1963) Suicide. A sociological and statistical study. Ronald, New York

Eichhorn H, Nitzsche M, Kliewe W (1985) Überlegungen zum Suizid im psychiatrischen Krankenhaus. Psychiatr Neurol Med Psychol (Leipz) 37:573−581

Ernst H (1979) Die Zunahme der Suizide in den Psychiatrischen Kliniken − Tatsachen, Ursachen, Prävention. Soz Präventivmed 24:34−37

Ernst K, Kern R (1974) Suizidstatistik und freiheitliche Klinikbehandlung 1900−1972. Arch Psychiatr Nervenkr 219:255−263

Evenson RC, Wood JB, Nutall EA, Cho DW (1982) Suicide rates among public mental health patients. Acta Psychiatr Scand 66:254−264

Farberow NL (1972) Follow-up study of high risk suicidal neuropsychiatric patients. Proposal of cooperative studies program. V.A. Wadsworth Hospital Center, Central Research Unit, Los Angeles, California USA, October 1972

Farberow NL, MacKinnon D (1975) Status of suicide in the Veterans Administration. Report III − Revised. Central Research Unit V.A., Wadsworth Hospital Center Los Angeles, California, February 1975

Farberow NL, Ganzler S, Cutter F, Reynolds D (1971) An eight-year survey of hospital suicides. Suicide Life Threat Behav 1:184−202

Finzen A (1983) Psychiatrische Behandlung und Suizid. Methodenprobleme bei der Untersuchung des Suizids unter psychiatrischer Behandlung. Psychiatr Prax 10:103−108

Finzen A (1984) Psychiatrische Behandlung und Suizid − Kann psychiatrische Behandlung den Patienten-Suizid verhindern? Psychiatr Prax 11:1−5

Gale SW, Mesnikoff A, Finde J, Talbott JA (1980) A study of suicide in state mental hospitals in New York City. Psychiatr Q 52:201−213

Gering AD (1985) Zur Abschätzung der Suizidalität unter besonderer Berücksichtigung von Suiziden psychiatrischer Klinikpatienten. Dissertation, University of Basel, Switzerland

Goldney RD, Positano S, Spence ND, Rosenman SJ (1985) Suicide in association with psychiatric hospitalisation. Aust NZ J Psychiatry 19:177−183

Gorenc KD, Bruner CA (1985) Suicidal behavior among patients in Bavarian mental hospitals. Acta Psychiatr Scand 71:468−470

Gorenc-Krause KD (1980) Der Suizid in den bayerischen Bezirkskrankenhäusern. Dissertation, University of Munich/FRG

Graaf AC de (1979) Zelmoord in psychiatrische Ziekenhuis (Suicide in psychiatric hospitals). Tijdschr Psychiatr 11−12:814−820

Grandel S (1978) Selbstmord und psychiatrische Behandlung. I. Suizide an psychiatrischen Krankenhäusern. Werkstattschriften zur Sozialpsychiatrie, no 21. Psychiatrie-Verlag, Wunstdorf

Haynes RL, Marques JK (1984) Patterns of suicide among hospitalized mentally disordered offenders. Suicide Life Threat Behav 14:113−125

Hessö R (1977) Suicide in Norwegian, Finnish and Swedish psychiatric hospitals. Arch Psychiatr Nervenkr 224:119−127

Hillard JR, Ramm D, Zung WWK et al. (1983) Suicide in a psychiatric emergency room population. Am J Psychiatry 140:459−462

James JP, Levin S (1964) Suicide following discharge from psychiatric hospital. Arch Gen Psychiatry 10:43−46

Jensen L (1966) Nosocomial suicides and suicides among discharged patients. Acta Psychiatr Scand 42 [Suppl 191]:149−170

Koester H, Engeles G (1970) Gelungene Suizide im psychiatrischen Krankenhaus. Z Präventivmed 15:19−26

Kramer M, Pollack ES, Redick RW, Locke BZ (1972) Mental disorder/suicide. Harvard University Press, Cambridge, Mass

Lange E (1966) Die Suizidgefahr beim Open-Door-System (ODS) in stationären psychiatrischen Einrichtungen. Soc Psychiatry 1:64−72

Langley GE, Bayatti NN (1984) Suicides in Exe Vale Hospital, 1972−1981. Br J Psychiatry 145:463−467

Lerer B, Avni J (1976) Suicide in a general hospital psychiatric department. Psychiatr Clin (Basel) 9:106−111

Levy S, Southcombe RH (1953) Suicide in a state hospital for the mentally ill. J Nerv Ment Dis 117:504−514

Lipschutz LS (1942) Some administrative aspects of suicide in the mental hospital. Am J Psychiatry 99:181−187

Lönnqvist J, Niskanen P, Rinta-Mänty R, Achte K, Kärhä E (1974) Suicides in psychiatric hospitals in different therapeutic eras. Psychiatr Fenn:265−274

Maier C (1981) Die Suizide in der Klinik Beverin 1920−1979. Ein Beitrag zur Diskussion über die Zunahme von Suiziden in psychiatrischen Kliniken. Schweiz Arch Neurol Neurochir Psychiatr 128:75−84

Malzberg B (1940) Mortality among patients with mental disease. State Hospital Press, Utica, New York

Medlicott RW, Medlicott PAW (1969) Suicide in and after discharge from a private psychiatric hospital over a period of eighty-six years. Aust NZ J Psychiatry 3:137−144

Mitterauer B (1981) Können Selbstmorde in einem psychiatrischen Krankenhaus verhindert werden? Psychiatr Prax 8:25−30

Modestin J (1982) Suizid in der psychiatrischen Institution. Nervenarzt 53:254−261

Morrison JR (1982) Suicide in a psychiatric practice population. J Clin Psychiatry 43:348−352

Morrison JR (1984) Suicide in psychiatric patients: age distribution. Suicide Life Threat Behav 14:52−58

Mülberger F (1887) Über die Bedeutung der Irrenanstalten für die Verhütung des Selbstmordes der Geisteskranken. Allg Z Psychiatrie 43:104−123

Nathan RG, Rousch AF (1984) Which patients commit suicide? Am J Psychiatry 141:1017

Neumann M (1971) Suicide proness. Isr Ann Psychiatry Relat Discipl 9:39−51

Niskanen P, Lönnqvist J, Achte K, Rinta-Mänty R (1974) Suicides in Helsinki hospitals in 1964−1972. Psychiatr Fenn:275−280

Ödegard O (1951) Mortality in Norwegian mental hospitals 1926−1941. Acta Genet 2:141−173

Perris C, Beskow J, Jacobsson L (1980) Some remarks on the incidence of successful suicide in psychiatric care. Soc Psychiatry 15:161−166

Pokorny AD (1960) Characteristics of forty-four patients who subsequently committed suicide. Arch Gen Psychiatry 2:314−323

Rabiner CJ, Wegner JT, Kane JM (1982) Suicide in a psychiatric population. Psychiatric Hospital 13:55−59

Retterstøl N (1979) Suicide in psychiatric hospitals in Norway. In: Achte K, Lönnqvist J (eds) Psychopathology of direct and indirect self-destruction. Psychiatria Fennica [Suppl 1978] pp 89−92

Ritzel G (1974) Beitrag zum Suizid in psychiatrischen Kliniken. Fortschr Neurol Psychiatr 42:38−50

Ritzel G, Kornek G (1983) Fördern freizügige und individuelle Therapie und Klinikführung den Suizid? Psycho 9:77

Roy A (1982) Risk factors for suicide in psychiatric patients. Arch Gen Psychiatry 39:1089−1095

Sayil J, Ceyhun B (1981) A study on successful suicide. In: Soubrier JP, Vedrinne J (eds) Depression and suicide. Pergamon, Paris, pp 496−501

Schlosser J, Strehle-Jung G (1982) Suizide während psychiatrischer Klinikbehandlung. Psychiatr Prax 9:20−26

Schwartz DA, Flinn DE, Slawson PL (1975) Suicide in the psychiatric hospital. Am J Psychiatry 132:150−153

Schwartz RS, Eisen SV (1984) The risk of suicide in young psychiatric patients hospitalized out of state. Psychiatry 47:342−350

Sletten JW, Brown ML, Evenson RC et al. (1972) Suicide in mental hospital patients. Dis Nerv Syst 33:328−334

Speijer D (1938) Overzicht der zelfmoordpoginge met dooddijken afloop in de nederlandsche krankzinnigengestichten gedurende het tijdvak 1882−1932 (Overview on suicides in the psychiatric hospitals in the Netherlands 1882−1932). Ned Tijdschr voor Geneesk 82:2824−2827

Statistisches Landesamt (1980) Statistik der Psychiatrischen Landeskrankenhäuser Baden-Württembergs 1980. Statistisches Landesamt, Stuttgart

Walk D (1967) Suicide and community care. Br J Psychiatry 113:1381−1391

100   M. G. Wolfersdorf et al.: Suicide in Psychiatric Hospitals

Wall HJ (1944) The psychiatric problem of suicide. Am J Psychiatry 101:404−406
Wiedmer L (1982) Die Suizide in der Psychiatrischen Universitätsklinik Basel von
    1900−1979. Dissertation, University of Basel, Switzerland
Wolfersdorf M (1983) Zum Suizidproblem in der psychatrischen Klinik. Neuropsychiatria
    Clinica 2:161−173
Wolfersdorf M (ed) (1984) Suizide psychiatrischer Patienten. Weissenhof, Weinsberg/FRG
Wolfersdorf M, Vogel R (1984) Depressionen bei Suiziden stationärer psychiatrischer Patien-
    ten. In: Welz R, Möller J (eds) Bestandsaufnahme der Suizidforschung. Epidemiologie,
    Prävention und Therapie. Roderer, Regensburg/FRG, pp 230−248 R
Wolfersdorf M, Vogel R, Hole G, Dreher R, Faulstich H, Freeman G, Geldmacher C, Herr
    W, Jonen B, Kirschmann J, Neef J, Stoppa H, Weisskittel C, Wohlt R, Zlatnikova J (1984)
    Ergebnisse einer retrospektiven Verbundstudie zum Suizid stationärer psychiatrischer
    Patienten. In: Weilz R, Möller J (eds) Bestandsaufnahme der Suizidforschung. Epidemio-
    logie, Prävention und Therapie. Roderer, Regensburg/FRG, pp 158−177
Wolfersdorf M, Schmidt-Michel PO, Weisskittel C, Keller F (1987) Reports on hospital
    suicides in the older German psychiatric literature (19th century). Is there a difference in
    the suicide rates compared to nowadays? Social Psychiatry 1988, in press
Wolpert E, Pickel H, Häfner H (1976) Zur Suizidproblematik psychiatrischer Patienten wäh-
    rend stationärer Behandlung. Presented at the 7th Donau-symposium for psychiatry. 30
    September 1976, Vienna, Austria

Suicides Among Patients Treated in a Ward Specializing in Affective Disorders

R. Metzger and M. G. Wolfersdorf

Introduction

Since the ancient time of the Hippocratic physicians, the close connection between depression or melancholia and suicide has been a well-known fact (Leibbrand and Wettley 1962).

The assessment of suicidal intent is one of the most important responsibilities of the psychiatrist treating patients with a depression disorder (Sainsbury 1968). Fifteen per cent, or every sixth patient, with a depressive disorder can be expected to die from suicide. This is the consistent result of many follow-up studies of patients with depressive disorders, as reviewed by Miles (1977).

Psychiatrists examining coroners' reports of suicides have also noted the high risk of depressive disorders. Considering only those suicides found to be mentally ill, there were 30% – 50% suffering from an affective disorder (Kraft and Babigian 1976; Lonnquist et al. 1981; Müller 1978; Robin et al. 1959; Roy 1981).

Clinical and Environmental Characteristics of Depressives at Risk for Suicide

In clinical practice, it is a difficult task to assess suicidal intent and to recognize in a group of depressives, who are mostly high-risk persons, those at special risk to die from suicide. For some types of depressive illness or depressive patients (e.g., subtype of depression, sex, age, mental status, clinical symptoms), a connection with suicide risk could be expected, but findings like those referred to below are inconsistent.

Subtypes of Depression

The question of whether patients with primary affective illness and neurotic or psychoneurotic depression bear the same risk of suicide has not been answered consistently.

Miles (1977), in reviewing the suicide risk for different psychiatric disorders, found the suicide risk in primary depressive illness to be as high as in neurotic or reactive depression. Comparing neurotic and personality disorders, he stated that "neurotic depressives are distinct suicidal risks." He, like Farberow and

McEvoy (1966), concluded "that the two types of depression from the standpoint of suicide do not differ." Some reports question this, comparing either depressive neurosis with other neurotic disorders (Zauner 1970) or with endogenous depression (Scharfetter et al. 1979).

These differences may be due to the fact that depressive neurosis may not be as valid a diagnosis as primary depressive disorders seem to be.

Sex, Age, and Marital Status

Since the work of Emil Durkheim, it has been a well-known fact in suicidology that suicide risk increases with age, is higher in males than females, and is connected with being divorced or widowed (Kreitmann 1980; Sainsbury 1968; Stengel 1969).

In depressive patients, the findings with respect to sex are contradictory. In his follow-up study of manic-depressive patients, Stenstedt (1952) found more suicides in men than in women; Perris and D'Elia (1966) noted only a slight tendency to a higher incidence of male suicides; Till and Kapamadzija (1981) found more female suicides in their follow-up study.

According to Robin et al. (1959), the suicide risk in depressives increases with age, but this increase resembles the distribution in the general population. The same assumption can be made concerning marital status.

Clinical Symptoms

Table 1 provides a survey of some items found to be connected with a high suicide risk in depressed persons. The various points were cited by different studies and are mentioned without value judgement. Clinical symptoms which are usually found to be associated with increased suicide risk are feelings of hopelessness (Kuhnt and Welz 1983; Wetzel 1976) and guilt (Hole 1971, 1973), and high anxiety (Pöldinger 1972), which could be associated with agitation (Pöldinger 1972; Sainsbury 1968).

Table 1. Items connected with a high suicide risk in depressed patients

Symptoms	Course of illness
Hopelessness	Lack of response to treatment
Feelings of guilt	Chronic course of illness
Delusion	Prior suicide attempts
Hostility	First year after discharge from hospital
Absence of hypochondria	
Lack of somatic equivalents of anxiousness	Social factors
Hysteroid personality (in women)	Unemployment
Anxiousness	Social isolation
Agitation	Broken home

Hostility, especially in dealing with therapeutic personnel, is a behavioral peculiarity found in some studies (Farberow et al. 1966; Farberow and McEvoy 1966; Yesavage 1984). A lack of somatic equivalence of anxiety could, as pointed out by Farberow (1966), show a relative ineffectiveness of somatic complaints in binding anxiety or depression. This could explain the absence of hypochondria as found by Stenback et al. (1965) and McDowall et al. (1968).

Course of Illness

The patient with a high suicide risk shows a chronic course of illness or, what might be the same, has a poor prognosis, "with no appreciable alleviation of psychological problems" (Farberow and McEvoy 1966; Roy 1981). Later suicides among depressed patients were consistently found to be associated with previous suicide attempts (Farberow and McEvoy 1966; Farberow 1981; McDowall et al. 1968; Bürk and Möller 1985). In addition, patients with depressive disorders who had attempted suicide were found to have a higher risk of dying by suicide (Häfner et al. 1983). The 1st year after discharge from hospital is a high-risk period for depressed patients as well as for all psychiatric patients (Lonnquist et al. 1981; Robin et al. 1968; Perris and D'Elia 1966).

The environmental factors mentioned in Table 1 are well known and will not be explained further (Farberow and McEvoy 1966; McDowall et al. 1968; Roy 1981; Kraft and Babigian 1976; Walton 1958).

Weissenau Depression Ward

The Weissenau Depression Ward is a specialized unit for the treatment of affective disorders. Nowadays, diagnosing and treating depressive illness is a task of the general practitioner and the psychiatrist practicing privately in the community (Kielholz 1974). Therefore, patients in such a specialized unit are suffering from acute severe depression, suicidal crisis, and depressions resistant to the usual therapeutic approaches (Wolfersdorf et al. 1981, 1983, 1985).

The suicide risk with respect to suicide attempts and suicidal thoughts is high: 20% are admitted to the hospital after a suicide attempt, 30% have a history of previous suicide attempts, and 50% of all patients at admission are thought to be suicidal by the therapist.

With this background, recognizing suicidal intent and preventing suicide is one of the priorities of the whole treatment plan. The treatment cannot be described in detail, but it should be mentioned that the therapeutic program includes pharmacotherapeutic treatment and a psychotherapeutic approach to the patient. The latter tries to combine the viewpoints of psychoanalysis, cognitive therapy, and behavioral therapy.

On a ward with patients having a high suicide risk, death from suicide is a very regrettable but unavoidable event. If suicide occurs during treatment, the responsible therapist together with the staff works up the case history and the feelings following the loss of a patient by suicide. There are also special therapeutic groups with surviving patients on the ward.

Material and Methods

Between the beginning of 1977 and the end of 1984, 1619 patients were treated in the Weissenau Depression Ward. During this time, 25 suicides occurred, 12 cases while under treatment and 13 after discharge from the hospital.

The social and clinical characteristics of the suicide group were compared with two representative groups of depressed inpatients. One group included all inpatients (523) from the beginning of 1977 to the end of 1981 and overlapped with the suicide group.

The second group was a representative group of 99 patients in 1983. In this group, no hospital suicides occurred and one suicide was committed after treatment. We used this group for a statistical comparison with the suicide group using the chi-squared test. A statistical comparison was also made between suicides while under treatment and after discharge using the chi-squared test with Yates correction and the Fisher test.

Results

Table 2 shows items not found to be different between the group of suicides and the representative group. These were sex and religion and what may be more surprising, the suicidal intent at admission as stated by the therapist in the record. Patients who later committed suicide also did not seem to be admitted more often after a suicide attempt than patients of the representative group.

Table 3 shows characteristics found to be different between the groups. Most often, the suicides were married; this proportion exceeds the proportion of married patients in the representative groups. In addition, it can be said that, of the 21 married patients, seven lived with the partner and 13 together with the partner and children. Family conflicts were found in 17 patients. There was no significant difference between the two subtypes of depression with respect to family conflicts.

The age distribution (Fig. 1) shows, especially in the females, a distinct over-representation of patients between 30 and 50 years of age.

The differences in the distribution of the depressive subtypes do not achieve statistical significance but do show a trend ($P = 0.2$). Psychotic depression was much more frequent at the last admission in the later suicides. The symptoms as stated by therapists at admission are in accordance with this (Table 4). In 13 cases, we found delusion at admission, but only in one case in the days before the suicide.

In contrast to the representative group which exhibited cardiac complaints such as palpitation in 30% and shortness of breath or headaches in 50%, somatic complaints were seldom stated by therapists for those who subsequently committed suicide.

The only significant difference between the suicides and the representative group was the history of prior suicide attempts. Suicide attempts during inpatient treatment seemed to be very high in the suicide group, but the small number of cases allows no statistical comparison.

Table 2. Items exhibiting no differences between a group of suicides ($n = 25$) and two representative groups of depressed inpatients (1977 – 1981, $n = 513$; 1983, $n = 99$)

| | Suicides | | Depressed inpatients | | | |
| | | | 1977 – 1981 | | 1983 | |
	(%)	(n)	(%)	(n)	(%)	(n)
Sex						
Males	20	5	21.2	109	27.3	27
Females	80	20	78.8	404	72.7	72
Religion						
Rom. Catholic	64				62	
Protestant	32				29	
Admission caused by suicide attempt	24	6	19.3		20.2	20
Suicidal intent at admission						
No signs of suicidal intent	32	8			36.3	36
Suicide intent denied by patient, but supposed by therapist	16	4			6.1	6
Thought of death or suicide, desire for pause	49	11			42.4	42
Not stated					15.2	15

Table 3. Items exhibiting differences between a group of suicides ($n = 25$) and two representative groups of depressed inpatients (1977 – 1981, $n = 513$; 1983, $n = 99$)

| | Suicide group | | Depressed inpatients | | | |
| | | | 1977 – 1981 | | 1983 | |
	(%)	(n)	(%)	(n)	(%)	(n)
Marital status						
Married	84		62.7		60	
Single	12		14.5		20	
Widowed	4		10.5		14	
Divorced	–		11.3		6	
Depressive subtype						
Psychotic depression	60	15	31.7	141	31.9	32
Neurotic depression	40	10	56.4	288	59.8	58
Prior suicide attempts [a]	68	17			34.7	34
Suicide attempts during inpatient treatment	28	7			2.7	2
Age distribution						
Mean: males	44.8 years		45.1 years			
females	37.8		47.1			
total	39.2		46.6			
Range	20 – 56		16 – 91			

[a] Significant difference, using the chi-squared test $P < 0.01$

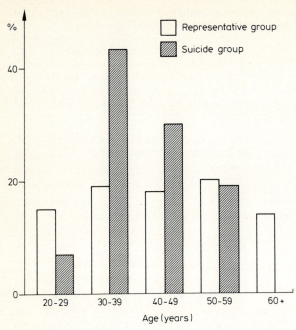

Fig. 1. Age distribution of 25 suicides and a representative group (*n* = 523) of depressed in-patients

Table 4. Symptoms upon hospital admission in a representative group of depressed inpatients (*n* = 99) and a group of suicides (*n* = 25)

	Suicide group		Representative group 1983	
	(*n*)	(%)	(*n*)	(%)
Delusion	13	52	11	12
Anxiousness	12	48	46	46
Hopelessness	13	52		−
Sleeplessness	15	60	68	68
Lack of self-esteem	16	64		−
Somatic complaints	3	9		30 − 50

   With respect to the cause of illness, we could not compare the suicides with the representative group. Within the suicide group, there were suicides during or after the first admission (Kielholz 1974) as well as after three or more admissions (Kraft and Babigian 1976). However, there were several patients with a long history of depressive episodes that became very severe and for which treatment was not very effective.

   Suicides after discharge occurred commonly in the 1st year: four patients died within 4 weeks, ten patients within 12 months, and three patients more than 1 year after discharge. The longest time was 6 years, the shortest 1 day after discharge.

Discussion

The number of patients discussed here is relatively small, and the 'clientele' of a special unit for affective disorders may be a very highly selected group. Perhaps in such a highly selected group, the influence of factors such as age, sex, and marital status is not the same as in the general population. Usually marriage should protect against suicide (Sainsbury 1968; Stengel 1969), but it did not in our cases.

For some characteristics, such as sex, marital status, prior suicide attempts, suicide in the 1st year after discharge, and the relative lack of somatic complaints, our findings are consistent with the studies mentioned above. Surprisingly, a trend to ward more psychotic depressions in the suicide group is to be seen. It should be remembered that all patients except for one were not stated to be paranoid at the time of suicide. Mitterauer (1981) found similar results. He concluded that, in these cases, the suicide could be "a special variety of balance suicide."

However, by working through the case notes, we gained the impression that possibly therapists can better deal with the suicidal impulses of neurotic depressives who form more binding ties with therapist or staff and exhibit more overt indications of suicide risk. Most psychotic depressive suicides were known to be suicidal over a long period of treatment and there were very few signs to indicate a heightened suicide risk before the suicide.

A retrospective study such as this offers limited evidence. The results indicate a need for further investigation and could prompt therapists involved in daily therapeutic work to increase the attention paid to the patients and their problems.

References

Bürk F, Möller HJ (1985) Prädiktoren für weiteres suizidales Verhalten. Fortschr Neurol Psychiatr 53:259–270

Farberow NL (1981) Suicide and depression in the United States. In: Soubrier JP, Vedrinne J (eds) Depression and suicide. Pergamon, Paris

Farberow NL, McEvoy TC (1966) Suicide among patients with diagnosis of anxiety reaction or depressive reaction in general medical and surgical hospitals. J Abnorm Psychol 71:287–299

Farberow N, Shneidman ES, Neuringer C (1966) Case history and hospitalization factors in suicides of neuropsychiatric hospital patients. J Nerv Ment Dis 142:32–44

Häfner H, Welz R, Gorenc K, Kleff F (1983) Selbstmordversuche und depressive Störungen. Schweiz Arch Neurol Neurochir Psychiatr 133 (2):283–294

Hole G (1971) Some comparisons among guilt feelings, religion, and suicidal tendencies in depressed patients. Suicide Life Threat Behav 1 (2):138–142

Hole G (1973) Suizidalität und Selbstwertverluste im Erleben depressiver Patienten. Grenzen der phänomenologischen Erfaßbarkeit. Z Psychother Med Psychol 23:233–238

Kielholz P (1974) Die Depression in der täglichen Praxis. Huber, Bern

Kraft DP, Babigian HM (1976) Suicide by persons with and without psychiatric contacts. Arch Gen Psychiatry 33:209–215

Kreitmann N (1980) Die Epidemiologie von Suizid und Parasuizid. Nervenarzt 51:121–138

Kuhnt S, Welz R (1983) Hilflosigkeit und Hoffnungslosigkeit bei Individuen mit suizidalen Handlungen. In: Pohlheimer H, Schmidtke A, Welz R (eds) Suizidales Verhalten. Methodenprobleme und Erklärungsansätze. Roderer, Regensburg

Leibbrand W, Wettley A (1962) Der Wahnsinn. Geschichte der abendländischen Psychopathologie. Alber, Freiburg

Lonnquist J, Koskenvuo M, Kaprio J, Langinvainio H (1981) The mortality in psychiatric disorders: a three year prospective follow-up study. In: Soubrier JP, Vedrinne J (eds) Depression and suicide. Pergamon, Paris

McDowall AW, Brooke EM, Freeman-Browne DL, Robin AA (1968) Subsequent suicide in depressed inpatients. Br J Psychiatry 114 (511):749—754

Miles C (1977) Conditions predisposing to suicide: A review. J Nerv Ment Dis 164 (4):231—246

Mitterauer B (1981) Können Selbstmorde in einem psychiatrischen Krankenhaus verhindert werden? Psychiatr Prax 8 (1):25—30

Müller D (1978) Selbstmord unter psychiatrischer Behandlung. Psychiatrie-Verlag, Wunstorf

Perris C, D'Elia G (1966) A study of bipolar and unipolar recurrent depressive psychosis. X. Mortality, suicide and life cycles. Acta Psychiatr Scand [Suppl] 194:172—183

Pöldinger W (1972) Suizidalität, Depression und Angst. In: Kielholz P (ed) Depressive Zustände. Huber, Bern

Robin AA, Brooke EM, Freeman-Browne DL (1968) Some aspects of suicide in psychiatric patients in Southend. Br J Psychiatry 114:739—747

Robins E, Murphy GE, Wilkinson R, Grassner S, Kayes J (1959) Some clinical considerations in the preventation of suicide based on a study of 134 successful suicides. Am J Public Health 49:888—898

Roy A (1981) Depression and suicide in psychiatric patients: Cause and prevention. In: Soubrier JP, Vedrinne J (eds) Depression and Suicides. Pergamon, Paris

Sainsbury P (1968) Suicide and depression. Br J Psychiatry (Special Publications, no 2). Headley, London

Scharfetter C, Angst J, Nüsperli M (1979) Suizid und endogene Psychose. Soz Präventivmed 24:37—42

Stenback A, Achte KA, Rimon RH (1965) Physical disease, hypochondria and alcohol addiction in suicides committed by mental hospital patients. Br J Psychiatry III:933

Stengel E (1969) Selbstmord und Selbstmordversuch. Fischer, Frankfurt

Stenstedt A (1952) A study in manic-depressive psychosis. Acta Psychiatr Neurol Scand [Suppl] 79:1—111

Till E, Kapamadzija B (1981) Endogenous depressions and suicidal behaviour. In: Soubrier JP, Vedrinne J (eds) Depression and suicide. Pergamon, Paris

Walton HJ (1958) Suicidal behaviour in depressive illness. J Ment Sci 104:884—891

Wetzel ED (1976) Hopelessness, depression, and suicide intent. Arch Gen Psychiatry 33:1069—1073

Wolfersdorf M, Straub R, Helber I, Kopittke W, Metzger R, Hole G, Faust V (1981) Depressive Patienten in stationärer Behandlung. Psychiatr Clin (Basel) 14:226—244

Wolfersdorf M, Straub R, Helber I, Kopittke W, Metzger R, Studemund B, Vock B, Hole G, Faust V (1983) Zur Hospitalisation Depressiver — Erste Ergebnisse einer epidemiologischen Studie der Weissenauer Depressionsstation. In: Faust V, Hole G (eds) Depression. Hippokrates, Stuttgart

Wolfersdorf M, Keller F, Wohlt R (1985) Zur Klientel der Weissenauer und Reichenauer Depressionsstation. In: Wolfersdorf M, Wohlt T, Hole G (eds) Depressionsstationen. Roderer, Regensburg

Yesavage JA (1984) Direct and indirect hostility and self-destructive behaviour by hospitalized depressives. Acta Psychiatr Scand 68 (5):345—350

Zauner J (1970) Study of the causes of death of former patients of a psychotherapeutic hospital on the basis of a catamnestic examination. Z Psychosom Med Psychoanal 16 (3):223—230

Types of Clinical Suicide

J. MODESTIN

Introduction

A considerable increase in clinical suicides has been registered over the last 10−20 years in Europe (Ernst and Kern 1974; Loennqvist et al. 1974; Retterstøl 1978; Modestin 1982; Wolfersdorf et al. 1984). Accordingly, psychiatric hospital inpatients were designated in 1982 by the WHO as a special group "meriting particular attention for the improvement or development of methods of care to prevent suicide." To meet these requirements, an improved knowledge of characteristics of certain groups of clinical suicides is desirable, as it could enable more specific therapeutic actions to be taken.

Methods

The present investigation was performed as part of an extended study on institutional suicide. With the help of police files, which encompass the most complete registration of suicides, 149 patients were identified who had all committed suicide while being on the hospital rolls of two different Swiss psychiatric hospitals in the years 1960−1981. The clinical charts of these inpatient suicides were thoroughly examined and demographic, psychosocial, and clinical data were extracted. For many patients, psychiatric expert opinions and clinical records from other psychiatric institutions were also available. All variables investigated were either primarily clearly determinable (such as sex and age) or defined and operationalized as exactly as possible. The last episode of the illness was diagnosed with the help of Research Diagnostic Criteria (Spitzer et al. 1978). Suicide attempts were evaluated using the classification of Motto (1965). Life events were investigated and classified according to Paykel et al. (1971, 1975). This report deals with the mutual comparison of individual diagnostic groups of suicides within the inpatient suicide population.

Results

Of the 149 inpatient suicides, 49 (33%) were diagnosed as schizophrenia, 75 (50%) as depression, and 9 (6%) as alcoholism. Compared with a control group of 149 clinical nonsuicides, representative of the entire inpatient population, schizophrenic and depressive patients were overrepresented, whereas alcoholic patients were significantly underrepresented in the suicide group. The most important results of the comparison of these three diagnostic groups of clinical suicides are presented in Table 1, which demonstrates that there are many differences between the schizophrenic, depressive, and alcoholic clinical suicides.

Schizophrenic suicides were of a younger age, mostly single, and childless. They frequently presented signs of disturbed social adjustment before the age of 25 years in terms of delinquency and/or vocational difficulties and/or relational difficulties. At the time of the index admission, the majority were in a more or less dependent status: they lived either with their parents or in various kinds of institutions. Their vocational situation was less favorable than that of depressed suicides. More than half of them were put under tutelage, and the majority were chronically disabled, i.e., they were unable to work, and/or institutionalized for more than half of the previous 5 years. The vast majority had

Table 1. Comparison of schizophrenic ($n = 49$), depressive ($n = 75$), and alcoholic ($n = 9$) inpatient suicides with regard to some demographic, psychosocial, and clinical variables

	Schizophrenic suicides		Depressive suicides		Alcoholic suicides		Significance ($df = 2$)	
	(n)	(%)	(n)	(%)	(n)	(%)		
Young age (<30 years)	16	33	11	15	0	0	$\chi^2 = 8.38$	$P=0.015$
Single	42	86	28	37	4	44	$\chi^2 = 28.60$	$P<0.001$
Childless	41	84	14	19	5	54	$\chi^2 = 51.05$	$P<0.001$
Disturbed social adjustment before 25 years of age	32	65	22	29	3	33	$\chi^2 = 16.02$	$P<0.001$
Dependent living situation	31	63	28	37	2	22	$\chi^2 = 10.20$	$P=0.006$
Unfavorable vocational situation	14	29	5	7	4	44	$\chi^2 = 14.92$	$P<0.001$
Chronically disabled	38	78	21	28	0	0	$\chi^2 = 37.19$	$P<0.001$
Tutelage	26	53	10	13	3	33	$\chi^2 = 22.65$	$P<0.001$
Onset of disease before 30 years of age	41	84	27	36	1	11	$\chi^2 = 33.41$	$P<0.001$
Duration of illness >5 years	39	80	39	52	3	33	$\chi^2 = 12.56$	$P=0.002$
More than 5 hospitalizations	24	49	18	24	3	33	$\chi^2 = 8.26$	$P=0.016$
Index hospitalization >1 year	29	59	13	17	1	11	$\chi^2 = 25.71$	$P<0.001$
Previous suicide attempts	21	43	51	68	5	56	$\chi^2 = 7.71$	$P=0.021$
Suicidal behavior at index admission	10	20	47	63	4	44	$\chi^2 = 21.32$	$P<0.001$
Suicidal behavior during index hospitalization	27	55	42	56	1	11	$\chi^2 = 6.68$	$P=0.035$
Considered suicidal	5	10	21	28	0	0	$\chi^2 = 8.31$	$P=0.016$
Undesirable life events	23	47	42	56	9	100	$\chi^2 = 8.68$	$P=0.013$
Stressful life events	21	43	35	47	8	89	$\chi^2 = 6.60$	$P=0.037$

become ill before the age of 30 and experienced an illness career characterized by a long duration of illness and many long hospitalizations. At the time of their suicide, 59% were chronic hospital patients, their index hospitalization lasting more than 1 year. In the long term, schizophrenic suicides presented less suicidal behavior than depressed ones.

The majority of the depressed clinical suicides were married and had families, and their early social adjustment was much better than that of schizophrenic suicides. At the time of the index admission, they were better socially adjusted and were much less frequently chronically disabled. The course of their illness was more favorable than that of schizophrenic suicides. On the other hand, they much more frequently presented previous suicidal behavior. Almost two-thirds of them were suicidal at the index admission. As in schizophrenic suicides, their suicide potential was frequently evident during the index hospitalization.

Alcoholic suicides resembled the depressive much more than the schizophrenic suicides as far as their marital status and early social adjustment were concerned. Their job situation was relatively poor at the index admission; however, none of the alcoholic suicides were chronically disabled. Alcoholic suicides apparently did not come into contact with psychiatric services until a later age, and again, as far as the characteristics of the course of their illness were concerned, they presented more similarities to depressed than schizophrenic suicides. Alcoholic suicides manifested suicidal behavior in their past history more frequently than schizophrenic but less frequently than depressed suicides, and they seldom manifested suicidal behavior during their index hospitalization. Thus, none was considered as suicidal at the time of his suicide. All alcoholic suicides had experienced undesirable life events during the last year of their lives and had also suffered significantly more stressful life events than had schizophrenic or depressed suicides.

Discussion

The majority of clinical suicides have been reported to be committed by schizophrenic and depressive patients (Farberow et al. 1971; Gale et al. 1980), which was confirmed in this study. An under-representation of alcoholics among hospital suicides has also been observed (Grandel 1978; Schlosser and Strehle-Jung 1982).

Many common characteristics of suicide are applicable to almost every conceivable situation of self-destruction (Shneidman 1985). On the other hand, there are considerable differences between individual suicides. The results presented here clearly demonstrate that there are many important differences between the clinical suicides on a group level, the groups in question being defined by the clinical diagnosis.

Schizophrenic inpatient suicides are characterized by a disturbed early social adjustment, a high degree of later disability, and an unfavorable course of their psychiatric illness. Generally, the risk of suicide appears to be correlated to illness virulence and to the magnitude of the loss of healthy functioning

(Dingman and McGlashan 1986). Depressive suicides are socially much less handicapped and their illness career is less disadvantageous. In the long term, however, they present a much higher and a more persistent suicide potential (Barraclough and Pallis 1975; Roy 1983). Alcoholic suicides are socially well adjusted for long periods of time. They demonstrate no signs of suicidal behavior while being in the hospital. They commit suicide unexpectedly after having suffered negative life events (Murphy et al. 1979; Robins 1981).

These differences have therapeutic implications. When evaluating the suicide danger in schizophrenic patients, their global life situation and previous development, including their illness career and the degree of the ensuing disability, must be paid full attention. In treating the patients, they must be helped to accept their disability and to develop adequate goals which are adapted to their reduced capacities (Mundt 1984). Thus, the importance of psychotherapy in preventing schizophrenic suicide has to be stressed. In depressive patients, suicidal behavior represents to a much greater extent a direct expression of their psychiatric illness. Our therapeutic efforts therefore have to be directed toward intensive treatment of the depressive illness, including intensive psychopharmacotherapy. Many depressed clinical suicides were not treated pharmacotherapeutically in an optimal way, and it seems that suicide might be a rare phenomenon in an adequately treated depressive patient (Beskow 1979; Modestin 1985). In none of the other diagnostic categories is there such a close relationship between negative life events and suicide as is found in alcoholics. Thus, these patients must be helped to cope with negative life experiences. Identifying such experiences, evaluating the importance of them for the patient, and improving his coping capacity make an active psychotherapeutic approach in these patients indispensable.

References

Barraclough B, Pallis DJ (1975) Depression followed by suicide: a comparison of depressed suicides with living depressives. Psychol Med 5:55–61

Beskow J (1979) Suicide and mental disorder in Swedish men. Acta Psychiatr Scand [Suppl] 277:1–138

Dingman CW, McGlashan TH (1986) Discriminating characteristics of suicides. Acta Psychiatr Scand 74:91–97

Ernst K, Kern R (1974) Suizidstatistik und freiheitliche Klinikbehandlung 1900–1972. Arch Psychiatr Nervenkr 219:255–263

Farberow NL, Ganzler S, Cutter F, Reynolds D (1971) An eight-year survey of hospital suicides. Suicide Life Threat Behav 1:184–202

Gale SW, Mesnikoff A, Fine J, Talbott JA (1980) A study of suicide in state mental hospitals in New York City. Psychiatr Q 52:201–213

Grandel S (1978) Selbstmord und psychiatrische Behandlung. Werkstattschriften zur Sozialpsychiatrie, no 21. Psychiatrie-Verlag, Wunstorf

Lönnqvist J, Niskanen P, Rinta-Mänty R, Achté K, Kärhä E (1974) Suicides in psychiatric hospitals in different therapeutic areas. A review of literature and own study. Psychiatr Fenn 5:265–273

Modestin J (1982) Suizid in der psychiatrischen Institution. Nervenarzt 53:254–261

Modestin J (1985) Antidepressive therapy in depressed clinical suicides. Acta Psychiatr Scand 71:111–116

Motto JA (1965) Suicide attempts. Arch Gen Psychiatry 13:516–520

Mundt C (1984) Suizide schizophrener Patienten. Überlegungen zur Genese und Prävention anhand einiger Fallbeispiele. Psychother Pychosom Med Psychol 34:193−197

Murphy GE, Armstrong JW Jr, Hermele SL, Fischer JR, Clendenin WW (1979) Suicide and alcoholism. Interpersonal loss confirmed as a predictor. Arch Gen Psychiatry 36:65−69

Paykel ES, Prusoff BA, Uhlenhuth EH (1971) Scaling of life events. Arch Gen Psychiatry 25:340−347

Paykel ES, Prusoff BA, Myers JK (1975) Suicide attempts and recent life events. Arch Gen Psychiatry 32:327−333

Retterstøl N (1978) Suicide in psychiatric hospitals in Norway. Psychiatr Fenn [Suppl] 9:89−92

Robins E (1981) The final months − study of the lives of 134 persons who committed suicide. Oxford University Press, New York

Roy A (1983) Suicide in depressives. Compr Psychiatry 24:487−491

Schlosser J, Strehle-Jung G (1982) Suizide während psychiatrischer Klinikbehandlung. Psychiatr Prax 9:20−26

Shneidman E (1985) Definition of suicide. Wiley, New York

Spitzer R, Endicott J, Robins E (1978) Research Diagnostic Criteria (RDC) for a selected group of functional disorders, 3rd edn, updated 6/1980. New York State Psychiatric Institute, New York

WHO Working Group (1982) Changing patterns in suicide behavior. WHO Regional Office for Europe, Copenhagen

Wolfersdorf M, Vogel R, Dreher D, Faulstich H et al. (1984) Suizide in psychiatrischen Landeskrankenhäusern − Einige Ergebnisse einer Untersuchung der Suizide in 4 süd-baden-württembergischen psychiatrischen Landeskrankenhäusern 1970−1981. In: Wolfersdorf M (ed) Suizide psychiatrischer Patienten. Weissenhof, Weinsberg, pp 147−183

Empirical Evaluation Studies Concerning Completed Suicide and Addiction

A. STÖTZER, W. POSER, and R. BECKER

Introduction

There are two theories concerning the causal connection between suicide and addiction: the common cause theory, meaning that suicide and addiction result from common underlying causes, and the processual cause interpretation, meaning that suicidal actions result from specific problems caused by addiction (Feuerlein 1975; Rushing 1969). In the latter case, we should also look for the significance of the pharmacological effect of drugs (e.g., alcohol) as a cause of depression (Bleuler 1975; Mayfield and Montgomery 1972).

Study

Three studies on the connection between addiction and suicide were carried out in Göttingen in the Federal Republic of Germany (Stötzer 1983).

Suicide Group

For the first study, 134 suicides committed between 1977 and 1979 in the region of Göttingen were identified with the help of forensic medical records. Concerning 63 of these 134 suicides, we discovered additional documents in psychiatric and general hospitals and in psychiatric offices in Göttingen. For the classification of the suicides as addicts, the criteria of Table 1 were used.

Of the suicides, 93 were male and 41 female; 33 (24%) were addicts (Table 2). Alcohol was the most important substance: it had been abused by 26 persons; 9 of them were also dependent on other drugs. Five suicides were due to

Table 1. Criteria for the classification of the suicides as addicts

1. The NCA Criteria for the Diagnosis of Alcoholism (Criteria Committee 1972)
2. The Criteria of Kemper et al.: addiction to drugs of the alcohol-barbiturate group (Kemper et al. 1980)
3. Suicide with an overdose of heroin
4. A concentration of bromide in plasma of 40 mg/dl and more in cases of known intake of bromides (Mayfield and Montgomery 1972)

illegal drugs only. Altogether, 25 persons (19%) had been dependent on drugs of the alcohol-barbiturate group only (Table 3).

At the time of the suicide, a greater percentage of addicts had been intoxicated than nonaddicts. The addicts had made suicide attempts more often than the other suicides.

The results show analogies to those of previous studies, e.g., James (1966) and Barraclough et al. (1974). Concerning the method employed, this study can be compared to that of Rossel (1969). He found 13% alcoholics among suicides autopsied in West Berlin (Rossel 1969) (Table 4). The individual histories of the suicides indicate that the connection between suicidal behavior and addiction may be explained by a synthesis of the processual cause interpretation and the common cause theory.

Table 2. Suicides $(n = 134)$ in the region of Göttingen (1977–1979)

	Suicides	
	(n)	(%)
Male	93	
Female	41	
Addiction certain	19	14
Addiction highly probable	14	10
Total	33	24

Table 3. Substances abused by the 33 suicides

Alcohol	17
Alcohol and sedatives (incl. benzodiazepines)	7
Alcohol and illegal drugs	2
Sedatives (incl. benzodiazepines)	1
Illegal drugs	5
Illegal drugs and sedatives (incl. benzodiazepines)	1

Table 4. Studies on addiction in suicides

Author	Suicides (n)	Addicts among the suicides (%)
Robins et al. (1959)	134	23
Palola et al. (1962)	114	31
James (1966)	193	17
Rossel (1969)	143	13
Barraclough et al. (1974)	100	21
Habermann and Baden (1978)	336	29
Own results (1983)	134	24

Psychiatric Inpatients

The second study was an evaluation of 107 patients who had died when hospitalized in the psychiatric clinic of Göttingen University. These patients had been admitted to the hospital between 1 January 1966 and 1 September 1980.

The distribution of age and sex among the deceased corresponds to the distribution of age and sex in the population of the Federal Republic of Germany (Statistical Yearbook 1980). The causes of death are shown in Table 5. Pneumonia, delirium tremens, and especially suicide were found more often as causes of death than in the general population.

Of the 107 patients, 20 were alcoholics and 4 were addicted to sedatives (including benzodiazepines). There were only two addicts among the suicides, both of them politoxicomaniacs and under psychiatric treatment for many years. Thus, addicted inpatients were more likely to die from delirium tremens than from suicide.

The increasing number of suicides during a hospital stay had been observed in this hospital too. Patients with addictions did not contribute to the hospital suicides. On the contrary, there were clearly less addicts among suicides than expected from their proportion among inpatients.

Patients with Substance-Use Disorders from a Case Register

In the third study, the mortality of patients with a history of abuse or dependence was analyzed. In a longitudinal study, started in 1977, the course of the disease in inpatients and outpatients with substance-use disorders was followed according to the Diagnostic and Statistical Manual of Mental Disorders III (DSM III, see American Psychiatric Association 1980). The patients were diagnosed in the psychiatric or neurological departments of the University Hospital of Göttingen (outpatients included).

After initial diagnosis, the patients were re-examined about 6 years later. In January 1986, 1167 patients could be located. Table 6 shows the types of substance-use disorder. There were four main groups: pure alcoholics, patients with isolated use of legal drugs, patients with combined use of legal drugs with alcohol and illegal drugs, and politoxicomaniacs. Isolated dependence on illegal drugs was rare. The expected deaths were calculated and compared with the observed deaths. In the main group, more deaths occurred than expected from the normal population. The ratio of observed to expected deaths was a measure for relative excess mortality. This ratio was highest in politoxicomaniacs and lowest in patients with abuse of or dependence on legal drugs only.

Table 7 shows the cause of death in the total sample. In 29 patients, the cause was unknown. In 93 cases, the information was available through the following sources: death certificates, autopsies, hospital records, police notes, relatives, general practitioners, and friends. Suicide was by far the most frequent cause of death, especially in patients with abuse of legal or illegal drugs. The majority of patients who committed suicide died during withdrawal or drug intoxication, only very few patients during abstinence. Thus, the common cause

Table 5. Causes of death ($n = 107$) in the psychiatric clinic of Göttingen University (1/1966 – 8/1980)

Circulatory diseases	36
Pneumonia	24
Neoplasms	14
Delirium tremens	14
Suicide during hospitalization	13
At home (during the weekend when allowed to leave clinic)	4
In the clinic	9
Cause of death unknown	6
	107

Table 6. Mortality in patients with substance-use disorders

Substance-use group	n	Years under observation	Deaths		Observed/ Expected
			Observed	Expected	
Alcoholism (isolated)	411	5.6±4.6	38	10.7	3.6
Legal drugs only	272	4.9±4.7	25	9.9	2.5
Illegal drugs only	11	3.7±5.4	0	0.3	–
Alcohol and legal drugs	356	7.8±5.8	45	12.4	3.6
Polytoxicomania	107	7.4±4.1	9	0.9	9.9

Table 7. Causes of death in patients with substance-use disorders

	(n)	(%)
Total cases	122	
Cause of death unknown	29	
Cause of death known	93	100
Suicide	34	37
Accident, intoxication	15	16
Malignancies	14	15
Cardiac infarction	7	8
Liver cirrhosis	5	5
Intracranial hemorrhage	4	4
Crime	4	4
Withdrawal syndrome	3	3
Pneumonia	3	3
Others	4	4

theory (Feuerlein 1975) does not explain the suicides. The pharmacological effect of addictive drugs or a withdrawal depression are the most probable explanations for this finding.

Malignancies, liver cirrhosis, and intracranial hemorrhage were most frequent in alcoholics, whereas accidents occurred with the same frequency in all groups. Crime as a cause of death was confined to illegal drugs.

References

American Psychiatric Association (1980) Diagnostic and statistical manual of mental disorders III (DSM III). APA, Washington, DC

Barraclough B, Bunch J, Nelson B, Sainsbury P (1974) A hundred cases of suicide: clinical aspects. Br J Psychiatry 125:355−373

Bleuler E (1975) Lehrbuch der Psychiatrie. Springer, Berlin Heidelberg New York

Criteria Committee, National Council on Alcoholism (1972) Criteria for the diagnosis of alcoholism. Am J Psychiatry 129:127−135

Feuerlein W (1975) Sucht und Suizidhandlungen. MMW 117:197−200

Haberman PW, Baden MM (1978) Alcohol, other drugs and violent death. Oxford University Press, New York

James IP (1966) Blood alcohol levels following successful suicide. Q J Stud Alcohol 27:23−29

Kemper N, Poser W, Poser S (1980) Benzodiazepin-Abhängigkeit. Dtsch Med Wochenschr 105:1707−1712

Mayfield DJ, Montgomery D (1972) Alcoholism, alcohol intoxication and suicide attempts. Arch Gen Psychiatry 27:349−353

Palola EG, Dorpat TL, Larson WR (1962) Alcoholism and suicidal behaviour. In: Dittmann DJ, Snyders CR (eds) Society culture and drinking habits. Wiley, New York, pp 511−534

Robins E, Gassner S, Kayes J (1959) The communication of suicidal intent: a study of 134 consecutive cases of successful (completed) suicide. Am J Psychiatry 115:724−733

Rossel U (1969) Todesumstände, Todesursachen und Obduktionsbefunde bei chronischen Alkoholikern. Thesis, Freie Universität Berlin

Rushing WA (1969) Suicide as a possible consequence of alcoholism. In: Rushing WA (ed) Deviant behaviour and social process. Rand-McNally, Chicago, pp 323−327

Stötzer A (1983) Zum Zusammenhang zwischen Suizid und Abhängigkeit von Alkohol, Medikamenten und illegalen Drogen. Thesis, Georg-August-Universität, Göttingen

World Health Statistics (1980). Vital statistics and causes of death. WHO, Geneva

Part II   Course and Prediction of Suicidal Behavior

Part II   Cause and Prediction of Animal Behavior

Catamnestic Studies on Patients Who Attempted Suicide: An Overview

H. WEDLER

Introduction

The efficiency of suicide prevention measures has not been well established up to the present time. Many different reasons may contribute to this fact.

While the extent of suicidal behavior still cannot be measured by objective methods, only catamnestic studies seem to give appropriate information for the evaluation of suicide prevention. Many catamnestic studies have been performed in the last 2 or 3 decades. While, in former times, they were used only as a type of follow-up observation, catamnestic studies are now used regularly as an instrument to control the efficacy of special programs of crisis intervention and suicide prediction. Unfortunately, due to certain methodological problems of previous studies, their scientific value has been minimized (Marten 1981).

Methodological Considerations

One main factor determining all the results of catamnestic studies concerns the selection of patient samples. Many outstanding differences found in earlier studies may be explicable in view of the fact that this has been neglected. Even the definition of the term "parasuicide" has proved to be subject to considerable variation. Some studies have focused only on "serious" suicidal attempts (e.g., Rosen 1970). Other studies have excluded just this group (Hofmann 1971). Regional structures of medical care and traditional ways of treating parasuicides may play an additional role.

Unselected samples have been assembled by including all patients who have been treated within a definite interval (Udsen 1966; Gardner et al. 1977) or have been seen consecutively in a special department (Hove 1953; Baert 1974). Many studies, however, fail to give any information on whether nonhospitalized patients have been included or not.

Further differences concern the optimal catamnestic period. Continuous observation during the time of follow-up might be the best way to get sufficient information. Continuous observation, however, may produce echo effects because repeated contact with patients yields therapeutic side effects. A short catamnestic period will only yield results of little prognostic value. Significant numbers of fatal repetition rates may be found only by use of longer intervals. A longer period, however, may increase the loss of patients, minimizing the validity of all results. In addition, the increasing number of new life events during a prolonged catamnestic interval will exert much influence on the final results. A judgment on earlier crisis intervention measures may be hazardous. Wilkins (1970) has emphasized an optimal catamnestic period for parasuicides of about 1.5 years.

The experimental design of catamnestic studies is greatly influenced by the number of patients. High numbers will provide more significant results, but more intensive instruments cannot be used (or can be used only within narrow limits). In many earlier studies, information about death by suicide was obtained only from official coroner's lists, while in other studies, all hospitals of the region and/or house physicians were asked, both being methods of little scientific value. Uncertain death certifications were or were not included. Some follow-up observations have shown not only a cumulation of suicide deaths after parasuicides, but also increased numbers of deaths for other reasons. Jokinen and Lehtinen (1977) found multiple accidents in about 50% of their male parasuicides, with or without death, within 5 years.

Retterstøl (1974) has emphasized that only the personal interview may be a valuable method of follow-up. The objective number of repeated parasuicides, however, may be not revealed even by this procedure. Some investigators used psychological interviews and tests to determine the psychosocial situation of their clients. This way of follow-up often includes a high rate of nonresponders. Furthermore, it seems uncertain whether a realistic picture of the patient's actual situation and the worth of earlier crisis intervention measures will be obtained with these instruments. Further studies have used questionnaires or structured interviews. The information obtained may have been influenced by the actual feeling of the patient as well as by the kind and number of questionnaire tasks.

Many differences between several catamnestic studies are concerned with the criteria for a good outcome. There is only one "strong" criterion for the evaluation of therapeutic interventions: death by suicide or not. This finding is relatively rare. Another criterion, repeated parasuicide, should not always be considered as a sign of ineffective crisis intervention with respect to its "strategic function." Other forms of deviant behavior should also be regarded in the evaluation of outcome, as in some catamnestic studies of the past years. Further studies have tested whether the patient learned to use other, nonsuicidal strategies to cope with new crisis situations. Last but not least, the patient's individual satisfaction with life has been regarded as an outcome criterion in some studies.

Prospective analyses to evaluate specific therapeutic strategies have often been performed without control groups. Randomized studies include a number of ethical problems (Kennedy 1972; Kreitman 1980). A strict randomization might fail because it seems nearly impossible to find control groups without any form of crisis help that might be given, e.g., during the somatic therapy by a nurse. This single contact may be extremely valuable for one or another patient in the actual situation.

Furthermore, it seems difficult to establish two or more alternative therapeutic regimes in one institution without side effects. Some investigators used different crisis intervention regimes one after the other (Ettlinger 1975; Wul-liemier et al. 1977). Due to the changing suicidal behavior of the population as well as the oscillating therapeutic climate, in one institution, the results of these studies seem to be uncertain.

Niskanen et al. (1974) pointed out that reinterviewing parasuicides after a few years provokes several ethical problems. Many patients refused such an interview, neglected the dark period of their lives, and did not wish to be reminded. Thibault et al. (1980) stated that alcoholics and parasuicides were the largest groups of patients in a general hospital who refused any follow-up.

To date, there is no general agreement concerning the methods and criteria of catamnestic studies, despite the fact that they are keenly needed for more and better information about the outcome of parasuicides.

Examples of Catamnestic Studies (Meta-analysis)

The number of catamnestic studies with quite different aims and designs has increased during the past years to a large extent (Tables 1 and 2). This has yielded a wide variety of different results. The following types of studies can be distinguished for analysis.

Classic Follow-up Studies

This kind of catamnestic study deals with a long-term follow-up after nonfatal suicidal acts. Dahlgren (1975) performed an extended study of all the investigations to date in this field. Continuous records were kept of 230 patients who had made suicide attempts in the years between 1933 and 1943, with only 1 person lost. Within 31−42 years, death by suicide was found in 14% of males and 8.8% of females. After the first 4 years, suicides were registered in 9.7% of males and 3.7% of females. Similar results were found in a study by Paerregaard (1974): 5% suicides after 3 years, 8% after 5 years, and 10% after 10 years.

A further follow-up study by Böhme (1984) included nearly all parasuicides who had been treated between 1948 and 1969 in a large German town (230 000 inhabitants). Of 3346 patients, 82.3% could be identified from official resources after an interval of 1−22 (median 7) years: 13.9% had died, 5.3% by suicide; 48.7% of the suicides happened within 1 year, 61.1% within 2 years, and 17.6% more than 5 years after the suicidal attempt. Psychotic patients demonstrated a much higher suicide rate (11.8%) than nonpsychotics (4.9%).

Repetition of Parasuicide

Other studies focused on the repetition rates, fatal or nonfatal, during a definite follow-up period. In a sample of 4628 patients, Udsen (1966) found 4.5% suicides and 22.4% nonfatal repetitions within 1−7.5 years. The parasuicides were registered only by admission lists of the same hospital.

Table 1. Catamnesis after suicide attempts: rate of fatal suicidal acts

Author	Country	Year of publi- cation	Type of clinic	Sample no.	No info. (%)	Interval (years)	Suicide death (%)
Ettlinger	S	1964		227		12	13.2
Ettlinger	S	1975	G	1351		5−6	11.6
Motto	USA	1965	G	193	30.6	5−8	11.2
Paerregaard	DK	1974	T	484		10	11.0
Jokinen and Lehtinen	SF	1977	G	175	30	5−6	11
Dahlgren	S	1975		229		31−42	10.9
Bahr	GDR	1971	P	104	19.2		10.7
Ekblom and Frisk	S	1959		138		6−8	8.7
Schneider	CH	1954		372		9−18	8
Retterstøl	N	1974a	G	74		4−11	6.8
Baert	B	1974	G	60	6.7	5	6.5
Dahlgren	S	1945		230		12	6.1
Eisenthal et al.	USA	1966		912		8	6
Rüegsegger	CH	1963	P	132	1.5	2+7	5.4
Böhme	FRG	1984	P	3346	17.7	1−22	5.3
Pino et al.	FRG	1979	G	100	27	6	5
Hove	DK	1953	T	500	1.2	2−3	4.8
Bernasconi	CH	1972	G	225	4.9	3−4.5	4.7
Udsen	DK	1966	T	4628		1−7.5	4.5
Katschnig et al.	A	1980	G	276	5	5	4.2
Hofmann	CH	1971	G	84	2.4	8	3.8
Otto	S	1971		1727		10−15	3.8
Greer and Lee	GB	1967		52		1−4.5	3.8
Ettlinger and Flordh	S	1955	G	457		0.6−2	3.5
Pokorny	USA	1966	G	615		0.1−14.5	3.4
Buglass and McCulloch	GB	1970		511		3	3.3
McCarthy et al.	IRL	1965		159		2−3	3.1
Stengel et al.	GB	1958	P	72	1.4	3−5	2.8
Wolf et al.	FRG	1979	A	292	3.4	2	2.7
Bratfos	N	1971		316		8	2.6
Wulliemier et al.	CH	1977	G	326	11.7	2	2.4
Sakinofsky	CN	1974	G	158	20.3	1	2.4
Batchelor and Napier	GB	1954	G	200	0.5	1	2.1
Greer and Bagley	GB	1971	T	211	3.3	1−2	2.0
Gardner et al.	USA	1964		387		1	2
Schmidt et al.	USA	1954		109		0.3−0.9	1.8
Kessel and McCulloch	GB	1966	G	511		1	1.6
Tuckman and Youngman	USA	1968		1112		1	1.4
Jansson	S	1962	P	476	1.3	1	1.3
Rosen	USA	1970	P	886		0.5−1.5	0.9
Stengel et al.	GB	1958	G	138	7.3	5−6	0.9
Kennedy	GB	1972	T	204		0−1	0.5
Gardner et al.	GB	1977	G	246	14.6	1	0.5
Wedler	FRG	1984	A	294	4.1	2	0.3
Ringel	A	1952		2879		1−3	0.05

Type of clinic: *G*, general hospital; *T*, toxicologic unit; *P*, psychiatric unit or hospital.

Table 2.   Catamnesis after suicidal attempts: nonfatal repetition rate

Author	Country	Year of publication	Type of clinic	Sample nr.	No info (%)	Interval (years)	Repara-suicide (%)
Barter et al.	USA	1968	P	63	28.6	0.3 – 3.6	42.2
Retterstøl	N	1974a	G	74	33.8		38.8
Motto	USA	1965	G	193	46.6	5 – 8	34
Pino et al.	FRG	1979	A	100	27	6	31
Gardner and Hanka	GB	1977	G	246	14.6	1	30
Greer and Bagley	GB	1971	T	211	7.1	1 – 2	27
Stengel et al.	GB	1952	G	138	33.3	5 – 6	26.1
Udsen	DK	1966	T	4628		1 – 7.5	22.4
Wedler	FRG	1984	A	294	38	2	20.5
Kennedy	GB	1972	T	204		0 – 1	19
Bernasconi	CH	1972	G	225	33.3	3 – 4.5	18.2
Stengel et al.	GB	1958	P	72	11.1	3 – 5	17.2
Rüegsegger	CH	1963	P	132	38.6	2+7	14.8
Wulliemier et al.	CH	1977	G	326	11.7	2	14.6
Gibbons	GB	1980	G	400		1	14
Greer and Lee	GB	1967	G	52	9.6	1 – 4.5	12.8
Hofmann	CH	1971	G	84	21.4	8	10.6
Hove	DK	1953	T	500	1.2	2 – 3	9.7
Jansson	S	1962	P	476	11.6	1	8.8
Wolf et al.	FRG	1979	A	292	18	2	8.2
Schmidt et al.	USA	1954		109	8.3	0.3 – 0.9	8.0
Batchelor and Napier	GB	1954	G	200	14	1	4.1

Type of clinic: *G*, general hospital; *T*, toxicologic unit; *P*, psychiatric unit or hospital.

Psychosocial Follow-up

This kind of catamnestic study deals not only with repetition rates of para-suicides, but also looks for the psychosocial development of each patient. In one study, Hofmann (1971) asked his patients 8 years later about their actual feeling and personal development. Subsequent psychiatric explorations were performed. Most of the patients exhibited a good course; only 12% demonstrated several psychosocial deficiencies. Similar results were found in a follow-up study by Wolf et al. (1979).

Gibbons (1980) used the results of personal catamnestic interviews for an evaluation of earlier crisis intervention therapy. In particular, new coping behavior and the patient's satisfaction with life were used as outcome criteria.

Evaluation of Diagnostic Instruments

Some catamnestic studies have been performed to certify the value of diagnostic instruments. Katschnig et al. (1980) found in their catamnesis a good confirmation of high-risk groups, identified 5 years earlier by cluster analysis.

A randomized trial by Gardner et al. (1977) tested the (diagnostic) evaluation of parasuicide patients by physicians and nurses vs psychiatrists. No significant differences concerning aftercare and outcome were found.

Evaluation of Therapeutic Regimes

Several studies have used catamnesis for the evaluation of specific therapeutic strategies of crisis intervention and aftercare. Greer and Bagley (1971) tested the effect of psychiatric aftercare in contrast to those patients who had refused any therapy. A much better outcome could be demonstrated in the first group, but, of course, the 'refusing' patients could not be regarded as realistic controls. •A similar study was started by Kennedy (1972).

Retterstøl (1974b) demonstrated a much better outcome for patients who had been treated in the psychiatric department of a general hospital in contrast to those treated in psychiatric district hospitals. The author concluded that the better sociotherapeutic facilities of the general hospital may have contributed to these results.

Ettlinger (1975) used two different patient groups: one treated before and one after the introduction of an intensive program of aftercare. The outcome after 5−6 years was not different.

Wulliemier et al. (1977) tested by catamnesis the effect of continuous aftercare. Patients treated 1 year before initiating this program were used as controls. The better outcome of the patients with more intensive aftercare was regarded as an effect of continuously contacting these patients after hospital discharge. The worth of continuous contact had also been demonstrated by Motto (1974).

Catamnestic observation of patients treated at different times by different methods was also used by Wedler (1984) to evaluate a crisis intervention scheme performed by the medical team of a general hospital without a psychiatrist's help. The author found a better therapeutic climate on the wards, better information of co-workers, and more intensive crisis intervention measures, but no striking differences concerning the outcome of patients.

Möller et al. (1984) tested the effect of different ways of initiating aftercare after self-poisoning. In addition to initial crisis intervention, a sample of patients was motivated by intensive measures to accept aftercare. This was performed randomly by psychiatrists, who had made the first contact, or other institutions outside the clinic. The authors found a much better level of compliance in these patients, who had no change of therapists, but their catamnestic outcome was even worse.

Conclusions

1. The repetition rate after suicidal acts is high. About 10% of all parasuicides will later die by suicide. The death rate increases with increasing years of follow-up, with most deaths occurring during the first few months after the first

parasuicide. On the other hand, the global psychosocial development in the majority of parasuicides is favorable.

2. Although many catamnestic studies have been performed, the effectiveness of crisis intervention and aftercare after suicide attempts has not been well established.

3. Catamnestic studies have shown that parasuicides are heterogeneous groups which need quite different crisis therapies and psychosocial aftercare. Continuous contact after hospital discharge seems to be worthwhile.

4. Results from one region cannot be transferred to others. Regional differences of suicidal behavior and the organization of psychosocial help may play a more important role.

5. Catamnestic studies include several unsolved methodological problems. Future studies should be planned prospectively, with well-defined samples of patients in both the experimental and the control groups. Randomization seems to be suitable only in some studies with a special design and special tasks. Generally, for an evaluation of therapeutic schemes, alternating periods should be used. Catamnesis needs personal contact. All patients included should be asked to agree to some further contact at the end of the catamnestic period. Besides suicide and parasuicide, further well-definable psychosocial events should be used as outcome criteria, e.g., development of psychosomatic disorders, addiction, psychosocial deviance. The uniform "basic documentation scale" (as described on p. 446ff. in this book) may offer a suitable base line for all data collection.

References

Baert AE (1974) A five year follow-up study of 50 consecutive suicide attempters. 7th International Congress on Suicide Prevention, Amsterdam, pp 88−92

Bahr J (1971) Stationär behandelte Suizidversuche aus katamnestischer Sicht. Psychiatr Neurol Med Psychol 23:247−252

Barter JT, Swaback DO, Todd D (1968) Adolescent suicide attempts. Arch Gen Psychiatry 19:253−257

Batchelor IRC, Napier MB (1954) The sequelae and short-term prognosis of attempted suicide. J Neurol Neurosurg Psychiatry 17:261

Bernasconi R (1972) Etude statistique et catamnestique de cas de tentative de suicide. Rec Med Suisse Romande 92:85−130

Böhme K (1984) Wie geht es weiter? − Eine katamnestische Untersuchung zu Überlebenszeiten und Todesursachen nach Selbstmordversuchen. In: Faust V, Wolfersdorf M (eds) Suizidgefahr. Hippokrates, Stuttgart

Bratfos O (1971) Attempted suicide. Acta Psychiatr Scand 47:48

Buglass D, McCulloch JW (1970) Further suicidal behaviour. The development and validation of predictive scales. Br J Psychiatry 116:483−491

Dahlgren KG (1945) On suicide and attempted suicide. A psychiatrical and statistical investigation. Lindstedts Univ bokhandel, Lund

Dahlgren KG (1975) Attempted suicides − 35 years afterwards. 8 Int congr suic prev, Jerusalem, p 32

Eisenthal S, Farberow NL, Shneidman ES (1966) Follow-up of neuropsychiatric patients in suicide observation status. Public Health Rep 81:977−990

Ekblom B, Frisk M (1959) Den vid suicidförsök omedelbart angivna subjektiva orsakens relation till recidivfrekvensen (The relationship of the subjective cause stated immediately in attempted suicides to their frequency of recurrence). Nord Med 62:1176

Ettlinger R (1975) Evaluation of suicide prevention after attempted suicide. Acta Psychiatr Scand [Suppl] 260

Ettlinger RW (1964) Suicides in a group of patients who had previously attempted suicide. Acta Psychiatr Scand 40:363–378

Ettlinger RW, Flordh P (1955) Attempted suicide: experience of 500 cases at a general hospital. Acta Psychiatr Neurol Scand [Suppl] 103:5–45

Gardner EA, Bahn AK, Mack M (1964) Suicide and psychiatric care in the aging. Arch Gen Psychiatry 10:547–555

Gardner R, Hanka R, O'Brien VC et al. (1977) Psychological and social evaluation in cases of deliberate self-poisoning admitted to a general hospital. Br Med J II:1567–1570

Gibbons JS (1980) Management of self-poisoning: social work intervention. In: Farmer R, Hirsch S (eds) The suicide syndrome. Croom Helm, London, pp 237–245

Greer S, Bagley C (1971) Effect of psychiatric intervention in attempted suicide: a controlled study. Br Med J 1:310–312

Greer S, Lee HA (1967) Subsequent progress of potentially lethal attempted suicides. Acta Psychiatr Scand 43:361–371

Hofmann T (1971) Katamnesen nach Suizidversuch – Hinweise für die Behandlung. Schweiz Rundschau Med (Praxis) 60:433–444

Hove H (1953) Reddede selvmordspatienters skaebne. Ugesk Laeger 115:645–646

Jansson B (1962) A catamnestic study of 476 attempted suicides with special regard to the prognosis for cases of drug automatism. Acta Psychiatr Scand 38:183–198

Jokinen K, Lehtinen V (1977) Suicidal poisonings treated in the medical ward in the year 1970, with 5–6 years follow-up. 9th int congr suic prev, Helsinki, pp 156–163

Katschnig H, Sint P, Fuchs-Robertin G (1980) Suicide and parasuicide: identification of high- and low-risk groups by cluster analysis with a 5-year follow-up. In: Farmer R, Hirsch S (eds) The suicide syndrome. Croom Helm, London, pp 154–166

Kennedy P (1972) Efficacy of a regional poisoning treatment centre in preventing further suicidal behaviour. Br Med J 4:255–257

Kessel N, McCulloch W (1966) Repeated acts of self-poisoning and self-injury. Prov R Soc Med 59:89–92

Kreitmann N (1980) Services for parasuicide and the place of a poisonings unit. In: Farmer R, Hirsch S (eds) The suicide syndrome. Croom Helm, London, pp 259–262

Marten RS (1981) Probleme und Ergebnisse von Verlaufsuntersuchungen an Suizidanten. In: Henseler H, Reimer C (eds) Selbstmordgefährdung. Frommann-Holzboog, Stuttgart

McCarthy PD, Walsh D (1965) Attempted suicide in Dublin. J Irish Med Ass 57:8

Möller HJ, Bürk F, Kurz A, Torhorst A, Wächtler C, Lauter H (1984) Stationäre und poststationäre psychiatrische Versorgung von Patienten nach Suizidversuch durch Intoxikation. In: Deutsch E et al. (eds) Diagnose, Verlaufskontrolle und Therapie schwerer exogener Vergiftungen. Schattauer, Stuttgart, pp 233–241

Motto JA (1965) Suicide attempts. Arch Gen Psychiatry 13:516–520

Motto JA (1974) Suicide prevention by long term contact. 7th Int congr suic prev, Amsterdam, pp 426–434

Niskanen P, Lönnqvist J, Achte K (1974) Methodological difficulties in a follow-up study concerning attempted suicides. 7th Int congr suic prev, Amsterdam, pp 93–96

Otto U (1971) Barns och Ungdomars självmordshandlingar. Seelig, Stockholm

Paerregaard G (1974) Suicide frequency among persons who have attempted suicide. A 10 years follow-up. 7th Int congr suic prev, Amsterdam, pp 97–100

Pino R, Kockott G, Feuerlein W (1979) Sechs-Jahres-Katamnese an hundert Patienten mit Suizidversuchen durch Tabletteneinnahme. Arch Psychiatr Nervenkr 227:213–226

Pokorny A (1966) A follow-up study of 618 suicidal patients. Am J Psychiatry 122:1095

Retterstøl N (1974a) The future fate of suicide attempters. 7th Int congr suic prev, Amsterdam, pp 101–109

Retterstøl N (1974b) Personal follow-up examination of patients admitted to a psychiatric hospital. 7th Int congr suic prev, Amsterdam, pp 110–113

Ringel E (1952) Der Selbstmord. Maudrich, Vienna

Rosen DH (1970) The serious suicide attempt: epidemiological and follow-up study of 886 patients. Am J Psychiatry 127:764–770

Ruegsegger P (1963) Selbstmordversuche. Klinische, statistische und katamnestische Untersuchungen an 132 Suizidversuchspatienten. Psychiatr Neurol 146:81−104

Sakinofsky I (1974) A domiciliary follow-up of suicide attempters: conclusions regarding prediction and treatment. In: Speyer N et al. (eds) 7th Int conf suicide prevention. Swets and Zeitlinger, Amsterdam

Schmidt EH, O'Neal P, Robins E (1954) Evaluation of suicide attempts as guide to therapy. J Am Med Assoc 155:549

Schneider PB (1954) Recherches catamnestiques sur la tentative de suicide. Bull Schweiz Akad Med Wiss 10:143−155

Stengel E (1952) Enquiries into attempted suicide. Proc R Soc Med 45:613−620

Stengel E, Cook N, Kreeger RI (1958) Attempted suicide, Maudsley monograph, no 4. Chapmann and Hall, London

Thibault GE, Mulley AG, Barnett GO et al. (1980) Medical intensive care: indications, interventions and outcomes. N Engl J Med 302:938−942

Tuckman J, Youngman WF (1968) Assessment of suicide risk in attempted suicide. In: Resnik HL (ed) Suicidal behaviors. Little Brown, Boston

Udsen P (1966) Prognosis and follow-up of attempted suicide. Int Anaesthiol Clin 4:379−388

Wedler HL (1984) Der Suizid-Patient im Allgemeinkrankenhaus. Enke, Stuttgart

Wilkins J (1970) A follow-up study of those who called a suicide prevention center. Am J Psychiatry 127:155−161

Wolf R, Gräf T, Wedler HL (1979) Über die Änderung der Lebenssituation nach Suizidversuchen. Med Welt 30:1431−1435

Wulliemier F, Kremer P, Carron R (1977) Vergleichende Studie über zwei Interventionsarten bei Suizidanten, die im allgemeinen Krankenhaus aufgenommen worden sind. Suizidprophylaxe 4:248−250

Sociopsychological Adjustment and Family History of Depressives with and without a Suicide Attempt

T. Bronisch and H. Hecht

Introduction

To our knowledge, up to now, only five studies (Walton 1958; Paykel and Dienelt 1971; Crook et al. 1975; Sonneck et al. 1976; Slater and Depue 1981) have been concerned with the question of differences between depressives with and without a suicide attempt in their past history.

To look for such differences, we compared two groups, one consisting of 24 inpatients with the diagnosis of brief or prolonged depressive reaction (International Classification of Diseases, ICD-9) who had never made a suicide attempt but needed psychiatric treatment because of an acute life crisis (nonsuicide attempters — NSA), and the other of 48 inpatients with the diagnosis of brief or prolonged depressive reaction whose suicide attempt (also related to a life crisis) was the reason for their admission (suicide attempters — SA).

The four following hypotheses to be verified concern background factors, social integration in the family of origin, social functioning, and social support. Moreover, certain personality features and personality disorders are examined:

1. *Background Factors.* There are more psychiatric disorders in first-degree relatives of SA than of NSA.
2. *Social Integration in the Family of Origin.* SA report less social integration in the family of origin than the NSA do (divorce, separation, etc.).
3. *Social Functioning and Social Support.* SA show less social functioning and have less social support than NSA do. The more chronic interpersonal maladjustment is reflected clinically in withdrawal from social contact.
4. *Personality Factors.* SA show more frustration intolerance as well as personality disorders from narcissistic, borderline, or histrionic types than NSA do.

Instruments

To assess psychiatric disorders and the degree of social integration in the family of origin, an observer's rating check list was filled out by the therapist. Social functioning and social support were assessed by the Social Interview Schedule (SIS) (Clare and Cairns 1978; German version Faltermaier et al. 1985; Hecht et al. 1987). The premorbid personality features were assessed by the Premorbid Personality Inventory (PPI) (von Zerssen 1979, 1982).

Subjects

Table 1 shows the sociodemographic characteristics of both groups (SA and NSA). Significant differences could not be ascertained. The average age for SA (34.2 years) and NSA (35.5 years) was comparable. Since two-thirds of the NSA did not belong to the 20−30 year age group − an age range including the highest number of suicide attempters (Bille-Brahe 1982; Hawton et al. 1982) − it could be ruled out that, because of the younger age, most NSA would attempt a suicide later on. The SA were predominantly lower class, whereas the NSA were middle class. However, this is only a tendency since the differences did not reach statistical significance.

Table 1. Sociodemographic characteristics of suicide attempters ($n = 48$) and nonsuicide attempters ($n = 24$)

		ICD-9:309.0/1 Suicide attempters ($n = 48$)		ICD-9:309.0/1 Nonsuicide attempters ($n = 24$)	
Age	20−29 years	23	48%	7	29%
	30−39 years	9	19%	7	29%
	40−49 years	11	23%	9	38%
	50−59 years	4	8%	1	4%
	≧ 60 years	1	2%	−	−
	x̄ SD	34.2	10.8	36.0	10.0
Sex	Male	12	25%	3	13%
	Female	36	75%	21	88%
Marital status	Never married	20	42%	9	38%
	Married	15	31%	12	50%
	Separated/divorced	12	25%	3	13%
	Widowed	1	2%	−	−
Occupational status	Employed (full/half-time)	32	67%	11	46%
	Unemployed	4	8%	1	4%
	Prematurely retired	1	2%	−	−
	In training	3	6%	2	8%
	Housewife	7	15%	9	38%
	Other status	1	2%	1	4%
Social class[a]	Upper class	6	13%	4	17%
	Middle class	17	35%	13	54%
	Lower class	23	48%	7	29%
	Unknown	2	4%	−	−

[a] According to Moore and Kleining (1960).

Results

Background Characteristics

Of 48 SA, 27 reported psychiatric disorders of first-degree relatives compared with only 7 of 24 NSA ($P\,0.05$). Predominantly suicide attempts and alcoholism were found in relatives of SA.

Social Integration of the Families of Origin

More SA experienced their parents' divorce in early childhood than NSA did ($P < 0.01$).

Social Functioning and Social Support

Figure 1 shows psychosocial functioning of the SA in comparison with matched controls. The scores concern the three dimensions assessed by the SIS: "O" means objective material conditions. "M" = management, which assesses the patients' coping and management behavior, while a subjective dimension, "satisfaction" (S), is evaluated by the patient himself. Figure 1 shows the em-

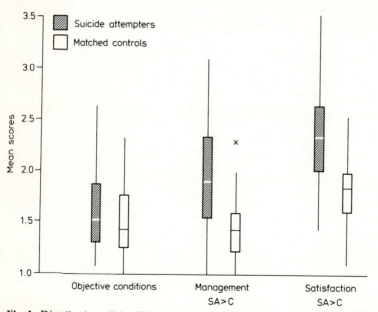

Fig. 1. Distribution of the SIS global scores (objective conditions, social management, satisfaction) for suicide attempters ($n = 48$) and matched controls, demonstrated by a boxplot. 3rd quartile (Q 3), median, and 1st quartile (Q 1). $p \le .01$. X, outlier: scores $\ge Q 3 + \frac{3}{2}$ (Q 3 − Q 1). *Horizontal lines* of boxes indicate, from top to bottom.

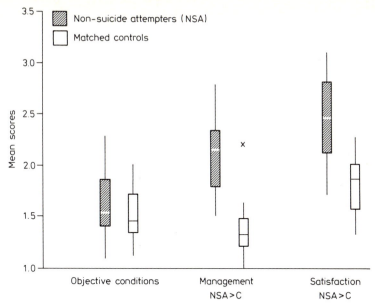

Fig. 2. Distribution of the SIS global scores (objective conditions, social management, satisfaction) for nonsuicide attempters ($n = 24$) and matched controls, demonstrated by a boxplot (see Fig. 1)

pirical distribution of data demonstrated by boxplots (Emerson and Strenio 1983). A value of 4 indicates severe objective restrictions, management difficulties, or dissatisfaction, a value of 1 indicates no objective restrictions, management difficulties, and great satisfaction with social life. The boxplots show the location, spread, tail length, and outlying data points. The location is summarized by the median, the crossbar in the interior of the box. The length of the box indicates the spread, using the fourth spread. The plot indicates tail length by the lines and by the outliers. The plot demonstrated that SA were significantly more handicapped by management difficulties and dissatisfaction than matched controls.

NSA in Fig. 2 displayed the same pattern of social dysfunctioning as SA did. Management as well as satisfaction scores were significantly more pathological than those of matched controls. SA who lived alone were handicapped by management difficulties and discontent, whereas the corresponding values of NSA were comparable with those of their controls.

Figure 3 shows the social support system of SA, NSA, and matched controls. Social support is divided into "close social support" and "diffuse social support." Close social support comprises the quality and number of close ties, diffuse social support comprises the quality and number of superficial contacts. The scores indicate that the values of a social network found in both patient groups were comparable with those in matched controls. Regarding diffuse social support, NSA displayed even lower values than the matched control group.

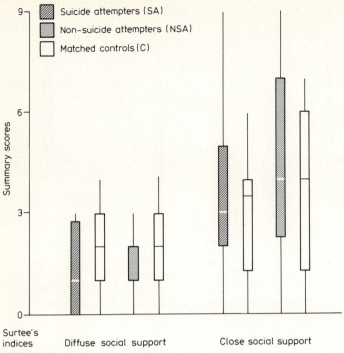

Fig. 3. Diffuse and close social support (SIS) indices for suicide attempters ($n = 48$), nonsuicide attempters ($n = 24$), and matched controls, demonstrated by a boxplot (see Fig. 1)

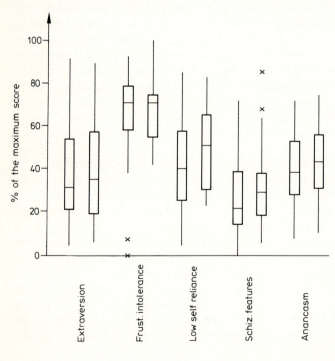

Fig. 4. Premorbid personality patterns (PPI) of suicide attempters (*left columns, n = 48*) and nonsuicide attempters (*right columns, n = 24*) demonstrated by a boxplot

Personality Factors

Figure 4 shows the personality features (frustration intolerance, low self-reliance, schizoid features, extraversion) of the SA and the NSA. No significant differences between these two groups could be ascertained, but both groups scored significantly higher in frustration intolerance, low self-reliance, and schizoid features than matched controls did. The diagnosis of a personality disorder according to ICD-9 was made in 46% of SA and 58% of NSA (no significant difference). In the group of NSA, the diagnosis of a hysterical personality disorder dominated with 45%, followed by 13% recording the diagnosis of another personality disorder. In the group of SA, 15% received the diagnosis of a hysterical personality disorder followed by 10% with the diagnosis of an affective personality disorder; the diagnosis of another personality disorder without any further clustering in specific categories was made in 21%.

Discussion

Summing up our findings, alcoholism and suicide attempts in first-degree relatives and divorce or separation of the patient's parents could be regarded as risk factors for depressives to attempt suicide in an acute life crisis.

Contrary to our hypothesis, both groups were socially integrated. Due to our cross-sectional data, we cannot say if the demonstrated management difficulties and dissatisfaction with social life are consequences of the illness or precipitate depression. A similar problem arises regarding our self-rating data of premorbid personality features. The pathological personality patterns of both groups indicate an unspecific effect, but state-dependent influences cannot be excluded. We expected a higher percentage of subjects with a concurrent hysterical personality disorder in the group of SA since such subjects are prone to manipulative suicide attempts. Our results, however, indicate the contrary — more subjects with hysterical features were in the group of NSA.

References

Bille-Brahe U (1982) Persons attempting suicide as clients in the Danish Welfare System. Soc Psychiatry 17:181—187

Clare A, Cairns V (1978) Design, development and use of a standardized interview to assess social maladjustment and disfunction in community studies. Psychol Med 8:598—604

Crook T, Raskin A, Davis D (1975) Factors associated with attempted suicide among hospitalized depressed patients. Psychol Med 5:381—388

Emerson JD, Strenio J (1983) Boxplots and batch comparison. In: Hoaglin DC, Mosteller F, Tukey JW (eds) Understanding robust and exploratory data analysis. Wiley, New York, pp 558—596

Faltermaier T, Wittchen H-U, Ellmann R, Lässle R (1985) The Social Interview Schedule (SIS) — content, structure and reliability. Soc Psychiatry 20:115—124

Hawton K, Fagg J, Marsack P, Wells P (1982) Deliberate self-poisoning and self-injury in the Oxford area: 1972—1980. Soc Psychiatry 17:175—179

Hecht H, Faltermaier T, Wittchen H-U (1987) Social Interview Schedule (SIS). Roderer, Regensburg

Moore H, Kleining G (1960) Das soziale Selbstbild der Gesellschaftsschichten in Deutschland. Köln Z Sociol Sozialpsychol 12:124−140
Paykel ES, Dienelt MN (1971) Suicide attempts following acute depression. J Nerv Ment Dis 153:234−243
Slater J, Depue RA (1981) The contribution of environmental events and social support to serious suicide attempts in primary depressive disorder. J Abnorm Soc Psychol 90:275−285
Sonneck G, Grünberger J, Ringel E (1976) Experimental contribution to the evaluation of the suicidal risk of depressive patients. Psychiatr Clin 9:84−96
Walton HJ (1958) Suicidal behaviour in depressive illness. A study of aetiological factors in suicide. J Ment Sci 104:884−891
Zerssen D von (1979) Klinisch-psychiatrische Selbstbeurteilungs-Fragebögen. In: Baumann U, Berbalk H, Seidenstücker G (eds) Klinische Psychologie, Trends in Forschung und Praxis, vol 2. Huber, Bern, pp 130−159
Zerssen D von (1982) Personality and affective disorders. In: Paykel ES (ed) Handbook of affective disorders. Churchill Livingstone, Edinburgh, pp 214−228

Psychopathological Course of Depressives with and without a Suicide Attempt

H. HECHT and T. BRONISCH

Introduction

The present study aims to explore the possible association between certain psychopathological characteristics and suicide inclination. Hostility and depression are important factors associated with suicide attempts. Suicide attempters (SA) are usually depressed; difficulty in regulating and expressing hostility is another characteristic common to suicide attempters (Weissman et al. 1973). Paykel and Dienelt (1971) and Weissman et al. (1973) compared depressed patients who had attempted suicide with those who had not and found that overtly expressed hostility was the most important distinguishing feature of the attempters. Whereas depressed SA and nonsuicide attempters (NSA) were equally depressed in the study of Weissman et al. (1973), van Praag and Plutchik (1985) found a significant postsuicidal decrease in depression compared with the level in the week prior to the suicide attempt. Such a drop in depression could not be found by the authors in patients who were also depressed but not suicidal.

The procedure adopted in our study was to compare a diagnostically homogeneous group of psychiatric patients with and without a history of suicidal behavior according to their psychopathological state during inpatient stay.

Methods

Subjects

The study included 72 patients with the International Classification of Diseases (ICD-9) diagnosis of a brief or prolonged depressive reaction (309.0 or 309.1) at admission and discharge; 48 of these had attempted suicide immediately before the index admission to the crisis intervention ward of the Max Planck Institute of Psychiatry, 24 patients had never attempted suicide in the past, and 11 subjects of the SA (23%) had made repeated suicide attempts.

According to the operationalized diagnostic criteria of the Diagnostic and Statistical Manual of Mental Disorders (DSM-III) (APA 1980), most subjects in both groups (60% of SA, 71% of NSA) were classified as having Major Depression. One subject (4%) of the NSA received a diagnosis of Panic Disorder. One patient (2%) of the SA was diagnosed as having a Simple Phobia or an obsessive Compulsive Disorder and two subjects (4%) as having a Dysthymic Disorder.

Table 1. Sociodemographic characteristics of suicide attempters and nonsuicide attempters

		ICD-9:309.0/1 Suicide attempter (n = 48)		ICD-9:309.0/1 Nonsuicide attempter (n = 24)	
Age	Mean (years)	34.2		35.5	
	SD	10.8		10.3	
Sex	Male	12	25%	3	13%
	Female	36	75%	21	88%
Marital status	Never married	20	42%	10	42%
	Married	15	31%	12	50%
	Separated/divorced	12	25%	2	8%
	Widowed	1	2%	–	–

Table 1 shows the sociodemographic characteristics of the samples. The mean ages of both groups were comparable. Differences with regard to sex distribution and marital status – there were more male and separated or divorced subjects in the group of suicide attempters – were not statistically significant. These two groups of patients were compared regarding the psychopathological course during index treatment.

Instruments

Severity of symptomatology was assessed by self-rating scales and observer's ratings. The observer's rating of psychopathology was measured by the Inpatient Multidimensional Psychiatric Scale (IMPS) (Lorr and Klett 1967) at admission and discharge.

The self-rating of psychopathology was threefold:

1. Assessment of paranoid and depressive tendencies by the Paranoid Depression Scale (PDS) (von Zerssen 1986) at admission and discharge
2. Assessment of somatic complaints by the Complaint List (CL) (von Zerssen 1986), also at admission and discharge
3. The course of the depressive mood was measured daily during the inpatient stay by the Adjective Mood Scale (AMS) (von Zerssen 1986)

The diagnoses according to DSM-III were assessed by a standardized interview, the Diagnostic Interview Schedule, Version II (DIS) (Robins et al. 1981; Semler and Wittchen 1983; Wittchen and Rupp 1982). The DSM-III diagnosis of an adjustment disorder with depressed mood was additionally based on the therapist's judgment about precipitating life events.

Results

Figure 1 shows the Inpatient Multidimensional Psychiatric Scale (IMPS) syndrome profile at index admission of SA (n = 48) and NSA (n = 24). Both

IMPS SCORES AT ADMISSION

DISTRIBUTION (%)

Scale	Percentage of the maximum score		normal scores	slightly abnorm.	severly abnorm.
EXC		SA	41.7	25.0	33.3
		NSA	20.8	50.0	29.2
HOS	SA (N=48)	SA	22.9	45.8	31.3
	NSA (N=24)	NSA	20.8	50.0	29.2
PAR		SA	100.0	0.0	0.0
		NSA	95.8	0.0	4.2
GRN		SA	75.0	10.4	14.6
		NSA	75.0	16.7	8.3
PCP		SA	97.9	2.1	0.0
		NSA	100.0	0.0	0.0
ANX		SA	12.5	29.2	58.3
		NSA	4.2	29.2	66.7
RTD		SA	27.1	27.1	45.8
		NSA	25.0	25.0	50.0
DIS		SA	100.0	0.0	0.0
		NSA	100.0	0.0	0.0
MTR		SA	41.7	16.7	41.7
		NSA	25.0	20.8	54.2
CNP		SA	54.2	20.8	25.0
		NSA	41.7	37.5	20.8
IMP		SA	45.8	35.4	18.8
	**	NSA	20.8	29.2	50.0
OBS		SA	97.9	2.1	0.0
		NSA	100.0	0.0	0.0

Fig. 1. IMPS scores for suicide attempters (SA) and nonsuicide attempters (NSA) at admission. *EXC*, excitement; *HOS*, hostile belligerence; *PAR*, paranoid projection; *GRN*, grandiose expansiveness; *PCP*, perceptual distortion; *ANX*, anxious depression; *RTC*, retardation and apathy; *DIS*, disorientation; *MTR*, motor disturbances; *CNP*, conceptual disorganization; *IMP*, impaired functioning; *OBS*, obsessive-phobic. ** $P \leq 0.01$ one-tailed U-test

groups had higher scores in the syndromes "excitement," "hostile belligerence," "anxious depression," and "retardation and apathy" than a control group (the dotted line represents the data from a representative community sample). Whereas 50% of NSA showed highly pathological scores in the syndrome "impaired functioning," most SA displayed normal or only slightly abnormal scores. Impaired functioning is a typical syndrome of depressive disorders and includes depressive symptoms and items concerning social dysfunctioning (lacks sex interest, cannot work, cannot concentrate, sleeping difficulties, fatigued, no interest in people). Whereas only 38% of SA were handicapped by three or more of these symptoms, 75% of NSA showed such a pattern.

Figure 2 shows the IMPS syndrome profile at discharge. Although the values of the two syndromes concerning depressive symptomatology (anxious depression and impaired functioning) were reduced, values for anxious depression, excitement, and hostile belligerence were still abnormal compared with the scores of control subjects (dotted line). The higher mean score of suicide attempters in the syndrome "grandiose expansiveness" ($P = 0.07$) was mainly due to a high percentage of subjects (38%) with attitudes of superiority.

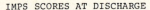

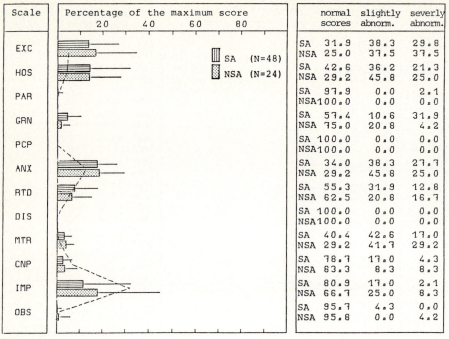

Fig. 2. IMPS scores for suicide attempters (SA) and nonsuicide attempters (NSA) at discharge (for abbreviations, see Fig. 1)

Figure 3 shows the scores of the Paranoid Depression Scale and the Complaint List at admission and discharge for both groups. There was a tendency for higher scores in the group of NSA, but the differences were not statistically significant.

Figure 4 demonstrates the median scores of the AMS during index treatment. At index admission, both groups were handicapped by severe depressive mood (scores above 25 are abnormal). During the next 3 days, depressive mood improved quickly in both groups. Whereas the median score was normal for SA after the 4th day, recovery in nonsuicide attempters remained incomplete. Before discharge, a tendency toward worsening emerged in both groups.

Our preliminary results are based upon a small sample of NSA. Therefore, replication studies would be necessary to confirm our findings. We could only replicate a small part of our results — the IMPS data of admission — by a cross-validation design (109 SA vs 17 NSA). Although the sample size of NSA was rather small, we could replicate our finding concerning the significantly higher scores for the syndrome "impaired functioning" for the NSA. In contrast to our study results, however, the SA of our cross-validation group scored significantly higher in "hostile belligerence" than did NSA.

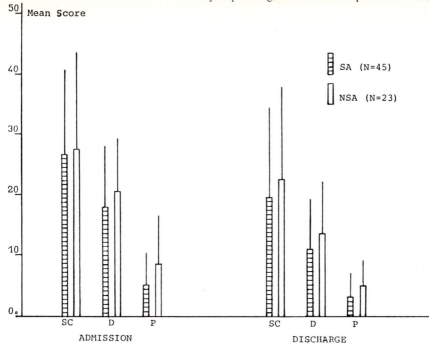

Fig. 3. Self-report measures: somatic complaints (SC), depressive (D), and paranoid (P) tendencies for suicide attempters and nonsuicide attempters. (Abnormal values: SC > 21, D > 10, P > 4)

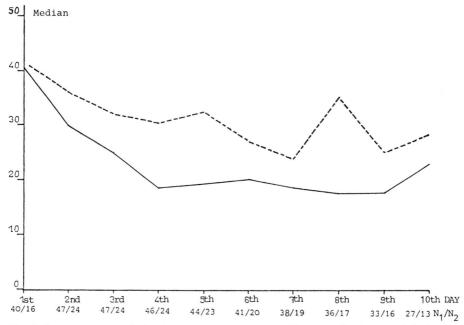

Fig. 4. Symptom course during index treatment, measured by the Adjective Mood Scale, for suicide attempters (*solid line*) and nonsuicide attempters (*dashed line*)

Discussion

We found some moderate differences for SA and NSA with regard to psycho-pathology and symptom course during inpatient stay. At admission, depressive symptomatology, especially impaired functioning, was less pronounced for SA in our study sample and in subjects of our cross-validation group, and the drop in depression during index treatment (both groups received psychotherapy) was more pronounced in the suicidal patients than in nonsuicidal subjects. This result confirms the findings of van Praag and Plutchik (1985) and is in contrast to those of Weissman et al. (1973). The higher degree of impaired functioning of the NSA at admission is in contrast to the results of our other report (Bronisch and Hecht, this volume), where we report a comparable degree of social dysfunction in both groups. We attribute this to differences between the applied instruments. Whereas the impaired functioning score of the IMPS included items regarding social function *and* depressive symptoms (such as "sleeping difficulties"), the data of our first paper were collected by a "pure" social interview.

Contrary to the results reported in the literature (Pallis and Birtchnell 1976; Weissman et al. 1973; Yesavage 1983), we failed to find a higher degree of overt hostility in SA than in NSA. We explain this with the higher percentage of NSA with a concurrent ICD-9 diagnosis of hysterical personality disorder (38% vs 15% in SA), a subgroup which is also characterized by a high degree of overt hostility. This hypothesis is supported by the significantly higher hostility score of SA than NSA in our cross-validation group. These samples included fewer subjects (only 13%) with pronounced hysterical features, and the percentage of subjects with a concurrent hysterical personality disorder was balanced between the two groups.

References

American Psychiatric Association (1980) Diagnostic and Statistical Manual of Mental Disorders, 3rd edn. APA, Washington

Lorr M, Klett CJ (1967) Inpatient Multidimensional Psychiatric Scale (IMPS), revised. Consulting Psychologists Press, Palo Alto

Pallis DJ, Birtchnell J (1976) Personality and suicidal history in psychiatric patients. J Clin Psychol 32:246–253

Paykel ES, Dienelt MN (1971) Suicide attempts following acute depression. J Nerv Ment Dis 153:234–243

Praag H van, Plutchik R (1985) An empirical study on the "cathartic effect" of attempted suicide. Psychiatry Res 16:123–130

Robins LN, Helzer JE, Croughan I, Ratcliff KS (1981) Diagnostic Interview Schedule. Its history, characteristic and validity. Arch Gen Psychiatry 38:381–389

Semler G, Wittchen H-U (1983) Das Diagnostik-Interview-Schedule. Erste Ergebnisse zur Reliabilität und differentiellen Validität der deutschen Fassung. In: Kommer D, Röhrle DB (eds) Gemeindepsychologische Perspektiven. Deutsche Gesellschaft für Verhaltenstherapie (DGVT), Köln, pp 109–117

Weissman M, Fox K, Klerman GL (1973) Hostility and depression associated with suicide attempts. Am J Psychiatry 130:450–459

Wittchen H-U, Rupp H-U (1982) Diagnostic Interview Schedule. Deutschsprachige Version II. Max-Planck-Institut für Psychiatrie, Munich (unpublished)

Yesavage JA (1983) Direct and indirect hostility and self-destructive behavior by hospitalized depressives. Acta Psychiatr Scand 68:345–350

Zerssen D von (1986) Clinical self-rating-scales (CSRS) of the Munich Psychiatric Information System (PSYCHJS München). In: Sartorius N, Ban TA (eds) Assessment of depression. Springer, Berlin Heidelberg New York, pp 270–303

Preliminary Results of a Study Concerning the Evaluation and Evolution of Patients Having Attempted to Commit Suicide

D. Cremniter, A. Meidinger, H. Thénault, and J. Fermanian

Introduction

Suicidal acts can be categorized according to their seriousness. In this study, we were primarily concerned with suicide attempts leading to *no serious somatic harm*. They resulted from crisis situations.

The patients committing such acts are generally kept under hospital surveillance for only 1 or 2 days; after a systematic psychiatric interview, most of them are sent home. As few of these patients are directed toward psychiatric treatment, we rarely have much information about their evolution over time. Our study aimed at collecting as much data as possible concerning patients whose suicide attempts were of medium seriousness. These patients were hospitalized at moments of crisis, and psychiatric pathologies were rarely clearly recognized. In addition, psychiatric follow-ups were seldom performed. Our goal in this study was thus to obtain information about the evolution of these patients so as to evaluate the therapeutic decisions made by their consulting psychiatrists.

Review of the Literature

Singer and Jolibois (1976) found that suicide attempts were often made as a reaction to the loss of important love objects and involved minimally structured neurotic states in which depression was not very intense and neurotic elements were hysterical in type. He also spoke of indeterminate states in this context, but insisted above all on the high long-term risk of *recurrence* of the act (at its highest during the first few months) due to neurotic and triggering elements.

Daumezon (1976) considered that the patient's prognosis depended upon his context, i.e., upon his implicit or explicit rejection by family and friends.

Wilmotte and Charles (1983) proposed a risk/rescue test designed to pinpoint patients likely to make another attempt within a year's time; they collected data concerning the suicide procedure employed, the degree of change in consciousness achieved, the reparability of the damage done, and the nature of the required treatment.

Methodology

We studied the symptomatology of patients that had attempted to commit suicide who were admitted to the "short-term emergency service" of a general hospital in the eastern suburbs of Paris. We excluded patients whose suicide attempts necessitated revival and/or surgical measures, as for example, when the attempt involved a serious overdose or violent methods (by hanging, firearms, jumping out of windows, etc.). The population studied thus constituted a homogeneous grouping from the point of view of the evaluation methods used.

The data were collected by two psychiatrists who saw the patients separately. The first collected clinical facts through the use of several evaluative tests: the Brief Psychiatric Rating Scale (BPRS) provided an overall idea of the patient's symptomatology, and a self-evaluation scale (the SCL 90, the Hopkins Symptom Checklist revised by Derogatis) filled out by each patient allowed us to study different factors reflecting the patient's subjective experience.

Evaluations of psychiatric symptomatology in patients that have attempted to commit suicide are rarely made just after their arrival and can create certain problems in an emergency service. Although we had anticipated that the drug overdose patients would have trouble filling out the self-evaluation — requiring, as it does, their active participation — we found that once the phase of toxic confusion had passed, most of them seemed to be favorably motivated in filling out this test. In fact, only 1 of 30 patients refused to do so.

The second psychiatrist collected clinical and diagnostic information during a standard psychiatric interview. It was his responsibility to decide upon the patient's therapeutic orientation. He had three choices open to him:

1. He could send the patient home with or without suggesting outpatient psychiatric help
2. He could hospitalize the patient on the psychiatric ward
3. He could assign the patient to the short-term emergency service if the appropriate orientation could not be immediately determined

The last step in the collection of data consisted in a follow-up study of the patients' evolution over time. They were all recontacted twice: (1) 2 weeks after their discharge to determine if they had complied with the recommended therapeutic orientations and (2) 5 months later. Given the virtual impossibility of getting these patients to return to the hospital for a consultation, we adopted the strategy of telephoning them or contacting their general practitioners or relatives if we could not speak with them personally. This provided us, nonetheless, with enough information to determine whether they had improved, deteriorated, or remained the same. Some of the patients have not yet, in fact, been contacted for the second time, as they were first seen less than 5 months ago.

The results presented here thus concern 30 patients seen at the very outset of the study. Sample groups were determined as follows: a week was chosen at random every 2 months, and the patients that had attempted to commit suicide during that week who were seen in the emergency room or admitted into the short-term emergency service at the hospital made up one sample group. We hoped in this way to obtain a representative patient population. These results reflect certain characteristics of the evaluation and short- and medium-term evolution of these patients, but are not statistically significant given the limited number of patients in the sample.

The *preliminary results* concern 30 patients who attempted to commit suicide, all of whom underwent the above-mentioned tests except for an 85-year-old woman who was unable to fill out the self-evaluation. We were able to recontact 29 of the 30 patients seen 2 weeks after discharge and 17 of the 20 patients making up our first sample group 5 months after discharge.

Results

Demographic Data

The 30-person sample included 23 women and 7 men, thus showing a clear predominance of women in anxiodepressive syndromes. The patients ranged in age from 16 to 85, and the median age was 34. Eighteen of the patients were under 35, five of whom were adolescents. Twenty-one of the patients were single, and only nine were married — these are the same proportions found in related studies.

Diagnosis

The diagnoses made by the second psychiatrist, on the basis of the clinical interview he had with each patient, can be broken down into a number of categories. Among the patients presenting a *clear psychiatric disorder*, we found:

5 anxiodepressive syndromes
4 depressive syndromes
5 alcoholics
2 neurotics
2 psychotics

The other patients were far more difficult to diagnose: certain patients were only just within the bounds of normality. The majority of them showed signs of pathological personality disorders — whose precise nature was not easy to determine — and these signs varied from one interview to the next. We decided, therefore, to classify these patients as suffering from pathological personality disorders and to subdivide them into (1) *simple* pathological personality disorders, i.e., those involving *no* previous pathological experiences or serious socioemotional or professional adjustment problems, and (2) *complex* pathological personality disorders, i.e., those involving one or more psychopathological experiences or serious socioprofessional adjustment problems. We found:

10 simple disorders
 4 complex disorders

We correlated diagnostic categories with the evaluation test data and the patients' evolution over time.

Let us now examine the results of the evaluative tests: the BPRS and the SCL 90 (see Fig. 1). We found average scores in the cases of personality dis-

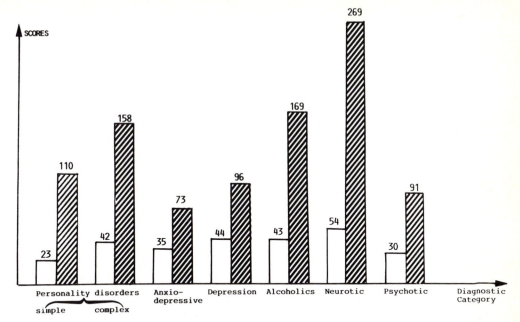

Fig. 1. Average scores on the BPRS (*open*) and SCL 90 (*hatched*) for the different diagnostic categories

orders, with higher scores for the complex disorders than for the simple ones. The BPRS showed relatively homogeneous results, and the items most frequently checked concerned anxiety, suicidal thoughts, depression, impulsiveness, and denial. The SCL showed a greater range of scores, as the overall scores for the group of personality disorders ranged from 8 to 246. The most frequently checked items concerned anxiety, paranoiac traits, hostility, depression, and hypersensitivity.

In the case of anxiodepressive syndromes, we found average scores on the BPRS but low scores on the self-evaluation scale. These patients thus seemed to minimize their pathology. The most important features here were anxiety and depression on the BPRS and hostility and depression on the SCL.

Among the patients manifesting more specific psychiatric pathologies, we found that the BPRS scores corresponded well to the pathologies: the low scores obtained by the two psychotics can be explained by the paucity of symptom expression, characteristic of psychosis; the two neurotics, on the other hand, scored quite highly, displaying abundant symptomatology.

The SCL 90 also showed an accentuation of symptom expression in neurotics, their scores being even higher than those given by the BPRS. Alcoholics also scored highly on the SCL 90, while psychotics' and depressives' scores were rather average (analogous to those of patients with anxiodepressive syndromes). These latter groupings included too few patients for us to pick out significant factors. We will simply mention that, while paranoiac traits were salient in psychosis, depression was most salient in the depressive syndromes. We found a greater number of factors represented in the other two diagnostic categories.

Therapeutic Orientations

Of the 30 patients in our sample, 22 (73.3%) were sent home, 4 (13.3%) were put in a short-term emergency service, and 4 were hospitalized on the psychiatric ward. These therapeutic orientations are represented in Fig. 2. Certain features here are striking:

All of the patients falling under the heading "*simple* personality disorders" were sent home without hospitalization. And only one of the four patients considered to be suffering from a *complex* personality disorder was sent to the short-term emergency service. On the whole, only outpatient care was prescribed for these two groupings of patients. These categories thus covered more patients than any of the others and corresponded most closely to suicidal behavior. The considerable number of patients sent directly back to their homes can be explained by the fact that these patients generally asked to go home immediately after emergency treatment. Outpatient care was proposed according to the particular case.

Hospitalization was prescribed far more often for those falling into other diagnostic categories, especially for the anxiodepressives and those characterized by neurotic and psychotic states. In Fig. 2, we distinguish hospitalization on the psychiatric ward from hospitalization in the short-term emergency service. This service often treats anxiodepressives who frequently must be observed for some time before a decision can be made as to the appropriate therapeutic orientation. The three alcoholics were not hospitalized because of their recalcitrant

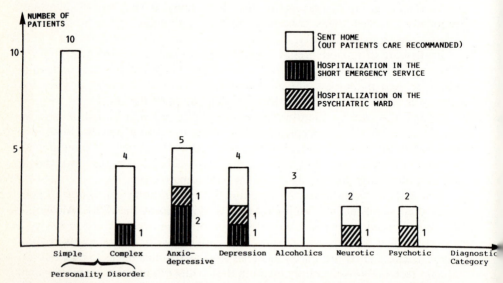

Fig. 2. Therapeutic orientations (therapeutic decisions made for each diagnostic category)

attitude to treatment and their ability to disguise their pathology; alcoholics often present a clinical picture akin to that seen in personality disorders.

In summarizing our considerations concerning therapeutic orientation, we must emphasize the importance of the personality disorders of patients that have attempted suicide who we discussed earlier: we have very little information at our disposal concerning the evolution and risk of recurrence of this predominant group of patients.

Evolution Over Time

Short-Term Compliance with Prescribed Therapeutic Orientation

Figure 3 summarizes the information obtained by recontacting, after 2 weeks, the patients who had not been hospitalized. We determined whether the patient had complied with the recommended therapeutic orientation (to return home or to consult a general practitioner or a psychiatrist). Figure 3 shows that the alcoholics and patients with complex personality disorders fulfilled the proposed orientations less often than any of the others, followed closely by patients with simple personality disorders. The others were relatively compliant.

Short-term Evolution

Two weeks after discharge, we found that, of the 30 patients in our sample, 11 (36.6%) had improved, 14 (46.6%) remained the same, and 5 (16.6%) deteriorated.

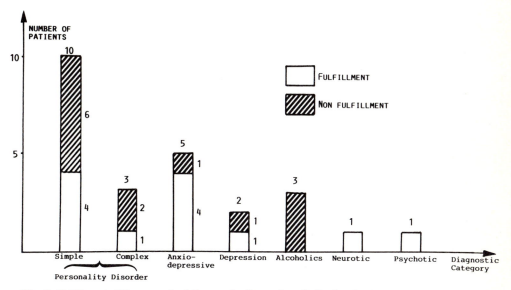

Fig. 3. Fulfilment of the prescribed therapy by the nonhospitalized patients

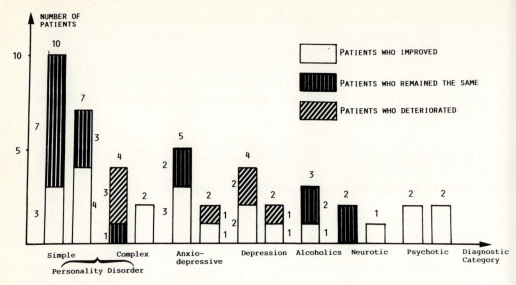

Fig. 4. Patients' short- and medium-term evolution. For each diagnostic category, the short-term and medium-term evolution is indicated in the first and second columns, respectively

Medium-Term Evolution

The medium-term evaluation (approximately 6 months after the attempted suicide) was not sufficient, in and of itself, to fully assess the patients' evolution. It is but the first stage in a long-term evaluation which will take place, approximately 2 years after the original act.

Approximately 6 months after discharge, we found that, of the 20 patients in our first sample group, 11 (55%) had improved, 3 (15%) had remained the same, and 2 (5%) had deteriorated (the evolution of 25% of these patients could not be determined). Figure 4 shows that patients with personality disorders had improved more after 6 months than after only 2 weeks. For the anxio-depressives, however, we had no indication of improvement after 6 months.

Correlation of Patient Evolution with Test Scores

If we compare patient evolution with the BPRS and SCL 90 test scores, we find (see Table 1) that the patients who improved the most — on a short-term as well as a long-term basis — scored the lowest on both of these tests. The patients who remained the same over time got markedly higher scores; their median score on the self-evaluation scale, for example, was twice as high. There were too few patients whose condition deteriorated to be able to draw any definite conclusions about them.

Table 1. Correlation between scale scores and short-term and medium-term evolution[a]

	BPRS		SCL 90	
	Short-term	Medium-term	Short-term	Medium-term
Improved	31	26	70	106
Remained the same	37	46	150	175
Deteriorated	41	48	159	85

[a] Each number represents the mean scores obtained on the BPRS and the SCL 90 by the patients who improved, remained the same, and deteriorated.

Prognosis

It thus seems that the BPRS and the SCL 90 provide us with a reliable criterion with which to determine certain patients' prognosis. Our results must, of course, be confirmed by a larger population sample. A statistical study of a large population would enable us to isolate more specific factors predicting an unfavorable prognosis. This preliminary study provides but a qualitative notion of the factors which seem important in the case of patients whose condition deteriorated. We found, notably, paranoia, hostility, and anxiety.

Discussion and Conclusion

These preliminary results obviously do not enable us to draw definitive conclusions, for our sample is still too small, and our data concerning patients' evolution are not yet complete. A number of points can, however, be made here:

Concerning methodology, it seems possible to make in-depth assessments of symptomatology in an emergency service context thanks to evaluative tests – most notably the self-evaluation scale (the SCL 90), which all but one of our patients filled out. These tests furnish valuable information.

The simple and complex personality disorders were the most difficult to evaluate clinically and deserve more scientific study. The majority of the patients discussed here, i.e., those who attempted suicide, suffered no serious somatic harm and were brought to a general hospital, fell into these categories.

The evaluative tests help us deal with this liminal pathology whose symptomatic manifestation is sometimes poor and imprecise: the BPRS is a reliable tool, as the scores agreed relatively well with the different diagnostic categories. Simple disorder scores, for example, varied between 18 and 24, while complex disorder scores varied between 37 and 53. The SCL 90 allows us to recognize certain factors concerning patients who are often classed under the rubric "indeterminate pathology," especially concerning the simple disorders. Patients with complex disorders, alcoholics, and neurotics scored very highly in this test, while the anxiodepressives had quite low scores. Patient evolution provides encouraging results, allowing us to anticipate the use of the SCL 90 in predicting recurrence of the suicidal act. We must first, of course, apply our methodology to a larger patient population and gather more information about long-term patient evolution.

It would be interesting to compare this methodology with one which uses risk tests, such as that of Pallis and Sainsbury (1976). The study done by Pino and Kockott (1979) characterizes patients who try to commit suicide a second time with such factors as degree of solitude, family status, anxiety, alcoholism, and high neurotic scores. Martin et al. (1985) found high suicide risks in antisocial people, alcoholics, and drug addicts. Their results agree substantially with our own.

References

Bürk F, Möller HJ (1985) Prädiktoren für weiteres suizidales Verhalten bei nach Suizidversuch hospitalisierten Patienten. Fortschr Neurol Psychiatr 53:259−270

Cloninger CR, Martin RL, Clayton P, Guze SB (1981) A blind follow-up and family study of anxiety neurosis: preliminary analysis of the St. Louis 500. In: Klein DF, Rabkin T (eds) Anxiety: new research and changing concepts. Raven, New York, pp 137−150

Corten P (1982) Attitude face aux suicidants et gardes d'hôpitaux généraux. Etude statistique. Psychol Méd 14/4:593−595

Craig TJ (1981) Mortality among psychiatric inpatients. Arch Gen Psychiatry 38:935−938

Daumezon G (1976) Les urgences psychiatriques. Rev Méd 17:729−736

Ettlinger RW (1955) Attempted suicide: experience of 500 cases at General Hospital. Acta Psychiatr Scand [Suppl] 103

Kessel H, McCulloch W (1966) Repeated acts of self-poisoning and self-injury. Proc R Soc Med 59:89−92

Kockott G, Heise H, Feverlein W (1970) Der Selbstmordversuch durch Intoxication. Fortschr Neurol Psychiatr 36:414−419

Kreitman N (1977) Parasuicide. Wiley, London

Martin RL, Cloninger CR, Guze SB (1979) The evaluation of diagnostic concordance in follow-up studies: II. A blind prospective follow-up of female criminals. J Psychiatr Res 15:107−125

Martin RL, Clayton PJ, Cloninger CR, Guze SB (1985) Mortality in a follow-up of 500 psychiatric outpatients: II. Cause-specific mortality. Arch Gen Psychiatry 42:58−66

Möller HJ, Versen D (1980) Probleme und Verbesserungsmöglichkeiten der psychiatrischen Diagnostik. In: Biefang S (ed) Evaluationsforschung in der Psychiatrie. Fragestellungen und Methoden. Enke, Stuttgart, pp 167−207

Pallis DJ, Sainsbury P (1976) The value of assessing intent in attempted suicide. Psychol Med 6:487−492

Pascalis G (1969) Tentatives de suicide des adolescents. Données statistiques françaises. Rapp congr de neurol et psychiat. Masson, Paris

Pino R, Kockott G (1979) Sechs-Jahres-Katamnese an hundert Patienten mit Suizidversuchen durch Tabletteneinnahme. Arch Psychiatr Nervenkr 227:213−226

Singer L, Jolibois M (1976) La menace de suicide. Rev Méd 17:744−753

Wilmotte J, Charles G (1983) Detection des suicidants susceptibles de récidive dans l'année. Acta Psychiatr Belg 83:558−568

A Follow-up Study 1 Year After Attempted Suicide: A Comparison Between Individuals Younger and Older Than 55 Years

J. Bäuml, C. Wächtler, A. Pilz, and H. Lauter

Introduction

Seen from an epidemiologic viewpoint, suicide and parasuicide are, as far as their respective numbers are concerned, definitely age-specific phenomena (Wächtler 1984; Lauter 1974). It was our intention in this study to compare two age groups − younger and older than 55 years − using the adult population of the city of Munich as a data base.

The adult residents of Munich who committed suicide in 1980 can be divided into three age groups: those 20−40, those 40−60, and those over 60 years of age. Quite conspicuous is the fact that the number of suicides in each group was very similar, namely, 91 for those 20−40 years old (32.7%), 94 for those 40−60 (33.8%), and 82 for those over 60 (29.5%). However, comparing the total number of deaths by all causes with the number of persons who committed suicide in each age group, one finds that death by suicide diminishes with increasing age: 19.2% of suicides are between 20 and 40 years old, 15.6% are between 40 and 60, and 0.7% are over 60 (Stadt München, Statistisches Handbuch, 1981). Thus, although those over 60 years of age comprise one-third of the total of suicides, death by suicide (0.7%) is only the 17th leading cause of death for this age group.

Although the ratio of successful suicides to suicide attempts is generally considered to be about 1:10, a closer look at this statistical generalization reveals a disturbing fact: whereas this ratio for individuals under 25 years of age is 1:20, the relationship of successful to attempted suicide reverses with increasing age so that, among the elderly, there are two successful suicides for every attempt (Wächtler 1984; Kreitman 1980).

Nevertheless, despite a very large number of publications relating to suicide and parasuicide, there are only relatively few which focus on the suicidal behavior of the elderly (Wächtler 1984; Kreitman 1976; Sainsbury 1965). In a 1-year follow-up study, we aimed to determine whether or not there are significant differences between younger and older parasuicidal individuals with respect to the following points: psychiatric diagnosis, main motives for attempting suicide, and the state of physical health at the time of the suicide attempt. In addition, the individual's present living situation, postepisodal suicidal behavior, and alterations in his/her situation at the time of follow-up were considered.

Methods

In the 12-month period from June 1979 to May 1980, 698 individuals were treated following a suicide attempt in the intensive care toxicology ward of the Hospital rechts der Isar of the Technical University of Munich: 623 of these were younger than 55 years, and 75 were 55 years of age or older. A sample population of 48 individuals from each age group was chosen for this study. Since 48 of the 75 older patients had been managed very closely during the index hospitalization, an equally large sample was randomly selected from the younger group. The decision to establish 55 years of age as the dividing line was influenced by the need for an adequate number of cases in the older group. Sex distribution was very similar in the two groups, there being 18 men and 30 women in the younger and 20 men and 28 women in the older group (Table 1). Approximately 1 year after the parasuicide event, these individuals were, without advance notice, visited in their homes.

Whenever possible, information from relatives and friends was also utilized. During the interview, a semistructured questionnaire was employed, which the patients had to answer verbally. Finally, the interviewees were asked to complete various self-evaluation questionnaires: somatic complaints, paranoid depressivity (von Zerssen 1976), hopelessness scale (Krampen 1979), and life satisfaction scale (Wiendieck 1970). Detailed data were obtained from 85% of those under 55 and from 91% of those of 55 and older.

Results

Endogenous psychosis was diagnosed for 12% of the younger and for 15% of the older patients; 8% of the older patients showed signs of a mild organic personality syndrome. Most frequent in both groups were the reactive disturbances, from which 40% of the younger and 54% of the older individuals suffered. Neuroses, psychopathic disturbances, and addiction problems were found twice as often in the younger group (Table 2).

The motive for suicide in 77% of the younger and 42% of the older individuals had involved problems in interpersonal relationships or the loss of a close relationship. The second most frequent reason (19%) among the older persons was concern about physical health. This was the case for only 2% of the younger persons (Table 3). Of the younger persons, 74% were in good physical condition, but this was true of only 23% of the older patients. On the other hand, only 5% of the younger, but 58% of the older patients were in poor physical health.

The living arrangements of both groups were compared with those of the average population of Munich. Of the younger patients, 28% were living alone. This number increased to 38% for the older persons. In Munich, 19% of the average population was living alone at this time. On the day of follow-up, 70% of the younger and 50% of the elderly group were found to have visitors (Table 4).

Table 1. Total number of patients and sample size

	< 55 years	≧ 55 years	Total
Total number	623	75	698
Sample size	48	48	96
♂:♀	18:30	20:28	
Average age	33	65	

Table 2. Psychiatric diagnoses

Diagnosis	ICD 9	< 55 years		≧ 55 years	
		(n)	(%)	(n)	(%)
Affective psychosis	296.1	5	12	4	15
Schizophrenic psychosis	295.3	1		3	
Organic personality syndrome, mild	310.1	0	0	4	8
Adjustment disorder	309.0/.1	19	40	26	54
Neuroses	300.0/.4	7	29	3	15
Personality disturbances	301.1/.3	7		4	
Alcohol abuse/dependence	305.0/303.0	5		4	
Drug abuse/dependence	305.4/.9	1	19	0	8
Polytoxicomania	304.8	3		0	
Total		48	100	48	100

Table 3. Main motives for suicide

Motives	< 55 years		≧ 55 years	
	(n)	(%)	(n)	(%)
Interpersonal problems, separation from partner	37	77	20	42
Health-related anxiety	1	2	9	19
Occupational worries	3	6	6	12
Fear of dependency	0	0	3	6
Other or no conflict	7	15	10	21
Total	48	100	48	100

Table 4. Living conditions at the time of follow-up

Living conditions	< 55 years (%)	≧ 55 years (%)	Population of Munich (%)
Living alone, one-person households	28	38	18.9
With others, two-or-more-person households	66	–	75.8
Other, living in institutions	6	–	5.3
Contact person found at home during interview	70	50	–

Suicides had not occurred in either group in the interim. However, two older patients had died from the delayed consequences of their attempted suicide. One patient of the younger and one of the older group had meanwhile died from independent causes; 38% of the younger and 16% of the older patients had a history of an attempted suicide in the past. After having been discharged from the hospital, 10% of the younger and 2% of the older patients had again attempted suicide.

During the period prior to follow-up, 39% of the younger and more than 50% of the older patients reported having suicidal thoughts. The patients also performed a self-evaluation for their feelings of hopelessness and pessimism. The result was that 54% of the younger and 65% of the older patients had pathologically increased ratings (Table 5).

Subsequent to the index parasuicide, 42% of the persons younger than 55 years had changed their place of residence, whereas a distinctly lower percentage (14%) of the older individuals had moved. The corresponding rate for the general Munich population amounted to 13.7% in 1980.

Almost half of the younger patients (46%) had changed their place of employment, whereby two-thirds of these reported to have improved their situation; for only one patient had it deteriorated.

All of the older patients (7%) spoke of a negative change in their lives. A separation from their partner had taken place for 54% of the younger and 7% of the older parasuicides (Table 6).

Table 5. Suicidal behavior prior to follow-up

	<55 years (%)	≧55 years (%)	Population of Munich (%)
Suicides	0	0	0.02
Deceased prior to follow-up	2	6	1
History of suicide attempt	39	16	–
Suicide attempt prior to follow-up	10	2	0.2
Suicidal thoughts prior to follow-up	39	50	20[a]
Pathologically increased scores for hopelessness and pessimism	54	65	–

[a] Suicidal thoughts among elderly people (Wiendieck 1972).

Table 6. Changes in social situation prior to follow-up

	<55 years (%)	≧55 years (%)	Population of Munich (%)
Change in residence	42	14	13.7
Change in employment	46	7	–
	⅔ with improvement	All with deterioration	
Change in partner	54	7	–

Discussion

Endogenous psychosis was found more often among the older patients, but still did not represent the bulk of diagnosis obtained; a similar result can be seen from other workers in this field (Kockott 1981; Feuerlein 1977). The younger individuals suffered more often from neurotic disturbances and addiction problems; among the older ones reactive disturbances predominated. It appears that the problems faced by younger persons are more of a long-term nature. On the other hand, older people undergo a suicide crisis when they are suddenly confronted with acute problems of aging (Wächtler 1983).

Problems in interpersonal relationships were prevalent in both age groups; concern about physical health was more predominant among the elderly than is described in the literature (Kockott 1981). These concerns were not unfounded, but due to a depressed attitude of the patients, a cognitive dissonance existed between the objective state of health and the fearful expectations arising from the respective ailment (Wächtler 1982; Kreitman 1976). In keeping with the descriptions of other authors, one cannot speak of a general isolation among persons who have attempted suicide. This holds true for young and old alike (Wächtler 1982).

On the basis of the various results from the self-evaluation tests and of the different rates of parasuicide repeaters in the two age groups, the following summary can be made:

Depression and concomitant recurring suicidal behavior are more dominant in older people. At the same time, there is a low rate of attempted and a high rate of successful suicide for this group (Wächtler 1984). The latter could not be confirmed as the period of time elapsed since the parasuicide event − 1 year − was too short.

In comparison with the average population and the group of the older persons, the younger ones showed a high rate of social change; most of them were correlated to a positive course (Bäuml 1986). This high frequency of change among the younger individuals appears to be a sign of vitality and a release of healthy, adaptive energy and indicates a positive development (Wolf et al. 1979).

Changes among the older persons were more of a negative nature. For instance, the move to an old-age home means giving up lifelong independence, or the loss of a dear one corresponds to feelings of being left alone, connected with a reduction of self-reliance (Gröschke-Bachmann 1982).

Considering the persistent chronic suicidal behavior, above all among the older patients, a long-term and intensive postevent management should be planned as has been suggested by many authors (Breucha and Möller 1982; Möller 1981, 1985; Wächtler 1982; Wolf et al. 1979; Kockott 1981).

References

Bäuml J (1986) Kurzzeitkatamnese von Patienten nach einem Suizidversuch im jüngeren und mittleren Erwachsenenalter − Ergebnisvergleich mit einer Untersuchung zu Suizidversuchspatienten im höheren Lebensalter. Technical University Munich

Breucha HP, Möller HJ (1982) 3-Jahres-Katamnese an 100 von der „ARCHE" nachbetreuten Parasuizidenten: Nachbetreuung, soziale und psychische Situation. Crisis 12:78−87

Feuerlein W (1977) Ursachen, Motivationen und Tendenzen von Selbstmordhandlungen im Alter. Aktuel Gerontol 7:67−74

Gröschke-Bachmann D (1982) Der Altersselbstmord in der Bundesrepublik − eine soziologische Betrachtung. Aktuel Gerontol 12:60−63

Kockott G (1981) Der Selbstmordversuch im Alter. Fortschr Med 26:1049−1056

Krampen G (1979) Hoffnungslosigkeit bei stationären Patienten − ihre Messung durch einen Kurzfragebogen (H-Scale). Med Psychol 5:39−49

Kreitman N (1976) Age and parasuicide ("attempted suicide"). Psychol Med 6:113−121

Kreitman N (1980) Die Epidemiologie von Suizid und Parasuizid. Nervenarzt 51:131−138

Lauter H (1974) Übersichten Alterspsychiatrie: Epidemiologische Aspekte alterspsychiatrischer Erkrankungen. Nervenarzt 45:277−288

Möller HJ, Geiger V (1981) Möglichkeiten zur „Compliance"-Verbesserung bei Parasuizidenten. Crisis 10:122−129

Möller HJ, Lauter H (1985) Der psychiatrische Liaisondienst. Münch Med Wochenschr 36:842−845

Sainsbury P (1965) Der Altersselbstmord. In: Zwingmann CH (ed) Selbstvernichtung. Akademische Verlagsgesellschaft, Frankfurt, p 9

Stadt München (1981) Statistisches Handbuch. Gerber, Munich

von Zerssen D (1976) Beschwerde-Liste, Paranoid-Depressivitäts-Liste. Beltz-Test, Weinheim

Wächtler C (1982) Suizidversuche im höheren Lebensalter − eine katamnestische Nachuntersuchung. Aktuel Gerontol 12:64−66

Wächtler C (1983) Suizidalität im Alter: auf die Probleme des alten Menschen eingehen. Psycho 9:506−519

Wächtler C (1984) Suizidalität. In: Oswald WD, Herman WM, Kanowski S, Lehr UM, Thomae H (eds) Gerontologie. Kohlhammer, Stuttgart, p 8

Wiendieck G (1970) Entwicklung einer Skala zur Messung der Lebenszufriedenheit im höheren Lebensalter. Aktuel Gerontol 3:215−224

Wiendieck G (1972) Zur appellativen Funktion des Suizidversuchs. Diss, Cologne

Wolf R, Gräf T, Wedler HL (1979) Über die Änderung der Lebenssituation nach Suizidversuchen. Med Welt 39:1413−1435

Three-Year Follow-up of 150 Inpatients After a Suicide Attempt by Drug Overdose

S. Bronisch, C. Bothge, and H.-J. Möller

Introduction

In 1976 Möller et al. (1978) examined 150 patients who had been admitted to the general hospital in München-Schwabing after a suicide attempt by drug overdose. Despite the fact that a general register of suicide attempts does not exist in Munich, the sample seems to be rather representative since in a study from Kockott et al. (1970) in another general hospital in Munich, patients after a suicide attempt by drug overdose displayed the same sociodemographic (for example age, sex, marital status) and similar psychiatric characteristics (suicide attempt in the previous history, severity of the suicide attempt, diagnosis) as our group did. These 150 patients were reexamined 3 years after the suicide attempt. The main objects of the follow-up study were:

1. What was the subsequent course of the patients after the suicide attempt?
2. Are there prognostic factors for further suicidal behavior?
3. Did the patients benefit from outpatient treatment after the attempt?

Study

Subjects

Information was obtained about 106 (71%) of 150 patients for an average follow-up period of 3 years. Seventy-eight (52%) filled in a questionnaire devised by us as well as three standardized self-rating instruments, whereas 28 (19%) refused to fill in these questionnaires but gave information about repeated suicide attempts and the utilization of psychiatric/psychotherapeutic services. No information could be collected from 44 (29%).

Instruments

Symptomatology and personality features were assessed by three self-rating questionnaires:

1. Assessment of paranoid and depressive tendencies by the Paranoid Depression Scale (PDS) (von Zerssen 1986),
2. Assessment of somatic complaints by the Somatic Complaints List (SC-L) (von Zerssen 1986),

3. The personality features of extroversion and neurotic tendency by the Extroversion Neuroticism Rigidity Questionnaire (ENR) (Vogt et al. 1960).

Data about outpatient aftercare, social adjustment within the follow-up period, general well-being (e.g., satisfaction with life), and repeated suicide attempts were collected by a self-constructed questionnaire. The self-rating scales and the self-constructed questionnaire were mailed to the patients. Patients who failed to respond were recontacted by letter, phone call, or personal visit.

The psychiatric diagnoses were assessed by the International Classification of Diseases, 8th revision, psychiatric diagnoses (ICD 8) (WHO 1979, German version Degkwitz et al. 1980).

Results

Of the whole sample who could be reexamined, 4 patients (3.8%) committed suicide, 17 patients (16%) repeated a suicide attempt, and 28 patients (27%) utilized psychiatric/psychotherapeutic services.

Seventy-eight patients filled in the whole battery of self-rating questionnaires. The sociodemographic characteristics were the following: 74% (58) were female, 26% (20) were male, 63% (49) were younger than 40, 37% (29) older than 40, 37% (29) had a history of previous suicidal behavior, 63% (49) had no history, 35% (27) were married, 5% (4) were widowed, 27% (21) were divorced, and 33% (26) were single.

On the basis of 11 criteria which originated from the data of the 150 patients, these 78 patients were compared with the remaining 72. No differences could be seen concerning sex, age, marital status, history of previous suicidal behavior, severity of the suicide attempt, recommending outpatient treatment, lasting of suicide intention, and moment of drug provision. The following variables differed from the original sample of 150 patients: there were more neurotic disorders (ICD 8: 300) as well as substance addiction (ICD 9: 303 and 304), there were more housewives and less blue-collar workers, and there were more people living together.

Table 1 shows the frequency of suicides and of repeated suicide attempts within the 3-year follow-up period. Four patients (5%) − all of them male − committed suicide. Fourteen patients (18%) repeated a suicide attempt at least once. The temporal distribution of the repeated attempts showed an elevated frequency in the 2 years following the index suicide attempt. Thirty-five patients (45%) reported suicidal intentions, which were present throughout the follow-up period in 14 (18%) cases. The frequency of suicidal ideation was evenly distributed over the years. Twenty-nine patients (37%) said that they had been dissatisfied with their lives at some time during follow-up; 20 (26%) of these patients had been chronically dissatisfied with their lives during the entire follow-up period, and also 20 patients (26%) had been chronically socially isolated. At follow-up 40 patients (51%) reported suffering from problems, and 21 patients (27%) reported having the same problems as at the time of the index suicide attempt. Half of the patients showed pathological depression scores in the self-rating scale.

Table 1. Status of patients ($n = 78$) during the 3-year follow-up period

	%	n
Suicide	5	4
Suicide attempts	18	14
Suicidal intentions	45	35
Dissatisfaction with life	26	20

Table 2. Number of psychiatric/psychotherapeutic sessions of patients treated ($n = 25$)

	Sessions (h)						No information
	1−2	3−5	6−10	11−20	21−30	30	
Patients treated	1	9	4	3	1	6	1
%	4	36	16	12	4	24	4

Risk groups for further suicide attempts during the follow-up period were:

Transient situational disturbance
Alcoholism and/or drug dependence
Single
Chronically socially isolated
Under 30 years of age
Change of jobs
Unemployment for a longer period

The following predictors of further suicidal behavior were examined: suicide attempts in the past history, the severeness of the suicide attempt using the Reed Scheme (Reed et al. 1952), age, sex, marital and occupational status as well as diagnostic groups. A diagnosis of transient situational disturbance (ICD 8: 307) or of substance addiction (ICD 8: 303, 304), age under 30, being single, being socially isolated, a frequent change of jobs, or being unemployed for a longer period were associated with an elevated rate of repetition.

The data on outpatient aftercare were obtained only from 25 (32%), whereas 53 (68%) patients remembered at follow-up that some kind of aftercare had been recommended to them while still in the hospital. Therefore, only 32% had been compliant with the recommendation.

Table 2 shows the number of psychiatric/psychotherapeutic sessions of the patients treated ($n = 25$). Ten patients (40%) terminated treatment after less than five therapeutic sessions. Including the four patients who remained in therapy for up to a maximum of 10 h, only 14 (44%) of the patients continued outpatient treatment for more than ten therapeutic sessions. The patients treated were distinguished from untreated patients only by the fact that they had made the more severe suicide attempts.

Discussion

Despite the fact that our sample originated from a general hospital, and subsequently the number of psychoses (6.6%) was small (Möller et al. 1978), the course and outcome was rather poor: 3.8% of the patients committed suicide and 16% made another suicide attempt, which is in agreement with the literature (Kessel, McCulloch 1966). Half of the patients were suffering from severe problems, 21 having the same problems as at the time of the index suicide attempt, and 45% reported suicidal intentions. The results show that many of the patients were not able to solve their problems and that the difficulties in a high percentage were chronic (Schmid-Bode et al. 1984).

Certain diagnostic groups were associated with the risk of further repeated suicide attempts: age under 30, being single, being chronically isolated socially, a frequent change of jobs, or being unemployed for a longer period of time.

Bürk and Möller (1985) reviewed 70 follow-up studies of patients hospitalized after attempted suicide which tried to find predictors for further suicidal behavior by statistical methods. The following predictors for patients were found: previous suicide attempt (risk of repetition of attempted suicide as well as suicide), previous psychiatric treatment (risk of repeated suicide attempt), addiction (suicide or repetition of attempted suicide), old age, and male sex (suicide).

The diagnosis of transient situational disturbance in our sample could perhaps replace the diagnosis of a personality disorder in the literature, which as a more serious diagnosis is often not given in the first diagnostic assessment if not enough information is available. Being single, a frequent change of jobs, or being unemployed for a longer period of time seem to be rather specific for our sample.

Although a large number of patients had a mental disorder and one-fifth had as a high risk group committed a suicide attempt before the index treatment, only one-third made use of aftercare treatment. Moreover, a large number of patients (56%) terminated their outpatient treatment prematurely. It can therefore be concluded that the readiness of the patients to utilize aftercare facilities was only poor or that perhaps the manner of treatment did not meet their requirements (Kurz et al. 1985). Since there was no difference between treated and untreated patients, new concepts of treatment concerning suicide attempters using psychiatric/psychotherapeutic services have to be developed (Hirsch et al. 1982).

References

Bürk F, Möller HJ (1985) Prädiktoren für weiteres suizidales Verhalten bei nach einem Suizidversuch hospitalisierten Patienten. Fortschr Neurol Psychiatr 53:259–270

Degkwitz R, Helmchen H, Kockott G, Mombour W (eds) (1980) Diagnosenschlüssel und Glossar psychiatrischer Krankheiten. Deutsche Ausgabe der internationalen Klassifikation der WHO: ICD, 8th revision, Springer, Berlin Heidelberg New York, chap V

Hirsch SR, Walsh C, Draper R (1982) Parasuicide. A review of treatment interventions. J Affective Disord 4:299–311

Kessel N, McCulloch W (1966) Repeated acts of self-poisoning and self-injury. Proc R Soc Med 59:89−93

Kockott G, Heyse H, Feuerlein W (1970) Der Selbstmordversuch durch Intoxikation. Fortschr Neurol Psychiatr 9:441−465

Kurz A, Möller HJ, Bürk A, Torhorst A, Wächtler C, Lauter H (1985) Determination of treatment disposal for parasuicide patients in a German university hospital. Soc Psychiatry 20:145−151

Möller HJ, Werner V, Feuerlein W (1978) Beschreibung von 150 Patienten mit Selbstmordversuch durch Tabletten unter besonderer Berücksichtigung des Selbstmordverhaltens und der Inanspruchnahme von Beratungsmöglichkeiten für Suizidgefährdete. Arch Psychiatr Nervenkr 226:113−135

Reed CE, Driggs MR, Foote CC (1952) Acute barbiturate intoxication: a study of 300 cases based on a physiologic system of classification on the severity of the intoxication. Ann Intern Med 37:290

Schmid-Bode W, Breucha HP, Möller HJ (1984) Ergebnisse einer 3-Jahres-Katamnese an 100 ambulant nachbetreuten Parasuiziidenten. In: Welz R, Möller HJ (eds) Bestandsaufnahme der Suizidforschung. Epidemiologie, Prävention und Therapie. Roderer, Regensburg

Vogt A, Revenstorf D, Brengelmann JC (1960) Analyse und Eichung des Extraversion-Neurotizismus-Fragebogens nach Brengelmann JC und Brengelmann L. Unpublished manuscript of the Psychology Department of the Max-Planck-Institute for Psychiatry, Munich

von Zerssen D (1986) Clinical self rating-scales (CSR-S) of the Munich Psychiatric Information. In: Sartorius N, Ban TA (eds) Assessment of depression. Springer, Berlin Heidelberg New York, pp 270−303

Survey and Follow-up of Patients Admitted to Innsbruck University Hospital for Attempted Suicide in 1983

W. W. Fleischhacker, C. Haring, C. H. Miller, and C. Barnas

Introduction

Appropriate preventive measures against suicidal behavior can only be taken after the identification and thorough investigation of the groups at risk. The following are known to be high-risk groups: depressives, alcoholics and other addicts, elderly and lonely people, persons announcing their suicide attempt, and persons having attempted suicide before (Sonneck 1983). A number of papers (Bancroft and Marsack 1977; Möller et al. 1982; Feuerlein 1984) document that a large proportion of the patients with attempted suicide in their histories tend to repeat the attempts or to commit suicide successfully.

In 1985, we analyzed the consultation activities of a psychiatric department for the years 1983 and 1984 (Fleischhacker et al. 1986). During these 2 years, 2048 patients were examined at different departments of the Innsbruck University Hospital. About 25% ($n = 507$) of the patients we examined had been admitted to the hospital for attempted suicide. This high percentage led us to take a closer look at this particular group of patients.

Methods

We tried to locate all patients who had been admitted for attempted suicide in 1983. Those whom we could reach on the telephone were asked to come for an interview. The following data were collected by a semistructured interview: stress situation before the suicide attempt, availability of persons to talk about problems before attempting suicides, feelings after the attempt, judgment of the contact with our consultant, environmental reaction to the attempted suicide, changes in stressors after the attempt, and further suicidal acts. The psychiatric diagnosis established at the time of follow-up was recorded. The names of those patients who had successfully committed suicide in the meantime were obtained from the reports filed by the police.

Results

This paper presents the preliminary results of our study. Of the 213 suicide attempters of 1983 who had been examined by our consultants, we were able to reach 62 patients (29.1%) on the telephone: 91.9% of them were prepared to come to our hospital for a semistructured interview, 4.8% refused information, and 3.2% convinced us that they had never attempted suicide.

Please note that the sum of percentages mentioned below is considerably higher than 100, since most patients experienced more than one stressor. The most common stressors were parental conflicts and family problems, as well as various forms of alcohol or drug abuse. Among the 64.9% who reported conflicts with their parents, we roughly discriminated between the acute problems of young patients and broken-home situations. Family problems were recorded in 45.6% of the cases, abuse of or addiction to alcohol or drugs in 42.1%, occupational problems in 29.8%, and death of or separation from partners in 26.3% (Fig. 1).

We also investigated with whom the patient had tried to talk about his problems before he attempted suicide. It turned out that the partners had hardly ever shown sympathy. Patients had commonly met with more sympathy from their colleagues at work and from psychiatrists they had consulted before. Another interesting finding was the fact that public advisory services had rarely been used (Fig. 2).

Furthermore, we tried to explore the patients' feelings after they had attempted suicide and realized that they would go on living. More than 32% of the patients reported having felt relief, 36% regret, and 31% did not remember a particular feeling.

At follow-up, we also asked the patients about their opinion as to the communication with the consultant psychiatrist following their suicide attempt: 44.2% made a positive judgment, 21% considered the contact with the psychiatrist unnecessary, and 34% regarded it as neutral. Statements such as sym-

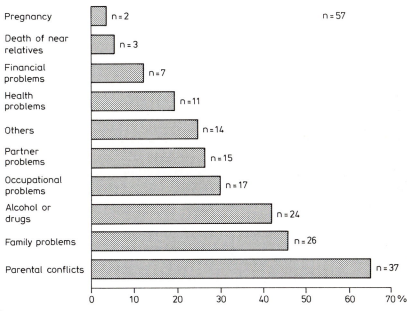

Fig. 1. Stressors

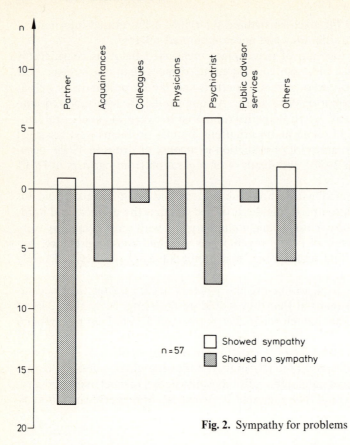

n = 57

☐ Showed sympathy

▨ Showed no sympathy

Fig. 2. Sympathy for problems

pathetic, understanding, encouraging, and constructive were rated as positive. If we could conclude from the interview that the patient could not or did not want to see any support by psychiatric care, we rated it as unnecessary. The neutral judgments also included those patients who could hardly remember the conversation due to organic mental disorder at the time of examination.

An assessment of the environmental reaction to the suicide attempt (Fig. 3) showed that the sympathy was greater when compared with the situation before the attempt. However, parents (64% negative reaction, 46% positive reaction) and partners (68% negative reaction, 32% positive reaction) still demonstrated prevailingly negative reactions. The suicide attempter could still expect more sympathy from his children (54% negative reaction, 46% positive reaction), his colleagues at work (47% negative reaction, 53% positive reaction), and his friends (46% negative reaction, 54% positive reaction).

At follow-up, the negative parental relations had improved in only 16.2% of the cases. A more favorable development was noted for the stressors, family problems (37% improvement), alcohol or drug abuse (37.5% improvement), and occupational problems (42.9% improvement). Nevertheless, the majority of problems had persisted or become even more serious also in these cases.

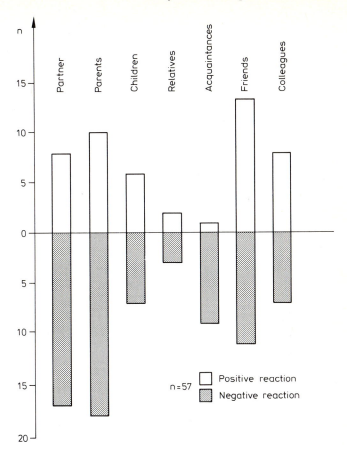

Fig. 3. Environmental reaction to the suicide attempt

A marked improvement was observed only in patients where the stressors before the suicide attempt had been death of near relatives or pregnancy, with a rate of 66.6% in either case, and for the stressor death of or separation from partners, with an improvement of 70.6%.

To get a better idea about the significance of stressors concerning further suicide risk, we differentiated between patients in whom the attempted suicide had not been followed by any further attempts up to the time of follow-up (66.6%), those who had made one further attempt (21.1%), and those with several further attempts (12.3%). The classification into these three subgroups demonstrated considerable differences concerning stress situations. Patients with more than two attempted suicides in their history at the time of follow-up reported more stressors than the total sample we examined, except for the factors, occupational problems and physical illness. Stressors of particular importance seemed to be negative parental relations, drug or alcohol abuse, and partner problems.

The psychiatrists making the follow-up examinations recorded the actual diagnoses valid on the day of interview, classified according to the International Classification of Diseases (ICD 9): 19.3% of the sample showed no signs or symptoms of mental illness at that time. As had been the case at the time of evaluation by the psychiatric consultant in 1983, the majority of psychiatric illnesses were personality disorders also at follow-up (26.3%). Other important disturbances were various different forms of addiction (22.8%), neurotic reactions (7.0%), and chronic depressive illness (3.5%). One patient presented with residual schizophrenia (1.4%), and four patients suffered from manic-depressive illness (7.0%).

A comparison of our list of suicide attempters with the suicide files of the police showed that 3.3% of the patients our consultants had interviewed in 1983 had actually committed suicide in the meantime. This adds up to 1.32% suicides per year or a suicide rate of 1315/100 000.

Discussion

Of the 213 patients who had been admitted to the Innsbruck University Hospital for attempted suicide in 1983, 29.1% underwent follow-up examination. Originally, we had expected that the low migration tendency of the Tyrolean population would make a follow-up examination easy. However, it turned out that the occupational situation – particularly in the hotel and restaurant business – was favorable to young people coming from other federal states, a subgroup with a high migration tendency.

Concerning the presuicidal stressors, we should like to refer to Henseler (1980), who doubts the value of statistics covering conscious motives. However, the stressors we collected were not precipitants, but should rather be regarded as contributors to some kind of situational constriction (Ringel 1984). The item sympathy is of particular interest. The majority of patients interviewed seemed to have experienced environmental help as insufficient. It therefore has to be concluded that the environment of the patients we examined showed little sensitivity to the severity of their problems. Another remarkable finding was that only one of the patients we interviewed had made use of a public advisory service. It will be necessary to make the availability of public services more commonly known to the public.

As has already been mentioned, the stress situation had hardly ever improved up to the day of follow-up when it was related to parental conflicts. This is most probably due to the fact that this stressor may be considered of acute importance only in young suicide attempters, whereas the trauma the other patients had suffered from their parental conflict seemed to have had no more acute impact on their suicidal ideation.

Those who had made several suicide attempts were commonly found to have difficulties with their parents and partners, as well as some kind of alcohol or drug problem. The importance of the factors, negative parental relations and alcohol or drug abuse, needs no further explanation. However, we were surprised to find that partner problems were so important in this subgroup, since this stressor had shown the most frequent improvement in the total sample. Our data seem to suggest that two forms of partner conflicts can be discriminated with regard to suicidal behavior: patients with actual neuroses had one attempted suicide in their histories, whereas patients with a chronic partner conflict related to their personality disturbance had made repeated attempts.

At the time of follow-up, 3.3% of the 213 patients had actually committed suicide. This corresponds with a rate of 1.32% per year, which is in agreement with the rates reported in the literature, e.g., 4% in 5 years (Katschnig et al. 1981), 1% in 1 year (Reimer 1982), and 3.3% in 3 years (Kreitman 1977).

However, it is important that — based on a suicide rate of 1315 — the suicide risk of the group of suicide attempters was 57 times higher than the suicide risk of the general Tyrolean population. This value is above the one reported by Katschnig et al. (1981), who found the suicide risk to be 43 times higher in a comparable population.

References

Bancroft J, Marsack P (1977) The repetitions of self-poisoning and self-injury. Br J Psychiatry 131:394
Feuerlein W (1984) Rezidivgefahr bei Suicidversuchen. Lebensversicherungsmedizin 3:56–59
Fleischhacker WW, Barnas CH, Haring CH, Stuppäck CH, Unterweger B, Wagner R (1986) Der Psychiatrische Konsiliardienst. Nervenarzt 57:589–592
Henseler H (1980) Narzißtische Krisen. Rowohlt, Hamburg
Katschnig A, Siut P, Fuchs-Robetin G (1981) Gibt es verschiedene Typen von Selbstmordversuchen? In: Welz R, Pohlmeier H (eds) Selbstmordhandlungen. Belz, Weinheim, p 13
Kreitman N (1977) Parasuicide. Wiley, London
Möller HJ, Torhorst A, Wächtler C (1982) Versorgung von Patienten nach Selbstmordversuch – Aufgaben, Probleme und Verbesserungsmöglichkeiten. Psychiatr Prax 9:106–112
Reimer C (1982) (ed) Suizid. Springer, Berlin Heidelberg New York
Ringel E (1984) Neue Gesichtspunkte zum praesuizidalen Syndrom. In: Ringel E (ed) Selbstmordverhütung. Fachbuchhandlung für Psychologie, Verlagsabteilung Eschborn
Sonneck G (1983) Krisenintervention und Selbstmordverhütung. Öst. Ärzteztg 38/20:1419–1422

Changes in Hopelessness and Dissimulation Tendencies in Patients After a Suicide Attempt

A. Schmidtke and S. Schaller

Problem

Previous studies dealing with the interrelationships between patients' self-reports concerning the intention of their suicide attempt and the estimated suicidal intent as well as the estimated lethality of the suicidal act have produced contradictory findings. Several factors may account for such discrepancies. In most previous studies, the suicidal intent and the lethality of the suicide attempt were only assessed using cross-sectional methods. However, the results of other studies have suggested that self-reports concerning the seriousness of a suicide attempt change with time after the attempt due to the influence of several factors (Wetzel 1976; Götze et al. 1979).

Several studies, for example those of Linehan and co-workers (Linehan and Nielsen 1981; Linehan and Nielsen 1983; Linehan et al. 1983), involving normal subjects and patients with suicide attempts have indicated that tendencies toward socially desirable reporting have a moderating effect on patients' statements concerning their hopelessness and their wishes not to die as well as their coping beliefs. However, it is possible that such dissimulation tendencies vary during the time period after a suicide attempt. In a previous study (Schmidtke and Schaller 1985) in which measurements were made at three time points after suicide attempts, we were able to demonstrate that dissimulation tendencies and acceptance of the failure of the attempt increased with time, whereas hopelessness, suicidal-depressive tendencies, and ratings of the intent to die decreased with time. In agreement with the results obtained by Linehan and co-workers, it was also found that dissimulation tendencies had the greatest effect on the covariation between hopelessness and suicidal-depressive tendencies.

In the present study, we extended the scope of our previous study by investigating whether, for a specific subgroup of patients, a stay in a psychiatric hospital after a suicide attempt had any influence on these values. We assumed that patients with suicide attempts who had been admitted to a psychiatric hospital must have been considered to be especially prone to further suicidal behavior or other psychic problems, whereas the suicide behavior of patients who had been discharged after medical treatment must have been regarded as being less serious.

Study

Design and Sample

We studied 41 male patients with a mean age of 34 years and 55 female patients with a mean age of 37 years who were receiving treatment in four psychiatric institutions. All of the patients had been diagnosed by psychiatrists and had been classified into International Classification of Diseases (ICD) groups 300 to 309. The patients had been admitted to a psychiatric hospital directly after their suicide attempt or immediately after medical treatment in a general hospital. Patients who had first been allowed to go home after treatment in a general hospital and had then been admitted to or had volunteered to enter a psychiatric hospital were not included in the study.

The time at which the first measurement was made varied from 0 to 17 days after admission to the psychiatric hospital and 0 to 19 days after the suicide attempt. Due to the longitudinal character of the investigation, the measurements were repeated twice after the first assessment. Figure 1 shows the design of the investigation. This design can be used to study both the different time periods after the suicide attempt and the different time periods after admission to a psychiatric hospital. Thus, by comparing various categories, it is possible to estimate whether the point of measurement or the repeating of measurements has an influence on the values. Hence, the design is similar to an extended fourfold table design according to Solomon (1949).

Instruments

The procedure included a questionnaire designed to estimate the lethality and intent of the suicidal act (Häfner et al. 1983) and seven-point rating scales to assess the patients' judgment of their suicide intent and need for help. The dissimulation tendency was measured using a questionnaire constructed for this

Days after suicide attempt/admittance to hospital

1st–4th day 1st testing	5th–8th day 2nd testing	> 9th day 3rd testing		
	5th–8th day 1st testing	9th–12th day 2nd testing	> 13th day 3rd testing	
		9th–12th day 1st testing	13th–16th day 2nd testing	> 17th day 3rd testing
			13th–16th day 1st testing	17th–20th day 2nd testing . . .
				17th–20th day 1st testing . . .

Fig. 1. Design of the study

purpose. It consisted of items derived from scales that had been developed to measure similar tendencies. The questionnaire included the factors "trustworthiness and helpfulness," "energy," and "weakness of character." The reliability, validity, and factor structure of the questionnaire had been examined in preliminary studies. Hopelessness was measured using the Hopelessness Scale of Beck (translated by Krampen 1979); suicidal-depressive tendencies were assessed using the Questionnaire to Assess Suicide Risk (*Fragebogentest zur Beurteilung der Suizidgefahr*) (Stork 1977).

Results

Preliminary analyses revealed no statistically significant differences between sexes, although female patients had higher dissimulation values and suicidal-depressive tendencies than males. Therefore, data were collapsed across sex.

Table 1 shows the values obtained at three time points (1) after admission to a psychiatric hospital and (2) after the suicide attempt. The data demonstrate that, during the 1st week after admission to hospital, hopelessness and suicidal-depressive tendencies decreased, while dissimulation tendencies increased. We found only small and non-significant changes in the values obtained at the three time points when more than 5 days had elapsed between admission to the hospital and the first measurement (i.e., more than 9 days after the suicide attempt). However, owing to the small number of patients in these groups, these findings are only of a preliminary nature.

Although exhibiting similar dissimulation tendencies, patients who had been quickly discharged from the hospital had significantly lower values for hopelessness ($P<.01$) and suicidal-depressive feelings ($P<.05$) than patients who had stayed in the hospital for a longer period.

Table 1. Means and standard deviations of hopelessness, suicidal-depressive tendencies, and dissimulation tendencies taken at three time points after admission to hospital and after the suicide attempt

Days	1−4		5−8		>9	
1. After admission to hospital (time lapse after the suicide attempt > 5 days)						
H	32.00	(4.73)	30.40	(5.77)	29.00	(7.52)
S	34.83	(11.58)	30.00	(8.80)	32.00	(12.98)
D	11.33	(3.50)	11.60	(3.71)	13.20	(3.70)
2. After the suicide attempt						
H	31.45	(5.00)	27.82	(4.32)	27.35	(4.11)
S	34.80	(10.97)	31.41	(12.65)	26.40	(11.83)
D	11.40	(3.94)	11.71	(3.75)	12.90	(3.89)

H, hopelessness; *S*, suicidal-depressive tendencies; *D*, dissimulation tendencies.

Discussion

The present results support our previous findings that hopelessness and suicidal-depressive feelings change with time after a suicide attempt (Schmidtke and Schaller 1985). This change was observed regardless of whether the computations were based on time categories after the suicide attempt or on the time after admission to a psychiatric hospital.

With regard to dissimulation tendencies, it is not yet clear whether the increased dissimulation tendencies were primarily caused by admission to hospital or whether they were caused by the time lapse after the suicide attempt. Because of the relatively low dissimulation tendencies of the patients who had been quickly discharged from hospital, we assume that the stay in hospital had a greater influence.

Nevertheless, these results demonstrate the necessity of taking into account the moderating effects of socially desirable reporting when interpreting self-reports of suicidal tendencies and hopelessness.

References

Götze P, Reimer C, Dahme B (1979) Zur Phänomenologie und Dynamik der Aufwachphase von Suicidpatienten. Psychiatr Clin 12:9–22

Häfner H, Welz R, Gorenc K, Kleff F (1983) Selbstmordversuche und depressive Störungen. Schweiz Arch Neurol Neurochir Psychiatr 133:283–294

Krampen G (1979) Hoffnungslosigkeit bei stationären Patienten – Ihre Messung durch einen Kurzfragebogen (H-Skala). Med Psychol 5:39–49

Linehan MM, Nielsen SL (1981) Assessment of suicide ideation and parasuicide: Hopelessness and social desirability. J Consult Clin Psychol 49:773–775

Linehan MM, Nielsen SL (1983) Social desirability: its relevance to the measurement of hopelessness and suicidal behavior. J Consult Clin Psychol 51:141–143

Linehan MM, Goodstein JL, Nielsen SL, Chiles JA (1983) Reasons for staying alive when you are thinking of killing yourself: the reasons for living inventory. J Consult Clin Psychol 51:276–286

Schmidtke A, Schaller S (1985) Changes over time and covariations in the rated intentions of suicide attempts, hopelessness and dissimulation tendencies in patients after a suicide attempt. Paper presented at the 13th congress for suicide prevention, Vienna

Solomon BL (1949) An extension of control group design. Psych Bull 46:137–150

Stork J (1977) Fragebogentest zur Beurteilung der Suizidgefahr (FBS). Müller, Salzburg

Wetzel RD (1976) Hopelessness, depression and suicide intent. Arch Gen Psychiatry 33:1069–1073

Validation of Six Risk Scales for Suicide Attempters*

A. KURZ, H.-J. MÖLLER, A. TORHORST, and H. LAUTER

Introduction

Any kind of therapy can only be effective in preventing suicide if it is available to persons who require it at a time when they require it. Methods of ascertaining the presence of suicide risk are therefore urgently needed. A considerable amount of research work has been directed to this problem in recent years. These efforts have largely concentrated on the question of who is at risk. They have started from two basic assumptions:

1. Suicide is associated with certain dispositional factors, which include age, personality traits, mental illness, and social circumstances (biological factors have not been considered so far)
2. Presence of such factors in a person at one point in time indicates a high probability of suicide

On these grounds, a number of suicide-risk estimation scales have been developed. Typically, they consist of a list of dispositional variables, a scoring system, and an algorithm which serves to classify individual scores into categories of risk. In most instances, the items have been empirically derived from comparisons of suicidal and nonsuicidal subjects. Various statistical procedures have been applied to extract from the differences the variable which most powerfully discriminated between the groups.

Only in a few studies has the validity of risk estimation been examined. Most scales performed poorly in the task of distinguishing suicides from non-suicides in new patient samples (Bürk et al. 1985). We have used six suicide-risk scales to identify suicides and repeated attempts in a 1-year follow-up study of over 400 suicide attempters.

Methods

The study sample included 485 patients who had been admitted to a poisoning-treatment unit after deliberate self-harm, mostly by drug overdose. The patients have been shown to be representative of suicide attempters in Western European cities (Kurz et al. 1985). Following medical treatment and careful

---

* Supported by a grant from the Federal Ministry for Youth, Family Affairs, and Health.

Table 1. Characteristics of six suicide-risk estimation scales selected for validation

Author(s)	Number of items	Items matched	Criteria [a]	Item content								
				Demo-graphic data	Mental illness	Previous suicidal behavior	Anti-social behavior	Severity of current suicide attempt	Presence of psycho-logical symptoms	Social isolation	Poor physical health	Recent loss
Cohen et al. (1966)	14	13	S, AS	+	+	+	+	+			+	+
Van de Loo and Diekstra (1970)	14	13	AS	+	+	+		+	+	+	+	+
Buglass and Horton (1974)	6	6	S, AS		+	+	+					
Pallis et al. (1982)												
Short list	7	7	S	+						+		
Long list	20	16	S	+	+				+	+	+	
Patterson et al. (1983)	10	10	AS	+	+	+			+	+	+	+

[a] S, suicide; AS, attempted suicide.

psychiatric examination, the majority were referred for outpatient aftercare. A personal follow-up investigation included 421 subjects or 82% of the original sample: 13 patients had committed suicide and 51 had made another suicide attempt within 1 year after discharge from the hospital.

Six suicide-risk estimation scales were chosen from the literature according to the following criteria: they had to be devised for use with suicide attempters and their items had to correspond to our data. The item content of the six scales, the criterion of risk (suicide, attempted suicide, or both), and the number of variables that were successfully matched are shown in Table 1.

According to the authors' instructions, individual risk scores were obtained on each scale. Patients were then divided into a low-risk and high-risk group. This was done separately for each scale using the original cutoff score. In addition, several other cutoff scores were tried to find out whether the original value was appropriate to the present patient sample. Finally, we examined how many of the patients who were rated at high risk had actually committed (or attempted) suicide within the follow-up period and how many of the low-risk subjects had remained alive (or relapse-free). The accuracy of prediction was

Table 2. Accuracy of prediction of six suicide-risk scales

Cutoff	Suicide		Attempted suicide		Combination	
	Sens.	Spec.	Sens.	Spec.	Sens.	Spec.
Cohen et al. 1966						
4	0.85	0.38	0.83	0.45	0.91	0.45
5	0.54	0.61	0.59	0.64	0.82	0.64
6	0.23	0.79	0.41	0.76	0.44	0.76
Van de Loo and Diekstra 1970						
4	0.92	0.47	0.87	0.37	0.86	0.37
5	0.62	0.70	0.57	0.60	0.54	0.68
6	0.31	0.83	0.26	0.77	0.21	0.77
Buglass and Horton 1974						
1	0.54	0.50	0.74	0.57	0.71	0.57
2	0.31	0.76	0.42	0.80	0.39	0.80
3	0.08	0.93	0.12	0.95	0.09	0.95
Pallis et al. 1982, short scale						
−0.75	0.46	0.49	0.81	0.34	0.81	0.34
−0.5	0.46	0.61	0.56	0.54	0.54	0.55
−0.25	0.31	0.77	0.40	0.65	0.40	0.65
Pallis et al. 1982, long scale						
0.0	0.61	0.38	0.74	0.40	0.72	0.40
0.25	0.54	0.62	0.57	0.64	0.57	0.64
0.5	0.31	0.78	0.36	0.80	0.35	0.80
Patterson et al., 1983						
3	0.69	0.57	0.73	0.61	0.72	0.61
4	0.38	0.75	0.48	0.79	0.46	0.79
5	0.23	0.89	0.19	0.90	0.16	0.90

expressed in terms of sensitivity and specificity (sensitivity is the ratio of correctly predicted suicides to the total number of suicides; specificity is the ratio of correctly predicted nonsuicides to the total number of nonsuicides).

Results

Sensitivity and specificity of prediction are shown for different cutoff values and for different criteria of outcome in Table 2 (original cutoff values in italics). A sensitivity of 0.75 or better was uniformly combined with a poor specificity lower than 0.50, i.e., 75% of the suicides (or attempted suicides) were correctly identified at the cost of misclassifying the majority of nonsuicides as suicides. Scales that had been developed with sound statistical analysis were not superior to instruments of simpler construction. The original cutoff values were inappropriate for the present sample in four scales. The accuracy of prediction was no better for the criteria that the scale had been devised for than for other criteria in five scales.

Discussion

As was found in previous validation studies, the suicide-risk scales did not predict suicidal behavior with reasonable accuracy. This failure has been mainly explained by statistical limitations in the prediction of infrequent events (Rosen 1954; Murphy 1983). It is certainly true that if the event to be predicted is very rare, as with suicide and attempted suicide, even a good predictor will produce a large number of false-positive forecasts. A high rate of false-positives, however, does not make the prediction completely worthless because the practical consequence will only be that patients will receive treatment who do not need it. What rate of false-positive predictions can be tolerated is largely a question of treatment availability and of economy.

Apart from statistical problems, some other reasons could account for our inability to make accurate judgments of suicide risk.

Factors that predispose to suicide and the way they interact may vary between diagnostic groups. Risk estimations which are based on the concept of a uniform disposition would then inevitably be imprecise. It is desirable that specific rating instruments be developed for the assessment of suicide probability in the most important risk groups, such as depressives and alcoholics.

The method of validation which was used in this and previous investigations may be inappropriate because it confuses risk estimation and prediction of suicidal behavior. Estimating the probability of suicide in a particular person at a particular time means deciding whether or not the person is presently inclined to carry out a suicidal act. Predicting suicidal behavior means forecasting the occurrence of such behavior in the future. The problem of prediction is that it can only be based on the patient's present state. This state, however, is subject to changes which may invalidate the prediction. The most important intervening variable is, of course, treatment. Thus, the assessment of risk can be correct while the long-term prediction may be wrong.

The fact that suicide risk scales fail to identify the persons who will attempt or commit suicide in the future does not mean that they are useless in the estimation of suicide risk. How well suicide-risk scales can accomplish this task must be determined by methods other than the validation procedure described in this study.

References

Buglass D, Horton J (1974) A scale for predicting subsequent suicidal behaviour. Br J Psychiatry 124:573–578

Bürk E, Kurz A, Möller HJ (1985) Suicide risk scales: do they help to predict suicidal behaviour? Eur Arch Psychiatr Neurol Sci 235:153–157

Cohen E, Motto JA, Seiden RH (1966) An instrument for evaluating suicide potential: a preliminary study. Am J Psychiatry 122:886–891

Kurz A, Möller HJ, Bürk F, Torhorst A, Wächtler C, Lauter H (1985) Determinants of treatment disposal for parasuicide patients in a German university hospital. Soc Psychiatry 20:145–151

Murphy GE (1983) On suicide prediction and prevention. Arch Gen Psychiatry 40:343–344

Pallis DJ, Barraclough BM, Levey AB, Jenkins JS, Sainsbury P (1982) Estimating suicide risk among attempted suicides. I. The development of new clinical scales. Br J Psychiatry 141:37–44

Pallis DJ, Gibbon JS, Pierce DW (1984) Estimating suicide risk among attempted suicides. II. Efficiency of predictive scales after the attempt. Br J Psychiatry 144:139–148

Patterson W, Dohn HH, Birg J, Patterson GA (1983) Evaluation of suicidal patients: the SAD PERSONS scale. Psychosomatics 14:434–439

Rosen A (1954) Detection of suicidal patients: an example of some limitations in the prediction of infrequent events. J Consult Psychiatry 18:397–403

Van de Loo KJ, Diekstra RW (1970) The construction of a questionnaire for prediction of subsequent suicidal attempts: a preliminary study. Ned Tijdschr Psychol Grensgebieden 25:96–100

A Simple Method to Predict Crises After Suicide Attempts (Parasuicides)

G. Sonneck and W. Horn

Introduction

In many hospitals, the treatment and adequate care of patients after a parasuicide is — from a quantitative viewpoint — a growing problem and, seen qualitatively, one which remains unsolved. The separation of somatic therapy from the ensuing psychiatric examination, while omitting the psychosocial problems involved here, generally leads to unsatisfactory results (Wedler 1984). For this reason, an integrated treatment program within the hospital is to be recommended.

To focus appropriate measures, particularly on those groups of people who continue to run a high suicide risk, one has to pay particular attention to the assessment of further danger from suicide. Research on this problem is characterized by methodological problems that are present in studies of suicidal behavior in general (Lester 1970).

This study is concerned with the following question: Is it possible to predict whether, immediately after his attempt, a certain person out of the large number of people who attempt suicide

1. Will repeat his suicide attempt or
2. May eventually die by suicide?

Method

Five-hundred-and-eighty-one people who had attempted suicide were investigated 10 years after the index suicide. Of this number, 5% had died by suicide and 12% by natural death. Of the remaining group, 35% had experienced further crises, and of these, 18% had repeated the suicide attempt.

Results

Using the "multiple linear regression of binary items" (Trappl 1977), we tried to find variables allowing the prediction of suicides or suicide attempts. These, however, could not be found.

In a further step, the same method was used for predicting new crises. Of 183 items, 6 characteristics were found which proved to be the best possible indicators for a prediction. Table 1 shows these characteristics with their respec-

Table 1. Characteristics and weightings for the mathematical prediction of new crises after suicide attempts

Repeated suicide attempt	30
Suicide attempt under the influence of alcohol	−21
Panic action suicide attempt	−32
Diagnosis: depressive reaction	−15
No religious confession	29
Independent profession	−68
Additive constant	69

Table 2. Numeric example for predicting new crises after parasuicide

	No new crises	New crises	Total
Actual number	654	346	1000
Correct prediction	559	181	740
Incorrect prediction	95	165	260

tive weighting factors. If, after summarizing all pertinent factors (not counting the nonpertinent ones), the total value, including the additive constant, was higher than 50, then the probability of new crises was high.

By means of this method, a smaller group of the total number, representing only 25% of the cases, could be specified, in which, however, the number of those facing new crises was twice as high as in the whole group (increasing from 35% to 70%), while in the remaining group, the percentage decreased from 35% to 22%. The importance of this result is shown in a numerical example in Table 2.

By this method, of 654 persons expected to have no new crisis, 559 were correctly defined. The remaining 95 were wrongly classified since they had new crises. Of 346 persons who had a new crisis, the prediction was correct for 181, while in 165 cases the classification was wrong, which means less than 50%, however.

By applying the same method to alcoholics after suicide attempts − a group defined as having a higher risk − corresponding results were obtained. (A significant fact was that this prediction could not be improved by using data recorded 2, 4, or 6 years after the index suicide attempt.)

Assuming that every suicide is preceded by a crisis, the data of those 5% who died by suicide were subjected to this examination procedure. Again, a specific subgroup of only a quarter of the whole group was identified, of which 15% had died by suicide, while in the rest of the group, the percentage dropped from 5% to 2%.

Conclusion

In a risk collective, determined by this method, two of three recorded persons will experience crises again, yet only one of seven persons is at risk of dying by suicide. However, of the whole sample of the 581 people who attempted suicide, every second new crisis as well as one of every three actual suicides would not have been predicted. This means that rather unspecific events such as a "new crisis" are relatively easily and accurately predictable. Specific actions such as suicides (and suicide attempts?) are far more difficult to foresee, as in general, human behavior cannot be predicted for longer periods ahead of time (Ingenkamp 1974).

The readiness to stumble in crisis, implying a higher vulnerability, does not allow one to conclude whether suicidal actions will be committed in the course of a crisis. Most probably, this depends on a number of different circumstances. With regard to suicide attempts, these are most probably connected with interpersonal conditions which are hard to determine and which could not be recorded in this study, even though it was extensive.

References

Ingenkamp K (1974) Tests in der Schulpraxis. Beltz, Weinheim
Lester D (1970) Attempts to predict suicidal risk using psychological tests. Psychol Bull 74:1–17
Trappl R (1977) Ein einfaches Verfahren zur Vorhersage des Verlaufes von Krankheiten. Wien Klin Wochenschr 89:371–375
Wedler HL (1984) Der Suizidpatient im Allgemeinkrankenhaus. Enke, Stuttgart

Estimating Suicide Risk Among Inpatients Treated for Depressive Disorders

R. VOGEL and M. G. WOLFERSDORF *

Introduction

Patients with depressive disorders belong to those most at risk for suicide. Pöld-inger (1980) even calls them the groups having the highest risk of all. Thus, one of the most important problems concerning the inpatient treatment of patients with depressive disorders is the question of how to deal with suicidal patients to make suicidal behavior superfluous. An important step in this direction is the attempt to recognize suicidal impulses and signals early. We have to ask on which basis or according to which criteria a potential risk may be recognized fairly exactly in patients with depressive disorders. With regard to the identification of such criteria, one could fall back upon the following categorized methods:

1. Standard psychological tests
2. So-called risk scales
3. Clinical assessment usually based on the presence or absence of psychopathological symptoms

Considering only the two last methods, the following problems with regard to the usefulness of their application may be stated: First, the existing results are partly based on very different samples, e.g., hospitalized psychiatric patients (e.g., Farberow and MacKinnon 1974; Zung 1974; Motto and Heilbron 1976), subjects from the general population (e.g., Tuckman and Youngman 1968), and clients of a suicide prevention center (Lettieri 1974). One mostly proceeds from subjects who attempted suicide and less from subjects who committed suicide. Second, the criteria of prediction are different. There are scales designed to predict any inclination toward suicide, scales to predict attempts, scales to predict suicides, and scales to predict the risk for repeating. Investigators often do not differentiate between (repeated) attempts and committed suicides (e.g., Cohen et al. 1966; Buglass and McCulloch 1970). Other problems concern the different methodologies (e.g., retrospectively vs prospectively, different follow-up periods, different records) and the different statistical procedures (univariate, multivariate). These factors clearly restrict the value of the scales and thus their general usefulness. This can be demonstrated by the fact that the use of the

---

* Assisted by the work "Suicidal Behavior and Psychiatric Hospital".

scales produces unstable results (cf. also Pöldinger and Sonneck 1980; Bürk et al. 1985 b). This is very similar to the clinical method which is usually based on the presence or absence of specific symptoms or symptom profiles (cf. Wolfersdorf 1983). According to van Egmond and Diekstra (1984), the results of this method are similarly far from clear.

Proceeding from these findings, it seems necessary to consider each major high-risk group separately to improve predictive accuracy. This investigation is such an attempt and focuses on patients with depressive disorders. We thought, in this context, that it would not be very convenient to evaluate single methods or scales (cf., e.g., Kielholz 1974; Pierce 1981; Tuckman and Youngman 1968; Pallis et al. 1982; Henseler et al. 1983; Pöldinger 1982) with regard to their usefulness for this specific 'clientele'. Because of practical considerations (many of the scales named are too complex or cumbersome for practical and routine use), we extracted from the existing scales more or less global categories which have proved to be risk factors in almost all studies. We analyzed in detail factors which may be related to the categories "actual suicide topic and suicide indicators," "social environmental relations and conditions," and "characteristics of current psychopathology" (cf. Kielholz 1974). Additionally, we were interested in the question of the extent to which the categories named were independent from each other. This applies especially to the association between the category "characteristics of current psychopathology," which according to our findings, is often the basis for the clinical assessment, and the two other categories, which are based on rather objectifying methods. The successful prediction of suicidal behavior demands that a relationship be established between the attributes of a patient and his suicidal acts. In the present study, we present detailed information about some attributes of depressed psychiatric inpatients who committed suicide in our institutions. A control sample will be investigated in a further study. The following statements are therefore to be regarded as preliminary.

Methods and Sample

On the basis of a standardized questionnaire, all suicides were registered that had been committed during treatment in five psychiatric hospitals in southern Germany since 1970 (cf. Wolfersdorf et al. 1982, 1984 a – c). The questionnaire included 116 items. In constructing the questionnaire with regard to the character of the study (study with a series of investigators), the retrospective method, and the source of the data (usually clinical records), we paid special attention to the clarity of the questions and instructions, and restricted ourselves to the recording of objective facts and facts which were most likely to be documented in most clinical records. To achieve this aim, a pretest was carried out before the actual documentation.

The sample encompassed 249 suicides. From this sample, suicides which could be related to the diagnostic categories 296, 298.0, and 300.4 (International Classification of Diseases, ICD 8) were chosen (62 patients). The subject of the analysis was the three categories named, which we indexed as shown in Fig. 1.

184   R. Vogel and M. G. Wolfersdorf

Category I: Actual suicide topic and suicide indicators

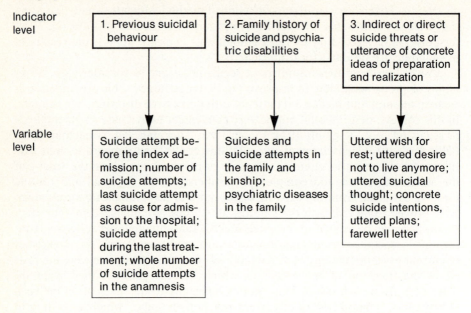

Indicator level

| 1. Previous suicidal behaviour | 2. Family history of suicide and psychiatric disabilities | 3. Indirect or direct suicide threats or utterance of concrete ideas of preparation and realization |

Variable level

| Suicide attempt before the index admission; number of suicide attempts; last suicide attempt as cause for admission to the hospital; suicide attempt during the last treatment; whole number of suicide attempts in the anamnesis | Suicides and suicide attempts in the family and kinship; psychiatric diseases in the family | Uttered wish for rest; uttered desire not to live anymore; uttered suicidal thought; concrete suicide intentions, uttered plans; farewell letter |

Category II: Special symptoms and syndrome patterns/characteristics of the disease before the suicide

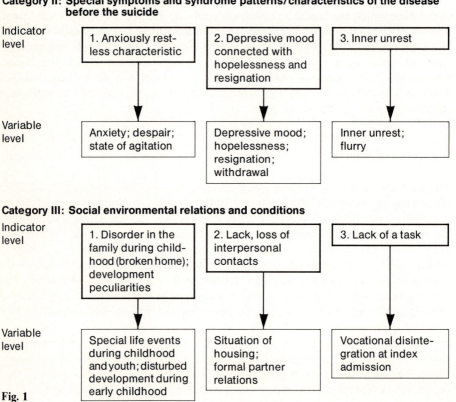

Indicator level

| 1. Anxiously restless characteristic | 2. Depressive mood connected with hopelessness and resignation | 3. Inner unrest |

Variable level

| Anxiety; despair; state of agitation | Depressive mood; hopelessness; resignation; withdrawal | Inner unrest; flurry |

Category III: Social environmental relations and conditions

Indicator level

| 1. Disorder in the family during childhood (broken home); development peculiarities | 2. Lack, loss of interpersonal contacts | 3. Lack of a task |

Variable level

| Special life events during childhood and youth; disturbed development during early childhood | Situation of housing; formal partner relations | Vocational disintegration at index admission |

Fig. 1

Results

Actual Suicide Topic and Suicide Indicators

Prior to the suicides of depressive inpatients, factors belonging to the "actual suicide topic" or to "actual suicide indicators" were often found (category I). Only in four subjects were no such indicators found (6.5% of all who committed suicide). Approximately one-third showed only one characteristic, two characteristics were known in another third, and all three of the characteristics named were found prior to the suicide in approximately 5%. The average was 1.5 features, indicating a suicide risk of the depressive inpatients within the scope of this global category. Prior attempts, including attempts during the index admission, were known in 60% of the depressive individuals. The last attempt led to admission to hospital in 31% (19 subjects). Sixteen subjects (26%) communicated direct or indirect suicide threats or concrete ideas of preparation and realization; concrete plans were extremely rare (3.4%). Thirteen subjects (21%) had a family history of suicide, and 27 subjects (44%) had a history of diagnosed and treated psychiatric diseases in their families.

Special Symptoms and Syndromes (in the Last 14 Days)

The psychopathological pattern which can be described, according to the files, prior to the suicide — especially with respect to the three syndromes named (anxiously restless, depressive mood associated with hopelessness and resignation, inner unrest) — confirms the importance of the clinical judgment of suicide risk of depressive inpatients (category II). The symptoms or syndromes named could be observed prior to the suicide in almost every second subject (43.5% of all who committed suicide): 16% exhibited only one symptom/syndrome, 14.5% two, and 13% all three. The average was 0.85 characteristics, indicating — on the basis of clinical assessment — a suicide risk of depressive inpatients. A depressive mood (34%) and feelings of hopelessness (29%), more rarely anxious restlessness (24.2%) and inner unrest (18%), were the most potential discriminators.

Social Environmental Relations and Conditions

The assessment of characteristics that are relatively unspecific for suicidal behavior, such as a broken home, lack or loss of social contacts and tasks, was another important potential discriminator (category III). In all, almost two-thirds of the persons who committed suicide (59.7%) had such characteristics. In 29%, the disturbance was restricted to one characteristic, and in 24%, to two; in 6.5%, all three of the characteristics were evident that define the category "social environmental relations and social conditions." The average was 1.3 characteristics, indicating — on the basis of disturbances unspecific for a suicide — a suicide risk of the depressive inpatients. Most frequently, a broken home or a record of juvenile offenses (48.4%) was found. The lack or loss of interpersonal contacts (34%), categorized here as rather formal aspects such as the living conditions (living alone) and the formal partner relationship (living without a partner), was rarer. Another third of the persons who committed suicide had been affected by the lack or loss of a central function in their life plans, their work, and thus subjected to tendencies of social disintegration (Vogel et al. 1984).

Association Between the Three Global Categories

The association between the categories was examined on the basis of dichotomized characteristics (χ^2 test). The three categories proved to be statistically independent. This result shows that the three areas for estimation of suicide risk for depressive inpatients offer useful, nonredundant information. For example, almost all subjects giving no indication of potential or probable suicidal behavior on the basis of clinical assessment (34 subjects or 55% of the overall sample) showed characteristics in the two other areas indicating a suicide risk (26 subjects with hints from the area "actual suicide topic and suicide indicators" and 21 subjects with hints from the area "social environmental relations and conditions"). This tendency of increasing information, which significantly increases as soon as a second or even third category is taken into account when estimating the suicide risk, was confirmed by another analysis (t-test).

Discussion

Evaluating the frequency of a certain characteristic prior to a suicide as an − even if preliminary − indication of its prognostic relevance, the three categories named for the estimation of suicide risk of depressive inpatients proved to be of differing importance. Indications from the area "actual suicide topic" were found most frequently. Almost every person who committed suicide had drawn attention to himself, showing a form of suicidal communication before his suicide. Previous suicide attempts were extremely important in this respect (60%). This result harmonizes with many follow-up studies, which almost all show prior suicide attempts to be an indicator of further suicide risk (cf. among others, the survey report by Bürk and Müller 1985a). Previous suicide attempts belong to the small number of risk factors − almost totally independent from the nature of the sample, the criterion of prediction, the follow-up period − which are able to validly predict (further) suicidal behavior. Thus, the frequent experience made in other areas (psychopathological state, vocational and social adaptation, frequency and length of inpatient treatment) that behavior shown in the past usually is the best predictor for a similar behavior in future is also confirmed for this field. Variables which are generally considered "unspecific for a suicide" were not found as frequently within the defined clientele as these "suicide-specific" variables. In this connection, broken-home situations and maladjustment of the individual who committed suicide were found most frequently (48%). Despite its lacking specificity, this area also gave a useful indication of a higher suicide risk. The persons who committed suicide were most inconspicuous with respect to the psychopathological pattern existing prior to the suicide: 43.5% were described as being conspicuous; in this respect, a depressive mood associated with hopelessness and resignation dominated. This fact together with the fact that our three categories proved independent shows that a clinical assessment essentially oriented toward psychopathologically conspicuous behavior can be advantageously complemented by rather objectifying methods to which the two other categories may be attached. Doing this definitely does not need much effort. In this connection, one should not overlook that there is a limit to predicting the degree of suicide risk in individual patients even on the basis of the method described because of the relative infrequency of completed suicide and finally because events may occur after the identification of risk factors which can influence the appearance of suicidal behavior, such as those events studied in life-event research. With respect to the clientele examined here, however, it is more important from our point of view that many suffer from "chronic crises" (cf. also Pöldinger and Sonneck 1980) and thus are often no longer able to cope with additional burdens. For example, a change of ward, a change of the physician, holiday or illness of the therapist, and the forthcoming discharge of the patient have to be regarded as situations which increase the probability of the occurrence of suicidal behavior. Thorough observation must be carried out as well as a thorough inquiry. The above considerations surely cannot prevent all suicides. Nevertheless, we expect a reduction of the number of suicides among depressive patients in our hospitals if a screening method comprising the above categories is applied continuously and systematically and if subsequent systematic observation of the above aspects is carried out. Further studies of our work group will show whether these expectations are realistic.

References

Buglass D, McCulloch JW (1970) Further suicidal behaviour: the development and validation of predictive scales. Br J Psychiatry 116:483−491

Bürk F, Möller HJ (1985a) Prädiktoren für weiteres suizidales Verhalten bei nach einem Suizidversuch hospitalisierten Patienten. Fortschr Neurol Psychiatr 53:259−270

Bürk F, Kurz A, Möller HJ (1985b) Suicide risk scales: do they help to predict suicidal behaviour? Eur Arch Psychiatr Neurol Sci 235:153−157

Cohen E, Motto JA, Seiden JH (1966) An instrument for evaluating suicide potential: a preliminary study. Am J Psychiatry 122:886−891

Farberow NL, MacKinnon DR (1974) The suicide prevention schedule for neuropsychiatric hospital patients. J Nerv Ment Dis 158:408−419

Henseler H, Marten RF, Sodemann U (1983) Kriterienliste als Screening-Instrument zur Erfassung von chronischer Suizidalität. Nervenarzt 54:33−41

Kielholz P (1974) Diagnose und Therapie der Depressionen für den Praktiker, 3rd edn. Lehmanns, Munich

Lettieri DJ (1974) Suicidal death prediction scales. In: Beck AT, Resnick HLP, Lettieri DJ (eds) The prediction of suicide. Charles, Bowie, Maryland

Motto JA, Heilbron DC (1976) Development and validation scales for the estimation of suicidal risk. In: Shneidman ES (ed) Suicidology: contemporary developments, Grune and Stratton, New York, pp 169−199

Pallis DJ, Barraclough BM, Leyey AB, Jenkins JS, Sainsbury P (1982) Estimating suicide risk among attempted suicides. Br J Psychiatry 141:37–44

Pierce DW (1981) The predictive validation of a suicide intent scale: a five year follow-up. Br J Psychiatry 139:391–396

Pöldinger W (1980) Die Beurteilung der Suizidalität. Ther Umsch 1 (37):9–16

Pöldinger W (1982) Suizidprophylaxe bei depressiven Syndromen. Neuropsychiatr Clin 1:87

Pöldinger W, Sonneck G (1980) Die Abschätzung der Suizidalität. Nervenarzt 51:147–151

Tuckman J, Youngman F (1968) A scale for assessing suicide risk of attempted suicides. J Clin Psychol 24:17–19

van Egmond M, Diekstra RFW (1984) Die Vorhersagbarkeit von suizidalen Verhaltensweisen: die Ergebnisse einer Meta-Analyse herausgegebener Studien. In: Welz R, Möller HJ (eds) Bestandsaufnahme der Suizidforschung. Roderer, Regensburg, pp 41–56

Vogel R, Wolfersdorf M et al. (1984) Die berufliche Integration stationär psychiatrischer Patienten vor ihrem Suizid. In: Welz R, Möller HJ (eds) Bestandsaufnahme der Suizidforschung. Roderer, Regensburg, pp 219–229

Wolfersdorf M (1983) Zum Suizidproblem in der psychiatrischen Klinik. Neuropsychiat Clin 2:161–173

Wolfersdorf M, Vogel R, Hole G et al. (1982) Suizide in vier psychiatrischen Landeskrankenhäusern Baden-Württembergs. Suizidprophylaxe 9 (2):83–93

Wolfersdorf M, Metzger R, Kopittke W et al. (1984a) Einige Aspekte des Suizidproblems in der psychiatrischen Klinik – Literaturübersicht und eigene Untersuchung. In: Faust V, Wolfersdorf M (eds) Suizidgefahr, pp 221–249

Wolfersdorf M, Vogel R, Hole G et al. (1984b) Suizide psychiatrischer Patienten. Weissenhof, Weinsberg

Wolfersdorf M, Vogel R, Hole G et al. (1984c) Ergebnisse einer retrospektiven Verbundstudie zum Suizid stationär psychiatrischer Patienten. Darstellung von 249 Kliniksuiziden. In: Welz R, Möller HJ (eds) Bestandsaufnahme der Suizidforschung. Roderer, Regensburg, pp 230–248

Zung WWK (1974) Index of potential suicide (IPS). In: Beck AT, Resnik HLP, Lettieri D (eds) The prediction of suicide. Charles, Bowie Maryland, pp 221–249

Clinical Prediction of Suicidal Behavior Among High-Risk Suicide Attempters

M. W. Hengeveld, J. van der Wal, and A. J. F. M. Kerkhof

Introduction

A central difficulty in the prediction of suicidal behavior is the so-called base-rate problem: the low incidence of suicide and attempted suicide presents us with the intractable problem of predicting infrequent events (Kreitman 1982; Pokorny 1982; Pallis et al. 1984; Motto et al. 1985). Even in a population of patients having attempted suicide, the risk of suicide is still low for predictive purposes. It would, therefore, be of interest to select a group of patients with a very high risk of suicidal behavior and then to try to estimate the suicide risk for each patient in this group. The authors recently succeeded in identifying such a high-risk group among the patients presented to a university hospital following a suicide attempt (Kerkhof 1985). This allowed us to study the possibility of clinically predicting future suicidal behavior within such a very high-risk group.

Method

The authors recently studied the management and aftercare of 173 patients consecutively presented, following an attempted suicide, to the University Hospital of Leiden. A representative selection of 120 patients was interviewed 4 to 6 weeks later. Follow-up by telephone, 7 months later, took place in 109 cases. By multivariate statistical analysis, the suicide attempters could be divided into two broad typological categories, a low-risk group and a high-risk group. The results of this analysis were presented by the third author in his doctoral thesis (Kerkhof 1985). The main characteristics of the patients of the high-risk group were: previous suicide attempts, previous psychiatric hospitalization or hospitalization at the time of the suicide attempt, and referral to a psychiatric hospital after emergency treatment in our hospital. They also often showed a strong intention and motivation to die, used more dangerous methods for the attempt, and had a high score on the Beck Depression Inventory at 4−6 weeks follow-up. Of this group of patients, exactly half attempted suicide again or committed suicide within the 7-month follow-up period. Eighteen months after the index suicide attempt, no less than 16 patients of the original group of 173 patients had killed themselves. Half of these patients had not been interviewed, but retrospectively also showed the main characteristics of the high-risk group.

The basic material used in the present study was reports of the psychiatric consultations with patients belonging to the high-risk group identified by the statistical analysis, completed with the interviews of patients who committed suicide. The most important reasons for exclusion of cases were: files that could not be found (10), patients not seen by the psychiatric consultant (7), psychiatric reports that presented too little information (3), or patients known to have attempted suicide after the follow-up period (3). Included were, eventually, the reports of 33 consultations with patients with a fairly proportional state of suicidal behavior: 9 (27%) eventually committed suicide and 8 (24%) attempted suicide. In addition to the psychiatric consultation reports, some data were gathered on the circumstances of the suicide attempts and on the patients' attitude toward the consultation and the patients' acceptance of the consultants' proposals. These data of the 33 consultations, made anonymous, were presented to four psychiatrists and four 3rd-year psychiatric residents employed in the Department of Psychiatry of the University Hospital of Leiden. They were asked to predict retrospectively whether each patient would commit suicide within 18 months, would attempt suicide within 7 months, or would do neither of the two. They were also asked to write down their arguments for their predictions.

Results

The predictive value for a completed suicide score was only 39%, and the predictive value of an attempted suicide score was even less, 32%. Even if both kinds of suicidal behavior were taken together, the percentage of accurate predictions appeared to be only 56% (the sensitivity was 71%, and the specificity was only 42%). That is to say, based on the clinical data written down by the psychiatric consultants, the experts were not at all able to reach a useful level of accuracy in predicting recurrent suicidal behavior within this group of very high-risk suicide attempters.

Taking a closer look at the experts' predictions in each of the 33 cases, the authors discovered an interesting phenomenon. As for the whole group of patients about half of the predictions of recurrent suicidal behavior were correct, one would have expected that in most individual cases also about half of the experts had given an accurate prediction. This appeared not to be true. In no less than 20 of the 33 cases, six or more experts shared the same opinion. Statistically, this is a highly significant finding ($z = 4.018$, $P < 0.001$). Particularly, in the group of nine patients who eventually committed suicide, in seven cases either almost all the experts were right or almost all were wrong in their predictions. Apparently, there is some pattern in the true or false scores made by the psychiatrists and psychiatric residents.

The arguments given by the experts for their predictions suggested some explanations for this pattern. Some patients who attempted suicide clearly without a strong intention to die, and who were readmitted to the psychiatric hospital, later committed suicide against the expectations of most of the eight experts. In other cases, most of the experts were too optimistic about the preventive effects of the psychiatric care given to the patients following the suicide attempt. If a suicide attempter used a very self-destructive method, had made one or more serious attempts shortly before, showed a strong intention to die, and had recently experienced a series of losses, most experts correctly predicted an eventual suicide. Patients who showed a pattern of recurrent nondangerous suicide attempts or self-inflicted injuries indeed kept following this pattern, as most experts expected. On the other hand, however, in some such cases where most experts predicted a suicide or an attempted suicide, they were wrong because either the patient was not able to commit suicide because of the physical handicap resulting from the suicide attempt or the psychiatric treatment prevented the patient from repeating suicidal behavior, at least temporarily or, hopefully, forever. If the patients' previous suicide attempts were long ago and if the index attempt appeared to have had some constructive effects, most experts were correct in their predicting no recurrent suicidal behavior within the next 7 months.

Discussion

Statistical analysis gave the authors a tool to identify, among patients referred to a university hospital following a suicide attempt, a very high-risk group of patients, of whom half attempted or committed suicide within 7 months. Clinically, it did not appear to be possible to predict the suicidal behavior of each individual patient of this high-risk group. This was not because of lack of skills of the experts. Here, one is confronted with some intractable problems hampering such predictions that are also mentioned in the literature (Kreitman 1982; Pallis et al. 1982; Pallis et al. 1984; Motto et al. 1985). Patients will be influenced by events and actions that nobody can predict. The more suicidal a patient is, the stronger the counteractions of the people surrounding him may be. Even if one were able to predict suicidal behavior more accurately, it would be impossible to predict the exact moment it would occur as well. Thus, one should be satisfied with the possibility of identifying a patient as very high risk, based upon general, not individual, characteristics. One then should treat these patients further as very high risk, although half of them will not actually attempt or commit suicide within the next months. Following the course of each individual patient's suicidal ideations will give us more tools for predicting and preventing his or her recurrent suicidal behavior.

References

Kerkhof AJFM (1985) Suicide en de geestelijke gezondheidszorg. Dissertation. Swets and Zeitlinger, Lisse

Kreitman N (1982) How useful is the prediction of suicide following parasuicide? In: Wilmotte J, Mendlewicz J (eds) New trends in suicide prevention. Karger, Basel, pp 77−84

Motto JA, Heilbron DC, Juster RP (1985) Development of a clinical instrument to estimate suicide risk. Am J Psychiatry 142:680−687

Pallis DJ, Barraclough BM, Levey AB, Jenkins JS, Sainsbury P (1982) Estimating suicide risk among attempted suicides. I. Development of new clinical scales. Br J Psychiatry 141:37–44
Pallis DJ, Gibbons JS, Pierce DW (1984) Estimating suicide risk among attempted suicides. II. Efficiency of predictive scales after the attempted suicide. Br J Psychiatry 144:139–148
Pokorny AD (1982) Prediction of suicide in psychiatric patients. Report of a prospective study. Arch Gen Psychiatry 40:249–257

Typology of Persons Who Attempted Suicide with Predictive Value for Repetition: A Prospective Cohort Study

A. J. F. M. KERKHOF, J. VAN DER WAL, and M. W. HENGEVELD

Introduction

Twenty-five years ago, Tuckman and Youngman were the first to empirically divide people who attempted suicide into one group with a low risk and another with a high risk for a fatal attempt in the future. Within the population of suicide attempters, the last group concerns mainly aged, divorced or widowed men who in their attempt used very dangerous methods and who had formerly received psychiatric treatment.

Nowadays, these findings from 1963 still appear to be valid. In numerous follow-up studies, from different countries and with different research designs, this pattern, in broad outline, continuously reappears, although some refinements have been made.

Thus, we now know that a history of previous suicide attempts means a comparatively bad prognosis, as well as alcohol, drugs, and/or medicine addiction (Hankoff 1976; Bürk and Möller 1985; Gezondheidsraad 1986). Moreover, the intention with which the suicide attempt was made (aimed at dying, stopping consciousness vs cry-for-help motives) is of prognostic value (Pallis and Pierce 1979; Pallis et al. 1982, 1984). Finally, a psychiatric admission after, and possibly as a result of an attempted suicide, is a strong predictor for future suicidal behavior (Hankoff 1976; WHO 1982; Gezondheidsraad 1986).

All in all, a very clearly defined high-risk group appears, within which hardly any differentiation is found. Within the relatively low-risk group, some nuances are still found, mainly based upon differences in the dynamics of the attempted suicide. Hawton (1987), for youngsters, postulates a simple but useful tripartition: acute, chronic, and chronic with serious behavioral disturbances (repeated truancy, stealing, drug taking, heavy drinking, fighting, being in trouble with police). Repeated nonfatal suicidal behavior occurs mainly in the last category.

All of this does not mean that we are capable of predicting which person will and which person will not become a repeater and who will or will not die from an attempt. As yet, instruments for prediction suffer from too large a number of false-positive predictions or a large number of missed true-positives (Bürk et al. 1985). The only prediction we can make is whether a person belongs to a high-risk group, i.e., that someone runs a high risk of becoming a repeater. Whether a particular person actually becomes a repeater cannot be said, this being too highly dependent on coincidence.

Method

All persons who, during the period February 1983 to September 1983, were treated for attempted suicide in the University Hospital in Leiden (UHL) were asked to attend an interview 4−6 weeks after discharge. Of the total group of 173 persons, we were able to ask 167 persons for their permission, and 120 interviews finally took place (72%). Six months later, i.e., an average of 7 months after being discharged from the UHL, 109 persons were interviewed for a second time (65%). In both interviews, questions were posed about repeated attempts. In a number of cases, relatives of respondents who had died in the meantime were interviewed. To verify the representativity of the group of persons interviewed, a nonresponse investigation was conducted through general practitioners of the persons who had not been interviewed. This took place on an average of 12 months after discharge from the hospital. Information was also obtained from psychiatric clinics in the region, which, on their own initiative, reported suicides to the researchers. In this way, of the 53 persons who were not interviewed, we were able to find out about 46 whether they were still alive or had died of suicide or some other cause. Even a considerable time after finishing the research, the researchers were informed (by attendants and relatives) of suicides of persons who had previously been interviewed.

Instruments

The data collected concerned demographic characteristics and characteristics of the suicide attempt, such as method, suicide intention (SIS; Beck et al. 1972), motives (Bancroft et al. 1976), and loss of consciousness. Inquiries were made about current and previous problems in life (AKTPRO and BIOPRO, Diekstra 1981), present and previous suicidal behavior, and present and previous mental-health treatment. A diagnosis was made by psychiatric consultants according to the Diagnostic and Statistical Manual (DSM III) (APA 1980), and the level of depression was measured by Beck's Depression Inventory (BDI; Beck et al. 1961), along with persistent suicidal ideation. Physical and mental well-being (VOEG, Dirken 1967), problem-solving strategies (UCL, Schreurs et al. 1983), and levels of social support were inquired about. The complete instrument is described in Kerkhof (1985).

Results

The group of suicide attempters ($n = 173$) was not described according to separate characteristics that were observed during treatment in the hospital or registered in interviews because we were not concerned with the prognostic value of separate risk factors, but with combinations of characteristics that can define subgroups in this perspective. By means of a nonlinear multivariate analysis, an empirical typology was constructed, which subsequently was linked with repeated suicidal behavior during the follow-up period.

Classification of Suicide Attempters

The selection of variables roughly corresponded with the variables normally used with classification research (demographic variables, treatment history, method of the attempted suicide, etc.). To include psychological variables such as depression, suicide intention, and motives in the classification at least in this way, is a new aspect. Unusually, here, variables measured during and related to the period after the attempted suicide were also involved in the classification.

New is also the technique used for this classification. A nonlinear principal components analysis (PRINCALS) (Gifi 1981, 1983) was used, a technique that enabled us to involve variables on nominal and ordinal measurement levels in a principal components analysis. The interpretation of the following can be compared with factor analysis. The difference from the techniques that are normally used for analysis, usually in the form of cluster analysis (Kiev 1976; Henderson et al. 1977; Paykel and Rassaby 1978) is that clusters of characteristics can now be placed against interpretative dimensions. PRINCALS is used here as an exploratory method to distinguish groups of persons with specific combi-

Table 1. Classification of suicide attempters by PRINCALS: selected variables, measurement levels, and loadings on two components

Variables	Level	Loadings	
1. Gender	s.n.	−.18	.11
2. Age	m.n.	−	−
3. Marital status/living conditions	m.n.	−	−
4. Professional level	m.n.	−	−
5. Treatment history	m.n.	−	−
6. Previous suicide attempts	m.n.	−	−
7. Planned (suicide intent scale)	s.o.	.64	−.09
8. Precautions (suicide intent scale)	s.o.	.51	−.15
9. Wish to die (suicide intent scale)	s.o.	.33	−.30
10. Cry for help (motives)	s.o.	−.12	.15
11. Stopping consciousness (motives)	s.o.	.30	−.37
12. Revenge (motives)	s.o.	.09	−.37
13. Wish to die (motives)	s.o.	.43	−.31
14. Level of consciousness (comatose)	s.o.	.28	−.09
15. BIOPRO (previous problems in life)	s.o.	.69	.01
16. Mode of suicide attempt (medicines-violent)	m.n.	−	−
17. Treatment after discharge	m.n.	−	−
18. VOEG (physical and mental well-being)	s.o.	.41	.06
19. BDI (level of depression)	s.o.	.79	−.06
20. AKTPRO (current problems in life)	s.o.	.69	−.13
21. Suicide ideation	s.o.	.74	−.26
22. Support I (social network)	s.o.	−.25	.21
23. Support II (social network)	s.o.	−.46	−.19
24. Contacts (social network)	s.o.	−.30	−.27
25. Depressive type (coping strategies)	s.o.	.47	−.44
26. Goal-directed (coping strategies)	s.o.	−.21	.18

Eigenvalues: .225 and .127; total fit = .352; total loss = 1.648.
Measurement level: *s.n.*, single nominal; *m.n.*, multiple nominal; *s.o.*, single ordinal.

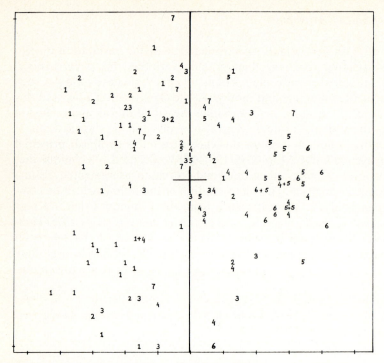

Fig. 1. Object scores labeled according to depression. *1*, no depression; *2*, on the edge of depression; *3*, mild; *4*, moderate; *5*, deep; *6*, severe depression; *7*, missing value

nations of characteristics. With this technique, the subgroups to be found do not necessarily have to be defined sharply from one another. They can, to a greater or lesser extent, overlap on one or more variables. The analysis presented here is the last one in a row, in which variables were successively left out that did not contribute to the typology. Thus, some problem-solving strategies were left out, as were income and religion, but also the variable "addiction." This variable did not appear to be of importance in the subdivision of suicide attempters.

The first dimension was dominated by depression. The BDI score had its highest loading on the first component (.79) and not on the second (−.06). The other variables with a high loading on this first component all presented a certain relation to depression, as is shown most clearly in continuous suicide ideation (.74), experience of actual problems (AKTPRO, .69), and of earlier problems (BIOPRO, .69). Also, the degree of *planning* and the degree in which measures of *precaution* were taken indicated a clear coherence with the degree of depression, measured at a point of time 4−6 weeks after the attempted suicide.

On the second dimension, only a few variables of single nominal or ordinal measurement levels had loadings higher than .35. Inspection of the category

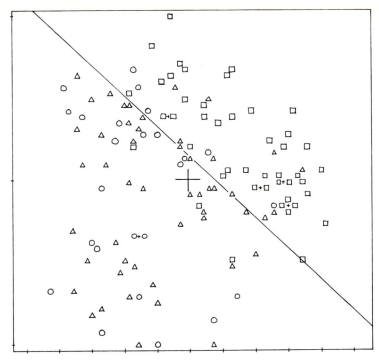

Fig. 2. Object scores labeled according to treatment after discharge from the hospital. □ , admitted to psychiatric hospital; △, outpatient mental health treatment; ○, no treatment or by general practitioner only

quantifications of the variables of multiple nominal measurement level showed that this component mainly reflects a combination of age, marital status/living situation, treatment history, and help received after discharge from the UHL.

The most important distinction between respondents was connected with the degree of depression. The plot of object scores, labeled after the score on the BDI (see Fig. 1), from left to right shows an increasing score. Left of the middle, we find the non- or slightly depressed respondents, right of the middle the moderate to highly depressed respondents. Apart from this bipartition in depressive or nondepressive respondents, inspection of the labeled object scores in Fig. 2 indicates another meaningful bipartition. There was a striking difference between respondents in the lower left triangle and respondents in the upper right triangle.

In the lower left, we find predominantly "first-evers," respondents who had never been admitted to a psychiatric hospital and who, after discharge from the UHL, were not admitted to a psychiatric hospital either. In the upper right, we find exclusively repeaters and mainly respondents who sometime earlier or shortly before the attempt had been admitted to a psychiatric hospital. After discharge from the UHL, in most cases, these respondents were readmitted or sent back to a psychiatric hospital (see Fig. 2).

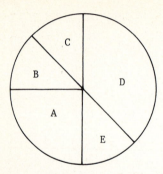

Fig. 3. Object scores grouped into clusters of persons with specific characteristics. Within types, subjects resemble each other for most variables, but not necessarily all. In type D, for instance, it is possible to find a young person living with parents who looks like type-D suicide attempters in all, or in nearly all, other respects (repeater, extensive treatment in history, violent method, etc.)

In the same way, according to scores on the other separate variables, object scores can be grouped differently every time. Consecutive groupings can, as it were, be placed on top of one another and thus bring out a certain pattern, as is shown in Fig. 3 in the form of a subdivided circle.

Segment A: Youngsters Living with Parents. This group included younger people under the age of 25 who usually lived with their parents. They had no strong suicide intention, but tried to mobilize others, especially parents, through the attempt. It was their first suicide attempt and the method they used was not very dangerous: exclusively pills. Most of them had never been treated, and some of them had only received outpatient mental health treatment. Presumably, we can speak here of young people who made a suicide attempt as a self-chosen form of crisis intervention. After the attempted suicide, most of them received outpatient mental health treatment, and some of them received no professional help at all. They were not depressed 4−6 weeks after the attempt, they had comparatively few current problems, experienced few psychosomatic complaints, stopped thinking of suicide, and received quite a lot of support from their social surroundings.

Segment B: Married/Cohabiting First-Evers. In this segment, we almost exclusively found married people and people who lived together. These were men and women over the age of 25. It was striking that, in this segment, the cry-for-help motive came strongly to the foreground. In other aspects, they resembled segment A: first-evers, never psychiatrically treated or exclusively on an outpatient basis, they took few precautions to prevent discovery, with little planning. They used somewhat more variety in their methods, either with or without alcohol, and were sometimes a little more violent.

After discharge from the UHL, they either received outpatient mental-health treatment or no professional aid at all. Some time later (4−6 weeks), they were no longer depressed, did not think of suicide anymore, had comparatively few current problems or psychosomatic complaints, and received a considerable amount of support from their social surroundings.

Segment C: Married/Cohabiting Repeaters. In this segment, we found also mainly married people who, in their suicide attempt, were especially led by cry-for-help motives. Also in these cases, very little suicide intention was involved, but this time there were only repeaters and mainly persons who had earlier or at the time of the attempted suicide been admitted to a psychiatric hospital. About 5 weeks later, they were not depressed. Their problem-solving strategies could not really be called goal oriented. They considered the chance that they would ever kill themselves very small, although they had at least two attempted suicides in the past.

Segment D: Repeaters Not Married or Cohabiting. In segment D, we found persons with characteristics contrary to those in segments A and B. This group included relatively many single men, but also single women, who earlier or at the time of the attempt had been admitted to a psychiatric hospital. They were all repeaters. At the time of the index suicide attempt, they had a relatively strong suicide intention and they used more dangerous methods. At the time of the interview, they were very depressed, continuously suicidal, and had, at that time numerous problems and physical/psychosomatic complaints. They received very little support from their social network, if there was any social contact outside the psychiatric hospital at all. Most respondents in this group (80%) were admitted to a psychiatric hospital after their discharge from the UHL.

Segment E: Young Adults with Behavioral Problems. In this segment, we found a number of young people (under the age of 30) who, in many cases, had already received outpatient treatment. There were just about as many first-evers as repeaters. Their suicidal intention was moderate. It was notable that, in these cases, motives of revenge were often present and that medicines were exclusively used without any danger to their lives. They either lived with parents, were cohabiting, or lived on their own.

Four to six weeks after discharge from the UHL, they were relatively depressed (but not very strongly), were still thinking of suicide, had many current problems and psychosomatic complaints, and received in their eyes little support from their social network. It was notable that the persons in this group, although depressed and also in other variables resembling those in segment D, were not admitted to a psychiatric hospital after discharge from the UHL, but predominantly received outpatient treatment.

Segment E distinguishes itself from segment A, the young people who were still living with their parents, in terms of their history of problems. Type E persons had had serious, long-lasting problems in numerous aspects of their lives (criminal offenses, prostitution, alcoholism). Presumably here, we can draw a parallel with Hawton's (1987) group "chronic with behavioral disorders," although type E is older.

In summary, five types of suicide attempters can be distinguished. The least problematic is type A, the young people still living with their parents, who because of interpersonal problems, undertake a first impulsive attempt. The most problematic is type D, the single repeaters, who have at some time been admitted to a psychiatric hospital. In between those two, there are two lines, the first one going from type A or B via C to D, in other words clockwise, and the second from type A via E to D, going counterclockwise, that show an increasingly serious nature. If it is correct to describe types of suicide attempters as more or less problematic in this way, then this should also be reflected in percentages of repetition during the follow-up period.

Repeated Suicidal Behavior

At follow-up, of the group of 120 persons interviewed, we knew whether 115 were still alive or had died: 5 respondents could not be traced anymore. Four of the respondents we traced appeared to have died of suicide in the meantime (see Table 2). Through attendants and relatives, an average of 24 months after discharge from the UHL, we were informed of another four suicides of ex-respondents.

From the nonresponse research we conducted among the general practitioners of persons who were not interviewed, it was found that within an average of 12 months after discharge from the UHL at least seven persons had died of suicide. Afterward, we were informed of one more suicide.

The nonresponse research suggested that the group that was not interviewed with respect to the risk of repetition was at higher risk than the group that was interviewed. This certainly held true for the first 12 months. After that time, the significant difference disappeared, but it should be noted that we were far more likely to be informed of suicides of interviewed persons than of those who were not interviewed.

Approximately 1 year after discharge, almost 7% of the cohort was found to have died of suicide, after 1½ years about 9%, and after 2 years at least 10% had died of suicide. In addition, another two persons had died of an unknown cause, whereby suicide could not be established, but on the other hand also could not be excluded.

A fatal repetition rate of 10% within 2 years in a prospective cohort study of suicide attempters has not yet been reported in similar research (WHO 1982).

Table 2. Repeated suicidal behavior in the follow-up period among interviewed and noninterviewed suicide attempters

	Interviewed (n)	(%)	Non-interviewed (n)	(%)	Total group (n)	(%)
Number	120	100	53	100	173	100
Traced	115	96	46	87	161	93
Suicide attempt						
Within 7 months	28	24	?	?	?	?
Suicide						
Within 7 months	4	3.5	?	?	?	?
Within 12 months	4	3.5[a]	7	15.2[a]	11	6.8
Within 18 months	7	6.1	7	15.2	14	8.7
Within 24 months	8	7.0	8	17.4	16	9.9

[a] Chi-squared with Yates' correction = 5.39; $df = 1$; $P < .05$.

Table 3. Repeated suicidal behavior for five types of suicide attempters within a follow-up period of 7 months for suicide attempts and 2 years for suicides

Type	Number	Suicide attempt	Suicide	Suicide +suicide attempt	Repetition (%)
A Youngsters living with parents	26	2	0	2	8
B Married/cohabiting first-evers	24	0	0	0	0
C Married/cohabiting repeaters	15	4	1	5	33
D Repeaters not married or cohabiting	40	14	6	20	50
E Young adults with behavioral problems	15	4	1	5	33
	120	24	8	32	27

This brings up the question of whether the group of suicide attempters that came to the attention of the UHL was to select a group compared with other cohorts that have been studied. Perhaps this can be explained by the fact that the UHL is surrounded by many psychiatric hospitals in the region. Most of the suicides took place among those who before and after the index suicide attempt had been admitted to a psychiatric hospital. There is also the possibility that the strict follow-up method in this study (personal contact and nonresponse analysis) revealed a higher mortality figure than comparable research. Also, the percentage of nonfatal repeated attempts (only among those interviewed) within 7 months of 24% is very high.

Repetition per Type

Concerning the group of persons interviewed per type, we determined what percentage repeated either with or without fatal outcome. Of the 120 interviewed, 28 persons made a new, nonfatal suicide attempt during the follow-up period, and 8 persons killed themselves within a period of 24 months after discharge from the UHL. Because of the fact that four persons who had died of suicide after the follow-up measurement (7 months) had also committed a nonfatal suicide attempt before this time, the total amount of persons came to 32 (= 26.7% of 120 interviewed, or 27.5% of the 115 traced).

Based on these percentages of repetition, we can roughly divide the group of suicide attempters into two large categories: a low-risk group, consisting of types A and B (together, 4% repetition), and a high-risk group, consisting of types C, D, and E (43% repetition all together), whereby especially type D brings with it a very high risk for repetition, at least 50% (see Table 3).

Discussion

Based upon this typology, it is fairly simple to place individual suicide attempters in either a low- or high-risk group. By doing this, we do not predict whether or not an individual will repeat.

As far as the group of individuals placed in the low-risk group is concerned, the chance of a new attempt is rather small, 4% within 7 months. A larger group (70 of 120), however, has a very high risk of repetition, at least 43%. Type D even has a risk of at least 50% (that is, within 7 months for suicide attempts and within 2 years for suicides).

Such a prediction on a group level can hardly be made more specific. In practice, it would be even handier if, within the high-risk group, a further differentiation could be made. A new PRINCALS analysis within the high-risk group (leaving out all first-evers) did not, however, provide any further useful refinements.

The known risk factors for repetition again show up in this typology. A combination of demographic characteristics, earlier suicide attempts, treatment history, and the intention with which the suicide attempt took place, is sufficient to place individuals in one of the types A to E or the high- or low-risk group. The prognosis is further sharpened by knowledge of continuous depression and suicide ideation. If a person, 1−2 months after an attempted suicide, is (still) depressed, then there is a fairly high chance that he will attempt again.

From this typology, another strong predictor emerges, namely, admission to a psychiatric hospital after an attempted suicide. The system of referral procedures and/or the help-seeking behavior of the respondents caused those with the highest risk of repetition to be admitted to psychiatric hospitals. This fact, in combination with the high repetition rate, however, leads us to suspect that the treatment in these psychiatric hospitals was not very successful in preventing repeated attempts.

Together with the fact that most of the persons involved were not very satisfied, either on a short- or a long-term basis, with treatment in psychiatric hospitals (Kerkhof 1985; Kerkhof and Jonker 1987) with respect to suicide prevention, it seems of the highest importance to try to improve the perspectives of treatment for this high-risk group because, after all, a considerable number of those who died of suicide in The Netherlands had made more than one earlier attempt and thus belonged to a high-risk group.

References

American Psychiatric Association (1980) DSM III: Diagnostic and statistical manual of mental disorders (3rd edn). Washington

Bancroft JHJ, Skrimshire AM, Simkin S (1976) The reasons people give for taking overdoses. Br J Psychiatry 138:538−548

Beck AT, Ward CH, Mendelson M, Mock J, Erbaugh J (1961) An inventory for measuring depression. Arch Gen Psychiatry 4:561−571

Beck AT, Schuyler D, Herman I (1972) Development of suicidal intent scales. In: Beck AT, Resnick HLP, Lettieri DJ (eds) The prediction of suicide. Charles, Bowie, Maryland

Bürk F, Möller HJ (1985) Prädiktoren für weiteres suizidales Verhalten bei nach einem Suizidversuch hospitalisierten Patienten. Fortschr Neurol Psychiatr 53:259−270

Bürk F, Kurz A, Möller HJ (1985) Suicide risk scales: do they help to predict suicidal behaviour? Eur Arch Psychiatr Neurol Sci 253:153−157

Diekstra RFW (1981) Over suicide. Samsom, Alphen a.d. Rijn

Dirken JM (1967) Arbeid en Stress: Het vaststellen van aanpassingsproblemen in werk-situaties. Wolters, Groningen

Gezondheidsraad (1986) Advies inzake Suicide. Report to the Minister of Health in the Netherlands, The Hague

Gifi A (1981) Non-linear multivariate analysis. Department of Datatheory, Faculty of Social Sciences, University of Leiden

Gifi A (1983) Princals user's guide. Department of Datatheory, Faculty of Social Sciences, University of Leiden

Hankoff LD (1976) Categories of attempted suicide: a longitudinal study. Am J Public Health 66:558–563

Hawton K (1987) Assessment and aftercare of adolescents who take overdoses. In: Diekstra RFW and Hawton K (eds) Suicide in adolescence. Martinus Nijhoff, Dordrecht

Henderson AS, Hartigan J, Davidson J, Lance GN, Duncan-Jones P, Koller KM, Ritchie K, McAuley H, Williams CL, Slaghuis W (1977) A typology of parasuicide. Br J Psychiatry 131:631–641

Kerkhof AJFM (1985) Suicide en de geestelijke gezondheidszorg. Swets and Zeitlinger, Lisse

Kerkhof AJFM, Jonker D (1987) Long term treatment following suicide attempts. Internal report. Department of Clinical Psychology, State University of Leiden

Kiev A (1976) Cluster analysis profiles of suicide attempters. Am J Psychiatry 133:150–153

Pallis DJ, Pierce DW (1979) Recognizing the suicidal overdose. J R Soc Med 72:565–571

Pallis DJ, Barraclough BM, Levey AB, Jenkins JS, Sainsbury P (1982) Estimating suicide risk among attempted suicides I: The development of new scales. Br J Psychiatry 141:37–44

Pallis DJ, Gibbons JS, Pierce DW (1984) Estimating suicide risk among attempted suicides II: Efficiency of predictive scales after the attempt. Br J Psychiatry 144:139–148

Paykel ES, Rassaby E (1978) Classification of suicide attempters by cluster analysis. Br J Psychiatry 133:45–54

Schreurs P, Tellegen B, Vromans I, van de Wllige G (1983) De ontwikkeling van de Utrechtse copinglijst. Psychologische Geschriften, PG 83.01. Institute for clinical and industrial psychology, Rijksuniversiteit, Utrecht

Tuckman J, Youngman WF (1963a) Suicide risk among persons attempting suicide. Public Health Rep 78:585–587

Tuckman J, Youngman WF (1963b) Identifying suicide risk groups among attempted suicides. Public Health 78:763–766

World Health Organization (WHO) (1982) Changing patterns in suicide behaviour. Euro-reports and studies. Regional Office for Europe, Copenhagen

Path Analytical Models for Predicting Suicide Risk

M. KUDA

Introduction

It is well-known that many of the difficult problems associated with suicide prediction still have not been clarified. I shall try to define several "criteria" of suicidality using the statistical method of path analysis. This task is related to my own professional work involving, for example, the prediction of suicidality among students, or more precisely, clients of a university psychotherapeutic counseling center. It is known that students have a significant suicide risk, as evidenced by numerous references in the literature (Friedrich 1974; Krüger 1982; Kuda and Kuda-Ebert 1981; Lungershausen 1968).

Methods

Criteria of Suicidality

Several criteria of suicidality were examined. From the therapist's viewpoint:

1. Fixation of expressed notions of suicidal ideas after the first therapeutic interviews
2. Ratings with regard to the prognosis of suicide risk.

   From the client's viewpoint:
3. Factual attempts at suicide

Besides assessing the overall reliability of predictions based on our variables, which will be described later, it is of interest to know which of the significant indirect paths chiefly determine suicide risk. Some of these indirect paths will be demonstrated.

Predictors of Suicidality

To define predictors, we utilized data from the basic documentation of the counseling center and therapists' evaluation of symptoms. There are five different sets of predictors: (1) sociobiography, (2) personality structure, (3) future perspectives, (4) study habits, and (5) categories of symptoms.

Sociobiography. This encompassed sex, number of semesters, broken home, number of siblings, and social mobility of the father. The corresponding information for the mother was invalid because too many data were missing.

Personality Structure. We used the Giessen Test (GT) (Beckmann and Richter 1974) and the FBS (questionnaire to assess suicide risk) (Stork 1972). The GT is based on a psychodynamic viewpoint and is composed of six standard scales (social resonance, self-control, dominance, depressive tendencies, permeability, and social potency). The FBS consists of 52 single statements which are combined to a sum score, according to the authors' key. The validity of the FBS has been examined by Kuda (1982) and Schmidtke and Schaller (1976). Contrary to our earlier intention, the FBS is used as a diagnostic and predictive instrument.

Future Perspectives. Besides a more global evaluation of pesonal future perspectives, combinations for estimating future developments of economic factors were used, such as common or personal unemployment now or in 10 years (optimism-A) and general perspectives for future developments (optimism-B). Another factor was the lack of concrete job conceptions and the sum score of our translation of the hopelessness scale (Beck et al. 1974). This is a valid indicator of general hopelessness vs optimism. The relevance of such "future orientations" as predictors of suicidality have previously been reported (Kuda 1985).

Study Habits. A more heterogeneous selection of components in work behavior (study habits) refers to working time/times per week, regularity of work, planning work time, time distribution of work, ability to concentrate, attitudes toward length of studies, test anxiety, and self-confidence in work.

Symptoms. Based on 40 single statements, four different sum scores were computed: somatic, achievement, social, and psychic disorders. Such compositions seem necessary because otherwise the number of predictors would be too large. Higher scores indicate more complexity and more serious disorders.

Statistical Method of Path Analysis

The principles of path analysis will be explained briefly. Extended descriptions and discussions are given by several authors (Blalock 1964; Brandstätter and Bernitzke 1976; Land 1969; Opp and Schmidt 1976; Weede 1972).

The aim of path analysis is to specify a model of causes based on information about covariation between variables listed.

"Causality" in this case merely refers to theoretically postulated dependencies of variables. According to the causalities postulated, two different types of models exist in principle:

1. The recursive model postulates one-sided causal connections and no feedback processes.
2. The nonrecursive model postulates reciprocal causal interactions and feedback processes.

We decided to choose the recursive model. The reason is a simplification in computer design. There is a general differentiation between *exogenous* and *endogenous* variables. *Exogenous* variables are not influenced by other variables: in our model, the sociobiographic components. *Endogenous* variables are explained by other variables, namely, exogenous or further endogenous variables. In each case, the model defines in advance which other variables are causal. Residual variables are not defined in this model. They determine the undefined variance. The total effect of one or more predictors on the explanation of the criterion may be divided into one direct and one or more indirect effects. In a statistical sense, path analysis is a multiple analysis or a sequence of multiple − correlation − analyses. A *path diagram* is the graphic presentation of the model with the direct paths between corresponding variables. The measures for the effects are the beta weights.

Path Models

General Model. The general model contains the complex "sociobiography" followed by the sets "personality structure," "future perspectives," "study habits," and "symptoms" as exogenous variables in this sequence (Fig. 1).

Specific Models. The specifications refer to changes in criterion variables whereas the placement of the other variables is the same. Therefore, we achieve three path models with the criteria: (1) suicidal ideas, (2) prognosis of suicide risk, and (3) former suicide attempts.

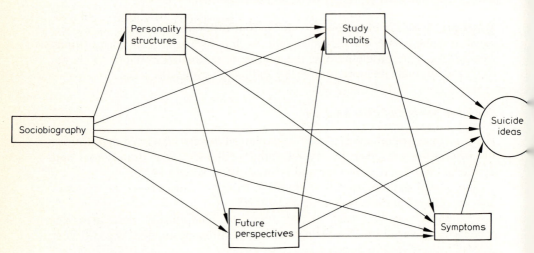

Fig. 1. Path diagram of the general model to predict suicide risk showing all possible direct and indirect paths

Results

Sample Characteristics

The sample included 306 students who had sought help in a psychotherapeutic counseling center during 1 year (Table 1). In comparison with the whole university, female students were overrepresented. For the other data, we have no comparable information from the university. With reference to our three criteria, 40 students (i.e., 13.1% of the sample) reported suicidal ideas during the

Table 1. Description of sample. $n = 306$ clients of a university counseling center

Male = 49%	Female = 51%
Number of semesters x̄ = 8.4	
Broken home 22.9%	
Siblings	
None	10.1
1	35.1
2	28.4
3 or more	26.4
Social mobility of father	
Descent	10.1
No change	68.2
Ascent	21.7

first therapeutic contact, and 18 students (i.e., 5.9%) had had one or more (up to four) suicide attempts. None of them attempted suicide in the course of the following psychotherapeutic contacts.

The prognosis of actual suicide risk by the therapists on a 7-point scale from 1 (no risk) to 7 (very strong risk) was rated as follows: no or very little risk (1 or 2) = 74.2%; some risk (3 or 4) = 16.4%; strong or very strong risk (5, 6, or 7) = 9.4%. Thus for the three criteria there were no normal distributions, but this was not expected.

Path Analysis

Direct Paths. Let us look first at the direct paths to the three criteria. It is striking that the sociobiography as well as the study habits hardly contribute anything to the explanation of variance in this way, and the symptoms have little relevance for prediction.

Suicidal Ideas. 21% of the variance is explained by the predictors (Fig. 2). Female students reported having had suicidal ideas earlier than male students, corresponding to more social inferiority (GT-1) and permeability (GT-5) as well as to less economic optimism and lower hope potential.

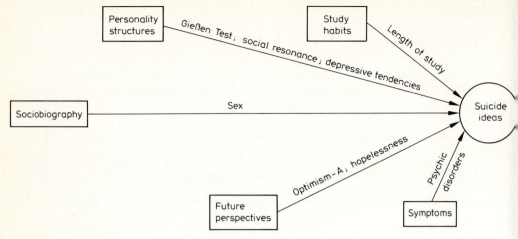

Fig. 2. Significant direct paths to the criterion "suicide ideas"

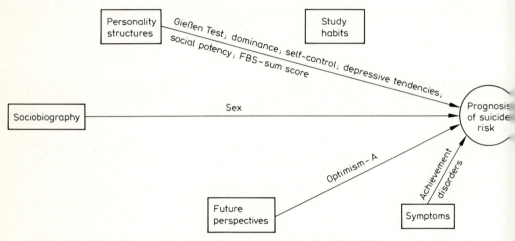

Fig. 3. Significant direct paths to the criterion "prognosis of suicide risk"

With regard to study habits, a long perspective is significant, more frequently indicating psychic disorders. These results are not surprising. Contrary to our expectation, neither a broken home nor global future perspectives were relevant, and there were also no achievement disorders, which could have been presumed especially in a sample of students. Even the FBS, which aims to predict suicide, was not significant.

Prognosis of Suicide Risk. This is primarily given by personality tests, but the common variance is low (14%) (Fig. 3). Significant predictors, in the sense of unfavorable are: less tendency to dominate (GT-2), less self-control (GT-3), higher permeability (GT-5), and less social potency (GT-6). The FBS is signifi-

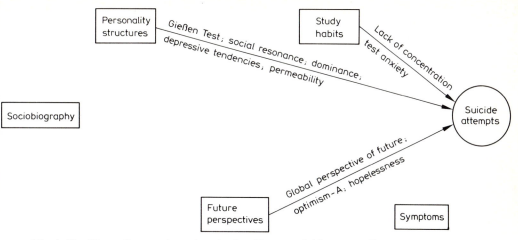

Fig. 4. Significant direct paths to the criterion "former suicide attempts"

cant in the exploration of strong depressive tendencies. Negative expectations about the development of employment (optimism-A) − especially among male students − and fewer disorders with regard to achievement are connected with an unfavorable prognosis. Very significant is the complex "study habits."

Suicide Attempts. The common variance of such attempts with the predictors is 10% (Fig. 4). Sociobiography and symptoms are not significant predictors in this criterion. In contrast, future perspectives have more importance for expectations concerning concrete job conceptions. Also the Giessen Test leads to a correlation of suicide attempts with less self-confidence (GT-1), less self-control, stronger depressive tendencies, and more permeability. In addition, subjective assessments of a low ability to concentrate and of lower self-confidence in work attitudes are prominent.

The low common variance between our three criteria may have various reasons, e.g., the low reliability of answers and/or different concepts of therapists. This demonstrates the necessity of gaining additional information by such path analyses. We attempt to do so by examining the so-called indirect effects.

Indirect Paths. Because the direct paths to the criteria had no extreme weight, we expected that the indirect explanation of variance would not particularly increase either.

In fact, they are not important for the prognosis, while they are more productive (with .272) for the suicide ideas. Half of the amount refers to the indirect path FBS → hope → suicide ideas. Nonetheless, the other indirect paths show the components of optimism or hopelessness or the expectations about economic conditions. The expectations about job enrichment are therefore important aspects which show if suicide ideas are present or not.

The indirect predictive effect is lower but likewise significant (.219). It is a composition of ten single components, none of which is prominent. This underlines the difficulty in prediction. Low social resonance (GT-1) and strong depressive tendencies indicated by the Giessen Test (GT-6) are prominent predictors, just like the FBS, optimism-A (labor market), and the hope scale.

Discussion

With the statistical method of path analysis, we tried to predict several criteria of suicidality using five sets of predictors. It is true that the results did not confirm our expectations but on the other hand the results also did not point to other explanations. That means our models have to be modified. Several different modifications are possible. First, the structure of the models may be changed, i. e., the sequences of the predictors may be varied. Another way is to regard the recursivity of the causal effects between the predictors and the criteria. Thus the assumption of linear additive correlations may be extended to curvilinear relations. With respect to the content of the variables, the validity of the criteria have to be tested. Also, the predictors have to be given a wider range, perhaps through methods other than questionnaires, with particular reference to psychodynamic aspects of the personal history. Likewise, cross-validations by further samples are necessary. Nevertheless, we think it is useful and necessary to pursue this way of predicting suicide tendencies.

References

Beck AT, Weissman A, Lester D (1974) The measurement of pessimism. The hopelessness scale. J Consult Clin Psychol 42:861−872

Beckmann D, Richter HE (1974) Der Gießen-Test. Huber, Bern

Blalock HM (1964) Causal inferences in nonexperimental research. Chapel Hill, University of North Carolina Press

Brandstätter J, Bernitzke F (1976) Zur Technik der Pfadanalyse. Psychol Beitr 18:12−34

Friedrich V (1974) Selbstmord und Selbstmordversuch unter Göttinger Studierenden. In: Sperling E, Jahnke J (eds) Zwischen Apathie und Protest, vol 2. Huber, Bern, pp 111−226

Krüger HJ (1982) Studentenprobleme − Psychosoziale und institutionelle Befunde. Campus, Frankfurt/M

Kuda M (1982) Dimensionsanalyse des „Fragebogentests zur Beurteilung der Suizidgefahr". Z Klin Psychol Psychother 30:12−24

Kuda M (1985) Economic, socio-biographic and psychodynamic aspects of suicidality. 13th International congress for suicide prevention and crisis intervention, Vienna

Kuda M, Kuda-Ebert M (1981) Zur Vorhersage der Selbstmordgefährdung bei Studierenden und Drogenabhängigen. Huber, Bern

Kuda M, Sperling E (1983) Psychotherapeutische Beratung und Hochschulpsychiatrie. In: Huber L (ed) Enzyklopädie Erziehungswissenschaften, vol 10. Klett-Cotta, Stuttgart, pp 415−426

Land KC (1969) Principals of path analysis. In: Borgatta EF (ed) Sociological methodology. Bass, San Francisco

Lungershausen E (1968) Selbstmord und Selbstmordversuch bei Studenten. Hüthig, Heidelberg

Opp KD, Schmidt P (1976) Einführung in die Mehrvariablenanalyse. Rowohlt, Reinbek

Schmidtke A, Schaller S (1976) Fragebogentest zur Beurteilung der Suizidgefahr. Kinderarzt 7:1161−1163

Stork J (1972) Fragebogentest zur Beurteilung der Suizidgefahr. Müller, Salzburg

Weede E (1972) Zur Pfadanalyse. Neuere Entwicklungen, Verbesserungen, Ergänzungen. Kölner Z Soziol Soz Psychol 24:110−117

A Computer Program for Exploring Depressive Patients with Suicidal Thoughts

R. KALB, I. FEHLER, R. GRABISCH, and J. DEMLING

Introduction

The estimation of suicide risk is a common task in psychiatry. Nearly every day, patients who have attempted suicide come from a medical hospital to our clinic for testing of their current suicide risk.

Even the general practitioner will have patients to treat who manifest suicidal thoughts. In every case, the physician will have to decide whether to admit the patient to a hospital or to give him an outpatient consultation.

The examination of suicide risk is generally supposed to be very difficult (Lungershausen 1968). Frequently, the decision is based on clinical experience of many years and not so much on psychological phenomena.

Therefore, early aid was developed to help physicians in their decision. After drawing up the characteristics of patients who later committed suicide (Pokorny 1960), so-called risk lists were developed (e.g. Devries 1966; Pöldinger 1968; Stork 1972; Kielholz 1974; Gustavson et al. 1977; Kreitman 1977; Lauter 1980).

However, these lists give little evidence because they only use statistical methods (Pöldinger and Sonneck 1980). Such statistical tools are too general and the patients are too different to allow an accurate statement about the individual patient. Thus, the deciding physician derives little profit from a method that predicts only 56% of the patients with and 76% without a later suicide act.

The probability of giving a wrong statement in an individual case is too high. Even the well-known risk list given by Pöldinger (1968) which recommends hospitalization if 100 points are reached and which claims no suicide risk if the number of points is less than 50 had no success in a test made by Padrutt (1970). Therefore, Padrutt concluded that the use of the risk list cannot be recommended in medical practice. Even Pöldinger himself stressed (1969) that the list should only be used within the (close) compass of an exploration that gives an entire judgment. Therefore, questionnaires which serve to estimate suicide risk have never succeeded. For example, Pöldinger characterizes (1984) depressive persons as risk group no. 1 and alcoholics and addicts to drugs and medicaments as risk group no. 2. Further risk groups are lonely and old people.

According to Robins (1985), all persons uttering suicidal thoughts, chronic alcoholics, or persons having major depressions should be treated by psychiatry.

Here is another possibility to use all this knowledge: with the help of a computer program, we could succeed in applying general knowledge to the individual patient and, with that, improve the possibilities of suicide – risk estimation.

Material

We investigated two groups of patients coming to our clinics. The patients of the first group were depressive and had suicidal thoughts without having attempted suicide. The patients of the other group were depressive too, had suicidal thoughts, and had attempted suicide the day before. The patients were randomly selected from patients admitted to the Poliklinik der Psychiatrischen Universitätsklinik Erlangen and the Bezirkskrankenhaus Erlangen. Patients with psychoses were not included. Our patients rather showed an acute situational reaction involving interpersonal conflicts.

To distinguish both groups, it was necessary to define a suicide attempt. In 1958, Stengel defined it as "every act of self-injury consciously aiming at self-destruction." Many survivors affirm that they did not want to die – we classify them in the group with a suicide attempt because they did try deliberate self-harm. Other patients have suicidal intentions such as standing on a skyscraper without jumping down – they too were included in the suicidal group.

Method

All patients were thoroughly interviewed; the interview was documented to answer the questions of the following program. Naturally, we avoided questions referring to a possible suicide attempt.

The program runs on a compatible 16-bit computer and mostly uses yes-or-no questions because these can be answered very fast. If more alternative answers are possible, they are mostly proposed by the program, but sometimes free answering is possible, too.

Examples of the dialogue are shown in the Appendix. This example makes it plain that, depending on the answers of the individual patient, each dialogue is different. This is possible because the program collects statements about the patient out of the dialogue and memorizes them. This short-time memory is observed by many so-called rules. Every rule is composed of a few premises and one conclusion. The premises contain the hitherto-existing knowledge; the conclusion can be a question, but also an internal conclusion or – at the end of the dialogue – a statement about the suicide risk of the current patient. Naturally, the personal data of the patient are not necessary for such a computer analysis. The program possesses, in addition to its dialogue mode, a learning mode. In this mode, the program can learn new rules to improve its predictions. Another mode is called an "explaining mode." In this mode, it explains why a question or a statement was chosen at this moment.

The set of all rules is called the knowledge of the program. Our rules use long-known knowledge such as the psychoanalytic model of suicidal tendency (Freud 1917). Freud viewed suicide as a failure to externalize aggressive feelings which are turned inward. He hypothesized that the individual turns back on himself the repressed aggression toward a person he otherwise needs .

Ringel (1969, 1974) refers to these thoughts of Freud with his ideas of the presuicidal syndrome. In the second point of his syndrome, aggression is (symptomatically) repressed and directed at one's own person. By preventing the satisfaction of aggression in the environment for a longer time (for example, by an inflexible rigorous "superego", or by illness with restriction of the psychic activity such as major depression, or by cultural prohibitions, or the lack of connections to other people), the impulse becomes stronger and stronger until it is directed at one's own person using it as a compensation object. This repression would prepare the described inversion of aggression.

The transition stage from inverted aggression to suicide attempt is filled with suicidal thoughts, coming rarely in the beginning, obtruding themselves onto the unfortunate later on.

After finding out many factors about the life, the current situation, and the psychic state of the patient, the question is how these factors are related to each other. A simple estimation of the factors and their summation to figure out the suicide risk rather blurs the outlines: it is too easy to disregard individual decisive factors. Therefore, our interest was to consider even those factors which may be preponderant over all others. That means, we had to model the behavior of decision instead of pursuing statistics.

In the end, all these factors form a network which should be able to give an individual decision for the patient. At that point, the program does not use all the features preceding a suicide attempt. That means that during a dialogue with the physician or the patient, the program pays particular attention to the social relations of the patient; if there are only very few, these few become especially important.

Many good social relations can be used to compensate for a bad one. This possibility does not exist for people who have only one or two real social relations. In this case − other reasons may exist in addition − the aggressions against a social partner have to be repressed and can be directed at the patient himself (inversion of aggression).

Another important thing is to estimate the probability of whether the situation can come to a head. Patients who have had suicidal thoughts for a long time without coming to a head are not as much endangered as those who have had intense problems in the recent past. An additional intensification is alcoholism or another addiction.

It is important that − unlike the questionnaires − only a fraction of the hundreds of possible questions have to be asked, namely, those which are important for the individual patient. The selection of the questions is made by the answers the patient gives.

The program should use the knowledge about risk factors provided by suicide research, but in contrast to the existing lists, apply this knowledge to the individual patient. In the end, the statement of the program should be testable and be confirmed by a number of patients.

Results

Buchanan and Shortliffe (1984) have taught us that the evaluation process of a computer program is a continual one that should begin at the time of system design, extended in an informal fashion through the early stages of development, and becoming increasingly formal as a developing system moves toward real-world implementation. It is useful to cite nine stages of system development, which summarize the evolution of an expert system (Table 1).

Our system is now in the third stage. We have gathered 40 case studies up to now. We have answered the questions of the program with the help of medical records and taught the system new rules if necessary. Each dialogue was recorded and criticized. When the system was right, we were delighted; when it was wrong, we taught it new rules (Table 2): 14 patients were successfully handled, for 10 patients the prediction was wrong, and 26 patients could not be handled until we added new rules.

Table 1.   Steps in the implementation of an expert system (Buchanan and Shortliffe 1984)

1. Top-level design with definition of long-range goals
2. First-version prototype, showing feasibility
3. System refinement in which informal test cases run to generate feedback
4. Structured evaluation of performance
5. Structured evaluation of acceptability to users
6. Service functioning for extended period in prototype environment
7. Follow-up studies to demonstrate the system's large-scale usefulness
8. Program changes to allow wide distribution of the system
9. General release and distribution with firm plans for maintenance and updating

Table 2.   The program's predictions of suicide attempts in patients with suicidal thoughts

	Suicide attempt	No suicide attempt	Total
Right prediction	11	3	14
Wrong prediction	5	5	10
No prediction	15	1	16
Sum	31	9	40

Discussion

The method we used is not quite new: Greist, Gustafson, and their associates (1973) used a computer program to predict suicide risk. Physicians and psychiatrists were given case histories of 20 patients, half of whom made a suicide attempt on their life within 3 months after first being seen by psychiatrists and half of whom did not.

The case histories were constructed from medical records and clinician's descriptions of the patient's first visit and first complaint of suicidal thoughts. In the experimental task, the physicians reviewed the case histories and predicted what was most likely to occur within the next 3 months: suicide attempt or no attempt. The same information was processed by the computer and Bayesian analysis assigned a probability to each possible outcome.

In their study, the computer identified attemptors more frequently (70% of the cases) than the average psychiatrist (38%). The computer was slightly less accurate in identifying nonattemptors (90% accuracy) than psychiatrists (93%). In a clinician-by-clinician comparison, the computer identified the correct outcome more frequently (85% of the time) than any individual physician (best was 80%).

The design of Gustafson et al. differs from our design because we prefer the dialogue between physicians and program and – what is more important – do not use statistical tools but a rule-based system.

We expect that our program will be useful because to predict the risk of a suicide attempt is one of the most responsible and difficult tasks a physician can be confronted with. On the other hand, it is well-known that many patients go to see a physician before making a suicide attempt. The corresponding percentage fluctuates between 22% and 82% (Kurz and Möller 1984). Linden (1969) discovered that 39% of his patients with a suicide attempt gave verbal suicide information to their environment and 56% conspicuous information generally. Of all patients who commit suicide, 50% – 80% talk about their intentions beforehand (Robins 1985).

We are now preparing the fourth stage of the evaluation of our system. The design of this stage will be the following:

1. We intend to investigate a great number of patients (more than 100), randomly selected, about one-half with, the other without a suicide attempt.
2. Besides the medical record, we will use a questionnaire answered by the patient, which poses the same questions as the program.
3. One must avoid the so-called halo effect, i.e., the influence on the answers of the physician to the program caused by knowing about the patient's attempt; therefore, the computer user must not know.
4. All patients will be reexamined several months or half a year later.
5. The knowledge base must remain constant or all medical records must, in the long run, be delivered to the program once more.

Appendix

Example of a dialogue between physician and program (partial). This program contains the knowledge to help you answer the question of whether a patient with suicidal thoughts and depression is endangered by a suicide attempt or not.

Why does the patient have suicidal thoughts?
    The patient has quarrels with his parents.

Why does the patient have quarrels with his parents?
  His parents don't like his girlfriend.

Does the patient have problems with his partner?
  Yes.

Does the patient have children?
  No.

Does the patient have other relatives or friends he can visit in case of need?
  No.

Is the patient dependent on his parents?
  Yes.

Is the patient dependent on his partner?
  Yes.

Does the patient have a job?
  No.

How long has the patient had suicidal thoughts (days, weeks, months, years)?
  The patient has had suicidal thoughts for years.

Has the patient made a suicide attempt before?
  Yes.

References

Buchanan BG, Shortliffe EH (1984) The problem of evaluation. In: Buchanan GB, Shortliffe EH (eds) Rule-based expert systems, Addison-Wesley, Reading
Devries AG (1966) A potential suicide personality inventory. Psychol Rep 18:731–738
Freud S (1917) Trauer und Melancholie. Fischer, Frankfurt
Greist IH, Gustafson DH, Strauss FF, Rowse GL, Laughren TP, Chiles JH (1973) A computer interview for suicide risk prediction. Am J Psychiatry 130:1327–1331
Gustafson DH, Greist JH, Strauss FF, Erdman H, Laughren TP (1977) A probabilistic system for identifying suicide attemptors. Comp Biomed Res 10:83–89
Kielholz P (1974) Diagnose und Therapie der Depressionen für Praktiker, 3rd edn. Lehmanns, Munich
Kreitman N (1977) Parasuicide. Wiley, London
Kurz A, Möller HJ (1984) Zur Wirksamkeit suizidprophylaktischer Versorgungsprogramme. In: Faust V, Wolfersdorf (eds) Suizidgefahr. Hippokrates, Stuttgart
Lauter H (1980) Akute psychiatrische Notfälle. Internist 21:40–49
Linden K-J (1969) Der Suizidversuch. Versuch einer Situationsanalyse. Enke, Stuttgart
Lungershausen E (1968) Suizidprophylaxe in der ärztlichen Praxis. Landarzt 44:27–29
Padrutt HP (1970) Die Abschätzung der Suizidalität. Überprüfung der Brauchbarkeit einer Risikoliste (Pöldinger). Schw Rundschau Med 59:403–404
Pokorny AD (1960) Characteristics of forty-four patients who subsequently committed suicide. Arch Gen Psychiatry 3:314–323
Pöldinger W (1968) Die Abschätzung der Suizidalität. Huber, Bern
Pöldinger W (1984) Suizidprophylaxe bei depressiven Syndromen. In: Faust V, Wolfersdorf M (eds) Suizidgefahr. Hippokrates, Stuttgart

Pöldinger W, Sonneck G (1980) Die Abschätzung der Suizidalität. Nervenarzt 51:147—151
Ringel E (1969) Selbstmordverhütung. Huber, Bern
Ringel E (1974) Selbstmord — Appell an die anderen. Kaiser, Munich
Robins E (1985) Suicide. In: Kaplan HJ, Sadock BJ (eds) Comprehensive textbook of psychiatry VI, vol II, 4th edn. Williams and Wilkins, Baltimore
Stengel E (1958) Untersuchungen zum Selbstmordversuch und seine Beziehungen zum Selbstmord. Schwabe, Basel
Stork J (1972) Fragebogentest zur Beurteilung der Suizidgefahr. Müller, Salzburg

Part III   Biological Factors of Suicidal Behavior

Biological Correlates of Suicidal Behavior*

M. ÅSBERG and P. NORDSTRÖM

Introduction

There has been a shift of focus in suicide research toward a psychobiological approach during the last 2 decades. The reason for this is the recent emergence of two clusters of biological factors which tend to correlate with suicidal behavior. These are associated with serotonergic neurotransmission and with certain neuroendocrine functions, particularly the release of cortisol.

The current research evidence relating suicidal acts to biological factors will be briefly reviewed in the present paper, and some methodological problems in this rapidly developing research field will be discussed.

Methodological Issues

Definition and Assessment of Suicidality

"Suicidal behavior" is a term which encompasses complex and heterogeneous phenomena such as suicidal ideation, attempted suicide, and completed suicide. Since only few suicide ideators and attempters go on to commit suicide, and acts and thoughts are likely to have different biological correlates, distinctions between different categories of suicidal behavior are particularly important in biologically oriented research. The time course of the suicidal behavior must be taken into account, and current suicidality must be distinguished from lifetime suicidal behavior, particularly with those biological markers which may be state dependent and not stable over time.

Suicide is often conceived of as an exclusively human behavior, which presupposes intentionality and a concept of death. In the light of this conception, biological research in suicide may appear as a futile endeavor, and this is probably the reason why the psychobiological approach is a late phenomenon in suicidology. The impetus was provided by accidental findings which, however, were found to be surprisingly reproducible and therefore could lay the ground for a more systematic exploration.

* Financial support was provided by the Swedish Medical Research Council (5454), the Söderström-König Foundation, the Torsten and Ragnar Söderberg Foundation, the Stockholm County Council, the Medical Research Council of the Swedish Life Insurance Companies, and the Karolinska Institute.

The definition of suicide is difficult, and many suicide researchers have struggled with the concept of intentionality. Although the validity of assessment of the intent to die is very often doubtful, "intent" has generally been crucial in the definition of suicide. Faced with this dilemma, some researchers focus on the intent to harm oneself, regardless of the intent to die. Others infer intent to die from the medical lethality of a suicide attempt, disregarding the patient's estimate of the risk, which in turn depends on his knowledge of the method involved. Because of these difficulties in definition and assessment of suicidality, a great proportion of self-inflicted deaths are registered as "uncertain" suicides, and in some settings, a diagnosis of suicide is not made unless there is a suicide note.

Similar problems are encountered in the definition and assessment of attempted suicide. Suicide attempts have been conceived of, not only as failed suicides, but also as "a cry for help" (Farberow and Shneidman 1961), and a "cry out of anger and confusion" (Rydin et al., unpublished). The clinical assessment is confounded by the patient's psychological coping mechanisms and explanatory style and by observer's bias.

Considering the heterogeneity of suicidal behavior, it is fairly obvious that any particular biological correlate cannot be expected to be relevant in all types of suicidality. We must examine correlations in subgroups. In the biological context, the heuristically most useful classification seems to be by simple behavior criteria, for example, according to the method used (active, violent, or passive, nonviolent) – perhaps because of its high reliability. Psychiatric diagnostic categories should also be taken into account since we know that certain psychiatric disorders are related to certain biological disturbances.

The concept of suicide risk is also ambiguous and used differently in statistical and clinical settings. In the general population, suicide is a rare event. The base rate in clinical groups is higher, but low enough to make prediction of suicide hazardous. Studies of possible biological, as well as psychological, predictors of suicide must therefore be performed in high-risk groups to be feasible and conclusive. Preferably, confounding factors such as sex, age, seasonal variations, psychiatric diagnosis, and medication and temporal relationship to any suicide attempt should be controlled for.

Markers of Monoaminergic Transmission

The markers used to assess the status of serotonergic neurotransmission in the living man are of necessity indirect. Precursors of the amine can be measured in blood and in CSF. The enzyme responsible for the degradation of serotonin, monoamine oxidase (MAO), exists in platelets as well as in neurons, and platelet MAO activity has been suggested to reflect some innate characteristic of the serotonin system, such as its size or capacity (Oreland and Shaskan 1983). Platelets have an uptake mechanism for serotonin, and they carry binding sites for imipramine as well as for serotonin. The consistent findings of deranged serotonin uptake and reduced number of imipramine binding sites on platelets from depressed patients sugggest that these measures reflect events in the central nervous system.

One of the most widely used methods for obtaining information about the turnover of the monoamines in the brain is to measure their metabolites in the CSF, usually obtained by lumbar puncture. The metabolite concentrations are in the nanomolar range, and highly sensitive and specific analytical methods are needed to measure them with sufficient accuracy.

An underlying assumption in the CSF studies is that the concentrations of neurotransmitter metabolites in CSF will reflect functionally important aspects of the parent transmitters in the brain. There has been some discussion as to whether concentrations of, e.g., the serotonin metabolite, 5-hydroxyindoleacetic acid (5-HIAA), in CSF reflects serotonin turnover in the spinal cord, rather than in the brain itself (Bulat and Zivkovic 1971). The demonstration by Stanley and coworkers (1985) that 5-HIAA in CSF, drawn after death, correlates strongly with 5-HIAA in brain cortex suggests, however, that brain events are indeed reflected in CSF metabolite concentrations.

A main advantage of the CSF technique is that spinal fluid is comparatively easy to obtain at little discomfort to the patient. There are many disadvantages as well. The concentrations of 5-HIAA and of the dopamine metabolite, homovanillic acid (HVA), depend, inter alia, on the subject's sex (men have lower concentrations), age (concentrations increase with age), and body height (the taller the subject, the lower the metabolite concentration) (Åsberg and Bertilsson 1979). The dependence on body height is presumably due to an active removal from CSF of the acid metabolites, as they flow from the brain ventricles down to the lumbar sac where the CSF is sampled. Metabolite concentrations also vary seasonally (Åsberg et al. 1981) and with the time of day (Nicoletti et al. 1981).

Most important in clinical studies, the monoamine metabolite concentrations are drastically altered by treatment with certain psychotropic drugs. The classic tricyclic antidepressants, for instance, reduce the CSF concentrations of the noradrenaline metabolite, 4-hydroxy-3-methoxyphenyl glycol (HMPG). Many antidepressants also lower the concentrations of 5-HIAA, and the interference with serotonin turnover appears to affect HVA concentrations as well (Bertilsson et al. 1974). The importance of an appropriate washout period before an individual is admitted to a research project is underlined by these findings. Lingering effects of previously given treatment might otherwise be misinterpreted as evidence of biological disturbances, when patients are compared with healthy control subjects.

There are only very few studies where different putative markers of the serotonin system have been measured simultaneously in the same subject. The little evidence there is does not support any strong correlations between the markers, suggesting that they may reflect different aspects of the system.

After death, serotonin and related enzymes and metabolites can be measured in the brain and CSF, but the methodological problems are tremendous. The time and mode of death, previous drug treatment, and decay of the amines or their metabolites between death and discovery of the body, and subsequent autopsy, are all important factors and difficult to ascertain.

The interpretation of low CSF concentrations of the serotonin metabolite is not clear. The decreased serotonin metabolism could indicate diminished serotonergic activity, or it might be thought of as a reflection of increased serotonergic function, i.e., hypersensitive postsynaptic receptors.

Markers of the Hypothalamic-Pituitary-Adrenal Axis

The activation of the hypothalamic-pituitary-adrenal axis (HPA axis) which occurs in stress states, as well as in some cases of depressive illness, is more easily measured than the serotonin system. HPA activation is reflected in increased concentrations of cortisol in plasma, CSF, and urine, as well as in a reduced ability to suppress cortisol secretion after administration of the synthetic steroid, dexamethasone. These measures tend to be correlated with each other.

In particular, the dexamethasone suppression test (DST) has been very widely used in recent psychiatric research. The test is simple to perform, but certain precautions must be taken to avoid error. Concomitant administration of benzodiazepines may normalize the DST. Defective compliance, that is, the patient does not ingest the dexamethasone as directed, is a potential cause of nonsuppression. It may be advantageous to check plasma concentrations of dexamethasone, in particular since a correlation between dexamethasone concentration and postdexamethasone cortisol has repeatedly been demonstrated (Holsboer et al. 1984; Morris et al. 1986).

The interpretation of an abnormal DST is not clear. Although it has been suggested to be specific for melancholia and recommended as a diagnostic test (Carroll 1982), there is much evidence to the contrary (Berger et al. 1984).

Biological Correlates of Suicidal Behavior – Studies of Suicide Attempters

Monoamine-Related Markers

CSF 5-HIAA. A relationship between low concentrations of CSF 5-HIAA and suicidal behavior was first described by Åsberg and coworkers (1976) who found, in a study of depressed patients, that the incidence of suicide attempts was significantly higher in patients with low than in those with high CSF 5-HIAA. Patients with low CSF 5-HIAA often used violent, active methods in their attempts in contrast to the patients with normal or high 5-HIAA, who had all taken overdoses of sedative drugs.

The relationship between low CSF 5-HIAA and suicidal behavior in depressed patients has been reproduced by several research groups in many countries (see summary in Table 1), including a country with a high suicide rate such as Hungary and a country with a low suicide rate such as Spain. Interestingly, the association with method was not found in Spain, while in Hungary, the relationship was confined to those who used violent methods. This difference suggests that the biological relationship may be important for a core group of suicide attempters, but not for a wider range of attempters who may be more influenced by the prevalent culture.

There are also some negative findings. The most interesting negative finding is the study by Roy-Byrne and coworkers (1983), who did not find any association in their bipolar patients, while there was a clear trend in their small unipolar group. There have been previous suggestions in small patient groups that the relationship may be absent in the bipolar (for instance, Ågren 1983).

On the other hand, the relationship is not confined to depressive illness. Low 5-HIAA in suicide attempters has been described in patients with personality disorders (Brown and coworkers 1979 and 1982), in minor affective disorders (Träskman et al. 1981), and in schizophrenia (van Praag 1983; Ninan et al. 1984).

This suggests that the psychobiological events that culminate in a suicide attempt or a suicide may not be the same in bipolar disorders and in other psychiatric disturbances. Possibly, the cognitive distortions and the profound hopelessness may be more important in the bipolar cases, while impulsiveness and hostility may be more important in the other disorders.

CSF HVA. Not only 5-HIAA, but also the dopamine metabolite has repeatedly been associated with suicidal behavior. The CSF concentrations of the two metabolites are strongly correlated, but interestingly, there is nevertheless a suggestion that the association between suicidal behavior and reduced CSF HVA is particularly strong in the setting of depressive illness and weaker outside this diagnostic category (cf. Träskman and coworkers 1981).

Platelet Markers. A low activity of MAO in platelets is well known to be associated with certain personality traits, particularly impulsiveness and related features such as sensation-seeking behavior (for review, see, e.g., Oreland and coworkers 1984). An association between low MAO and suicidal behavior has been demonstrated in a few studies. Buchsbaum and coworkers (1976) found a higher incidence of psychosocial problems, including suicidal behavior, among relatives of probands with low platelet MAO (which is under genetic control). Gottfries and coworkers (1980) found lower MAO in patients who had made violent suicide attempts in contrast to other depressed patients including those who had taken drug overdoses.

Although a series of studies has suggested that the number of binding sites for tritiated imipramine on platelets is reduced in major depressive disorders (see review by Åsberg and Wägner 1986), there appears to be only one report with a (weak) association with suicide. Thus, Wägner and coworkers (1985) found a marginally *higher* number of imipramine binding sites in depressed patients who had attempted suicide with violent methods in contrast to nonsuicidal depressives.

Postsynaptic Effects. In a very interesting study of serotonin function beyond the postsynaptic receptor, Meltzer and coworkers (1984a) measured the response in blood cortisol concentration to administration of the serotonin precursor, 5-hydroxytryptophan. Normally, this procedure results in a slight increase in serum cortisol. The cortisol release is exaggerated in depressive illness. When the depressed patients were subdivided into those who had attempted suicide, those

Table 1. Studies of CSF 5-HIAA and suicidal behavior

Author	Subjects	Measure of suicidality	Result
Åsberg et al. 1976	68 hospitalized depressed patients	Attempted or completed suicide within index illness episode	Low 5-HIAA in the 15 attempters, particularly those using violent methods
Brown et al. 1979	22 men with personality disorder	Lifetime history of suicide attempt	Lower 5-HIAA in the 11 suicide attempters
Ågren 1980	33 depressed patients	SADS suicidality scales	Negative correlation between 5-HIAA and suicidality scores
Träskman et al. 1981	30 suicide attempters and 45 healthy controls	Recent attempted or completed suicide	5-HIAA lower in attempters than in controls
Leckman et al. 1981	132 psychiatric patients	Rated suicidal ideation	Negative correlation with suicidal ideation in the 76 psychotic patients
Brown et al. 1982	12 patients with borderline personality disorder	Lifetime history of suicide attempt	Lower 5-HIAA in the 5 attempters
Montgomery SA and Montgomery D 1982	49 patients with endogenous depression	History of suicidal act	More attempters among patients with low 5-HIAA
van Praag 1982	203 depressed patients	Recent suicide attempt	More suicide attempters among patients with low CSF 5-HIAA
Palaniappan et al. 1983	40 hospitalized depressed patients	Suicide item in the Hamilton Rating Scale	Negative correlation between CSF 5-HIAA and suicide score
Ågren 1983	110 depressed patients	SADS suicidality scales	Low 5-HIAA associated with recent or current suicidal ideation
Roy-Byrne et al. 1983	32 bipolar and 13 unipolar patients	Lifetime history of suicide attempt	No association with 5-HIAA in bipolar patients
van Praag 1983	10 nondepressed schizophrenic suicide attempters, 10 nonsuicidal schizophrenics and 10 controls	Recent suicide attempt	Lower CSF 5-HIAA in suicide attempters
Banki et al. 1984	141 female psychiatric inpatients	Recent suicide attempt	Negative correlations with 5-HIAA particularly with violent attempts

Study	Sample	Measure	Findings
Ninan et al. 1984	8 suicidal and 8 nonsuicidal schizophrenics	Lifetime history of suicide attempt	Lower 5-HIAA in suicide attempters
Lopez-Ibor et al. 1985	21 depressed patients	Suicide attempt and suicidal ideation rated on the Hamilton Scale	More attempts and higher suicidality scores in patients with low 5-HIAA
Roy et al. 1985	54 patients with chronic schizophrenia	Lifetime history of suicide attempt	No difference in 5-HIAA between 27 attempters and 27 non-attempters
Edman et al. 1986	7 psychiatric patients who attempted suicide and 7 healthy controls	Recent suicide attempt	Lower 5-HIAA in attempters
Roy et al. 1986	27 depressed patients and 22 healthy controls	Lifetime history of suicide attempt	A low CSF HVA/5-HIAA ratio was more common among the 19 attempters
Secunda et al. 1986	132 unipolar and bipolar primary major depressive disorder patients	SADS suicidality scales	No difference in 5-HIAA between 19 current suicide attempters and 38 nonattempters

who had suicidal thoughts and those who were not suicidal, the cortisol re-action was clearly enhanced in the attempters (Meltzer et al. 1984b). This find-ing is in line with the hypothesis of a reduced release of serotonin in suicide attempters, which would tend to cause hypersensitivity of serotonin receptors.

Melatonin and Magnesium. Recently, two studies have emerged where two further biological variables that are related with serotonin have been found to correlate with suicidal behavior. The serum concentration of melatonin, which is formed by enzymatic transformation of serotonin, is decreased in depressive disorders but was shown to be closer to normal in suicidal than in nonsuicidal depressed patients by Beck-Friis and coworkers (1985).

Magnesium concentrations in CSF are strongly correlated to melatonin in CSF (Beckman et al. 1984) and to 5-HIAA in CSF. Banki and coworkers (1985) found lower CSF magnesium in suicide attempters than controls.

Endocrinologic Markers

HPA Axis. In 1965, Bunney and coworkers reported that the excretion of cor-tisol metabolites in urine was unusually high in patients who went on to at-tempt or complete suicide. In 1969, Bunney and coworkers reproduced their findings and suggested that the measurement of cortisol might be useful to identify people at risk for suicide. Although there has been some doubt about the clinical usefulness of the test, the association between high cortisol and suicidality has been reproduced by several later investigators (see summary in Table 2).

With the introduction of the DST, interest in the relationship between sui-cide and HPA-axis activation increased. Thus, Carroll and coworkers (1981) found abnormal DSTs more often in suicidal than in nonsuicidal patients, but the relationship was confined to patients with melancholia. Several investiga-tors have reproduced these associations, while others failed to do so (for sum-mary, see Table 2). Most authors agree that DST nonsuppression is in-dependent of CSF 5-HIAA (Mårtensson et al., unpublished).

Thyroid Axis

Blunted thyroid-stimulating hormone (TSH) responses to injection of thy-rotropin-releasing hormone (TRH) are seen in 25%−50% of patients with de-pressive disorders and in occasional alcoholic patients (even when they have been abstinent for years). There is no correlation between cortisol suppression by dexamethasone and increase in TSH in response to TRH (Arato et al. 1983; Prange and Loosen 1984).

The blunted TSH response to TRH in depression has been associated both with an increased incidence of suicide and of suicide attempts (Linkowski and coworkers 1983, 1984; Kjellman and coworkers 1985). Banki et al. (1984), how-ever, reported a *higher* TSH response to TRH in suicidal than in nonsuicidal

Table 2. Studies of the HPA axis and suicidal behavior

Author	Subjects	Index	Result
Bunney et al. 1965	33 depressed patients	17-OH-CS/u[a]	Three patients who ultimately committed suicide had concentrations close to the upper end of the distribution
Bunney et al. 1969	62 normal subjects, 31 normal subjects under stress, and 52 depressed patients	17-OH-CS/u	Nine patients who later attempted or committed suicide hat significantly higher concentrations than the controls
Levy and Hansen 1969	"General spectrum of severe psychiatric illnesses"	17-OH-CS/u	Two subsequent suicides of patients with concentrations within the normal range when corrected for body size
Fink and Carpenter 1976	Two completed suicides	17-OH-CS/u	Low mean levels in one suicide, moderately elevated in the other suicide
Ostroff et al. 1982	22 male psychiatric inpatients	Cortisol/u	Three patients with high levels made serious suicide attempts, two of which were lethal
Prasad 1985	32 male suicide attempters	Cortisol/u	The 13 patients who had used violent means had a higher mean level compared with 19 wrist-slashers
Krieger 1974	Psychiatric inpatients admitted because of suicide risk	Cortisol/p	The 13 patients who committed suicide within 2 years had higher mean 8:30 a.m. serum levels than 39 suicide-risk patients who did not commit suicide
Platman et al. 1971	Single case study	Cortisol/p	Elevated concentration 4 days preceding a serious suicide attempt
Greden et al. 1980	14 endogenous depressives	Repeated DSTs	One of four nonnormalizers committed suicide 2 months later
Papakostas et al. 1981	14 male unipolar melancholic patients	Repeated DSTs	One of ten nonnormalizers after ECT committed suicide within 1 month
Carroll et al. 1981	250 melancholic patients	DST	Five completed suicides, all with abnormal DSTs. Eleven suicide attempters had abnormal DSTs. Three patients with other diagnoses who completed suicide had normal DSTs
Yerevanian et al. 1983	14 primary, endogenous major depressive disorder patients	Repeated DSTs	Three of ten nonnormalizers suicided; two within 3 days of discharge and another one after 8 months

Table 2. (continued)

Author	Subjects	Index	Result
Coryell and Schlesser 1981	243 unipolar depression inpatients	DST	Four patients with primary unipolar depression and abnormal DSTs subsequently committed suicide, while one secondary unipolar patient with normal DST also committed suicide
Ågren 1983	60 patients with major depressive disorders	DST	The proportion post-/predexamethasone plasma cortisol level at 11:00 a.m. correlated positively with measures of past suicidality, especially with medical lethality
Targum et al. 1983	49 primary unipolar depressed patients	DST	Significantly more patients admitted for suicide attempts (14 of 17) than nonsuicidal patients (9 of 32) had abnormal DSTs. All five patients who made subsequent attempts (one completed) within 6 months had had abnormal DSTs
van Wettere et al. 1983	51 suicide attempters	DST	No association with type of suicide attempt (violent vs nonviolent), no association with suicidal behavior rating scales
Chabrol et al. 1983	20 adolescent suicide attempters	DST	Four had abnormal DSTs
Banki and Arato 1983	57 female psychiatric inpatients	DST	86% abnormal DSTs in those admitted after attempted suicide (12 of 14); 58% nonsuppressors among nonattempters
Banki et al. 1984	111 female psychiatric inpatients	DST	Violent and nonviolent suicide attempters had comparable but significantly higher rates of abnormal DST (12 of 15: 80% and 17 of 24: 71%) than nonsuicidal patients (38 of 72: 53%)
Robbins and Alessi 1985	45 adolescent psychiatric inpatients	DST	All six of those with normal DST attempted suicide on admission, while 17 of the 22 with normal DST made nonsevere attempts. Four of the six nonsuppressors made serious attempts. Two nonserious suicide attempters had nonsuppression and subsequently made serious attempts – one fatal

Ennis et al. 1985	DST	72 patients admitted for assessment of suicidal risk	The distribution of the 31 abnormal DSTs among those with and without history of self-harm and the ones admitted after an overdose or self-injury is not reported
Wilmotte et al. 1986	DST	54 nonendogenous depressives admitted after attempted suicide	A high proportion of abnormal DSTs but no correlation with the lethality of the attempt
Secunda et al. 1986	DST	132 primary major depressive disorder patients (85 unipolar and 47 bipolar patients)	Among 28 suicide attempters as compared with 60 nonattempters, a reduction in evening pre-DST plasmacortisol was found, restricted to the unipolar suicide attempters (16) as opposed to nonattempters (44)
Brown et al. 1986	DST	65 primary major depressive disorder patients	No significant differences in cortisol nonsuppression could be found between 13 recent (2 violent), 9 past, and 42 nonattempters
Roy et al. 1986	DST	27 depressed inpatients and 22 normal control subjects	Ten of 19 patients with prior suicide attempts (four current) and four of eight nonattempters had abnormal DSTs, i.e., no difference. Three out of four female patients who comitted suicide within a year had been melancholic DST-nonsuppressors
Zimmerman et al. 1986	DST	187 primary unipolar depressed inpatients	The frequency of serious suicide attempts among the 60 DST-nonsuppressors (3.3%) did not differ from that among suppressors (9.4%). However, nonserious attempts were significantly more frequent in the suppressors (24.4% as compared with 8.3%); 31 of 36 (86%) of such attempts were made by this group
Brooksbank et al. 1972	Cortisol/brain	23 suicides and 7 controls	As low as or lower than in the frontal cortex of controls
Träskman et al. 1980	Cortisol/CSF	19 depressed patients, 12 nondepressed patients admitted after a suicide attempt and 30 healthy volunteers	No significant difference between 5 suicidal and 14 nonsuicidal depressed patients. The nondepressed suicidal patients did not differ from controls

Table 2. (continued)

Author	Subjects	Index	Result
Banki et al. 1984	141 female psychiatric inpatients	Cortisol/CSF	No difference between 18 violent, 34 nonviolent recent suicide attempters and nonattempters
Secunda et al. 1986	132 depressed patients	Cortisol/CSF	No difference between 19 current suicide attempters and 34 nonattempters
Meltzer et al. 1984b	47 major affective disorder psychiatric inpatients	5-HTP challenge[b]	The mean peak-minus base line serum cortisol response to 5-HTP of the 7 suicide attempters was significantly greater than that of the 33 who had not attempted suicide

[a] 17-Hydroxy-corticosteroids in urine.
[b] 5-Hydroxytryptophan, 200 mg orally.

patients. Although the reason for this discrepancy is not obvious, it may be relevant that Ågren (1981) found that base line plasma TSH correlated in different directions with different suicide scales from the Schedule for Affective Disorders and Schizophrenia (SADS) inventory in his large group of patients with major depressive disorders.

Biological Correlates of Suicidal Behavior — Autopsy Studies of Suicide Victims

In the light of the biological findings in suicide attempters, there has been an upsurge in the interest in autopsy studies of suicide victims. The results of the studies performed during the 1960s and early 1970s of serotonin and 5-HIAA in suicide brains are conflicting, presumably due to the difficulties in finding adequate controls matched for such factors as time of death, drug treatment, and agonal state. The general trend would, however, seem to be that slightly lower concentrations of the parent amine were often found in suicide brains. Of particular interest is the report from Lloyd and coworkers (1974) of a significantly lower concentration of serotonin in some, but not all of the raphe nuclei in the brainstem where the serotonin neurons of the brain originate. The advantage of studying relatively discrete brain regions was also demonstrated by the study of Korpi and coworkers (1986), who found *lower* serotonin content in the hypothalamus and *higher* serotonin content in the basal ganglia from suicide victims compared with controls.

Receptor binding sites seem to be less vulnerable to decomposition after death, and there have been several studies of the binding of imipramine, serotonin, and other relevant ligands to brain membranes from suicide victims. Although not all investigators agree, there is a tendency for the number of imipramine binding sites to be reduced, while the number of serotonin-2 receptors is, if anything, increased (for summary, see Åsberg et al. 1987).

Of particular interest but difficult to explain in terms of reduced release of serotonin in suicidal individuals is the finding by Kauert and coworkers (1984 and the present volume) of *increased* concentration of serotonin in CSF from suicide victims. It is, however, matched by the report from Gjerris and coworkers (1986) of increased CSF serotonin in depressive disorders and suggests that the disturbance of serotonin transmission seen in this illness may have a more complicated explanation than previously thought.

Biological Markers and Suicide Risk

Those who commit suicide and those who attempt it are well-known to differ in many important respects, even if there is an overlap between the two populations. The mortality from suicide within a year after a suicide attempt is usually around 2% (Ettlinger 1975). Although this is a substantial increase compared with the population rate, completed suicide remains a rare event even in this group. The low base rate is probably one of the reasons why attempts to create instruments for the prediction of individual suicides have largely been failures (cf. Pokorny 1983; Burk et al. 1985; Cohen 1986).

There is some evidence, however, that biological measures may help to define a group of suicide attempters where the risk of completed suicide is very much higher. Thus, in the follow-up study by Träskman and coworkers (1981), the 1-year mortality from suicide was 22% in those psychiatric inpatients who had made a suicide attempt and had a CSF 5-HIAA below the median of the attempter group. Very similar findings have been reported by Roy and coworkers (1986), who also underline the predictive power of low CSF concentrations of HVA.

The prevalence of suicide in this group is so high that special suicide precautions may be warranted whenever a patient of this type appears in the clinic. It is, however, by no means clear exactly how these patients should be treated. It is somewhat discouraging to note that the high suicide mortality was found regardless of the antidepressant treatment given to the patients, and it is clear that some innovations in treatment are badly needed for this group. There is yet no compelling evidence that serotonin-uptake inhibitors should be particularly effective in patients with low CSF 5-HIAA (cf. review by Åsberg et al. 1986), although they may have the advantage of being relatively atoxic in overdose.

Genetics of Sucide

The consistent finding of a relationship with certain biological variables suggests the possibility of a genetic basis for some cases of suicide. The genetic studies of suicide have been reviewed by Rainer (1984), who concluded that, on the whole, the empirical evidence does not favor a genetic hypothesis. A family history of suicide is found more often than expected among those who attempt or commit suicide (Roy 1983). This is usually explained as a consequence of psychological identification and of a shared genetic vulnerability to depressive illness.

Strong evidence in favor of a genetic component has, however, recently emerged from the series of adoption studies performed in collaboration between Danish and American investigators. Thus, Kety and coworkers (1975) and Schulsinger (1972) found a significantly increased prevalence of suicide in biological relatives of adoptees with schizophrenia and psychopathy, respectively, when compared with biological relatives of adopted, matched healthy controls. Wender et al. (1986) reported a 15-fold increase in suicide in biological relatives of adoptees with depressive disorders compared with controls. Schulsinger et al. (1979), starting from 57 identified suicide victims who had been adopted, reported a significant increase in suicide mortality in the biological relatives compared with adopted relatives and controls, regardless of whether the suicide victims had a psychiatric diagnosis or not.

Toward a Psychobiology of Suicide

The evidence that associates suicidal behavior with biological variables has grown impressively over the last 10 years. Although many of the findings are in apparent conflict, some quite clear lines may be discerned and perhaps also the contours of an emerging picture.

The most reproducible and impressive evidence concerns two factors, namely, serotonin neurotransmission and the regulation of cortisol secretion. These are likely to be relatively independent and associated with suicide via different mechanisms.

The HPA activation and the resulting cortisol hypersecretion, and the abnormal reaction to dexamethasone, may be related to emotional pain and failing defenses, as originally suggested by Bunney and co-workers. In animals, hypercortisolism accompanies defeat and submission (Henry and Stephens 1978). Defeat and submission is also accompanied by decreasing testosterone levels in male animals (Rose et al. 1971; Keverne et al. 1982) and in men (Elias 1982), and interestingly, Mason and co-workers (1984) reported a dramatic decrease in plasma testosterone in three psychiatric patients who shortly afterward committed suicide by violent methods.

Support for the stress hypothesis of abnormal DST was provided by Ceuleman and coworkers (1985), who found almost 50% abnormal DSTs immediately prior to surgery for herniated discs in otherwise healthy, nondepressed individuals. The nonsuppressors had higher scores in state, but not in trait anxiety inventories, suggesting that anticipatory anxiety may indeed have been related to the HPA activation.

If the HPA activation reflects the emotional suffering and subjective helplessness associated with depressive illness, the relationship with suicide makes intuitive sense. The abnormal DST may function as an alert signal that the emotional pain is approaching unbearable levels.

A low CSF 5-HIAA is a different matter. Low concentrations of the metabolite occur in mentally healthy people who have never been depressed or seriously contemplated suicide. The low concentrations are, however, connected with a family history of depressive illness, and there is evidence that they reflect a *vulnerability* to illness, rather than the illness state itself.

If the low CSF 5-HIAA reflects a more or less enduring trait, it might be interesting to search for intervening variables in temperament or personality features. The importance of serotonin for regulation of certain aggressive behaviors in animals, and the association initially postulated by Freud and the classic psychoanalysts (cf. Abraham 1927) between aggression and suicide, led to the suggestion by Åsberg and coworkers (1976) that dysregulation of aggression might be important.

In line with this hypothesis, Linnoila and coworkers (1983) and Lidberg and coworkers (1984, 1985) found an association between low CSF 5-HIAA and violent crime (unpremeditated homicide). Virkkunen and coworkers (1987) found low concentrations of 5-HIAA in another criminal behavior, thought to be more closely connected with failing impulse control than with aggression as such, namely, arson. Associations have been found between impulsiveness measured by questionnaires and low 5-HIAA in psychiatric patients. In normal young men, low CSF 5-HIAA was associated with dominance, lack of fear, and easily aroused and expressed anger (Åsberg et al. 1987).

A low output serotonin system (or perhaps more likely, a poorly regulated or low stability system) may thus be a factor which may render an individual more vulnerable to impulsive action, of a self-destructive or aggressive nature, in times of crisis. Although there is some evidence of a constitutional basis of this vulnerability, it may also be acquired. There is, for instance, evidence from animal studies that serotonin activity may be changed by environmental stimuli [cf. Anisman and coworkers' studies of the effects on the monoamine systems of learned helplessness in rats (1980) and Valzelli's studies of the reduced serotonin turnover during isolation-induced aggression in mice (1981)].

Research Priorities

The findings reviewed above suggest several lines for further research. There is, for instance, a need for new, more easily accessible serotonin markers that could be used in a clinical setting. 5-HIAA measurements require hospitalization and highly standardized procedures, and above all, the patient must not be taking antidepressant or neuroleptic drugs when the test is performed. There is furthermore a need to understand in detail what aspects of the serotonin system are reflected by the different markers. How do we, for instance, explain the high levels of the parent amine in CSF from suicide victims against the background of low levels of its metabolite in suicide attempters? What is the relationship, if any, between platelet markers such as MAO activity and the corresponding brain MAO activity? What do imipramine binding sites reflect, in the periphery and in the brain, and why do they seem to be altered in different directions in suicidal individuals?

There is also a need to study high risk groups longitudinally and in great detail. The high-risk strategy is the obvious solution to the problem of prospective studies of rare events, but they are time- and effort-consuming and place the investigator in the dilemma of having a moral obligation to do his best to prevent the occurrence of that which he intends to study.

The potential rewards of such studies are, however, also obvious since a better understanding of links between biology and suicide may open up new approaches to the prevention of suicide. Serotonin transmission can be manipulated, with drugs but perhaps also with dietary changes, and it would seem important to test treatment regimens intended to potentiate serotonin function in patients with a high suicide potential. It is also plausible that an increased understanding of the psychological processes that are controlled by serotonin neurons could be used to create more focused psychotherapeutic interventions than have hitherto been available for work with the suicide-prone patient.

Acknowledgement. The secretarial assistance of Marie Skjöldebrand is gratefully acknowledged.

References

Abraham K (1927) Versuch einer Entwicklungsgeschichte der Libido auf Grund der Psychoanalyse seelischer Störungen. In: Neue Arbeiten zur ärztlichen Psychoanalyse, vol 2, Internationaler Psychoanalytischer Verlag, Leipzig

Ågren H (1980) Symptom patterns in unipolar and bipolar depression correlating with monoamine metabolites in the cerebrospinal fluid: II. Suicide. Psychiatry Res 3:225−236

Ågren H (1981) Biological markers in major depressive disorders. A clinical and multivariate study. Thesis, Acta Univ Upsaliensis, abstracts of Uppsala, dissertations from the faculty of medicine 405, Uppsala

Ågren H (1983) Life at risk: markers of suicidality in depression. Psychiatric Developments 1:87−104

Anisman H, Pizzino A, Sklar LS (1980) Coping with stress, norepinephrine depletion and escape performance. Brain Res 191:583−588

Arato M, Rihmer Z, Banki CM, Grof P (1983) The relationships of neuroendocrine tests in endogenous depression. Prog Neuro-Psychopharmacol Biol Psychiatry 7:715−718

Åsberg M, Bertilsson L (1979) Serotonin in depressive illness − studies of CSF 5-HIAA. In: Saletu B (ed) Neuropsychopharmacology. Pergamon, Oxford, pp 105−115

Asberg M, Wägner A (1986) Biochemical effects of antidepressant treatment − studies of monoamine metabolites in cerebrospinal fluid and platelet 3H-imipramine binding. In: Porter R, Bock G, Clark S (eds) Antidepressants and receptor function. Wiley, Chichester (Ciba Foundation symposium No 123), pp 57−83

Asberg M, Träskman L, Thoren P (1976) 5-HIAA in the cerebrospinal fluid: a biochemical suicide predictor? Arch Gen Psychiatry 33:1193−1197

Åsberg M, Bertilsson L, Rydin E, Schalling D, Thorén P, Träskman-Bendz L (1981) Monoamine metabolites in cerebrospinal fluid in relation to depressive illness, suicidal behaviour and personality. In: Angrist B, Burrows G, Lader M, Lingjaerde O, Sedvall G, Wheatley D (eds) Recent advances in neuropsycho-pharmacology. Adv Bio Sci 31:257−271

Åsberg M, Eriksson B, Mårtensson B, Träskman-Bendtz L, Wägner A (1986) Therapeutic effects of serotonin uptake inhibitors in depression. J Clin Psychiatry 47 (4 Suppl):23−35

Åsberg M, Schalling D, Träskman-Bendz L, Wägner A (1987) Psychobiology of suicide, impulsivity and related phenomena. In: Meltzer HY (ed) Psychopharmacology, the third generation of process. Raven, New York, pp 655−668

Banki CM, Arato M (1983) Amine metabolites and neuroendocrine responses related to depression and suicide. J Affective Disord 5:223−232

Banki CM, Arato M, Papp Z, Kurcz M (1984) Biochemical markers in suicidal patients. Investigations with cerebrospinal fluid amine metabolites and neuroendocrine tests. J Affective Disord 6:341−350

Banki CM, Vojnik M, Papp Z, Balla KZ, Arato M (1985) Cerebrospinal fluid magnesium and calcium related to amine metabolites, diagnosis and suicide attempts. Biol Psychiatry 20:163−171

Beck-Friis J, Kjellman BF, Aperia B, Undén F, von Rosen D, Ljunggren JG, Wetterberg L (1985) Serum melatonin in relation to clinical variables in patients with major depressive disorder and a hypothesis of a low melatonin syndrome. Acta Psychiatr Scand 71:319−330

Beckman H, Wetterberg L, Gattaz WF (1984) Melatonin immunoreactivity in cerebrospinal fluid of schizophrenic patients and healthy controls. Psychiatry Res 11:107−110

Berger M, Pirke KM, Doerr P, Krieg JC, von Zerssen D (1984) The limited utility of the dexamethasone suppression test for the diagnostic process in psychiatry. Br J Psychiatry 145:372−382

Bertilsson L, Åsberg M, Thorén P (1974) Differential effects of chlorimipramine and nortriptyline on cerebrospinal fluid metabolites of serotonin and noradrenaline in depression. Eur J Clin Pharmacol 7:365−368

Brooksbank BWL, Brammall MA, Cunningham AE, Shaw DM, Damps FE (1972) Estimation of corticosteroids in human cerebral cortex after death by suicide, accident, or disease. Psychol Med 2:56−65

Brown GL, Goodwin FK, Ballenger JC, Goyer PF, Major LF (1979) Aggression in humans correlates with cerebrospinal fluid metabolites. Psychiatry Res 1:131−139

Brown GL, Ebert MH, Goyer PF, Jimerson DC, Klein WJ, Bunney WE, Goodwin FK (1982) Aggression, suicide, and serotonin: relationships to CSF amine metabolites. Am J Psychiatry 139:741–746

Brown RP, Mason B, Stoll P, Brizer D, Kocsis J, Stokes PE, Mann JJ (1986) Adrenocortical function and suicidal behavior in depressive disorders. Psychiatry Res 17:317–323

Buchsbaum MS, Coursey RD, Murphy DL (1976) The biochemical high-risk paradigm: behavioral and familial correlates of low platelet monoamine oxidase activity. Science 194:339–341

Bulat M, Zivkovic B (1971) Origin of 5-hydroxyindoleacetic acid in the spinal fluid. Science 173:738–740

Bunney WE Jr, Mason JW, Roatch JF, Hamburg DA (1965) A Psychoendocrine study of severe psychotic depressive crisis. Am J Psychiatry 122:72–80

Bunney WE Jr, Fawcett JA, Davis JM, Gifford S (1969) Further evaluation of urinary 17-hydroxycorticosteroids in suicidal patients. Arch Gen Psychiatry 21:138–150

Bürk F, Kurz A, Möller HJ (1985) Suicide risk scales: do they help to predict suicidal behaviour? Eur Arch Psychiatry Neurol Sci 235:153–157

Carroll BJ (1982) The dexamethasone suppression test for melancholia. Br J Psychiatry 140:292–304

Carroll BJ, Greden JF, Feinberg M (1981) Suicide, neuroendocrine dysfunction and CSF 5-HIAA concentrations in depression. In: Angrist B, Burrows G, Lader M, Lingjaerde O, Sedvall G, Wheatley D (eds) Recent Advances in Neuropsychopharmacology. Advances in the Bio-Sciences 31:307–313

Ceuleman DLS, Westenberg HGM, van Praag HM (1985) The effect of stress on the dexamethasone suppression test. Psychiatry Res 14:189–195

Chabrol H, Claverie J, Moron P (1983) DST, TRH test, and adolescent suicide attempts. Am J Psychiatry 140:265

Cohen J (1986) Statistical approaches to suicidal risk-factor analysis. In: Mann JJ, Stanley M (eds) The Psychobiology of Suicidal Behavior. Ann NY Acad Sci 487:34–41

Coryell W, Schlesser MA (1981) Suicide and the dexamethasone suppression test in unipolar depression. Am J Psychiatry 138:1120–1121

Edman G, Åsberg M, Levander S, Schalling D (1986) Skin conductance habitation and cerebrospinal fluid 5-hydroxyindoleacetic acid in suicidal patients. Arch Gen Psychiatry 43:586–592

Elias M (1982) Serum cortisol, testosterone and testosterone-binding globulin responses to competitive fighting in human males. Aggressive Behav 7:215–224

Ennis J, Barnes RA, Kennedy S (1985) The dexamethasone suppression test and suicidal patients. Br J Psychiatry 147:419–423

Ettlinger R (1975) Evaluation of suicide prevention after attempted suicide. Acta Psychiatr Scand [Suppl] 260

Farberow NL, Shneidman ES (1961) The cry for help. McGraw-Hill, New York

Fink EB, Carpenter WT Jr (1976) Further examination of a biochemical test for suicide potential. Dis Nerv Syst 37:341–343

Gjerris A, Christensen NJ, Linnoila M, Rafaelsen OJ (1986) Amines and their metabolites in cerebrospinal fluid (CSF) in depression. Clin Neuropharmacol 9 (suppl 4):72–73

Gottfries CG, von Knorring L, Oreland L (1980) Platelet monoamine oxidase activity in mental disorders: 2. Affective psychosis and suicidal behavior. Prog Neuro-Psychopharmacol 4:185–192

Greden JF, Albala AA, Haskett RF, James NM, Goodman L, Steiner M, Carroll BJ (1980) Normalization of dexamethasone suppression test: a laboratory index of recovery from endogenous depression. Biol Psychiatry 15:449–458

Henry JP, Stephens PM (1978) Stress, health and the social environment. Springer, Berlin Heidelberg New York

Holsboer F, Haack D, Gerken A, Wecsei P (1984) Plasma dexamethasone concentrations and differential suppression response of cortisol and corticosterone in depressives and controls. Biol Psychiatry 19:281–293

Kauert G, Gilg T, Eisenmenger W, Spann W (1984) Post mortem biogenic amines in CSF of suicides and controls. Presented to the Collegium Internationale Neuro-Psychopharmacologicum at its 14th Congress in Florence 1984

Kety SS, Rosenthal D, Wender PH, Schulsinger F, Jacobsen B (1975) Mental illness in the biological and adopted families of adopted individuals who have become schizophrenic: a preliminary report based on psychiatric interviews. In: Fieve RR, Rosenthal D, Brill H (eds) Genetic Research in Psychiatry. The Johns Hopkins University Press, Baltimore, pp 147 – 165

Keverne EB, Meller RE, Eberhart JA (1982) Social influences on behavior and neuroendocrine responsiveness in Talapoin monkeys. Scand J Psychol suppl 1:37 – 47

Kjellman BF, Ljunggren JG, Beck-Friis J, Wetterberg L (1985) Effect of TRH on TSH and prolactin levels in affective disorders. Psychiatry Res 14:353 – 363

Korpi ER, KLeinman JE, Goodman SI, Phillips I, DeLisi LE, Linnoila M, Wyatt RJ (1986) Serotonin and 5-hydroxyindolacetic acid in brains of suicide victims. Comparisons in chronic schizophrenic patients with suicide as cause of death. Arch Gen Psychiatry 43:594 – 600

Krieger G (1974) The plasma level of cortisol as a predictor of suicide. Dis Nerv Syst 35:237 – 240

Leckman JF, Charney DS, Nelson CR, Heninger GR, Bowers MB Jr (1981) CSF tryptophan, 5-HIAA and HVA in 132 patients characterized by diagnosis and clinical state. Rec Adv Neuropsychopharmacol 31:289 – 297

Levy B, Hansen E (1969) Failure of the test for suicide potential. Analysis of urinary 17-OHCS steroid findings prior to suicide in two patients. Arch Gen Psychiatry 20:415 – 418

Lidberg L, Åsberg M, Sundqvist-Stensman UB (1984) 5-hydroxyindoleacetic acid levels in attempted suicides who have killed their children. Lancet II:928

Lidberg L, Tuck JR, Åsberg M, Scalia-Tomba GP, Bertilsson L (1985) Homicide, suicide and CSF 5-HIAA. Acta Psychiatr Scand 71:230 – 236

Linkowski P, van Wettere JP, Kerhofs M, Brauman H, Mendlewicz J (1983) Thyrotrophin response to thyreostimulin in affectively ill women: relationship to suicidal behaviour. Br J Psychiatry 143:401 – 504

Linkowski P, van Wettere JP, Kerhofs M, Gregoire F, Brauman H, Mendlewicz J (1984) Violent suicidal behavior and the thyrotropin-releasing hormone-thyroid-stimulating hormone test: a clinical outcome study. Neuropsychobiology 12:19 – 22

Linnoila M, Virkunnen M, Scheinin M, Nuutila A, Rimon R, Goodwin FK (1983) Low cerebrospinal fluid 5-hydroxyindoleacetic acid concentration differentiates impulsive from nonimpulsive violent behavior. Life Sci 33:2609 – 2614

Lloyd KG, Farley IJ, Deck JHN, Hornykiewicz O (1974) Serotonin and 5-hydroxyindoleacetic acid in discrete areas of the brainstem of suicide victims and control patients. In: Costa E, Gessa GL, Sandler M (eds) Serotonin: new vistas. Advances in Biochemical Psychopharmacology 11. Raven, New York, pp 387 – 397

Lopez-Ibor JJ Jr, Saiz-Ruiz J, Pérez de los Cobos JC (1985) Biological correlations of suicide and aggressivity in major depressions (with melancholia): 5-hydroxyindoleacetic acid and cortisol in cerebral spinal fluid, dexamethasone suppression test and therapeutic response to 5-hydroxytryptophan. Neuropsychobiology 14:67 – 74

Mason JW, Giller EL, Ostroff RB (1984) Relationships between psychological mechanisms and the pituitary-gonadal system. Curr Clin Practice Series 26:215 – 228

Meltzer HY, Umberkoman-Wiita B, Robertson A, Tricou BJ, Lowry M, Perline R (1984a) Effect of 5-hydroxytryptophan on serum cortisol levels in major affective disorders. I. Enhanced response in depression and mania. Arch Gen Psychiatry 41:366 – 374

Meltzer HY, Perline R, Tricou BJ, Lowy M, Robertson A (1984b) Effects of 5-hydroxytryptophan on serum cortisol levels in major affective disorders. II. Relation to suicide, psychosis, and depressive symptoms. Arch Gen Psychiatry 41:379 – 387

Montgomery SA, Montgomery D (1982) Pharmacological prevention of suicidal behaviour. J Affective Disord 4:291 – 298

Morris H, Carr V, Gilliland J, Hopper M (1986) Dexamethasone concentrations and the dexamethasone suppression test in psychiatric disorders. Br J Psychiatry 148:66 – 69

Nicoletti F, Raffaele R, Falsaperla A, Paci R (1981) Circadian variation in 5-hydroxyindoleacetic acid levels in human cerebrospinal fluid. Eur Neurol 20:834 – 838

Ninan PT, van Kammen DP, Scheinin M, Linnoila M, Bunney WE Jr, Goodwin FK (1984) CSF 5-hydroxyindoleacetic acid in suicidal schizophrenic patients. Am J Psychiatry 141:566 – 569

240   M. Åsberg and P. Nordström

Oreland L, Shaskan EG (1983) Monoamine oxidase activity as a biological marker. Trends Pharmacol Sci 4:339–341

Oreland L, von Knorring L, Schalling D (1984) Connections between monoamine oxidase, temperament and disease. In: Paton W, Mitchell J, Turner P (eds) Proc IUPHAR 9th international congress of pharmacology. Macmillan London, pp 193–202, vol 2

Ostroff R, Giller E, Bonese K, Ebersole E, Harkness L, Mason J (1982) Neuroendocrine risk factors of suicidal behavior. Am J Psychiatry 139:1323–1325

Palaniappan V, Ramachandran V, Somasundaram O (1983) Suicidal ideation and biogenic amines in depression. Indian J Psychiatry 25:286–292

Papakostas Y, Fink M, Lee J, Irwin P, Johnson L (1981) Neuroendocrine measures in psychiatric patients: course and outcome with ECT. Psychiatry Res 4:55–64

Platman SR, Plutchik R, Weinstein B (1971) Psychiatric, physiological, behavioral and self-report measures in relation to a suicide attempt. J Psychiatr Res 8:127–137

Pokorny AD (1983) Prediction of suicide in psychiatric patients. Arch Gen Psychiatry 40:249–257

Prange AJ Jr, Loosen PT (1984) Peptides in depression. In: Usdin E, Åsberg M, Bertilsson L, Sjöqvist F (eds) Frontiers in biochemical and pharmacological research in depression. Advances in Biochemical Psychopharmacology 39. Raven, New York, pp 127–145

Pradad AJ (1985) Neuroendocrine differences between violent and non-violent parasuicides. Neuropsychobiology 13:157–159

Rainer JD (1984) Genetic factors in depression and suicide. Am J Psychother 38:329–340

Robbins DR, Alessi NE (1985) Suicide and the dexamethasone suppression test in adolescence. Biol Psychiatry 20:94–119

Rose RM, Holaday JW, Bernstein IS (1971) Plasma testosterone, dominance rank and aggressive behaviour in male rhesus monkeys. Nature 231:366–368

Roy A (1983) Family history of suicide. Arch Gen Psychiatry 40:971–974

Roy A, Ninan P, Mazonson A, Pickar D, van Kammen D, Linnoila M, Paul SM (1985) CSF monoamine metabolites in chronic schizophrenic patients who attempt suicide. Psychol Medicine 15:335–340

Roy A, Ågren H, Pickar D, Linnoila M, Doran AR, Cutler NR, Paul SM (1986) Reduced CSF concentrations of homovanillic acid and homovanillic acid to 5-hydroxyindoleacetic acid ratios in depressed patients: relationship to suicidal behavior and dexamethasone nonsuppression. Am J Psychiatry 143:1539–1545

Roy-Byrne P, Post RM, Rubinow DR, Linnoila M, Savard R, Davis D (1983) CSF 5-HIAA and personal and family history of sucide in affectively ill patients: a negative study. Psychiatry Res 10:263–274

Schulsinger F (1972) Psychopathy: Heredity and environment. Int J Ment Health 1:190–206

Schulsinger F, Kety SS, Rosenthal D, Wender PH (1979) A family study of suicide. In: Schou M, Strömgren E (eds) Origin, prevention and treatment of affective disorders. Academic, London, pp 277–287

Secunda SK, Cross CK, Koslow S, Katz MM, Kocsis J, Maas JW, Landis H (1986) Biochemistry and suicidal behavior in depressed patients. Biol Psychiatry 21:756–767

Stanley M, Träskman-Bendz L, Dorovini-Zis K (1985) Correlations between aminergic metabolites simultaneously obtained from human CSF and brain. Life Sci 37:1279–1286

Targum SD, Rosen L, Capodanno AE (1983) The dexamethasone suppression test in suicidal patients with unipolar depression. Am J Psychiatry 140:877–879

Träskman L, Tybring G, Åsberg M, Bertilsson L, Lantto O, Schalling D (1980) Cortisol in the CSF of depressed and suicidal patients. Arch Gen Psychiatry 37:761–767

Träskman L, Åsberg M, Bertilsson L, Sjöstrand L (1981) Monoamine metabolites in CSF and suicidal behavior. Arch Gen Psychiatry 38:631–636

Valzelli L (1981) Psychobiology of aggression and violence. Raven, New York

van Praag HM (1982) Depression, suicide and the metabolism of serotonin in the brain. J Affective Disord 4:275–290

van Praag HM (1983) CSF 5-HIAA and suicide in non-depressed schizophrenics. Lancet II:977–978

van Wettere JP, Charles G, Wilmotte J (1983) Test de freination à la dexaméthasone et suicide. Acta Psychiatr Belg 83:569–578

Virkunnen M, Nuutila A, Goodwin FK, Linnoila M (1987) Cerebrospinal fluid monoamine metabolite levels in male arsonists. Arch Gen Psychiatry 44:241−247

Wägner A, Åberg-Widstedt A, Åsberg M, Ekqvist B, Mårtensson B, Montero D (1985) Lower ^{3}H-imipramine binding in platelets from untreated depressed patients compared to healthy controls. Psychiatry Res 16:131−139

Wender PH, Kety SS, Rosenthal D, Schulsinger F, Ortmann J, Lunde I (1986) Psychiatric disorders in the biological and adoptive families of adopted individuals with affective disorders. Arch Gen Psychiatry 43:923−929

Wilmotte J, van Wettere JP, Depauw Y, Charles G (1986) Tests de freination à la dexamethasone repètes apres une tentative de suicide. Acta Psychiatr Belg 86:242−248

Yerevanian BI, Olafsdottir H, Milanese E, Russotto J, Mallon P, Baciewicz G, Sagi E (1983) Normalization of the dexamethasone suppression test at discharge from hospital. Its prognostic value. J Affective Disord 5:191−197

Zimmerman M, Coryell W, Pfohl B (1986) The validity of the dexamethasone suppression test as a marker for endogenous depression. Arch Gen Psychiatry 43:347−355

Postmortem Neurochemical Investigation of Suicide

M. ARATÓ, A. FALUS, P. SÓTONYI, E. SOMOGYI, L. TÓTHFALUSI, K. MAGYAR, H. AKIL, and S. J. WATSON

Introduction

Several neurochemical mechanisms can be implicated in suicidal behavior — not as causal factors but rather as biological components of this very complex phenomenon. Most investigators have measured levels of various monoamine metabolites and hormones in body fluids of suicide attempters only. However, completed suicide and attempted suicide have been shown to be statistically distinct on demographic and diagnostic grounds. Another shortcoming of these studies is the various time intervals between the suicidal act and the timing of sampling. In this way, only permanent neurochemical abnormalities could be detected — trait markers. With postmortem sampling shortly after death, we can obtain more accurate information about the actual condition of the central nervous and endocrine systems at the time of death. Encouraged by a recent study (Stanley et al. 1985) and our own preliminary findings (Arató et al. 1985a), we have tried to use postmortem measurements as a new research tool to explore the neurochemical background of suicides.

Three different systems were investigated:

1. Serotonin metabolism by measuring CSF levels of 5-hydroxyindoleacetic acid (5-HIAA). Serotonin is called the "civilizing neurohormone" which inhibits hetero/autoaggression. Reduced serotonin turnover has been repeatedly reported in suicide attempters, especially in violent cases (Åsberg et al. 1984; Bánki et al. 1984). Low CSF 5-HIAA levels have also been found as an indicator of aggressivity and impulsivity (Brown et al. 1982; Linnoila et al. 1983).

2. Hypothalamic-pituitary-adrenal axis ("stress system"). Several studies have suggested an association between adrenal axis dysregulation and suicidial behavior (Bunney and Fawcett 1965; Krieger 1974).

3. Endogenous opioid regulation by measuring CSF levels of β-endorphin. The opiates as endogenous analgesics of physical and psychic pain may also have a role in suicidal behavior. As far as we know, this is the first attempt to investigate this postulated relationship.

Study

We obtained postmortem CSF samples within the first few hours after death from 22 suicide victims as well as from controls (sudden natural and accidental death). The two groups were comparable regarding sex, age, postmortem in-

Table 1. Subjects characteristics

Suicides				Controls		
Age	Suicide method	PMI[a]		Age	Cause of death	PMI[a]
Males						
44	Hanging	5		25	Traffic accident	6
53	Hanging	6		66	Acute cardiac death	6
59	Hanging	3		39	Acute cardiac death	6
44	Hanging	6		52	Acute cardiac death	7
21	Hanging	3		30	Acute cardiac death	8
53	Hanging	7		69	Acute cardiac death	5
38	Hanging	8		72	Acute cardiac death	3
65	Hanging	7		58	Acute cardiac death	8
28	Hanging	8		54	Acute cardiac death	5
43	Hanging	7		49	Acute cardiac death	3
51	Hanging	8		72	Acute cardiac death	4
66	Hanging	8		47	Acute cardiac death	7
78	Hanging	5		58	Acute cardiac death	6
33	Cutting	7		62	Acute cardiac death	6
53	Drug OD	6		67	Acute cardiac death	6
39	Drug OD	8		21	Aorta rupture	5
Females						
59	Hanging	8		35	Traffic accident	4
37	Hanging	7		54	Traffic accident	5
80	Jumping	3		65	Traffic accident	5
26	Drug OD	6		78	Acute cardiac death	2
38	Drug OD	4		44	Acute cardiac death	3
47	Drug OD	6		24	Acute cardiac death	8

[a] Postmortem interval in hours.

terval, and clock time of death (see Table 1). The sampling was done by suboccipital cisternal puncture, and the first 10 ml divided in aliquots was used for neurochemical measurements.

5-HIAA levels were measured by HPLC using electrochemical detection (Palfreyman et al. 1982). Cortisol was determined by a competitive protein-binding method (Murphy 1967), and adrenocorticotropic hormone (ACTH) concentrations by a CIS-SORIN radioimmunoassay kit. β-endorphin immunoreactivity was assayed using a validated radioimmunoassay (Cahill et al. 1983) in Ann Arbor, MI.

Results

The cortisol and ACTH results are shown in Fig. 1. In agreement with the study of Träskman et al. (1980) and with our previous investigations (Arató et al. 1985b), CSF cortisol levels did not differ between suicides and controls. There was no difference between the groups in CSF ACTH levels either. In the control group, we found high β-endorphin levels in some cases of acute cardiac death.

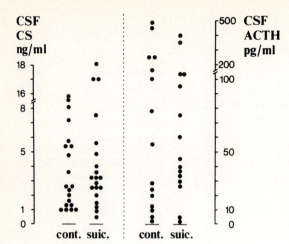

Fig. 1. Cortisol and ACTH levels in postmorten CSF from controls and suicides

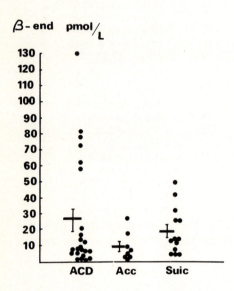

Fig. 2. β-endorphin immunoreactivity in CSF of controls (*ACD*, acute cardiac death; *Acc*, traffic accident) and suicides

The suicides, however, did not differ from the control group of sudden accidental deaths (Fig. 2).

In contrast to our expectations, we found a significantly higher mean CSF 5-HIAA value in suicides compared with the controls (Fig. 3). This finding also contradicts the results of studies on suicide attempters, but it is in good agreement with a similar postmortem study by Kauert et al. (1984) − their data are also presented in this book − which showed significantly higher serotonin levels in postmortem CSF on suicides compared with nonsuicide cases. It cannot be excluded, however, that changes in the serotonin metabolite levels are due to the metabolic changes in the brain that occur during agony. In an ongoing study, we are investigating the possible effect of various methods of suicide on

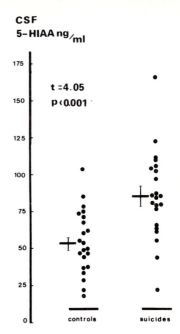

CSF
5-HIAA ng/ml

t =4.05
p‹0.001

controls   suicides

Fig. 3. 5-HIAA levels in the cisternal CSF of controls and suicides

neuroendocrine and neurochemical parameters. If our finding of an elevated serotonin turnover at the time of death is confirmed by further investigations, it could be postulated that instability instead of weakness of the serotonergic system may have a role in suicidal behavior. A reformulation of the classic monoamine deficiency hypothesis of affective disorders and related syndromes has been suggested by Siever and Davis (1985). Our data in concert with some recent studies (Träskman-Bendz et al. 1984; Roy et al. 1986) tend to support the proposed concept of dysregulation of serotonin mechanisms in suicidal behavior.

References

Arató M, Falus A, Tóthfalusi L, Magyar K, Sótonyi P, Somogyi E (1985a) Postmortem cerebrospinal fluid measurements in suicide. 13th Congress Int Acad Legal Med Soc Med, September 1985, Budapest

Arató M, Bánki CM (1985b) Hypothalamic-pituitary-adrenal axis and suicide. Conf Psychobiol Suic Behav. The New York Academy of Science, September, New York

Åsberg M, Edman G, Rydin E, Schalling D, Träskman-Bendz L, Wagner A (1984) Biological correlates of suicidal behaviour. Clin Neuropharmacol 7 (suppl 1):758−759

Bánki CM, Arató M, Papp Z, Kurcz M (1984) Biochemical markers in suicidal patients. Investigations with cerebrospinal fluid amine metabolites and neuroendocrine tests. J Affective Disord 6:341−350

Brown GL, Ebert MH, Goyer PF, Jimerson DC, Klein WJ, Bunney WE, Goodwin FK (1982) Aggression, suicide and serotonin: relationship to CSF amine metabolites. Am J Psychiatry 139:741−746

Bunney WE, Fawcett JA (1965) Possibility of a biochemical test for suicidal potential: an analysis of endocrine findings prior to three suicides. Arch Gen Psychiatry 13:232−239

Cahill CA, Matthews JD, Akil H (1983) Human plasma β-END like peptides: a rapid, high recovery extraction technique and validation of radioimmunoassay. J Clin Endocrinol Metab 56:992−997

Kauert G, Gilg T, Eisenmenger W, Spann W (1984) Postmortem biogenic amines in CSF of suicides and controls. College Int Neuro-Psychopharmacol 1984, Florence

Krieger G (1974) The plasma level or cortisol as a predictor of suicide. Dis Nerv Syst 35:237−240

Linnoila M, Virkkunen M, Scheinin M, Muutila A, Rimon R, Goodwin FK (1983) Low cerebrospinal fluid 5-hydroxyindolacetic acid concentration differentiates impulsive from nonimpulsive violent behaviour. Life Sci 33:2609−2614

Murphy BEP (1967) Some studies of the protein-binding of steroids and their application to the routine micro and ultra-micro measurement of various steroids in body fluids by competitive protein-binding radioassay. J Clin Endocrinol Metab 27:973−990

Palfreyman MG, Huout S, Wagner J (1982) Value of monoamine metabolite determinations in CSF as an index of their concentrations in rat brain. J Pharmacol Methods 8:183−196

Roy A, Pickar D, Linnoila M, Doran AR, Paul SM (1986) Cerebrospinal fluid monoamine and monoamine metabolite levels and the dexamethasone suppression test in depression. Arch Gen Psychiatry 43:356−360

Siever LJ, Davis KL (1985) Overview: toward a dysregulation hypothesis of depression. Am J Psychiatry 142:1017−1031

Stanley M, Träskman-Bendz L, Dorovin-Zis K (1985) Correlation between aminergic metabolites simultaneously obtained from human CSF and brain. Life Sci 37:1279−1286

Träskman L, Tybing G, Åsberg M, Bertilsson L, Lantto O, Schalling D (1980) Cortisol in the CSF of depressed and suicidal patients. Arch Gen Psychiatry 37:761−767

Träskman-Bendz L, Åsberg M, Bertilsson L, Thoren P (1984) CSF monoamine metabolites of depressed patients during illness and after recovery. Acta Psychiatr Scand 69:332−342

Corticotropin-Releasing Factor in Depression and Suicide

C. M. Banki, G. Bissette, C. B. Nemeroff, and M. Arató

Introduction

Hypothalamic-pituitary-adrenocortical (HPA) axis hyperactivity is one of the most consistent findings in major depression (Carroll 1982; Halbreich et al. 1985; Carroll 1985). However, the regulation of HPA activity in humans is highly complex, and the mechanism of cortisol overproduction together with impaired suppressibility by exogenous steroids is far from being understood. One possibility is a primary overproduction of the principal adrenocorticotropic hormone (ACTH)-stimulating hypothalamic substance: corticotropin-releasing factor (CRF), a 41-amino acid peptide isolated and characterized by Vale et al. (1981). At present there are two lines of evidence favoring this hypothesis: first, Gold et al. (1984) showed that depressed patients responded with a lower ACTH rise to intravenously administered CRF than nondepressed patients or healthy controls, consistent with a down regulation of the pituitary CRF receptors. Second, our group reported that in psychiatric patient groups from different countries (including the USA, Sweden, and Hungary) there was a fairly specific increase in lumbar CSF CRF concentration in subjects with major unipolar and bipolar depression compared with other diagnostic groups (schizophrenia, senile dementia, anxiety disorders, etc.) or with healthy controls (Nemeroff et al. 1984; Bissette et al. 1985).

Since earlier studies on CSF monoamine metabolites raised the question of whether the changes observed were due to the presence of a major depressive syndrome or to a more specific symptom or behavior such as suicide (Träskman et al. 1981; Van Praag 1984; Banki et al. 1984), our interest in this study was aimed at separating two possible sources of variance in CRF concentrations in CSF of patients with psychiatric disorders, namely, major depression and actual suicide attempts shortly before admission.

Patients and Methods

A relatively large group of psychiatric inpatients from a Hungarian mental hospital were studied. One hundred thirty-eight subjects were from a neurological unit consisting of 65 males and 73 females, with a mean age of 42.4 ± 13.0 years and no difference between the sexes; they had various peripheral neurological disorders but no primary CNS disease such as Parkinson's disease, multiple sclerosis, or epilepsy. None of them had any major psychiatric disorder, but 28 female patients had mild adjustment disorders or generalized anxiety disorders as identified by Diagnostic and Statistical Manual (DSM III) criteria, and 27 males had abused alcohol before admission.

Fifty-four patients (all but one females) had major depression and 17 of them also met criteria for melancholia while 26 others had psychotic features. Four females were in a manic phase of their bipolar disorder; finally, 23 female patients had a schizophrenic disorder excluding schizo-affective conditions. All patients were tested for any major medical illness and pregnancy before inclusion. They had been free from antidepressant, neuroleptic, or anticonvulsant medication for at least 2 weeks and free from lithium or steroid hormones for at least 6 months before admission.

Twenty-two female patients were hospitalized following a recent (within 1 week) suicide attempt using either violent ($n = 8$) or nonviolent (psychotropic drug overdose, $n = 14$) methods. Seventeen of the attempters had major depression, two had schizophrenia, and three had an adjustment disorder without symptoms fulfilling criteria for major depression. The attempter group was not different from the non-attempters regarding age, number and duration of previous treatments, body measures (weight, height, etc.), or other clinical variables.

After obtaining informed consents, lumbar punctures were performed after controlled fast and bed rest at $9:00 - 10:00$ a.m., and the first 6-ml sample was used for CRF assay. The samples were stored and transported on dry ice within 4 months to the United States. The CRF-like immunoreactivity was measured by a sensitive and specific radioimmunoassay using the antiserum provided by Dr. Wylie Wale from the Salk Institute, La Jolla, CA (Nemeroff et al. 1984).

Results

As reported earlier there was no significant relationship between the CSF concentration of CRF immunoreactivity and several background variables such as age, body weight, height, duration of illness, and days of hospitalization in this reasonably sized population. No difference between males and females could be detected: males had a mean concentration of 40.9 ± 14.3 pg/ml and females 40.6 ± 12.2 pg/ml in the neurological subgroup.

Minor psychiatric disorders in the same group appeared to be largely without effect on the mean CSF concentration of CRF: those with a history of alcohol abuse had 38.6 ± 16.1 pg/ml and those with anxiety disorders 43.3 ± 17.3 pg/ml; in subjects without any symptoms, 40.8 ± 12.2 pg/ml was found.

Manic patients ($n = 4$) had mean CSF CRF levels almost identical to controls: 42.9 ± 15.9 pg/ml. The schizophrenic subgroup showed a moderate, although statistically significant elevation with a mean concentration of 57.8 ± 30.0 pg/ml. Patients with major depression had markedly elevated CRF levels in their CSF, their mean being almost twice as high as the controls: 80.1 ± 51.9 pg/ml; this group was also significantly higher compared with the schizophrenics ($P < .001$, Newman-Keuls test following ANOVA, corrected for unequal sample sizes).

On the other hand, there were no major differences among subgroups separated according to the presence and type of the previous suicide attempts (Table 1). Because of the established difference between depressed and non-depressed patients, the comparison was made within major depression and non-depressed patients separately by a nested ANOVA design: the difference between the diagnostic groups was significant as shown above [$F(1,3) = 17.65$; $P < .05$] but the difference between suicidal and non-suicidal patients within the main groups was not [$F(3.177) = 0.89$; NS]. Similarly there was no difference whatsoever between the violent and nonviolent attempters (see Table 1).

Standard 1-mg dexamethasone suppression tests (DST) were carried out following the CSF investigation in the psychiatric patients; 21 depressed patients, 6 schizophrenics, and 1 manic patient failed to suppress below 5 µg/ml at both 8:00 a.m. and 15:00 p.m. after dexamethasone. Surprisingly, there was no correlation between postdexamethasone plasma cortisol and CSF CRF immunoreactivity at either 8:00 a.m. or 15:00 p.m. ($r = 0.11$ and 0.13, respectively). The DST results did not correlate with the suicide attempts.

Finally, we performed a multivariate regression analysis to quantify the effects of age, sex, depression, and suicide on the CSF CRF concentration (Table 2). This was made including only the subjects having psychiatric symptoms (i.e., omitting the neurological controls without any psychiatric disorders), just as we did when comparing suicidal and nonsuicidal patients. In the patient group, age and sex together explained only 6.6% of the CSF CRF variance; the presence of major depression added another 7% which was statistically significant, but the addition of suicide did not improve this regression further.

Table 1. CSF CRF immunoreactivity in psychiatric patients with an without suicide behavior. Values are mean $\pm$ SD (pg/ml)

Depression ($n = 54$):	Violent suicide attempt ($n = 8$)	74.5 ± 55.2
	Nonviolent attempt ($n = 10$)	78.9 ± 64.1
	No suicidal behavior ($n = 36$)	81.3 ± 57.3
Nondepressed ($n = 81$)	Violent suicide attempt ($n = 1$)	44
	Nonviolent attempt ($n = 4$)	48.2 ± 39.8
	No suicidal behavior ($n = 76$)	47.9 ± 30.4

Table 2. Multiple regression analysis of CSF CRF immunoreactivity on clinical factors

Factor	R^2	F	P	R^2 increase	F	P
Age	0.003	0.21	NS	–		
Sex	0.066	2.33	NS	0.063	3.45	NS
Depression	0.135	3.38	$< .05$	0.069	5.18	$< .0.5$
Suicide	0.136	2.52	$< .0.5$	0.001	0.07	NS

Discussion

The results from this laboratory indicate that in fact there is an overproduction of the major HPA-stimulating neuropeptide CRF within the CNS in psychiatric patients with major depression (Nemeroff et al. 1984; Bissette et al. 1985; Banki et al. 1987). The present depressive patients were all severely ill, most were psychotic or melancholic, and all were recently hospitalized inpatients; this may restrict the above conclusion to patients of this degree of severity until further studies are done on other samples. However, our schizophrenic and manic patients were equally psychotic, often with extreme agitation and marked productive symptoms while their CRF elevation in the CSF, if at all present, was significantly less pronounced.

The main conclusion from this study is that unlike certain monoamine findings (Träskman et al. 1981; Banki et al. 1984) the CSF CRF immunoreactivity appears to be unrelated to the actual suicidal behavior and is only parallel with the depressive syndrome. Other psychiatric symptoms were also investigated for their possible correlation with CRF (Banki et al. 1987), but none were found in the total group. This corresponds well with many studies made with another HPA variable, namely the DST, in depression: none of the separate symptoms, but the major (endogenous-type) depressive syndrome in its complexity appears to be related to the endocrine dysfunction.

One question to be answered in the future is why CSF CRF levels do not correlate with pre- or postdexamethasone plasma cortisol (Bissette et al. 1985). As a matter of fact, very little is known about the origin of CRF found in the lumbar CSF: immunoreactive CRF is present in several brain and spinal areas outside the hypothalamus and while the DST may reflect CRF hypersecretion in the median eminence only, there can be other large contributions of CRF in the spinal fluid from elsewhere, obscuring local − hypothalamic − changes.

The relationship between depression and suicide is necessarily a highly complex one and to separate biological variables as correlates of one or the other is a delicate issue (Van Praag 1984). Our results indicate that suicidal behavior in nondepressed (female) patients usually does not involve significant CRF overproduction and the HPA hyperfunction in depressed patients is not more evident in those who attempt suicide compared with those who do not. On the other hand, it is evident that major depression is one important cause of suicidal acts and therefore its biological basis, including HPA axis overactivity probably due to primary CRF excess, must be kept in mind in both prevention and treatment of suicide.

References

Banki CM, Arato M, Papp Z, Kurcz M (1984) Cerebrospinal fluid amine metabolites and neuroendocrine findings: biochemical markers in suicidal patients. J Affect Disord 6:341−350
Banki CM, Bissette G, Arato M, O'Connor L, Nemeroff CB (1987) Cerebrospinal fluid corticotrophin-like immunoreactivity in depression and schizophrenia. Am J Psychiatry 144:873−877.

Bissette G, Spielman F, Stanley M, Banki CM, Finke M, Träskman L, Arato M, Nemeroff CB (1985) Further studies of CRF-like immunoreactivity in patients with affective disorders. Soc Neurosci Abstr 11:133

Carroll BJ (1982) The dexamethasone suppression test for melancholia. Br J Psychiatry 140:292–304

Carroll BJ (1985) Dexamethasone suppression test: a review of contemporary confusion. J Clin Psychiatry 46:13–24

Gold PW, Chrousos G, Kellner C, Post RM, Roy A, Avgerinos P, Schulte H, Loriaux LD (1984) Psychiatric implications of basic and clinical studies with corticotropin-releasing factor. Am J Psychiatry 141:619–627

Halbreich U, Asnis GM, Schindledecker R, Zumoff B, Nathan S (1985) Cortisol secretion in endogenous depression. Arch Gen Psychiatry 42:904–908

Nemeroff CB, Widerlöv E, Bissette G, Walleus H, Eklund K, Kilts CD, Vale W, Loosen PT (1984) Elevated concentrations of CSF corticotropin-releasing factor-like immunoreactivity in depressed patients. Science 226:1342–1344

Träskman L, Åsberg M, Bertilsson L, Sjöstrand L (1981) Monoamine metabolites in CSF and suicidal behavior. Arch Gen Psychiatry 38:631–637

Vale W, Spiess J, Rivier C, Rivier J (1981) Characterization of a 41-residue ovine hypothalamic peptide that stimulates secretion of corticotropin and beta-endorphin. Science 213:1394–1397

Van Praag HM (1984) Depression, suicide, and serotonin metabolism in the brain. In: Post RM, Ballenger JC (eds) Neurobiology of mood disorders. Williams and Wilkins, Baltimore, pp 601–618

Measurements of Biogenic Amines and Metabolites in the CSF of Suicide Victims and Nonsuicides

G. Kauert, T. Zucker, T. Gilg, and W. Eisenmenger

Introduction

In 1983 we started a study by measuring biogenic amines in postmortem CSF from suicide victims and nonsuicides. What prompted us to do that? The reasons first were of a practical nature: In forensic medicine one of the main purposes is the detection of causes of death. However, in many cases there are no anatomic or morphological signs. Especially for those cases in which a differentiation between suicide and accident or homicide is not possible, other diagnostic criteria must be found. The monoamine hypothesis of the pathogenesis of depressive disorders and particularly the findings of decreased 5-hydroxyindoleacetic acid (5-HIAA) levels in lumbar CSF of depressive suicidal patients (Åsberg et al. 1976) prompted us to assess serotonin (5-HT) and other biogenetic amines in the postmortem CSF to look for quantitative differences in suicides and controls regardless of mental disorders. For detailed reviews about biological factors of suicidal behavior see Åsberg et al. (1986).

Analyzing the amines or neurotransmitters themselves instead of their acidic and neutral metabolites has practical reasons: We have a routine method for detecting biogenic amines simultaneously from biological fluids and tissues (Kauert 1986). Up to now measurements of biogenic amines in postmortem CSF have not been performed.

Methods

Sampling of CSF from the Corpse

The CSF samples were taken during legal autopsies. To obtain cranial CSF, the calvarium was opened, the chiasma opticum carefully cut avoiding injury to the arteriae carotis internae, the brain then slightly lifted, and with a long cannulated syringe CSF aspirated from the subarachnoid space in the area of the cisterna interpeduncularis and downward at the height of the pons (Fig. 1a, b). We could not perform suboccipital puncture for forensic reasons.

The lumbar puncture was performed by ventral perforation of the intervertebral disk L3/L4 or L4/L5 after removal of the intestinal tract (Fig. 1c). The volume of CSF ranged from 2 to 6 ml. The samples were kept frozen at $-20°$ C until analysis.

Analyses

The isolation of biogenic amines from CSF consists of a combined ion exchange and derivatization step. In general, we took 2 ml of CSF and used etilefrine as an internal standard for quantification. The derivatives formed were detected by capillary gas chromatography mass spectrometry using an ammonia chemical ionization mode to get intensive quasi molecular ions for multiple ion detection (Fig. 2).

For more detailed description of the analytical procedure see Kauert 1986.

Casuistics

The causes of death for the controls and the modes chosen for suicide are listed in Table 1 according to the frequency of the number of cases in which we obtained cranial *plus* lumbar or cranial CSF alone.

Table 1. Frequency with which cranial *plus* lumbar CSF or cranial CSF alone was obtained

	No. of cases	
	Cranial	Lumbar
Causes of death in controls		
Cardiac	17	6
Pneumonia	4	1
Suffocation	4	1
Thrust of knife	3	2
Pulmonary embolism	2	–
Hyperglycemia	1	1
Electric shock	1	1
Thorax trauma	1	–
Carbon monoxide	1	1
Bathing accident	1	–
Drowning	1	–
Shooting	1	–
Total	37	13
Methods chosen for suicide		
Hanging atypical	21	10
Hanging typical	1	1
Cutting of wrist arteries	4	–
Shooting	2	–
Falling from height	1	–
Drowning	2	–
Suffocation (plastic bag)	–	1
Drug overdose	7	4
Cyanide intoxication	3	1
Carbon monoxide intoxication	3	4
Parathion intoxication	2	1
Total	46	22

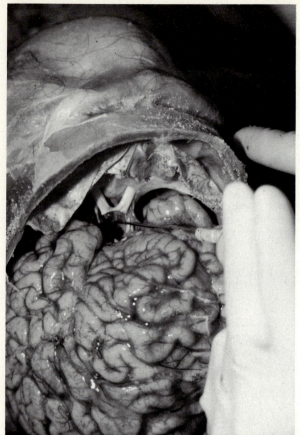

Fig. 1 a

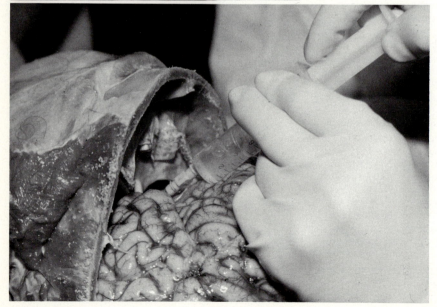

Fig. 1 b

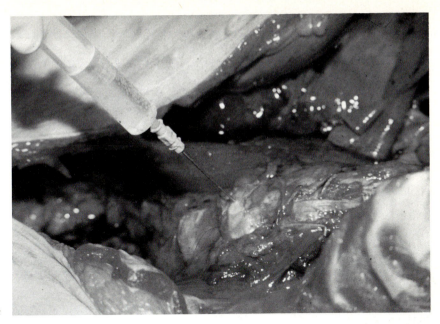

Fig. 1 c

Fig. 1a–c. Technique of cranial puncture of CSF after opening of the scull (**a, b**) and technique of lumbar puncture of CSF (**c**)

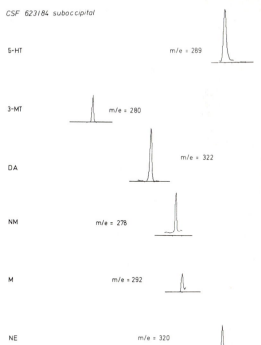

CSF 623184 suboccipital

5-HT   m/e = 289

3-MT   m/e = 280

DA   m/e = 322

NM   m/e = 278

M   m/e = 292

Fig. 2. Mass fragmentogram of ▶ biogenic amine derivatives isolated from CSF. *5-HT,* serotonin; *3-MT,* methoxytyramine; *DA,* dopamine; *NM,* normetanephrine; *M,* metanephrine; *NE,* norepinephrine; *E,* epinephrine

NE   m/e = 320

E   m/e = 334

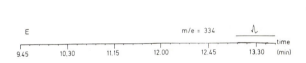

9.45   10.30   11.15   12.00   12.45   13.30   (min)

Table 2 a.   Parameters of cases with 5-HT determination in cranial CSF

		Controls	Suicides	P
Age	$\bar{x}$/SD	51.9/20.1	51.3/18.9	NS
(yrs)	range	6−85	26−95	
	n	27	46	
Body weight	$\bar{x}$/SD	64.9/15.3	63.2/12.5	NS
(kg)	range	24.0−86.3	43.5−88.8	
	n	36	46	
Body height	$\bar{x}$/SD	168.4/11.4	167.4/9.6	NS
(cm)	range	126−186	145−185	
	n	36	45	
Postmortem delay	$\bar{x}$/SD	44.6/29.6	31.8/19.9	<.05
(h)	range	3−122	5.5−88	
	n	37	45	
Ethanol in blood	$\bar{x}$/SD	0.29/0.61	0.56/0.96	NS
(‰)	range	0.0−1.98	0.0−3.06	
	n	37	45	

Table 2 b.   Parameters of cases with 5-HT determination in cranial CSF

		Controls	Suicides	P
Age	$\bar{x}$/SD	42.9/20.5	46.9/16.6	NS
(yrs)	range	6−85	25−95	
	n	13	22	
Body weight	$\bar{x}$/SD	61.4/16.7	64.3/10.4	NS
(kg)	range	24.0−78.3	44.7−88.8	
	n	12	22	
Body height	$\bar{x}$/SD	167.3/15.0	168.5/7.9	NS
(cm)	range	126−186	145−185	
	n	12	22	
Postmortem delay	$\bar{x}$/SD	45.1/34.7	38.3/26.8	<.05
(h)	range	3−122	5.5−88	
	n	13	22	
Ethanol in blood	$\bar{x}$/SD	0.39/0.67	0.68/0.99	NS
(‰)	range	0.0−1.75	0.0−2.81	
	n	7	9	

In the controls about half of the cases derived from cardiac failures and in the suicides the largest group were due to atypical hanging. Besides other violent methods, we also included cases from drug overdoses as well as intoxications by poisons such as cyanide, carbon monoxide, or organophosphates.

A comparison of the demographic data in suicide victims and controls separated according to cranial and lumbar 5-HT determinations is demonstrated in Table 2 a, b.

Results

The most striking findings among the amines investigated showed 5-HT both in cranial and lumbar CSF (Fig. 3). In suicides the 5-HT levels were significantly increased by a mean factor of about 3 for both cranial and lumbar CSF.

The data available from the literature for basal 5-HT levels in lumbar CSF are very inconsistent, obviously because of different analytical methods employed. The most probable level is in a range of 1 ng/ml. The distribution of frequency of 5-HT levels is demonstrated in Fig. 4. In cranial CSF there was a rather broad overlapping of values between suicides and controls, but we found that 50% of the values of the controls showed levels lower than 10 ng/ml and only 15% of the suicide values were within this range.

Moreover, there was no case of suicide below the 5-ng limit. The relative frequency of distribution of 5-HT levels in lumbar CSF is plotted in Fig. 5. Again we found a simular situation compared with the cranial 5-HT levels: about 50% of the control values were below the 5-ng limit, and no case of suicide could be found there.

The other amines which we analyzed, i.e., dopamine, epinephrine, norepinephrine, and the 3-methoxy metabolites of these amines, showed no or no significant differences between the groups.

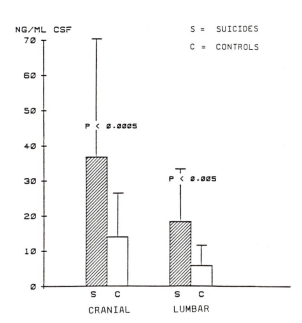

Fig. 3. Serotonin concentrations in cranial and lumbar CSF of suicide victims and controls

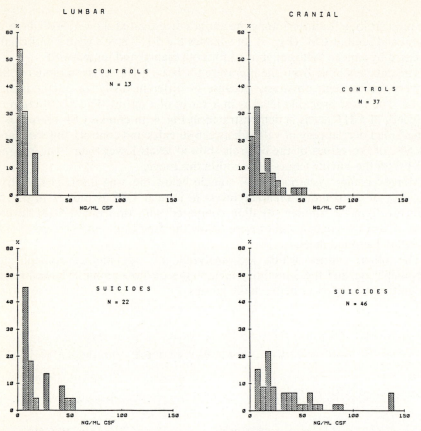

Fig. 4. Distribution of relative frequency of the cranial serotonin concentrations in suicide victims and controls

Fig. 5. Distribution of relative frequency of the lumbar serotonin concentrations in suicide victims and controls

Discussion

Postmortem biochemical investigations of mental disorders often are regarded with skepsis by some clinicians because of potential artifacts. In fact, for many endogenous substrates there is evidence for postmortem alterations, e.g., because of sustained enzymatic activities. Table 3 lists some possible factors of influence on CSF of biogenic amines.

The most often discussed and greatest factor of influence is believed to be the postmortem delay, which either may include an enzymatic activity within the pathway or a chemical degradation process of the amines. However, we could not find any correlation between postmortem delay and the concentrations, for instance, of 5-HT and/or norepinephrine (Fig. 6), although we have to make one limitation: we were not able to observe the time immediately after

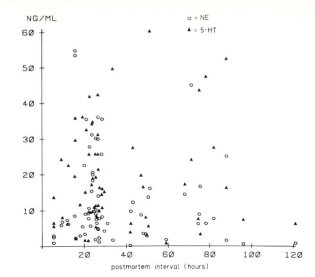

Fig. 6. Postmortem interval
(= time elapsed between time
of death or discovery of the
corpse and autopsy) vs cranial
CSF serotonin and norepi-
nephrine concentrations of
both suicide victims and
controls. *NE*, norepinephrine;
5-HT, serotonin

Table 3. Theoretical and practical aspects of factors influencing postmortem biogenic amine
levels in CSF

1. Postmortem delay	5. Age, sex, height, weight
2. Duration of death agony	6. Chemical stability
3. Handling of the corpse	7. Sampling technique
4. Previous drug treatment	8. Seasonal/diurnal rhythms

death. The duration of agony may influence the amine levels. We were able to
find in previous investigations of peripheral postmortem blood that cat-
echolamines are extremely high in prolonged agony (Kauert 1986). If that
would be the case, however, we must assume that people committing suicide
respond more powerfully to agonal stress than those who died without any intention.

The position of the corpse and its handling before autopsy are potential factors influencing the biogenic amine levels, particularly in regard to the craniocaudal gradient of concentration. One would expect that an equilibration
process during transfer of the corpse may occur. On the other hand, from our
results we were able to show a marked gradient between cranial and lumbar
CSF levels of 5-HT (Fig. 7). Because of the involvement of 5-HT in dark-light-
dependent pathways of the pineal gland hormone melatonin, an influence of
this biorhythm on CSF 5-HT was thought to exist by Åsberg (personal communication, 1985). Taylor et al. (1985) reported about diurnal rhythms of serotonin in Rhesus monkey CSF rising at the beginning of the dark period and
falling to base line at the appearance of light. However, the authors mentioned
that there is a marked variation in the amplitude of the serotonin elevations.
We therefore examined a possible influence of biorhythms on our results and
plotted the levels of cranial and lumbar CSF vs clock time of death so far as
this was possible (Fig. 8). Only those cases are illustrated in Fig. 8 for which we

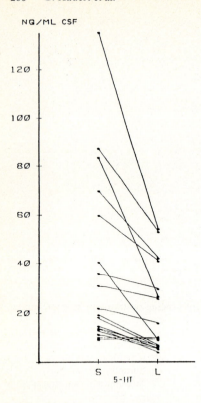

Fig. 7. Postmortem craniocaudal gradient of CSF serotonin concentrations. *S*, Suboccipital; *L*, lumbar CSF

have nearly exact time data, and there were no hints of any correlation between dark-light periods and 5-HT levels, either in cranial or in lumbar CSF. Beyond that, there is no evidence that suicides are preferably committed at night.

On examination of all factors we have discussed, we now have to take into account that all but a previous drug treatment, especially with antidepressives, have to be referred to both suicide victims and controls so that none of these factors gives an explanation for the differences of 5-HT levels in CSF of suicides and controls. The demographic data for both collectives listed in Table 2a, b do not differ with the exception of postmortem delay, which is shorter in suicide cases because autopsies are performed as soon as possible after discovery for criminalistic investigations.

What can we conclude from our studies up to now? First of all, we may suggest that in suicide cases a deficit of 5-HT does not exist *at least* in CSF. In contrast, some authors reported *decreased* postmortem 5-HT levels in specific brain sections (Lloyd et al. 1974; Korpi et al. 1983; Pare et al. 1969). We are presently not able to confirm whether or not these observations are perhaps negatively correlated with our findings. A decreased monoamine oxidase activity, as observed by some authors in suicidal behavior and suicides with previous alcoholism, does not seem to be responsible for our findings when we keep in mind the results of increased 5-HIAA levels in suicides reported by Arato (1986).

It might be that suicide has its own nosologic criteria, which are independent of mental disorders; however, up to now we are not able to give an

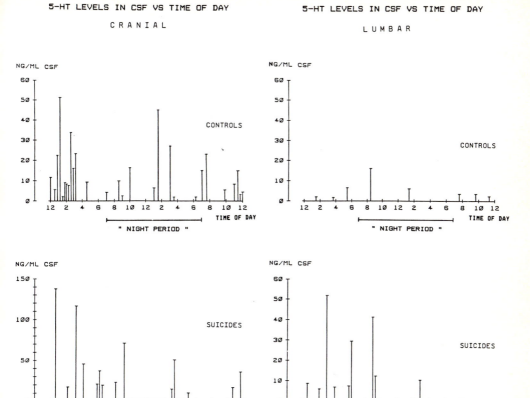

Fig. 8 a, b. Distribution of serotonin levels in cranial (**a**) and lumbar (**b**) CSF vs time of day

explanation for our findings with regard to the monoamine hypothesis of depressive disorders. Many potential influences, e.g., drugs and poisons on serotonin turnover, remain to be clarified which is why we are going to enlarge the number of cases to obtain sufficient collectives for statistical work. For forensic purposes as mentioned at the beginning of our paper, we are hopeful of having available a biochemical marker for differentiation between suicide and nonsuicide.

References

Arato M (1986) Post mortem neurochemical investigations of suicidal behavior. First Eur symposium on empirical research of suicidal behaviour, March 1986, Munich

Åsberg M, Träskman L, Thoren P (1976) 5-HIAA in the cerebrospinal fluid − a biochemical marker? Arch Gen Psychiatry 33:1193−1197

Åsberg M, Nordström P, Träskman-Bendz L (1986) Biological factors in suicide. In: Roy A (ed) Suicide. Williams and Wilkins, Baltimore, pp 47−71

Kauert G (1986) Katecholamine in der Agonie. Enke, Stuttgart

Korpi ER, Kleinmann JE, Goodman SI, Phillips J, Delisi LE, Linnoila M, Wyatt RJ (1983) Serotonin and 5-Hydroxyindolacetic acid concentrations in different brain regions of suicide victims: comparison in chronic schizophrenic patients with suicide as cause of death. Int Soc Neurochem, Vancouver

Lloyd KG, Farley IJ, Deck JHN, Hornykiewicz O (1974) Serotonin and 5-Hydroxyindolacetic acid in discrete areas of the brainstem of suicide victims and control patients. Adv Biochem Psychopharmacol 11:387−397

Pare CMB, Yeung DPH, Price K, Stacey RS (1969) 5-Hydroxytryptamine, noradrenaline and dopamine in brainstem, hypothalamus and caudate nucleus of controls and of patients committing suicide by coal-gas poisoning. Lancet II:133−135

Taylor PL, Garrick NA, Burns RS, Tamarkin L, Murphy DL, Markey SP (1982) Diurnal rhythms of serotonin in monkey cerebrospinal fluid. Life Sci 31:1993−1999

Plasma Amino Acids and Suicidal Behavior: An Investigation of Different Groups of Patients Who Attempted to Commit Suicide

J. DEMLING, K. LANGER, W. STEIN, R. HÖLL, and R. KALB

Introduction

Biochemical findings in depressed (Coppen 1967) and suicidal patients as well as the results of studies on neuronal activity of psychotropic drugs (Fuxe et al. 1977) permit the conclusion that certain subgroups of depressions are due to some functional deficiency of central serotonergic neuronal systems.

In 1976, Åsberg and co-workers, in a catamnestic study of depressed patients, found the 5-hydroxyindoleacetic acid (5-HIAA) levels in the CSF of patients who later attempted suicide to be predominantly within the lower range of the bimodally distributed CSF 5-HIAA concentrations; this was especially obvious in violently suicidal patients and persons who eventually committed suicide.

Tryptophan, an essential amino acid which (besides 5-hydroxytryptophan) is a serotonin precursor, circulates in plasma in a free fraction (about 10%), whereas a major part is noncovalently bound to albumin (McMenamy and Oncley 1958); all other plasma amino acids exist only in free form. Therefore, it seemed of interest to investigate the concentrations of free and total (free and albumin-bound) tryptophan in the plasma of depressed patients in comparison with levels found in healthy controls. Meanwhile, about 25 studies devoted to this question have been conducted (for references, see Møller et al. 1983): about half of them yielded decreased free plasma tryptophan levels in depressed patients or special subgroups of depressions. Almost all of these studies showed normal plasma concentrations of total tryptophan.

In penetrating the blood-brain barrier, free tryptophan shares a transport carrier competitively with five or six other amino acids (the aromatic amino acids phenylalanine and tyrosine, the branched-chained amino acids valine, leucine, and isoleucine, and possibly methionine). Therefore, the uptake of tryptophan into the CNS is determined, besides its plasma concentration, by the molar ratio of tryptophan to the sum of the concentrations of the competing amino acids (Fernstrom and Wurtman 1972). DeMyer and co-workers (1981) found significant differences in the total tryptophan ratio in a population of 18 depressed patients compared with a group of healthy controls. In the same study, the difference of the free tryptophan ratio was less, but also still significant.

Branchey and co-workers (1984), investigating the total tryptophan ratio in alcoholic patients, observed significantly lower values in depressed patients with a history of aggressive and suicidal behavior compared with depressed alcoholics without such a history and alcoholics lacking disturbances of mood and (nondrinking) behavior.

The CSF findings in suicide patients and the changes in amino acid levels described in depressed and alcoholic patients led us to investigate possible changes of amino acid patterns in the plasma of patients who had tried to commit suicide.

Methods

Patients

Fifty-nine patients who had attempted suicide were investigated. Most of the attempts were intoxications of a mild or moderate degree, mainly with psychotropic and/or analgetic drugs, partly combined with alcohol intake. According to the state of treatment and the time interval between suicide attempt and blood collection, we distinguished between two groups of patients. Group A patients were studied in the morning after taking the overdose when the detoxication treatment in the intensive care unit was about to be finished. Patients belonging to group B had, after the initial medical treatment, been examined by a psychiatrist and were sent to the closed psychiatric ward still being suspected as suicidal. In these patients, the time elapsed between the suicide attempt and blood drawing (see below) was a median of 21 days (minimum 3, maximum 94 days). Using the International Classification of Diseases (ICD, ninth revision), 39 patients were diagnosed as reactive depressives (ICD 309), neurotics (ICD 300.4), or personality disorders (mainly ICD 301.6), whereas 20 suicide patients had signs and symptoms of endogenous depression (mainly ICD 296.1), schizophrenia (mainly ICD 295.3), or schizo-affective psychosis (ICD 295.7). Group A consisted of nonpsychotic patients only, in one of whom chronic alcoholism was diagnosed. All were free from metabolic, liver, or kidney diseases. Patients were carefully interviewed for diagnostic classification and features of self-aggression by two trained psychiatrists independently. Blood parameters investigated were levels of total tryptophan, free tryptophan, the sum of the concentrations of the six competing large neutral amino acids (LNAA) (valine, leucine, isoleucine, methionine, phenylalanine, and tyrosine), and the ratios of total and of free tryptophan, as described in the introduction.

Control persons were students of medicine and dental medicine as well as members of the nursing staff of our clinic. In all of them psychiatric as well as physical diseases could be ruled out, and none of these persons was on a special diet or had medication prescribed regularly.

Group A comprised 28 suicide attempters (4 male, 24 female) with a mean age of 29.7 years (SD $\pm$ 8.8 years, range 18–53 years), and group B consisted of 31 patients (14 male, 17 female) with a mean age of 31.8 years (SD $\pm$ 13.1 years, range 17–65 years). Controls were 21 male and 33 female volunteers with a mean age of 27.5 years (SD $\pm$ 7.8 years, range 17–53 years).

Blood Samples

Blood samples were collected between 7 and 7:30 a.m. after an overnight fast of at least 10 h. Not all of the intensive care patients had been completely detoxified at that time (having attempted suicide the day before), and for those group B patients who were on drugs, no washout period was kept as we drew blood as soon as possible after admission. However, none of these patients was on drugs known to decrease plasma total tryptophan levels. Blood was collected in 10-ml plastic syringes that contained ethylenediaminetetraacetate (EDTA). After immediate centrifugation, the plasma samples were divided into 2-ml aliquots and stored frozen ($-20°$ C) in Eppendorf plastic tubes until analyzed.

As we took blood from patients and controls over the same period of the year (June until December), we regarded possible seasonal variations (Wirz-Justice and Richter 1979) of amino acid levels negligible.

Statistical Analysis

All differences of means were tested by the two-tailed Student's t-test for independent samples. P values exceeding 0.05 were considered nonsignificant (NS in Table 1). Comparisons of means for the competing LNAA had not been planned at the outset of the study so that the P values of the referring tests are just a more objective method of describing the data obtained (to be understood as explorative data analysis).

Biochemical Analysis

Concentrations of the amino acids valine, leucine, isoleucine, methionine, phenylalanine, and tyrosine were measured by cation exchange chromatography with ninhydrine postcolumn derivatization (based on the method described by Moore and Stein 1951). Total tryptophan levels were determined by HPLC with fluorescence detection, after sulfosalicylic acid (SSA) deproteinization of plasma. The same method was applied for measuring free tryptophan, after molecular filtration of plasma.

Results

The essential results of the study are summarized in Table 1. For both groups of patients, the mean levels of *total tryptophan* were lower than the control value to a very significant degree. Comparing group B patients with controls, we were not able to find significant differences in the mean values of plasma free tryptophan and the free tryptophan ratio. Group A even showed a slight but significant ($P = 0.029$) increase of the free tryptophan ratio compared with controls.

The mean value of the *sum of the competing LNAA* showed a sharp and very significant decrease for group A in comparison with the control value. In group B patients, the difference did not reach significance.

Table 1. Mean values with standard errors of means (SEMs) of the main variables studied and statistical differences for corresponding parameters between patient groups and controls, respectively

Amino acids[a]	Group A (n = 28)			Group B (n = 31)			Controls (n = 54)	
	Mean	SEM	t-test[b]	Mean	SEM	t-test[b]	Mean	SEM
Total tryptophan	40.9	2.2	$P \ll 0.001$	46.4	1.9	$P \ll 0.001$	56.8	1.1
Free tryptophan	6.1	0.5	$P = 0.765$ NS[c]	6.4	0.5	$P = 0.521$ NS[c]	6.0	0.4
Sum of competing LNAA	450.3	19.9	$P < 0.001$	554.2	21.9	$P = 0.890$	551.9	14.4
Tryptophan ratios								
Total tryptophan ratio	0.094	0.006	$P = 0.051$ NS[c]	0.087	0.007	$P < 0.001$	0.105	0.002
Free tryptophan ratio	0.014	0.001	$P = 0.029$	0.012	0.001	$P = 0.476$ NS[c]	0.011	0.001

[a] Amino acid concentrations are given as μmol/liter plasma.
[b] Against controls, resp.; two-tailed t-test for independent samples was used.
[c] NS, nonsignificant ($P > 0.05$).

When the large neutral amino acids in group A were compared separately with the control mean levels (data not shown in Table 1), the differences were most pronounced for the branched-chained amino acids isoleucine ($P \ll 0.001$), valine ($P < 0.001$), leucine ($P = 0.003$), and for methionine ($P = 0.001$); the aromatic amino acids phenylalanine ($P = 0.011$) and tyrosine ($P = 0.020$) also showed, albeit to a lesser degree, significantly lower mean values. By far the greatest difference, however, was found for total tryptophan ($P \ll 0.001$). As for group B, we found the decrease of competing LNAA levels to be significant only for methionine ($P < 0.002$). Again there was a marked difference for total tryptophan ($P \ll 0.001$).

The *total tryptophan ratio* was significantly lower in group B ($P < 0.001$), whereas group A patients did not exhibit a significant difference ($P = 0.051$) against controls regarding this variable.

Comparing the means of total and free tryptophan and the corresponding ratios for *nonpsychotic* and for those of *psychotic* (endogenously depressed, schizophrenic, schizo-affective) patients, the difference did not prove to be significant between these two groups of suicide attempters.

We also considered the data for the male and female patients against sex-matched controls. For the female patients (n = 24) of group A (n = 28), we found the differences described hitherto confirmed (total tryptophan: $P \ll 0.001$, total tryptophan ratio: NS). The females of group B, however, did not show a marked decrease in any one of the amino acids studied but presented a slightly yet significantly ($P = 0.036$) lower total tryptophan ratio when compared with female controls. In contrast, the male patients of group B differed very significantly from sex-matched controls in total tryptophan ($P \ll 0.001$) and total tryptophan ratio ($P < 0.002$).

Discussion

In our suicide population we could not show, in comparison with controls, a diminution of plasma free tryptophan or a lower free tryptophan ratio. The increase of the free tryptophan ratio in group A patients was mainly due to the diminished sum of competing LNAA (denominator of the ratio, cf. Table 1). In addition, mean levels of free tryptophan found in group B patients even had a tendency to exceed the control level. This was an unexpected finding because, as described above, it is the free tryptophan fraction that penetrates the blood-brain barrier to be enzymatically transformed to serotonin which, according to the underlying hypothesis, is less available in the CNS of suicidal persons. However, equivocal results have been obtained by working groups studying free tryptophan levels in plasma of depressed patients (see above). Moreover, Fernstrom and co-workers (1976) claimed that the *total* tryptophan ratio is the predominant factor for tryptophan uptake into the brain. There is also evidence that the relation between free and bound tryptophan in the peripheral plasma does not exactly reflect the conditions at the blood-brain barrier (Pardridge 1979).

In contrast to free tryptophan, total tryptophan levels differed very significantly for both suicide groups A and B in comparison with controls, respectively. The lowest value was found in group A patients who, at the time of blood drawing, were under intensive care treatment. This finding might indicate an intensified metabolic degradation of tryptophan and the LNAA due to the stress situation to which these patients were more exposed than group B patients at the time of blood collection. For instance, it is known that glucocorticoids enhance the oxidative metabolism of tryptophan by inducing the rate-limiting enzyme of this pathway, tryptophan pyrrolase (Mehler et al. 1958). However, a preliminary study did not reveal a marked increase of plasma cortisol (and human growth hormone) in this group of patients compared with our controls. In spite of the overnight fast, nutritional factors may contribute to the plasma findings in this group of patients who were investigated between 10 and 15 h after taking the overdose.

In group B patients whose blood was collected several days or weeks (mean = 21 days) after the suicide attempt, the sum of competing amino acids lay within the control range whereas the mean level of total tryptophan was significantly lower ($P \ll 0.001$) than the control values. Consequently, a total tryptophan ratio for group B patients far smaller than the control ratio ($P \ll 0.001$) was calculated. According to our present data, this holds true especially for male patients; female suicide attempters of this group did not show significant changes in single amino acid levels, although their total tryptophan ratio ranged slightly, yet significantly, below the control value. The results could indicate that in suicidal persons, especially males, the low plasma tryptophan level outlasts − and thus may be independent of − the stress-mediated influences inherent in the acute situation of an autoaggressive act or intensive care treatment.

The mainly psychotropic drugs taken with suicidal intention (acute effects, groups A and B) or for medical reasons (chronic effects, mainly group B) could have exerted influences on the amino acid levels; these influences are, however, difficult to estimate, due not least of all to the fact that only few studies have been devoted to these questions. Badawy and Evans (1982) described for a number of antidepressants and other psychotropic drugs an inhibitory effect on tryptophan pyrrolase activity; tryptophan levels would, therefore, be expected to rise rather than be diminished in patients treated or intoxicated (if a short-term effect is assumed) with drugs of this kind.

If a deficiency of central serotonergic systems gives rise to an affective disorder with features of suicidality, it cannot, from our findings, be ruled out that this kind of disturbance is in part due to an insufficient supply of the plasma precursor, tryptophan. This may be a specific deficiency, taking into account that total tryptophan levels were, in contrast to our results, nearly always found to be normal in the plasma of depressives, irrespective of suicidal behavior (Møller 1985).

Very recently, Hanssen and co-workers (1986) presented data on the enzymatic activity of tryptophan pyrrolase in postmortem liver homogenates. In suicides, an extended induction of the enzyme was found in comparison with other sudden death victims. This is in agreement with our results and may give an explanation for the lower mean concentrations of plasma tryptophan that we saw in our suicide patients.

The findings presented here, seen in the light of the pertinent literature, favor the hypothesis that a diminution of plasma total tryptophan and a smaller total tryptophan ratio could be, besides other factors, a biological marker for a tendency to − or vulnerability for − autoaggressive behavior. Whether this is an indicator of an acute mental state or a biological feature of the suicidal personality in general or related to a subgroup of suicidal patients requires further investigation.

References

Åsberg M, Träskman L, Thorén P (1976) 5-HIAA in the cerebrospinal fluid − a biochemical suicide predictor? Arch Gen Psychiatry 33:1193−1197

Badawy AA, Evans M (1982) Inhibition of rat liver tryptophan pyrrolase activity and elevation of brain tryptophan concentration by acute administration of small doses of antidepressants. Br J Pharmacol 77 (1):59−67

Branchey L, Branchey M, Shaw S, Lieber CS (1984) Depression, suicide, and aggression in alcoholics and their relationship to plasma amino acids. Psychiatry Res 12 (3):219−226

Coppen A (1967) The biochemistry of affective disorders. Br J Psychiatry 113:1237−1264

DeMyer MK, Shea PA, Hendrie HC, Yoshimura NN (1981) Plasma tryptophan and five other amino acids in depressed and normal subjects. Arch Gen Psychiatry 38 (6):642−646

Fernstrom JD, Wurtman RJ (1972) Brain serotonin content: physiological regulation by plasma neutral amino acids. Science 178:414−416

Fernstrom JD, Hirsch MJ, Faller DV (1976) Tryptophan concentrations in rat brain: failure to correlate with serum free tryptophan, or its ratio to the sum of other serum neutral amino acids. Biochem J 160:589−595

Fuxe K, Ogren S, Agnati L, Gustafsson JA, Jonsson G (1977) On the mechanism of action of the antidepressant drugs amitryptiline and nortriptyline. Evidence for 5-hydroxy-tryptamine receptor blocking activity. Neurosci Lett 6:339−343

Hanssen HP, Agarwal DP, Gerdes S, Goedde HW (1986) Studies on tryptophan pyrrolase activity in post-mortem liver homogenates. Abstract (F8), International Study Group for Tryptophan Research, 5th international meeting, Cardiff, July 28 – August 1

McMenamy RH, Oncley JL (1958) The specific binding of L-tryptophan to serum albumin. J Biol Chem 233:1435 – 1447

Mehler AH, McDaniel EG, Hundley JM (1958) Changes in the enzymatic composition of liver: (II) influence of hormones on picolinic carboxylase and tryptophan peroxydase. J Biol Chem 232:331 – 335

Møller SE (1985) Tryptophan to competing amino acids ratio in depressive disorder: relation to efficacy of antidepressive treatments. Acta Psychiatr Scand [Suppl 325] 72:3 – 31

Møller SE, Kirk L, Brandrup E, Hollnagel M, Kaldan B, Odum K (1983) Tryptophan availability in endogenous depression – relation to efficacy of L-tryptophan treatment. In: van Praag HM, Mendlewicz J (eds) Advances in biological psychiatry, vol 10: management of depression with monoamine precursors. Karger, Basel, p 30

Moore S, Stein WH (1951) Chromatography of amino acids on sulfonated polystyrene resins. J Biol Chem 192:663 – 681

Pardridge WM (1979) Tryptophan transport through the blood-brain barrier: in vivo measurement of free and albumin-bound amino acid. Life Sci 25:1519 – 1528

Wirz-Justice A, Richter R (1979) Seasonality in biochemical determinations: a source of variance and a clue to the temporal incidence of affective illness. Psychiatry Res 1:53 – 60

Review of Imipramine Binding in Platelets from Psychiatric Patients: Its Relevance to the Biology of Suicide

D. Marazziti and G. M. Pacifici

Biological research in the field of suicidology is strictly linked to biological aspects of depressive illness. About half of suicides are retrospectively diagnosed as having suffered from depression, while most of them had had depressive symptoms prior to death (Beskow 1979; Van Praag 1982). The biochemical mechanisms at the basis of depressive illness are not yet fully understood. Several studies suggest an involvement of noradrenaline and serotonin. Low levels of serotonin, or its metabolite 5-hydroxyindoleacetic acid (5-HIAA), have been observed in the brain of suicides (Lloyd et al. 1974). Van Praag (1977) suggested that low concentrations of 5-HIAA in the CNS could be a marker for the vulnerability to depression. Several groups have studied the relationship between suicidal behavior and the concentrations of 5-HIAA in the CNS (Åsberg et al. 1976; Träskman et al. 1981; Van Praag 1982; Roy et al. 1984). Many, but not all of the investigators, observed a correlation between low levels of 5-HIAA and suicidality. Considering that 2% of those who attempt suicide are successful, it is important to predict the risk of suicide to prevent it.

Platelets and serotoninergic neurons have in common the active transport of serotonin. Platelets accumulate serotonin by an active process, store the neurotransmitter in granules, and possess the monoamine oxidase (MAO) that inactivate serotonin (Stahl 1977). Although some difference may exist in the transport of serotonin between platelets and neurons, the ease of obtaining platelets and the possibility of repeating studies in these cells from the same subject may constitute a suitable approach for evaluating the time course of psychiatric disorders. Therefore, platelets have been extensively investigated in depression. A low activity of MAO in platelets was found in college students attempting suicide (Buchsbaum et al. 1976) and in depressed patients who committed suicide (Gottfries et al. 1980). Many authors have described a defect in the velocity of serotonin uptake in platelets from depressed patients (Coppen et al. 1978; Meltzer et al. 1981; Healy et al. 1986).

After the discovery of the existence of imipramine (IMI) binding sites in the brain, specific and high-affinity IMI binding sites were demonstrated also in blood platelets (Briley et al. 1979; Raisman et al. 1979; Paul et al. 1980; Rehavi et al. 1980). The importance of IMI binding in psychiatry derives from findings that show a correlation between the number of sites and the rate of serotonin uptake. It was then demonstrated that the IMI binding sites represent another common attribute of the outer membrane of presynaptic serotoninergic neurons and platelets (Paul et al. 1981 a). It was also suggested that the binding of IMI might influence the serotonin uptake by an allosteric mechanism (Wennogle

Table 1. Studies on imipramine binding in human platelets

Authors	Controls			Depressed patients		
	n^a	B_{max}	Kd	n^a	B_{max}	Kd
Asarch et al. (1980)	16	703 ± 190	1.9 ± 0.7	22	548 ± 160	2.0 ± 0.5
Baron et al. (1983)	15	991 ± 347	3.4 ± 1.2	15	775 ± 287	2.5 ± 0.7
Berrettini et al. (1982)	12	440 ± 168	3.1 ± 1.6	12	450 ± 151	3.0 ± 1.6
Briley et al. (1980)	21	604 ± 192	2.6 ± 1.8	16	275 ± 24	2.5 ± 0.3
Hrdina et al. (1986)	17	1000 ± 201	1.3 ± 0.3	20	894 ± 332	2.6 ± 1.0
Langer et al. (1983)	70	562 ± 250	1.6 ± 1.6	48	318 ± 124	2.4 ± 2.4
Lewis & McChesney (1985)	20	1238 ± 201	0.7 ± 0.4	45	1009 ± 239	0.8 ± 0.4
Mellerup et al. (1982)	33	1010 ± 280	0.6 ± 0.2	19	1190 ± 230	0.6 ± 0.2
Paul et al. (1981b)	28	450 ± 122	1.5 ± 0.7	14	318 ± 75	0.9 ± 0.8
Raisman et al. (1981)	39	581 ± 231	2.4 ± 1.9	10	300 ± 122	2.8 ± 2.1
Raisman et al. (1982)	27	539 ± 208	1.2 ± 1.0	14	368 ± 153	1.8 ± 1.4
Suranyi-Cadotte et al. (1982)	17	658 ± 136		3	306 ± 69	
Waegner et al. (1985)	53	1123 ± 178	1.0 ± 0.3	63	1012 ± 295	1.0 ± 0.4
Whitaker et al. (1984)	17	764 ± 468	1.6 ± 0.3	16	798 ± 484	1.9 ± 0.8
Wood et al. (1983)	17	658 ± 136	3.0 ± 0.1	56	543 ± 166	3.1 ± 1.4

[a] n, number of subjects investigated.

and Meyerson 1982). Platelet IMI binding sites may be used as a model to better understand the biochemistry of psychiatric disorders. A decrease of density of IMI binding sites (B_{max}) was observed in platelets from depressed patients compared with healthy subjects (Asarch et al. 1980; Briley et al. 1980; Paul et al. 1981b; Raisman et al. 1981, 1982; Suranyi-Cadotte et al. 1982, 1984; Baron et al. 1983, 1986; Langer and Raisman 1983; Wood et al. 1983; Lewis and McChesney 1985). However, no difference in B_{max} was found between controls and depressed patients in the euthymic phase (Berrettini et al. 1982) or bipolar patients in the depressed phase (Mellerup et al. 1982). Gentsch et al. (1985) also confirmed the lack of a difference in B_{max} and in dissociation constant (Kd) when different categories of psychiatric patients were compared. In addition, these authors also reported a lack of difference in B_{max} between controls and depressed patients. The presence of conflicting results suggests that the matter is complex because of the multitude of uncontrollable factors.

B_{max} and Kd exhibit a wide range when various studies are compared (Table 1). Several hypotheses for such a variability may be considered:

1. The heterogeneity of the depression.
2. The differences in the methods employed for the preparation of platelet membranes (Friedl et al. 1983).
3. The age of the platelets (Arora and Meltzer 1984); B_{max} is higher in heavier (young) than in lighter (old) platelets.
4. The existence of a seasonal variation for IMI binding in groups of normal and depressed subjects (Egrise et al. 1983; Whitaker et al. 1984). Egrise et al. (1983) reported the highest B_{max} for IMI binding in autumn and the lowest in spring, whereas Whitaker et al. (1984) found the highest B_{max} in January and the lowest in September. A circadian rhythm was found by Gentsch et al.

(1985) in platelets from normal donors; the highest B_{max} was found at 3 p.m. and 11 p.m. Seasonal and diurnal rhythms have also been described for serotonin uptake (Arora et al. 1983).

5. Aging also influences the B_{max} for IMI; B_{max} is lower in older people than in the young (Langer et al. 1980; Marazziti et al. 1987).

Information on the effects of previous treatments with tricyclic antidepressants on IMI binding sites is limited and controversial. It is not yet possible to establish whether chronic treatment with tricyclics influences the binding of IMI to platelet membranes (Briley et al. 1982; Braddock et al. 1984; Gentsch et al. 1984).

Langer and Raisman (1983) and Baron et al. (1986) suggested that the decreased density of IMI binding sites in platelets might represent a "state-independent biological marker" for depression and reflect a susceptibility to this disease. Suranyi-Cadotte et al. (1982, 1984) observed that B_{max} for IMI tends to increase in depressed patients in the remission phase. These authors thus concluded that the decrease of B_{max} may represent a state-dependent marker. Langer et al. (1986) recently noted a tendency of B_{max} to increase in the platelets of depressed patients after treatment with electroconvulsive shock therapy.

Few studies have been performed on IMI binding in postmortem tissues from normal and depressed patients. Stanley et al. (1982) observed a decreased IMI binding in the frontal cortex and Perry et al. (1983) in the hippocampus and occipital cortex of depressed patients. In contrast, a normal (Crow 1985) or an increased IMI binding (Meyerson et al. 1982) was observed in the frontal cortex of depressed subjects.

The studies concerning platelet IMI binding in suicidal patients are few, Waegner et al. (1985) described a higher B_{max} in the platelets of depressed patients who attempted suicide by violent than by nonviolent means. An interesting investigation on this topic was recently performed by Paul (1986) who measured both B_{max} for IMI and serotonin uptake in platelets and in the brain of depressed patients and controls. He observed a decreased serotonin uptake and a decreased number of IMI binding sites in the hypothalamus of depressed patients compared with nonpsychiatric subjects. To our knowledge, this is the first demonstration that IMI binding sites in platelets and in the brain are subjected to similar changes in depression. Paul (1986) also demonstrated a relationship between the probability of committing suicide and the decrease of B_{max} for IMI and serotonin uptake.

Low IMI binding sites have also been described in schizophrenia (Meltzer et al. 1984), panic attacks (Lewis et al. 1985; Marazziti et al., in press), anorexia nervosa (Weizman et al. 1986b), and obsessive-compulsive disorders (Weizman et al. 1986a).

Looking for a concept to unify all of this body of knowledge, we tentatively state that a variation in B_{max} may represent an unspecific sign of brain dysfunction. In the light of these results, it seems interesting to study the IMI binding in platelets from a large number of depressed patients to assess whether the binding of IMI decreases in a similar way in different disorders. Future research in this area should provide a reliable marker to predict the risk of suicide.

References

Arora RC, Meltzer HY (1984) Imipramine binding in subpopulations of normal human blood platelets. Biol Psychiatry 19:257–262

Arora RC, Kregel L, Meltzer HY (1983) Seasonal variation of serotonin uptake in normal controls and depressed patients. Biol Psychiatry 19:795–804

Asarch KB, Shih JC, Kulcsar A (1980) Decreased 3H-imipramine binding in depressed males and females. Commun Psychopharmacol 4:425–432

Åsberg M, Traskman L, Thoren P (1976) 5-HIAA in the cerebrospinal fluid: a biochemical suicide predictor? Arch Gen Psychiatry 33:1193–1197

Baron M, Barkai A, Gruen R, Kowalik S, Quitkin F (1983) 3H-imipramine binding sites in unipolar depression. Biol Psychiatry 18:1403–1409

Baron M, Barkai A, Gruen R, Peselow E, Fieve RR, Quitkin F (1986) Platelet 3H-imipramine binding sites in affective disorders: trait versus status characteristics. Am J Psychiatry 143:711–717

Berrettini WH, Nurnberger JI, Post RM, Gershon ES (1982) Platelet 3H-imipramine binding in euthymic bipolar patients. Psychiatry Res 7:215–219

Beskow J (1979) Suicide and mental disorder in Swedish men. Acta Psychiatr Scand [Suppl] 277

Braddock LE, Cowen PS, Elliot SM, Frazer S, Stump K (1984) Changes in the binding to platelets of 3H-imipramine and 3H-yohimbine in normal subjects taking amitryptiline. Neuropharmacol 23:285–288

Briley MS, Raisman R, Langer SZ (1979) Human platelets possess high-affinity binding sites for 3H-imipramine. Eur J Pharmacol 58:347–348

Briley MS, Langer SZ, Raisman R, Sechter D, Zarifian E (1980) Tritiated imipramine binding sites are decreased in platelets from untreated depressed patients. Science 209:303–305

Briley MS, Raisman R, Arbilla S, Casadamont M, Langer SZ (1982) Concomitant decrease in 3H-imipramine binding in cat brain and platelets after chronic treatment with imipramine. Eur J Pharmacol 81:309–314

Buchsbaum MS, Coursey ED, Murphy DL (1976) The biochemical high-risk paradigm: behavioral and familial correlates of low platelet monoamine oxidase activity. Science 194:339–341

Coppen A, Swade C, Wood K (1978) Platelet 5-hydroxytryptamine accumulation in depressive illness. Clin Chim Acta 87:165–168

Crow T (1985) Monoamine neurons and reward: can they be related to clinical syndrome? Proc 14th Ann Meeting Soc Biol Psychiatry. Dallas, May 15–19

Egrise D, Desmedt D, Schoutens A, Mendlewicz J (1983) Circannual variations in the density of tritiated imipramine binding sites on blood platelets in man. Neuropsychobiol 10:101–102

Friedl W, Propping P, Weck B (1983) 3H-imipramine binding in human platelets. Influence of varying proportions of intact platelets in membrane preparations on binding. Psychopharmacol 80:96–99

Gentsch G, Lichsteiner M, Feer H (1984) Regional distribution of 3H-imipramine and 3H-cyanoimipramine binding in rat brain tissues: effect of long-term antidepressant administration. J Neural Transmission 59:257–261

Gentsch G, Lichsteiner M, Gastpar M, Gastpar G, Feer H (1985) 3H-imipramine binding sites in platelets of hospitalized psychiatric patients. Psychiatry Res 14:177–187

Gottfries CG, Knorring L von, Oreland L (1980) Platelet monoamine oxidase activity in mental disorders. II. Affective disorders and suicidal behavior. Prog Neuropsychopharmacol 4:185–192

Healy D, O'Halloran A, Carney PA, Leonard BE (1986) Platelet 5-HT uptake in delusional and non delusional depression. J Affective Disord 10:233–239

Hrdina PA, Lapiere YA, Horn ER, Bakish D (1986) Platelet 3H-imipramine binding: a possible predictor of response to antidepressant treatment. Prog Neuropsychopharmacol Biol Psychiatry 9:619–623

Langer SZ, Briley MS, Raisman R, Henry JF, Morselli PL (1980) Specific 3H-imipramine binding in human platelets: influence of age and sex. Naunyn Schmiedebergs Arch Pharmacol 313:189–194

Langer SZ, Raisman R (1983) High-affinity binding of 3H-imipramine and 3H-desipramine: biochemical tools for studies in depression. Life Sci 29:211−220

Langer SZ, Sechter D, Loo H, Raisman R, Zarifian E (1986) Electroconvulsive shock therapy and maximum binding of platelet tritiated imipramine binding in depression. Arch Gen Psychiatry 43:949−952

Lewis DA, McChesney C (1985) Tritiated imipramine binding distinguishes among subtypes of depression. Arch Gen Psychiatry 42:485−488

Lewis DA, Noyes RJ, Coryell W, Clancy S (1985) Tritiated imipramine binding to platelets is decreased in patients with agoraphobia. Psychiatry Res 16:2−9

Lloyd KG, Farley IJ, Deck JHN, Hornykiewicz O (1974) Serotonin and 5-hydroxyindoleacetic acid in discrete areas of the brain stem of suicide victims and control patients. Adv Biochem 11:387−398

Marazziti D, Giusti P, Rotondo A, Placidi GF, Pacifici GM (1987) Imipramine receptors in human platelets: effect of age. Clin Pharmacol Res VII(2):145−148

Mellerup EG, Plenge P, Rosenberg R (1982) 3H-imipramine binding sites in platelets from psychiatric patients. Psychiat Res 7:221−227

Meltzer HY, Arora RC, Baber R, Tricou BJ (1981) Serotonin uptake in blood platelets of psychiatric patients. Arch Gen Psychiatry 38:1322−1326

Meltzer HY, Arora RC, Robertson A, Lowy M (1984) Platelet 3H-imipramine binding and platelet 5-HT uptake in affective disorders and schizophrenia. Clin Neuropharmacol [Suppl 1] 7:320−321

Meyerson LR, Wennogle LP, Abel MS, Coupet J, Lippa AS, Rau CE, Beer B (1982) Human brain receptor alterations in suicide victims. Pharmacol Biochem Behav 17:157−163

Paul SM (1986) Serotonin reuptake in platelets and human brain: clinical implications. Proc WPA Regional Symposium, Copenhagen, 19−22 May

Paul SM, Rehavi M, Skolnick P, Goodwin FK (1980) Demonstration of specific high-affinity binding sites for 3H-imipramine in human platelets. Life Sci 26:953−959

Paul SM, Rehavi M, Rice KC, Ittah Y, Skolnick P (1981 a) Does high affinity 3H-imipramine binding label serotonin reuptake sites in brain and platelets? Life Sci 28:2753−2760

Paul SM, Rehavi M, Skolnick P, Ballenger JC, Goodwin FK (1981 b) Depressed patients have decreased binding of tritiated imipramine to platelet serotonin transporter. Arch Gen Psychiatry 38:1315−1317

Perry EK, Marshall EF, Blessed G, Tomlinson BE, Perry RH (1983) Decreased imipramine binding in the brains of patients with depressive illness. Br J Psychiatry 142:188−192

Raisman R, Briley R, Langer SZ (1979) High affinity imipramine binding in rat cerebral cortex. Eur J Pharmacol 54:307−308

Raisman R, Secther D, Briley MS, Zarifian E, Langer SZ (1981) High affinity 3H-imipramine binding in platelets from untreated and treated patients compared to healthy volunteers. Psychopharmacology 75:368−371

Raisman R, Briley MS, Bouchami F, Sechter D, Zarifian E, Langer SZ (1982) 3H-imipramine binding and serotonin uptake in platelets from untreated depressed patients and control volunteers. Psychopharmacology 77:332−335

Rehavi M, Paul SM, Skolnick P, Goodwin FK (1980) Demonstration of specific high-affinity binding sites in human brain. Life Sci 26:2273−2276

Roy P, Post RM, Rubinow DR, Linnoila M, Savard R, Davis D (1984) CSF 5-HIAA and personal and family history of suicide in affectively ill patients: a negative study. Psychiatry Res 10:263−274

Stahl SM (1977) The human platelets. A diagnostic and research tool of the study of biogenic amines in psychiatric and neurological disorders. Arch Gen Psychiatry 34:509−516

Stanley M, Virgilio J, Gershon S (1982) Tritiated imipramine binding sites are decreased in the frontal cortex of suicides. Science 216:1377−1379

Suranyi-Cadotte BE, Wood PL, Nair NPV, Schwartz G (1982) Normalization of platelet 3H-imipramine binding in depressed patients during remission. Eur J Pharmacol 85:357−358

Suranyi-Cadotte BE, Quirion R, McQuide P (1984) Platelet 3H-imipramine binding: a state dependent marker in depression. Prog Neuropsychopharmacol Biol Psychiatry 8:731−741

Traskman L, Åsberg M, Bertilsson L, Sjostrand L (1981) Monoamine metabolites in CSF and suicidal behavior. Arch Gen Psychiatry 38:631−636 van Praag HM (1977) Significance of biochemical parameters in the diagnosis, treatment and prevention of depressive disorders. Biol Psychiatry 8:311–325

van Praag HM (1982) Depression, suicide and the metabolism of serotonin in the brain. J Affective Disord 4:275–290

Waegner A, Aberg-Wistedt A, Åsberg M, Ekqvist B, Martenson B, Montero D (1985) Lower 3H-imipramine binding in platelets from untreated depressed patients compared to healthy controls. Psychiatry Res 16:131–139

Weizman A, Carmi M, Hermesh H, Shahar A, Apter A, Tyano S, Rehavi M (1986a) High-affinity imipramine binding and serotonin uptake in platelets of eight adolescent and ten adult obsessive-compulsive patients. Am J Psychiatry 143:335–339

Weizman R, Carmi M, Tyano S, Apter A, Rehavi M (1986b) High-affinity 3H-imipramine binding and serotonin uptake to platelets of adolescent females suffering from anorexia nervosa. Life Sci 38:1235–1242

Wennogle LP, Meyerson LR (1984) Serotonin modulates the dissociation of 3H-imipramine from human platelet recognition sites. Eur J Pharmacol 86:303–307

Whitaker PM, Warsh IJ, Stancer HC, Persad E, Vint CK (1984) Seasonal variation in platelet 3H-imipramine binding: comparable values in control and depressed populations. Psychiatry Res 11:127–131

Wood PL, Suranyi-Cadotte BE, Schwartz G, Nair PV (1983) Platelet 3H-imipramine binding and red blood cell choline in affective disorders: indications of heterogenous pathogenesis. Biol Psychiatry 18:715–719

Part IV   Psychosocial Factors of Suicidal Behavior

Broken Home and Suicidal Behavior: Methodological Problems

S. Schaller and A. Schmidtke

Introduction

It has often been hypothesized that life events and family factors are "causes" of suicidal behavior. In this context, the influence of a broken home has been the subject of a great deal of discussion, and it has been suggested that this variable results in a "predisposition" toward suicidal behavior (Haffter 1979), or that it is a "causal factor" (Kitamura 1982) of such behavior. Thus, for example, Biener (1978, p. 115) stated that a broken home is the primary cause or a contributing factor in 60% of cases of suicides among adolescents.

Previous Findings

Most studies indicate that a high proportion of patients with a record of suicidal behavior come from broken homes. In a survey of 69 studies published since 1941 (Table 1) − in which the methodological problems discussed below are not taken into account − previous findings concerning the incidence of broken homes among suicides can be seen to have ranged from 23% to 85% (weighted mean for all investigations, 40%), while among patients with suicide attempts, the rate ranged from 9% to 92% (weighted mean, 47%). These rates are indeed considerably higher than might have been expected from the base rate for the incidence of broken homes among the population as a whole. Ac-

Table 1. Incidence of broken homes among various sample groups

Sample group	Number of studies	Total number of subjects in the sample group	Broken-home rate	
			Range (%)	Weighted mean (%)
Suicides	8	988	23−85	40
Suicide attempters	61	8182	9−92	47
Patients with psychiatric disorders	78	33609	4−55	24
Drug abusers/addicts	17	8288	19−70	43
Alcoholics	16	3314	9−71	28
Delinquents	30	61492	19−81	44
Controls	26	42937	7−41	17

cording to various sources, it would appear that in the Federal Republic of Germany the incidence of broken homes among children and adolescents up to 18 years of age lies between 6% and 19% (cf. Schaller and Schmidtke 1983); however, due to the increasing divorce rate, this figure can be expected to rise. In Great Britain, the available evidence suggests that the broken-home rate is about 12%. According to figures published by the American Census Office for 1985, 23.3% of families with children in the United States are one-parent families, 60% of which are to be found among the black population (Frankfurter Allgemeine Zeitung 6. 11. 86).

However, to be able to make a critical assessment of the widely claimed connection between a broken home and suicidal behavior, it is necessary to take into account a number of general methodological problems as well as specific problems inherent in the study of the causes of suicidal behavior.

General Methodological Problems

Definition and Operationalism of a Broken Home

In previous studies, many different definitions of the term "broken home" have been put forward. Some investigators have only applied this term to structurally incomplete families, i.e., a family lacking at least one natural parent. Others have considerably extended this definition to include "dysfunctional families" (i.e., "functionally incomplete") in the broadest sense, e.g., disharmony between the parents, adoptive children, upbringing in an institution or by relatives, drug addiction or mental illness among one or both of the parents, or rejection of the child by its parents. Several authors have even emphasized that the effects of a broken home are not confined to one generation, for they may have an important influence on the psychological development of children whose parents themselves have experienced parental loss; thus, such investigators have given combined figures for the number of parental losses for both the parents (first generation) and the children (second generation; cf. Langenmayr 1975).

Even if the term broken home is only applied to structurally incomplete families, a number of aspects need to be carefully differentiated, i.e., the absent parent, the reason for the absence (type of loss), the duration and starting point of the absence, and the resulting situation (cf. Lösel 1971). Moreover, interactions between these variables and the sex of the child have to be taken into account.

Absent Persons. In empirical studies, the sex and number (i.e., mother, father, or both) of the absent parent(s) are frequently ignored, even though it would seem reasonable to suppose that these variables have differential effects. For example, it remains a matter of controversy as to whether the loss of a father or a mother has the greatest effect. According to the psychoanalytic view (e.g., Bowlby 1969; Munro 1966a, b), the early loss of the mother has more far-reaching consequences than that of the father. However, apart from investigations of the so-called hospitalization syndrome among children who have been brought up in institutions, there is a scarcity of empirical studies dealing with the effects of maternal absence. In a study of female adolescents who had remained in the custody of their father after a divorce (age at the time of divorce, 11.7 ± 3.8 years), Stephens and Day (1979) did not detect any negative effects of the maternal loss with respect to self-concept and identification compared to girls from intact families. On the other hand, recent studies have increasingly emphasized the negative effects resulting from the loss of a father. For example, Matussek and May (1981) concluded that, with regard to depressive illnesses, the loss of the father alone has more serious consequences than simultaneous separation from both parents. Meyer-Krahmer (1980) also stressed the particular significance of paternal loss, especially in connection with the normal development of boys.

Of course, the objective fact of a "paternal loss" cannot be regarded in isolation from certain accompanying factors, i.e., the way in which the loss is subjectively experienced, and the situation brought into being by the loss. Thus, for example, it is conceivable that, in the event of a divorce, "paternal loss" might be so serious because it results in "maternal loss" due to the greater demands made on the divorced mother. In a study of 16000 children utilizing information provided by the National Child Bureau in Great Britain, Ferri (1973) found that fathers who had raised their children alone had received considerably more support in bringing up their children (usually from a grandmother or eldest daughter) than mothers in the same situation (24% vs 5%). The percentages of fathers and mothers who had brought up their children without any other support after the loss of the spouse were 41% and 61%, respectively.

It is also possible that the reported covariation between (emotional) disturbances and the absence of a relationship with the father is due to statistical artifacts. After a divorce or separation, it is most usual for children to remain with their mother (cf. Hetherington 1979). In addition, among the age groups most frequently investigated, the effects of the Second World War were such that paternal death was far more prevalent than maternal death (e.g., Weyerer 1984: 14.4% vs. 7.6%).

Reasons for Absence. Many previous investigators have made no attempt to distinguish between different reasons for the absence of one or both of the parents (e.g., death, separation, divorce, illegitimate birth, long stays in hospital or in prison). Also, it is necessary to differentiate very precisely the cause of the death of a parent. Clearly, one would expect the effects of paternal loss to vary according to whether the father has died as a result of an accident, illness, or suicide or is regarded as a "war hero." Above all, among suicidal patients who have experienced the loss of a parent by suicide, it is difficult to determine to what extent ensuing stigmatization within their social environment should be taken into account (cf. Cain and Fast 1966; Dorpat 1972; Shepherd and Barraclough 1976; Rudestam 1977; Rogers et al. 1982; Rudestam and Imbroll 1983; Goldney 1985 a). Irrespective of this, the picture has begun to emerge − partly due to experiences during and after the Second World War − that a child's social development is generally less damaged when a family loses a parent as a result of death (particularly in a "harmonious" family) than when the family is split by divorce (cf. Lehr 1973; Rutter 1977; Hetherington 1979). Indeed, when comparing adolescents who had attempted suicide with a control group, Goldney (1981) found no significant differences in adolescents with a dead parent, whereas a significant difference was observable for those who had experienced the divorce or separation of their parents. It is possible that the conflict between parents before their separation/divorce is of crucial importance (Herzer et al. 1981). For example, in support of this hypothesis, it has been found that emotionally disturbed children from disharmonious families show a stronger tendency to have relapses than children from broken homes (Power et al. 1974). Children who exhibit adjustment disturbances before a divorce also tend to experience longer-lasting disturbances after the divorce (Kelly 1978, cited in Hetherington 1979). However, it remains unclear whether such disturbances are the product of pathogenic conditions existing before the divorce or can be attributed to the experience of loss; it is even possible that such manifestations are independent of these conditions, the child having previously exhibited such disturbances. Rutter (1971), summarizing the results of his studies, concluded that separation in itself has no negative effects, but that the reason for the separation is of critical importance.

Time Considerations. In previous studies, the assignment of age limits, i.e., the maximum age of a child before which the occurrence of parental death or separation can be considered as resulting in a pathogenous broken-home situation, has shown wide variation, often with no clear reason being given for the choice of a particular age; the lowest upper limit that has been applied is 5 years, the highest being 19 years. Furthermore, the minimum period of parental absence that can be considered to constitute a broken-home situation has been variously defined, ranging from 6 months to over 4 years. These varying assignments of upper age limits and minimum time periods in definitions of broken homes further exacerbate the difficulties of providing a satisfactory definition of this theoretical concept. In a review of the available literature, Rutter (1979) concluded that, when a child is separated from an adult to whom it has close emotional ties, the time factor is not as important as the nature and closeness of the relationship with that person. Also, there has been a tendency to ignore the fact that the stress agents resulting from the loss of a parent may differ according to the age of a child. Older children are often called upon to take over the role and functions of the missing partner; although, in certain cases, this may even have a beneficial effect (e.g., early assumption of responsibility), it can also have serious negative effects (e.g., coping with demands beyond a child's capabilities). On the other hand, younger children are often less able to cope with a divorce (especially when they have a good relationship with their parents) because they are unable to regard the problems of their parents as being separate from their own person, thus leading to the possibility of developing feelings of guilt (Tessman 1978).

The Situation Following Loss. Few studies have given information concerning the way in which a suicidal youth has been brought up after parental loss or divorce (by the mother or father alone, by one parent plus a stepfather/mother, by grandparents, by adoptive parents, or in an institution), even though investigations of nonsuicidal adolescents have shown this variable to be of crucial importance (Young and Parish 1977). For example, Parish and Taylor (1979) found that children whose mothers did not remarry after a divorce had a significantly lower self-concept than children from intact families, whereas this was not the case when the mother remarried. According to the results of several American studies, it appears that, particularly for boys, the presence of a stepfather or an elder brother has a beneficial influence (Stephens and Day 1979). In contrast, German investigations have indicated the opposite to be the case: for example, in the Tübingen study of juvenile delinquents, Dolde (1978) found the presence of a stepfather to have a negative effect with respect to non-recidivism. Furthermore, Weyerer (1984) reported that children brought up by step-parents or adoptive parents belonged to the second highest risk group with respect to the likelihood of developing psychiatric illnesses or requiring psychiatric treatment during adulthood (see below).

It seems probable that these factors covary with the problems of the remaining parent. Indeed, it has been found that the incidence of physical illness and emotional problems is higher among divorced adults than among married adults (Bloom et al. 1978; Bojanovsky 1983; Bojanovsky and Wagner 1985). Moreover, it is possible that the feelings of a divorced mother/father toward the father/mother of her/his child(ren) will be different than those of a mother/father toward a dead partner, and this may significantly influence her/his ability to cope with the divorce as well as her/his attitude toward the child(ren). It has also been reported that the proportion of adoptive children who are admitted to psychiatric institutions is very high (cf. Stephenson 1975; Huth 1978; Jungmann 1980a, b); however, in such cases, it is unclear to what extent the findings are affected by specific selection mechanisms resulting from increased social control by social welfare authorities.

Another factor which has been given very little attention is the possible occurrence of a "multiple" broken-home effect, i.e., additional losses of influential adults resulting from temporary accommodation or the changing of partners by the remaining parent. In the Tübingen study of juvenile delinquents, Dolde (1978) found a higher incidence of youths with a number of "stepfathers" among jailed adolescents than in the control group.

When investigating children placed in institutions as a result of a broken family, differential factors must also be carefully considered. In a recent study, Stober et al. (1982) used the variables age, sex, religion, and socioeconomic status to match adolescents who had received treatment after a suicide attempt with those with no record of suicidal behavior; 25% of the broken-home adolescents with a record of suicidal behavior had grown up in an institution or had lived with adoptive or foster parents, whereas all except three of the control subjects with a broken home had been brought up by the mother (the three others having been raised by a stepmother, a grandmother, and relatives, respectively). In the Tübingen investigation (Göppinger 1983), it was also found that many of the juvenile offenders had been placed in an institution during their school years and had spent longer periods in institutions than the subjects in the comparison group. However, most of those who had become offenders at an early age had been placed in an institution as a result of asocial behavior or due to neglect by their parents, whereas those who had become offenders when adults (along with the members of the comparison group) had been put in an institution, often on a temporary basis, as a result of the illness or death of the parent(s).

Interaction with the Sex of a Child. Cantor (1972) emphasized the particular importance of the loss of a father among female adolescents who attempt suicide, while Brown and Epps (1966) obtained similar findings with regard to female delinquency. In contrast, Weyerer (1984) reported that paternal loss before 15 years of age causes an elevated relative risk of psychiatric illness only among men, with maternal loss causing a similar increase among women.

A series of investigations have attempted to elucidate the influence of paternal loss on the concept of self as well as on cognitive styles (e.g., Young and Parish 1977; Parish and Copeland 1980). Although the results exhibit a number of discrepancies, they do indicate that the sex of a child, the nature of the loss/separation, and the ensuing circumstances are moderating influences.

Disharmony within a family and divorce also appear to have a more persistent effect on boys than on girls (Hetherington 1979), which in part can be attributed to differing reactions and attitudes toward boys and girls after a divorce, i.e., boys tend to be regarded in a more negative way than girls (Santrock and Trace 1978). Divorced mothers of boys report more stress and depressive feelings than those of girls (Colletta 1978, cited in Hetherington 1979; Hetherington et al. 1978). However, in a 10-year follow-up, Wallerstein (1984) found long-lasting effects among girls as well.

Reliability of Subjects' Reports Concerning Broken Homes

A particular problem encountered in studies of broken homes is the unreliability of subjects' reports concerning the experience of separation during childhood. In a study in which adults (average age, 38 years) were twice asked to answer questions about parental loss experienced before the age of 14 years (interval between questioning, 8 months), Finlay-Jones et al. (1981) found an acceptable correspondence between the two sets of answers only in cases of parental death (100%) and separation (92%). With respect to the active military service of the father during the war, only in 73% of cases were corresponding answers given at the two times of questioning. For other types of separation and loss, the two sets of answers were found to agree in only about 50% of cases. Also, Barraclough and Bunch (1973) found that subjects' attempts to date the death of a parent tended to be relatively inaccurate, with the inexactitude increasing with the length of time that had elapsed after the event; indeed, for 11% of the subjects tested, the discrepancy between the actual and remembered date of the decease of a parent amounted to 3 years or more. Only 60% of those questioned were able to recall correctly the year of parental death. Possibly for these reasons, Farmer (1979) found that, when the number of patients who were unable to give any information concerning a "broken-home variable" was taken into consideration, the difference between the criterion (suicidal patients) and control groups ceased to be significant.

Subjects' reports are even more unreliable when not only structurally damaged but also functionally disturbed families are taken into account. On the one hand, this broader concept further hinders any possibility of making meaningful comparisons of the body of literature dealing with broken homes because the operational definitions are different. On the other hand, subjects' reports concerning functionally disturbed families are, due to their necessarily more subjective nature (e.g., concerning the attitude of the parents or the manner of upbringing), more likely to be distorted and misleading. Particularly among socially deviant patients, several investigators have found extremely idealistic and unrealistic expectations of parents and partners (e.g., Lazarus 1976; Zimmer-Höfler et al. 1985). Failure of the parents to live up to these expectations can result in negative attitudes toward the parents and their upbringing methods. Thus, Goldney (1981, 1985b) found that patients with suicide attempts regarded their parents' characters in a more negative light than control subjects. These patients reported that, on the one hand, their parents were less caring, while on the other hand, they were overprotective. Similar results have been obtained for adolescents with an alcohol problem (Jacobsen and Stallmann 1985).

Socioeconomic Status

The reported incidence of structurally incomplete families appears to covary inversely with socioeconomic status. In a sample of patients receiving treatment in a department of child and adolescent psychiatry in Berlin ($n = 1040$), Petri (1979) found a broken-home rate of 33.4%. When these broken-home patients were subdivided according to social class, substantial differences become clear, with the proportion of those from lower-class backgrounds being 42.4%, while the middle and upper classes accounted for 29.4% and 26.6%, respectively. Also, in a random sample of the population in Bavaria, Weyerer (1984) found that, of the people who had experienced a broken home before the age of 15 years, the highest proportion came from the lower classes (27.5% vs 24.4%). Similar evidence has been presented in a study of the Deutsches Institut für Wirtschaftsforschung (DIW); German Institute of Economic Research) (1980) and in the Third Family Report of the Federal Republic of Germany (1979), both of which showed that "incomplete" families have a lower average income than structurally complete families. It has also been suggested that unhappy marriages and divorces may occur more frequently among families with a low or unstable income (Brandwein et al. 1974; Ross and Sawhill 1975).

It is also reasonable to assume that, in some cases, a broken home can lead to a decline in social status because divorce often results in the loss of one partner's salary. According to the figures for 1967 published by the American Census Bureau (1968), the proportion of white families in the United States with an income of less than $ 3000 was over three times higher for those in which the father was absent than for families with a father (32% vs 10%); among the black population, the corresponding proportions were 53% and 24%.

When a divorce compels a mother to take on a job, her child(ren) may suffer a double loss. However, the fact of a mother taking employment would appear to have less influence than the mother's attitude toward work (discussed as early as 1962 by Yarrow et al.). Whereas Rutter (1979) was unable to detect any negative effects stemming from mothers holding a job, Sander et al. (1983) found that the problems arising from divorces were much more negatively evaluated by mothers who had unskilled or semiskilled jobs. A further problem that often arises from a divorce is the necessity of moving home (in the case of socioeconomic decline, usually to cheaper accommodation), resulting in yet more experiences of separation (loss of friends, neighbors, schoolfriends). The possibility cannot be excluded that a move to problem areas with higher rates of delinquency and psychiatric problems may produce further negative effects.

The higher broken-home rate among persons with a record of suicidal behavior may therefore be a statistical artifact arising from the greater likelihood of persons from the lower classes being included in sample groups. Bearing in mind the problems surrounding the discrepancy between the reported and actual number of suicide attempts (cf. Schmidtke 1984), it seems that a suicide attempt by a member of the lower classes is more likely to come to light than such an act by a member of the upper classes.

Direction of Effects

Another methodological problem encountered when attempting to evaluate reports obtained from subjects with emotional disorders concerns the direction of effects. In general, in investigations dealing with the influences of a broken home, it is assumed that unfavorable conditions within a family are the cause of deviant behavior. However, the available statistics (most being of a correlative and a posteriori nature) do not appear to bear out such interpretations with regard to effect direction. At least since the publication of the studies by Bell (1968, 1979), developmental psychologists have recognized that parents and children have reciprocal influences on each other. Thus, it has been suggested that, in certain instances, disharmony within a family may, in fact, have its origins in the deviant behavior of a child (cf., for example, Göppinger 1976).

Another aspect that has received too little attention is the possibility that the likelihood of a doctor/therapist diagnosing "depression" may be influenced by knowledge of a broken home in a patient's history, as depressive behavior is expected in such cases (cf. Berlinsky and Biller 1982).

Specific Methodological Aspects

Selection of Criterion Samples

The selection of related criteria groups is the source of further methodological problems, as most studies have focused on patients who are already in institutions or on subjects whose behavior is conspicuously deviant.

Even though the importance of a broken home in patients who have exhibited suicidal behavior has long been a source of discussion and controversy, there is a striking paucity of representative and systematic studies in which an attempt has been made to establish the incidence of psychiatric disturbances among children from structurally or functionally disturbed families. Gebert (1975) reported that 1.2% of children who experienced the divorce of their parents attempted suicide, while Bühler and Kächele (1978) reported a figure of 2.5%. In a study of children and adolescents receiving psychiatric treatment, Lempp (1980) found a higher rate of suicide attempts among those with divorced parents (3%) compared with those with no experience of divorce (0%). Haffter (1979) found the incidence of suicide and suicide attempts to be 3% among children of divorced parents.

It would appear that, when attempting to determine such rates, the behavior criteria (i.e., suicide attempts) need to be more precisely differentiated. For example, Kurz et al. (1982) reported that the most important factor distinguishing those patients with more than one suicide attempt from those with only one suicide attempt was a broken-home background.

Age of the Criterion Sample

The age of the subjects in a sample will greatly affect the percentage of broken-home situations encountered, this being due to a number of factors such as varying levels of risk of parental death and of paternal death caused by war. For example, in the United States between 1920 and 1963, the probability of a parent dying before a child's 18th birthday fell from 16.3% to 4.4% (Dennehy 1966). A series of studies have revealed considerable differences in the rate of broken homes among different age groups (with socioeconomic status also exerting a noticeable influence; e.g., Brown et al. 1977). Thus, Beck et al. (1963) found that the covariation between parental loss during childhood and severe depression was much less pronounced when the age of their subjects was partialled out.

It also remains to be elucidated how long a broken home can still be regarded as representing a vulnerability factor with regard to suicidal behavior (cf. Bühler and Kächele 1978). For example, Bruhn (1962) proposed that this factor exerts such effects primarily on younger people (i.e., up to 30 years of age), while tending to be overshadowed by other influences with increasing age.

Selection Processes

In certain cases, specific selection processes may account for an apparent connection between suicidal behavior and broken homes. For example, due to more frequent and more intensive contact with youth authorities (e.g., adoptive children, cf. Hersov 1977; Jungmann 1980a, b) or greater social control as a result of being placed in an institution (cf., for example, v. Hauff and Henckel 1981), adolescents from a broken home who attempt suicide are more likely to be referred to qualified persons (i.e., in close-knit family units, a suicide attempt has more chance of being covered up). Also, in families with a low income, the social services play a greater supporting role (Colletta 1978, cited in Hetherington 1979), so that the likelihood of stronger social control is similarly increased. In a comparative study of patients with suicide attempts and a control group in the same hospital (the socioeconomic status being deduced from the way in which the hospital costs were paid), Deykin et al. (1985) demonstrated that the suicidal patients were more frequently included in records of the Department of Social Services than the controls (females, 15.4% vs 4.9%; males, 16.6% vs 2.7%). The reasons for their inclusion could not be precisely ascertained, although it appeared that the majority of cases handled by this department were victims of child abuse or neglect.

When considering the composition of sample groups, ethnic differences also have to be taken into account, particularly in American studies. In one study aimed at investigating general broken-home rates, Shaw and McKay (1932) found the highest broken-home rate among Blacks (48%), the lowest being among Jews (20%; both figures corrected for age). From this, they concluded that any results concerning broken-home rates that provide no information about the distribution of ethnic or national groups within the sample must be considered as being virtually worthless.

Control Groups

In the light of the above-mentioned aspects, it would appear to be useful not only to compare the broken-home rate within sample groups of suicidal patients with demographic data obtained for the population as a whole, but also to make a differentiated comparison with samples matched according to specific aspects. Most previously published studies have involved comparisons of ad hoc sample groups of a more or less chance composition. For example, Shaw and McKay (1932), in a survey of 29 schools (comprising a total of 7278 children), found the broken-home rate in the individual schools to range from 16% to 53%, the mean being 29%.

For methodological reasons, groups of patients with various psychiatric disturbances often have to be used as comparison groups. However, in many such studies, the previously mentioned criticisms are also applicable, as the control groups appear to have been assembled more or less by chance, and the criterion groups often consist of mixed groups of patients with a broad spectrum of psychiatric diagnoses. Consequently, the results of previous studies concerning comparative broken-home rates among groups of suicidal and delinquent or psychiatrically disturbed subjects exhibit remarkably wide variations (Table 1).

The incidence of other psychiatric and social disturbances among subjects from broken homes has also been little investigated. In one study, Markusen and Fulton (1971) examined a group of 11 450 15-year-olds twice over a period of 12 years; for 2267 of the males, it was possible to obtain information about whether or not they had a record of delinquency. Of the 131 males whose parents were divorced, 21% were delinquents (34% of these having committed serious crimes), while of the 161 males who had lost a parent by death, 16% were delinquent (23% having committed serious crimes). Of the 1976 males from structurally intact families, 11% were found to be delinquent (18% of whom had committed serious crimes). In another investigation, Bendiksen and Fulton (1975) sent a questionnaire containing questions about serious illnesses, severe emotional problems, and prison stays to a total of 409 subjects from the original Minnesota Multiphasic Personality Inventory (MMPI) study of 1954, whose family background was known. In all, 256 subjects filled in and returned the questionnaire, and these were divided into three groups as follows: (1) those with a dead parent ($n = 70$), (2) those with divorced parents ($n = 46$), and (3) those from an intact family ($n = 140$). Of the subjects comprising group 1, 17% reported serious illnesses, 33% reported severe emotional stress, and 6% had spent time in prison. The corresponding rates for group 2 were 20%, 35%, and 2%, respectively, while for group 3, they were 9%, 20%, and 2%, respectively. It should, however, be noted that, of the total subsample of the MMPI study, Bendiksen and Fulton (1975) were only able to trace the whereabouts of 30% of the divorced-family subjects, 50% of those with a dead parent, and 60% of the intact-family subjects. In addition, the intact-family group showed a 70% response to the questionnaire compared with a 68% response from both broken-home groups.

In a study of a group of 1340 subjects taken from the general population of Bavaria, Weyerer (1984) found that 27% had experienced a broken home before the age of 15 years. He also found that those who had not been brought up by their natural parents exhibited an elevated relative risk of having a psychiatric illness, the highest relative risk being among those who had grown up with stepparents or adoptive parents or in an institution. Subjects who had experienced parental death during childhood exhibited only a marginally increased relative risk. It should be pointed out, however, that Weyerer did not investigate whether there was any connection between upbringing with adoptive/stepparents or in institutions and socioeconomic status.

In a study involving the questioning of pupils attending a German gymnasium (grammar/high school), Zimmermann (1974) reported a broken-home rate of 9.9% (parental death and divorce); 13.2% of those with a dead father and 16.7% of those with a dead mother or divorced parents admitted to having tried soft drugs (hashish), the corresponding figures for the adolescents from intact families being 10.9%.

In a comparison between children of divorced or separated parents and children from intact families, McDermott (1970) found an increased incidence of various disturbances (i.e., running away from home, school problems, "depression") among the former group. However, it is of interest that the disturbances reported for the broken-home group seemed to be specific stress reactions and, in general, were of a shorter duration than the behavioral problems experienced by the children from intact families.

Discussion

Previous studies have consistently reported that the broken-home rate among groups of subjects with a history of suicidal behavior is significantly higher than the base rate for the population as a whole. However, due to the methodological objections that can be raised to many of these studies, it can safely be assumed that the covariation between the variable "broken home" and suicidal behavior as compared with other psychiatric disturbances has, in most cases, been overestimated. This conclusion is further supported by the fact that, in studies of samples of depressive subjects, the partialling out of other influencing variables has resulted in only slight differences, with respect to the occurrence of a broken home, between the criterion and control groups.

To the best of our knowledge, no existing study of the incidence of suicidal behavior among samples of broken-home subjects has dealt with other influential factors in sufficient detail to allow existing hypotheses concerning the differential effects of various broken-home situations to be tested. Furthermore, few studies investigating the problem of a broken home in connection with suicides or suicide attempters have indicated any awareness of the methodological problems outlined above. In the study of Stober et al. (1982), the only investigation in Germany known to us in which subjects were differentiated according to age, sex, socioeconomic status, and religion, it was found that the situation following parental loss was markedly different in the case of patients with suicide attempts compared with the control group. It is conceivable that the probability of the occurrence of the suicidal acts might have been influenced by these circumstances.

In a meta-analysis of articles that included, among others, nine studies involving samples of patients after suicide attempts, Berlinsky and Biller (1982) found that only five of these studies attained the second highest level (II) of methodological adequacy, with two studies reaching level III. (Level I indicates the highest standards of methodological adequacy, e.g., the type of loss is specified, the data are statistically analyzed, the sample is homogeneous, the comparison group is matched, the methods of assessment are reliable and valid, the time that has elapsed between the time of assessment and the time when the loss occurred is considered, the characteristics of the family structure are controlled for or analyzed when interpreting the results.)

It has been proposed that, in some cases, other factors which have their origins in the subject him/herself (perhaps affecting a person's ability to cope with parental loss) may be of greater importance in the development of subsequent psychological problems than the variable broken home. This view is supported by the results of a study concerning the psychological effects of parental loss among the brothers and sisters of psychiatrically disturbed patients, in which it was found that siblings who had been equally exposed to the same stressors did not exhibit a higher incidence of psychiatric illness or deficiency than that observed among the population as a whole (Granville-Grossman 1966; Perris et al. 1986).

This would also seem to be confirmed by the findings of the few studies that have dealt with the prevalence of suicide attempts among children and adolescents from broken homes, for the percentages recorded are very close to published estimates of the general rate of attempted suicide among adolescents (cf. Schmidtke 1981, 1984; Schmidtke and Häfner 1986). Further evidence in favor of this hypothesis is provided by the results of several epidemiologic studies showing that, in spite of differing increases in the divorce rate in various countries, no corresponding increases in the suicide rate among adolescents can be demonstrated (cf. Berman and Cohen-Sandler 1982). When interpreting published findings, it is necessary to take into account changes in broken-home rates (in part due to the effects of wars) with time as well as increases in the number of broken homes resulting from divorce. It is also open to question as to how long the effects of a broken home can still be regarded as having any influence on subsequent suicidal behavior (cf. Bühler and Kächele 1978).

Moreover, differing operational definitions of the term, broken home, represent a further obstacle to any attempt to define the concept with respect to the effects that this factor may exert. Divergent views with regard to what actually constitutes a "broken home" would appear to be responsible for the considerable discrepancies between previous findings concerning the incidence of broken homes among suicides and patients with suicide attempts; as a consequence, any comparisons between the results of previously published studies are bound to be of debatable value.

Bearing these methodological considerations in mind, it remains questionable as to whether the variable, broken home, specifically predisposes a person to suicidal behavior. It seems more likely that a broken home, in combination with the simultaneous and subsequent emergence of adverse circumstances, increases the probability of the appearance of deviant behavior in general. Therefore, it would appear to be of little use only to compare groups of suicidal subjects with "control" groups, as in most cases, this only provides an insight into the circumstances and variables affecting "emotional disturbances" in general rather than suicidal behavior in particular.

Furthermore, several investigators have put forward the view that, with respect to suicidal acts, there are no marked differences between adolescents from intact families and those from disturbed family units (cf. Schneer et al. 1975). Using the broken-home variable alone, it is impossible to devise any empirically demonstrable theory concerning the conditions specific for suicidal behavior (as is also the case for other forms of "deviant" behavior).

Although many investigators have regarded a one-parent family as being a pathogenous factor (cf. Hetherington 1979), the loss of a parent may, in certain cases, signify the end of a long-standing conflict and thus result in an improvement in a child's situation. All in all, it would seem that the most useful approach for understanding suicidal behavior is to analyze the learning history and background of patients who have exhibited such behavior. Therefore, within the general framework of more broadly based theoretical models of suicidal behavior (e.g., those explaining such behavior in terms of learning and coping processes, cf. Schmidtke 1988), the variable, broken home, should be regarded as being only one of several factors conditioning the failure to develop or apply adequate coping strategies and to receive adequate social support.

References

Barraclough BM, Bunch J (1973) Accuracy of dating parent deaths: recollected dates compared with death certificates. Br J Psychiatry 123:573−574

Beck AT, Sethi BB, Tuthill RW (1963) Childhood bereavement and adult depression. Arch Gen Psychiatry 9:295−302

Bell RQ (1968) A reinterpretation of the direction of effects in studies of socialization. Psychol Rev 75:81−95

Bell RQ (1979) Parent, child, and reciprocal influence. Am Psychol 34:821−826

Bendiksen R, Fulton R (1975) Death and the child: an anterospective test of the childhood bereavement and later behavior disorder hypothesis. Omega 6:45−59

Berlinsky EB, Biller HB (1982) Parental death and psychological development. Lexington Books, Lexington

Berman AL, Cohen-Sandler R (1982) Childhood and adolescent suicide research: a critique. Crisis 3:3−15

Biener K (1978) Ursachen und Auslöser von Selbstmorden und Selbstmordversuchen Jugendlicher. Caritas 79:114−117

Bloom BL, Asher SJ, White SW (1978) Marital disruption as a stressor: a review and analysis. Psychol Bull 85:867−894

Bojanovsky J (1983) Psychische Probleme bei Geschiedenen. Enke, Stuttgart

Bojanovsky J, Wagner G (1983) Scheidung − ein Trauma? Psycho 11:782−791

Bowlby J (1969) Attachment and loss. Hogarth, London

Brandwein RA, Brown CA, Fox CM (1974) Women and children last: the social situation of divorced mothers and their families: J Marriage Family 36:498−514

Brown F, Epps P (1966) Childhood bereavement and subsequent crime. Br J Psychiatry 112:1043−1048

Brown G, Harris T, Copeland J (1977) Depression and loss. Br J Psychiatry 30:1−18

Bruhn JG (1962) Broken homes among attempted suicides and psychiatric outpatients: a comparative study. J Ment Sci 108:772−779

Bühler H, Kächele S (1978) Die Ehescheidung als pathogener Faktor − Eine kinder- und jugendpsychiatrische Untersuchung. Prax Kinderpsychol Kinderpsychiatr 27:296−300

Cain AC, Fast I (1965) Children's disturbed reactions to parent suicide. Am J Orthopsychiatry 36:873−880

Cantor P (1972) The adolescent attempters: Sex, sibling position, and family constellation. Life Threat Behav 2:252−261

Dennehy CM (1966) Childhood bereavement and psychiatric illness. Br J Psychiatry 112:1049−1069

Deutsches Institut für Wirtschaftsforschung (DIW) (1980) Die aktuelle Einkommenslage der Familien in der Bundesrepublik Deutschland auf der Grundlage des DIW-Einkommensmodells. Gutachten im Auftrage des Bundesministeriums für Jugend, Familie und Gesundheit

Deykin EY, Alpert JJ, McNamara JJ (1985) A pilot study of the effect of exposure to child abuse or neglect on adolescent suicidal behavior. Am J Psychiatry 142:1299−1303

Dolde G (1978) Sozialisation und kriminelle Karriere. Minerva, Munich

Dorpat TL (1972) Psychological effects of parental suicide on surviving children. In: Cain AC (ed) Survivors of suicide. Thomas, Springfield, p 121

Farmer RDT (1979) The differences between those who repeat and those who do not. In: Farmer RDT, Hirsch SR (eds) The suicide syndrom. Croom Helm, London, p 187

Ferri E (1973) Characteristics of motherless families. Br J Soc Work 3:91−100

Finlay-Jones R, Scott R, Duncan-Jones P, Byrne D, Henderson S (1981) The reliability of reports of early separations. Aust N Z J Psychiatry 15:27−31

Gebert K (1975) Neuropsychiatrische Erkrankungen bei Kindern aus geschiedenen Ehen. Psychiatr Neurol Med Psychol 27:668−675

Goldney RD (1981) Parental loss and reported childhood stress in young women who attempt suicide. Acta Psychiat Scand 64:34−49

Goldney RD (1985a) Survivor victims and crisis care. Crisis 6:1−9

Goldney RD (1985b) Parental representation in young women who attempt suicide. Acta Psychiat Scand 72:230−232

Göppinger H (1976) Kriminologie, 3rd edn. Beck, Munich

Göppinger H (1983) Der Täter in seinen sozialen Bezügen. Springer, Berlin Heidelberg New York

Granville-Grossman KL (1966) Early bereavement and schizophrenia. Br J Psychiatry 112:1027−1034

Haffter C (1979) Kinder aus geschiedenen Ehen. Huber, Bern

Hersov L (1977) Adoption. In: Rutter M, Hersov L (eds) Child psychiatry. Blackwell, Oxford, p 136

Herzer R, Herzer H, Perlwitz R (1981) Familiäre Beziehungsstörungen und Suizidversuche im Kindes- und Jugendalter. Ärztl Jugendkd 72:298−303

Hetherington EM (1979) Divorce. A child's perspective. Am Psychol 34:851−858

Hetherington EM, Cox M, Cox R (1978) The aftermath of divorce. In: Stevens JH, Matthews M (eds) Mother-child, father-child relations. National Association for the Education of Young Children, Washington

Huth W (1978) Psychische Störungen bei Adoptivkindern − Eine Übersicht über den Stand der klinischen Forschung. Z Klin Psychol Psychother 26:256−270

Jacobsen G, Stallmann M (1985) Alkoholkonsum von Berliner Jugendlichen − Ergebnisse einer Repräsentativbefragung von Schülern der 10. Jahrgangsstufe. Suchtgefahren 31:394−401

Jungmann J (1980a) Forschungsergebnisse zur Entwicklung von Adoptivkindern. Z Kinder Jugendpsychiat 8:184−219

Jungmann J (1980b) Adoption unter Vorbehalt? − Zur psychischen Problematik von Adoptivkindern. Prax Kinderpsychol Kinderpsychiat 29:225−230

Kitamura A (1982) Eine vergleichende Untersuchung der Suizidversuche deutscher und japanischer Jugendlicher. Prax Kinderpsychol Kinderpsychiatr 31:191−201

Kurz A, Torhorst A, Wächtler C, Möller HJ (1982) Vergleichende Untersuchung von 295 Patienten mit erstmaligem und wiederholtem Suizidversuch. Arch Psychiatr Nervenkr 232:427−438

Langenmayr A (1975) Personenverluste und ihre Wirkung bei der Entstehung von Neurosestrukturen. Prax Kinderpsychol Kinderpsychiat 24:136−145

Lazarus H (1976) Subjektive Familienstruktur und Jugendkriminalität. Schindele, Rheinstetten

Lehr U (1973) Die Bedeutung der Familie im Sozialisationsprozeß. Kohlhammer, Stuttgart

Lempp R (1980) Ehescheidung und psychische Störungen bei Kindern. In: Remschmidt H (ed) Psychopathologie der Familie und kinderpsychiatrische Erkrankungen. Huber, Bern, p 106

Lösel F (1971) Evidenz und Problematik empirischer Zusammenhänge zwischen "broken home" und Delinquenz. Sonderforschungsbereich 22, Nürnberg

Markusen E, Fulton R (1971) Childhood bereavement and behavior disorders: a critical review. Omega 2:107−117

Matussek P, May U (1981) Verlustereignisse in der Kindheit als prädisponierende Faktoren für neurotische und psychotische Depressionen. Arch Psychiatr Nervenkr 229:189−204

McDermott JF (1970) Divorce and its psychiatric sequelae in children. Arch Gen Psychiatry 23:421−427

Meyer-Krahmer K (1980) Die Rolle des Vaters in der Entwicklung des Kindes. Psychol Erzieh Unterr 27:87−102

Munro A (1966a) Some familial and social factors in depressive illness. Br J Psychiatry 112:429−441

Munro A (1966b) Parental deprivation in depressive patients. Br J Psychiatry 112:443−457

Parish TS, Copeland TF (1980) Locus of control and father loss. J Genet Psychol 136:147−148

Parish TS, Taylor JC (1979) The impact of divorce and subsequent father absence on children's and adolescents' self-concepts. Manuscript, Kansas State University

Perris C, Holmgren S, Knorring L v, Perris H (1986) Parental loss by death in the early childhood of depressed patients and of their healthy siblings. Br J Psychiatry 148:165−169

Petri H (1979) Soziale Schicht und psychische Erkrankungen im Kindes- und Jugendalter. Vandenhoeck and Ruprecht, Göttingen

Power MJ, Ash PM, Shoenberg E, Sirey EC (1974) Delinquency and the family. Br J Soc Work 4:13−38

Rogers J, Sheldon A, Barwick C, Letofsky K, Lancee W (1982) Help for families of suicide: survivors support program. Can J Psychiatry 27:444−449

Ross HL, Sawhill IV (1975) Time of transition: The growth of families headed by women. Urban Institute, Washington DC

Rudestam KE (1977) Physical and psychological responses to suicide in the family. J Consult Clin Psychol 45:162−170

Rudestam KE, Imbroll D (1983) Societal reactions to a child's death by suicide. J Consult Clin Psychol 51:461−462

Rutter M (1971) Parent-child separation: Psychological effects on the children. J Child Psychol Psychiatry 12:233−260

Rutter M (1977) Separation, loss and family relationships. In: Rutter M, Hersov L (eds) Child psychiatry. Blackwell, Oxford, p 47

Rutter M (1979) Separation experiences: A new look at an old topic. J Pediatr 95:147−154

Sander E, Berger M, Isselstein-Mohr D (1983) Die Wahrnehmung der eigenen Problemsituation durch alleinerziehende Mütter. Psychol Erz Unterr 30:16−23

Santrock JW, Trace RL (1978) Effect of children's family structure status on the development of stereotypes by children. J Educ Psychol 70:754−757

Schaller S, Schmidtke A (1983) Broken home − ein beweisbarer Zusammenhang? In: Pohlmeier H, Schmidtke A, Welz R (eds) Suizidales Verhalten. Roderer, Regensburg, p 123

Schmidtke A (1981) Entwicklung der Häufigkeit suizidaler Handlungen im Kindes- und Jugendalter in der Bundesrepublik Deutschland. Kinderarzt 12:697−714

Schmidtke A (1984) Zur Entwicklung der Häufigkeit suizidaler Handlungen im Kindes- und Jugendalter in der Bundesrepublik Deutschland 1950 bis 1981. Suicidprophylaxe 11:45−79

Schmidtke A (1988) Verhaltenstheoretisches Erklärungsmodell suizidalen Verhaltens. Roderer, Regensburg

Schmidtke A, Häfner H (1986) Suizide und Suizidversuche in der Bundesrepublik Deutschland: Häufigkeiten und Trends. In: Specht F, Schmidtke A (eds) Selbstmordhandlungen bei Kindern und Jugendlichen. Roderer, Regensburg, pp 27−49

Schneer HI, Perlstein A, Brozovsky M (1975) Hospitalized suicidal adolescents. Two generations. J Am Acad Child Psychiatry 14:565−567

Shaw CR, McKay HD (1932) Are broken homes a causative factor in juvenile delinquency? Social Forces 10:514−524

Shepherd DM, Barraclough BM (1976) The aftermath of parental suicide for children. Br J Psychiatry 129:267−276

Stephens N, Day HD (1979) Sex-role identity, parental identification, and self-concept of adolescent daughters from mother-absent, father-absent, and intact families. J Psychol 103:193−202

Stephenson PS (1975) The emotional implications of adoption policy. Compr Psychiatry 16:363−367

Stober B, Göhring J, Günzler G (1982) Suizidale Verhaltensweisen und deren familiäre Bedingungen bei Schülern. Acta Paedopsychiatr 48:239−248

Tessman LH (1978) Children of parting parents. Aronson, New York

von Hauff M, Henckel D (1981) Heimkinder als Problemgruppe der Sozialpolitik. Kinderarzt 12:993−998

Wallerstein JS (1984) Children of divorce: preliminary report of a ten-year follow-up of young children. Am J Orthopsychiatry 54:444

Weyerer S (1984) Der Einfluß des Verlustes von Vater oder Mutter in der Kindheit auf das Auftreten psychischer Erkrankungen im Erwachsenenalter. Manuscript, Central Institute of Mental Health, Mannheim

Yarrow MR, Scott P, de Loeuw L, Hernig C (1962) Childrearing in families of working and non-working mothers. Sociometry 25:122

Young ER, Parish TS (1977) Impact of father absence during childhood on the psychological adjustment of college females. Sex Roles 3:217–227

Zimmer-Höfler D, Uchtenhagen A (1985) Wie "normal" ist Heroinabhängigkeit? Eine zweijährige Verlaufsuntersuchung mit repräsentativer Kontrollgruppe. Drogalcohol 9:83–104

Zimmer-Höfler D, Uchtenhagen A, Christen S, Meyer-Fehr P (1985) Normal oder Opiatabhängig – ein empirischer Gruppenvergleich. In: Uchtenhagen A, Zimmer-Höfler D (eds) Heroinabhängige und ihre "normalen" Altersgenossen, Bern

Zimmermann R (1974) Drogenkontakt bei Oberschülern einer Großstadt. Ergebnisse einer Untersuchung an Oberschulen der Stadt Essen. Z Klin Psychol Psychother 22:169–179

"Broken-Home"-Related Data from Patients Following an Attempted Suicide: Comparison with Data from Psychiatric and Nonpsychiatric Patients

T. Riehl, A. Kurz, A. Torhorst, and H.-J. Möller

Introduction

After Zilboorg (1936a, b, 1937) pointed out in 1936 the association between suicide and disturbed family life during childhood, thus introducing the concept of a "broken home," there have been a number of investigations concerning this topic. As is the case with other social conditions of suicide and similar to affective disorders (Hudgens et al. 1967; Matussek and May 1981; Munro 1966), the significance of a "broken home" as a social risk factor of suicide has been judged differently.

A general comparison of the various studies in this field is not possible because of the differences in the sample groups, e.g., bipolar patients (Johnson and Hunt 1979), female prisoners (Climent et al. 1977), wrist-cutters (Rosenthal et al. 1972), veterans (Pokorny 1960), children (Pfeffer et al. 1979), or black and white race (Stein et al. 1974).

The main reason for the diverging results is probably to be found in the varying definition of broken home. There is no agreement concerning the description of parental loss only as a parental death (Birtchnell 1970; Bunch et al. 1971; Schneer et al. 1975) or a separation from parents as well (e.g. Kearney and Taylor 1969; Oliver et al. 1971). Others have included separation from siblings (McConaghy et al. 1966; Palmer 1941) and illegitimacy (Dorpat et al. 1965; Lobos and Battegay 1974; Reitman 1942).

The time of loss is applied to the period up to an age of 12 years (Crook and Raskin 1975) to 20 years (Oliver et al. 1971). Comparability becomes even more difficult if concepts such as "family stability" (Adam et al. 1982), "closeness to parents" (Thomas and Duszynski 1974), "parental strife" (Lobos and Battegay 1974; Walton 1958), "history of violence" (Pfeffer et al. 1979; Rosen 1970), or "severe discipline" (Crook and Raskin 1975; Pfeffer et al. 1979) are brought into the investigation.

Methods

The data to be presented here stem from two investigations carried out in our clinic in 1981.

The first study is a project entitled "Outpatient Aftercare Following a Suicide Attempt." The initial sample consisted of 485 patients who were admitted for inpatient detoxification to the toxicology ward of the University Clinic rechts der Isar and who fulfilled Kreitmann's criteria (Kreitmann 1977) for "parasuicide." By applying definite diagnostic or organizational exclusion criteria, for example, to exclude psychoses, a smaller project sample of 247 patients was obtained. Although the smaller sample differed from the original sample in the exclusion of psychotics and a part of the drug addicts, it was, however, representative of the original sample. The main psychiatric diagnoses at the initial as well as the second patient examination were obtained according to the International Classification of Diseases, 9th Rev. (ICD 9), revealing the distribution shown in Table 1.

Table 1.   Random samples of comparison

247 patients following an attempted suicide	
28%	Neurotic disorder
44%	Reactive disorder
15%	Drug-alcohol abuse-dependency
11%	Personality disorder
2%	Others
119 psychiatric inpatients	
36%	Schizophrenic illness
29%	endogenous depression
35%	Neurotic disorder
64 surgical inpatients (control group)	

In the second study, which sought to analyze early childhood development and premorbid personality using standardized questionnaires, 119 psychiatric inpatients from our clinic comprised the original sample; these patients were for the most part in remission of an acute psychiatric disease and were about to be released. Patients with less than average intelligence, gross defects, or an organic personality alteration were excluded. Sixty-four surgical inpatients, chosen to correspond to the psychiatric sample with regard to age and sex distribution, served as controls. The distribution of the main psychiatric diagnoses are shown in Table 1.

The samples containing patients having a suicide attempt and psychiatric inpatients were comparable with respect to demographic data. In both studies we employed, among other things, a self-evaluation questionnaire designed by our clinic originally to determine neurotic etiologies. This questionnaire contains 123 items meant to detect important childhood-selected factors contributing to the development of neurosis. The first ten questions relate to the form of family life experienced by the individual patients. Those items are listed in Table 2.

In the first study − involving patients following a suicide attempt − the items could be answered with "yes" or "no." In the second study − involving the psychiatric and surgical patients − there were four possible answers. For the sake of comparison with the first study, the four-stage answers were evaluated dichotomously.

Table 2.   Self-evaluating questionnaire aimed at establishing neurotic etiologies

---

1. Until my 15th year I lived for the most part with *my parents*
2. ... with *my mother*
3. ... with *my father*
4. ... with *close relatives or with foster parents*
5. ... in a *home for children*
6. ... in *more than one home for children*
7. My *parents divorced* before I was *6 years* old
8. My *parents divorced* when I was *between 6 and 15 years* old
9. One or both of my *parents died* before I was *6 years* old
10. One or both of my *parents died* when I was *between 6 and 15* years old

---

Of the 247 self-evaluation questionnaires of the patients having a suicide attempt 225 could be interpreted, whereas all of the questionnaires of the psychiatric sample and the controls could be used.

Results

Table 3 shows the respective frequencies in the three samples for the answers to the broken-home-related questions. The contents of the individual items appear in abbreviated form.

According to the chi-square test, there was no significant increase in frequency for *any* item when the suicide attempt sample was compared either with the inpatient psychiatric group or the control sample. Only for items 3 (more with father) and 5 (children's home) could we observe trends at significance levels of 25% and 28%, respectively, for the comparison between the suicide attempt group and the controls.

Table 3.   Broken-home-related data: comparison of samples

1. More with patients		2. More with mother		3. More with father		4. More with relatives	
A:	24%	A:	26%	A:	9%	A:	6%
P:	25%	P:	22%	P:	11%	P:	10%
C:	23%	C:	20%	C:	5%	C:	3%
5. Children's home		6. > 1 children's homes		7. Parental divorce before 6 years		8. Parental divorce between 6 and 15 years	
A:	11%	A:	5%	A:	7%	A:	9%
P:	8%	P	2%	P:	6%	P:	8%
C:	6%	C	5%	C:	4%	C:	8%
9. Parental death before 6 years		10. Parental death between 6 and 15 years					
A:	7%	A:	7%				
P:	3%	P:	6%				
C:	8%	C:	5%				

A, attempted suicide; *P*, psychiatric inpatients, *C*, control group.

Discussion

On the basis of the data taken from the self-evaluation questionnaires of our clinic, we could find no significant increase in the frequency of broken-home histories in patients having a suicide attempt.

Even if we take into consideration the methodological difficulties inherent in the self-evaluation scales, for example, errors caused by improper completion of the questionnaires, or, as in our situation, the subsequent dichotomization of the data of the second sample, one cannot assume that these difficulties will have a negative effect specifically on the broken-home hypothesis.

The results of this investigation are in agreement with those of several other studies (Bunch et al. 1971; Lobos and Battegay 1974; Retterstøl and Stype 1973; Rorsman 1973; Thomas and Duszynski 1974; Weissman et al. 1973).

In Greer's publication (Greer 1964) the incidence of parental deprivation ranged from 32% to 74% in studies about attempted suicides with a control group. In an overview Lester listed seven studies (Lester 1971) which noted an increased frequency of parental deprivation for cases of suicide as opposed to ten studies which could not determine an increased frequency. Lester cited in his more recent overview (Lester 1983) 13 studies appearing in the 1970s reporting an excess of childhood loss of parents in suicidal individuals as opposed to 12 studies reporting no excess of parental loss.

The review of the entire literature on this subject, however, reveals that the majority of studies do indicate a tendency toward an increased frequency of the broken-home situation in suicidal persons (Lester 1983, Welz 1983).

Regardless of these considerations, it remains to be investigated — which factors ultimately predispose those individuals having a history of a broken home to suicidal behavior since, as the control group of our study demonstrates, a large number of *non*suicidal individuals likewise come from broken homes.

References

Adam KS, Bouchons A, Streiner D (1982) Parental and family stability in attempted suicide. Arch Gen Psychiatry 39:1081 – 1085

Birtchnell J (1970) The relationship between attempted suicide, depression and parental death. Brit J Psychiatry 116:307 – 313

Bunch J, Barraclough B, Nelson B, Sainsbury P (1971) Early parental bereavement and suicide. Soc Psychiatry 6:200 – 202

Climent C, Plutchik R, Ervin F, Rollins A (1977) Parental loss, depression and violence. Acta Psychiatr Scand 55:261 – 268

Crook T, Raskin A (1975) Association of childhood parental loss with attempted suicide and depression. J Consult Psychol 43, No. 2:277

Dorpat TL, Jackson JK, Ripley HS (1965) Broken homes and attempted and completed suicide. Arch Gen Psychiatry 12:213 – 216

Greer S (1964) The relationship between parental loss and attempted suicide, a control study. Brit J Psychiat 110:698 – 705

Hudgens RW, Morrison JR, Barehta RG (1967) Life events and onset of primary affective disorders. Arch Gen Psychiatry 16:134 – 145

Johnson G, Hunt G (1979) Suicidal behavior in bipolar manic-depressive patients and their families. Compr Psychiatry 20:159 – 164

Kearney T, Taylor C (1969) Emotionally disturbed adolescents with alcoholic parents. Acta Paedopsychiatr 36:215–221

Kreitman N (ed) (1977) Parasuicide. Wiley, London

Lester D (1972) Why people kill themselves: a summary of research findings of suicide behavior. Thomas, Springfield

Lester D (1983) Why people kill themselves: a summary of research findings of suicide behavior. Thomas, Springfield, Ill

Lobos R, Battegay R (1974) The suicidal attempt. Proc. 7th Int. Congr. for Suicide Prevention. Swets & Zeitlinger, Amsterdam, pp 232–242

Matussek P, May U (1981) Verlustereignisse in der Kindheit als prädisponierende Faktoren für neurotische und psychotische Depressionen. Arch Psychiatr Nervenkr 229:198–204

McConaghy N, Linane J, Buckle RC (1966) Parental deprivation and attempted suicide. Med J Aust 1:886–892

Munro A (1966) Parental deprivation in depressive patients. Br J Psychiatry 112:443–457

Oliver R, Kaminski Z, Tudor K, Hetzel B (1971) The epidemiology of attempted suicide as seen in the casualty department. Med J Aust 1:833–839

Palmer DM (1941) Factors in suicidal attempts: a review of 25 consecutive cases. J Nerv Ment Dis 4:421–442

Pfeffer C, Conte H, Plutchik R, Jerret I (1979) Suicidal behavior in latency age children. J Am Acad Child Psychiatry 18:679–692

Pokorny AD (1960) Characteristics of 44 patients who subsequently committed suicide. Arch Gen Psychiatry 2:314–323

Reitman F (1942) On the predictability of suicide. J Ment Sci 88:580–582

Retterstøl N, Strype B (1973) Suicide attempters in Norway. Life Threat Behav 3:283–297

Rorsman B (1973) Suicide in psychiatric patients. Soc Psychiatry 8:55–66

Rosen D (1970) The serious suicide attempt. Am J Psychiatry 127:764–770

Rosenthal R, Rinzler C, Wallsh R, Klausner E (1972) Wrist-cutting syndrome. Am J Psychiatry 128:1363–1368

Schneer H, Perlstein A, Brozovsky M (1975) Hospitalized suicidal adolescents. J Am Acad Child Psychiatry 14:268–280

Stein M, Levy M, Glasberg M (1974) Separations in black and white suicide attempters. Arch Gen Psychiatry 31:815–821

Thomas C, Duszynski K (1974) Closeness to parents and the family constellation in a prospective study of five disease states. Johns Hopkins Med J 134:251–270

Walton HJ (1958) Sucidal behavior in depressive illness. A study of aetiological factors in suicide. J Ment Sci 104:884–891

Weissman M, Fox K, Klerman G (1973) Hostility and depression associated with suicide attempts. Am J Psychiatry 130:450–455

Welz R (1983) Drogen, Alkohol und Suizid; strukturelle und individuelle Aspekte abweichenden Verhaltens. Enke, Stuttgart

Zilboorg G (1936a) Differential diagnostic types of suicide. Arch Neurol Psychiat 35:270–291

Zilboorg G (1936b) Suicide among civilized and primitive races. Am J Psychiatry 92:1346–1369

Zilboorg G (1937) Considerations on suicide. Am J Orthopsychiatry 7:15–31

Life Events, Current Social Stressors, and Risk of Attempted Suicide

R. WELZ

Introduction

That severe strain and adverse experiences can cause a person to become ill or emotionally disturbed is a well-known fact of life. Psychological and sociologic surveys on the aftereffects of catastrophes such as earthquakes, hurricanes, and fires (Birnbaum 1976), war captivity (Biderman 1964), long-term imprisonment (Spaulding and Ford 1976), and mining accidents (Ploeger 1974) all take this fact as their starting point and go on to reveal a basic connection between extremely distressing situations and subsequent emotional/mental health problems.

In addition to these surveys of catastrophes involving many individuals simultaneously, there have been other studies investigating single events such as the move to a new area (Mechanic 1986), changes at work (Berkanovic and Krochalk 1977), and the death of a spouse (Bojanowski 1977). These surveys also deal with the consequences of the situations on a person's mental health.

It is the aim of life-event research to systematize the available data and to prove the existence of a connection between life events and the onset of illness.

Life events are defined as "objective" events experienced by an individual (e.g., death of a spouse, move to a new area, promotion at work) which result in a change or imbalance in the person's level of adjustment to his environment, requiring a reorganization of the relevant behavior patterns either partly or in whole. Life events are rated according to an "item list" (Holmes and Rahe 1967; Brown 1974) which catalogues occurrences which could constitute a change in a person's life. The frequency of such occurrences within a certain period of time is also to be considered when rating them.

A direct link has been established between life events and subsequent illness in the case of chronic heart disease (Hinkle 1974; Kaplan and Kimball 1982; Siegrist et al. 1980), leukemia in children (Holmes and Masuda 1974), acute schizophrenia (Brown 1974), depression (Hudgens 1974), and neurotic symptoms (Möller et al. 1984). These findings were confirmed and modified in later studies (cf. Dohrenwend and Dohrenwend 1978; Katschnig 1980; Badura 1981, 1985).

Investigations into the role of life events in connection with attempted suicide are sporadic (Paykel et al. 1975; Paykel 1980; Luscomb et al. 1980; Tegeler and Platzek 1987) and do not differentiate within the group of suicide attempters.

Theoretical Development of an Existing Life-Event Concept

Criticism of life-event research has been aimed less at the conclusions drawn (i.e., the link between life events and subsequent illness) than at the methods employed to rate the relevant life events.

Many items are linked with occurrences either in connection with the onset of an illness or as a consequence of illness (Dohrenwend and Dohrenwend 1978). This is especially the case with mental illness or emotional disturbances, where accompanying social complications are the rule.

Furthermore, the categories into which life events are divided were found to be too general and not sufficiently differentiated. Suggested improvements include: a more subjective emphasis (Dohrenwend 1974), consideration of whether or not the life events could be anticipated (Redfield and Stone 1979), and a differential between positive and negative events (Horowitz et al. 1977).

Illfield (1976) investigated the role of current social events in addition to that of life events. Social stressors exist in such fields of a person's life as family, work, home, and other social situations involving social interactions. The stressors are a permanent and current feature in a person's life which appear again and again and which are experienced as unpleasant or as a problem. Anticipated events which a person fears or feels threatened by can also play a role in the cause of an illness, mental and physical. Lazarus and Launier (1978) saw the cognitive assessment of such events and the individual's method of coping with them as central to his theory.

The quality of an individual's interaction with his environment is dependent on two factors: his cognitive ability to assess a problem and the person's resources to deal with it. The process of cognitive assessment and evaluation of a problem situation is decisive for the intensity and quality of the emotional reaction to it, whereby every emotional reaction is dependent upon the individuals own system of values. Both the individual's ability to assess a life event and his emotional reaction to it are constantly being modified through his interaction with his environment, personal coping strategies, group contact, and social support received. Coping is the sum of all cognitive and behavioral efforts made to deal with and master problem situations arising from life events. Lazarus and Launier (1978) described various coping strategies such as inhibition of action, information seeking, intrapsychological processes, and direct action (Fig. 1).

Fig. 1. Hypothetical model of relationship between environment, perceived stress, and illness

New information and the rational analysis of known facts can result in a revised assessment of a problem situation, thus lightening the burden for the person involved. Coping strategies need not be logical or rational however. Refusal to acknowledge information and other strategies such as self-deception or intellectualization can equally reduce the burden in the eyes of the person involved causing relief, while the situation remains objectively unchanged. Cohen and Lazarus (1973) reported how denial of an operation beforehand or suppression of that situation resulted in the patient suffering significantly less post-operative complications than patients who had been very preoccupied with the operation they were to have. Lazarus and Launier (1978) referred to the inactivity following problem situations as action inhibition. Although inactivity and passive toleration of a problem situation is not generally regarded as a suitable coping strategy, it can be justified in cases where direct action would result in extremely negative consequences and a worsening of the situation. The term intrapsychological processes is used to describe a heterogeneous group of cognitive coping strategies, e.g., defense mechanisms, self- deception, reaction structures, and attempts at avoidance.

In the case of direct action, the individual tries to influence the effects he experiences as the result of an occurrence through his own immediate action. There are several possibilities: losing one's temper, attempt at revenge, aggression, escape through activities offering distraction, escape through alcohol or drugs. Last but not least suicide and attempted suicide can be seen as the most misdirected way of coping with a crisis.

Life Events, Perceived Stress and the Risk of Attempted Suicide

Research into the connection between life events and current social stressors and suicidal behavior has been, up to now, sporadic, with little or no differentiation of the group of suicide attempters. The findings of this research (Paykel et al. 1975; Paykel 1980; Luscomb et al. 1980) can be summarized as follows: persons who attempt suicide experienced more negative events than persons in a control group.

In a study on attempted suicide (Welz et al. 1988) a dual concept was evolved providing data on classic life events, current social stressors, and anticipated events. This study set out to answer the following three questions:

1. Is there a difference in the number of life events and current social stressors experienced by persons who attempt suicide in the 6 months before the attempt compared with a control group?
2. Can a typical problem pattern be identified in persons who have attempted suicide?
3. Is there a difference between problem patterns found in the control group and those of the persons who have attempted suicide?

Sample and Method

The data were collected by carrying out a cumulative random survey of patients who had attempted suicide and been treated either as outpatients or inpatients in psychiatric institutions or as emergency cases in the casualty department of the main regional hospital in Mannheim within a time period of 18 months.

Of 101 patients interviewed, 91 completed the total interview including the life-event list. The majority was female (66%). The patients were interviewed for the most part in the 1st week after their suicide attempt, a few were interviewed in the 2nd week. The control group was made up of members of the general population corresponding in age and sex to the patients interviewed. To determine the frequency of live events and current social stressors, a problem list was used which contained 58 items (Welz et al. 1988). Roughly half of these items concerned long-term problems and subjective assessment of pressure experienced and the other half life events.

The items were divided a priori into fields of life such as work, education/training, personal relationships, everyday life and health. Each person interviewed was asked to state which of the stressors he had experienced in the 6 months prior to the interview.

Results

As Table 1 illustrates, the patients who attempted suicide experienced twice as many life events and current social stressors as the control group.

There was hardly any difference between male and female scores. The results confirmed the hypothesis of earlier studies that persons who attempt suicide feel themselves under considerably more pressure from problems in the time before their attempt than other people.

The results shown in Table 1 can, however, offer no basis for conclusions regarding the actual details of everyday circumstances in the time prior to the suicide attempt. For this reason, a separate evaluation of results was carried out according to different areas of life events and current social stressors defined a priori. As shown in Fig. 2, there was hardly any difference in the frequency of problems and life events in the field of education/training between the two groups.

Table 1.   Critical life events and current social stressors experienced by persons who attempted suicide and by a control group

	Attempted suicide	Control group
Male	11.90	6.04
Female	11.60	5.60
Total	11.71	5.76

Significance:	$t = 4.32$	$P < 0.01$
	$t = 6.51$	$P < 0.01$
Total	$t = 8.03$	$P < 0.01$

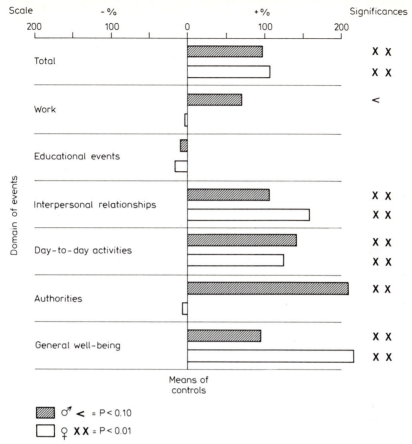

Fig. 2. Differences between patients with suicide attempts and controls

   In contrast, male members of the attempted suicide group experienced more problems in the field of work than their control group counterparts. Women experienced problems most frequently in the field of close personal relationships and partnership, as well as in connection with their general well-being. The greatest difference in results between male attempted suicide group members and the control group was in the field of problems with the authorities.

   To establish how far it is possible to divide current problems and life events into various fields of life, and whether or not there are patterns and connections between them, a factor analysis was carried out.

Factor Analysis

Factor analysis was carried out according to the principal axis method. The squares of multiple correlation coefficients were taken as estimations for communalities and several literations were carried out so that the estimated communalities converged with the actual communality values. To ascertain the number of extracting factors, Guttman (1954) and Kaiser and Dickman (1959) criteria were used. After the dimensions were fixed, factor scores based on the results of the respective factor analyses were calculated for each respondent and used in further calculations.

To prove that the differences between groups apparent in the respective test of the hypothesis do in fact represent differences in values on the recorded dimensions and to counter assumptions that the differences were due to variance in the methods of measuring, an additional test of equivalence of the determined dimensions was carried out through similarity rotations of factors and total factor matrices. For these calculations, two samples (separated according to different criteria) were rotated in pairs to maximum similarity to eliminate random variance. Similarity coefficients (factor congruence coefficients) were averaged after z-transformation to calculate the mean similarity coefficient. The square of the similarity coefficient showed to what extent the variance in each matrix could be due to the general variance.

To ascertain "substantial" factors, the loading matrices of the various analyses were also compared in the course of determination with the number of factors. This was done by recording the intersecting set of variables fulfilling the Fürntratt criteria to test the "stability" of the factors. In the case of a "stable" factor, the variables fulfilling the Fürntratt criteria should split up less randomly into other factors, i.e., they should split up into meaningful factors which can be interpreted as additional factors.

After conducting various analyses and calculating similarities, we decided on a five-factor solution. The factors can be defined as follows in the light of certain indicative items:

Factor 1: Difficulties in education/training
Indicative items:
− I was afraid I could not meet the requirements of the course (.75).
− I experienced conflicts with people who played an important role in my training/education (.63).
− I was dissatisfied in general with my education/training (.60).

Factor 2: Isolation
Indicative items:
− I feel isolated in my area of residence (.61).
− I feel deserted or neglected by the persons closest to me in matters which are of importance to me (.49).
− I have had an unpleasant feeling of being generally ill at ease recently (.45).

Factor 3: Subjective difficulties at work
Indicative items:
− I was working in difficult circumstances (.61).
− High demands were made of me at work (.58).
− I was afraid of criticism from superiors and colleagues or was treated by them in another humiliating way (.53).

Factor 4: Partnership problems
Indicative items:
− My marriage/partnership broke up (.69).
− My partner showed little affection (.68).
− I suffered from the partnership being unbalanced (.56).

Factor 5: Social and financial difficulties
Indicative items:
− I or close relatives was/were involved in either criminal law proceedings or
civil law proceedings (.48).
− My financial situation deteriorated (.47).
− My well-being was adversely affected, mainly by alcohol (.45).

For each person in the different groups, factor scores were estimated for resulting factors and distribution values were calculated.

Group Comparison

Group results were compared both according to the separate dimensions of
problems and life events defined a priori and in the light of the total factor
scores. Table 2 shows the results of the groups in each separate field.

Table 3 shows the comparison of the factor scores. Both male and female
members of the attempted suicide group differed significantly from the control
group. As seen in Fig. 2, both had scores higher by 100%. In certain dimensions,
the male members of the attempted suicide group compared differently with
their control group counterparts from the female members of the attempted
suicide group and theirs.

Table 2. Frequency of problems and critical life events in the suicide attempt group and control group according to fields of life and sex[a]

Field		Suicide attempt group	Control group	Significance
Work	Male	2.48 (1.65)	1.46 (1.24)	NS
	Female	1.09	0.29	NS
Education/Training	Male	0.26 (0.29)	0.29 (0.36)	NS
	Female	0.33	0.40	NS
Personal relationships	Male	3.68 (4.34)	1.79 (1.80)	$P<0.01$
	Female	4.69	1.80	$P<0.01$
Everyday life	Male	1.90 (1.96)	0.79 (0.87)	NS
	Female	2.04	0.91	NS
Public life/probs. with authorities	Male	0.65 (0.44)	0.21 (0.32)	$P<0.01$
	Female	0.35	0.38	NS
Gen. well-being	Male	2.93 (3.04)	1.50 (1.17)	$P<0.01$
	Female	3.11	0.98	$P<0.01$

[a] Figures in parentheses for comparison of total scores of both sexes.

Table 3. Differences in factor scores between suicide attempt group and control group

	Factor 1 Difficulties in education/ training		Factor 2 Isolation		Factor 3 Difficulties at work		Factor 4 Partnership problems		Factor 5 Social and financial problems	
	♀	♂	♀	♂	♀	♂	♀	♂	♀	♂
Suicide attempt	−.021	1.06	.326	.873	.013	.947	.348	.936	.170	.904
Control	−.035	.76	−.396	.668	−.011	.806	−.419	.569	−.201	.701
Significance	$t = -.10$		$t = 6.12**$		$t = 0.18$		$t = 6.46**$		$t = 3.02**$	

** $P < 0.01$.

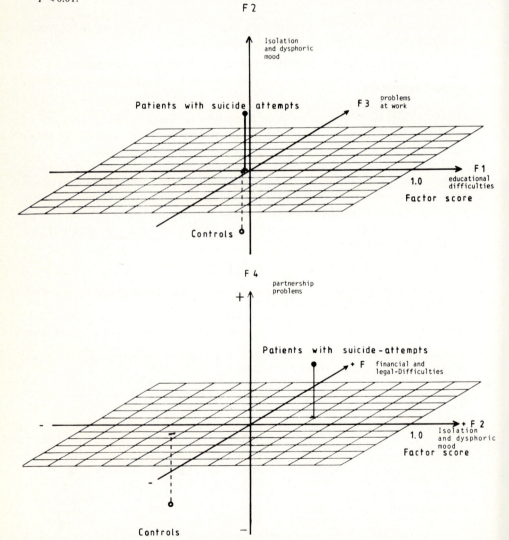

Fig. 3. Means of factor scores in three-dimensional space

For instance, in the field of work, only the male members of the attempted suicide group had higher scores than the control group; females in both groups scored about the same. In the field of education/training, neither male nor female members of the attempted suicide group differed significantly from the control group. However, in the field of personal relationships and everyday life, members of the attempted suicide group again scored higher than the control group, rating over 100% more. A further significant difference between the sexes was apparent in the field of public life/problems with authorities. Here the male members of the attempted suicide group had 210% higher scores than those of the control group. Females in both groups scored about the same. In the field of general well-being, another trend was apparent: while members of the attempted suicide group in toto rated higher scores than the control group, the scores of female members of the attempted suicide group were in turn higher than the scores of male members of that group.

There was no difference in factor scores for factors 1 (education/training) and 3 (difficulties at work) between the groups. However, there were very significant differences for factors 2 (feelings of isolation and unpleasantness), 5 (social/financial difficulties), and 4 (partnership problems).

As illustrated in Fig. 3, the two groups are easily distinguishable from each other on the factor space.

Considering these partly very significant differences in scores between the sexes, it might be worth investigating in future research whether or not other subdivisions exist, differing in their problem frequency and in their life-event structures and problem patterns.

This seems especially worthy of thought since it has been shown by Schmidtke (1988) that there is no uniform behavior pattern in suicide and attempted suicide, but that the group as such can be divided according to sociodemographic, clinical, and biopsychological aspects, as well as according to the seriousness of the attempt and the degree of the risk of dying.

References

Badura B (ed) (1981) Soziale Unterstützung und chronische Krankheit. Zum Stand sozial-epidemiologischer Forschung. Suhrkamp, Frankfurt

Badura B (1985) Zur Soziologie der Krankheitsbewältigung. Soziologie 14:339−348

Berkanovic E, Krochalt PC (1977) Occupational mobility and health. In: Kasl S, Reichsman F (eds) Epidemiological studies in psychosomatic medicine. Advances in psychosomatic medicine, vol 9. Karger, Basel

Biderman AD (1964) Captivity love and behavior in captivity. In: Grosser, Wechsler, Greenblatt (eds) The threat of impeding disaster. Cambridge

Birnbaum F, Caplan J, Scharff T (1976) Crisis intervention after a natural disaster. In: Moos RH (ed) Human adaptation, coping with life crises. Lexington

Bojanovski J (1977) Morbidität und Mortalität bei Verwitweten. Fortschr Med 95:593−596

Brown GW (1974) Meaning, measurement and stress of life events. In: Dohrenwend BS, Dohrenwend BP (eds) Stressful life events: their nature and effects. Wiley, New York, pp 217−243

Cohen F, Lazarus RS (1973) Active coping processes, coping disposition and recovery from surgery. Psychosom Med 35:375−389

Dohrenwend BP (1974) Problems in defining and sampling the relevant population of stressful life events. In: Dohrenwend BS, Dohrenwend BP (eds) Stressful life events: their nature and effects. Wiley, New York, pp 275–310

Dohrenwend BS, Dohrenwend BP (1978) Some issues in research of stressful life events. J Nerv Ment Dis 166:7–15

Guttman L (1954) Some necessary conditions for common factor analysis. Psychometrica 19:149–161

Hinkle LE (1974) The effects of exposure to culture change, social change, and changes in interpersonal relationships on health. In: Dohrenwend BS, Dohrenwend BP (eds) Stressful life events: their nature and effects. Wiley, New York, pp 9–44

Holmes TH, Rahe RH (1967) The social readjustment scale. Psychosom Med 11:213–218

Holmes TH, Masuda M (1974) Life change and illness susceptibility. In: Dohrenwend BS, Dohrenwend BP (eds) Stressful life events: their nature and effects. Wiley, New York, pp 45–72

Horowitz M, Schaefer C, Hiroto D, Wilner N, Levin B (1977) Life events questionnaires for measuring presumptive stress. Psychosom Med 6:413–431

Hudgens RW (1974) Personal catastrophe and depression. In: Dohrenwend BS, Dohrenwend BP (eds) Stressful life events: their nature and effects. Wiley, New York, pp 119–134

Illfeld FW (1976) Characteristics of current social stressors. Psychol Rep 39:1231–1247

Kaiser HF, Dickman K (1959) Analytic determination of common factors. Am J Psychol 14:425

Kaplan W, Kimball C (1982) The risk and course of coronary artery disease: A biopsychosocial perspective. In: Millon T, Green C, Meagher R (eds) Handbook of clinical health psychology. Plenum, New York

Katschnig H (ed) (1980) Sozialer Streß und psychische Erkrankungen. Urban and Schwarzenberg, Munich

Luscomb RL, Clum GA, Patsiokas AT (1980) Mediating factors in the relationship between life stress and suicide attempting. J Nerv Ment Dis 168:644–650

Lazarus RS, Launier R (1978) Stress related transactions between person and environment. In: Pervin LA, Lewis M (eds) Perspectives in international psychology. Plenum, New York

Mechanic D (1986) Social factors affecting the mental health of the elderly. In: Häfner H, Moschel G, Satorius N (eds) Mental health in the elderly. Springer, Berlin Heidelberg New York

Möller HJ, Grießhammer C, Hacker H (1984) Einschneidende Lebensereignisse im Vorfeld von akuten psychischen Erkrankungen. Eur Arch Psychiatr Neurol Sci 234:118–124

Paykel ES (1980) Recent life events and attempted suicide. In: Farmer R, Hirsch S (eds) The Suicide Syndrome. Croom Helm, London

Paykel ES, Prusoff BA, Myers JK (1975) Suicide attempts and recent life events. Arch Gen Psychiatry 32:327–333

Ploeger A (1974) Lengede – zehn Jahre danach. Psychother Med Psychol 24:137–143

Redfield J, Stone A (1979) Individual viewpoints of stressful life events. J Consult Clin Psychol 47:147–154

Schmidtke A (1988) Verhaltenstheoretisches Erklärungsmodell suizidalen Verhaltens. Roderer, Regensburg

Siegrist J, Dittmann K, Ritter K, Weber J (1980) Soziale Belastungen und Herzinfarkt. Eine medizin-soziologische Fall-Kontroll-Studie. Enke, Stuttgart

Spaulding RC, Ford CV (1976) Psychological reactions to the stresses of imprisonment and repatriation. In: Moos RH (ed) Human adaptation: coping with life crisis. Heath, Lexington

Tegeler J, Platzek M (1987) Recent life Events and Sucidal Attempts. In this volume

Welz R, Schmidtke A, Häfner H (1988) Lebensverändernde Ereignisse, wahrgenommener Streß und Suizidversuchsrisiko. Suizidprophylaxe 15, in press

Recent Life Events and Suicide Attempts

J. Tegeler and M. Platzek

Introduction

Recent life events have been regarded as important factors in the aetiology of suicide attempts. Despite this recognition, only few systematic studies have examined life events in suicide attempters in comparison with depressives, schizophrenics and controls from the general population. Discrepant results reported by Paykel et al. (1975), Cochrane and Robertson (1975), O'Brien and Farmer (1980), and Luscomb et al. (1980) may be due to different criteria for selecting subjects and differing methods of assessing life stress.

In our previous study, 20 depressives and 20 schizophrenics did not differ concerning the total number of life events experienced 6 months preceding admission to the hospital, but the amount of readjustment necessary to cope with the events and the response to different stress situations were significantly higher for depressives than for schizophrenics (Tegeler and Pastors 1982). In this report results from a study with a larger sample of suicide attempters, depressives, schizophrenics, and controls from the general population are presented.

Method

The group of suicide attempters included 64 persons admitted to the Department of Psychiatry. Parasuicide was defined as intentional self-injury, where a high degree of suicidal intent had been expressed. Only patients who had no symptoms of a major or minor depressive disorder according to Research Diagnostic Criteria (RDC) were included. The other groups consisted of 59 first-episode schizophrenics, 40 neurotic depressives, 38 endogenous depressives with repeat episodes, and 47 subjects from the general population.

General demographic data were recorded. Patients and controls were assessed using the brief psychiatric rating scale (BPRS), Hamilton psychiatric rating scale for depression (HAMD), and paranoid-depressive scale (PDS). The Life Events Inventory consists of a list of 92 individual events which were assigned to the following nine categories or subscales: marital relationship or relationship with the opposite sex, employment, accidents, finances, legal problems, health, sudden serious events, changes in life habits, and children. The time period covered by the interview were 1 month, 2–6 months, and 7–12 months before the suicide attempt or onset of illness. For the depressives and schizophrenics, the onset of illness was defined in terms of an exacerbation of symptoms at a separate interview. Because it is important to assess the personal meaning of life events, patients and controls were asked to scale the events experienced according to expected or unexpected, influenced or not influenced, pleasant or unpleasant, and upsetting or not upsetting. The patients and controls were then asked to scale the events, regardless of whether or not they had experienced these, according to the categories pleasant or unpleasant, and to estimate the individual amount of readjustment necessary to cope with the event (Holmes and Rahe 1967). Finally, using a Stress Response Inventory, 16 different modes of response to 16 explicitly described situations were evaluated.

The ratings of BPRS, HAMD, and PDS were completed in the first 3 days after admission and again at the time of the interviews. These interviews, scaling of experienced life events, and ratings of the Stress Response Inventory were completed after improvement to minimize distortions due to psychiatric disorder. Analyses of variances and subsequent Scheffé tests were performed.

Results

The demographic characteristics of the patients and controls are recorded in Table 1. A similar distribution of life events in the age intervals ≤ 20 years, $20-29$, $30-39$, $40-49$, $50-59$, and ≥ 60 years was found in all samples of patients. Only in the control group did the youngest (≤ 20 years, $n = 2$) reported significantly more life events than the oldest persons (≥ 60 years, $n = 5$).

After admission to the hospital, endogenous and neurotic depressives showed significantly higher total scores of BPRS, HAMD, and PDS than suicide attempters and controls. At the time of the interviews on life events according to improvement of symptoms, the patients had total scores of BPRS between 19 and 25 points and total scores of HAMD between 3 and 11 points, which did not differ from the ratings of the control group.

The total number of events reported by patients and controls are shown in Table 2. In the month prior to the attempt, the event rate was approximately that of the controls, but in the 2- to 6-month period suicide attempters experienced a significantly higher rate of events. Suicide attempters and neurotic depressives did not differ in the total number of life events, but in comparison

Table 1. Demographic characteristics of patients and controls

	SA	ED	ND	C
Female	29	33	28	25
Male	35	5	12	22
Age (years)				
Mean	30.9	53.1	42.6	38.0
SD	9.3	7.5	12.5	14.1
Range	18 – 54	41 – 65	21 – 62	18 – 64

SA, suicide attempters; *ED*, endogenous depressives; *ND*, neurotic depressives; *C*, controls.

Table 2. Total number of life events (analysis of variance and Scheffé tests, $P<0.05$)

Time period	SA x̄ (SD)	ED x̄ (SD)	ND x̄ (SD)	C x̄ (SD)	P
1 month	1.94 (1.90) SA>ED	0.50 (1.08) ED<SA ED<C	1.25 (1.63)	1.47 (1.59) C>ED	0.00
2−6 months	7.25 (3.90) SA>ED SA>C	2.55 (2.06) ED<SA ED<ND	6.20 (5.24) ND>ED	3.53 (2.80) C<SA	0.00
7−12 months	7.45 (4.28) SA>ED	3.55 (1.91) ED<SA ED<ND	6.60 (4.30) ND>ED	5.17 (2.25)	0.00

SA, suicide attempters; *ED*, endogenous depressives; *ND*, neurotic depressives; *C*, controls.

Table 3. Life events in time period 1−12 months (analysis of variance and Scheffé tests, $P<0.05$).

	SA Mean SD		ED Mean SD		ND Mean SD		C Mean SD		P
Marital relationship	5.50	2.82	1.82	1.43	4.27	3.46	3.04	2.03	0.00
Employment	3.50	2.35	0.90	1.57	2.45	2.26	1.70	1.61	0.00
Accidents	0.89	0.94	0.32	0.52	0.50	0.60	0.81	0.77	0.00
Finances	1.47	1.41	0.61	0.95	1.32	1.18	0.85	1.08	0.00
Legal problems	0.39	0.66	0.05	0.23	0.32	0.76	0.11	0.31	0.00
Sudden serious events	1.47	0.96	0.53	0.60	1.52	1.42	0.77	0.84	0.00
Health	0.87	1.06	0.82	0.86	0.72	0.88	0.79	0.91	0.95
Changes in life habits	2.25	1.76	0.97	0.68	2.50	1.54	1.60	1.03	0.00
Children	0.30	0.68	0.60	0.75	0.42	0.75	0.53	0.88	0.34

SA, suicide attempters; *ED*, endogenous depressives; *ND*, neurotic depressives; *C*, controls.

with endogenous depressives suicide attempters reported significantly more events in the three time periods.

In the 1-month period suicide attempters experienced more events in the areas of marital relationship or relationship with the opposite sex, employment, finances, and accidents than endogenous depressives but not in comparison with controls. In the time period 2−6 months suicide attempters had significantly more life events than endogenous depressives in the following subscales: marital relationship or relationship with the opposite sex, employment, accidents, finances, and changes in life habits. In comparison with controls suicide attempters experienced more life events in the areas of marital relationship or relationship with the opposite sex, employment, sudden serious events, and changes in life habits. Differences between suicide attempters and neurotic depressives were found only in the areas of employment and accidents.

Concerning the time period 7−12 months suicide attempters reported more events than endogenous depressives in the subscales of marital relationship, employment, finances, legal problems, and sudden serious events. In comparison with controls suicide attempters experienced more events concerning marital relationship or relationship with the opposite sex, finances, and legal problems.

Results concerning time period 1−12 months are presented in Table 3. In comparison with endogenous depressives, suicide attempters experienced significantly more events during this time period in all but the two subscales of health and children. Parasuicides reported more events than controls in the following subscales: marital relationship or relationship with the opposite sex, employment, finances, legal problems, and sudden serious events. No differences were found between suicide attempters and neurotic depressives.

Discussion

There are three main sets of findings from this study. First, suicide attempters reported significantly more life events in the time period 2−6 months in comparison with controls. Endogenous depressives experienced fewer events than suicide attempters in all three time periods, whereas no differences could be found between suicide attempters and neurotic depressives. Second, in contrast to the results reported by Paykel et al. (1975) and Power et al. (1985), we could not find a marked peak of events in the month prior to the suicide attempt. In our sample the event rate in suicide attempters as well as in the other samples showed an approximately constant increase over the first 6 months and the following 6 months. These results suggest that the influence of life events on suicidal behavior and neurotic depression may extend over a considerable length of time. Selection of the samples may explain this difference in comparison with the results reported by Paykel et al. (1975) and Power et al. (1985) who studied suicide attempters in a general emergency service, whereas in our study only patients with high suicidal intent who had been admitted to the psychiatric hospital were included. Consistent with the findings of Paykel (1974) and Möller et al. (1984), neurotic depressives reported significantly more life events than endogenous depressives. Third, events in the areas of marital relationship or relationship with the opposite sex, employment, legal problems, and finances may have a special impact on suicidal behavior and may act as a stimulus variable. Their effects on suicidal intent are mediated through other variables such as hopelessness and coping resources, i.e., social support.

References

Cochrane R, Robertson A (1975) Stress in the lives of parasuicides. Soc Psychiatry 10:161−171

Holmes TH, Rahe RH (1967) The social readjustment rating scale. J Psychosom Res 11:213−218

Luscomb RL, Clum GA, Patsiokas AT (1980) Mediating factors in the relationship between life stress and suicide attempting. J Nerv Ment Dis 168:644−650

Möller HJ, Griesshammer C, Hacker H (1984) Einschneidende Lebensereignisse im Vorfeld von akuten psychischen Erkrankungen. Eur Arch Psychiatr Neurol Sci 234:118−124

O'Brien SEM, Farmer RDT (1980) The role of life events in the aetiology of self-poisoning. In: Farmer RDT, Hirsch SR (ed) The suicide syndrome. Croom Helm, London
Paykel ES (1974) Recent life events and clinical depression. In: Gunderson E, Rahe R (ed) Life stress and illness. Thomas, Springfield
Paykel ES, Prusoff BA, Myers JK (1975) Suicide attempts and recent life events. Arch Gen Psychiatry 32:327−333
Power KG, Cooke DJ, Brooks DN (1985) Life stress, medical lethality and suicidal intent. Br J Psychiatry 147:655−659
Tegeler J, Pastors W (1982) Unterschiede von Lebensereignissen und Streß-Reagibilität bei schizophrenen und depressiven Patientinnen vor der stationären Aufnahme. In: Heinrich K (ed) Der Schizophrene außerhalb der Klinik. Huber, Bern

A Description of Behavioral Patterns of Coping with Life Events in Suicidal Patients

C. THOMSSEN and H.-J. MÖLLER

Introduction

Whenever a person attempts to commit suicide, the people in his environment generally search for the reasons for this act. One would first ask about the relationships of the attempted suicide to events in his preceding history.

Modern psychology tries to describe the links between life events and the changes and the development of the individual personality (Filipp 1981). Coping strategies and different mediating factors are seen to be essential in the individual's reaction to his life events (Lazarus 1979).

There have been many studies in clinical psychology on the links between – on the one hand – life events, social support, and coping behavior and – on the other hand – onset of somatic, psychosomatic, and psychiatric illness (Dohrenwend et al. 1974; Gunderson and Rahe 1974; Filipp 1981).

The "stress-buffering role of social support" was emphasized in the studies by Dean and Lin (1977), Miller and Ingham (1976), Surtees (1980), and others and various types of coping behavior have been described in the studies by Coyne et al. (1981), Parker and Brown (1982), and others. In this study we tried to find the relations between these parameters and suicide attempts. We imagined a simply structured model of the stress process (Fig. 1). Similar models were described by Miller (1980), Dohrenwend BP and Dohrenwend BS (1979), and others:

Life events produce stress, which is mediated by distinct factors; one of the most important of these would be social support. In the literature (Miller and Ingham 1979) we found evidence that ineffective coping with stress is related to the onset of minor or major illness or, for example, to attempted suicide (Cochrane and Robertson 1975; Papa 1980).

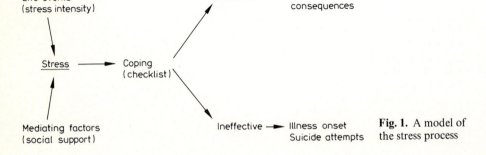

Fig. 1. A model of the stress process

Methods

We examined a cohort of fifty 20- to 60-year-old patients who were taken into the hospital for attempted suicide and a randomized control group of 73 surgical and gynecological patients matched by age and sex.

The attempted suicides were divided into two groups: 24 patients with a severe suicide intent and 26 patients with a mild suicide intent. This distinction was made on the basis of the Suicide Intent Scale by Beck (1974).

The two groups of suicide attempters and the control group were compared on the basis of the model in Table 1. Life events and the amount of stress were measured in the Item List of Stress Intensity designed by Kuhnt et al. (1982). Social interactions and personal relationships were measured using the Social Support Index of Surtees (1980). Finally, to describe coping behavior, we used the "Ways of Coping Checklist" of Folkman and Lazarus (1980) in the German version by Braukmann and Filipp (1983).

Results and Discussion

Item List of Stress Intensity

In the evaluation of the Item List of Stress Intensity we found a clear and significant difference between the control group and the attempted suicides as a whole (Table 1). In the attempted suicides, we found more highly stressed life events in the past, a higher mean stress intensity, and a higher mean frequency of the stress experienced.

At the time of the interview, they felt more stress in general, not only from current life events, but also from previous ones.

We found a similar distribution in the intervals between the events and the interview, although the attempted suicides were found to have more life events at any given time. The whole inquiry did not show any evident difference be-

Table 1. Item List of Stress Intensity designed by Kuhnt et al. (1982)

Parameter	Significant differences between	
	Controls ($n = 72$) and attempted suicides ($n = 46$)	Mild ($n = 24$) and severe ($n = 22$) suicide intent
Life events [a]	***	NS
Stress intensity [a]	**	NS
Frequency of stress experienced [a]	***	NS
Present increased stress [b]	***	NS
Influence on other spheres of life [a]	***	**

*** $P<0.001$; ** $P<0.01$; * $P<0.05$; NS, no significant difference.

[a] t-test

[b] χ^2-test

tween patients with a severe suicide intent and those with a mild one. We only found that patients with a severe suicide intent claimed the stress had more influence on other spheres of life. Furthermore, a separate evaluation of chronic and current problems did not show any difference between severe and mild attempted suicides either.

Our results differ from the findings of the authors of this Item List. They found more chronic difficulties and more stress caused by them in patients with severe suicide attempts rated by clinical appraisal and more current problems in the low-risk group (Kuhnt et al. 1982). Our results are similar to those in the literature. Paykel et al. (1975), for example, concluded from his findings comparing suicides and a control group of depressive patients that there is a "strong and immediate relationship between suicide attempts and life events." In line with our results, too, Papa (1980) did not find any correlation between the amount of stress experienced by an individual and the suicide intent.

Social Support Index

The evaluation of the Social Support Index when applied to the three groups described produced the following significant results (Table 2): The more severe the suicide intent was, the higher the scores reached by these patients were, i.e., the worse the social relationships were. These differences were particularly evident regarding close relations, whereas the diffuse social relations exhibited only differences between the control group and the attempted suicides as a whole. Comparing severe and mild attempted suicides point for point the only difference in fact is in the existence of a confidant.

These results demonstrate a strong association between poor social support and the severity of the suicide intent. These findings are confirmed in the literature. The extensive statistical data evaluation by Schubert and Summa (1984) showed that the less contact the people had, the more severe their suicide attempt was. Slater and Depue (1981) found this link between social support and suicide intent too. They examined primary depressive patients with and without suicide attempts and found significantly more often a lack of confidential relationships in the group of the attempted suicides.

Ways of Coping Checklist

The results of the Ways of Coping Checklist are shown in Table 3. The attempted suicides showed significantly more emotion-focused coping strategies than the control group. In the ratio of emotion-focused coping to problem-focused coping they showed a reciprocal proportion compared with the control group.

Regarding the control group, our results correspond to the results found by the authors of the German version of this list even though the levels we found were slightly higher. In the literature on the "stress process" (Lazarus 1979; Miller and Ingham 1979), we find that coping effectively with highly stressed life events seems to depend on well-balanced coping strategies, for example, an

Table 2. Social Support Index designed by Surtees (1980)

Support components	Significant differences between	
	Controls ($n = 71$) and attempted suicides ($n = 49$)	Mild ($n = 26$) and severe ($n = 23$) suicide intent
1. Confidant	***	***
2. Close relations		
3. Living group		
4. Work contacts	*	
5. Neighbors		
6. Friends	*	
7. Club/church	*	
Close support (comp. 1, 2, 3, 6)	***	***
Diffuse support (comp. 4, 5, 7)	**	
Overall support	***	***

t-test, *** $P<0.001$; ** $P<0.01$; * $P<0.05$.

Table 3. The Ways of Coping Checklist designed by Folkman et al. (1980) and Braukmann et al. (1983). The individual and global strategies are defined according to the factor analysis studies by Braukmann et al. (1983)

Coping strategies	Controls	Attempted suicides	Mild intent	Severe intent
	$n = 133$	$n = 93$	$n = 49$	$n = 44$
Global strategies				
Problem-focused	9.1	8.4	9.5	7.2**
Emotion-focused	7.6	9.8***	10.2	9.4
Individual strategies				
Problem-focused	4.4	3.5**	4.3	2.8**
Resigned wishful thinking	7.3	8.8***	8.8	8.8
Denial and avoidance	2.2	2.9***	3.0	2.9
Indecision	4.1	4.0	4.2	3.7
Self-blame	1.8	2.6***	2.6	2.7
Cognitive self-regulation	4.9	4.0***	4.2	3.7

t-test, *** $P<0.001$; ** $P<0.01$; * $P<0.05$.

adequate ratio of problem-focused and emotion-focused strategies. Too little problem-focused behavior could mean that the individual had given up a real solution to the problem. Denial without problem-solving would mean the recurrent presence of just this problem. Thus, this coping manner would not be effective and, if there were no change in this process, the consequence would be minor or major illness.

Our results are in line with the hypothesis that in attempted suicides the patterns of coping have become imbalanced. Also, in the analysis of the individual strategies as described in the factor analysis studies by Braukmann and

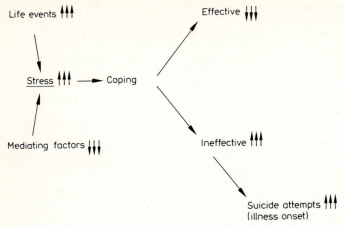

Fig. 2. The model of the stress process complemented by our results of the studies on stress and the coping resources of attempted suicides

Filipp (1983), we found the state of imbalance described above: In the group of attempted suicides as a whole we found more coping strategies considered to be ineffective such as resigned wishful thinking, denial, avoidance behavior, and self-blame. In contrast, we found less cognitive self-regulation, considered to be an effective coping strategy.

Conclusion

To summarize our findings on the basis of our model (Fig. 2): Attempted suicides had more life events in their preceding history than the control group. Furthermore, they felt more stress and simultaneously were not able to cope with the stress in a well-balanced and effective manner. Additional coping resources such as social support play a mediating role in this process. Thus, the lack of a confidential relationship produced a worse situation in the attempted suicides. These results confirm the conclusion of Papa (1980) who said that "it may not be the amount of stress experienced by an individual that predicts suicide but the manner in which stress is handled."

References

Beck AT et al. (1974) Development of suicidal intent scales. In: Beck AT et al. (eds) The prediction of suicide. Charles, Bowie, MD, pp 45–56

Braukmann W, Filipp SH et al. (1983) Die Skala zur Erfassung des Bewältigungsverhaltens (SEBV). Forschungsbericht Nr. 27/1983, Entwicklungspsychologie des Erwachsenenalters, Department of Psychology, The University of Trier

Cochrane R, Robertson A (1975) Stress in the lives of parasuicides. Soc Psychiatry 10:161–171

Coyne JC, Aldwin C, Lazarus RS (1981) Depression and coping in stressful episodes. J Abnorm Psychol 90 (5):439–447

Dean A, Lin N (1977) The stress-buffering role of social support. J Nerv Ment Dis 165:403−417

Dohrenwend BP, Dohrenwend BS (1974) Stressful life events: their nature and effects. Wiley, New York

Dohrenwend BP, Dohrenwend BS (1979) The conceptualization and measurement of stressful life events: an overview of the issues. In: Depue RA (ed) The psychobiology of the depressive disorders. Implications for the effect of stress. Academic, New York, pp 105−121

Filipp SH (1981) Ein allgemeines Modell für die Analyse kritischer Lebensereignisse. In: Filipp SH (ed) Kritische Lebensereignisse. Urban and Schwarzenberg, Munich, pp 1−52

Folkman S, Lazarus RS (1980) An analysis of coping in a middle-aged community sample. J Health Soc Behav 21:219−239

Gunderson E, Rahe RH (1974) Life stress and illness. Thomas, Springfield

Kuhnt S, Kleff F, Welz R (1982) Stressbelastung und Stressbewältingungsressourcen bei suicidalen Handlungen. In: Luer G (ed) Bericht über den 33. Kongreß der Deutschen Gesellschaft für Psychologie. Hogrefe, Göttingen

Lazarus RS (1979) Positive denial: the case for not facing reality. Psychol Today 13 (6):44−60

Miller PMcC (1980) Problembewältigungsverhalten. In: Katschnig H (ed) Sozialer Streß und psychische Erkrankung. Fortschritte der Sozialpsychiatrie 5. Urban and Schwarzenberg, Munich, pp 250−261

Miller PMcC, Ingham JG (1979) Reflections on the life-events-to-illness link with some preliminary findings. In: Sarason IG, Spiel-Berger CD (eds) Stress and anxiety, vol VI. Hemisphere, New York, pp 313−363

Papa LL (1980) Responses to life events as predictors of suicidal behavior. Nurs Res 29 (6):362−369

Parker GB, Brown LB (1982) Coping behaviours, that mediate between life events and depression. Arch Gen Psychiatry 39:386−391

Paykel ES, Myers JK (1975) Sucide attempts and recent life events. Arch Gen Psychiatry 32:327−333

Schubert R, Summa JD (1984) Suizidprophylaxe durch frühzeitige Erkennung exogener und endogener Risikofaktoren. Bundesgesundheitsblatt 27 (6):1984

Slater J, Depue RA (1981) The contribution of environmental events and social support to serious suicide attempts in primary depressive disorder. J Abnorm Psychol 90 (4):275−285

Surtees PG (1980) Social support, residual adversity and depressive outcome. Soc Psychiatry 15:71−80

Social Support and Suicidal Behavior

R. WELZ, H. O. VEIEL, and H. HÄFNER

The Concept of Social Support

Essential elements of the social support concept can already be found in the work of Emil Durckheim, who, 90 years ago, examined the influence of societal factors on suicide frequencies. These studies gave rise to the theory of social disintegration. Durkheim (1952, p. 210) explained the integrating function of groups by basically psychological concepts:

These is, in short, in a cohesive and animated society a constant interchange of ideas and feelings from all to each and each to all, something like a mutual *moral support*, which instead of throwing the individual on his own resources, leads him to share in the collection energy and support his own when exhausted.

Subsequent to the studies of Durkheim, the concept of "social isolation," rather than his original concept of "social disintegration," became ever more important in research on social and psychological conditions of suicide and mental disorders.

Faris and Dunham (1939) found high incidence rates of certain categories of mental disorders in those areas of Chicago with a high proportion of single households. Sainsbury (1955) found in London a high correlation between the suicide rate and the proportion of persons living alone as well as between the suicide rate and the proportion of people living in communal housing, such as old-age homes. Epidemiologic research on schizophrenia, depression, and on mental illness in old age consistently showed higher rates of social isolation as typical for these conditions.

On the basis of empirical results showing the relationships between social isolation and mental disorders, a new research area developed during the 1970s in epidemiology: the investigation of social network integration and of social support and their effects on incidence, course, and rehabilitation of mental and physical illness. Nuckolls et al. (1972) were among the first to examine the specific importance of social support with regard to coping with stressful life events. In their sample of pregnant women, the authors found that subjects who had sufficient "social assets" showed fewer pregnancy complications than those without. Cobb and Gore (1973) showed that in men who had lost their job the severity of depression correlated with the extent of social support from their friends and families. Similar effects were found with regard to more general psychological problems and also with regard to physical illness (Siegrist et al. 1980).

In spite of the generally comparable results concerning the beneficial effects of social support, either via a direct effect on health or via a buffering effect in the face of stress, the great differences in conceptualization, definition, and operationalization of social support make a detailed comparison of the various results very difficult. Lin et al. (1979) conceptualized the social support of an individual as a function of his ties to other individuals, groups, or to society at large. Cobb (1976) emphasized subjective aspects defining social support as information leading the individual to believe that he or she is loved, cared for, and esteemed and that he or she belongs to a system of mutual obligations and expectations. George (1980) differentiated between supportive transactions in everyday situations and in crises. Thoits (1982) distinguished between the amount, the type, and the source of support. Pearlin et al. (1981) seemed to regard the essence of social support as the accessibility of other individuals and groups as the accessibility of other individuals and groups and their mobilization against the vicissitudes of life. Other authors differentiated between objective and subjective aspects of social contacts, and even finer differentiations based on empirical analyses have been made by Norbeck and Tilden (1983) and Schaefer et al. (1981).

The different and often incompatible definitions and operationalizations of the term "social support" to be found in the empirical and theoretical literature made it necessary to define and clarify what was meant by it.

Veiel (1985) proposed a differentiated and comprehensive conceptual framework for research on social support, which was taken as a basis for the analyses reported below. It postulates an objective/subjective and a structural/interactional assessment dimension. The structural aspect refers to parameters such as size, density, and interconnectedness of the social network, while the interactive aspect refers to the actual transactions that take place within these structures. The objective/subjective dimension refers to whether support is quantified by the subject him- or herself or by the investigator. Further differentiations concern the type of support (psychological, instrumental, everyday/crisis support), and the overall relationship that exists between the provider and the recipient of support (Veiel 1985).

Method and Sample

The aim of this study was to examine the pattern of social support of suicide attempters in comparison with a sample of control subjects. It is part of a larger project on psychological, social, and medical factors influencing the risk of committing suicidal attempts. The role of life events and difficulties and of coping behavior, hopelessness, and anomie in bringing about suicidal behavior have been examined and, partly, already published (Häfner et al. 1983; Kuhnt and Welz 1983; Welz and Häfner 1984). The data were collected in a cumulative sample of suicide attempters who, during a period of 18 months, were treated in the emergency or psychiatric facilities of the Mannheim General Hospital. The sample included 101 subjects who completed the interview; 34 of the subjects were male, 67 were female. The interview was conducted, in most cases, within the 1st week, in a few cases within 2 weeks, after the suicide attempt.

A control sample matched for age and sex was drawn from the general population. Objective dimensions of social support were assessed by collecting information on:

1. The number of family members, friends, and acquaintances in regular contact with the subjects
2. Memberships in social organizations and groups
3. The frequency of contact with these persons and organizations

These data yielded objective information concerning supportive structures and interactions as well as concerning the role of relationships between subjects and the providers of social support.

Qualitative aspects of support were assessed by asking subjects who they could ask for help and support regarding certain categories of needs. These were: instrumental help with everyday problems, instrumental help in crisis situations, everyday common activities and small talk, psychological and emotional support in crisis situations, and the subjects' need of being important for other persons (positive appraisal).

Results

Regarding the number of persons in regular contact with the subjects, suicide attempters named significantly fewer persons than controls (Table 1).

Comparable to the smaller social networks repeatedly found to be typical for psychiatric patients, suicide attempters, as a group, were characterized by a smaller circle of persons in regular contact. The differences were significant both regarding the number of friends and acquaintances and regarding the number of family members, irrespective of whether the subject was living alone or with a partner. The difference, however, was particularly great with regard to friends and acquaintances: controls had, on average, twice as many friends and acquaintances as suicide attempters. Also, other characteristics of the social network such as membership in groups, availability of telephones, and frequency of telephone calls or of mail differentiated between the two groups (Table 2).

In Tables 1 and 2 an interesting effect can be observed which, as will be seen later, also appears in the qualitative support categories. While attempters who were not living with a spouse or partner had fewer friends and acquaintances and were less frequently members in groups and organizations than those who were, the opposite held true for the control group. Controls not living with a partner appeared more active and more successful at maintaining and establishing social contacts.

A similar finding regarding qualitative aspects of support was that controls without a partner named more persons in the six different qualitative support categories than those living with a partner.

In the attempter group, those without a partner perceived themselves as less supported. Overall, attempters had significantly fewer persons who would sup-

Table 1. Size of the social network of suicide attempters and controls

	Attempters		Controls		Level of significance
	Without partner	With partner	Without partner	With partner	
Number of acquaintances	3.3	3.5	8.7	6.3	$P<0.0001$
Number of relatives	4.1	4.9	6.4	5.6	$P<0.005$

Table 2. Social network of suicidal attempters: objective indicators[a]

	Attempters		Controls		Level of significance
	Without partner	With partner	Without partner	With partner	
Group membership	0.25	0.44	1.1	0.75	–
Contact frq. grp.	0.83	2.97	5.5	3.5	$P<0.05$
Phone available	0.81	0.66	0.92	0.97	$P<0.05$
Frq. calls/week	6.6	9.0	9.6	10.2	–
Frq. of private mail/month	2.8	2.48	3.92	3.58	–

[a] Values are *proportions* of the subsamples with the characteristic in question.

port them in crisis situations, with whom they interacted socially, and who would come to their assistance in conflicts with third persons. The same held true for emotional problems. If one distinguishes, in the six support categories, between friends and acquaintances on the one hand, and family members on the other, again significant differences between attempters and controls appear. Whereas the control group had a circle of friends and acquaintances that was twice as large as the attempters', but had only marginally more contacts to family members, they had in all five qualitative categories significantly and substantially more support by their families than the suicide attempters.

To sum up, one can state that suicide attempters have a smaller social network than general population controls, whose larger network results primarily from the much greater circle of friends and acquaintances. Suicide attempters belong less frequently to groups and organizations, have less frequently access to a telephone, and receive fewer calls and letters than the controls. Regarding specific functional categories of support, the difference between attempters and controls, however, is particularly large regarding family members.

Henderson (1984), in an editorial on the results of social support research, once stated:

Social support is obtainable only through social relationships which are themselves achieved only by having competence in establishing and maintaining them. Such competence is an attribute of the individual, not of his social environment ... Individuals who lack social support lack social relationships and this must often be due to personality defects.

Table 3. Perceived support in different areas by friends and family members

		Suicide attempters		Control group		F values	
		Without partner (n = 40)	With partner (n = 61)	Without partner (n = 13)	With partner (n = 69)	1 3	2
Instrumental everyday support	All	1.23	1.69	2.15	1.84	–	–
	Acquaintances	0.53	0.46	0.77	0.36	–	–
	Family	0.55	1.21	1.39	0.45	5.5	5.5
Instrumental crisis support	All	1.88	2.16	3.39	3.06	29.6**	
	Acquaintances	0.93	0.44	1.15	0.62	–	8.1*
	Family	0.95	1.69	2.23	2.39	20.9**	28.1**
Emotional everyday support	All	1.90	1.93	3.39	3.26	49.4**	
	Acquaintances	1.23	0.85	2.39	1.55	19.2**	33.8**
	Family	0.65	1.08	1.00	1.69	11.4**	25.4**
Emotional crisis support	All	1.25	1.44	2.62	2.44	39.2**	
	Acquaintances	0.73	0.51	1.62	0.75	8.2*	14.3**
	Family	0.50	0.91	1.00	1.64	23.8*	30.3**
Positive appraisal	All	1.43	1.98	2.85	2.77	21.7**	
	Acquaintances	0.78	0.23	1.08	0.44	–	5.4
	Family	0.63	1.72	1.69	2.31	15.1**	17.5**

* $P < 0.01$; ** $P < 0.001$.

1 F values and significance levels are based on discriminant analysis and refer to the power on the respective variable to discriminate between attempters and controls over and above partnership status, which was treated as a covariate. They may also be interpreted as reflecting main effects of group membership (attempters/controls) on the respective variables.

2 F values in this column refer to the effects of the family and acquaintance variables when the effects of both the respective other variables and of partnership status are partialled out.

3 F values < 4 are not shown.

This statement may be accurate regarding the number of friends and acquaintances, i.e., regarding the availability of supportive persons, but even where relationships do exist − in families − they are less frequently perceived as sources of social support in the group of suicide attempters.

References

Cobb S (1976) Social support as a moderator of life stress. Psychosom Med 38:300−315

Cobb S, Gore S (1973) Unemployment, social support and health. University of Michigan, Ann Arbor, Michigan

Durkheim E (1952) Suicide. Routledge and Kegan, London

Faris REL, Dunham WH (1939) Mental disorders in urban areas. University Chicago Press, Chicago

George LK (1980) Role transition in later life. Brooks/Cole, Monterry

Häfner H, Welz R, Gorenc K, Kleff F (1983) Selbstmordversuche und depressive Störungen. Schweiz Arch Neurol Neurochir Psychiatr 133:283−294

Henderson AS (1984) Interpreting the evidence of social support. Soc Psychiatry 19:49−52

Kuhnt S, Welz R (1983) Hilflosigkeit und Hoffnungslosigkeit bei Individuen mit suizidalen Handlungen. In: Pohlmeier H et al. (ed) Suizidales Verhalten. Roderer, Regensburg, pp 39 – 51

Lin N, Simeone RS, Ensel WM, Kuo W (1979) Social support, stressful life events and illness. J Health Soc Behav 20:108 – 119

Norbeck JS, Tilden VP (1983) Life stress, social support, and emotional disequilibrium in complications of pregnancy: a prospective, multivariate study. J Health Soc Behav 24:30 – 46

Nuckolls KB, Cassel J, Kaplan BH (1972) Psychosocial assets, life crisis, and the prognosis of pregnancy. Am J Epidemiol 95:431 – 441

Pearlin LI, Menaghan EG, Lieberman MA, Mullan JT (1981) The stress process. J Health Soc Behav 22:337 – 356

Sainsbury P (1955) Suicide in London. Chapman and Hall, London

Schaefer C, Coyne JC, Lazarus RS (1981) The health-related functions of social support. J Behav Med 4:381 – 406

Siegrist J, Dittmann K, Ritter K, Weber J (1980) Soziale Belastungen und Herzinfarkt. Eine medizinsoziologische Fall-Kontroll-Studie. Enke, Stuttgart

Thoits PA (1982) Conceptual, methodological and theoretical problems in studying social support as a buffer against stress. J Health Soc Behav 23:145 – 159

Veiel HOF (1985) Dimensions of social support: a conceptual framework for research. Soc Psychiatry 20:136 – 162

Welz R, Häfner H (1984) Imitation und Kontagiosität bei Selbstmordhandlungen. Eine empirische Untersuchung über Selbstmordhandlungen im Freundes- und Familienkreis von Individuen mit Suizidversuchen. In Welz R, Möller HJ (ed) Bestandsaufnahme der Suizidforschung. Roderer, Regensburg, pp 63 – 76

Description and Prognostic Value of Standardized Procedures for Determining Remarkable Personality Traits in Patients Following a Suicide Attempt

T. Dietzfelbinger, A. Kurz, A. Torhorst, and H.-J. Möller

Introduction

Among the psychological risk factors predisposing to suicidality, personality traits play a not unimportant role. The work of Henderson (1983) involving patients with reactive or neurotic depression indicates that as regards the evolution of depressive symptoms it is not so much the variables of social environment, e.g., life events or social support, that are responsible, but rather the manner in which an individual having a particular personality reacts to these variables.

In planning this study involving suicidal patients, which was launched in 1981 in the University Hospital of the Technical University in Munich and which deals primarily with the evaluation of different follow-up management strategies, it seemed sensible and appropriate to pay special attention to the detailed diagnosis of personality.

The following discussion considers on three levels the data derived from either self-evaluation or examiner-oriented personality questionnaires completed at the time of admission:

1. Correlation analysis of the different questionnaires on the scale level
2. Comparison of the personality profiles of suicidal patients with those of other psychiatric diagnostic groups and of control samples
3. Evaluation of the prognostic (predictive) value of personality dimensions with respect to repeat rate and to change in the estimate of psychopathological behavior and of the disturbances in social adjustment.

Description of the Patient Collective

Of the 485 patients admitted to the Toxicology Department of the Technical University Hospital for inpatient detoxification following a suicide attempt, the present study includes those 247 patients who met the requirements for ambulatory psychotherapy programs and who were therefore not affected by the following exclusion criteria:

1. Intoxication judged as stemming from drug-abuse behavior
2. Diagnosis of psychosis
3. Necessity of inpatient psychiatric follow-up treatment
4. Long-term ambulatory psychotherapy prior to suicide attempt

5. Poor language skills (foreign patients)
6. Residence not in the range of the Munich metropolitan railway system
7. Lacking patient consent
8. Other organizational reasons

Table 1 gives an overview of the essential characteristics of the collective under consideration here. The sociodemographic data and the primary psychiatric diagnoses − excluding the psychoses − of this collective were largely in agreement

Table 1.   Overview of sample population

	n	%
Primary psychiatric diagnosis		
Neurosis	69	28
Personality disorder	28	11
Substance abuse/dependence	37	15
Reactive disorder	108	44
Other diagnoses	5	2
	247	100
History		
Earlier suicide attempts	65	26
Earlier outpatient psychiatric treatment	53	21
Earlier inpatient psychiatric treatment	21	9
Problem focus		
None	123	50
Partner relationship	88	35
Family	19	8
Other	17	7
	247	100
Age		
15−19	49	20
20−39	139	56
40−59	50	20
60 and older	9	4
	247	100
Family status		
Unmarried	127	51
Married	78	32
Widowed	6	2
Divorced	36	15
	247	100
Sex		
Male	91	37
Female	156	63
	247	100
Unemployed		
Yes	30	12
No	217	88
	247	100

with the data presented in two earlier studies concerning suicidality in Munich (Kockott et al. 1970; Möller et al. 1978). However, in comparison with the general population of Munich, the following subgroups within the collective were clearly overrepresented: persons under 40 years of age (76% of the collective compared with 43% of the general population), females (63% vs 52%), unmarried persons (51% vs 41%), divorced persons (15% vs 6%), and unemployed persons (12% vs 4%).

Methods

The following statistical tools served as the basis for personality diagnosis:

Anancasm-Hystericism-Orality Scale (AHOS)

The AHOS questionnaire (v Zerssen 1980) employs the patient's self-evaluation in determining premorbid personality. Along with a general Neuroticism Scale (20 items), this questionnaire includes 20 items for each of the following three personality dimensions derived from psychoanalysis: (a) anancasm (obsessive-compulsive traits), (b) hystericism (extroverted-egocentric traits), and (c) orality (passive-dependent traits). Reference values were obtained from patients having other psychiatric diagnoses as well as from psychologically unremarkable control persons.

Freiburg Personality Inventory (FPI)

This standardized questionnaire likewise aims at determining premorbid personality on the basis of the patient's self-evaluation (Fahrenberg et al. 1978); it comprises nine standard scales ascertained by factor analysis as well as three item analytically construed supplemental scales (cf. Table 3). For the present study, the abbreviated form FPI-A consisting of 114 items was used. An accompanying manual offers comparison values for a number of clinical and nonclinical diagnostic groups.

Psychological and Social Communication Findings (PSCF)

The PSCF (Rudolf 1979, 1986) is a standardized questionnaire employed by the examining physician as a means to describe quantitatively the personality of neurotic patients. It consists of 84 individual traits which have been classified on the basis of factor analysis into ten personality dimensions (cf. Table 4). Reference values exist for a large collective of unselected outpatients with neurotic and psychosomatic complaints.

Personality Profiles of Suicidal Patients in Comparison with References

Table 2 summarizes the comparison between the mean values in the four AHOS dimensions obtained from the suicidal patients and those reference values obtained from other psychiatric diagnostic groups and from somatically ill persons (Kurz 1984) or from persons without psychiatric symptoms (v Zerssen 1979). These findings should be very cautiously interpreted, especially since there were significant differences between the two groups of mentally well persons as regards the mean values in the Hystericism Scale. If as the differentiating criterion a difference of more than 50% of the standard deviation is accepted, then only in the Neuroticism Scale did the suicidal patients achieve values which were clearly above those of the two reference groups. The values for the suicidal patients were in any case lower than those for the patients having other psychiatric diagnoses, especially for the neurotic depressives. In the Orality Scale, the suicidal patients had the lowest values of all the psychiatric patients, these values being on the level of those for the control groups. The suicidal patients reached the lowest value of all the collectives considered in the Anancasm Scale; the restricted validity of this scale has been discussed elsewhere (v Zerssen 1979). With regard to the dimensions defined by the AHOS, the suicidal patients were on the whole hardly remarkable, especially when compared with neurotic-depressive patients.

In contrast, the comparison between the mean values in the FPI dimensions obtained from suicidal patients and the values obtained from Kurz's data (1984), or from the FPI Manual covering healthy controls, showed a relatively consistent trend, corresponding to the results described for the Neuroticism Scale of the AHOS questionnaire (Table 3): in 8 of the 12 FPI dimensions, the scores of the suicidal patients lay between those of both control groups and those of the neurotic depressives, whereby these latter patients demonstrated the most pathological values in these eight dimensions (with the exception of FPI 2, where schizophrenics dominated). The FPI dimensions under discussion here are: "nervousness" (FPI 1), "spontaneous agressivity" (FPI 2), "depressiveness" (FPI 3), "excitability" (FPI 4), "inhibition" (FPI 8), and "emotional

Table 2. Comparison of mean AHOS values for suicidal patients and references

Scale	Suicidal patients		Other psychiatric diagnoses					
			S $n = 43$	ED $n = 35$	ND $n = 42$	Total $n = 120$	C $n = 64$	Norm Z
	$\bar{x}$	σ	$\bar{x}$	$\bar{x}$	$\bar{x}$	$\bar{x}$	$\bar{x}$	$\bar{x}$
Anancasm	26.3	9.0	27.4	28.9	30.3	28.8	28.2	31.2
Hystericism	23.7	8.6	28.1	20.3	23.5	24.3	23.1	31.2
Orality	25.6	8.0	30.5	27.6	30.7	29.7	23.5	27.0
Neuroticism	28.6	9.5	29.9	31.0	35.2	32.0	23.5	24.0

S, schizophrenics; *ED*, endogenous depressives; *ND*, neurotic depressives; *C*, controls; *Norm Z*, reference values from mentally healthy individuals after v. Zerssen.

Table 3. Comparison of mean FPI values for suicidal patients and references

Scale	Suicidal patients		Other psychiatric diagnoses					
			S $n = 43$	ED $n = 35$	ND $n = 42$	Total $n = 120$	C $n = 64$	Norm
	$\bar{x}$	σ	$\bar{x}$	$\bar{x}$	$\bar{x}$	$\bar{x}$	$\bar{x}$	$\bar{x}$
1 Nervousness	7.6	4.6	7.9	8.1	10.4	8.8	6.4	6.0
2 Spontaneous aggressivity	3.6	2.4	4.5	3.0	4.2	4.4	2.9	3.3
3 Depressiveness	8.8	3.4	8.5	8.1	10.1	8.1	5.6	6.0
4 Excitability	5.9	2.7	5.2	4.5	6.1	5.8	5.0	4.8
5 Sociability	7.6	3.5	7.2	5.3	6.4	6.5	7.8	7.0
6 Stability	4.3	2.6	4.8	4.4	3.2	4.1	5.2	5.4
7 Reactive aggressivity/dominance striving	2.8	1.7	3.2	3.0	3.1	3.1	3.9	3.8
8 Inhibition	5.5	2.4	5.8	5.8	6.9	3.1	4.5	4.7
9 Frankness	5.5	2.6	8.9	8.0	8.8	8.6	9.0	4.5
E Extroversion	6.1	2.7	6.3	3.9	5.3	5.3	5.8	5.6
N Neuroticism	7.5	3.0	7.1	6.8	8.4	7.5	5.7	5.8
M Masculinity	4.7	2.6	5.0	4.4	3.0	4.1	6.1	6.4

S, schizophrenics; *ED,* endogenous depressives; *ND,* neurotic depressives; *C,* controls; *Norm,* reference values of mentally healthy individuals as given by the FPI Manual.

lability" (FPI N), where the mean scores of the neurotic depressives were higher than those of the controls, and "stability" (FPI 6) and "masculinity" (FPI M), where the controls' scores were higher. Compared with the two collectives of psychotically ill patients, the suicidal patients evaluated themselves as being less "nervous" (FPI 1) and "inhibited" (FPI 8), but more "depressed" (FPI 3), "excitable" (FPI 4), "neurotic" (FPI N), and "unstable" (FPI 6). In the FPI supplemental scale "extroversion", the suicidal patients − in contrast to those with neurotic depression − reached a somewhat higher value than the groups of mentally well individuals; in the scale "sociability" (FPI 5), however, the suicidal patients had the highest mean score of all the psychiatric diagnostic groups, thereby attaining a level comparable to that of the controls. Surprisingly, when compared with all reference groups, the suicidal patients demonstrated the lowest degree of "reactive aggressivity/dominance striving" (FPI 7). Thus, the results of Angst and Clayton (1986), who in a prospective study concluded that increased aggressiveness is a predictor of suicidal behavior, cannot be unequivocally reproduced by the data presented here. Within the framework of their study, these two authors employed factor analysis to generate from the unabrigded FPI three new FPI dimensions, designated "aggressivity", "extroversion", and "autonomous lability". In this so-defined aggressiveness dimension, which is closely related to the FPI-standard scales 2, 4, and 7 (spontaneous aggressivity, excitability, and reactive aggressivity/dominance striving, respectively), patients not classified by psychiatric diagnosis who later attempted suicide achieved significantly higher scores than the mentally unremarkable control persons.

Summarizing the results presented thus far, it can be seen that suicidal patients are especially remarkable in precisely those FPI dimensions which represent the fundamental personality factor "emotional lability" – "neurotic tendency" – described by Eysenck in 1960; in this respect, however, suicidal patients are less remarkable than patients suffering from a symptomatic neurotic depression.

The reference values given by Rudolf (1986) for a comprehensive collective of unselected patients, who because of neurotic and psychosomatic complaints were admitted to outpatient psychotherapy, demonstrated after their transformation into t values a mean of 50, with a standard deviation of 10, in all scales of the PSCF. Viewing the data presented in Table 4, one sees that the suicidal patients reached similar scores in the dimensions "narcissistic-combatant" (PSCF 3) and "protestation of disappointment" (PSCF 4), combined by Rudolf into the concept of "combatant resistance", as well as in "social disintegration" (PSCF 10). On the other hand, the scores of the suicidal patients were clearly lower than those of the references in the PSCF dimensions 1 ("compulsive orderliness") and 2 ("oversolicitousness and sense of obligation"), which describe overconforming and oversocialized behavior, 5 ("emotionally distant") and 6 ("fear of others"), in which disturbed interpersonal communication and an impaired ability to make contacts are expressed, as well as in 7 ("anxiety symptoms"). The suicidal patients had higher scores only in the two dimensions which Rudolf combined in the term "depressed-disappointing basic attitude", namely, "depressed helplessness" (PSCF 8) and "failed relationships" (PSCF 9). It would certainly be rash to conclude from these comparisons that those persons who in a specific life situation consult a physician to treat mental complaints are in the manner described above fundamentally different from patients who in a comparable situation attempt suicide. The relatively high score of the suicidal patients in the PSCF dimension 9, "failed relationships", could be related, for example, to the fact that approximately one-third of these patients stated that a problematic partner relationship triggered the suicide attempt. The discrepancy between the scores of the two patient collectives in the PSCF scale depressed helplessness, which serves to indicate earlier or immediate suicidality or depression, was also rather small. However, no data are avail-

Table 4. Mean PSCF values and standard deviations for suicidal patients

Scale	$\bar{x}$	σ
1. Compulsive orderliness	43.9	11.7
2. Oversolicitousness and sense of obligation	45.8	12.8
3. Narcissistic-combatant	48.9	11.4
4. Protestation of disappointment	50.7	8.9
5. Emotionally distant	44.5	10.3
6. Fear of others	44.6	11.4
7. Anxiety symptoms	43.9	10.1
8. Depressive helplessness	52.5	7.0
9. Failed relationships	53.2	11.7
10. Social disintegration	49.4	11.6

able concerning suicidal behavior or partner conflicts among the patients of the reference collectives. Beyond this, before risking a definite conclusion in this regard, one would certainly wish to have scores from a population of mentally unremarkable individuals. In any case, the present results could serve as the basis for further studies examining the validity of the PSCF.

Correlations Between the Individual Personality Dimensions

Pearson's product moment correlation coefficients were determined for all paired comparisons and subsequently submitted to significance testing with the two-tailed t test. The correlation matrix for the 12 FPI dimensions (Table 5) largely reproduces the intercorrelation pattern appearing in the FPI Manual. A correlation analysis involving the comparison of the AHOS scales among each other and with the scales of the FPI was first carried out by Kurz (1984); his results were for the most part confirmed by the data presented in Table 5. Considering only the correlation coefficients determined from the comparison of the AHOS dimensions, it can be observed that orality is relatively closely related not only to the other scales of this inventory, but also to almost all of the FPI dimensions. However, an even stronger correlation can be seen between the Neuroticism Scale of the AHOS and the FPI dimensions.

With regard to the PSCF scales, the same tight correlations between scales 1 and 2 (Compulsive orderliness and oversolicitousness and sense of obligation), between 3 and 4 (narcissistic-combatant and protestation of disappointment), and between 5 and 6 (emotionally distant and fear of others) can be seen in

Table 5. Correlations between the individual personality dimensions of the self-evaluation questionnaires AHOS and FPI. Only those coefficients appear for which $P < 0.001$

Scale	AHOS				FPI											
	A	H	O	N	1	2	3	4	5	6	7	8	9	E	N	M
AHOS A	1	.65	.29	.28	.28		.25			-.30	.25			-.25		
AHOS H		1	.55		.44	.26	.29				.25		.32		.25	
AHOS O			1	.60	.45	.26	.50	.37		-.30	.31	.45			.46	-.39
AHOS N				1	.48		.65	.43	-.56	-.58		.64		-.45	.61	-.64
FPI 1					1	.39	.56	.42	-.31	-.26	.36	.53	.25		.53	-.62
FPI 2						1	.46	.52		.56		.51		.37	.47	
FPI 3							1	.63	-.46	-.47	.43	.56	.45		.82	-.62
FPI 4								1		-.30	.53	.38	.45		.80	-.39
FPI 5									1		.34		-.56	.84	-.32	.44
FPI 6										1			-.45	.25	-.55	.61
FPI 7											1		.36		.50	
FPI 8												1	.24	-.45	.49	-.67
FPI 9													1		.43	
FPI E														1		.34
FPI N															1	-.58
FPI M																1

Table 6. Intercorrelation matrix for the PSCF dimensions. Only those correlation coefficients appear for which $P < 0.001$

	PSCF									
	1	2	3	4	5	6	7	8	9	10
PSCF 1	1	.78			.25	.51	.27	.24		−.26
PSCF 2		1				.42				−.32
PSCF 3			1	.69			.27		.25	.50
PSCF 4				1	.23		.35	.34	.26	.42
PSCF 5					1	.60	.25	.38		.30
PSCF 6						1	.46	.53		
PSCF 7							1	.67		.30
PSCF 8								1	.23	.47
PSCF 9									1	
PSCF 10										1

Table 7. Correlations between self-evaluated personality dimensions (AHOS, FPI) and dimensions evaluated by the examining physician (PSCF). Coefficients as in Tables 5 and 6

	PSCF									
	1	2	3	4	5	6	7	8	9	10
AHOS A							.26			.27
AHOS H			.26							.33
AHOS O				.28			.27			
AHOS N	.30					.38	.24	.31		
FPI 1							.27	.33	.31	
FPI 2										.30
FPI 3				.30	.30	.36	.28	.36		.29
FPI 4				.26						
FPI 5					−.34	−.44				
FPI 6	−.31					−.42		−.41		
FPI 7										
FPI 8						.41		.27		
FPI 9										
FPI E	−.25					−.37				
FPI N						.32	.28	.31		
FPI E	−.27	−.24				−.42	−.25	−.34		

Table 6 as have been previously described by Rudolf (1986) on the basis of a second-order factor analysis. In contrast to Rudolf's results, however, no such close correlation could be established between the PCSF scales 8, 9, and 10 (depressed helplessness, failed relationships, and social disintegration, respectively); on the contrary, the PSCF dimension 9 appears to be largely independent of all other PSCF dimensions, while scale 10 is significantly related to nearly all other PSCF dimensions, with PSCF 8 correlating more specifically with scales 6 and 7 (anxiety symptoms). These latter three could be united under the term "helpless-anxious self-doubt."

Rather lose correlations are the rule in the comparison of the self-evaluation scale AHOS and FPI on the one hand and the examination scale PSCF on the other (Table 7). In only five cases did the value of the correlation coefficient exceed ±0.40, as evidenced by the relatively close correlation between PSCF 6 (fear of others) and several FPI scales (inhibition and − negatively − stability, sociability, and masculinity). Nonetheless, with the exception of PSCF 9 (failed relationships), all PSCF dimensions correlated with one or more of the self-evaluation scales in a respectively sensible fashion. At this point, the fact that one is dealing here with very different types of inventories should not be overlooked: in the one type, the patient him-/herself, using preformulated statements, is describing his/her own premorbid personality, in the other, the examining physician, usually employing classificatory terms, is documenting his/her findings relating to the patient's personality. It should also be pointed out here that the correlation coefficients from comparisons between two fully compatible scales, one a self-evaluation, the other an evaluation by a close relative, lay in the same range as above, i.e., ±.40 (Dietzfelbinger 1985). Thus, the results presented in this paper do not speak against the validity of the PSCF scales and should encourage further validity studies concerning this statistical tool.

Prognostic Value of Personality Dimensions in Assessing Suicidal Patients

To test the prognostic value of the individual personality dimensions described above, correlation analysis was carried out to establish the relationship of these dimensions to the frequency of suicidal behavior and to the difference in the index and follow-up scores of a global assessment scale concerned with determining aspects of psychopathology and disturbances in social adjustment. Specifically, correlation analysis was applied to the comparison of the questionnaire scales with the following criteria (Table 8):

1. Recurrence of suicidal behavior, i.e., suicide attempt ($n = 25$) or suicide ($n = 6$) within 1 year subsequent to the index examination, classified according to the categories "yes" ($n = 31$) and "no" ($n = 204$).

2. Frequency of suicidal behavior during the year subsequent to the index examination, classified according to the number of suicide attempts without consideration of the suicides; 7 of the 25 patients who reattempted suicide during this time did so more than once; and the total number of suicide reattempts was 44.

3. Global estimation or mental health status, as measured by the Global Assessment Scale (GAS) (Endicott et al. 1976), at the time of the index examination (mean: 58.7, standard deviation: 12.2).

4. GAS score 1 year subsequent to the index examination (mean: 65.5, standard deviation: 18.0).

5. Difference of the two GAS scores (3−4, mean: 6.8, standard deviation: 17.6).

Follow-up data could be gathered from 235 patients, i.e., 95% of the original collective. With regard to recurrent suicidal behavior within 1 year after the in-

Table 8. Correlations of personality dimensions with the frequency of recurrent suicidal behavior and with the GAS data

		Recurrent suicidal behavior	No. of suicide attempts	Index GAS	Follow-up GAS	GAS difference
AHOS	Anancasm	.16*	.22**	−.17*	−.27***	−.18*
AHOS	Hystericism	.08	.09	−.16*	−.12	−.02
AHOS	Orality	.11	.17*	−.20**	−.23**	−.12
AHOS	Neuroticism	.08	.14	−.16*	−.16*	−.06
FPI 1	Nervousness	.16*	.20**	−.19**	−.19**	−.07
FPI 2	Spontaneous aggressivity	.20**	.20**	−.11	−.13	−.06
FPI 3	Depressiveness	.18**	.19**	−.23***	−.20**	−.04
FPI 4	Excitability	.07	.05	−.08	−.07	−.01
FPI 5	Sociability	−.11	−.08	.21**	.09	−.05
FPI 6	Stability	.05	.00	.18**	.02	−.11
FPI 7	Reactive aggressivity/ dominance striving	.19**	.13	−.08	−.14*	−.08
FPI 8	Inhibition	.11	.09	−.14*	−.09	.00
FPI 9	Frankness	.09	.07	−.09	−.07	.00
FPI E	Extroversion	−.05	−.04	.09	−.01	−.07
FPI N	Neuroticism	.07	.07	−.17**	−.14*	−.02
FPI M	Masculinity	.03	−.09	.12	.11	.03
PSCF 1	Compulsive orderliness	−.20**	−.02	−.03	.13	.16*
PSCF 2	Oversolicitousness and sense of obligation	−.20**	−.03	.07	.11	.07
PSCF 3	Narcissistic-combatant	.10	.02	−.32***	−.18*	.02
PSCF 4	Protestation of disappointment	−.02	.00	−.37***	−.18*	.05
PSCF 5	Emotionally distant	.08	.06	−.48***	−.26***	.04
PSCF 6	Fear of others	−.05	.06	−.35***	−.04	.17*
PSCF 7	Anxiety symptoms	.03	.05	−.44***	−.22**	.07
PSCF 8	Depressive helplessness	.11	.09	−.56***	−.24***	.10
PSCF 9	Failed relationships	−.26**	−.05	−.21**	−.08	.05
PSCF 10	Social disintegration	.32***	.21**	−.58***	−.39***	−.03

* $P < 0.05$; ** $P < 0.01$; *** $P < 0.001$.

dex attempt, the closest correlation (0.32, $P < 0.001$) was achieved by the PSCF dimension social disintegration. In good agreement with this result was the negative correlation with this criterion of the PSCF scales 1 and 2, which represented overly conforming social behavior. The scale failed relationships (PSCF 9) also possessed a statistically significant relationship to a low frequency of reattempted suicide or of suicide during the follow-up period. This latter result can hardly be interpreted on the basis of the present data since it is possible that additional variables played a role here, e.g., whether or not a partner relationship existed during the year following the index suicide attempt.

The dimensions of the AHOS and the FPI appear to have little prognostic value as regards recurrent suicidal behavior: the correlation coefficients did not exceed 0.20. Still, significant correlations with this criterion can be observed for the self-evaluations compulsive (AHOS A, $P < 0.05$), nervous (FPI 1, $P < 0.05$), spontaneously aggressive (FPI 2, $P < 0.01$), depressed (FPI 3, $P < 0.01$). In the light of theoretical considerations, the finding that aggressiveness is a risk factor with regard to suicidal behavior, albeit on a low level, is remarkable. This result would seem to support the findings of Angst and Clayton (1986) described above.

Considering now the correlations of the mean values from the personality scales with the number of suicide reattempts during the follow-up period, one sees that the absolute values of the correlation coefficients, in particular with respect to the PSCF, are even lower than in the above cases. On the basis of this small collective of suicide reattempts ($n = 7$), however, it would be premature to conclude that the degree to which remarkable personality traits are described by standardized procedures possesses no prognostic significance as regards the recurrence of suicidal behavior; rather, this question should be the object of an investigation incorporating an appropriately large sample population.

With the exception of the PSCF scales 1 and 2, the values of all dimensions of this inventory correlated well – usually highly significantly ($P < 0.001$) – with the scores of the GAS completed at the time of the index examination; this correlation is closest for PSCF 10 (social disintegration). Of all the self-evaluation scales, the FPI scale 3 (depressiveness) demonstrated the most significant correlation with the initial GAS survey. In contrast to this, the absolute values of correlation coefficients from the comparison between the self-evaluated personality dimensions and the GAS scores at the time of follow-up were clearly lower. Nonetheless, very high correlations ($P < 0.001$) with the follow-up GAS scores were found for the Anancasm Scale of the AHOS as well as for the PSCF scales 5, 8, and 10 (emotionally distant, depressed helplessness, and social disintegration, respectively), whereby PSCF 10 once again showed the closest relationship. Only the Anancasm Scale of the AHOS demonstrated a significantly negative correlation ($P < 0.05$) with the numerical difference between the initial and follow-up GAS scores, indicating that with regard to this criterion this scale is most indicative of an unfavorable prognosis. On the other hand, the scales PSCF 1 and 6 (compulsive orderliness and fear of others) both correlated significantly ($P < 0.05$) with this overall slight improvement of the patients' global mental state during the follow-up period.

Recapitulating, it seems that the prognostic value of the personality dimensions as predictors for the above outcome criteria is rather small. The greatest relative importance in this respect would have to be assigned to the scale PSCF 10 (social disintegration), which correlated highly significant with both recurrent suicidal behavior within the follow-up period (positive correlation) and the follow-up GAS score (negative correlation). On the basis of these results alone, however, no unequivocal statements relating to individual patients can be made. An essential contribution in this direction is the PSCF-10-oriented comparison between patients who on the one hand made no further suicide attempt and those who on the other made one or more attempts or actually committed suicide (Table 9). From these data, it can be seen that none of the patients showing recurrent suicidal behavior possessed a t value of less than 50.5 (raw value less than 6) in the PSCF 10 scale social disintegration, while 80 patients (= 48%) who did not reattempt suicide had t values below this mark. These facts support the hypothesis that in individual cases very low values for

Table 9. PSCF dimension 10 (social disintegration): frequency distribution of recurrent suicidal behavior or absence thereof during the year subsequent to the index suicide attempt

	PSCF score													
Raw value	0	1	2	3	4	5	6	7	8	9	10	11	12	>12 (max. 33)
t value	22.9	32.7	38.5	42.6	45.8	48.3	50.5	52.4	54.1	55.6	56.9	58.2	59.3	>59.3 (max. 73.0)
No. of patients attempting/ committing suicide during the follow-up period	0	0	0	0	0	0	2	1	1	5	2	3	2	9
No. of patients who made no suicide attempt during the follow-up period	14	10	19	11	10	16	16	13	15	7	2	4	8	20

this personality dimension may relate to a favorable prognosis with regard to the criterion recurrent suicidal behavior, a hypothesis which, of course, needs to be tested.

References

Angst J, Clayton P (1986) Premorbid personality of depressive, bipolar, and schizophrenic patients with special reference to suicidal issues. Comp Psych 27, No. 6:511–532

Dietzfelbinger T (1985) Quantifizierende Erfassung biographischer Aspekte und prämorbider Persönlichkeitsdimensionen bei Neurosen und endogenen Psychosen. Thesis, Technische Universität, Munich

Endicott J, Spitzer RL, Fleiss JL, Cohen J (1976) The global assessment scale. A procedure for measuring overall severity of psychiatric disturbance. Arch Gen Psychiatry 33:766–771

Eysenck HJ (1960) The structure of human personality. Methuen, London

Fahrenberg J, Selg H, Hampel R (1978) Das Freiburger Persönlichkeitsinventar FPI. Hogrefe, Göttingen

Henderson AS (1983) Vulnerability to depression. The lack of social support does not cause depression. In: Angst J (ed) The origins of depression: current concepts and approaches. Springer, Berlin Heidelberg New York, pp 107–119

Kockott G, Heyse H, Feuerlein W (1970) Der Selbstmordversuch durch Intoxikation. Fortschr Neurol Psychiatr 38:441–456

Krauss W (1972) Objektivierende Untersuchungen zur prämorbiden Persönlichkeit von Neurotikern. Thesis, Ludwig-Maximilians-Universität, Munich

Kurz A (1984) Skalierte Erfassung von frühkindlichen Entwicklungen und Erfahrungen, sowie prämorbide Persönlichkeitszüge psychiatrischer Patienten. Thesis, Technische Universität, Munich

Möller HJ, Werner V, Feuerlein W (1978) Beschreibung von 150 Patienten mit Selbstmordversuch durch Tabletten unter besonderer Berücksichtigung des Selbstmordverhaltens und der Inanspruchnahme von Beratungsmöglichkeiten für Suizidgefährdete. Arch Psychiatr Nervenkr 226:113–135

Rudolf G (1979) Der psychische und sozialkommunikative Befund, ein Instrument zur standardisierten Erfassung neurotischer Befunde. Z Psychosom Med 25:1−16
Rudolf G, Porsch U (1986) Neurotische Interaktionsmuster. Die Bildung von Befundskalen aus dem PSKB. Zschr Psychosom Med 32:117−139
von Zerssen D (1979) Klinisch-psychiatrische Selbstbeurteilungsfragebögen. In: Baumann U, Berbalk H, Seidenstucker G (ed) Klinische Psychologie − Trends in Forschung und Praxis Bd II. Huber, Bern
von Zerssen D (1980) Persönlichkeitsforschung bei Depressionen. In: Heimann H, Giedke H (ed) Neue Perspektiven in der Depressionsforschung. Huber, Bern, pp 155−178

Imitation Effects After Fictional Television Suicides

A. SCHMIDTKE and H. HÄFNER

Introduction

Many of the hypotheses that have been put forward to explain suicidal behavior have pointed to the possibility that such behavior is transmitted by imitation (Diekstra 1974; Häfner 1980; Schmidtke 1981, 1988; Welz and Häfner 1984; Phillips 1985). Among the empirical studies performed to investigate such hypotheses, two fundamentally different approaches can be distinguished.

1. Several investigations have involved determining the rates of actual or attempted suicide in the social environment of persons who have previously committed or attempted suicide (e.g., Kreitman et al. 1969, 1970; Murphy and Wetzel 1982; Welz and Häfner 1984). However, the value of this approach remains questionable, as persons of the same family may suffer from the same hereditary mental illnesses that cause suicidal behavior (e.g., depression; Egeland and Sussex 1985). Also, persons living in the same environment may be subject to the same stressors, and the suicide of a close relative or friend may result in stigmatization and/or a psychological disorder that might itself lead to depression and suicidal behavior (Schmidtke and Häfner 1986, 1987).

2. The other main approach has been to test the imitation hypothesis by examining the effects of the mass media (Häfner and Schmidtke 1986; Schmidtke and Häfner 1986). Most investigations concerning the impact of newspaper reports of suicides (e.g., Motto 1967, 1970; Blumenthal and Bergner 1973; Phillips 1974; Barraclough et al. 1977; Bollen and Phillips 1981, 1982; Wasserman 1984; Littman 1985) have demonstrated covariations between reports and suicide rate, e.g., increased suicide rates immediately (within 8 – 10 days) after the publication of such stories (Phillips 1974; Bollen and Phillips 1981, 1982). Phillips (1977, 1979) has also reported increases in the number of road accidents after newspaper reports of suicides, as well as increases in the number of multifatality airplane crashes after newspaper stories concerning homicide-suicide cases (Phillips 1978, 1980). However, Phillips' classification of certain airplane accidents as homicidal-suicidal acts has been seriously called into question by Altheide (1981).

In some studies, television news reports of "normal" suicides have also been found to result in short-term increases in suicide rates among adults (Bollen and Phillips 1982) and adolescents (Phillips and Carstensen 1986); in contrast, the study of Horton and Stack (1984) revealed no relationship between the number of seconds of coverage of suicide stories on the 6 o'clock national (USA) news and the monthly suicide rate over the period 1974 – 1980. Also, effects comparable to those produced by newspaper reports have not been detected after television coverage of homicide-suicide cases (Phillips 1980). In a study of the effects of fictional suicidal behavior in American soap operas broadcast in 1977, Phillips (1982) found increases in the number of suicides after the broadcasting of such "model suicidal behavior." However, Kessler and Stipp (1984) have questioned the validity of this study by pointing out Phillips' incorrect determination of the base line and experimental time periods, as well as the questionable nature of some of the suicidal models included. An increase in the number of suicide attempts by adolescents after the broadcasting of a television movie (showing the suicide of a young couple and its effects on their parents) was reported by Ostroff et al. (1985). Similar effects were observed in three English cities after the broadcasting of an episode of a soap opera in which a suicide attempt by a female character was shown (Ellis and Walsh 1986; Fowler 1986; Sandler et al. 1986); in another city, however, no effects were detected (Daniels 1986). In a study of four films dealing with suicide and showing suicide models, Gould and Shaffer (1986) found, after three of the films, an increase in the number of suicide attempts and suicides among adolescents in the New York area.

Mass suicides, which are usually given a great deal of publicity (e.g., Jonestown), have been found to have no influence on suicide rates, this probably being attributable to the involuntary character of such suicides (cf, for example, Stack 1983).

To the best of our knowledge, no studies dealing with the effect of TV coverage of suicides or potential TV suicide models have been performed in any European country. Furthermore, the differential effects of imitation have received, at best, only cursory treatment in previous studies concerning suicidal behavior. The results of basic research into imitation suggest that suicide transmission probably depends on the number of models available as well as the degree to which certain attributes of the model(s), e.g., age, sex, and status, approximate those of the observer (Groffmann and Schmidtke 1977).

Study

In the Federal Republic of Germany, a six-episode TV serial entitled *Tod eines Schuelers* (Death of a Student) was broadcast in 1981. The outcome of the suicidal act was repeated at the beginning of each episode, and the beginning of the suicidal act was shown in episodes 2–6. The serial was broadcast again in 1982. Using this "natural experiment" as a basis, we attempted to study differential imitation effects in suicide behavior.

Design

The six episodes of the serial were first broadcast in January and February 1981 (January 18 and 25 and February 1, 8, 15, and 22 on Sundays at 8:15 p.m.). The serial was repeated in October and November 1982 (October 24 and 31 and

November 7, 14, 17, and 21 on Sundays at 4:00 p.m.: the fifth episode was shown on a Wednesday, which was a national holiday). By including a corresponding time period before and after the period of broadcasting, we obtained a "natural" ABABA design (A, baseline phase; B, intervention phase), with an A phase of approximately 1.5 years between the two periods of broadcasting. To investigate trends over time, the period 1976–1984 was studied, with the first A phase being from 1976 to 1980 and the last A phase being from 1983 to the end of 1984.

Model Variables

As model variables, we used the *method of suicide* (to be run over by a train), the *age* (19 years), and the *sex* (male) of the model. As information concerning the social status of train suicides was unobtainable, we were unable to investigate this aspect.

Data

The Statistics Office of the Federal Republic of Germany does not provide information concerning the exact date of a suicidal act or the specific method, because the suicides are classified according to the International Classification of Diseases (ICD). Therefore, to investigate railway suicides for the years 1976–1984, we ourselves collected data concerning the sex and age of all railway suicides and the date of the suicidal acts in nine of the ten administrative districts of the German Federal Railways. The staff of the remaining district collected the data themselves. For this research, we had the cooperation of the Central Transport Office in Mainz.

Data Analysis

For methodological reasons, we investigated two overlapping time periods to be able to show the effects more clearly. The first period extended from the day of the broadcasting of the first episode up to the second Sunday after the broadcasting of the last episode (correspondingly, the same 49 days in the control years). The longer period of observation extended up to the fifth Sunday after the last episode and thus comprised a further 21 days. The corresponding time periods for the second broadcast were 42 and 68 days (up to December 31), these being shorter because the fifth episode was shown on a Wednesday.

Results

By comparing the period of the *first broadcast* plus the following 2 weeks with the same periods in the control years, a clear increase was evident in the suicide

NUMBER OF
SUICIDES

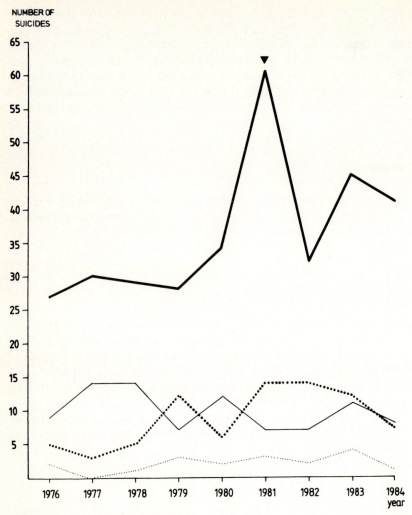

Fig. 1. Suicides in the age group of 15- to 29-year-olds during and after the first period of broadcasting (observation period January 18, 10 p.m. + 70 days; *bold solid line,* males; *bold dotted line,* females) and in the control period (January 1 – January 18, 8 a.m.; *solid line,* males; *dotted line,* females)

figures for 15- to 29-year-olds, i.e., the group closest in age to the model. The same trends were observed for the period extending to 5 weeks after the last episode. The results obtained for the combined age group of 15- to 29-year-olds for this longer time period are shown in Fig. 1.

In comparison with the control years, the difference was 86% for males (62 suicides during the period of broadcasting plus 5 weeks after the last episode: mean for the control years, 33.25), while for females, a difference of 75% was observed (14: mean, 8 suicides). Both figures were significantly different from the mean values for the control years. When, for the purpose of testing specific

NUMBER OF
SUICIDES

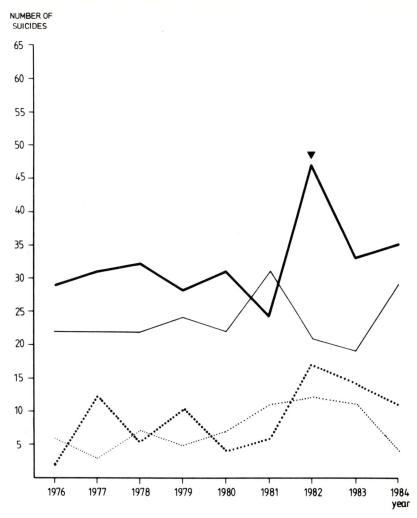

Fig. 2. Suicides in the age groups of 15- to 29-year-olds during and after the second period of broadcasting (observation period October 24, 6 a.m. + 68 days; *bold solid line*, males; *bold dotted line*, females) and in the control period (September 5 – October 24, 4 a.m.; *solid line*, males; *dotted line*, females)

effects, further age groups were differentiated, i.e., 15 – 19 years, 20 – 24 years, and 25 – 29 years, the effect was clearest in the youngest age group. For males in this age group, we found 21 suicides in comparison with a mean of 7.6 suicides for the same time periods in the control years. This difference is highly significant ($P < 0.01$). Among young females, a peak in the suicide figures was also found in the corresponding period during and after the first broadcasting, i.e., 6 suicides in comparison with a mean of 2.3 suicides in the control years. In the other age groups, the effect was slighter. No effect was observable in groups aged over 40 years.

Similar results were also obtained for the *second period of broadcasting*. Figure 2 shows the results obtained for 15- to 29-year-old males during and 5 weeks after the period of rebroadcasting.

The number of male suicides increased to 47 (54%), the mean for the control period being 30.28. The females in this age group exhibited a similar trend. For the second period of broadcasting, further differentiation of age groups also revealed that the effect was strongest in groups consisting of younger males. While the mean for the control years was 8.4, suicides among this age group during and after the second broadcasting rose to 18. Neither for other male age groups nor for females were such clear-cut effects detected.

The differential imitation effect becomes most pronounced when the various time periods of broadcasting are considered simultaneously within the framework of the ABABA design. As Fig. 2 illustrates, the group consisting of 15- to 29-year-old males exhibited clearly increased values in the periods during and after the broadcasting of the serial. The first period of broadcasting has rank 1 (suicides per day), the second period having rank 2. The ratio of the increases observed for 15- to 29-year-old males during and after the two periods of broadcasting corresponded to the ratio of the audience figures for this group for the two broadcasts (19% vs 8.9%).

Discussion

In agreement with the findings of Phillips (1978, 1980), we observed significant imitation effects with regard to a specific type of suicidal behavior after the broadcasting of a serial dealing with a fictional suicide model and a specific suicide method. The effect was most pronounced in the group whose members most closely resembled the model with respect to age and sex, i.e., 15- to 19-year-old males. The effects became progressively weaker as the similarities between the characteristics (i.e., age and sex) of the suicides diverged from those of the model, so that no effect was detectable in males aged over 40 years (cf. Schmidtke and Häfner 1986). These results thus confirm the findings of basic research that imitation effects depend on similarities between the model and observer.

Although several American studies have stated that imitation effects are only detectable for a relatively short period of time, i.e., 8−10 days after a broadcast or report (e.g., Bollen and Phillips 1982), our findings indicate that such effects can be traced over a considerably longer time span. Indeed, the figures obtained for the 5 weeks immediately following the broadcasting of the last episode of the serial revealed trends closely resembling those observed for the 2 weeks after the last episode. Therefore, the concept that imitation effects are confined to a period of 8−10 days would appear to be no longer tenable. Further analysis of the data and comparisons with the analogous time series of other suicide methods should enable us to determine the period over which increases in model-like suicidal behavior are detectable.

References

Altheide DL (1981) Airplane accidents, murder, and the mass media: comment on Phillips. Soc Forces 60:593−596

Barraclough B, Shepherd D, Jennings C (1977) Do newspaper reports of coroner's inquests incite people to commit suicide? Br J Psychiatry 131:528−532

Blumenthal S, Bergner L (1973) Suicide and newspapers: a replicated study. Am J Psychiatry 130:468−471

Bollen KA, Phillips DP (1981) Suicidal motor vehicle fatalities in Detroit: a replication. AJS 87:404−412

Bollen KA, Phillips DP (1982) Imitative suicides: a national study of effects of television news stories. Am Social Rev 47:802−809

Daniels RG (1986) Emotional crises imitating television. Lancet i:856

Diekstra RFW (1974) A social learning approach to the prediction of suicidal behaviour. In: Speyer N, Diekstra RFW, v de Loo KJM (eds) Proceedings 7th International Conference for Suicide Prevention, Amsterdam, August 27−30, 1973. Swets and Zeitlinger, Amsterdam, pp 55−66

Egeland JA, Sussex JN (1985) Suicide and family loading for affective disorders. JAMA 254:915−918

Ellis SJ, Walsh S (1986) Soap may seriously damage your health. Lancet i:686

Fowler BP (1986) Emotional crises imitating television. Lancet i:1036−1037

Gould MS, Shaffer D (1986) The impact of suicide in television movies − evidence of imitation. N Engl J Med 315:690−694

Groffmann KJ, Schmidtke A (1977) Persönlichkeitspsychologische Grundlagen. In: Pongratz LJ (ed) Klinische Psychologie. Hogrefe, Göttingen, pp 664−714 (Handbuch der Psychologie, vol 8/1)

Häfner H (1980) Attempted suicide − a contagious behavior? In: Symposium on priorities in psychiatry today. Abstract book, Hong Kong

Häfner H, Schmidtke A (1986) Effects of the mass media on suicidal behaviour and deliberate self-harm. WHO Paper ICP/-PSF 017/10 for the working group on preventive practices in suicide and attempted suicide, York

Horton H, Stack S (1984) The effect of television on national suicide rates. J Soc Psychol 123:141−142

Kessler RC, Stipp H (1984) The impact of fictional television suicide stories on U.S. fatalities: a replication. AJS 90:151−167

Kreitman N, Smith P, Tan ES (1969) Attempted suicide in social networks. Br J Prev Soc Med 23:116−123

Kreitman N, Smith P, Tan ES (1970) Attempted suicide as language: on empirical study. Br J Psychiatry 116:465−473

Littmann SK (1985) Suicide epidemics and newspaper reporting. Suicide Life Threat Behav 15:43−50

Motto JA (1967) Suicide and suggestibility − the role of the press. Am J Psychiatry 124:252−256

Motto JA (1970) Newspaper influence on suicide. Arch Gen Psychiatry 23:143−148

Murphy GE, Wetzel RD (1982) Family history of suicidal behaviour among suicide attempters. J Nerv Ment Dis 170:86−90

Ostroff RB, Behrends RW, Kinson L, Oliphant J (1985) Adolescent suicides modeled after television movies. Am J Psychiatry 142:989

Phillips DP (1974) The influence of suggestion on suicide: substantive and theoretical implications of the Werther effect. Am Sociol Rev 39:340−354

Phillips DP (1977) Motor vehicle fatalities increase just after publicized suicide stories. Science 196:1464−1465

Phillips DP (1978) Airplane accident fatalities increase just after newspaper stories about murder and suicide. Science 201:748−749

Phillips DP (1979) Suicide, motor-vehicle fatalities and the mass-media: evidence towards a theory of suggestion. AJS 84:1150−1174

Phillips DP (1980) Airplane accidents, murder, and the mass media: towards a theory of imitation and suggestion. Soc Forces 58:1001−1024

Phillips DP (1982) The impact of fictional television stories on U.S. adult fatalities: new evidence on the effect of the mass media on violence. AJS 87:1340−1359

Phillips DP (1985) The Werther effect. Suicide, and other forms of violence, are contagious. Science 7/8:32−39

Phillips DP, Carstensens LL (1986) Clustering of teenage suicide after television news stories about suicide. N Engl J Med 315:685−689

Sandler DA, Connell PA, Welsh K (1986) Emotional crises imitating television. Lancet i:856

Schmidtke A (1981) Verhaltenstheoretische Erklärungsmodelle suizidalen Verhaltens. In: Welz R, Pohlmeier H (eds) Selbstmordhandlungen. Beltz, Weinheim, pp 125−167

Schmidtke A (1988) Verhaltenstheoretisches Erklärungsmodell suizidaler Handlungen. Roderer, Regensburg

Schmidtke A, Häfner H (1986) Die Vermittlung von Selbstmordmotivation und Selbstmordhandlung durch fiktive Modelle. Die Folgen der Fernsehserie „Tod eines Schülers". Nervenarzt 57:502−510

Schmidtke A, Häfner H (1988) The Werther effect after television films. Psych Med (in press)

Stack S (1983) The effect of the Jonestown suicides on American suicide rates. J Soc Psychol 119:145−146

Wasserman IM (1984) Imitation and suicide: a reexamination of the Werther effect. Am Sociol Rev 49:427−436

Welz R, Häfner H (1984) Imitation und Kontagiosität bei Selbstmordhandlungen. In: Welz R, Moeller HJ (eds) Bestandsaufnahme der Suizidforschung. Roderer, Regensburg, pp 63−76

Background Factors of Parasuicide in Denmark

U. BILLE-BRAHE

Introduction

In Denmark, as in most other Western countries, the increasing rates of parasuicide have given rise to growing concern, and a considerable part of the research on suicidal behavior in recent years has been concentrating on this special type of self-destructive behavior. The aim of this paper is to review some of the results of research carried out at the Institute of Psychiatry at Odense University Hospital.

Methods

The difficulties in monitoring data on parasuicide is well-known. Danish cause-of-death statistics, giving detailed information on *suicide*, go back more than 150 years, but when it comes to the "unsuccessful suicides", that is, attempted suicide or *parasuicide*, no such official records exist.

A research project dealing with suicidal behavior in a Danish county (the county of Fyn) was launched in 1977, under the supervision of Professor Niels Juel-Nielsen of the Department of Psychiatry, Odense University Hospital (Juel-Nielsen 1980).

The county of Fyn (the seat of Odense University) is an administrative and geographically well-delimited region, which in area and population corresponds to roughly 10% of Denmark. Analyses of demographic, economic, social, and health conditions in the county show that the inhabitants comprise a representative sample of the Danish population (Bille-Brahe 1982). It is therefore contended that information on parasuicide, collected in Fyn, provides a sound basis for estimating the incidence of parasuicide in the whole of Denmark, as well as the characteristics of the Danish parasuiciders in general.

The purpose of the first phase of the project was to estimate the incidence of parasuicide. To that end, the rates of parasuicide were calculated from particulars obtained from case sheets of all admissions to the departments of psychiatry in the county and also admissions to somatic departments where the diagnoses might cover up a suicidal act (Bille-Brahe and Juel-Nielsen 1986).

The second phase was aimed at determination and analyses of a series of demographic, social, psychiatric, and psychological features that can be helpful in identifiying groups at risk for suicidal behavior. For this purpose, an interview investigation was carried out covering patients admitted to the Department of Psychiatry, Odense University Hospital, following a parasuicide (Bille-Brahe et al. 1982; Hansen and Wang 1984; Bille-Brahe et al. 1985; Wang et al. 1985).

Results

Incidence of Parasuicide

Figure 1 gives an overall picture of suicidal behavior in the county of Fyn during the period 1976–1980. The curves show that the incidence of both parasuicide and threatened suicide increased rapidly in the latter years of the decade. The rates for parasuicide shown in Fig. 2 regarding the period 1976–1979 were calculated on the above-mentioned scrutinizing of case sheets; the rates for 1980 were estimated on the basis of material from an investigation carried out over a 6-month period. The latter figures must be accepted with some reservations, as the investigation did not include the "high season" (late spring), and the estimated rates are therefore probably lower than the actual rates.

As the uncertainty of the estimates for 1980 would increase if the data were distributed according to sex and age, rates for sex and for the various age

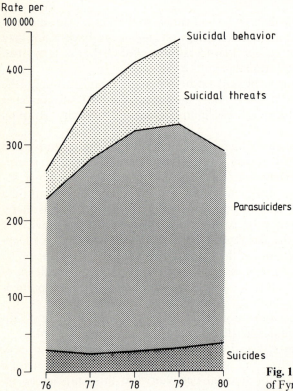

Fig. 1. Suicidal behavior in the county of Fyn, 1976–1980 per 100 000 inhabitants aged 15 years and over

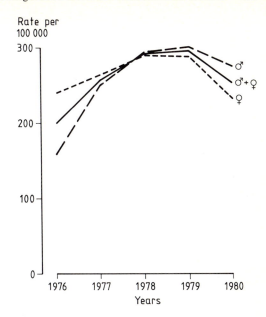

Fig. 2. Rates of parasuicide by sex. (Bille-Brahe and Juel-Nielsen 1986)

groups were calculated (see Fig. 3), and trend analyses carried out for the period 1976–1979 only.

From 1976 to 1979 the mean rates of parasuicide for men increased by 91%, and a chi-square test for trends showed an ascending trend over the period ($P > 0.01$). The rates were higher in 1979 than in 1976 for all male age groups except those over 69 years, although ascending trends could only be proved for men aged 15–19 and 30–59.

The mean rates for women increased by 20% only, and no trend could be found. The highest increase in the female rates was among the 15- to 29-years-olds; the rates showed an ascending trend ($P > 0.01$) for this age group only.

Social Characteristics of Parasuicides

The parasuiciders could not be unequivocally described as being in poor financial circumstances. The extent of their satisfaction with their income did not differ significantly from that of the normal population described in a Report on Living Conditions, compiled in 1976 by the Danish National Institute for Social Research (Hansen 1978). Further, they themselves very rarely mentioned financial problems as precipitating the suicidal act. Their situation could, however, be characterized by a lack of association with the labor market and a level of vocational training decidedly lower than that in the population as a whole (Fig. 4). On the other hand, the parasuiciders could not be defined as coming mainly from the lower social classes; the social status profile of the parasuiciders was close to that of the suiciders with its relatively large number of persons from both lower *and* upper classes (Fig. 5).

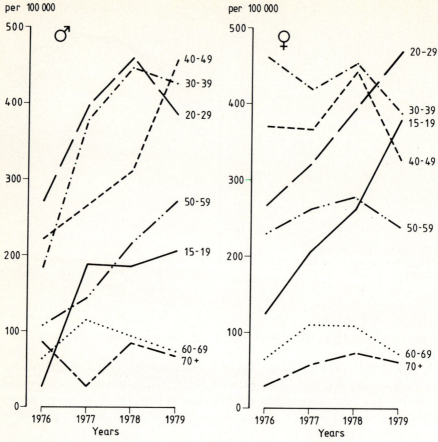

Fig. 3. Rates of parasuicide by age and sex. (Bille-Brahe and Juel-Nielsen 1986)

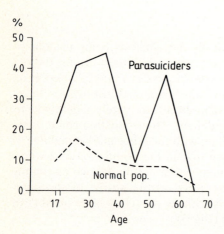

Fig. 4. Parasuiciders and the normal population by age-standardized rates of unemployment. (Bille-Brahe et al. 1985)

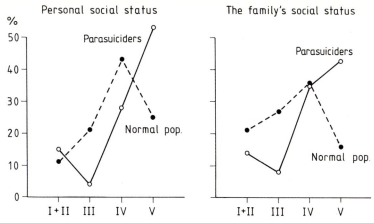

Fig. 5. Parasuiciders and the normal population by social status. (Bille-Brahe et al. 1985)

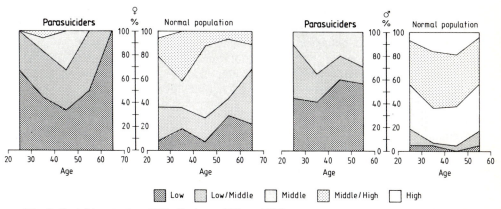

Fig. 6. Social integration. (Bille-Brahe and Wang 1985)

Less than half of the parasuiciders were married or had a steady partner. Significantly more unmarried or formerly married persons were present in all age groups of parasuiciders than in the corresponding groups in the normal population; this also applied to both sexes.

Three times as many parasuiciders as in the normal population lived alone and more than five times as many were single parents: 19% of the female parasuicides lived alone with small children as against only 2% of the women of the same age in the catchment area.

To see if the Durkheimian theories on the inverse correlation between *suicide* and social integration also apply to *parasuicide*, indices showing the level of integration in three main spheres of man's life were calculated for the parasuiciders and for the normal population, using information from the previously mentioned Report on Living Conditions. The results showed that parasuiciders were not only more isolated in the context of family, friends, and neighbors, but also more poorly situated with regard to integration into the work environment and less engaged in community and social events. Figure 6 shows the level of social integration, based on an aggregation of the three indices, and demonstrates that the level of social integration was significantly lower for all ages and both sexes in the parasuicide population than in the Danish population generally.

This result is supported by the fact that 86% of the parasuiciders interviewed stated that they had felt lonely during the period leading up to the suicidal act: 43% reported that they were often alone, although they would have preferred to be in the company of others, and 46% said they had no one to confide in. The corresponding figures in the Report on Living Conditions amounted to not quite 5% and 17%, respectively.

Attempts were made to identify high-risk groups in a 3-year follow-up study of the parasuiciders (first-timers and repeaters). Of 99 parasuiciders 36% repeated the act, and 10% of the 99 committed suicide during the follow-up period. The following risk indicators emerged:

1. For repetitive nonfatal suicidal behavior (parasuicides): female sex, age 30−40, loneliness, suicidal behavior in relatives, suicidal rumination, and help-seeking behavior around the time of the index attempt.
2. For fatal suicidal behavior (suicide): male sex, age 50−60, previous psychiatric record, somatic complaints, previous suicidal behavior, and suicidal rumination. The study showed that around the time of the parasuicide, many experienced hopelessness, isolation, and suicidal ideation.

Discussion

Apparently the frequency of parasuicide in Denmark did not, as in most other countries (Diekstra 1982), peak during the mid-1970s. On the contrary, rates continued to increase throughout the decade, especially among young people. The increase in the average rates of parasuicide has mainly been due to the fact that more and more men, especially very young men and men aged 30−59, attempt suicide.

Some have tried to explain the increase in rates of parasuicides by the general economic recession and the increasing rates of unemployment, but the increase in suicidal behavior cannot be put down to "hard times" alone. Firstly, the increase in the rates of parasuicide − and this applies to other types of so-called deviant behavior as well − started back in the booming 1960s. Secondly, it cannot be proved that parasuiciders have encountered more difficulties than others from the recession, and finally, parasuicide − as other types of deviant behavior − is becoming more and more evenly distributed among the social classes.

An important fact in this context is, of course, that the changes which have taken place during the last few decades can be neither described nor explained in economic terms only. The changes in our society − in the fields of economy and technology, in general living conditions, in norms and values, in social life and the social interaction setting, in family structure − have developed through a complicated interplay of cause and effect. The adverse effects of these changes, and perhaps especially of the violence and the accelerating speed of the development, have been tendencies toward egoism and anomie, and, according to Durkheim (1979), thereby predispositions to suicidal behavior.

Albeit several reports indicate a growing imbalance between the individual "I" and the collective "we," our study does not purport to explain the upward trend in parasuicide by a general increase in egoism and anomie. All that our results do show is that the level of social integration is lower among parasuiciders than in the population in general. The results also indicate that parasuiciders are, characteristically, incapable of compensating for poor integration in one sphere of life by better integration in another. Instead it appears to be a question of "social derout" in which a low level of integration in one area leads to accelerated disintegration in others.

It has been said that suicidal behavior is the ultimate consequence of loneliness. As mentioned above, 86% of the parasuiciders stated that they had felt lonely. However, it was not at all clear just how the parasuiciders defined "being lonely." The usual parameters such as living with somebody, contact with family, friends, etc. did not yield any differences between the lonely parasuiciders and those not lonely.

An attempt was made, using various forms of factor analyses, to define this loneliness in terms of existing typologies such as physical, emotional, social loneliness, "loneliness of the inner self", "spiritual loneliness" (Bille-Brahe 1984, working paper). The results tended to show that variables indicating "emotional loneliness" could be aggregated into a factor of some importance, but the main conclusion was that although the parameters used allowed distinction of the lonely from those not lonely, no clear patterns or types of loneliness emerged. However, vague outlines of one type of loneliness, manifesting itself in passivity and indifference, did emerge from detailed study of the total material and all the analyses. This "type" of loneliness would, in clinical psychiatry, probably be termed a neurosis; a psychologist would speak of deficient ego strength, and it would, to a social scientist, recall Durkheim's concept of egoism.

References

Bille-Brahe U (1982) Levekårene i Fyns Amt. Odense University

Bille-Brahe U, Juel-Nielsen N (1986) Trends in attempted suicide in Denmark, 1976–1980. Suicide Life Threat Behav 16 (1):46–55

Bille-Brahe U, Wang AG (1985) Attempted suicide in Denmark II. Social Integration. Soc Psychiatry 20:163–170

Bille-Brahe U, Kolmos L, Hansen W, Parnas W, Wang AG (1982) Suicide attempts in Fyn 1980–1981. An interview study. Danish Data Archive, Odense University, DDA-401

Bille-Brahe U, Hansen W, Kolmos L, Wang AG (1985) Attempted suicide in Denmark I. Some basic social characteristics. Acta Psychiatr Scand 71:217–226

Diekstra RFW (1982) Epidemiology of attempted suicide in the EEC. Biol Psychiatry 162:1–16

Durkheim E (1979) Suicide. A study in sociology. Routledge and Kegan, London

Hansen EJ (1978) The Danish welfare study. Danish Data Archive, Odense University DDA-070

Hansen W, Wang AG (1984) Suicide attempts in a Danish region. Soc Psychiatry 19:197–201

Juel-Nielsen N (1980) Forskning vedrørende suicidal adfærd. Ugeskr Laeger 142:31–32

Wang AG, Nielsen B, Bille-Brahe U, Hansen W, Kolmos L (1985) Attempted suicide in Denmark III. Assessment of repeated suicidal behavior. Acta Psychiatr Scand 72:389–394

Suicide and Unemployment in Italy

P. CREPET and F. FLORENZANO

Introduction

During the last few decades much research has been done on the health risks involved in certain kinds of work and exposure to toxic substances emplyoed in industry as well as the more general issue of the changes brought about in the style and quality of workers' lives. Rather less attention has, however, been paid to the social, health, and psychological conditions of the jobless, and this general neglect spans the age brackets most suited for productive work. Nevertheless, various international organizations (OECD, WHO, EEC) have for some time been drawing attention to the great influence these conditions can have on physical and mental health.

Although the level of unemployment in Italy is among the highest in Europe, and there are some situations with no parallel elsewhere in the world (the "Cassa Integrazione Guadagni,"[1] for example, which is often the first step toward unemployment), it has yet to receive the concentrated attention of researchers in the health field.

In addition to this shortcoming, the various difficulties standing in the way of research can be summed up under three headings:

1. *Cultural.* The experience of being jobless assumes different features in the north and the south, and whether or not it is accepted depends on social "compatibility"; obviously, there is a wide range of individual reactions.

2. *Methodological.* A sample of unemployed subjects shows far more heterogeneity than emerges from studies on the employed; moreover, the data sources (and therefore the denominators) are readily available but not entirely reliable.

3. *Sociopolitical.* Lacking representation and defense on the part of the official unions, the unemployed have limited social status.

However, the authorities, unions, and researchers who daily have to deal with problems deriving from loss of work are now realizing the links between unemployment and health problems. Taking the lead from work done in this field abroad (Platt and Kreitmann 1985; Probsting and Till 1985; Smith 1985), above all on attempted suicide (Platt 1986a, 1986b), and the results of the recent workshop organized by the European region of the WHO in York (Crepet

---

[1] Ordinary or extraordinary intervention on the part of the "Istituto di Previdenza Sociale" (INPS) in support of companies facing crises, entailing payment of workers with the equivalent of about 80% of the previous salary.

1986), significant inquiry has also been developing in Italy (Florenzano 1985a, 1985b; William et al. 1986).

This report on the phenomenon of suicide as it emerges from indicators currently available on the national scale is, in fact, based on the study of the probable links between unemployment and mental health problems.

Quality of the Data

Statistics on suicide in Italy are collected and published by Istat (Istituto Centrale di Statistica) and are based on data from two sources:

1. *Medical,* based on death certificates
2. *Legal,* based on police reports

Unfortunately, the two sources do not tally; for example, in some years the legal documentation reports over 30% fewer suicides than the medical sources. The quality of the data employed is also very uneven. The medical statistics are undoubtedly more reliable, but published with a considerable time lag (4−5 years) and arranged in only three categories: sex, age group, and cause of death. For socially significant factors we have to look to the legal statistics, which offer information on working conditions, motives, education, civil status, and position. The fact that recent breakdowns are in general readily available makes this source particularly useful.

Another problem is the lack of classified data at the local level; for example, at this level such significant details as working conditions and motives are not classified, and this makes any reliable analysis of the north-south discrepancies particularly difficult, above all for cases of attempted suicide. Figures provided by the police alone, in fact, vastly underestimate the number of attempted suicides (in 1985, 1826 attempts vs 3679 actual suicides); although no legal action is taken against the person, there is a tendency, abetted by doctors, not to report these cases.

Allowing for these difficulties, contradictions, and inaccuracies, only the legal figures can therefore be used to study the relationship between unemployment and suicide.

In the following analyses, reference was made to these statistics (Table 1) with the conviction that it is more important to analyze trends than to concentrate on precise figures, even though this may involve "chronic" underestimation of the phenomenon.

Sex, Unemployment, and Suicide

Table 2 shows the increase in specific suicide rates among the unemployed in Italy. Analysis of these specific rates for all the unemployed showed that the specific rate rose from 4.6 per 100000 inhabitants in 1978 to 9.4 in 1985; while the phenomenon is rare among women (although the specific rate has doubled, it remains very low), the situation is rather more serious for men, with a rate rising from 9.3 in 1978 to 19.4 in 1985.

Table 1. Number of unemployed and suicides: specific rates of unemployment and suicide rates by sex (Italy trend 1973–1985)

Year	Unemployed (×1000)			Suicides			Unemployed rate/100			Suicide rate/100000		
	M	F	Total	M	F	Total	M	F	Total	M	F	Total
1973	604	701	1305	1759	765	2524	4.2	11.6	6.4	6.6	2.7	4.0
1974	524	589	1113	1628	693	2321	3.6	9.6	5.4	6.3	2.5	4.2
1975	558	672	1230	1633	706	2339	3.8	10.7	5.9	6.0	2.5	4.2
1976	624	802	1426	1609	665	2274	4.2	12.2	6.7	5.9	2.3	4.1
1977	675	871	1545	1783	720	2503	4.6	12.5	7.2	6.5	2.5	4.5
1978	691	880	1571	1879	739	2618	4.7	12.6	7.2	6.8	2.5	4.7
1979	730	968	1698	1565	760	2635	4.9	13.3	7.7	6.7	2.6	4.7
1980	715	982	1698	1847	784	2631	4.8	13.1	7.6	6.6	2.7	4.7
1981	808	1104	1913	2003	752	2755	5.4	14.4	8.4	7.2	2.6	4.9
1982	919	1149	2068	2093	851	2944	6.1	14.9	9.1	7.5	2.9	5.2
1983	1001	1277	2278	2004	847	2851	6.6	16.2	9.9	7.2	2.9	5.0
1984	1013	1377	2391	2252	920	3172	6.8	17.1	10.4	8.2	3.1	5.6
1985	1054	1418	2471	2642	1037	3679	7.2	17.4	10.6	9.5	3.5	6.4

Table 2. Suicide rates among employed and unemployed (in search of the 1st and of new employment) (specific rate/100000)

Year	A Employed			B In search of 1st employment			C In search of new employment			B + C Unemployed		
	M	F	Total	M	F	Total	M	F	Total	M	F	Total
1978	6.0	2.5	4.9	9.6	1.2	5.3	8.8	0.6	3.8	9.3	0.9	4.6
1979	6.4	2.2	5.1	5.8	1.5	3.6	13.9	1.0	5.9	9.3	1.2	4.7
1980	6.1	1.7	5.0	9.7	0.8	5.1	25.8	2.5	11.0	16.4	1.7	7.8
1981	6.5	1.7	5.0	8.5	1.5	4.8	20.5	1.2	8.4	13.6	1.4	6.5
1982	6.7	1.9	5.2	6.3	1.0	3.5	26.1	2.0	11.6	13.6	1.4	6.5
1983	5.6	1.6	4.3	4.7	0.6	2.6	25.7	3.5	12.3	12.9	2.0	6.8
1984	6.5	1.8	5.0	6.9	1.9	4.3	25.7	2.0	11.0	15.6	2.0	7.7
1985	7.2	1.9	5.5	7.1	1.8	4.3	34.0	1.8	14.2	19.4	1.8	9.4

Analysis of the specific rates according to the type of employment, as in the case of those seeking their first situation (mainly young subjects) or those seeking a new one having lost their jobs, revealed striking differences. The suicide rate of males seeking a *new* job rose from 8.8 per 100000 in 1978 to 34.0 in 1985. This fourfold increase in specific rates again showed that our main concern should not be the relationship between the young (seeking *first* jobs) and suicide, but should focus in particular on those who have lost jobs.

Analysis of specific suicide rates among the employed showed fairly steady rates for the period concerned: a slight increase in the case of males (6.0 in 1978, 7.2 in 1985) which is somewhat offset by a decrease for women (2.5 in 1978, 1.9 in 1985).

Table 3. Suicide by categories of people working and not working (rates/100 000)

Year	People working			People not working		
	M	F	Total	M	F	Total
1976	5.8	1.9	4.6	13.0	3.5	6.2
1977	6.5	2.0	5.1	14.0	3.8	6.6
1978	5.7	2.2	4.6	17.6	3.8	7.6
1979	6.1	1.9	4.7	16.4	4.1	7.5
1980	5.8	2.2	4.6	16.4	4.1	7.6
1981	6.2	1.5	4.6	18.2	4.2	8.2
1982	6.3	1.7	4.8	19.3	4.9	8.9
1983	6.1	1.7	4.7	17.3	4.7	8.4
1984	7.1	1.8	5.3	19.3	5.2	9.3
1985	8.2	1.8	5.9	18.2	5.4	9.5

Above and beyond the question of suicide among the unemployed, there is a case for paying more general attention to the role played by nonemployment in various circumstances (pensioners, the category of housewives, etc.). In fact, suicide rates for the *nonwork force* are double those of the *work force*.

Table 3 shows suicide rates for the two conditions: apart from the notably high rates for males, the increase in the suicide rate among housewives was the major factor boosting the specific rates for women to a far higher level than appeared in other categories.

These figures alone suffice to confirm the real importance of the WHO campaign to bring down the number of suicides, in Italy as elsewhere, while dealing with the conditions, including unemployment, that lead to suicide. It must, however, be borne in mind that suicide is an extreme indicator of the state of mental health of the unemployed, and the upmost caution must be applied if we are to avoid oversimplification and exaggerated fears.

Correlation Between Suicide and Unemployment

The correlation between suicide and unemployment can be demonstrated statistically. Table 4 shows the correlation coefficients obtained by comparing suicide rates for the employed with those for the unemployed.

Table 4. Correlation among suicide rate, unemployment rate, and employment rate

Suicide rate	Unemployment rate			Employment rate		
	M	F	Total	M	F	Total
M	.895***	.861***	.869***	−.771***	.720**	.559*
F	.874***	.826***	.841***	−.679*	.662*	.497
Total	.921***	.896***	.907***	−.857***	.839***	.695**

DF = 11; * P < 0.05; ** P < 0.01; *** P < 0.001.

The correlation coefficient was particularly high in all combinations of unemployment and suicide rates (from a minimum of $r = 0.826$ in female unemployment and suicide rates to a maximum of $r = 0.921$ for male unemployment rates and total suicide rates) and in all cases appeared positive and extremely significant ($P < 0.001$).

The most interesting features emerge from the correlation between employment and suicide rates:

1. The negative correlation between male employment and suicide rates
2. The positive correlation between male employment rates and those for the sexes taken together
3. The noncorrelation between female employment and suicide rates
4. The negative correlation between male employment and female unemployment rates ($r = -0.679$)

These correlations applied to a relatively short period (1973—1985). Although they did not indicate any causal relationship between unemployment and suicide, they did at any rate offer further confirmation of a time linkage between the two events. The simplistic approach based on concurrence (which could be extended at random to any sociomedical field) must, however, give way to careful analysis involving the application of epidemiologic research methods. We have, moreover, set alongside the correlations obtained the degree or *relative risk* (RR) and *attributable risk* (AR), which are analyzed below.

The correlation between the male employment rate and the female suicide rate (i.e., decrease in female suicide rates with increase in male employment rates), which is not observed in the case of female employment and male suicide rates, seems to confirm the hypothesis that the unemployment/health relationship exerts its influence on the weakest members of the families of the unemployed, above all wives, elderly parents, children without job prospects, etc. Even though this correlation does not necessarily have a causal basis, it lends support to the supposition that the conditions of economic dependence that hold for so many Italian women bear some relation to suicide rates; this in turn brings us back to the socioeconomic complexity of the suicide problem.

Relative Risk of Sucide for Unemployed and Employed

Analysis of the RR of suicide for the unemployed compared with the employed during the period under consideration provided direct confirmation of theories that see unemployment as a serious risk factor.

Taking the RR for the total of unemployed, our data revealed that the figure doubled from 1978 to 1985. While the suicide RR for the unemployed was lower than for the employed (RR% = 92 and 94, respectively) in 1978 and 1979, from 1980 onward it rose steeply until it had practically doubled by 1985, reaching 183. It is, however, necessary to take into account the differences in reference population (there are far more employed than unemployed so that the absolute values for suicides are much higher). The RR was much greater

Table 5. Relative risk (%) and attributable risk (%) of suicide among unemployed and employed

Year	Unemployment condition	Relative risk (%)			Attributable risk (%)		
		M	F	Total	M	F	Total
1978	Total unemployed	155	36	94	35	−178	− 6
	In search of new employment	147	48	77	30	−317	−29
	In search of 1st employment	160	24	108	37	−108	7
1979	Total unemployed	145	54	92	31	− 83	− 8
	In search of new employment	217	45	116	54	−120	13
	In search of 1st employment	91	68	70	−10	− 47	−42
1980	Total unemployed	69	100	156	63	0	36
	In search of new employment	423	147	220	76	32	54
	In search of 1st employment	159	47	102	37	−112	2
1981	Total unemployed	209	82	130	52	− 21	23
	In search of new employment	315	70	168	68	− 42	40
	In search of 1st employment	131	88	96	23	− 13	− 4
1982	Total unemployed	203	74	125	51	− 36	20
	In search of new employment	390	105	223	74	5	55
	In search of 1st employment	94	53	67	− 6	− 90	−48
1983	Total unemployed	230	125	158	57	20	36
	In search of new employment	459	219	286	78	54	65
	In search of 1st employment	84	37	60	−19	−166	−65
1984	Total unemployed	240	111	154	58	10	35
	In search of new employment	395	111	220	74	10	54
	In search of 1st employment	106	105	86	6	5	−16
1985	Total unemployed	292	72	183	66	− 38	45
	In search of new employment	508	83	284	80	− 20	65
	In search of 1st employment	118	61	84	15	− 64	−18

for males than for females, rising during this period from 155 to 292, i.e., practically double the initial RR.

On the whole, however, there was a *reverse* trend in women, the RR being higher among the employed as we saw when dealing with correlation. If, however, we analyze the RR using the total specific rates, we risk losing sight of some significant differences that point to a variety of ways of dealing with the condition of being nonemployed.

It can, in fact, be observed that the suicide RR among the "real" unemployed, i.e., those seeking a *new* job, is extremely high, reaching five times the rate for the employed in the case of males. While the RR for men and women seeking new jobs stood at 77 in 1978 (the specific suicide rates for this category being lower than the specific rates for the employed), it had more than doubled by 1985, reaching 284 (Table 5).

The RR trend among the female population was somewhat uneven; from a low lavel in 1978 and 1979, it rose in 1980, dropped in 1982, 1983, and 1984 (in 1983 the total RR was high, with the suicide RR among unemployed women standing at 219), and was again low in 1985.

On the whole, the nonemployed seemed to resort to suicide less frequently than the unemployed, and the rates therefore tended toward equality or showed less favorable trends among the employed.

Among nonemployed men and women, the inverse tendency seemed to hold: the RR for males showed an overall drop, while in the case of women it tended to be constant or to rise slightly. The suicide RR for the unemployed was, in fact, higher than for the employed, with peaks up to five times greater in the case of males seeking new jobs.

Attributable Risk of Suicide for the Unemployed

The AR% is a measure of the percentage risk attributable to unemployment in this case. In 1978 and 1979 the suicide risk attributable to unemployment was practically nonexistent, but subsequently the percentage of suicides among the unemployed with suicide attributable to this social condition rose as high as 45% in 1985.

Here, too, there were considerable variations according to sex and type of unemployment: in the case of males seeking new jobs, the AR for unemployment rose from 30% in 1978 to 80% in 1985, while the female population, in direct contrast, showed no unemployment AR.

AR measurements also showed the relation between unemployment and suicide, offering for the first time a percentage estimate of the number of unemployed that had committed suicide as a consequence of their condition.

Considerations

Our study has above all brought out four points concerning the relationship between unemployment and suicide:

1. The positive correlation between unemployment and suicide (and the negative correlation with employment) between 1973 and 1985 in Italy
2. The relative risk of suicide for men seeking new jobs has risen during the last 8 years
3. Unemployment is a likely cause of suicide among the unemployed in 66% of the cases (total attributable risk)
4. The different behavior of male and female suicides

While the contradictions shown by Italian sources of statistics certainly help allay concern about the effects of unemployment on the population, they by no means invalidate the link between unemployment and the probability of falling physically and mentally ill that emerges from analyses of the trends.

Given that unemployment has serious indirect effects on social and individual well-being, it is of vital importance to investigate the negative psychological and emotional effects arising from this condition.

The data presented here suggest a clear correlation between unemployment and suicide, especially in the case of those seeking new employment. They also tend to confirm Platt's hypothesis (1986b) that attempted suicide is more likely to ensue when loss of work occurs in a social and cultural context that inclines subjects to experience it as a "symptom" of personal shortcomings, and therefore as a personal stigma or handicap rather than as an effect of collective, social, and economic catastrophe. This could in part account for the different suicide behavior of the unemployed in search of their first jobs and those who have lost their jobs: for the young, with job prospects becoming bleaker and bleaker, there are so many in the same condition that joblessness can no longer be put down to individual incapability or weakness.

Above and beyond the interpretative hypotheses, valid as they may be, the figures show all too clearly that the scourge now afflicting growing sections of the Italian population is bound to create enormous problems for our health and social security services, which are ill-prepared to cope with new demands and needs. The risk of "medicalizing" or, even worse, "psychiatrizing" such a large section of the population is very real, and we must apply all our skill and understanding to the prevention of further social disaster.

References

Crepet P (1986) Suicide and Attempted Suicide: New Trends and Correlations in Italy. Working paper presented at the working group on preventive suicide and attempted suicide, WHO working group, York, 22−26 September 1986

Florenzano F (1985a) Lavoro, disoccupazione e suicidio in Italia. La correlazione positiva tra la disoccupazione e suicidio nel periodo 1973−1984. Medicina − Rivista dell'Enciclopedia Medica Italiana 5:460−462

Florenzano F (1985b) Lo stato di salute dei disoccupati in Italia. Isis news Mensile di Sanita' Pubblica 4/5:4−14

Platt S (1986a) Clinical and social characteristics of male parasuicides: variation by employment status and duration of unemployment. Acta Psychiatr Scand 74:24−31

Platt S (1986b) Parasuicide and unemployment. Br J Psychiatry 149:401−405

Platt S, Kreitmann N (1985) Parasuicide and unemployment among men in Edinburgh 1968−1982. Psychol Med 15:113−123

Probsting E, Till W (1985) Suizidalität und Arbeitslosigkeit. Crisis 6:19−35

Smith R (1985) "I couldn't stand it any more": suicide and unemployment. Br Med J 291:1563−1566

William P, De Salvia D, Tansella M (1986) Suicide, psychiatric reform, and the provision of psychiatric services in Italy. Soc Psychiatry 21:89−95

The British Anomaly: Suicide, Domestic Gas and Unemployment in the United Kingdom

N. KREITMAN

The trends of suicide rates in the United Kingdom during World War II and over the subsequent 10 years showed nothing very unexpected. The suicide rates fell steeply with the onset of war as is universally found, and in the subsequent peace showed a climbing rate which represented a gradual return to pre-war levels followed by a further progression upwards. However, from around late 1950s a curious change became apparent.

Figure 1 illustrates the suicide rates for a number of European countries between a base period of 1961–1963 and a later point some 15 years later, in 1975–1977. It is clear that in virtually every country the suicide rate has in-

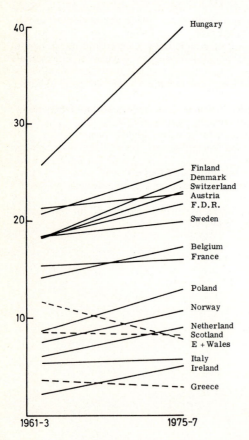

Fig. 1. European suicide rates per 100000: mean 1961–1963 and mean 1975–1977

creased, with only three exceptions (shown as dotted lines). Of these one down-ward decline can be discerned for Greece: I cannot speculate as to what the ex-planation might be for that country. The other two examples refer to two re-gions of the United Kingdom which collect their suicidal statistics in-dependently, namely Scotland, and England and Wales.

These divergent trends — between the United Kingdom on the one hand and the rest of Europe on the other — presented a paradox which contributed to a decision by the World Health Organisation to mount a study aimed in part at explaining these rather strange phenomena. The wider remit of the WHO en-quiry was to comment on the trends in Europe generally. The report of that study is now available (Sainsbury et al. 1980; WHO 1982). The study period be-tween 1961–1963 and 1971–1973 was selected and the authors analysed the changes in suicide rates between the beginning and end of that period in re-lation to changes in a number of social and demographic variables, employing a variety of statistical techniques which need not concern us here. They point to the importance *inter alia* of male unemployment as a correlate of suicide. The observation is undoubtedly correct for the majority of countries included in the survey, yet it does not accord with the experience in the United Kingdom; be-tween the beginning and end of the decade in question unemployment in the United Kingdom increased by 50%; yet, as we have seen, the suicide rate de-clined.

The paradox is underlined if one compares the United Kingdom with a dif-ferent set of industrialised nations, including some from outside Europe. The recent study by Boor (1980) correlated unemployment rates and suicide rates in nine countries. In the United States, France, Japan and Canada the correlations were positive and statistically significant even over a relatively small number of years. In Sweden and the Federal Republic of Germany the rates failed to reach statistically significant levels, but were still positive. Italy, which is probably the least industrialised of the nations in the series, showed a zero correlation. Great Britain, on the other hand, showed a large and significant *negative* correlation in contrast to the rest of the group (Table 1).

Table 1. Correlations between rates for unemployment and suicide in eight countries (from Boor, 1980)

Country	Period	Correlation
USA	1962–1976	+.79*
France	1962–1974	+.64*
Japan	1962–1976	+.53*
Canada	1962–1975	+.51*
Sweden	1962–1976	+.40
FRG	1962–1975	+.39
Italy	1962–1974	.00
Great Britain	1962–1975	−.59*

* $P<0.05$

The anomalous position in the United Kingdom also emerges when one looks back to earlier years in this century and examines the association between suicide and unemployment within the United Kingdom itself. It seems that in those years the association was precisely as one would imagine from the rest of the data which has been touched on so far. For example, a study by Swinscow (1951) produced the results illustrated in Fig. 2. Between 1923 and 1947 the pattern was precisely as would be anticipated from the world literature.

It seems then that the anomaly which requires explanation is localised to the United Kingdom and to a time between beginning in 1955 or 1960 and spanning the subsequent decade. It is reasonable to look for factors which might perturb the basis correlation and which would be unique to the United Kingdom within this time period.

The declining rates in the United Kingdom have of course attracted considerable comment from research workers in Britain, notably with respect to the notion that the detoxification of domestic gas might be responsible. The use of domestic gas as a method of suicide seems to have been particularly popular in Britain where it once accounted for up to 25% of all suicidal deaths, a proportion markedly in excess of that reported from other nations (the nearest rival in this respect was the Netherlands). In Britain the gas supplied to the domestic consumer traditionally contained about 14% of carbon monoxide. New methods of production and new sources of gas, such as the introduction of natural gas

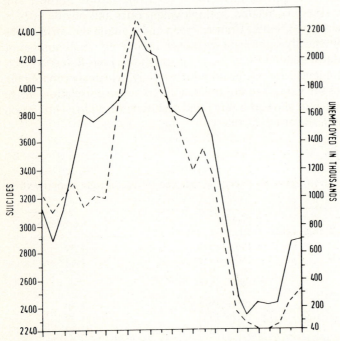

Fig. 2. Suicide and unemployment in Great Britain 1923–1947. Comparison between numbers of male suicides, shown thus ———, and numbers of unemployed males, shown thus - - - during 1923–1947 (Great Britain)

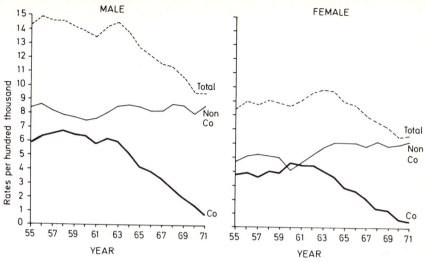

Fig. 3. England and Wales: Sex-specific suicide rates by mode of death

later in the 1960s, led to a decline in this proportion. From about 1958 to 1963 the decrease was very slow, but during the 1960s the fall in the concentration of carbon monoxide occurred steeply, and by 1971 or 1972 the CO content was approximately zero.

The consequence was that domestic gas ceased to be poisonous save under the most remarkable conditions. In parallel with this the proportion of suicides due to domestic gas also fell (Fig. 3) and there was much debate as to whether the decline in the total suicide rate over the period in question could be ascribed to that fall in domestic gas suicides. Figure 4, from a study by our own research group (Kreitman 1976), rather suggested that a direct and simple causal mechanism could be legitimately inferred, but others did not share this view. Perhaps with hindsight the position has become clearer in that if the thesis that reducing the availability of the popular means of suicide does lead to a fall in the total rate, i.e. with no compensatory increase from other causes, then one would suppose that after 1972, when the detoxification programme was completed, then the suicide rate should again resume its former upward drift. That does indeed appear to have been the case, as Fig. 4 indicates.

The question then arises as to how far the changes in domestic gas might act in the role of the "perturber" of the unemployment-suicide correlation discussed earlier. We have recently undertaken an analysis to explore this possibility (Kreitman et al. 1984). The basic hypothesis was that the suicide rate does indeed follow the traditional relationship to unemployment so amply documented in the literature, but that the suicide rate itself might be envisaged as containing two separate components. Of these the first is suicide by domestic gas, while the second is all other modes of suicide. It is further postulated that that part of the rate associated with the non-carbon monoxide deaths would follow the standard positive correlation with the unemployment rates. Changes of this kind would not of course be observed in connection with carbon monoxide

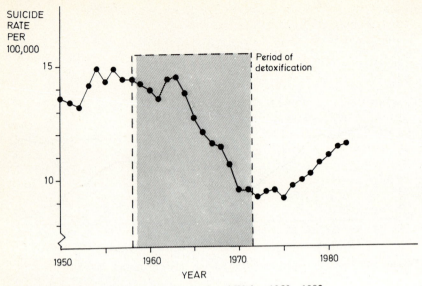

Fig. 4. Male suicide rate (all ages) England and Wales: 1950−1982

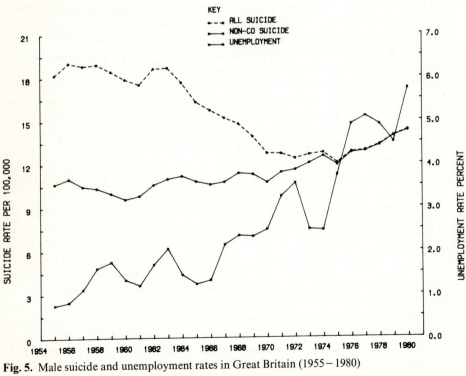

Fig. 5. Male suicide and unemployment rates in Great Britain (1955−1980)

suicides since any such basic association would be overwhelmed by the more important and opposite effect of the detoxification.

The relevant data are illustrated in Fig. 5. Calculation namely confirms what the eye discerns. Between 1955 and 1980 unemployment and the total suicide rate were negatively correlated (at $r = -0.73$) as already noted. However over the same period unemployment and non-carbon monoxide suicide correlated positively (at $r = +0.88$). The hypothesis does appear to be confirmed.

At this point it might be appropriate to step back, as it were, and consider more generally two aspects of the findings. The first concerns the role of availability of method on suicide. At first it would not appear that a simple matter such as the relative ease or difficulty of access to one particular mode of death would be likely to have any important influence on the suicide rates of a nation. However, this traditional view may require to be revised, not only because of the data presented here but also in view of the number of other sets of information now becoming available.

There is firstly a series of historical analyses, e.g. by Farmer et al. (1979) looking at method-specific rates over a sustained period of time such as the past century. His general conclusion was that there was a surprising degree of independence between the trends for at least the main groups of suicidal deaths; he identified violent methods including hanging and shooting, asphyxiation by domestic gas, and suicide by ingestion as the three main groups. It is, for example, of considerable interest that with the introduction of domestic gas in the first decade of this century a new group of suicidal deaths apparently emerged which were additional to, rather than replacements for, suicide by other methods. It seems with the removal of this mode of suicide the converse process has occurred.

Secondly, data from the United States is appearing contrasting those States in which the control of guns is strictly enforced by law to other states where access to firearms is comparatively easy (e.g. Lester et al. 1982). This work suggests not only that suicide by shooting differs between the two groups but that the total suicide rates also differ in the same direction, notwithstanding some minor degree of "compensation" by resort to other methods. These results of course have other possible interpretations, but they are certainly consistent with an availability model.

Thirdly, descriptive accounts have appeared of the use of famous suicide locations such as the Golden Gate Bridge in San Francisco or certain high cliffs around the coast of Great Britain. It seems that people will sometimes travel long distances to reach these spots, passing on the way many other locations which would have served their suicidal purpose equally well (Surtees 1982). Evidently there is some specific psychological connotation of such places, and there is evidence, albeit somewhat ill systematised, that if access to these spots is regulated potential suicides do not simply move to an adjacent area.

Perhaps as psychiatrists we should not be surprised that for many patients fantasy of death is highly specific with respect to the scene (as well as to the interpersonal context). Lastly we may note the curious phenomenon over the last decade or so of miniature epidemics of suicide occurring in certain political contexts; I have in mind the rash of political suicides by burning which occurred during and shortly after the Vietnam war, with deaths of this kind being reported right across Europe and the United States. The numbers were never very large, but it is I think of interest that they did not appear, so far as could be ascertained, to occur at the expense of "ordinary" suicides. In other words a new group of suicide victims had emerged in response to the popularly of a new if horrible method of dying.

All these strands of evidence do indeed appear persuasive, but it could not be claimed that the issue has been resolved. Clearly considerations of availability could only be expected to be relevant to that group of the population which may be designated as potentially suicidal and indeed actively involved with fantasies or plans of death. However if it is indeed the case that suicide does involve at least for some a highly specific yet popular mode of dying, then there might be possibilities through public health measures of prophylactic steps on a worthwhile scale.

The second component of the thesis which has been advanced here concerns the relation of suicide to unemployment. This is a very large and complex area, and it is possible only to point to the most obvious limitation of the data considered so far. The kind of correlations demonstrated in this paper are essentially of the ecological variety, with the units of study across time rather than place. Data are simply not available on the suicide rate *among* the unemployed nor conversely of the proportion of suicides who were unemployed at the material times. The causal connections here may be anything but straightforward. It has been shown, for example, that for parasuicide — which in many respects is radically different from suicide but may illustrate the present point nevertheless — the *rates* among the unemployed have steadily fallen as unemployment has ceased to represent personal pathology to a marked degree and has come more and more to be the result of impersonal economic factors. Nevertheless the absolute increase in the numbers of unemployed in recent years has more than offset this decline in the rate, so that the proportion of parasuicides attributable in the statistical sense to unemployment has in fact become greater. It seems quite possible that some such analogous mechanism may be operating in the area of completed suicide. Rather more certainly one can point to a number of indirect effects of unemployment as being relevant. It can be shown for example that there is a substantial correlation between *male* unemployment and *female* suicide. This could be because male and female unemployment are themselves correlated, but equally plausibly one could be seeing here the effects of male unemployment on family stability and the stresses falling on the wife and mother. None of this implies that unemployment is not important in a causal sense, but is does indicate that the causal chain may be highly complex.

Finally the point may be made that if the arguments presented here are correct the "British anomaly" in effect disappears. It seems that after all, we are good Europeans, at least in this respect.

References

Farmer RDT (1979) Suicide by different methods. Postgrad Med J 55:775−779

Kreitman N (1976) The coal-gas story. Br J Prev Soc Med 30:86−93

Kreitman N, Platt S (1984) Suicide, unemployment and domestic gas detoxification in Great Britain. J Epidem Comm Hlth 38:1−6

Lester D, Murel M (1982) The preventive effect of strict gun control laws on suicide and homicide. Suicide Life Threat Behav 12:131−140

Sainsbury P, Jenkins J, Levey A (1980) The social correlates of suicide in Europe. In: Farmer R, Hirsch S (eds) The suicide syndrome. Croom Helm, London

Surtees S (1982) Suicide and accidental death at Beachy Head. Br Med J 284:321−324

Swinscow D (1951) Some suicide statistics. Br Med J i:17−23

World Health Organisation (1982) Changing patterns in suicide behaviour. Euro Report and Studies 74, Copenhagen, WHO

Individuals and Social Factors in the Psychodynamics of Suicide

B. Temesváry

All over the world the question has been raised about what could be in the background of the very high Hungarian suicide mortality — which is not a new phenomenon. There are some who consider suicide as a "new morbus hungaricus," a term which was formerly used for tuberculosis. Although it is by no means a special Hungarian phenomenon, the increase in the incidence of suicide mortality and other self-destructive forms of behavior is an alarming phenomenon throughout the world. The fact that the suicide rate is conspicuously high in some areas which used to belong to the Austro-Hungarian Monarchy and among Hungarian emigrants emphasizes the importance of sociocultural factors although the problem has to be analyzed in a more complex way. Sociocultural factors act in the human psyche which (i.e., the psyche) is also complex but can be interpreted only in a sociocultural context. It is due to the importance of the social background that Hungarian suicide mortality shows a wavelike pattern with periodic peaks; the nearly linear rise, independent of social and frontier changes, speaks for the not negligible intrapsychic factors.

It is perhaps less known that even in such a relatively small country there are considerable intraterritorial differences in suicide mortality (Fig. 1); although the increasing tendency refers to the whole country, the mortality rate of the south-eastern part of Hungary is nearly twice as much as that of the north-western territories. Among regions showing different mortality rates, differences may be encountered in various respects: the structure of the settlements (solitary farms are characteristic of our region, while tiny villages are typical of the western part of our country). There are differences in the family structure.

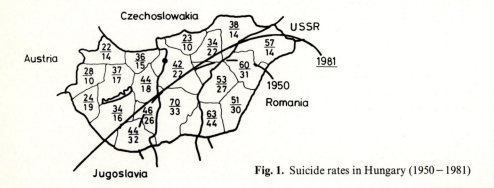

Fig. 1. Suicide rates in Hungary (1950 – 1981)

Their "mentality" as well as their systems of religion and traditions show variations, and various interpersonal and communicative characteristics hard to reveal by exact methods can also be observed.

Several generations, or accumulated suicides in the family or in the same environment, have hardly been dealt with in the literature; Durkheim (1897) did not attribute any importance to this phenomenon.

Some authors attack great importance to identification in the psychodynamics of accumulated suicides:

(a) direct identification with the parent in his suicidal act, (b) resignation to death by suicide, (c) fears of one's suicidal impulses, and (d) masked manifestations (Cain and Fast 1972).

Some authors, however, think that the "broken-home" situation can contribute to the occurrence of suicide among children (Zilboorg 1937; Andics 1938). Other authors explain the causes of suicide in behavioral terms (G. Lester and D. Lester 1971; D. Lester 1972; Motto 1967, 1970; Phillips 1974, 1985; Phillips and Carstensen 1986; Diekstra 1974; Ebstkamp et al. 1981; Schmidtke 1981; Schmidtke and Schaller 1984; Welz 1983; Welz and Hafner 1984; Gould and Schaeffer 1986).

At the end of the 1930s a world hit ("Gloomy Sunday") composed by a Hungarian songwriter induced a wave of suicide in Hungary (later the songwriter himself committed suicide), but according to the dynamics of the Werther effect (Phillips 1974), the suicide of famous artists always had "followers" (frequently at the same spot and with the same method) in Hungary. In the past few months a lot of suicide cases have been registered following the suicide of the 17-year-old Hungarian beauty queen. The patients made their attempts with the same rare cardiac drug. A young man who made his suicide attempt on the grave of the young girl completely unknown to him was treated at our clinic (these events happened after the European Congress on Suicidology in Munich).

Preliminaries of the Investigation

Our team has been engaged in suicide aftercare in Szeged since 1978. The suicide mortality of our county is especially high (63/100000) even compared with the country as a whole. About 450 patients attempting suicide are in need of emergency treatment every year. Patients with a suicide attempt are usually taken to the hospital. Following detoxication, I have treated them as an independent suicidologist counselor for 2 years. The most serious cases treated by internists or psychiatrists on duty get to our psychiatry ward anyway. At the moment we have no separate crisis intervention ward. About one-third of the 450 suicidal patients recorded per year in our town are treated at our clinic, one-third go to the suicide outpatient department, and the remaining one-third either do not wish to take part in the treatment or seek other sorts of help (in a lesser number).

In our district, where the suicide rate is well above the national average, completed and attempted suicides are frequent within the same family; cases of attempted suicides in smaller groups — sometimes with a ritual character — are not rare either.

In our earlier investigations (1985) we examined the occasional suggestive factors and the verbal attitude of 200 patients. We are well aware of the fact that the verbal attitude and the actual one do not always coincide, but we hope that our results following a detailed psychiatric exploration are objective.

The examinations were carried out at our suicide outpatient department on the basis of a semistructured questionnaire used at our clinic since 1978. In an in-depth interview, the patients were asked about the preliminaries, the motivation, and the circumstances of their suicide attempt (Ringel's presuicidal syndrome, cry for help, the seriousness of wanting to die). Data of their psychosocial development were also examined (family circumstances, development of character, sexuality, interpersonal links, etc.). Besides data referring to their bodily and psychic state of health, special attention was paid to factors which either through identification or suggestive effect might have played a role in the psychodynamics of their suicide attempt:

1. The occurrence of a suicide pattern in the environment = suicide or attempted suicide (within the family, in the circle of friends, among acquaintances).

2. What was the attitude toward suicide in the environment of the patients? If there was a suicide pattern, what was the connection with it; if not, what was the attitude toward suicide in his environment in general?

3. An attempt was made to categorize the verbal attitude of the patients toward suicide. In the course of years of practice, we received the following answers frequently (these are indicated in our questionnaire: if there are different answers, we quote them word for word): (a) suicide is a shame, (b) the person who chooses suicide can only be blamed, (c) nobody who chooses suicide can be blamed, (d) suicide is the same as dying of other causes, and (e) it is understandable if somebody chooses suicide.

In addition, the patients were asked whether there was any factor in their life which might have had an affect on their suicide attempt (a literary work, a film, a TV program).

Five categories were set up for our evaluation: (1) positive, (2) ambivalent, (3) negative verbal attitude, (4) taboo, and (5) no answer or the answer "I do not know." Considering blatant negative refusal and a blatant accepting attitude the evaluation was not difficult. The most frequent positive answer was: "There are situations in life when no other solution is possible." We found it remarkable that in many cases the answer — independently of the patient's educational and intelligence level — was the word "taboo," which is not frequent in colloquial Hungarian, or "this topic was taboo at home, we never spoke about it." We feel that there is a quantitative and not qualitative difference between the ambivalent or positive answers in the field of identification, but we find the strictly positive answers even more remarkable in a situation of a suicidal case of uncertain outcome which might even result in hospitalization. To determine whether it is those who seek help to the greatest extent, the ones who want to demonstrate a "cry for help" with their act, or whether the most endangered patients demonstrate the most positive attitude, we carried out examinations into the connections of the verbal attitude and the sex, age, occupation, illness, number of previous suicide attempts, possibility of a repeated suicide attempt, method of suicide attempt, and place of living. Besides the suicide pattern there was no significant connection between any other factor and the verbal attitude.

In the course of our examinations in 1985, randomized examination of 200 persons who attempted suicide was carried out: 50 male and 150 female. Sixty-nine patients had a suicide pattern in the environment; of them, there was a fatal suicide in the families of 36, and a suicide attempt in the families of 16. This ratio of suicide pattern was high in our material. In the control group of 200 patients with the same male-female ratio and with no suicide anamnesis, the suicide pattern in the family was 10%. Considering the data of our suicide outpatient department, the suicide pattern in the family was found to be 30%.

According to the survey, no significant interrelation (chi-square test) could be observed between the sex, age, qualification, illnesses, probability of further attempted suicides, and the verbal attitude of the patients investigated toward suicide. Similarly, in our investigations there was no significant relation between the suicide pattern and the verbal attitude of the observed patient's environment either. By the help of a comprehensive survey, the verbal attitude of the investigated patients having a suicide pattern was significantly more positive toward suicide than that of their environment (chi-square test, $P < 0.001$). The significance was encountered even in the subgroups of those with a pattern.

The subgroups of patients with a suicide pattern [namely, (1) the group of patients with suicide in the family, (2) with suicide and attempted suicide in the family, and (3) with suicide and attempted suicide in the family and in the environment] showed a significantly more positive verbal attitude toward suicide than the patients' environment (chi-square test: $P < 0.001$).

The significantly more negative attitude of the patients' environment − or more exactly, how this attitude toward suicide lives in the emotions and memory of the patients investigated − can be explained by a sense of guilt toward the deceased family member, or the fear that the suicide pattern may be passed along can play a role too (sometimes this is even verbalized). Perhaps the most remarkable result of these investigations was that the verbal attitude of the patients who have a suicide pattern in the family or in the environment was more positive than that of suicide patients with no suicide pattern and to the same significance.

Discussion

After these investigations, the question was raised whether there might be an accidental or a causal connection between the positive verbal attitude of the patients and the suicide pattern. In our present survey, we repeated the investigations where we had found significant interrelations last year (100 patients: 36 male, 64 female), and our new investigation shows the same results.

Patients with a suicide pattern had a significantly more positive verbal attitude toward suicide than patients with no suicide pattern (Figs. 2 and 3). With the help of a comprehensive survey, the verbal attitude of the patients with a

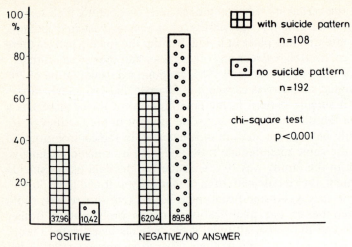

Fig. 2. Suicide pattern and the patients verbal attitude

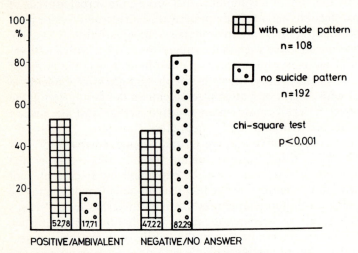

Fig. 3. Suicide pattern and the patient's verbal attitude

suicide pattern was significantly more positive toward suicide than the verbal attitude of their environment. The highest rate of positive verbal attitude was found if there was fatal suicide in the family (40.57%) (Fig. 4), blatantly accepting verbal attitude (53.70%) positive or ambivalent, but really accepting behavior (Fig. 5). The rate was somewhat lower if the suicide attempt and suicide as a suicide pattern in the family were examined together in connection with the verbal attitude (Figs. 6 and 7).

We compared the answers expressing their own attitude and the answers referring to the attitude of their environment (this latter examination was aimed at determining whether it was simply applying the positive attitude of the environment that results in the seemingly positive verbal attitude in these cases).

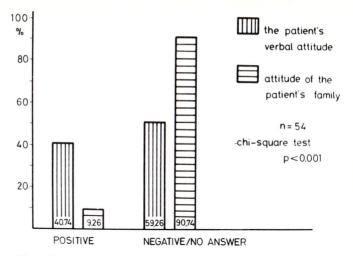

Fig. 4. Suicide in the family and verbal attitude

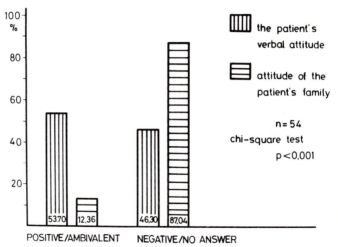

Fig. 5. Suicide in the family and verbal attitude

It is remarkable (similar to the examinations in 1985) that of 108 patients with a suicide pattern asked about the attitude in their environment 43 said that "they never talked about it, this topic was a taboo." In 37 of these cases, there was a suicide pattern in the family, 28 of which were fatal suicide acts. There were considerably fewer "covert" answers if the patients were asked about their own attitude: 16 of them answered: "I have never thought about this" (Fig. 8).

It may be asked what kind of answer can be found in the field where we got no reliable answers such as "taboo," "no answer," "he does not know." Of course, it is possible that in this field we can find more answers expressing a verbal positive attitude, but for fear of hospitalization the patients were afraid to give them. Perhaps it is more important that patients with a suicide pattern

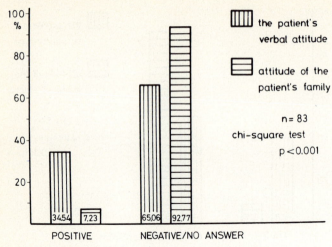

Fig. 6. Suicide pattern in the family and verbal attitude

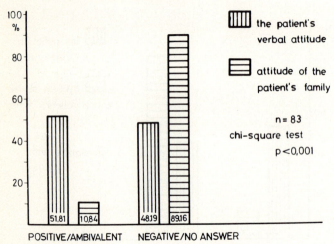

Fig. 7. Suicide pattern in the family and verbal attitude

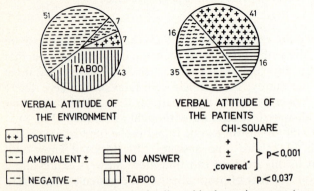

Fig. 8. Suicide pattern in the family and in the environment ($n = 108$)

gave an "unknown" answer/reaction in significantly fewer cases. Comparing this reaction with the large "taboo" field of the investigated persons' environment, we can suppose that the positive verbal attitude toward suicide can be passed on in a nonverbal way. The Hungarian attitude toward suicide is characteristically Janus-faced: the verbal attitude shows prejudiced disapproval, but the exceptionally high suicide rate in the country reveals nonverbal approval.

I do not think that we can give a sufficient explanation to the psychodynamics of suicide through behavioral models. Other individual factors, such as emotional identification or a feeling of ambivalency, also play a great role, besides the behaviorally interpretable factors.

Only in the first moment are we surprised by the occurrence of ambivalent feelings in the process of a detailed psychiatric exploration. We found ambivalent feelings toward the person (who had committed or attempted suicide) with whom our patient identified himself. Patients who had equivocally positive or negative emotional relations toward suicidal persons did not express in many cases a positive verbal attitude toward suicide. Analyzing the psychodynamics of some patients with completed suicide, we often found an extremely ambivalent feeling toward one of the parents, mostly the mother. We must analyze this question more deeply.

Our investigations do not give an answer to the following questions: which part of the psychodynamics of suicide can be interpreted by model learning and classic conditioning, how large is the field which can be explained by a behavioral model, and how large is the field of the socialization or psychoanalytic interpretation. We suppose that the future will be a "healthy" eclecticism of a complex multisided explanation.

References

Cain AC, Fast I (1972) Children's disturbed reactions to parent suicide: distortions of guilt, communication, and identification. In: Cain A (ed) Survivors of suicide. Thomas, Springfield

Diekstra RFW (1974) A social learning theory approach to the prediction of suicidal behaviour. In: Speyer N, Diekstra RFW, van der Loo KJM (eds) Proceedings of the 7th international conference for suicide prevention. Swets Zeitlinger, Amsterdam, pp 55–66

Diekstra RFW, Heuves W (1986) Recent trends in suicide rates. A social learning perspective. In: Specht F, Schmidtke A (eds) Selbstmordhandlungen bei Kindern und Jugendlichen. Roderer, Regensburg, pp 50–64

Durkheim E (1897) Le suicide. Etude de sociologie. Alcan, Paris

Ebstkamp CA, Schippers GM, Diekstra RFW (1981) Ein additives Zwei-Faktoren-Modell suizidalen Verhaltens. In: Welz R, Pohlmeier H (eds) Selbstmordhandlungen. Beltz, Weinheim, pp 211–221

Gould MS, Shaffer D (1986) The impact of suicide in television movies. N Engl J Med 315 (11):690–694

Lester D (1972) Why people kill themselves. Thomas, Springfield, pp 187–189

Lester G, Lester D (1971) Suicide, the gamble with death. Prentice-Hall, Englewood Cliffs, p 142

Motto JA (1967) Suicide and suggestibility the role of the press. Am J Psychiatry 124:252–256

Motto JA (1970) Newspaper influence on suicide. Arch Gen Psychiatry 23:143–148

Phillips DP (1974) The influence of suggestion on suicide: substantive and theoretical implications of the Werther effect. Am Sociol Rev 39:340–354

Phillips DP (1985) The Werther effect. Suicide and other forms of violence, are contagious. The sciences 25 (7–8:):32–39

Phillips D, Carstensen LL (1986) Clustering of teenage suicides after television news stories about suicide. N Engl J Med 315 (11):685–689

Schmidtke A (1981' Verhaltenstheoretische Erklärungsmodelle suizicalen Verhaltens. In: Welz R, Pohlmeier H (eds) Selbstmordhandlungen. Beltz, Weinheim, pp 125–167

Schmidtke A, Schaller S (1984) Adlers Suizidtheorie und verhaltenstheoretische Erklärungsmodelle suizidaler Handlungen. Z Individualpsychol 9:196–203

von Andics M (1938) Über Sinn und Sinnlosigkeit des Lebens. Gerold, Vienna

Welz R (1983) Drogen, Alkohol und Suizid. Enke, Stuttgart, pp 44–51

Welz R, Häfner H (1984) Imitation und Kontagiosität bei Selbstmordhandlungen. In: Welz R, Möller J (eds) Bestandsaufnahme der Suicidforschung. Roderer, Regensburg, pp 63–76

Zilboorg G (1937) Considerations on suicide. Am J Orthopsychiatry 15–31

Suicidal Patients' Comprehension of Significant Others' Attitudes Toward Them *

D. WOLK-WASSERMAN

Introduction

The significance of the attitudes of family members and friends for the development of the suicidal process in the suicidal patient has received far too little attention (Meerloo 1959; Richman and Rosenbaum 1970; Rosenbaum and Richman 1970) given the fact that several investigations (Robins et al. 1959; Murphy and Robins 1968; Rudestam 1971; Bernstein 1978, 1979; Kovacs et al. 1976; Beskow 1979) showed that in 30% – 80% of cases persons who contemplate taking their own lives communicated their suicidal intentions to the people closest to them, sometimes several times and often to several people.

One may assume that the development of the suicidal process in the direction of a suicidal action depends to a large extent not only on factors specific to the patient but also on the support afforded by the social network (Slater and Depue 1981) and all the help a suicidal patient who is desperate can obtain. However, the support provided by the social network should not only be gauged by the number of contacts which can be traced in the patient's surroundings (Welz et al. 1986); one should also take into account the quality of these contacts and the genuine support which suicidal patients can conceivably obtain from various people in their immediate proximity, as well as the patients' capacity to avail themselves of this support.

The purpose of this study was to account for the reactions of persons in the suicidal patient's immediate proximity and to show whether and, if so, how these reactions influenced the development of the patient's suicidal process before the suicide attempt in question and during the follow-up year. Particular emphasis was placed on how patients perceived significant others' responses to their suicidal communication, which were described in an earlier paper (Wolk-Wasserman 1986 a).

Material

Patients

The material comprises data on 40 suicide-attempt patients (18 men and 22 women) who were consecutively admitted to an intensive care unit (ICU) after

* The study was funded by the Ministry of Health and Social Affairs, the Commission for Social Research (DSF 303/76), and the Swedish Medical Research Council (B84-21P-6899-01A).

overdosing tablets, often in combination with alcohol. Diagnoses were as follows: neurosis (14 cases), abuse of alcohol and drugs (19), psychosis (3), and prepsychosis (4).

The neurosis diagnosis was used as an exclusion diagnosis (i.e., excluding patients who were alcohol/drug abusers, psychotic, or brain damaged). The median age in this group was 28 years (range: 18−81). Four of the 14 patients had previously attempted suicide, and only one patient did so during the follow-up year.

The diagnosis of *alcohol/drug abuse* was made when abuse was the chief symptom. Twelve abusers of alcohol were also dependent on drugs. The median age was 34 (range: 19−49); 14 of the 19 patients had previously attempted suicide, and 11 patients attempted suicide again during the follow-up year.

Of the three *psychotic* patients, two were schizophrenic and one was in a psychotic-depressive state. The anamnesis of the four patients with a diagnosis of *prepsychosis*, who exhibited schizoid, hypomanic, or paranoid symptoms, showed that all had previously been diagnosed as disturbed, with psychotic episodes. The median age in this group was 30 (range: 19−71). Six of the seven patients had previously attempted suicide, and five did so again during the follow-up year.

Most patients in the neurosis group belonged to social classes II and III (on a three-point scale). In the abuse group, most patients belonged to social class III, while all three classes were represented among the prepsychosis/psychosis patients.

Significant Others

Significant others were defined as persons in close and continuous contact with, and important to, the patient: 24 partners (spouse, financé(e), girl/boyfriend), 23 parents, and 23 other relatives (sibling, adult child, sister-/brother-in-law) or friends of 37 patients were interviewed. Three patients had no relatives or friends at all. Eight patients had no steady relationships with heterosexual partners.

Many partners proved to be mentally disturbed: nine, for example, had themselves attempted suicide, and a further nine were alcohol/drug abusers. The incidence of suicidal actions in the form of suicide attempts and suicides was noted among the parents and siblings of 21 of 40 patients.

Dropouts

Three patients could not be reached for follow-up interviews. Eight partners and two parents with whom interviews had been planned could not be interviewed, either because the patients withheld their permission or because the significant others themselves did not wish to cooperate. In these cases, use was made of material from medical records and interviews with care personnel who were in contact with patients and/or their significant others.

Method

The patients were interviewed in connection with their admission and then followed up in the subsequent year. In addition, relatives, friends, and persons involved in the patients' treatment were interviewed. All in all, 300 semistructured interviews were conducted, of which 149 were tape-recorded. Information from all somatic and psychiatric records and from social welfare offices' notes on the patients was analyzed. Details about theoretical background, definitions, material collection, interview method, documentation, and the processing of the material have been given in other publications (Wolk-Wasserman 1986a, b).

Results and Discussion

Dependency

The patients' relationships with partners, and even with other family members and close associates, were often characterized by strong and frequently explicit dependency needs. When conflicts arose, the patients felt unloved and were vulnerable and easily upset.

Thoughts of suicide afflicted the neurotic, alcohol-, and drug-abuse patients when their relationships deteriorated markedly, and there appeared to be a risk of their collapsing altogether. Patients in the prepsychosis/psychosis group experienced suicidal thoughts in similar situations and, moreover, when patients imagined that existing relationships were becoming unbalanced.

Suicidal thoughts may be seen as the individual's attempt to solve individual psychic conflicts; however, expressed in the form of suicidal communication to others, they acquire an interpersonal meaning in addition to the individual one. Suicidal thoughts were expressed either verbally (directly or indirectly) or nonverbally (directly or indirectly) by 37 of 40 patients, on several occasions and often to many people. In most cases the suicidal communication was a response to threatened or actual separation and was one of the means by which the patients strove to preserve existing relationships. This communication, and the intense anxiety, fear, despair, and sometimes chaos experienced and shown to significant others by patients when they faced the fact that their relationships − on which they were usually heavily dependent − might come to an end, had a profound impact on their interpersonal relations and a marked effect on significant others. Suicidal communication of one kind or another was recognized by significant others to 31 of the 37 patients.

Patients' Perception of Significant Others' Reactions to Suicidal Communication

Silence Interpreted as a Negative Attitude or Indifference. As described in a previous work (Wolk-Wasserman 1986a), significant others' responses to the patients' suicidal communication, in all three diagnostic groups, was near-total silence and evasion.

The fact that no open dialogue took place on the subject of suicide was due not only to the inexperience of both parties in dealing with family problems, but also to the distress and anxiety felt by significant others when the patients voiced, or otherwise expressed, their suicidal thoughts. This distress was probably exacerbated by the significant others' thoughts about their own problems and destruction coming to the fore. It must be mentioned in this connection that significant others in this material were a psychically labile group, with their own psychiatric and psychological problems which, in many cases, required psychiatric consultations or treatment (Wolk-Wasserman 1986 b). In addition, a very important factor contributing to the significant others' silence was their fear that discussing the patients' suicidal thoughts and utterances with them would precipitate their realization.

Only in a few cases did significant others try, by keeping silent, to control their irritation or conceal their aggressive feelings. In most cases, significant others reacted with silence because they were worried about the patient. They experienced anxiety or even anguish, but were unsure how to act and show their concern for the suicidal family member other than by silence. They also found it difficult to seek help actively from professional institutions (Wolk-Wasserman 1986 b; Wolk-Wasserman 1987 b).

Suicidal patients interpreted significant others' silence more often as indicating negative attitudes toward them than as a sign of concern, hesitation, and the significant others' individual stress. As depressive patients usually do, suicidal patients reacted with a negative interpretation of reactions in their surroundings. They also showed very little understanding of the fact that significant others might have individual problems which contributed to their difficulties in coping with interpersonal problems.

Patients' Incomprehension of Contradictory Tendencies in the Significant Others' Ambivalence: Comprehension of Hate but Not Love. The ambivalence demonstrated by significant others toward patients concerned the continuation of the relationship and the issue of helping the patient, for example, in concrete ways or by assisting the patient where contacts with somatic or social care services were concerned (Wolk-Wasserman 1986 a).

Ambivalence was most striking on the issue of whether to continue the relationship with the patient. Most partners to patients in all diagnostic groups, but even other significant others where patients in the abuse group were concerned, exhibited ambivalence on this point.

Except for partners, the neurosis and prepsychosis/psychosis patients' significant others did not appear to be ambivalent concerning the question of continuing the relationship.

Ambivalence on the issue of whether to help the patient was clearly exhibited among all significant others of patients in the abuse group. However, such ambivalence was shown only on a very small scale by the neurotic patients' significant others and not at all by those of the prepsychotic/psychotic patients.

In most cases, significant others were well aware of two components in their ambivalence vis-à-vis the suicidal patient. It meant the existence of two contradictory wishes – to stay with the patient and to leave him, to help and not to help.

The patients in all three diagnostic groups showed a tendency to stress only the negative component in the ambivalent reactions of significant others. For example, the significant others' desire both to break off and to continue the relationship was usually interpreted by the patients as an urge to abandon and separate from them. It was difficult for the patients to see that ambivalence had two poles: a positive pole, i.e., the desire to stay in the relationship and solve the difficulties, and a negative pole, i.e., the desire to break off the relationship. This manner of perception is characteristic of a depressive-narcissistic personality type (Wolk-Wasserman 1986 b). This type of patient is in desperate need of reinforcement for his self-esteem, and reinforcement is expected to be direct and powerful. All ambivalence, nuances, and hesitations are usually interpreted as rejection and confirmation of the patient's worthlessness. The negative component of ambivalence is therefore often given undue weight in patients' interpretation of significant others' reactions.

Most patients perceived their partners' and other significant others' ambivalence as an entirely negative attitude and, in turn, intensified their suicidal communication and other demanding forms of behavior, presumably further reinforcing the significant others' ambivalence – a vicious circle. This process varied in intensity and duration, lasting weeks or months for the neurotics and months or years for abusers and prepsychotics/psychotics. The situation often became unbearable, and the families were in great need of professional help in understanding and controlling these interactions.

Aggressiveness. A small number of significant others actually reacted to the patients' suicidal communication with manifest aggressiveness.

Aggressiveness may be defined as "a tendency or cluster of tendencies finding expression in real or fantasy behavior intended to harm other people or to destroy, humiliate, or constrain them, etc." (Laplanche and Pontalis 1980). In this study, the author concentrated on identifying the significant others' expressions of death wishes regarding the suicidal patient. Death wishes were used as an operational definition of aggressiveness because their incidence could be quantified (Table 1).

Death wishes could be expressed verbally, to the patient's face or others, for example, the interviewees, therapists, or friends and acquaintances, or as turning-away reactions, when significant others – although aware that a suicidal action was imminent or had already occurred – left patients to their fate, often leaving home, without helping to obtain medical help.

When significant others' remarks or reactions were classified as expressing death wishes, it was clear that their desire was to rid themselves of the patient and of responsibility for her or him. In these cases, the significant others believed the patient's death to be the only prospect of release from the relationship with the patient.

There seems to have been a strong correlation between the degree of aggressiveness shown by significant others and the length and intensity of the

Table 1. Incidence of death wishes regarding patients among significant others, classified by patients' diagnostic groups

	Neurosis group (n = 14)			Abuse group (n = 19)			Prepsychosis/psychosis group (n = 7)		
	Verbal		Turning-away	Verbal		Turning-away	Verbal		Turning-away
	To patient	To others		To patient	To others		To patient	To others	
Partners (n = 24)									
N (n = 7)	0	0	2	6	3	6	0	0	0
A (n = 13)									
P (n = 4)									
Parents (n = 23)									
N (n = 6)	0	0	0	1	3	0	0	0	0
A (n = 10)									
P (n = 7)									
Relatives/ friends (n = 23)									
N (n = 9)	0	2	0	1	3	0	0	0	0
A (n = 10)									
P (n = 4)									

N, neurosis group; A, alcohol/drug abuse group; P, prepsychosis/psychosis group.

patient's suicidal process. One simple measure of the latter was the number of previous suicide attempts.

In the neurosis group – in which the suicidal process had not been protracted and fewer suicide attempts had been made earlier – the significant others' aggressiveness never took the form of verbal death wishes regarding the patient, but two partners showed turning-away reactions (Table 1).

On the other hand, the significant others' failure to discuss the patient's suicidal communication and their ambivalence were often perceived by the patients as signs of negative or even aggressive attitudes toward them. However, it is also conceivable that, for example, ambivalence could include a growing component of aggressiveness.

In the abuse group, the suicidal process had been protracted, and many patients had a history of numerous suicide attempts. A large number of significant others – partners, parents, relatives, and friends – expressed death wishes in direct, verbal terms to the patients (Table 1), frequently when the patients, during arguments, directly threatened to commit suicide.

In the abuse group, the lack of a supportive network usually increased the patients' feelings of worthlessness and meaninglessness and was probably one of the most important causes of the abuse patients' great number of repeated suicidal actions in the follow-up year. Difficulties in treatment – which were marked in the abuse group — and the fact that hardly any significant others were offered or received treatment were additional reasons why the suicidal process was not arrested.

In the prepsychosis/psychosis group, significant others' aggressiveness in no case took the form of death wishes. On the other hand, it found expression in their complaints about public care institutions — which, in many cases, may be regarded as displaced aggressiveness — and in their wishes (sometimes expressed clearly in interviews) to escape the burden of responsibility for the patients. Far from being voiced to the patients, such wishes were probably disguised by intensified surveillance and a more than usually protective attitude when the patients' suicidal utterances became more frequent. Thus, the patients received a good deal of protection, which may have saved their lives, since significant others often contacted patients in time and arranged their transportation to the hospital.

Development of the Suicidal Process. The development of the suicidal process toward suicidal action was investigated partly in a retrospective manner (i.e., the author tried, by means of interviews immediately after the patients' suicide attempts, to elucidate the situation before the suicide attempt) and partly in a prospective manner (the author endeavoured, by means of interviews during the follow-up year, to elucidate the new presuicidal situation arising in 17 cases owing to the patients' repeating their suicide attempts).

Conceivably, the patients' sense of inferiority, feeling of desperation, self-hate, and self-accusations became more intense when people close to them reacted to their suicidal communication with silence, manifest ambivalence, and sometimes also aggressiveness. Silence and ambivalence were often interpreted by suicidal patients as signs of indifference or negative attitudes, probably in part because of the patients' negative feelings about themselves and tendency to look on the dark side. Presumably, significant others' reactions are more crucial when the patient is dependent on a single major relationship.

The escalation of suicidal thoughts and actions was hastened when other significant others in addition to partners displayed ambivalence, and when their aggressiveness became more marked (Table 1). This steady escalation was evident in the abuse group, in which there was a high incidence of repeated suicide attempts in the follow-up year. A contributory factor in this context was the difficulty in treating the patients successfully (Wolk-Wasserman 1986 b, 1987 a).

In the neurosis group, ambivalence and aggressiveness were only in exceptional cases exhibited by significant others who were not partners. In these cases, the significant others' silence and ambivalence were often interpreted by patients as negative attitudes, and this probably played a part in precipitating suicidal actions. In the follow-up year, patients and also some significant others received psychiatric treatment or attended consultations in which they cooperated relatively well (Wolk-Wasserman 1986 b, 1987 a). This was probably an important factor reducing the incidence of repeated suicidal actions.

In the prepsychosis/psychosis group, a relatively large number of repeated suicide attempts took place during the follow-up year, presumably owing to the patients' severe psychiatric problems and the therapists' difficulties in tackling and working through the patients' suicidal tendencies. The lack of cooperation between significant others and therapists was another contributory factor (Wolk-Wasserman 1987b).

Conclusions

Significant others' attitudes to the patients' suicidal communication are probably extremely important for the development of the suicidal process as is also the suicidal persons' interpretation of significant others' silence and ambivalence as solely negative attitudes toward them. The same applies to suicidal patients' difficulties in discerning the positive component of ambivalence and the concern aspect of silence.

If suicide-prevention programs are to succeed, the capacity to intervene in the dynamics of the suicidal family, and to provide treatment help and support not only to the patients but also to partners and other significant others, is vital. An effort to ease the dialogue between partners, and between patients and other significant others, and to correct the suicidal patients' interpretations of significant others' attitudes as solely negative, should be an essential element in the therapy. Helping the suicidal patients to comprehend the elements of concern, interest, worry, responsibility, and love in the significant others' feelings and helping to show significant others how to express these feelings seem to be very important.

References

Bernstein M (1978–1979) The communication of suicidal intent by completed suicides. Omega 9:175–182
Beskow J (1979) Suicide and mental disorder in Swedish men. Acta Psychiatr Scand [Suppl] 277:1–138
Kovacs M, Beck AT, Weissman MA (1976) The communication of suicidal intent. Arch Gen Psychiatry 33:198–201
Laplanche J, Pontalis J-B (1980) The language of psycho-analysis. Hogarth, London, pp 17–21
Meerloo JAM (1959) Suicide, menticide, and psychic homicide. Arch Neurol Psychiatry 81:360–362
Murphy GE, Robins E (1968) The communication of suicidal ideas. In: Resnik HLP (ed) Suicidal behaviors. Little Brown, Boston, pp 163–170
Richman J, Rosenbaum M (1970) A clinical study of the role of hostility and death wishes by the family and society in suicidal attempts. Isr Ann Psychiatry Relat Discip 8:213–231
Robins E, Gassner S, Kayes J, Wilkinson RH, Murphy GE (1959) The communication of suicidal intent: a study of 134 consecutive cases of successful (completed) suicide. Am J Psychiatry 115:724–733
Rosenbaum M, Richman J (1970) Suicide: the role of hostility and death wishes from the family and significant others. Am J Psychiatry 126:128–131 (1652–1655)
Rudestam KE (1971) Stockholm and Los Angeles: a cross-cultural study of the communication of suicide intent. J Consult Clin Psychol 36:82–90
Slater J, Depue RA (1981) The contribution of environmental events and social support to serious suicide attempts in primary depressive disorder. J Abnorm Psychol 90 (4):275–285

Welz R, Veiel H, Häfner H (1986) Social support and suicidal behaviour. First European symposion on empirical research of suicidal behaviour. Munich, 19–22, March 1986

Wolk-Wasserman D (1986 a) Suicidal communication of persons attempting suicide and responses of significant others. Acta Psychiatr Scand 73 (5):481–499

Wolk-Wasserman D (1986 b) Attempted suicide – the patient's family, social network and therapy. Dissertation, Graphic systems, Stockholm

Wolk-Wasserman D (1987 a) Some problems connected with the treatment of suicide attempt patients: transference and countertransference aspects. Crisis 8/1:69–82

Wolk-Wasserman D (1987 b) Contacts of suicidal neurotic and prepsychotic/psychotic patients and their significant others with public care institutions before the suicide attempt. Acta Psychiatr Scand 75:358–372

Suicide: Beyond the Regulation of Emotion

H. GUTSCHER

Introduction

This paper adresses two issues: (a) the utility of applying the coping paradigm to the study of suicide and other forms of self-damaging behavior and (b) the outline for a resource theory of the regulation of emotion.

There have been many attempts to find common underlying causes of diverse forms of self-damaging behavior (Menninger 1938; Lettieri 1978). The research set out here tries to give a new answer to the problem of establishing common determinants in self-damaging behavior. In their attempt to classify coping strategies, Lazarus and Launier (1978) postulated a distinction between instrumental or problem-oriented behavior on the one hand and palliative or emotion-oriented behavior on the other. Coping always involves some kind of change or adjustment in the transaction between man and his environment. The elements to be modified may be either external factors within a given situation or intraindividual factors such as cognition and emotion. In the first case, coping aims for changes in the real world by such means as direct action, support-seeking, and so forth. In the second case, coping implies either cognitive changes such as minimization, restructuring, and efforts to restore self-esteem (Wills and Shiffman 1985; p. 9; Taylor 1983) or is focused directly upon the negative emotion, with the aim of eliminating or reducing (at least temporarily) the impact of negative emotional states without recourse to objective changes in the transaction with the given situation. A considerable body of evidence indicates that many forms of substance abuse serve the function of minimizing negative moods (Grunberg and Baum 1985; Gutscher and Hornung 1986, p. 121).

A resource theory of the regulation of emotion has to be based upon the importance of emotions occurring within the wider context of psychic regulation processes. Negative emotional arousal in this context serves as an activating agent directing action toward a solution or mitigation of a real or imagined problem in the outside world. Successful action brings the negative emotional state to an end. The degree of success of direct action, however, depends on the availability of personal and social resources and skills. A lack of positive resources is expected to activate negative resources such as escape or avoidance tendencies. Under these conditions, maladaptive strategies reliant upon the substance-based regulation of emotion are easily acquired and learned (Tucker 1982). The real problems of the individual in the outside world remain unresolved, which eventually leads back to states of negative emotional arousal

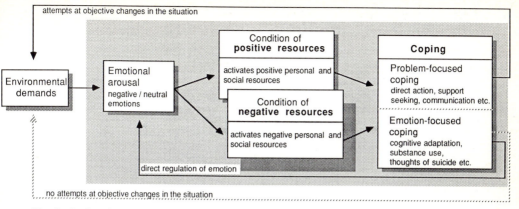

Fig. 1. Outline for a resource theory of the regulation of emotion

and new cycles of substance intake. A previous study (Gutscher 1985) has shown that the exploitation of positive social and personal resources has a buffering effect on the impact of life stress. The loss of this buffering function inherent in the employment of positive resources makes the use of modes of behavior that directly regulate the negative emotions all the more necessary.

The central point about a resource theory of the regulation of emotion is that the acquisition of direct forms of emotion regulation through substance use depends on the type and extent of social and personal resources (Fig. 1).

It seems to be important to emphasize the mitigating function of these types of maladaptive behavior as the possible beginning of a self-destructive career. In this theoretical context, suicide could then be seen as the ultimate answer to the demands and challenges of life when other strategies of emotion regulation have failed. The establishment of common determinants in different forms of self-damaging behavior might at least be partially derived from the highly developed but shortsighted kinds of functional approach aiming at subjective well-being that are mentioned above.

The relationship of presuicidal behavior (measured as the contemplation of suicide) to several forms of substance use, to personal and social resources, and to affective state will be investigated below. We will also consider whether these modes of behavior can in fact be ordered along a dimension that has the "direct regulation of emotion" at one pole and "problem-solving" at the other.

Methods

This research was conducted as part of a larger project on self-damaging behavior in Switzerland. Data were collected in 1977 by means of personal 1-h interviews with 3000 persons aged 16 to 90 in the German- and French-speaking parts of the country. The sample was a two-stage, proportionally stratified, random sample of individuals. The response rate was 78%. A standardized ques-

Table 1. Description of the 23 variables

Variables[a]	Label (see Fig. 2)	No. of items	Alpha
Situational variables			
Life stress	LIFE STRESS	55	–
Daily "hassles"	HASSLES	1	–
Daily "uplifts"	UPLIFTS	1	–
Affective state			
Negative emotions	NEG. EMOTIONS	5	.81
Feelings of depression	DEPRESSION	1	–
Positive personal resources			
Self-esteem	SELF-ESTEEM	5	.70
Communication skills	COMMUNICATION	3	.57
Negative personal resources			
Tendency to escape from problems	ESCAPE	3	.61
Tendency to avoid conflicts and rejection	AVOIDANCE	7	.68
Suppression of negative feelings	SUPPRESSION	3	.57
Positive social resources			
Quality of the social network, social support	SOCIAL SUPPORT	3	.61
Obligations within the social network	SOCIAL OBLIGATIONS	1	–
Job satisfaction	JOB SATISFACTION	5	.81
Negative social resources			
Feelings of isolation	ISOLATION	5	.68
Problem-focused coping			
Instrumental coping	INSTRUMENTAL COPING	7	.67
Emotion-focused coping			
Smoking	SMOKING	5	.96
Overeating	OVEREATING	5	.96
Alcohol	ALCOHOL	5	.93
Illegal drugs (cannabis, opioides, etc.)	DRUGS	5	.97
Stimulants (amphetamines)	STIMULANTS	5	.98
Analgesics	ANALGESICS	5	.98
Sedatives	SEDATIVES	5	.96
Thoughts of suicide	SUICIDE	5	.96

[a] The items exist in German and French versions only.

tionnaire was used which was partially handed out to and filled out by the respondents. The 23 variables are described in Table 1.

Unidimensionality of the scales was tested by factor analysis; additive unit weighting was applied to compute the factor scores. Multidimensional scaling (MINISSA) is a mathematical technique that enables the researcher to convert similarities between objects (i.e., correlations between variables) into distances between variables in either a metric or nonmetric dimensional configuration. Results from multidimensional scaling can be viewed as aggregated conceptual maps of the interviewed persons. This technique was used to answer the following questions: How is presuicidal behavior (measured as thoughts of suicide) related to other forms of self-damaging behavior? How are these behavioral patterns related to personal and social resources, affective state, and situational variables?

Results

Data from the program suggest that a two-dimensional configuration of the 23 variables is appropriate (Fig. 2).

The variables appeared to be clustered into two distinct groups at the two poles of the vertical dimension. Variables at the top end of the vertical dimension were closely associated with positive social and personal resources and with instrumental, problem-oriented coping. Variables at the lower end of the vertical dimension were thematically oriented toward negative personal and so-

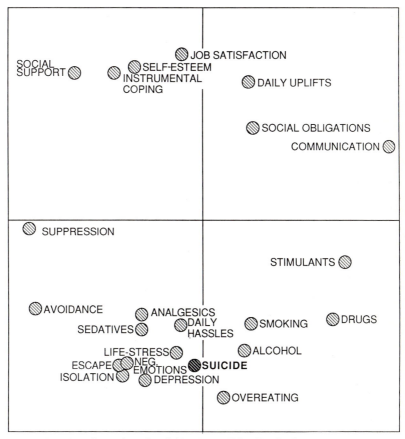

Fig. 2. Two-dimensional configuration of variables (stress DHAT = 0.15)

cial resources, negative evaluation of the situation, substance use, and thoughts of suicide. Thinking of suicide appeared to be closely embedded in the context of various forms of substance use. The emergent structure was repeated within various data subsets. A complete replication of the above as part of a new, extended study employing new data is currently underway.

Discussion

One of the purposes of this paper is to demonstrate the utility of applying the coping paradigm to the study of suicide and other forms of self-damaging behavior. The vertical axis in Fig. 2 can easily be interpreted in terms of the coping paradigm. Variables are vertically ordered along a problem-oriented vs emotion-oriented continuum. The horizontal dimension is much harder to interpret: the objects on the right side indicate the more socially oriented and visible modes of behavior (SOCIAL OBLIGATIONS, COMMUNICATION), whereas the behavior on the left side appears rather to be inward-directed (SUPPRESSION, AVOIDANCE).

The paper's secondary goal is to propose the concept of the regulation of emotion as the common, underlying determining factor of various forms of self-damaging behavior. The spatial relationship between several forms of substance-oriented behavior (ANALGESICS, SEDATIVES, SMOKING, DRUGS, ALCOHOL, STIMULANTS, OVEREATING) and negative personal resources such as the inability to express negative feelings (SUPPRESSION), the tendency to avoid conflicts (AVOIDANCE), to escape from interaction (ESCAPE) into isolation, and the proximity of these to subjective life stress and the pressures of everyday life ("HASSLES," cf. Lazarus and DeLongis 1983) indicate a close conceptual relationship between negative resources and the regulation of emotion as a coping strategy. On the other hand, positive resources such as self-esteem, communication skills, obligations within the social network, and reliance on social support are associated with instrumental coping (Fleishman 1984).

The spatial proximity of thoughts of suicide to substance-based methods of emotion emphasizes how closely related such concepts are (cf. Maris 1981, p. 316). Substance consumption as a means to temporarily manipulate one's mood is widely accepted in our culture, but it seems to be often abused as a general coping strategy that is substituted for direct instrumental coping. Where substance consumption is used more and more as a substitute for other coping strategies, it proves to be maladaptive and self-damaging.

Suicide can be regarded as behavior which becomes conceivable and learnable only as a direct result of coping resources that have failed. The results suggest that primary prevention should be aimed at maintaining and building meaningful network structures in families and other social institutions and organizations that promote rather than hinder the acquisition and development of positive personal and social resources. Only when suicide is more readily accepted as the culmination of a negative development in the context of declining coping resources within a suicidal career can the primary prevention of suicide by anything more than just the prevention of the act of suicide.

References

Fleishman JA (1984) Personality characteristics and coping patterns. J Health Soc Behav 25:229 – 244

Grunberg NE, Baum A (1985) Biological commonalities of stress and substance abuse. In: Shiffman S, Wills TA (eds) Coping and substance use. Academic, Orlando, pp 25 – 62

Gutscher H (1985) Verhalten unter Belastung – Wege in die Selbstgefährdung. In: Braun HJ (ed) Selbstaggression, Selbstzerstörung, Suizid. Artemis, Zurich, pp 125 – 139

Gutscher H, Hornung R (1986) Spezifische Probleme und Risiken des Medikationsverhaltens. In: Gutscher H, Hornung R, May U, Schaer M (eds) Medikamentenkonsum und Medikationsrisiken. Huber, Bern, pp 92 – 134

Lazarus RS, DeLongis A (1983) Psychological stress and coping in aging. Am J Psychol 38:245 – 254

Lazarus RS, Launier R (1978) Stress-related transactions between person and environment. In: Pervin LA, Lewis M (eds) Perspectives in interactional psychology. Plenum, New York, pp 287 – 327

Lettieri DJ (ed) (1978) Drugs and suicide. Sage, London

Maris RW (1981) Pathways to suicide. Johns Hopkins University Press, Baltimore

Menninger K (1938) Man against himself. Harcourt, Brace, and World, New York

MINISSA (Michigan-Israel-Nijmegen Integrated Smallest Space Analysis) From: Lingoes J et al, MDS (X) programs, version 3.2, Program Library Unit, University of Edinburgh

Taylor SE (1983) Adjustment to threatening events. Am J Psychol 38:1161 – 1173

Tucker MB (1982) Social support and coping: applications for the study of female drug abuse. J Soc Issue 38:117 – 137

Wills TA, Shiffman S (1985) Coping and substance use: a conceptual framework: In: Shiffman S, Wills TA (eds) Coping and substance use. Academic, Orlando, pp 3 – 24

Part V   Treatment Evaluation

Effectiveness of Suicide Prevention:
A Short Review of the Literature

A. Kurz and H.-J. Möller

Introduction

The abundant literature on the work of suicide prevention programs and institutions contains only a few investigations into the effectiveness of such services. Epidemiologic methods have been used to examine the influence of suicide prevention programs on the incidence of suicide in the area they serve. Clinical research has been directed to the evaluation of treatment schemes in patient samples. In this overview, problems and results of both types of investigations will be summarized and conclusions for future research will be drawn (Kurz and Möller 1982a, b).

Epidemiologic Studies

Researchers have followed two different approaches to assess the effect of anti-suicide programs and institutions on local suicide rates. Some have studied the geographical distribution of suicide rates according to whether or not a suicide prevention service was available in the area. Their main problem was to find towns or other geographical regions which were identical twins with respect to all ecological factors that contribute to the incidence of suicide. Others have looked at the variation of the suicide rate in one geographical area before and after a suicide prevention service had been introduced. The principal difficulty here was to exclude chance variations of the suicide rate and changes caused by other uncontrolled influences.

In a study of the first type, Bagley (1968) showed that the suicide rate was lower in British towns with a "Samaritan" branch than in towns without. (The Samaritan movement is a widespread organization of trained laymen who offer help, advice, and friendship to those who are tempted to commit suicide.) Using refined criteria of ecological similarity between towns, Barraclough et al. (1977) failed to confirm Bagley's results. In the United States, two studies were equally unable to demonstrate that the presence of a suicide prevention center was associated with a local reduction of suicides (Lester 1974; Bridge et al. 1977).

The introduction of a community psychiatric service in Southern England was not followed by a drop of the annual suicide rates (Sainsbury et al. 1966), neither was the opening of suicide prevention centers in Los Angeles (Weiner 1969) and in Cleveland (Sawyer et al. 1972). Ringel (1968) speculated that the activity of the suicide prevention center in Vienna (*Lebensmüdenfürsorge*) may have contributed to the significant decrease of suicides in the city between 1953 and 1967. In Edinburgh, the parasuicide rate remained constant over 2 years in one city ward where a Health, Welfare, and Advice Center had been established while parasuicide rates went up in other parts of the city (Kreitman 1977). Data on the frequency of suicides were not reported. The most impressive, though preliminary evidence for the effectiveness of a suicide prevention scheme comes from a Swedish study. After a community psychiatric center had started its work in Stockholm county, the annual suicide rate fell from 19.5 to 14.0 per 100 000 inhabitants (Cullberg 1978). No information is available on the development of the suicide rate in subsequent years.

Clinical Studies

The most important limit to clinical investigations into the effectiveness of suicide prevention programs is of an ethical nature. No patient who is at risk of committing suicide may be left without treatment. Therefore, clinical trials must compare one form of therapy with another. Differences in outcome, however, can only be expected if the two treatment schedules are sufficiently distinct. A second problem concerns the choice of outcome measures. The only convincing evidence for the effectiveness of a suicide prevention program would be a significant reduction of suicides within a certain follow-up period in the patients who were treated according to that program as compared with control cases. Given the low probability of future suicide even in high-risk groups, large patient samples are required to obtain interpretable differences in suicide rates. Researchers have sometimes resorted to other criteria of outcome, such as the frequency of suicidal attempts (or parasuicides) or ratings of psychopathology and social adjustment. Certainly these measures can reflect benefit from treatment. When prevention of suicide is at issue, however, they must be considered secondary.

Chowdhury et al. (1973) compared a special outpatient service for repeated suicide attempters with a routine schedule. The experimental treatment program included regular and frequent appointments and domiciliary visits in cases of nonattendance. Patients were advised to call the Samaritan 24-h emergency telephone service whenever necessary. Control cases were also given outpatient appointments but the initiative of maintaining contact was left with them. After 6 months, no significant difference was observed between the two groups in the proportion of patients with further suicidal attempts. No suicide occurred in either group.

Ettlinger's (1975) study was carried out on a large sample of over 1200 suicide attempters admitted to a general hospital. One-half of the patients were treated according to an experimental program. It consisted of three outpatient appointments within 1 year, home visits in cases of nonattendance, and motivation to make use of any therapy or counseling that was required. The remaining patients made up the control group. Half of them were discharged from the hospital without further treatment, one-third was referred for psychiatric out-patient therapy, and one-third was referred to other resources. A follow-up examination after 5 years showed no differences in the frequency of suicides or repeated suicidal attempts between the experimental and control groups.

Litman and Wold (1976) reported on a program of "Continuing Relationship Maintenance" for callers to an emergency telephone service. With the patients of the experimental group, trained volunteers kept weekly contact over 18 months mainly by telephone, supplemented by meetings at the suicide prevention center or in the subject's home. The volunteers referred the patients to professional treatment or counseling when necessary. Control cases were given appointments at the suicide prevention center for crisis intervention. The initiative of keeping the appointment was in the hands of the patients. After 2 years the suicide and suicide reattempt rates were not significantly different between the groups.

Welu (1977) described an outreach program for suicide attempters provided by nurses and social workers of a community mental health center. The members of this team kept at least biweekly contact with the patients over 4 months. They tried to motivate the patients to make use of any kind of treatment that was necessary. Control cases were given appointments at the community mental health center without exerting any influence on their compliance or were hospitalized. The frequency of repeated suicidal attempts was lower in the special outreach program after 4 months.

Gibbons et al. (1978) compared the routine treatment for suicide attempters admitted to a casualty ward with a special social work service. The experimental patients were referred to a social worker who tried to establish contact immediately and performed task-centered casework up to a maximum of 3 months. Control cases were referred to their general practitioner or to some other resource. The follow-up examination after 1 year revealed no difference in the proportion of patients who repeated self-poisoning.

Motto (1978) evaluated a program of long-term contact for patients who were admitted to a psychiatric hospital because of a depressed or suicidal state and who declined postdischarge treatment or dropped out of a treatment schedule in less than 1 month. The experimental patients were started on a schedule of regular communications from the research staff member who had interviewed them in the hospital by letter or telephone call, expressing concern and inviting response. The schedule included a total of 24 contacts within 5 years. With the controls no contact was established. The suicide rate was lower in the contact group than in the control cases. The difference reached statistical significance in the 3rd year after hospital discharge, but the rates tended to converge afterward.

In the study of Wulliemier et al. (1979) on suicide attempters at a general hospital all patients were proposed regular treatment. The experimental patients were told before discharge that the research team would get in touch with them several times over a period of 2 years if they were not in treatment. The control cases received no such surveillance. After 2 years the frequencies of suicides and of repeated suicidal attempts were lower in the experimental group, but the differences did not reach statistical significance.

Liberman and Eckman (1981) compared two inpatient psychotherapy programs of equal intensity and duration for nonpsychotic, nonaddicted patients who had repeatedly carried out suicidal attempts. Following discharge, aftercare was provided for all patients by a community mental health center or by private therapists. As judged from the rate of repeated suicidal attempts within 2 years, the insight-oriented therapy program was not superior to the behavior therapy scheme.

Comments

There is little evidence that suicide prevention services are effective in terms of reducing the incidence of suicide in the patient or population sample under study. On the other hand, the available data do not prove the failure of antisuicide programs.

Epidemiologic methods may be insensitive to the influence of preventive services. Even if an antisuicide program had an incredibly high success rate, its effect would reach epidemiologic magnitude only when a substantial percentage of persons at risk in the catchment area would be treated according to it. Regarding the large number of alternative treatment resources this seems unrealistic. Yet, for other reasons, epidemiologic investigations are unlikely to resolve the problem of effectiveness. Probably no geographical areas can be found which are identical in all ecological aspects influencing the suicide rate and differ only in the presence or absence of a suicide prevention service. Moreover, the catchment area of such a service is never confined to geographical limits. Finally, a statistical association between the introduction of a suicide prevention scheme and a drop in local frequency of suicides does not suggest a causal relationship unless all other possible influences on the suicide have been ruled out. For example, it is tempting to assume that the decrease of suicides in England and Wales from 1963 to 1970 was brought about by the growth of the Samaritan movement in those years (Fox 1976). In relating these two developments, it would be overlooked that the reduction of the suicide rates was mainly due to the detoxification of domestic gas within the same period of time (Kreitman 1980).

The results of clinical studies also remain inconclusive. In seven of eight investigations reviewed here, cases were defined by the presence of suicide risk. Apart from being difficult to assess, suicide risk is not a diagnosis and no specific treatment corresponds to it. Patient samples which are selected by this criterion must be highly heterogeneous regarding diagnosis, and the appropriate treatment will vary accordingly. In fact, the only description of therapy to be found in the seven studies is that it was adjusted to individual requirements. Under such conditions the focus of evaluation necessarily shifts from treatment proper to more general strategies of patient management, such as improving compliance. Without sufficient control of treatment variables, however, effectiveness of such strategies cannot be determined. Treatment-related variations of outcome are indistinguishable from differences depending on management. A comparable situation would exist in psychopharmacology research if drug effects were examined by manipulating the regularity of medication without knowing what drugs are involved. The only study of a suicide prevention scheme which gives account of therapy has compared two experimental programs and has not included a group of less intensively treated controls.

From the previous experience in the evaluation of suicide prevention services, conclusions may be drawn for future research. As the risk of suicide can arise in many psychiatric disorders and even in the absence of any mental abnormality, suicide prevention schemes must provide a broad range of specific treatments such as medication, psychotherapy and social work. Any suicide prevention program is composed of several steps of action, all of which may contribute to its success or failure. These include diagnosis, assessment of suicide risk, treatment disposal, treatment, strategies of management (e.g., control of compliance), and aftercare schedules (e.g., contact maintenance). Attempts to determine the effectiveness of such complex structures globally without due consideration of their constituents cannot be expected to yield clear results and should therefore be abandoned. It appears more promising if clinical studies were directed to the evaluation of antisuicide treatment programs for particular diagnostic groups. The elements of these programs will have to be exactly defined and documented.

References

Barraclough BM, Jennings C, Moss JR (1977) Suicide prevention by the Samaritans. A controlled study of effectiveness. Lancet ii:237–238

Bridge TP, Potkin SG, Zung WWK, Soldo BJ (1977) Suicide prevention centers – ecological study of effectiveness. J Nerv Ment Dis 164:18–24

Chowdhury N, Hicks RC, Kreitman N (1973) Evaluation of an after-care service of parasuicide (attempted suicide) patients. Soc Psychiatry 8:67–81

Cullberg J (1978) The Nacka project – an experiment in community psychiatry. In: Aalberg V (ed) 9th Int congr on suicide prevention. The Finnish Association for Mental Health, Oy Länsi Savo, pp 76–80

Ettlinger R (1975) Evaluation of suicide prevention after attempted suicide. Acta Psychiatr Scand [Suppl] 260:1–135

Fox R (1976) The recent decline of suicide in Britain: the role of the Samaritan suicide prevention movement. In: Shneidman ES (ed) Suicidology. Contemporary developments. Grune and Stratton, New York, pp 499–524

Gibbons JS, Butler J, Urwin P, Gibbons JL (1978) Evaluation of a social work service for self-poisoning patients. Br J Psychiatry 133:111–118

Kreitman N (ed) (1977) Parasuicide. Wiley, New York

Kreitman N (1980) Die Epidemiologie von Suizid und Parasuizid. Nervenarzt 51:131–138

Kurz A, Möller HJ (1982a) Ergebnisse der epidemiologischen Evaluation von suizid-prophylaktischen Versorgungsprogrammen. Psychiatr Prax 9:12–19

Kurz A, Möller HJ (1982b) Ergebnisse der klinisch-experimentellen Evaluation von suizid-prophylaktischen Versorgungsprogrammen. Arch Psychiatr Nervenkr 232:97–118

Lester D (1974) Effect of suicide prevention centers on suicide rates in the United States. Public Health Rep 89:37–39

Liberman RP, Eckman T (1981) Behavior therapy vs. insight-oriented therapy for repeated suicide attempters. Arch Gen Psychiatry 38:1126–1130

Litman RE, Wold CI (1976) Beyond crisis intervention. In: Shneidman ES (ed) Suicidology. Contemporary developments. Grune and Stratton, New York, pp 528–546

Motto JA (1978) Suicidal persons who decline treatment: a long-term program. In: Aalberg V (ed) 9th Int congr for suicide prevention. The Finnish Association for Mental Health, Oy Länsi Savo, pp 285−290

Ringel E (1968) Suicide prevention in Vienna. In: Resnik HLP (ed) Suicidal behavior. Diagnosis and management. Little and Brown, Boston, pp 381−390

Sainsbury P, Walk D, Grad J (1966) Evaluating the Graylingwell Hospital community psychiatric service in Chichester: suicide and community care. Milbank Memorial Fund Quarterly 44/II:243−245

Sawyer JB, Sudak HS, Hall SR (1972) A follow-up study of 53 suicides known to a suicide prevention center. Life Threat Behav 2:227−238

Weiner IW (1969) The effectiveness of a suicide prevention program. Ment Hygiene 53:357−363

Welu TC (1977) A follow-up program for suicide attempters: evaluation of effectiveness. Suicide Life Threat Behav 7:17−30

Wulliemier F, Bovet J, Maylan D (1979) Le devenir des suicidants admis à l'hôpital général. Etude comparative de deux formes de prévention des récidives et des suicides. Soz Präventivmed 24:73−88

On the Effect of Crisis Intervention in Suicidal Patients

K. Böhme, M. Gast, C. Kulessa, and E. Rau

Introduction

In the literature about the clinical treatment of patients who have been admitted into a hospital after a suicide attempt there is agreement concerning the necessity of a "tertiary" prophylaxis for suicides. The suicide attempt stands undoubtedly as one of the determining – possibly the most determining – risk factors for further suicidality. The efficiency, however, of tertiary prophylactic concepts in the aftercare and of aftercare institutions are differently judged, contrary to this almost trivial statement.

Several authors (Kennedy 1972; Greer and Blagley 1973; Sainsbury 1975; Wullemier et al. 1977; Sonneck 1982) demonstrated or based their writings on the fact that pointed prophylactic measures apparently curtail the suicide risk. Others, such as Ettlinger (1975) and Kurz et al. (1984) did not see any influence of treatment concepts on recidivism.

On the whole, in the area of suicide prevention, we have to differentiate today between the actually proven usefulness of a crisis intervention after a suicide attempt and the hypothesis about its efficiency. This statement does not mean that therapists after long years of intensive endeavours should relinquish their programs. It rather means that they need to critically observe their work and that attempts to better their techniques and to scientifically objectify results should continue. We would like to present the results of such an objectifying study and discuss them.

Study

The concept of a psychiatrically attended crisis intervention program for patients who went through detoxification in an intensive care unit (ICU) after a suicide attempt was first tried out in 1965 at the University of Heidelberg. From the beginning, there was very close cooperation between psychiatrists on the one hand and priests and social workers on the other. At that time it was difficult, though to stimulate interest in clinical institutions for the subject of suicide prevention and to generate willingness to finance such a program.

In 1974 it was possible to create within the ICU of the Medical University Clinic an integrated crisis intervention team. Included was one psychiatrist, one psychologist or a second psychiatrist, a psychiatric social worker, and two priests.

The structure and concept of this crisis intervention team was described in detail elsewhere (Böhme et al. 1978). Therefore, the description here will be brief: During the awakening phase, the first contact was made with one of the team members. This particular member stayed the main contact person for the patient during inpatient treatment, which usually lasted 2–5 days. Other team members, however, could also be included into treatment when special problems arose (church related, social work, psychiatric differential diagnosis). In the three to five meetings of 45–60 min duration, the presuicidal conflict situation was diagnosed, and together with the patient and his or her significant others, if possible, a strategic plan for the following procedure was made. This concerned either individual or family therapy or help in social, legal, or spiritual matters. For continued inpatient psychiatric treatment, which is more often necessary in the case of patients with a major psychotic disorder, two beds were available in the psychiatric clinic nearby.

In critical cases the crisis intervention team offered several meetings even after discharge. When the psychotherapeutic treatment was delegated to a therapist not belonging to the team, feedback about this treatment was given. In this way there was less risk of discontinuation and compliance was better.

In 1976 the team had stabilized, was familiar with the concept, and also had the necessary acceptance of the internists on the ward, which seemed at that stage of crucial importance. In 1979, the time span from 1 July 1976 to 30 June 1977 was regarded as a stable and representative phase to test the efficiency of the work of this crisis intervention team.

Aside from other aspects, this study was to test whether the above briefly described interventions and the ensuing therapy would effect a lowering of the recidivism rate of suicide attempts and suicides.

Results

During the reference period, a total of 650 patients with suicidal intoxication were admitted to the ICU of the Medical Clinic of the University of Heidelberg. Four patients died following intoxication; 596 patients (92%) were seen and treated by team members. Fifty patients left the clinic too fast, especially on weekends, so that contact with team members could not be established. Often with these patients, alcohol played a role as the contributing means of intoxication. Patients admitted with alcohol intoxication but no suicidal ideation were not included in this study.

Only 486 of the 596 patients who lived in or nearby Heidelberg could be personally interviewed. Among these 486 patients, 63 were depressives and schizophrenics who were excluded because of the difference to be expected in the postsuicidal phase, especially regarding the dynamics inherent in a psychosis. The study comprised 423 patients.

A survey questionnaire of 109 questions was developed to serve as the foundation for a semistructured interview. Details about the structure of this questionnaire can be found in the dissertations of Gast and Rau (1985). Table 1 shows an overview of the clusters of questions.

Table 1.   Overview of the content structure of the questionnaire

Personal data: sex, age, family status, marital relationship, education
(questions 8, 12, 16−22)

History of suicide attempts and therapies
(questions 23−28)

Index suicide attempt
(questions 10, 14, 29−31)

Crisis intervention of the suicide team
(questions 32−34)

Professional or occupational changes during the catamnesis
(questions 35−42)

Changes in living conditions during the catamnesis
(questions 43−45)

Changes in relationship to important others during the catamnesis
(questions 9, 46−48)

Aftercare and therapies during the catamnesis
(questions 40, 70)

Suicidal tendencies and relapses during the catamnesis
(questions 71−79, 87−99)

Problems of drug dependencies during the catamnesis
(questions 104−106)

Openness to therapy, suicidality, and prognosis estimated by the investigator
(questions 107−109)

In collaboration with the Institute for Medical Documentation, Statistics, and Data Processing of the University of Heidelberg a representative sample of 100 patients was drawn from the total sample of 423 patients. After the study began, though, difficulties arose with regard to the time span of 3 years for the catamnesis. More than 50% of those patients no longer lived at their old address, and it sometimes took several months to locate them. Many contacts had to be made by letter, phone, or personally if a meeting could take place. Several patents declined, others had moved away from Heidelberg, some died.

For these reasons, upon the advice of the statistical consultant, the representative sample had to be augmented to 160 about 1 year after the study began. In the end, 94 of the 160 patients of the reference sample (59%) were investigated. Table 2 gives an overview of what happened to the reference sample, showing clearly the great difficulties encountered in empirical suicide research. These difficulties already occurred on a methodically simple level despite having the facilities of a University Clinic at hand.

The duration of the catamnesis varied between 30 and 61 months; the mean was 3.5 years. Since we know from other investigations (Böhme et al. 1982) that the recidivism rate is highest in the first 2 years after the index suicide attempt (i.e., the suicide attempt for which the patient came to our attention), we do not consider the unintended prolongation of the catamnesis duration to be an essentially influencing factor regarding the interpretation of the results.

We have to point out, however, one special aspect of such a patient population. It is not only the index suicide attempt that turns this population into a

Table 2. General population sample at the end of the investigation

Patients	abs	%
Interviewed	94	58.8
Declined	29	18.1
Moved away	18	11.3
Unknown	10	6.3
Died	9	5.6
	160	100.1

Table 3. Amount of suicide attempts (recidivism) during catamnesis

Number of suicidal gestures during catamnesis	abs	%
None	66	70
1	18	19
2	2	2
3	4	4
Unclear	4	4
Total	94	99

risk group as was pointed out in many follow-up studies and cohort studies. Rather, a fraction of a little less than one-third (28%) of the patients investigated had already tried to commit suicide at an earlier date.

The index suicide attempt, then, cannot generally be seen as the clinically definable onset of a suicidal decompensation of individual problem-solving strategies. It becomes for many patients an indicator of a progressive disintegration process when other negative factors − in our population especially a drug dependency − are added.

Looking at the results, we have to report that nine patients died during the time span of the catamnesis. Four of those were suicides; two died of natural causes; for three patients the cause of death could not be determined despite the most intensive investigations. The average age of the suicides (three women, one man) was significantly higher (54) than that of the whole sample (31). The suicides happened 4 and 10 weeks and 2.4 and 2.7 years after the index suicide attempts.

Of the 94 patients investigated 28 (30%) tried once or several times to commit suicide during the time of the catamnesis. Table 3 shows the exact data. Figure 1 shows in a histogram the spread over time of the recidivism. It is easy

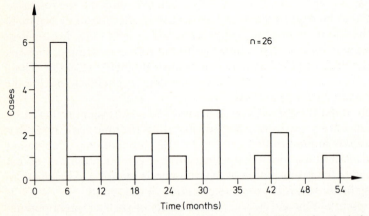

Fig. 1. Histogram of the time lapses for the cases of recidivism after the index suicide attempt

Table 4. Recidivism rate with respect to aftercare

Kind of aftercare	Recidivism rate (%)
Ambulatory	19
Inpatient	60
No aftercare	29

Table 5. Overview of the kind of aftercare and its relationship to the recidivism rate

Kind of aftercare	Suicidal relapses					
	Yes		No		Total	
	abs	%	abs	%	abs	%
Ambulatory	6	22	26	39	32	34
Inpatient	6	22	4	6	10	11
No aftercare	15	56	36	55	51	55
Sum total	27	100	66	100	93	100
No account	1				1	

Table 6. Relationship of recidivism rate and drug dependency

Dependency	Suicidal relapses					
	Yes		No		Total	
	abs	%	abs	%	abs	%
Degree of dependency (light/heavy/unclear)	11	39	6	9	17	18
Questionable dependency	5	18	1	2	6	6
No dependency	12	43	59	89	71	76
Sum total	28	100	66	100	94	100

to detect how dangerous in this populations, too, the 1st year after the suicide attempt was. During this time 13 of the 28 cases of recidivism occurred.

It is remarkable in this context that the recidivism rate in our patient population without a suicide attempt — prior to the index suicide attempt — was significantly higher than for patients with a suicide attempt in their medical history. It is our conviction that this constitutes an indicator for the process character in the suicidal development of part of our patients.

With the first interpretation of these results, we have to clarify that with a recidivism rate of 30% during the time of the catamnesis we certainly cannot refer to the total result in speaking about efficacy regarding the clinical work of our crisis intervention team. Of course, we were not satisfied with this result, and we tried to find out what happened to the efforts of our work and whether

Table 7. Overview of ten inpatients

Number	Facility of care	Diagnosis at time of index suicide attempt	Treatment voluntary	Treatment duration (weeks)	Termination	Therapy success
1	Psychiatric University Clinic	Alcohol abuse	Yes	5	Agreement on both sides	Yes
2	Psychiatric University Clinic	Drug dependency	Yes	3	Agreement on both sides	No
3	Psychiatric University Clinic	Polytoxicomania	No	12	By therapist	No
4	Psychiatric University Clinic	Adjustment reaction	No account	1	No account	No account
5	Psychiatric State Hospital	Alcohol abuse	Yes	3	By patient	No
6	Psychiatric State Hospital	Drug dependency	Yes	1	Agreement on both sides	Yes
7	Psychiatric State Hospital	Drug dependency	No	3	Agreement on both sides	No account
8	Ward for Children/Youth	Adjustment reaction	Yes	4	Agreement on both sides	Yes
9	"Zentralinstitut für seelische Gesundheit"	Other organic psychotic condition	Yes	40	Agreement on both sides	No account
10	Aftercare Clinic	Unclear	Yes	4	Agreement on both sides	No account

Table 8. Diagnoses for all 94 patients investigated

Psychiatric diagnosis	Suicidal relapses		
	Yes abs	%	No abs
Adjustment reaction	7	25	31
Neurotic development	3	11	11
Narcissistic disorder	4	14	6
Drug dependency	10	36	6
Organic psychotic conditions	2	7	2
Other diagnosis or diagnosis unclear	2	7	7
Sum total	28	100	63
No account			3

all the endeavors were in vain. Methodologically we had to be cautious because no one is more inclined to misinterpret false-positives in his favor than the person who wants to promote the usefulness of his concept.

In a first very simple step, we divided the patients into three subgroups according to the kind of aftercare they received. We differentiated between those who were taken care of by a team member or a therapist they were delegated to after the crisis intervention. A second subgroup comprised those who went directly into inpatient treatment during crisis intervention. And finally, all those who received no aftercare for whatever reason following the crisis intervention constituted the third subgroup.

Table 4 shows that the rate of recidivism differed a great deal for these subgroups. Table 5 differentiates recidivism in absolute terms and percentage wise for these three subgroups.

If one continues to ask in what ways patients with and without suicide relapses differ, the factor of drug and alcohol dependency takes on great importance. Table 6 poignantly shows that the recidivism rate was significantly higher for patients with a dependency problem (and here mostly with alcohol) in contrast to patients without relapses.

The high amount of patients with dependencies in the subgroups of patients with suicide relapses led us to investigate the question of whether (see Table 4) dependency could be used as a discriminating factor in the above-mentioned subgroups. Therefore, we listed separately the ten patients for whom continued inpatient treatment had been advised.

If we only look at the nine adults who received inpatient treatment right after the crisis intervention, we find that six of them, i.e., two-thirds, suffered from dependency. None of the other subgroups had such a percentage needing inpatient treatment (6 of 16!). Table 8 again points out clearly that the group of dependent patients ranked absolutely highest in recidivism (36% of all suicide attempts).

Discussion

In the light of these findings, we can expect a very negative effect regarding the success of a crisis intervention in cases of suicidality and dependency (together) just looking at their recidivism rate. For the methodological approach, on the other hand, this statement means that for measurements on efficiency not only psychotic patients, as we did beforehand, but also drug-dependent patients have to be excluded or considered separately in a subgroup.

We now have an explanation for the high recidivism rate for those receiving inpatient treatment after the crisis intervention. This sheds no light, however, on the reasons accounting for the lower recidivism rate for patients with aftercare. One could say, perhaps, that the offer of therapy was accepted more easily by less disturbed patients for whatever reasons and that in this way a selection for less risk occurred. On the other hand, Selkin and Morris (1971) pointed out that patients who declined aftercare were less depressed and burdened and had a more favorable outcome than the treatment group.

To investigate this question further, we had to leave the statistical analysis for a while to turn to the basic therapeutic situation in 1976/1977 when patients of this sample were treated by the crisis intervention team. Daily team conferences where all patients were thoroughly discussed were part of the clinical routine in the crisis intervention setting. Also, twice a week there was group supervision where problem patients were presented. In this fashion, it was possible to recognize early severely disturbed patients and patients with the most acute problem constellation and to offer an aftercare program. Already at that time, we had the conviction that chances for a successful crisis intervention were all the greater the more we were able to establish a personal relationship over the entire treatment time with one therapist. On account of this concept, we can now be sure, for the interpretation of the results, that the outpatients did not comprise a subgroup of patients with less disturbance and, only for this reason, had a better prognosis.

A methodically and therapeutically problematic subgroup consisted of those 24 patients who, despite advice from the team, did not receive aftercare. This part of the population had not been separately considered statistically so that we are not able to state whether there were differences compared with the subgroup of those patients who did receive aftercare.

In conclusion, we can say that the subgroup of those patients who underwent aftercare following the index suicide attempt in comparison with the subgroup of inpatients and in comparison with the subgroup with no aftercare showed a clearly lower recidivsm rate. Since there are no indications that the subgroup with ambulatory aftercare consisted of patients who, for other reasons, had a better prognosis, we are convinced that the lowering of the recidivism rate was a consequence of the aftercare through the crisis intervention team and other outside therapists. It became clear that this kind of therapeutic concept in efficiency research constitutes a methodological problem, i.e., previously defined subgroups need to be considered separately. After we had already excluded psychotic patients, there were patients, especially those with drug and alcohol dependencies, who without differentiation would have led to distinct distortion of the overall results of our research. Psychoses as well as dependencies have their own dynamics, when considering the process of the disease, which would not be influenced decidedly by a crisis intervention and the therapeutic measures of longer duration that normally follow.

Acknowledgement. We thank Professor Dr. H. Immich, former Director of the Institute for Medical Documentation, Statistics, and Data Processing at the University of Heidelberg, for his friendly support.

References

Böhme K, Kulessa C, Reiner A (1978) Suizidenten-Nachbetreuung. Psychosoziale Krisenintervention auf der Intensivstation der Medizinischen Universitätsklinik Heidelberg. Dtsch Ärzteblatt 75:3045 – 3047

Böhme K, Schönfeld H, v Weltzien J (1982) Suicide studies. Life expectancy and causes of death after suicide attempts. Psychiatr Fenn (International Edition) 127 – 141

Ettlinger R (1975) Evaluation of suicide prevention after attempted suicide. Acta Psychiatr Scand [Suppl] 260

Gast M, Rau E (1985) Evaluation einer stationären Krisenintervention am Beispiel des Suicidentendienstes an der Medizinischen und Psychiatrischen Universitätsklinik Heidelberg. Dissertation, Dept of Clinical Medicine II, Ruprecht-Karls-Universität, Heidelberg

Greer S, Blagley C (1973) Effect of psychiatric intervention in attempted suicide: a controlled study. Br Med J 1:310 – 312

Kennedy P (1972) Efficacy of a regional poisoning treatment centre in preventing further suicidal behaviour. Br Med J 4:255 – 257

Kurz A, Möller HJ, Bürk F, Torhorst A, Wächtler C, Lauter H (1984) Ein Versuch zur Verbesserung der psychiatrischen Versorgung von Suizidpatienten am Allgemeinkrankenhaus. In: Welz R, Möller HJ (eds) Bestandsaufnahme der Suizidforschung. Epidemiologie, Prävention und Therapie. Roderer, Regensburg, pp 128 – 141

Sainsbury P (1975) Suicide and attempted suicide. In: Kisker KP, Meyer JE, Müller C, Strömgren E (eds) Psychiatrie der Gegenwart. Forschung und Praxis, vol III, 2nd edn. Springer, Berlin Heidelberg New York, pp 557 – 606

Selkin J, Morris J (1971) Some behavioral factors which influence the recovery rate of suicide attempts. Bull Suicidol 8:29 – 38

Sonneck G (1982) Betreuungsmodelle für Suizidgefährdete. In: Reimer C (ed) Suizid – Ergebnisse und Therapie. Springer, Berlin Heidelberg New York, pp 103 – 116

Wullemier F, Kremer P, Carron R (1977) Vergleichende Studie über zwei Interventionsarten bei Suizidanten, die im allgemeinen Krankenhaus aufgenommen worden sind. Suizidprophylaxe 4:248 – 250

Evaluation of Two Different Strategies of an Outpatient Aftercare Program for Suicide Attempters in a General Hospital*

A. KURZ, H.-J. MÖLLER, F. BÜRK, A. TORHORST, C. WÄCHTLER, and H. LAUTER

Introduction

At the Klinikum rechts der Isar in Munich, approximately 500 patients per year are admitted to the poisoning treatment unit after suicidal attempts. Medical care is supplemented by psychiatric examination in each case. The majority of patients are referred for psychiatric hospital treatment or for some outpatient therapy or counseling. The determinants of treatment disposal have been discussed elsewhere (Kurz et al. 1985). From 1981 to 1982, we carried out an investigation which was aimed at the improvement of suicide prevention in this setting. From several studies, it is known that suicide attempters are reluctant to make use of counseling and therapy (Paykel et al. 1974; Morgan et al. 1976; Hankoff 1979). The poor compliance may be an important limitation to the efficacy of suicide prevention programs. The first hypothesis of our study was that the patients' compliance would be improved by providing a continuous therapeutic relationship in the transition from hospital treatment to outpatient care. The second hypothesis was that an improvement of compliance would result in a reduced frequency of further suicidal behavior.

Method

The study was concerned with 458 patients who fulfilled the criteria of parasuicide (Kreitman and Philip 1969). They were typical of suicide attempters in Western European cities. Patients who required psychiatric hospital treatment and patients who did not need any further therapy were excluded from the study. The remaining 226 patients were allocated to three different treatment programs. Group A, consisting of 85 patients, received the standard treatment. It included initial crisis intervention and subsequent referral for counseling or treatment outside the hospital.

Group A was recruited from January to April, 1981. Group B, including 73 patients, received the standard treatment plus 15 min of verbal motivation before discharge. Noncompliant patients were recontacted by phone or letter. Group C, consisting of 68 subjects, were offered outpatient treatment by the research psychiatrists who had examined them initially. Treatment was limited to 12 sessions within 3 months. Stimulation of compliance was the same as in

* Supported by the FRG Ministry for Youth, Family, and Health.

group B. The allocation of cases between groups B and C was randomized. It is important to note that the three treatment programs had in common the initial psychiatric examination and crisis intervention. The latter normally included an informant interview. Twelve months after hospital admission, a personal follow-up examination was carried out. Information on suicides was obtained from an informant or from local administrative authorities.

Results

Regarding all data collected at the initial psychiatric examination, there were no major differences between the groups. In particular, the randomized allocation of cases between groups B and C was unbiased. Figure 1 shows that the number of patients who kept their first outpatient appointment was lowest in group A, intermediate in group B, and highest in group C. The difference between groups B and C was significant. Apparently, the supplementary motivational efforts had only a minimal effect on the patients' compliance. When, however, continuity of care was provided in the transition from hospital to outpatient treatment, the patients' compliance increased considerably. Figure 1 also demonstrates that the patients in group C remained in therapy longer than did the patients in the other groups. The improvement of initial compliance was not annihilated by early termination. It should be mentioned that the continuation of therapy was not determined by the patients' compliance alone but

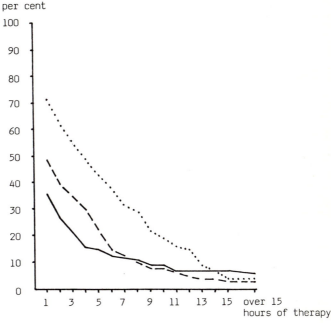

Fig. 1. Patients remaining in therapy. *Solid line,* group A; *dashed line* group B; *dotted line,* group C

also by the therapists' opinion on the necessity of further treatment. The standards of this judgment may well have been different between the treatment programs.

Information on suicides and repeated suicide attempts was obtained on 218 of the 226 patients: 6 patients had committed suicide within 12 months, which corresponds to a suicide rate of 2.8%, and 24 patients (11%) had repeated a suicide attempt at least once. Table 1 shows that the suicide rate did not differ greatly between the groups. The absolute figures are very small and cannot be interpreted statistically. The frequency of repeated suicide attempts, however, was clearly lower in group B than in the remaining groups. Taking suicides and attempted suicides together, the difference between groups B and C was significant. The special outpatient treatment program which was offered to group C attracted more patients than the other programs and kept them in treatment for a longer period of time but was not superior to the standard procedure and even inferior to the treatment program of group B in preventing further suicidal behavior.

If differences of outcome were brought about by the aftercare treatment and not by other factors, they should be more pronounced in treated than in untreated patients. In groups A and C, suicides occurred exclusively among treated patients, in group B only in untreated cases (Table 2). Regarding the small numbers, this finding should not be overestimated. The frequency of repeated suicide attempts was practically identical for treated and untreated patients in all three groups. Thus, there is some doubt as to whether the difference in outcome between the groups was brought about by a different efficacy of the aftercare programs. It is of course a puzzle why even the untreated patients of group B had a better outcome than the treated or untreated patients of the

Table 1. Outcome after 12 months

	Group A (n = 82)	Group B (n = 70)	Group C (n = 66)
Suicide	1 1%	2 3%	3 5%
Suicide attempt (not if preceding suicide)	11 13%	3 4%	9 14%
No further suicidal behavior	70 85%	65 93%	54 82%

Table 2. Outcome after 12 months in treated and untreated patients

	Group A		Group B		Group C	
	Treated (n = 31)	Untreated (n = 51)	Treated (n = 36)	Untreated (n = 37)	Treated (n = 49)	Untreated (n = 19)
Suicide	1 3%	–	–	2 5%	3 6%	–
Suicide attempt (not if preceding suicide)	5 16%	6 12%	2 6%	1 3%	6 12%	3 16%

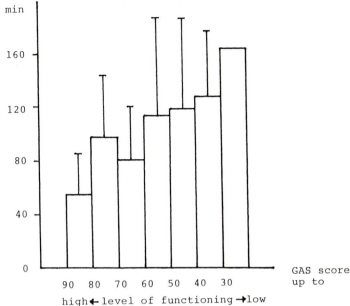

Fig. 2. Total time of psychiatric intervention related to global assessment score (GAS)

other groups. A possible yet unprobable reason is that the untreated patients of group B were positively selected when compared with the untreated patients of the other groups. Testing this hypothesis, we found no such selection.

How can it be explained that the outcome was the same for treated and untreated patients within each group? The first explanation is that all treatment programs were ineffective. Although we must assume that not all patients benefited from treatment, this hypothesis seems unlikely. The second explanation is a spontaneous selection of patients. The patients who came for therapy may have been negatively selected so that the effect of treatment was only compensatory. When looking at a large number of patient variables which are generally felt to be relevant for future suicidal behavior, we found some evidence for a negative selection of treated patients. Several suicide risk factors were clearly overrepresented in the treated cases, such as male sex, old age, previous suicidal behavior, and previous psychiatric treatment. The third explanation is that patients at high suicide risk had been excluded from the study. As a consequence, the probability of further suicidal behavior was low in all groups and the effect of the treatment may not have shown. The fourth explanation is that the outpatient treatment was not the only therapeutic factor. All patients received initial crisis intervention while in the hospital. Three interview sessions were provided for each patient on the average. This is about the same amount of treatment as the patients received in the subsequent outpatient care. In many cases the initial treatment may have been sufficient to resolve the crisis so that the aftercare program had no additional effect. This hypothesis can neither be confirmed nor rejected by the available data. It would be supported, however, if an association could be shown between the initial treatment efforts and the patients' degree of psychopathological and social disturbance. The total time of initial psychiatric intervention was positively related to the patients' disturbance as rated on the Globald Assessment Scale (GAS) (Fig. 2). Positive correlations were also seen between the amount of initial therapeutic efforts and social maladjustment, severity of psychopathological symptoms, severity of intoxication, and estimates of suicide risk. The amount of initial psychiatric care was somewhat lower in group C than in the other groups.

Discussion

The first hypothesis of the study was clearly confirmed. When the patients were offered outpatient aftercare by the research psychiatrist they were already acquainted with, instead of being referred to anonymous therapists, compliance increased significantly. The second hypothesis, however, had to be rejected. The improvement of the patients' compliance was not accompanied by a reduced frequency of suicidal behavior within a period of 1 year.

The interpretation of our data is impeded by methodological problems. The three treatment programs were distinguished not only by compliance rates, but also by the therapy variables. As a consequence, compliance-related effects cannot be separated from treatment-related effects. For various reasons, the outpatient treatment that was offered to group C may have been less effective than the treatment that was provided for the other groups. The effects of compliance would have been more clearly demonstrable if the treatment variables had been kept constant.

It is difficult to explain that the frequency of further suicidal behavior was no different between treated and untreated patients within each treatment group. A spontaneous negative selection of treated patients or a ceiling effect may have been involved.

The results of the study raise the question of whether time-limited psychotherapy, which was the type of treatment for group C and most probably for many patients in the other groups, has a prophylactic effect. Particularly in those cases where suicidal behavior is the result of a long-standing disturbance of personality and life-style, other forms of treatment may be more appropriate. We have adressed this issue in a subsequent study where we compared the efficacy of time-limited psychotherapy and long-term contact in a sample of parasuicide repeaters.

References

Hankoff LD (1979) Situational categories. In: Hankoff LD, Einsidler B (eds) Suicide – theory and clinical aspects. PSG, Littleton, pp 235 – 249
Kreitman N, Philip AE (1969) Parasuicide. Br J Psychiatry 115:746 – 747
Kurz A, Möller HJ, Bürk F, Torhorst A, Wächtler C, Lauter H (1985) Determinants of treatment disposal for parasuicidal patients in a German university hospital. Soc Psychiatry 20:145 – 151
Morgan HG, Barton J, Pottle S, Pocock H, Burns-Cox CJ (1976) Deliberate self-harm: a follow-up study of 279 patients. Br J Psychiatry 128:361 – 368
Paykel ES, Hallowell C, Dressler DM, Shapiro DL, Weissman MM (1974) Treatment of suicide attempters. A descriptive study. Arch Gen Psychiatry 31:487 – 491

Comparing a 3-Month and a 12-Month-Outpatient Aftercare Program for Parasuicide Repeaters *

A. TORHORST, H.-J. MÖLLER, A. KURZ, W. SCHMID-BODE, and H. LAUTER

Introduction

Previous efforts to demonstrate the effectiveness of outpatient treatment of patients after a suicide attempt have not led to convincing results (Gibbons et al. 1978; Wulliemier et al. 1979; overview in Kurz and Möller 1982). The present study deals (specifically) with that group of patients known to possess the highest risk of repeating a suicide attempt, namely, those patients who are suicide attempt repeaters. The basic hypothesis maintains that parasuicide repeaters are individuals suffering less from an episodic than from a more continuous psychosocial disturbance. From this, it seems logical to assume that especially for this clientele a long-term therapy would be more successful than a short-term, crisis-oriented therapy. In the present study, the effect of a short-term, crisis-oriented outpatient treatment program with research staff comprised of 12 weekly sessions extending over a maximum of 3 months is compared with a treatment program having a single 1-h session per month but extending over 12 months.

Methods

From a total of 422 patients (Table 1) who in 1984 had attempted suicide by intoxication, 203 were chosen who fulfilled the criteria of repeated parasuicide. Of these patients, 123 were excluded from the study for various reasons: endogenous psychosis, continuing psychotherapeutic treatment elsewhere, inpatient psychiatric therapy of a nonpsychotic condition, drug overdose, lack of understanding, too long a travel time to the outpatient center.

All patients were treated in the form of crisis intervention during hospitalization; they stayed in the hospital about 3 days. The remaining 80 parasuicide repeaters were randomly assigned to the group of either 3 months or 12 months of outpatient treatment.

Patients were described by a large number of standardized scales measuring psychopathology, especially depression and social adjustment, as well as sociodemographic variables.

---

* Supported by a grant from the FRG Ministry for Research and Technology.

Table 1.   Outpatient treatment for parasuicide repeaters

Project design		(n)	(%)
Total sample: Patients after parasuicide		422	100
Including: First parasuidice		219	52
Repeated parasuicide		203	48
Excluded from study (of 203 repeaters)		203	100
Psychosis	31		15
In current psychotherapy	30		15
No psychosis, hospitalized in psychiatry	33		16
Overdose in drug dependence	7		3
Not speaking German	5		2
Living outside the "S-Bahn" of Munich	17		8
Total excluded		123	29
Parasuicide repeaters in study		80	39
Randomization for outpatient treatment for 12 sessions within			
3 months (weekly sessions)		40	
12 months (monthly sessions)		40	

The investigation was carried out by three psychiatric attendants working in the liaison service on the toxicology ward of the Psychiatric Clinic of the Technical University in Munich. Patients were followed up personally 3 months and 12 months after the index parasuicide.

At 3 months 50% − 67% were followed up, at 12 months we could obtain information for 97.5%; complete self- and experts' ratings data from personal follow-up were available for 85%.

Results

Prerequisite for the determination of the effect of a treatment is that the groups to be compared be as similar as possible with regard to chosen comprehensive parameters. The two collectives of this study differed significantly from each other in but few sociodemographic, psychopathological, or other characteristics. A further prerequisite for judging the effect of a treatment is that the patient accepts the form of help being offered.

Although the attendance at the first session was about equal for both groups (about 60%), the participation of the 12-month group dropped drastically by the second session to under 40%, while the participation of the patients in the 3-month program remained higher. The average number of sessions was 3.9 for the 3-month group and 2.6 for the 12-month group.

This means that an essential prerequisite for the comparison of the two groups was not fulfilled since the treatment was not made use of equally by both collectives. The further interpretation of this study is thus restricted to a comparison of two groups of parasuicide repeaters who were offered differing forms of treatment.

How did the two groups progress in the year following the index parasuicide? The repeat rate for suicide attempts was identical for both groups (22.5%). One could conclude from this that there was no difference between the patients in the 3-month and 12-month programs.

If one considers along with this single criterion other characteristics (registered for all patients) of the course of therapy, the following results are obtained: the globally evaluated psychosocial situation of the individuals in both groups hardly changed in the period between the index parasuicide and the 1-year follow-up; there was no change at all for addictive behavior. Standardized evaluations psychopathology (Inpatient Multidimensional Psychiatric Scale, IMPS), self-evaluated depressivity (D-S), and complaint scores (B-L) (v. Zerssen and Koeller 1976) improved considerably more for the patients of the 3-month program than for those of the 12-month program (Fig. 1). Other criteria, such as duration of unemployment, inability to work, or job and partner conflicts, did *not* demonstrate unambiguous change. Using the Life-Events Scale, it could be shown that for both groups severe partner strife occurred *less* frequently and that a new employment commenced *more* frequently, but also that the patients in both groups were more frequently unemployed for more than 1 month following the index parasuicide. Social support hardly changed, although there was a slight downward tendency in the 12-month group. Social adjustment in the areas of employment and leisure activity remained unchanged in both groups. Patients in the 3-month group evaluated themselves according to the social adjustment scale (SAS) significantly more positively in the areas of employment and leisure activity, close family, and feelings for relatives than did the patients of the 12-month group. Taken together, these results indicate that regarding some parameters the patients of the 3-month program showed more improvement than the patients in the 12-month program.

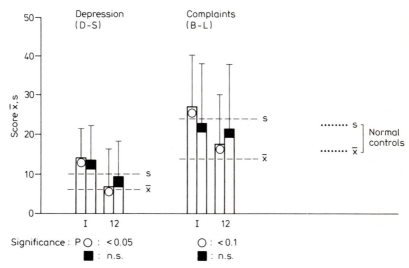

Fig. 1. Change of patients between index-parasuicide (I) and 1-year follow-up (12). *circles* 3-month program, $n = 37$; *squares* 12-month program, $n = 36$

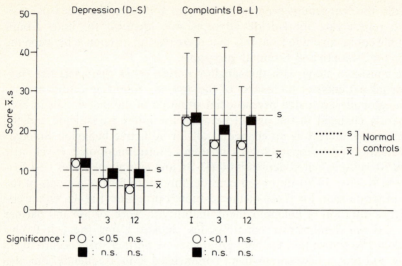

Fig. 2. Change of patients between index-parasuicide (I), 3-month (3), and 12- month (12) follow-up. *circles* 3-month program, $n = 24$; *squares* 12-month program, $n = 18$

A three-point evaluation is possible for part of the patients: in addition to the 12-month follow-up, a 3-month follow-up was carried out with half of the same patients so that the result implied earlier came out more clearly (Fig. 2). There were significant improvements for the patients of the 3-month program, but *not* for those of the 12-month group. These changes took place between the index parasuicide and the 3-month follow-up and appeared to hold steady over the next 9 months until the 12-month follow-up occurred.

How are these changes related to the treatment offered? The global evaluations by the physician and patient both revealed a greater improvement in those patients of the 3-month program who took advantage of the therapy offer in comparison with those who did not participate. A similar effect for the patients in the 12-month program was not observed. Furthermore, there were two quantitative criteria for the characterization of the treatment offered: (1) the number of sessions attended and (2) the number of months in which the patient remained in therapy.

With respect to the parasuicide repeater rate, there is an obvious relationship (Fig. 3): two-thirds of the repetitions occurred with patients who had not attended therapy at all, while for the remaining one-third there appeared to be no evident relationship to outpatient treatment attendance. There was, however, one restriction: after 3 months of treatment, there were only two new suicide attempts. The reattempt rate, depending on compliance, was: no compliance 35% − 45%, one to three sessions 0% − 8%, four to twelve sessions 18%.

Next, one would suppose that in the 3-month group there would be a positive relationship between the extent of therapy as measured by the number of sessions attended and the improvement of the patient as measured by self- and experts' rating scales for psychopathology.

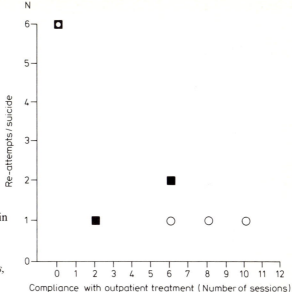

Fig. 3. Re-attempts/suicides within 1 year after index-parasuicide, depending on compliance with outpatient treatment. *circles,* 3-month program, $n = 40$, *squares,* 12-month program, $n = 40$

For patients who came to none or one session there was no significant improvement. The case, here, was different for those patients who had attended two or three to six sessions: for these latter, a lasting positive effect could be registered, which was significantly different from that in the 12-month group. For those attending more than six therapy sessions, no consistent tendency could be determined since the small number of cases did not allow the drawing of meaningful conclusions.

Thus, one might very cautiously conclude that a positive relationship existed between the number of sessions attended when the rate of attendance was one session per week *and* a positive change. Such a relationship was not demonstrated when the rate attendance was one session per month.

Table 2. Compliance (%) and outcome 1 year after index parasuicide (reattempts/suicides, %) depending on therapists

Therapists	Outpatient program	
	3 months	12 months
	Compliance 1 − 12 sessions (%)	
1	70	67
2	78	42
3	61	67
	Reattempts/suicides (%)	
1	15	17
2	22	45
3	29	14

Are there further indicators for the effectiveness of postparasuicidal therapy? It was shown in an earlier study (Torhorst et al. 1984) that the participation in treatment is dependent upon characteristics of the therapist. In the present study, there were also distinctive differences in the participation rate of the patients for different therapists (Table 2). The percentage of participation in the 12-month group varied between 67% and 42%. In agreement with the expectation that participation in a therapy program contributes to the prevention of reattempts, we found that for the one therapist whose patient participation rate was only 42%, the parasuicide repeater rate was 45%.

Conclusion

The following points serve to summarize the material presented here:

1. Both outpatient treatment programs failed to be accepted by suicide repeaters.
2. It appears urgently necessary to develop ways of motivating all patients with repeated suicide attempts to participate in a postepisodal treatment. Or is it possible that the indication for outpatient treatment did not meet the needs for intervention? Or was it the "free will" of patients to maintain self-destructive behavior for communication with others and for coping with their own hurting feelings?
3. The crisis-oriented, short-term therapy program with a high attendance rate appears to be more effective in improving psychosocial assessment of parasuicide repeaters than a low-frequency, long-term therapy program. As already examined in an earlier study, the therapist seems to represent one decisive variable with regard to the success of postparasuicidal treatment.

References

Gibbons JS, Butler J, Urwin P, Gibbons JL (1978) Evaluation of a social work service for self-poisoning patients. Br J Psychiatry 133:111−118

Kurz A, Möller HJ (1982) Ergebnisse der klinisch-experimentellen Evaluation von suizid-prophylaktischen Versorgungsprogrammen. Arch Psychiatr Nervenkr 232:97−118

Torhost A, Möller HJ, Dürk F, Kurz A, Wächtler C, Lauter H (1984) Ambulante Nachsorge nach Suizidversuchen − erste Ergebnisse einer experimentellen Studie. Suizidprophylaxe 11:254−273

von Zerssen D, Koeller DN (1976) Klinische Selbstbeurteilungsskalen (KS b-S) aus dem Münchner Psychiatrischen Informationssystem, Manuale. Beltz, Weinheim

Wulliemier F, Bovet J, Meylan D (1979) Le devenir des suicidants admis à l'hôpital général. Etude comparative des deux formes de prévention de récidif et de suicide. Sozial- und Präventivmedizin. Médecine sociale et préventive 24:73−88

Are There Differences Between Patients Who Were Seeking Help in a Suicidal Crisis and Patients Who Were Referred to a Suicide Prevention Center After Having Attempted Suicide?

I. Winter, A. Vogl, H. P. Breucha, and H.-J. Möller

Introduction

Suicidal thoughts and behavior demonstrate a characteristic ambivalence: on the one hand, autoaggression as the only or ultimate course of action, on the other, the desire for help and change in a life situation experienced as unbearable.

Accordingly, one part of those individuals threatened by suicide might seek professional help during a crisis *before* the autoaggressive tendencies are acted out, while others will take up a therapy offer only *after* a suicide attempt. The psychological circumstances regarding the initiation of therapy and the continuation of a therapeutic relationship (Kurz and Möller 1984) will likewise be different for these two groups (internal vs external motivation).

Beyond this, one can also find differences regarding the further development of suicidal individuals. Follow-up studies (review Marten 1981, Möller 1982) show that the further development among parasuicides is prognostically more unfavorable than among individuals having had a suicidal crisis alone (Luborsky et al. 1971, Butcher and Koss 1978). In the present study, we sought to answer the following questions:

1. Are individuals who have had a suicidal crisis and those who have actually attempted suicide subtypes of the "suicidal patient" which can be characterized by important and significantly different traits?
2. Do the data and results of follow-up investigations regarding the further development of these prospective subtypes permit the establishment of prognostically relevant characteristics for each subtype?

Methods

The data for this comparison were derived from two 3-year follow-up studies with initial samples of 100 patients each. All of these patients had been treated in 1976 on an outpatient basis at the *Arche*, which is a model institution in Munich entrusted with the outpatient care of suicidal individuals. The samples included, on the one hand, patients undergoing a suicidal crisis and, on the other, patients who had recently attempted suicide.

Both patient collectives were investigated using the same methods. First of all, relevant biographical and psychiatric data taken from the *Arche* files were collected. In the subsequent follow-up, the patients were then interviewed using a standardized questionnaire, which included items relating to postepisodal treatment, social adaption, as well as to psychopathological findings at the time of the follow-up interview. The Paranoid Depressivity Scale and the Complaint List of von Zerssen and Koeller (1976) as well as the Extroversion Neuroticism Questionnaire of Brengelmann and Brengelmann (1960) were applied.

Subgroup differences were tested with the chi-square test for statistical significance.

Results

These two initial samples did not differ significantly with regard to age, sex, marriage and educational status, periods of unemployment, family history of psychiatric illness, and of suicide or parasuicide. There was also no significant difference regarding remarkable childhood behavior or a history of a "broken home." Seventy percent of the patients were between 21 and 40 years of age; women were overrepresented, comprising 80% of both groups.

Those patients coming to the *Arche* after a suicide attempt did, however, demonstrate a significantly higher frequency of former suicide attempts in their histories. At the time of the most recent attempt, they suffered more often from partner conflicts as well as from mood depression. Such patients more frequently attended less than three subsequent therapy sessions at the *Arche* (Table 1).

With regard to a history of psychiatric or psychotherapeutic treatment, there was practically no difference between the two groups. However, the patients having a suicidal crisis more frequently had outpatient therapy experience (Table 2).

In both samples, in checking for the representativity of the groups followed up relative to the initial samples, there were no differences with respect to most sociodemographic and anamnestic characteristics. Other significant differences, however, did become evident, differences indicating for both samples an unfavorable tendency regarding therapy motivation and social stability. Among those patients who could not be interviewed, there were more individuals having a therapy duration of less than 6 h as well as more frequent changes of job and residence. The data of the patients followed up and interviewed cannot be applied without restriction to the total samples. The following refers only to those patients for whom the data collection was complete (Table 3).

Referring to the characteristic "history of suicide attempts," there were grave differences between the two collectives interviewed. In the patients with a suicide attempt, there were twice as many individuals with a history of at least one prior attempt (Table 4). Almost half of those patients experiencing a suicidal crisis came to therapy either on their own initiative or after being motivated by friends, while two-thirds of the patients attempting suicide were referred to the *Arche* by private practitioners or clinics. Partner conflicts at the time of the episode were overrepresented in the group of parasuicides (Table 5).

Table 1. Significantly varying characteristics of initial samples ($P \leq 0.05$)

	Patients with a suicide attempt ($n = 100$)	Patients in a suicidal crisis ($n = 100$)
History of suicide attempt	48% 18% of which repeatedly	30% 13% of which repeatedly
Partner conflict at time of crisis	66%	46%
Depressed mood at index time	43%	14%
Less than 3 h of therapy at the *Arche*	49%	26%

Table 2. Prior psychiatric/psychotherapeutic treatment in the initial sample (data from the files of the *Arche*)

	Patients with a suicide attempt ($n = 100$)	Patients in a sucidal crisis ($n = 100$)
Inpatient	10%	13%
In-/outpatient	4%	7%
Outpatient	10%	17%
Total	24%	37%

Table 3. Significant differences between initial sample and follow-up sample

	Patients with a suicide attempt ($n = 100$)		Patients in a suicidal crisis ($n = 100$)	
	Not interviewed ($n = 50$)	Interviewed ($n = 50$)	Not interviewed ($n = 51$)	Interviewed ($n = 49$)
Broken home	38%	10%	37%	37%
Therapy less than 6 h at the *Arche*	86%	52%	76%	23.5%
Change of residence	68%	20%	–	–
Change of employment	–	–	34%	19%

Table 4. History of suicide attempt

Pateints with a suicide attempt ($n = 50$)	Patients in a suicidal crisis ($n = 49$)
58%	28.6%
Repeated attempts: 24% of the above	Repeated attempts: 8.2% of the above More than 9 years previous

Table 5.   Significant data regarding the time of the crisis situation

	Patients with a suicide attempt ($n = 50$)	Patients in a suicidal crisis ($n = 49$)
Problem	72% partner conflict	75% problems in various areas, depressed mood
Admission through physician	64%	28.6%
Admission through friends	12%	34.7%
Self-initiative	–	12.2%

Table 6.   Duration of therapy at the *Arche*

	Patients with a suicide attempt ($n = 50$)		Patients in a suicidal crisis ($n = 49$)	
1– 2 h	42%	Less addiction	12.2%	More than half referred
2– 5 h	10%	problems	28.6%	to therapy elsewhere
6–30 h	48%		59.2%	

Half of the patients with a suicide attempt were so-called therapy in-terrupters, having less than 3 h of therapy. In contrast to patients who were in therapy longer, these patients had significantly fewer problems with substance dependence and a better social environment. Accordingly, the more severely disturbed patients in this group of parasuicides had longer therapies at the *Arche* (Table 6).

The assessment of the self-evaluation scales showed that two-thirds of the crisis patients in the sample interviewed had pathological complaint scores. This was the case for only one-third of the parasuicides. In light of the compa-rable scores in both groups for depression and neuroticism, there is reason to presume that such patients tend to overt plaintiveness.

For the period of follow-up, the parasuicides revealed clearly unfavorable characteristics with respect to the further development of their situation. Com-pared with those with a suicidal crisis, the frequency of substance dependence was twice as great, as was the occurrence of more or less extensive inpatient psychiatric treatment (Table 7). Although for both samples the frequency of suicidal thoughts during the follow-up period was the same, the repeat rate of suicide attempts was much higher among the parasuicides. Again, for both groups, the frequencies of suicidal thoughts and repeated suicide attempts had their respective peaks in the 1st year following the incident leading to help-seeking at the *Arche* (Table 8). The parasuicide repeaters were in comparison with the other parasuicides more often dissatisfied with their lives, were more often in psychiatric care, and demonstrated more often somatic illness and sub-stance dependence.

Table 7. Significantly varying characteristics during follow-up period

	Patients after a suicide attempt ($n = 50$)	Patients after a suicidal crisis ($n = 49$)
Substance dependence	42%	22.4%
Inpatient psychiatric/psychotherapeutic treatment	24% 16% longer than 1 month	10% 8% longer than 1 month
Outpatient psychiatric/psychotherapeutic treatment	52% 24% longer than 50 h	57% 28% longer than 50 h

Table 8. Suicidal thougths and suicide attempts during the follow-up period

	Patients after a suicide attempt ($n = 50$)	Patients in a suicidal crisis ($n = 49$)
Suicidal thoughts	50%	50%
Suicide attempts	30%	4.1%
Suicides	2 patients	1 patient

Discussion and Summary

In both samples, only 50% of the patients delivered sufficient data at the time of the follow-up. Among the other 50% the patients either refused the interview or could not be reached. The relatively low participation rate indicates the unfavorable conditions for an investigation within the framework of an outpatient care establishment, which is not primarily intended for research purposes and which treats its patients with much empathy and compassion.

One can maintain that the two follow-up collectives differ significantly in various points of relevance, especially as regards history of suicide attempts, help-seeking behavior, and active participation in therapy. We have seen that the parasuicides seek and accept help less often and that they tend more strongly to repeated suicide attempts, whereby this tendency is hardly witnessed among patients coming to the *Arche* in a suicidal crisis. One could therefore suppose that the parasuicides tend rather to "acting-out" behavior in the form of a suicide attempt as a "cry for help," while the crisis patients practice more constructive forms of conflict-solving, for example, by accepting therapy. In addition, one can deduce from the data concerning dependency and frequency of inpatient treatment that the parasuicides comprise a more severely disturbed clientele, while the − prognostically seen − better-off crisis patients display merely a greater degree of plaintiveness.

References

Brengelmann JC, Brengelmann L (1960) Deutsche Validierung von Fragebogen der Extraversion, neurotischen Tendenz und Rigidität. Z Exp Angew Psychol 7:291−331

Butcher JN, Koss MP (1978) Research on brief and crisis oriented therapies. In: Garfield SL, Bergin AE (eds) Handbook of psychotherapy and behavior change, 2nd edn. Wiley, New York, pp 725−767

Kurz A, Möller HJ (1984) Hilfesuchverhalten und Compliance von Suizidgefährdeten. Psychiatr Prax 11:6−13

Luborsky L, Chandler M, Auerbach AH, Cohen J, Bachrach HM (1971) Factors influencing the outcome of psychotherapy. A review of quantitative research. Psychol Bull 75/3:145−161

Marten RF (1981) Probleme und Ergebnisse von Verlaufsuntersuchungen an Suicidanten. In: Henseler H, Reimer CH (eds) Selbstmordgefährdung. Gremmann-Holzboog, Stuttgart, pp 65−81

Möller HJ (1982) Das Problem der Inanspruchnahme von Betreuungseinrichtungen für Suizidgefährdete. In: Reimer CH (ed) Suizid. Ergebnisse und Therapie. Springer, Berlin Heidelberg New York, pp 129−139

von Zerssen D, Koeller DM (1976) Klinische Selbstbeurteilungsskalen (KSb-S) aus dem Münchner Psychiatrischen Informationssystem, Manuale. Beltz, Weinheim

Influence of Crisis Intervention Telephone Services ("Crisis Hotlines") on the Suicide Rate in 25 German Cities

T. Riehl, E. Marchner, and H.-J. Möller

Introduction

In the 1950s, churches of both confessions founded crisis intervention services called *Telefonseelsorge* in many major cities of the Federal Republic of Germany (in the following presentation, we will often refer to these services by using the shorter designation "crisis hotlines"). By 1979 — the year in which this study began — 68 telephone services were operating in which committed lay persons working without remuneration offered advice per telephone, 24 h a day, to individuals experiencing a psychological crisis.

Every year approximately 200 000 telephone conversations, i.e., 3% of the total number of calls, were held with individuals who voluntarily admitted to thoughts of suicide as their reason for seeking help. It is safe to assume that in addition a large number of other callers were also involved in a suicidal crisis, even if the motives they stated were different. Although this leads to another assumption that "crisis hotlines" have an extensive effect in preventing suicide, the validity of this assumption has not yet been investigated as it has been for comparable organizations such as the Samaritans in the United Kingdom (Bagley 1968; Barraclough and Jennings 1977; Barraclough and Jennings 1979; Fox 1976; Jennings et al. 1978; Kreitman 1977) or similar groups in the United States (Bridge et al. 1977; Lester 1973; Weiner 1969) and Sweden (Cullberg 1978).

It was the aim of our study to arrive at an epidemiological evaluation of the effects of crisis hotlines with regard to suicide prophylaxis in the Federal Republic of Germany.

Methods

The suicide and population figures on which this study is based were drawn from data compiled from federal, provincial, and municipal statistics offices.

The commencement of effect of the crisis hotlines was considered to be in the year of their respective establishment as long as this took place in the first half of the year. If a crisis hotline was established in the second half of the year, commencement of effect was taken to be in the following year. In some cities, more than one crisis hotline was established at different times, for example, a Catholic and a Protestant one. In such situations, analysis proceeded in the fol-

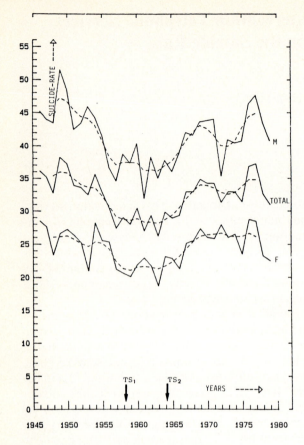

Fig. 1. Overview of the course of the suicide rate for the male, female, and total populations of Hamburg (FRG). Curves are calculated by gliding weighted 5-year averages (1958 and 1964, TS_1 and TS_2, establishment of the *Telefonseelsorge*)

lowing manner: first, the effectiveness of the one crisis hotline was examined, then that of the other separately, without taking the first one into consideration.

Changes in the population which related to the suicide rate were compensated by corresponding corrections of the calculations. When changes in the population regarding sex and age distribution occur within the period of observation, such corrections are appropriate since the suicide frequency is different for both sexes and is also dependent upon the age distribution in the population. In only six of the cities investigated could population standardization be carried out; for the other cities, no sufficiently differentiated data were available.

The fluctuations in the suicide rates for the individual years were smoothed out by the method of sliding averages. The disadvantages associated with this form of data presentation, such as the production of actually nonexistent short-term trends, was largely avoided by employing the method of weighted 5-year averages (Fig. 1).

To estimate a trend accurately, linear regression analysis was applied. Using the method of least squares after Murray, two trend-related regression plots could be determined. The first results from the suicide-rate data recorded up to

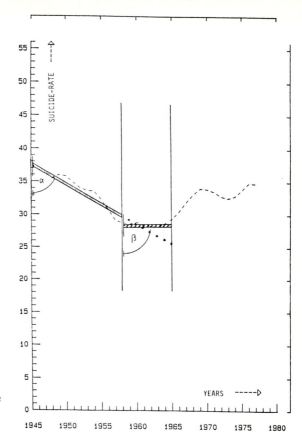

Fig. 2. Results of the statistical analysis of the suicidal behavior for the total population of Hamburg (FRG) with reference to the establishment of the *Telefonseelsorge* in 1958

15 years prior to the commencement of effect of a crisis hotline in the city concerned, the second can be determined from the data recorded up to 7 years following the establishment of this service. The differences between the angle of the second regression line and that of the first were used as a criterion for evaluating the effect of a crisis intervention telephone service on suicidal behavior, whereby a positive angle difference is equal to a rising trend, a negative difference to a falling trend (Fig. 2). The period of 15 years prior to the establishment of a crisis hotline was chosen to reduce as much as possible solitary or periodic interference factors. The evaluation of the effect during the 7 years following the establishment of a crisis hotline was chosen under the assumption that the years which are close to the year of establishment are of relatively greater importance for the trend analysis. If a shorter period of time were to be taken, coincidental suicide-rate fluctuations might give the appearance of a change in trend, particularly in smaller cities. In a longer period of time, there would be a greater probability of the occurrence of solitary or periodic interference factors. Finally, a comparison of the arithmetic averages of the observed and expected suicide rates was carried out. This comparison of averages is necessary because a falling trend can occur despite a generally high suicide

level. Only if it was possible to lower the suicide level during the time period following the establishment of a crisis hotline, while for the same period the suicide trend did not rise, is it possible to speak of a suicide-preventing influence of a crisis hotline.

Twenty-five medium-sized and large cities having more than 100 000 inhabitants were included in the study. The choice was restricted to those cities in which crisis hotlines had been operating for a sufficiently long time and for which the data necessary for analysis were available. For all the cities, the data were processed in the previously described manner and the corresponding characteristics defined according to male, female, and total population. Subsequently, the results were summarized in a general evaluation.

For reasons of statistical security, investigations were carried out to determine if the observed suicide rate deviated significantly from the expected rate once the crisis hotline had commenced effect. A measure of the deviation between the observed and expected suicide-rate values was furnished by the chi-square test. The expected suicide-rate results are based on the hypothetical assumption that the suicide-rate values will reflect the linear regression trend for the period prior to the establishment of a crisis hotline. If the observed suicide-rate values deviate significantly from the expected values as determined by the chi-square test, then this would indicate an influence of the respective crisis hotline.

Results

In general, the analyses were based on periods of observation of 15 years prior and 7 years following commencement of effect of the crisis hotlines.

In nine cities the period of observation prior to the establishment of the crisis hotline was somewhat shorter, in six other cities the period of observation following the establishment was also somewhat shorter. Incomplete (suicide-rate) data series were not utilized, if there were periods of observation of less than 9 years prior and less than 4 years following the establishment of a crisis hotline, respectively. This was the case for four cities as well as for the sex-related differentiation of effect of the crisis hotline in three of these four cities.

Seen for the total population of the respective cities, in only three was there a significant alteration of the suicide rate following the introduction of crisis hotlines. In these three cities, however, there occurred not a reduction, but rather an increase in the suicide rate (e.g., Hamburg, Fig. 2).

If one differentiates the data according to sex, significant alterations following the introduction of the crisis hotline are found for men in ten cities and for women in eight. Here, too, there occurred not a reduction, but rather an increase in the suicide rates. Only in three cities was there for men and in two cities for women a significant reduction of the suicide rate following introduction of the crisis hotline.

Discussion

The results of this investigation lead to the conclusion that a positive effect of crisis hotline is not demonstrated when the analytical methods described previously are employed. This conclusion is in agreement with several other epidemiological evaluations of the effect of similar services on suicide prevention (Barraclough and Jennings 1979; Bridge et al. 1977; Jennings 1977; Lester 1974 a, b; Lester 1979; Weiner 1969).

Although in the differentiation of the data according to sex there were in some few instances indications of a significant decrease in the suicide rate following the introduction of crisis hotlines, in the majority of cases an increase of the suicide rate was revealed. On the whole, these disappointing results have to be interpreted critically, especially with regard to inherent methodological problems.

Environment-oriented investigations have made clear the difficulties in controlling even the social structure variables alone (Barraclough and Jennings 1977, 1979; Jennings 1977; Jennings et al. 1978; Kreitman 1976; Lancet Editorial 1978; Lawton 1977). In the present study, as in most epidemiological studies, not enough attention is paid to known influences, for example, increase in the unemployment rate, superannuation of the population, detoxification of sewer gas, introduction of social-psychiatric services, so that only a very reserved interpretation of the association between a change in the suicide rate and a change in suicide prevention programs can be made.

One can, however, counter an overly critical interpretation of the present results with other, not less important arguments. Thus, one need not assume that the results of the individual analyses are qualified by one or more factors influencing the suicide rate, i.e., factors whose effects appear simultaneously with but are diametrically opposed to the effect of the crisis hotlines, which would lead to a compensation (nullification) of the latter. It is very difficult to imagine factors that would only take effect when a crisis hotline is established; moreover, such factors would have to be, with regard to their causes, intimately associated with the establishment of the crisis hotline. Such a hypothesis would be entirely justified, *if* this investigation had been restricted to only one city. The credibility of such a hypothesis vanishes, however, if one considers (1) that these "interference factors" would be taking effect in different cities at different times during an observation period of approximately 20 years, whereby this effect would have to be restricted to those cities where crisis hotlines were operating, and (2) that the diametrically opposed effect of these factors would have to develop at exactly the same time as the activity of the crisis hotlines.

Within the context of other investigations with similar outcomes, the results presented here allow various conclusions. On the one hand, one could assume that those seeking aid commit suicide despite the intervention of the crisis hotline. On the other hand, it could be that those callers judged by the crisis hotline to be suicidal are in reality not in a suicidal crisis. Finally, one can make the assumption that those persons who experience a crisis and who subsequently actually commit suicide do not beforehand make use of this crisis intervention service. Findings in the literature suggest that the results here are best explained by the fact that there are significant statistical differences with respect to different variables between the collectives of those who make use of crisis intervention services and that of suicides (Greer and Weinstein 1979; Stengel and Cook 1961).

In conclusion, it should be emphasized that it is not the intent of the investigation to call into question the work of crisis intervention telephone services. In any case, the uncertainties involved in analyzing the data prohibit such criticism. In addition, as was mentioned at the beginning of this presentation, suicide prevention is only one aspect in the broad spectrum of activity of the crisis intervention services.

References

Bagley C (1968) The evaluation of a suicide prevention schema by an ecological method. Soc Sci Med 2:1−14

Barraclough BM, Jennings C (1977) Suicide prevention by the Samaritans. A controlled study of effectiveness. Lancet ii:237−238

Barraclough BM, Jennings C (1979) Is suicide preventable by telephone counselling? A controlled study of the effectiveness of the Samaritans. 10th Int congr for suicide prevention and crisis intervention, Ottawa, pp 209−214

Bridge TP, Potkin SG, Zung WW, Soldo BJ (1977) Suicide prevention centers − ecological study of effectiveness. J Nerv Ment Dis 164:18−24

Cullberg J (1978) The Nacka project − an experiment in community psychiatry. 9th Int congr for suicide prevention, Helsinki, pp 76−80

Fox R (1976) The recent decline of suicide in Britain: the role of the Samaritan suicide prevention movement. In: Shneidman E (ed) Suicidology. Grune and Stratton, New York, pp 499−524

Greer FL, Weinstein RS (1979) Suicide prevention center outreach: callers and noncallers compared. Psychol Rep 44:387−393

Jennings C (1977) Letter to the editor. Lancet ii:706−707

Jennings C, Barraclough BM, Moss JR (1978) Have the Samaritans lowered the suicide rate? A controlled study. Psychol Med 8:413−422

Kreitman N (1976) The coal gas story. Br J Prev Soc Med 30:86−93

Kreitman N (ed) (1977) Parasuicide. Wiley, New York

Lancet editorial (1978) Suicide and the Samaritans. Lancet ii:772−773

Lawton A (1977) Suicide prevention by the Samaritans. Lancet ii:706

Lester D (1973) Prevention of suicide. JAMA 225:203

Lester D (1974a) Effect of suicide prevention centers on suicide rates in the United States. Public Health Rep 89:37−39

Lester D (1974b) Suicide prevention centers: data from 1970. JAMA 229:394

Lester D (1979) Preventing suicide: whether to, when and how. 10th Int congr for suicide prevention and crisis intervention, Ottawa, pp 246−252

Stengel E, Cook NG (1961) Contrasting suicide rates in industrial communities. J Ment Sci 107:1011−1019

Weiner IW (1969) The effectiveness of a suicide prevention program. Ment Hyg 53:357−363

Suicidal Callers on the Telephone Crisis Line in Ljubljana, Yugoslavia

O. Tekavčič-Grad and A. Zavasnik

Introduction

When crisis lines to help people in mental distress were first founded in the late 1950s and early 1960s, one of their main aims was to lower the suicide rate in their area. From then on we can read about all sorts of proof on the lowering of this rate (such as the Samaritans in the United Kingdom, Varah 1985; Williams et al. 1973; Cohen and Nelson 1983); on the other hand, there are several arguments that the problem of suicide is so complex and complicated that the eventual changes in its rate cannot be explained simply by the work of one service. Nevertheless, those persons with suicidal thoughts, wishes, threats, and attempts were, are, and will be the everyday "users" of the telephone crisis lines. They remain that kind of risk group for which it is known to be even more at risk when their suicidal behavior is more fixed (Sainsbury 1982). The telephone crisis lines are the kind of services which respond to these suicidal persons in the phase when their behavior pattern is only developing and that is probably the main preventive function of these services.

Suicide prevention work is very important in Slovenia, the most developed Yugoslav republic, as our suicide rate is extremely high — 35.5 per 100 000 inhabitants and still increasing (Milčinski 1985) — which in absolute numbers means more deaths due to suicide than car accidents (Virant-Jaklič 1985). The reflection of this particular situation is the significant number of suicidal callers on our telephone crisis line (26% of all the calls in 1984, for example). Our telephone service has been working for 7 years as a part of the University Psychiatric Hospital in Ljubljana, where the highly suicidal callers can immediately be admitted to the unit for crisis intervention.

We were interested in the differences and similarities among the callers with and the callers without suicidal intentions who asked for help at our telephone crisis line in the year 1984.

Methods

All the calls in 1984 were checked and we found 250 suicidal callers of 965 registered. We compared the following attributes: the number of contacts, sex, age, marital status, problems, was the caller drunk or not at the time of the call, state of depression, degree of the suicide risk, and if any referrals had been made.

Results

Figures 1–9 show the percentages of both the suicidal and all other callers separated by sex.

The results obtained confirm the hypothesis that there are some differences between both groups. We found differences between male and female callers in the number of contacts they made to our service (Fig. 1). The female callers were more prone to use this kind of help chronically, while male callers used it less frequently, but in a more serious life crisis. This is probably the reason why there are more first calls made by men with suicidal thoughts. It is obvious that suicidal behavior as a style of solving life problems becomes more quickly fixed in the female callers.

As claimed elsewhere (Williams et al. 1973), there were also more female callers on our crisis line – suicidal and others (Fig. 2). Concerning age, we found that the age group at risk among females (21–30 years old) coincided with the incidence of attempted suicide for the same age group in the whole Slovene population (Virant-Jaklič 1985) (Fig. 3).

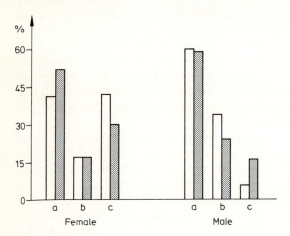

Fig. 1. Number of contacts. *a*, First call; *b*, calling 1–3 times; *c*, chronic caller. *Solid bar*, suicidal; *dotted bar*, all callers

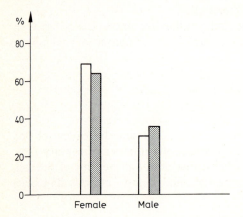

Fig. 2. Sex of callers. *Solid bar*, suicidal; *dotted bar*, all callers

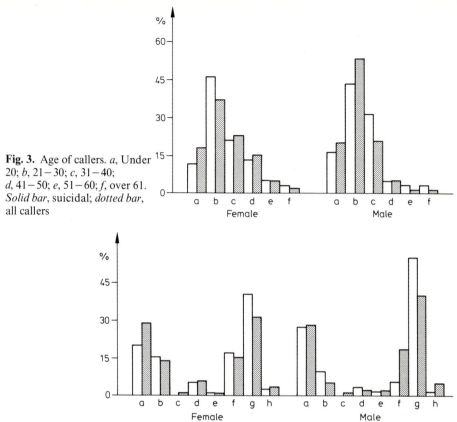

Fig. 3. Age of callers. *a*, Under 20; *b*, 21−30; *c*, 31−40; *d*, 41−50; *e*, 51−60; *f*, over 61. *Solid bar*, suicidal; *dotted bar*, all callers

Fig. 4. Marital status. *a*, Married; *b*, divorced; *c*, separated; *d*, widowed; *e*, living together; *f*, single with partner; *g*, single without partner; *h*, no data. *Solid bar*, suicidal; *dotted bar*, all callers

It is even more interesting for the males that our suicidal risk group of callers inclined to match the group at highest risk to commit suicide in the population (31 − 40 years of age, Virant-Jaklič 1985).

The callers at highest risk were the ones living alone without a partner (if they were female even with a partner but outside marriage), those divorced, and in the male group those widowed (Fig. 4).

Among the most popular problems chosen in the suicidal group of callers were loneliness, alcoholism, drug abuse, and in the group of female callers − problems related to the parent−child relationship. The most usual problems were connected to the partnership (Fig. 5). However, there were not as many suicidal callers dealing with this problem. This could possibly be explained with a different kind of style and intensity of reacting, including the possibility of projecting the reasons for troubles onto the partner if there is one. It is obvious that the problem of loneliness is much more difficult to bear for the male callers (as the suicide risk is also higher for males without a partner, Milčinski 1985).

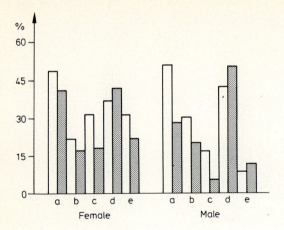

Fig. 5. Problems. *a*, Loneliness; *b*, alcohol; *c*, drug abuse; *d*, couple's problems; *c*, generation gab. *Solid bar*, suicidal; *dotted bar*, all callers

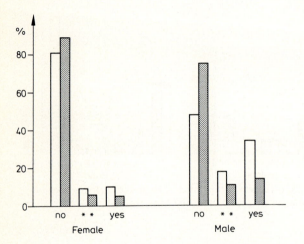

Fig. 6. Callers drunk. *Solid bar*, suicidal; *dotted bar*, all callers; **, possibly

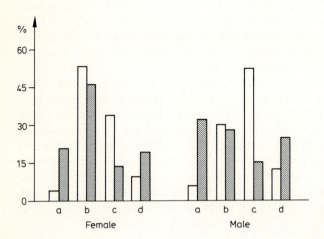

Fig. 7. Signs of depression. *a*, None; *b*, some; *c*, serious; *d*,cannot judge. *Solid bar*, suicidal; *dotted bar*, all callers

As is known, men try to solve their problems by drinking more often than women (Beckman et al. 1986; Cutter et al. 1984), and our male callers, often calling drunk, confirmed this observation (Fig. 6). Both male and female suicidal callers were assessed for depression (mild or severe). The male callers were less often assessed as depressive, but when they were, they were seriously depressed (Fig. 7). It is interesting that the assessment of depression of the suicidal callers was not of any problem for the counselors, which proves their adequate focusing and attention-paying to this important risk factor.

We know from theory and practice (Cohen and Nelson 1983) that people in a crisis usually have suicidal fantasies and thoughts rather than producing suicidal threats and attempts (Fig. 8).

Besides the relaxation and disburdening, the suicidal callers were more often referred to the psychiatrist than the others, especially the male suicidal callers. It was even more frequent than usual that they were offered the immediate help of a psychiatrist just after the call, followed by admission to our unit for crisis intervention (Fig. 9).

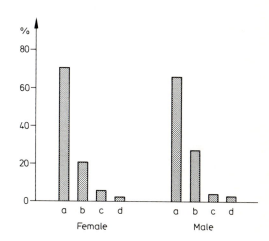

Fig. 8. Suicidal intentions. *a*, thoughts and fantasies; *b*, threat; *c*, suicidal attempt; *d*, very serious attempt

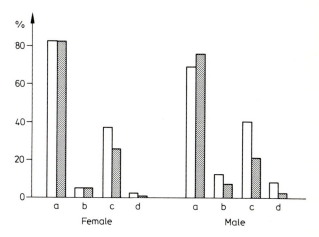

Fig. 9. Interventions. *a*, Disburdening conversation; *b*, referral to GP; *c*, referral to psychiatrist; *d*, immediate help. *Solid bar*, suicidal; *dotted bar*, all callers

It might be concluded from our population of 965 callers checked that the 250 suicidal callers were often 20—40 years old, not living with a partner, lonely, addicted to alcohol or drugs, drunk (male), and severely depressed. The counselors recognized the suicidal thoughts of the callers quickly and successfully, offering enough relaxation, support, acceptance, and helpful counseling. If this was not enough, they referred them to a psychiatrist in an outpatient clinic or to a general practitioner. If the caller was assessed as highly suicidal, the immediate help of a psychiatrist as well as admission into our hospital were arranged.

The results obtained show that the counselors were sensitive enough toward the suicidal callers. The purpose of future education for the counselors should be to pay even more attention to the callers with the above-mentioned risk factors, even if they do not explicitly show or announce their suicidal thoughts and threats while calling the telephone crisis line.

References

Beckman LJ, Amaro H (1986) Personal and social difficulties faced by women and men entering alcoholism treatment. J Stud Alcohol 47:135—145

Cohen LH, Nelson DW (1983) Crisis intervention: an overview of theory and technique. In: Cohen LH, Claiborn WL, Specter GA (eds) Crisis intervention, 2nd edn. Human Sciences, New York, pp 13—27

Cutter HSG, O'Farrell T (1983) Relationship between reasons for drinking and customary drinking behavior. J Stud Alcohol 45:321—325

Milčinski L (1985) Samomor in Slovenci, 2nd edn. Cankarjeva založba, Ljubljana, pp 141—159

Sainsbury P (1982) Depression and suicide prevention. In: Willmote J, Mendlewicz J (eds) New trends in suicide prevention. Karger, Basel, pp 17—32

Varah C (1984) Parasuicide. In: Varah C (ed) The Samaritans — befriending the suicidal, 2nd edn. Constable, London, pp 52—54

Virant-Jaklič M (1985) Samomor in samomorilni poskus v Sloveniji v letu 1984. Unierzitetna psihiatrična klinika, Ljubljana, pp 1—13

Williams T, Douds J (1973) The unique contribution of telephone therapy. In: Lester D, Brockopp GW (eds) Crisis intervention and counselling by telephone. Thomas, Springfield, pp 80—89

Effect of Deregistration of Drugs and Prescription Recommendations on the Pattern of Self-Poisonings

O. Ekeberg, D. Jacobsen, B. Flaaten, and A. Mack

Introduction

In Norway, the sales of narcotic drugs have been subject to increasingly rigorous control, especially since 1970 when a monitory system for the legal prescription and use of narcotics was introduced (Jøldal and Halvorsen 1982). Regulatory measures, however, have not been sufficient to prevent an increasing number of self-poisonings in Norway, self-poisoning becoming the most commonly used suicide method in Norway about 1980 (Ekeberg et al. 1985).

Four barbiturates (amobarbital, cyclobarbital, pentobarbital, and secobarbital) were formally withdrawn from the Norwegian market on 1 April 1980, reducing the number of barbiturates available in Norway to five (aprobarbital, enhexymal, enallymal, thiomebumal, and phenobarbital). Recommendations were subsequently made by health authorities for a more restrictive attitude when prescribing drugs that can be abused, particularly where patients unknown to the doctors were concerned. This coincided with our ongoing study to investigate the source of the drugs obtained by patients admitted for self-poisoning. The aim of the study was then extended also to investigate the effect of the regulatory measures. The study is more extensively described elsewhere (Ekeberg et al. 1987).

Methods

All patients admitted for self-poisoning 1 year before (first period) and 1 year after (second period) the regulatory measures were included in the study.

The drugs were classified in six categories: barbiturates, benzodiazepines, antidepressants, neuroleptics, "other hypnotics," and "others." Seven categories were adopted for the classification of the sources of the toxic agents: four representing doctors and three representing nonmedical sources (family, friends and "others"). "Family doctor" is the doctor regularly consulted by the patient. "Random doctor" is a doctor consulted for the first time. "Same compound from different doctors" is a classification referring to patients who intentionally consult different doctors to obtain the same drug. "Psychiatrist" refers to the specialist.

In the first period 654 patients were admitted and in the second 696. Patients poisoned by compounds obtainable without prescription and patients leaving the hospital before the interview could take place were excluded. The study included 354 patients (72% females) in the first period and 386 (70% females) in the second.

Results

Self-poisonings with barbiturates decreased from 101 to 45 ($P < 0.001$). There was a relative increase in barbiturates obtained from the family doctor, 30.7% and 57.8%, respectively ($P < 0.001$). The main reason for this is presumably that most of the remaining self-poisonings in this group were related to the anti-epileptic phenobarbital. Our hypothesis that benzodiazepines and "other hypnotics" would take over from the barbiturates was not confirmed; in fact, both categories decreased slightly but not significantly. However, antidepressants increased from 62 to 92 ($P < 0.01$) and neuroleptics from 75 to 106 ($P < 0.01$). The increase in self-poisonings by antidepressants calls for caution, due to the toxicity. In 1978 almost three times as many deaths were caused by barbiturates as by antidepressants in Oslo. Four years later, exactly the opposite held true, and antidepressants had become the most common cause of death by self-poisoning (Teige 1985).

The main group was "family doctor" comprising 35.9% and 35.5%, respectively, of the patients (Table 1). Patients consulting doctors randomly, either "random doctor" or "same compound from different doctors," decreased from 23.8% to 12.4% ($P < 0.001$). However, only the last category contributed to the decrease; drugs obtained from a "random doctor" did not change significantly. Drugs obtained from psychiatrists increased from 12.3% to 18.9% ($P < 0.01$). Drugs obtained from nonmedical sources increased from 28.0% to 33.2% ($P < 0.05$, one-tailed test). The great number of drugs obtained from non-medical sources constitutes a big problem in connection with drug control measures. In addition, 135 patients in the first period and 151 in the second were poisoned by compounds obtainable without prescription.

Neither the number of patients nor the total number of toxic agents taken changed significantly. This was in accordance with our hypothesis that the patients' drive for drugs and self-poisonings was unlikely to change.

Table 1. Sources of all the toxic agents in the first and the second period

	1st period (%)	2nd period (%)
Family doctor	35.9	35.5
Psychiatrist **	12.3	18.9
Random doctor	8.0	9.2
Same compound from different doctors ***	15.8	3.2
Family	9.2	11.0
Friends	16.5	19.3
Others	2.3	2.9
Sum	100.0	100.0
Total number (n)	576	555

** $P < 0.01$;   *** $P < 0.001$

Conclusion

1. Deregistration of four barbiturates was followed by a significant decrease in self-poisonings with barbiturates in general.
2. An increase in self-poisonings with antidepressants and neuroleptics was found, whereas benzodiazepines and "other hypnotics" did not change significantly.
3. Drugs obtained by doctors randomly consulted decreased, whereas drugs obtained from psychiatrists increased.
4. Almost one-third of the drugs in self-poisonings were obtained from nonmedical sources. This proportion increased after the regulatory measures.
5. Regulations made by health authorities can influence the pattern of self-poisonings, but does not seem to influence the general tendency to abuse drugs and to take an overdose.

References

Ekeberg Ø, Jacobsen D, Enger E, Frederichsen PS, Holan L (1985) The reliability of the official suicide statistics in Norway. Tidsskr Nor Lægeforen (Eng abstr) 105:123-7
Ekeberg Ø, Jacobsen D, Flaaten B, Mack A (1987) Effect of regulatory withdrawal of drugs and prescription recommendations on the pattern of self-poisonings. Acta Med Scand 221:483-7
Jøldal B, Halvorsen I (1982) Sales statistics in the control of drug abuse in Norway. Bull Narc 2:57−68
Teige B (1985) Fatal drug and alcohol intoxications outside hospital. Tidsskr Nor Lægeforen (Eng abstr) 105:1857−1859

Experiences with a Routine-Documentation-System for Parasuicides

H. WEDLER and F. KLEIN

Introduction

Management of suicide patients in general hospitals still remains a major problem. Three reasons may be responsible for this fact:

1. High number of parasuicides
2. Lack of crisis intervention facilities, including an unsatisfactory structure of management of parasuicides in many hospitals
3. Poor compliance of suicide patients

As Sonneck (1976) and others have indicated, these facts are not suitable to enable complete psychosocial care for all suicidal patients, but they stress the necessity of a possible evaluation for detecting patients at risk. Evaluation, however, requires a basic pool of continuously recorded, well operationable information. How is it possible to accomplish this at general hospitals?

Deficiencies of Data Collection on Medical Wards

Generally, some basic data are currently recorded from all patients admitted to general hospitals such as age, sex, and domicile. These data do not allow a sufficient evaluation of risk factors. Katschnig et al. (1980) have described a minimal program of basic data concerning parasuicides which proved to be able to distinguish between high- and lower-risk groups with respect to fatal repetition rates. Besides age and sex, the following items were included: actual working situation, motivation and mode of parasuicide, use of alcohol at the time of the suicidal act, state of conciousness when arriving at the hospital, number of previous suicidal attempts, and the psychiatric diagnosis.

At first glance, it seems easy to obtain all these data from all parasuicides in any emergency department, but in reality they are completed – in hospitals without scientific programs – only in a minority. In the course of an earlier study at the medical department of our hospital, it had been noted that only age, sex, and occupation had been regularly recorded. All other items were documented nonsystematically and only in a smaller number of cases.

Engelhardt et al. (1973) have stated that doctors and nurses working in general hospitals usually obtain little information concerning the psychosocial background of the somatically ill patients and then only in about 10% of cases. Apparently, this lack of information may be hazardous when concerning parasuicides because any evaluation or judgment of further suicidal risk and − more importantly − any indication of further treatment will fail without sufficient psychosocial data. Certainly, there may be many facts of the patient's personal history which surface casually during contact with members of the staff of the ward, but this information will not be available as a source for evaluation without routine documentation. Moreover, it seems that only those factors which are routinely present in mind and are well accepted will be used as relevant data for decision making.

On the other hand, neither simple authoritative instructions nor delegation of these tasks to psychosocial specialists have proved to be able to solve these problems in a sufficient way.

For example, in the United Kingdom where routine psychiatric evaluation of all parasuicides had been obligatory, Rabee and Watson (1978) as well as Blake and Mitchell (1978) stated that in contrast to official directions, little more than 50% reached the psychiatrist's attention. Linden (1969) noted in reviewing records from a psychiatric university hospital in Germany that even with the presence of a scientific program two-thirds of all male and one-third of all female parasuicides could not be evaluated because they had left the ward prematurely.

These experiences indicate that psychosocial evaluation of parasuicides should be immediately performed at the place of first contact.

Material and Methods

On the basis of a structured crisis intervention program, which included close cooperation of the medical team with social workers and psychologists (Wedler 1986), a special basic documentation scale of suicidal behavior was tested to obtain continuously sufficient information about patients treated after suicidal acts. This scale was developed by a German interdisciplinary working group from Munich, Heidelberg, Mannheim, and Darmstadt (Kulessa et al. 1984). It contains 131 items concerning psychiatric and somatic diagnosis, sociodemographic data, early history, the actual crisis and suicidal act, as well as strategies of treatment and aftercare.

In this pilot study, the purpose was to determine whether this strategy would be able to provide sufficient information about parasuicides in routine work at a general hospital not under the auspices of the better personal and instrumental resources of a specific scientific program.

The scale was used in 295 parasuicides consecutively admitted between 1983 and 1984. It was completed by medical ward doctors and social workers who made the first contact with parasuicides or performed crisis intervention. For each patient the documentation time took 8 − 15 min.

Results

In all 295 patients, 63% underwent complete crisis intervention. On an average, it entailed five meetings with each patient face-to-face, and an additional 1.5 meetings with family members. In 2% (six persons) no interview was possible.

Table 1 gives an example of the scale concerning some sociodemographic data. The distribution within the items of sex, nationality, and civil status seems to be typical for a nonselected population of parasuicides. The amount of missing information is small. In one item, however, concerning religion, no information was given in 83% of cases. Naturally, the distribution in this item is not representative for the whole sample.

A synopsis of the extent of noninformation for all other items can be seen in Table 2. A high information level concerning one item was recorded, when more than 90% of all clients had given information. A level of 60%−90% indicates moderate information and a level of less than 60% low information.

From 11 items concerning sociodemographic data, 6 reached a high information level, 3 a moderate one, and 2 a low level (these two concerned religion as well as the question of whether school education had been finished with a final examination).

Forty-eight items comprised data from the early history. In 13 the information level was high, in 22 moderate, and in 13 low. In particular, little information was given about earlier suicidal acts in the family and the surrounding area. One item concerning earlier parasuicides of the patient himself was not documented in 28% of cases. Another group of nine items dealt with the in-

Table 1. Distribution within some sociodemographic items and percentage of lack of information

Item	%	% no information
Sex		
Male	28.5	0
Female	71.5	
Nationality		
German	86.1	1.0
Other	12.9	
Civil status		
Unmarried	40.0	3.1
Married	36.9	
Widowed	6.4	
Divorced	9.1	
Remarried	2.4	
Married, living in separation	2.0	
Religion		
Protestant	4.7	83.1
Catholic	7.4	
Islamic	3.4	
Other	.3	
No religion	1.0	

Table 2. Percentage of high, moderate, and low information levels in severall groups of items

Groups of items	Information level		
	High > 90%	Moderate 60% – 90%	Low < 60%
Sociodemographic data (11 items)	6	3	2
Historical data (48 items)	13	22	13
Suicidal act: intention, motivation, attitudes (9 items)	7	2	0
Suicidal act: performance (4 items)	4	0	0

Table 3. Comparison of deficiencies of information by use of conventional documentation vs the basic documentation scale

Item	% no information		
	Conventional documentation		Basic documen- tation scale
	1969	1979	1983/1984
Sex	0	0	0
Age	5	1	0
Civil status	21	17	3
Occupation	3	4	2
Repeated attempt	59	67	28
Consciousness	1	1	1
Psychiatric diagnosis	84	94	48
Motivation	40 [a]	ND	4
Use of alcohol	ND	ND	9

[a] 1971. *ND*, no documentation.

tention, motivation, and attitudes of the actual suicidal act. In seven of them the information level was high, in two moderate.

All four items concerning the performance of the actual parasuicide and the use of alcohol reached a high level of information.

Comparison with Conventional Forms of Documentation

A comparison of these data, recorded by the basic documentation scale together with the results from two earlier studies where data were recorded in a conventional way, demonstrates a much higher level of information in nearly all items (Table 3). There are still some deficiencies, e.g. concerning the number of earlier parasuicides and the documentation of the psychiatric diagnosis. These shortcomings may be overcome in the future by improved training of doctors and social workers in these specific fields. The data listed in this table include all the items used by Katschnig et al. (1980).

Conclusions Concerning Identification of High-Risk Groups

It may be concluded that by making the basic documentation scale a part of the routine evaluation at general hospitals it will be possible to identify a greater percentage of high-risk groups of all suicidal patients. The following example is given to demonstrate that obtaining information from parasuicides may be not only a nice statistic match but that it will lead to further therapeutic consequences. Katschnig et al. (1980) described a group of parasuicides at very high risk, including the factors of age older than 59 years, lack of occupation, and unhappiness. Applying this to the sample of the 295 patients presented, 28 had been older than 59, of these, 22 were without an occupation, 12 had as a motive unhappiness, while 7 had one or more suicidal acts in their history. Ten of 28 fulfilled all risk items described previously. Regarding the mode of aftercare, as also recorded in our scale, it can be stated that 85% of all these elder patients and all of the ten high-risk persons were transferred to intensive aftercare after discharge from our hospital (Haensell et al. 1985).

On the basis of these results, it seems justified to claim that the basic documentation scale is a useful instrument for the management of suicides at general hospitals.

References

Blake DR, Mitchell JRA (1978) Self-poisoning: management of patients in Nottingham. Br Med J i: 1032–1035

Engelhardt K, Wirth A, Kindermann L (1973) Kranke im Krankenhaus. Enke, Stuttgart

Haensell A, Wedler H, Klein F (1985) Erste Ergebnisse einer standardisierten Dokumentation bei Suizidpatienten in der Medizinischen Klinik. Klin Wochenschr 63 (suppl IV):30

Katschnig H, Sint P, Fuchs-Robertin G (1980) Suicide and parasuicide: identification of high- and low-risk groups by cluster analysis with a 5-year follow-up. In: Farmer R, Hirsch S (eds) The suicide syndrome. Croom Helm, London, p 154

Kulessa C et al. (1984) Basisdokumentation suizidalen Verhaltens. Beltz, Weinheim

Linden KJ (1969) Der Suizidversuch. Enke, Stuttgart

Rabee SK, Watson JP (1978) The management of 100 cases of self poisoning referred to the accident and emergency department of a district general hospital in London, England. 8th internat congress on suicide prevention, Jerusalem (abstracts, p 104)

Sonneck G (1976) Krisenintervention und Suizidverhütung. Ars Med 66:419–424

Wedler H (1986) Die Rolle des medizinischen Teams bei der Betreuung von Suizidpatienten. Dtsch Med Wochenschr 111:342–344

General Structure of Single Interviews Coping with a Suicidal Crisis

P. Szabó

Introduction

In dealing with people in a suicidal crisis – especially in a first interview – one of the most important and exciting questions for professional helpers is the assessment of the actual level of the suicidal danger and how to recognize the turning point in an interview, when the danger of the self-destructive behavior is over.

We think that the crucial task for us is to find a way of better understanding communications during suicidal danger to be more effective both in prevention and treatment.

In our estimation, a crisis is an organic part of the human existence and most of them are managed without professional help, but there is a significant period in this process, when the problem-solving capacity has been damaged and everyone in a crisis gives a warning of the danger of self-destruction, almost automatically.

From a solution without external help to a presuicidal syndrome (Ringel 1969) or a decodable "cry-for-help" (Farberow 1961) signal, the way is quite the same concerning characteristics of the communicative behavior. The total ambivalence in connection with external help can sometimes result from being too quiet or having very noisy messages. Thus, the insufficient understanding between interaction partners is interpreted by people in a crisis as rejection so they are forced to send new messages about self-destructive behavior. The experiences from this process have an influence on patient's behavior in a face-to-face situation too, and the fear of being rejected can reproduce crisis signals in their communciation both verbally and nonverbally.

For that very reason and in agreement with what Shneidman has said (1985) "The common interpersonal act in suicide is communication of intention," we prefer focusing on the communication of people in a crisis.

Method

In an attempt to test the hypothesis that the structure and development of a single interview coping with a suicidal crisis show similarities, six subjects were randomly selected from patients who came for treatment to the Szigetvár crisis intervention ward of the Suicide Prevention Center in Baranya County. As is usual in our practice, all of the first clinical interviews were videotaped and audiotaped.

In spite of the technical instruments, the room is suitable for psychotherapeutic interviews; the video equipment is not hidden; the recording is automatic with a static camera. With the aim of studying the very nature of patient's communicative behavior, we avoid bargaining about consent before the conversation. From an ethical viewpoint, we think that it is not the fact of recording information that is most important but the handling of the materials recorded!

The next step was the transcription to prepare the recorded materials for content analysis. The method for evaluation of verbal content was based on results of Kézdi's research team (Kézdi and Balikó 1985; Szabó 1985).

Hundreds and hundreds of crisis and noncrisis speech material were analyzed with the help of the modified Weintraub's criteria (Weintraub 1981). All of the material contained 1000 words. The goal was to find a measurement of verbal content to separate crisis and noncrisis talks. The factor analysis separated two main factors among the grammatic and semantic manifestations (Fig. 1): (1) the "encounter factor," i.e., references to here and now, expression of actual feelings together with a low level of nonpersonal references, generalizations, distance and (2) the "crisis factor," i.e., negatives, ceasing, and suicidal ideations. The validity and reliability of these criteria have been well established.

The content analysis was followed by evaluation of videotaped facial expressions. The examination of the face was chosen because of the very specific and detailed information it provides about an emotional state (Ekman 1972). In this phase, we tried to digitalize the nonverbal cues in a simple way by catching depressed or nondepressed facial expressions which appeared at the same time as

---

Criteria
 1. Nonpersonal references, generalizations, distance
 2. References to I, WE, ME
 3. Negatives, ceasing
 4. Labeling
 5. Uncertainity, hesitation, withdrawal
 6. References to "hic et nunc"
 7. Rationalization
 8. Expression of actual feelings
 9. Expression of idiosyncratic feelings
10. Suicidal ideations

Structure of factors

Variables,	1st Factor	2nd Factor
1	-0.504	
3		0.471
6	0.5	
8	0.267	
10		0.459

* The figures denote the number of criteria applied

Fig. 1. Criteria for content analysis (Kézdi et al. 1985)

significant criteria. The scores of depressed facial expressions and the frequency of significant criteria were summarized, then computed, and the result of processing was a particular dialogogram, which showed the structure and dynamics of an interview.

Results

The dialogograms in Figs. 2−7 illustrate our preliminary results. When reading the pictures, it is useful to know the following:

1. The "crisis factor" is drawn vertically
2. The distance from the basic line in the horizontal plane informs us about the growing of the "encounter factor"
3. The upper band shows the changes of a depressed face in connection with saying coded grammatic and semantic units
4. There is, of course, a line for time.

In the first three dialogograms (Figs. 2−4), we can follow the characteristics of the similar development in problem-solving conversations, from the beginning to the end. Getting nearer to the end phase, we can see the growing of the encounter factor and the decreasing of the crisis factor. Changes of the two bands parallelly go to the turning point and after that the band of a depressed face goes together with the changes of the encounter factor.

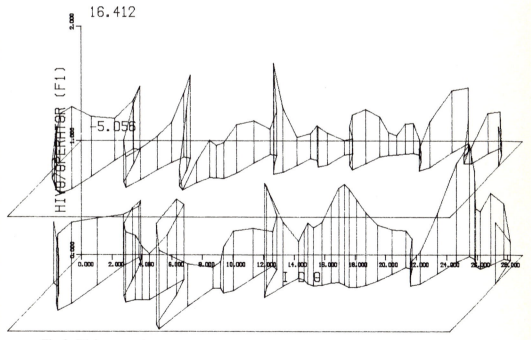

Fig. 2. Dialogogram 1

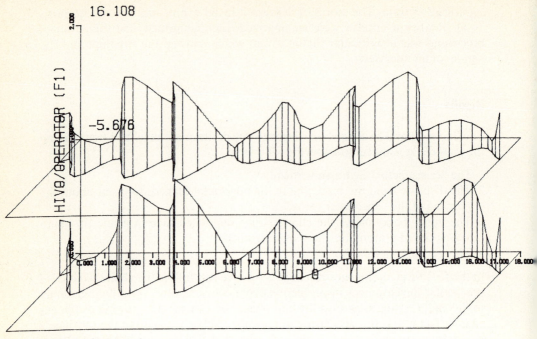

Fig. 3. Dialogogram 2

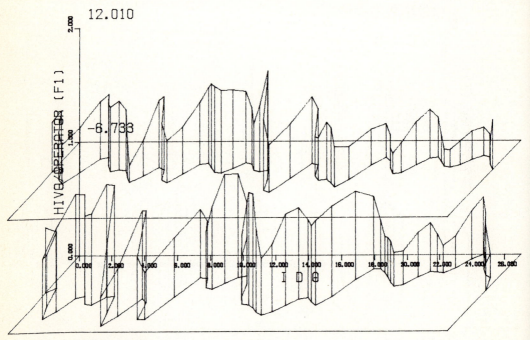

Fig. 4. Dialogogram 3

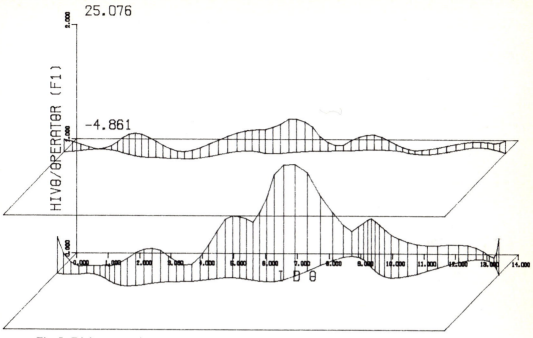

Fig. 5. Dialogogram 4

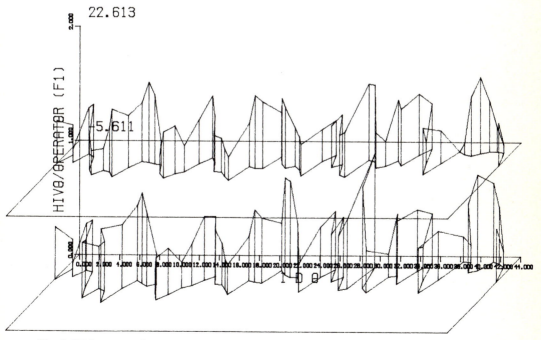

Fig. 6. Dialogogram 5

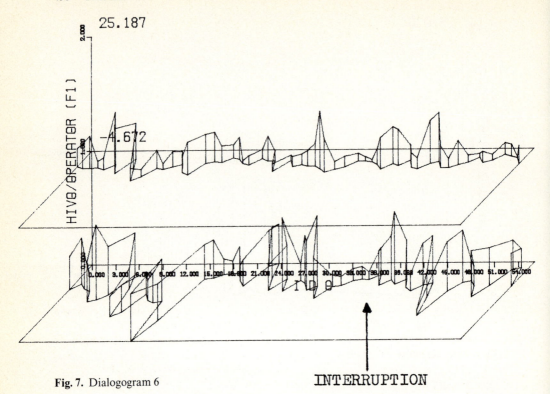

Fig. 7. Dialogogram 6   INTERRUPTION

The patient described in Fig. 5 was admitted after a self-destructive event, but the crisis was over. The high level of the encounter factor and the consistently low level of depressed manifestations, in contrast to the first three dialogograms, seem to prove it.

The hysterically communicated crisis illustrated in Fig. 6 demonstrates almost everything within itself.

Figure 7 is a particular dialogogram of an interrupted interview. Before the end of the conversation, it was disturbed by a telephone call and instead of finishing the talk the patient produced crisis signals again. That is why we can say that we can study two interview structures in one.

Discussion

We think that not only the general psychiatric interviews but all of the "efficient-in-one-session" crisis intervention interviews consist of three successive phases. This general structure is shown throughout the changes of the latent content of initial interviews (Fig. 8).

The opening phase (A) includes the ordinary rituals and greetings of a first meeting, and there is an impression management on both sides, i.e., deficiency of problem-solving capacity vs quasi-omnipotence. The middle phase is divided into three other parts: (1) bargaining on understanding (B), (2) turn (C),

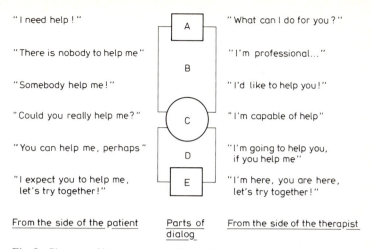

"I need help!"   "What can I do for you?"

"There is nobody to help me"   "I'm professional..."

"Somebody help me!"   "I'd like to help you!"

"Could you really help me?"   "I'm capable of help"

"You can help me, perhaps"   "I'm going to help you,
                                                   if you help me"

"I expect you to help me,   "I'm here, you are here,
let's try together!"   let's try together!"

From the side of the patient   Parts of   From the side of the therapist
                                dialog

Fig. 8. Changes of latent content of initial interviews

and (3) bargaining on solution (D). The last phase is the end phase (E) to finish or contract. Of course, the borderlines cannot be sharply distinguised and one sentence can symbolize more than one round within a given part.

We have found that the existence of the crisis factor together with depressed facial expressions in patient's communication is characteristic to the part of bargaining on understanding. The appearance of the encounter factor in verbal content and the parallel nondepressed behavior in facial expressions inform the therapist that not only the turning point has been reached but also that the acute suicidal danger is over.

We do not believe that a computer instead of a psychiatrist will deal with patients in the future, but the visualized information of interviews – such as these dialogograms – can help in his or her work. We would not like to overemphasize our primary results, but we think they are useful in recognizing crisis, controlling the strategic interview, and training for suicide prevention, both in telephonic work and clinical practice.

Acknowledgement. We thank I. Bártfai for the programs producing the dialogograms and the Computer Center of the Technical Institute at Pécs where the programs were run.

References

Ekman P et al. (1972) Emotion in the human face. Pergamon, New York
Farberow NL (1961) The cry for help. McGraw-Hill, New York
Gregory I, Smeltzer DJ (1977) Psychiatry: essentials of clinical practice. Little Brown, Boston
Kézdi B, Balikó M (1985) Semantic and grammatical characteristics of verbal behavior in suicidal crisis. LASP Congress, Vienna
Ringel E (ed) (1969) Selbstmordverhütung. Huber, Bern
Shneidman ES (1985) Ten commonalities of suicide and their implications for response. IASP Congress, Vienna
Szabó P (1985) Some data to verbal and non-verbal communication in suicidal crisis. IASP Congress, Vienna
Weintraub W (1981) Verbal behavior. Wiley, New York

Motivation for Compliance with Outpatient Treatment of Patients Hospitalized After Parasuicide

A. TORHORST, F. BÜRK, A. KURZ, C. WAECHTLER, and H.-J. MÖLLER

Introduction

Parasuicide attempters represent a high-risk group for repetition of para-suicides. Experts agree on the indication for aftercare for these patients at risk. Patients themselves do not share this point of view. Compliance with outpatient programs is very low, ranging from about 11% (Bogard 1970) up to under 50% (Paykel et al. 1974) (overview in Kurz and Möller 1984).

In general psychotherapy there is a positive correlation between high primary motivation and positive outcome of psychotherapy (Sifneos 1978). In suicidology there is one study indicating no positive correlation between primary motivation and compliance (Möller and Geiger 1982).

The aim of this study was to determine whether compliance and outcome can be predicted by the primary motivation of patients for psychotherapy (Torhorst et al. 1987).

Methods

Of 485 parasuicide attempters (Torhorst et al. 1984), 226 patients were offered outpatient psychotherapy for the time after hospitalization. The patients were described extensively with standardized measurements for sociodemographic data, psychopathology, social adjustment, etc. A personal follow-up was conducted 1 year after the index parasuicide. During this time span, 3% of the patients died by suicide and 13% were parasuicide repeaters.

Motivation was scored in self- and experts' ratings. For self-rating, a scale with 52 items was developed. Four factors proved to be clinically usable: (1) positive motivation for psychotherapy, (2) subjective obstacle to psychotherapy, (3) previous experience with psychotherapy, and (4) subjectively, no problems. The experts' ratings included seven different items.

There were three different ways of motivating patients to intensify compliance:

1. Of the 226 patients, 85 were cared for routinely. The patients were referred to an outpatient institution within the community, and they were not reminded to fix another date with this institution of the first interview was missed.

The remaining patients were randomized to one of the following two groups:

2. One group of 73 patients was motivated in a special motivation interview, dealing especially with the arguments against compliance with outpatient treatment. A date was fixed with the outpatient treatment institution, and compliance was controlled by telephone. If one patient did not come for the first interview, he was reminded by phone or by letter.

3. A total of 68 patients in the experimental group were treated the same as patients in the control group (2). In contrast to the patients of the control group (group 2), the patients were offered the outpatient treatment with the therapist, talking to them after awakening from the self-poisoning act. That means, within the experimental group the continuity of care was guaranteed.

Results

To answer the question of whether motivation for psychotherapy tells something about actual compliance and outcome there is one essential prerequisite: motivation has to be comparable within different groups of randomized patients.

Analysis of intercorrelations between the four factors of the self-rating scale proved a significant correlation between the positive expectations and the experience with psychotherapy. Analysis of the frequency distribution showed that 54% of the patients scored themselves as positively motivated for psychotherapy.

The experts' ratings of motivation included seven items: (1) suffering, (2) positive attitudes for psychotherapy, (3) positive expectations from psychotherapy, (4) reality of expectations from psychotherapy, (5) external obstacles to compliance, (6) external motivation, and (7) global assessment of willingness for compliance.

Analysis of intercorrelations showed close correlations (r between 0.75 and 0.88) for the criteria 2, 3, 4, and 7.

Analysis of the frequencies of the single items showed strong suffering in 75% of the patients; 47% of the patients seemed to be motivated for compliance positively. No motivation was scored for only 17%.

Self- and experts' rating scales showed different categories of "motivation." One would assume correlations between motivation and background variables such as age, sex, and profession as well as the personality items within standardized questionnaires measuring dimensions of personality and psychopathology.

Self- and expert-rated motivations showed no positive correlation to sex, age, inability to work, unemployment, housing situation, and intention of parasuicide.

Correlations with standardized dimensions of psychopathology showed, in summary (only significant correlations, $p < 0.001$), that positively motivated patients were more depressive and anxious. Patients with previous experience with psychotherapy were more disturbed.

Summarizing the results up to now, two main groups of patients can be distinguished: anxious depressive patients with positive motivation and socially deviant patients with poor motivation. One would expect that on the basis of these results compliance can be predicted. Against expectations there were no such correlations either in self- or in experts' ratings of motivation. These results were derived from all of the 226 patients within the three treatment groups.

In the current study, an attempt was made to increase compliance by different motivation strategies.

Prerequisite for comparing these strategies is the comparable "amount" of motivation at the beginning of the study. Patients of the routine group, the control group and the experimental group showed in self- and experts' rating scales nearly identical mean values.

Of the patients of the routine group − fixing a date with the outpatient institution without special motivation and without control of compliance − 39% of patients came for the first interview.

Additional motivation as well as control of compliance and mentioning to the patients to fix another date for the first interview did not increase the compliance for external outpatient treatment (control group) up to 48% significantly. In contrast, compliance could be increased significantly when the continuity of care was guaranteed: 72% of the patients came to the first outpatient interview when the therapist remained the same.

Another interesting result showed that these 72% represented the mean range of compliance of four different therapists. The range of actual compliance differed between 47% and 90% with the different therapists.

Discussion

It is well-known that patients after parasuicide often refuse outpatient postepisodal treatment. This study investigated whether compliance is a function of primary motivation for psychotherapy. The results showed no significant correlations between motivation and compliance. This result corresponded well with another study measuring motivation only on a global score value made by clinicians (Möller and Geiger 1982).

Patients who are more disturbed in terms of depression and anxiety are more positively motivated than patients with disturbances in social behavior. One should expect that these differences in motivation would result in different rates of compliance.

Against expectations compliance seemed to be independent of the personal variables of the patients. Compliance strongly depends on the personality of the therapist. This leads to the point that future studies should focus on therapeutic alliances such as in general psychotherapy research (Luborsky et al. 1983).

References

Bogard M (1970) Follow-up study of suicidal patients seen in emergency room consultation. Am J Psychiatry 126:1017−1020

Kurz A, Möller HJ (1984) Hilfesuchverhalten und Compliance von Suizidgefährdeten. Psychiatr Praxis 11:6−13

Luborsky L, Crits-Christoph P, Alexander L, Margolis M, Cohen M (1983) Two helping alliance methods for predicting outcomes of psychotherapy. A counting signs vs. a global rating method. J Nerv Ment Dis 171:480−491

Möller HJ, Geiger V (1982) Inanspruchnahme von Nachbetreuungsmaßnahmen durch Parasuizidenten: Probleme und Verbesserungsmöglichkeiten. In: Helmchen H, Linden M, Rüger U (eds) Psychotherapie in der Psychiatrie. Springer, Berlin Heidelberg New York

Paykel ES, Hallowell C, Dressler DM, Shapiro DL, Weissman MM (1974) Treatment of suicide attempters. Arch Gen Psychiatry 31:487−493

Sifneos PE (1978) Motivation for change. A prognostic guide for successful psychotherapy. Psychother Psychosom 29:293−298

Torhorst A, Möller HJ, Bürk F, Kurz A, Wächtler C, Lauter H (1984) Ein-Jahres-Katamnese bei einer Stichprobe von 485 Patienten nach Suizidversuch. In: Welz R, Möller HJ (eds) Bestandsaufnahme der Suizidforschung. Roderer, Regensburg, pp 142−152

Torhorst A, Möller HJ, Bürk F, Kurz A, Wächtler C, Lauter H (1987) Attempts to improve the psychiatric management of parasuicide patients. A controlled clinical study comparing different strategies of outpatient treatment. Crisis 8/1:53−61

Attitudes Toward Suicide: Development of a Suicide Attitude Questionnaire (SUIATT)

R. F. W. DIEKSTRA and A. J. F. M. KERKHOF

Introduction

Society may affect an individual's likelihood of committing or attempting suicide through the attitudes it inculcates toward it. Although few if any of the numerous sociologic, psychological, and anthropological authors on the subject of suicide over the last 100 years would disagree with such a statement, empirical studies comparing prevailing attitudes toward suicide in social groups that differ in their suicide rates are virtually nonexistent. Research of this kind would require the availability of a psychometrically sound scale for measuring attitudes toward suicide.

The only attempt thus far to construct such an instrument was undertaken by Domino et al. (1982). Their Suicide Opinion Questionnaire (SOQ) consists of 100 items that were empirically selected from a pool of 138 items, which were chosen by persons with varying levels of expertise in the field to be representative of the most important aspects of attitudes toward suicide. A factor analysis on the SOQ items yielded no less than 15 factors, indicating (according to the authors) the complexity of attitudes toward suicide. Based on the information provided by the authors, the psychometric and theoretical value of the SOQ is, however, difficult to assess and might even be questionable.

First, current theories about attitudes and attitude measurement were ignored in the process of item pool construction, the item formulation, and scale construction. The same seems to apply to prevailing theories on the etiology of suicide. Consequently, the SOQ items are very heterogeneous in structure and formulation. Second, only 61 of the 100 items have loadings > 0.30 on one or more of the 15 factors extracted, a fact that was not explicitly mentioned by the authors and that should have had considerable implications for the final version of the SOQ. Besides, the fact that the 15 factors account for 76.7% of the variance suggests that a considerable number of them must be of relatively little weight in terms of total variance explained (< 5%), but again the authors omitted providing the reader with information on this point. Clearly, the conclusive statement Domino et al. (1982, p. 262) make about the SOQ as having already proven to be a useful instrument for measuring attitudes toward suicide is premature.

The present study describes the construction and psychometric characteristics of a 63-item scale for measuring attitudes toward suicide (SUIATT) designed in such a way as to meet the criticisms leveled against the SOQ.

The SUIATT is proposed to be of use in comparative studies on differences in suicide rates across communities and for educational purposes.

Subjects and Methods

The construction of the suicide attitude questionnaire, SUIATT for short, was based on the program that Loevinger (1956) outlined for the construction of objective tests as instruments for psychological theory and which still has current value.

The theoretical concepts on suicide underlying the construction process and the definition of the universe of content were derived from the social learning theory of suicidal behavior (Diekstra 1973, 1974, 1985; Diekstra et al. 1980). This theory assumes that suicidal acts are chosen and goal-directed behaviors. This implies that whereas the suicidal individual may consider suicide to be the only alternative left to attain a certain goal or to solve a problem, the suicidal act itself and its consequences may be threatening and thwarting motives for close relatives or other persons in the direct or wider environment of the actor. Consequently, the attitude toward suicide may differ depending upon whether the (supposed) actor is the respondent himself, somebody else, e.g., the person most near and dear to the respondent, or someone unknown. The original item pool, therefore, had to be constructed in such a way as to include similar items for different referents, both as actors (suicide by respondent him/herself, by persons near and dear, and by people in general) and as recipients or bystanders (consequences of suicide by respondent for him/herself, for the person most near and dear, and for society, etc.).

The concept of attitude as used in this study was defined in terms of the well-known three-component model, differentiating between an affective cognitive and instrumental/conative component of attitude (e.g., Secord and Backman 1974; Schuman and Johnson 1976).

Using a facet analysis approach (Guttman 1954; Guttman and Elisur 1973), a syntactic sentence was composed consisting of three facets: actors, recipients, and attitude components, logically resulting in a $3 \times 3 \times 3 = 27$-item scale. However, since several of the combinations of these facets led to absurdities or tautologies in item content, they were removed. A substantial number of other combinations could only be formed using several items and/or content areas.

The resulting 133-item version of the SUIATT with likert-type 5-point response scales was filled out and commented upon by a group of 85 graduate students in clinical psychology. Based on these comments and on the results of a factor analysis, 70 items were removed and some of the remaining items were reformulated. Examples of the items in the final version are given in Table 1. The distribution of the items over the combinations of referents and attitude components subscales is shown in Table 2.

Fifteen items are formulated identically for each of the referents. The remaining items concern only one or two referents, for reasons mentioned earlier. Items are scored in such a way that the more restricting, rejecting, or negative the answer/attitude is, the lower the score (from 1 to 5).

The 63-item SUIATT was administered to a group of 712 persons; 308 (43.3%) of them were males and 404 (56.7%) females, with a mean age of 43.6 years (range $15-68$ years). This group formed 69.8% of a sample of 1071 persons drawn from the municipial registers of 11 medium-sized urban and 6 small

Table 1.   Examples of items from the SUIATT

Cognitive attitude component

Item 36: Do you think you have the right   1. Always
          to commit suicide?   2. Mostly
                                                     3. Never
                                                     4. Mostly not
                                                     5. Sometimes yes/sometimes not

Item 59: Do you think people have the right   1. Always
          to commit suicide?   2. Mostly
                                                     3. Never
                                                     4. Mostly not
                                                     5. Sometimes yes/sometimes not

Affective attitude component

Item 8:   If the person most near and dear to you would commit suicide, how would you feel
          about it?
          1. That would be the worst thing that could happen to me
          2. That would be one of the worst things that could happen to me
          3. That would be a fairly bad thing for me
          4. That would be a bad thing for me
          5. I don't know how I would feel about that

Item 12: How do you feel about the fact that people commit suicide?
          1. I don't know how I feel about that
          2. That's a fairly bad thing
          3. That's a bad thing
          4. That's one of the worst things that can happen
          5. That's the worst thing that can happen

Instrumental attitude component

Item 15: How probable is it for you to commit suicide in case you did suffere from severe and
          chronic pain?

5	4	3	2	1
Very probable	Probable	Maybe/ maybe not	Unprobable	Very unprobable

Item 47: How probable is it for people in general to commit suicide in case they suffer from
          severe and chronic pain?

5	4	3	2	1
Very probable	Probable	Maybe/ maybe not	Unprobable	Very unprobable

Item 71: How probable is it for the person most near and dear to you to commit suicide in
          case he/she did suffere from severe and chronic pain?

1	2	3	4	5
Very unprobable	Unprobable	Maybe/ maybe not	Probable	Very probable

---

rural communities in the eastern part of the Netherlands, comprising a population of nearly 630 000 inhabitants.

The total sample essentially formed a conglomerate of subsamples stratified by gender and age (15–65 years) so as to be representative of the respective municipalities.

Table 2. Number of items per referent and attitude components

	Referent			
	Respondent	Beloved	People	Total
Attitude component				
Affective	2	2	1	5
Cognitive	6	3	8	17
Instrumental	14	13	14	41
	22	18	23	63

Selected subjects were invited by mail to participate in a study on "life problems and attitudes toward life and death" and, if necessary, received two reminders (after 2 and 4 weeks); 8.2% explicitly refused to cooperate for various reasons. The remaining 22% did not reply at all. The relatively high response rate must probably be attributed to the fact that during the mailing period several regional and local newspapers and periodicals published articles on the project stressing its importance and the desirability for people to cooperate.

Comparison of the final investigation group on the one hand and the sample and catchment area population on the other hand showed the gender distribution to be somewhat different (% males in sample/catchment area 49.95). Age groups above 55 years were somewhat underrepresented (difference of 2.1%) and below 20 years of age overrepresented (difference of 3.08%). To assess test-retest reliability the SUIATT was administered a second time, approximately 6 weeks later to a group of 256 persons. This group formed 85.3% of a subsample of 300 subjects drawn at random from the total investigation group and invited to have a follow-up interview. Differences between the follow-up group and the total group in terms of age and sex were negligible.

Results

Are the main theoretical facets upon which the SUIATT and its subscales are based reflected in the empirical properties of the data? This question was examined for both facets successively through inspection of the correlation structure and through analysis of the internal consistencies (Cronbach's α) of the alleged subscales.

Referents

Inspection of the correlation structure revealed that the mean inter-item correlations within referents were all higher, except one, than those between referents (see Table 3).

Table 3(a) shows that only the mean inter-item correlation within the referent "someone" was lower than the mean of the inter-item correlations between the referents "beloved" and "respondent."

Table 3. Mean inter-item correlations (Pearson r) within and between referents (a): all items (63) and (b) identically formulated items only (45)[a]

Referents	a				b			
	No. of items	Respon-dent	Beloved	Someone	No. of items	Respon-dent	Beloved	Someone
Respondent	(22)	.17			(15)	.22		
Beloved	(18)	.14	.21		(15)	.18	.27	
Someone	(23)	.09	.11	.13	(15)	.09	.14	.22

$n = 511$ all correlations significant $P < .05$

[a] In computing mean inter-item correlations within and between referents, all correlations between pairs of identically formulated items have been deleted.

Table 4. Psychometric properties of scales "respondent", "beloved" and "someone"

Scale	No of.			Mean interitem		Interscale correlations of sum scores t-test			
	Items	Mean	SD	corr.	Stand.	Resp.	Bel.	Some-one	Coeffi-cient
Respondent	22	40.3	9.4	.17	.79	.82	–	.70	.55	.81
Beloved	18	33.8	8.0	.21	.79	.83	.70	–	.59	.65
Someone	23	57.2	9.1	.13	.77	.78	.55	.59	–	.67
SUIATT	63	131.3	22.6	.13	.90	.91	.88	.87	.83	.82

When, as in Table 3 b, only the set of similar items for all referents was considered, all within-referent mean correlations were higher than those between referents.

Table 4 shows for each "referent scale" the numbers of items, means and standard deviations, mean inter-item correlations, Cronbach's and standardized, the inter-scale correlations, and test-retest correlations, which proved to be satisfactory both for the referent subscales and the total scale. Inspection of all corrected item-total correlations revealed that all but two items had a higher correlation with the sum of the other items in the scale to which they belong than with the sum score of the other two scales. In the two instances in which this was not the case, the difference was only minor (0.02).

Analysis of variance (one-way, unbalanced) performed on item (mean) scores with "referent" as factor showed a significant effect [F (2,262) = 35.19, $P < 0.001$). This effect was mainly due to differences between the referent "someone" on the one hand and "respondent" and "most beloved" on the other hand. This finding seems to indicate increasing permissiveness toward suicide with increasing social distance between actor and respondent, thus lending support to what the social learning approach of suicidal behavior predicts (Diekstra 1973). It also points out the necessity of distinguishing clearly between referents when measuring attitudes toward suicide.

Attitude Components

The second step in the internal validation of the SUIATT was to assess whether the distinction between (groups of) items supposed to measure affective, cognitive, and instrumental attitude components was to be found in the inter-item correlation matrix. Therefore, the effects of the referents was controlled by combining all pairs and triplets of identically formulated items over the referents and considering the sum scores obtained as separate variables.

Table 3b shows that the mean inter-item correlations within each of the three attitude components were satisfactory if compared with between components. The same can be said of the reliability coefficients (α and split half, see Table 4) for each of the component scales.

An exploratory principal components analysis was run on the matrix of inter-item correlations between attitude component subscales with numbers of factors extracted determined by number of eigenvalues > 1. The result was a five-factor solution accounting for 55% of the total variance, which was rotated according to varimax criterion (see Table 5).

Table 5. Principal components analysis (varimax rotation) on 16 "referent-free" sets of items

Description of sets of items	No. of items	Defined attitude component	I	II	III	IV	V
1. Right to commit suicide	(2)	Cognitive	.61	.12	.34	.14	.07
2. Willingness to assist	(2)	Instrumental	.54	.06	.17	.06	.03
3. Desirability of suicide hospices	(1)	Instrumental	.45	.04	.09	.05	.15
4. Worst thing to happen	(3)	Affective	.36	.37	.04	.14	.11
5. Physical impairment as condition for suicide	(12)	Instr. circumstances	.34	.04	.14	.67	.20
6. Rank order of suicide as cause of death	(2)	Affective	.33	.16	−.03	.14	.14
7. Consequences for society	(2)	Cognitive	.16	.80	.09	−.01	.04
8. Consequences for relatives	(2)	Cognitive	.08	.73	−.00	.04	.10
9. Consequences for person him/herself	(1)	Cognitive	.22	.17	.13	−.05	−.05
10. Seriousness of suicidal communication	(2)	Cognitive	.07	−.07	.59	.04	.07
11. Impulsivity of suicidal behavior	(3)	Cognitive	.11	.02	.59	.05	.06
12. Rationally vs (mental) abnormality of suicide	(2)	Cognitive	.12	.14	.46	.05	.13
13. Cowardice/bravery of suicide	(3)	Cognitive	.27	.09	.38	.15	.00
14. Social disruption as condition for suicide	(24)	Instrumental circumstances	.03	.02	.11	.75	.11
15. Likelihood of committing suicide by resp.	(1)	Instrumental	.09	.08	.08	.08	.67
16. Suicidal ideation by resp.	(1)	Instrumental	.12	.05	.15	.14	.41
Remaining variance			49.3	19.9	14.0	9.0	7.9

Interpretation of single factors based on variable loadings < 0.40 revealed two pure cognitive factors: factor II (consequences of suicide) and factor III (rationality of suicide); two factors reflected only instrumental attitude components: factor IV (physical impairment and social disruption as circumstances for committing suicide) and factor V (present and past suicidal ideation); and one factor on which both cognitive and instrumental items had high loadings: factor I (right to commit suicide/willingness to assist with suicide/desirability of suicide hospices).

The affective component did not appear as a single factor but the affective subscales had moderate loadings on both factors I and II. Similar relations between affective and other attitude components were reported by other researchers (e.g., Azjen and Fishbein 1980).

These findings confirm the original hypothesized three-component model of attitude toward suicide only to a certain degree. Closer study of the solution suggested that both the cognitive and the instrumental attitude component should preferably be divided into three factors/subscales. The cognitive component was divided into (1) consequences of suicide, (2) right to commit suicide, and (3) rationality/abnormality of suicide. The instrumental component was devided into (1) present and past ideation, (2) willingness to assist with suicide, and (3) probability of suicide in adverse (physical/social) conditions. With regard to the latter, careful study of the factor matrix suggested that a further distinction between physical and social circumstances could be meaningful.

Formation of Scales

The result of the analyses carried out thus far generally seem to justify the formation of scales based on combinations of referent with attitude components. Given the proposed subdivision of the cognitive and instrumental components outlined in the previous section this would lead logically to (3 × 8) 24 subscales.

However, for the referent "most near and dear," no items were included in the SUIATT from the cognitive subscales right to commit suicide and consequences of suicide.

The reasons for this were already explained in the methods section. Moreover, the instrumental subscale "past and present ideation" necessarily referred only to one referent (self), and the subscale willingness to assist only applied to the referents "most near and dear" and "people in general." For the resulting 19 subscales, the number of items in each scale, means and standard deviations, mean inter-item correlations, consistency coefficients, and test-retest correlations are shown in Table 6.

A final check on scale consistency was done by comparing all corrected item-total correlations of the same scale with the correlations of each item with the corrected subtotals of the remaining scales.

In only 26 of 1062 cases, items had a slightly but not significantly higher correlation with another subscale than with the corrected sum total of the subscale to which they belong. Therefore, subscale consistency was considered to be satisfactory.

Table 6. Formation of scales: number of items n, means m and standard deviations sd, mean inter-item correlations $\bar{r}$, consistency-coefficient α, and test-retest correlations tr

Scale	Referents																								
	Resp. him/herself						Most near and dear						People in general						Total					
	n	m	sd	$\bar{r}$	α	tr	n	m	sd	$\bar{r}$	α	tr	n	m	sd	$\bar{r}$	α	tr	n	m	sd	$\bar{r}$	α	tr
Affective	2	4.1	2.1	.26	.42	.60	2	3.9	1.9	.20	.33	.50	1	2.4	1.1	–	–	.40	5	10.3	4.0	.29	.66	.65
Cognitive																								
Compos mentis	3	8.7	2.8	.16	.36	.66	3	9.1	2.6	.25	.50	.68	4	12.2	2.9	.22	.52	.64	10	30.0	7.3	.27	.78	.76
Consequences	2	4.4	1.5	.56	.72	.59	–	–	–	–	–	–	3	7.6	1.7	.23	.45	.62	5	12.0	2.8	.29	.66	.66
Right to	1	2.2	1.6	–	–	.63	–	–	–	–	–	–	1	2.6	1.5	–	–	.66	2	4.8	2.6	.70	.82	.72
Instrumental																								
General	2	2.7	1.2	.27	.39	.61	1	1.4	0.8	–	–	.68	2	3.9	1.6	.23	.36	.53	5	8.0	2.6	.18	.51	.66
Physical	4	7.7	3.3	.53	.82	.68	4	7.6	3.1	.55	.83	.66	4	11.2	2.9	.40	.72	.59	12	26.4	7.6	.35	.87	.76
Social	8	10.7	3.2	.32	.75	.71	8	11.9	4.1	.41	.82	.51	8	17.7	4.9	.37	.82	.56	24	40.1	9.5	.24	.87	.65
Total	22	40.3	9.4	.17	.79	.81	18	33.8	8.0	.21	.79	.65	23	57.2	9.1	.13	.77	.67	63	131.3	22.6	.13	.90	.82

Moreover, most of the exceptions concerned items of the subscale rationality/abnormality, which had higher correlations with the subscales right to commit suicide and physical impairment. In terms of content, this finding is not so surprising since both rationality, right to commit suicide, and physical illness are essential notions in the ongoing discussion on (the relationship between) suicide and euthanasia. The fact that three items of the subscale instrumental-general (willingness to assist/desirability of suicide hospices) had also somewhat higher correlations with the subscales right to commit suicide and physical impairment underlines this interpretation.

The remaining item that had a lower correlation with its own (social disruption) than another subscale (physical impairment) was "the probability of suicide by respondent in case of admission to a mental hospital."

Relationship Between Subscales

The question then arises as to how the resulting 19 subscales are related to one another. For it is on the basis of these relationships that we shall be able to describe in its most elementary form the attitudes toward suicide held among the general public. To this end, a principal component analysis was carried out on the matrix of intercorrelations of the 19 subscales with the number of factors equal to the number of eigenvalues > 1.

The six factors extracted account for 65% of the total variance. Table 7 shows the component loadings of the subscales after rotation to the varimax criterion.

Table 7. Principal components analysis (varimax rotation) on 19 SUIATT scales

Scales	I	II	III	IV	V	VI
Affective-self	.16	.21	.07	.63	−.01	.16
Affective-beloved	.08	.13	.04	.56	.08	.11
Affective-people	.06	.14	.01	.47	−.03	.28
Rationality-self	.11	.22	.63	.14	.02	.10
Rationality-beloved	.09	.21	.79	.04	.06	.03
Rationaliy-people	.04	.18	.88	−.01	.08	.03
Consequences-self	.06	.12	.02	.20	.02	.62
Consequences-people	−.01	.11	.10	.20	−.02	.67
Right to-self	.14	.75	.22	.10	−.00	.14
Right to-people	.15	.68	.23	.08	.01	.14
Instrumental-self	.23	.16	.13	.18	.06	.06
Instrumental-beloved	.01	.50	.14	.20	.10	.04
Instrumental-people	.04	.50	.10	.22	.08	.07
Physical-self	.55	.38	.10	.17	.20	.01
Physical-beloved	.62	.31	.05	.05	.27	.09
Physical-people	.22	.20	.02	.04	−.88	−.00
Social-self	.76	.00	.02	.16	.01	−.03
Social-beloved	.79	−.01	.08	.01	.15	.06
Social-people	.34	−.02	.17	.04	.44	−.00
Remaining variance	46.2%	18.7%	14.8%	8.6%	7.0%	4.8%

Inspection of the factor loadings above 0.40 suggests the following interpretation:

Factor I: *Probability of suicide by respondent and the person most near and dear to respondant in case of severe physical impairment and/or social disruption.* This factor accounted for almost 30% of the total variance and half the common variance. The emergence of this factor once again underlines the importance of distinguishing between referents (actors) in measuring attitudes toward suicide. The subscales physical impairment – people in general and social impairment – people in general have only moderate loadings on this factor and highest loadings on factor V.

It is also important to notice that the subscale instrumental-respondent (with items such as: "did you ever think of committing suicide"? and "how probable do you think it is that you will ever commit suicide"?) had of all factors its highest loading, though still moderate (0.23), on this factor. This might indicate that this factor is most closely related to the probability of suicidal behavior by the respondent.

Factor II: *Right to commit suicide and willingness to assist with suicide (euthanasia).* This factor explaining 12.4% of the total variance had its highest loadings on the two right to suicide subscales and two instrumental subscales (instrumental-beloved and instrumental-people) that contained items such as: "are you willing to assist people/your most beloved to commit suicide, when he/she asks for it"?

It is worth noting that the subscales physical impairment-respondent and physical impairment-most beloved had their all but one highest loading (0.38 and 0.31) on this factor. This seems to indicate that respondents limit the right to suicide and their willingness to assist with it to cases of terminal or incurably physical illness.

Since it is under such circumstances that (assisting with) suicide and euthanasia are almost identical in the opinion of both the public and health professionals, a further interpretation of this factor as "euthanasia" seems warranted.

Factor III: This factor, explaining almost 10% of the total variance, had its highest loadings on the three cognitive subscales containing items on (mental) abnormality, impulsivity, and cowardice in relation to suicidal acts.

This clearly suggests an interpretation of this factor as *"rationality vs (mental) abnormality of suicide."*

Factor IV: This factor explained 5.6% of the total variance and had its highest loadings on the affective subscales.

They contained items such as: "suicide is the worst thing one can do" (agree-disagree) and "what is in your opinion the worst way to die ..." (followed by causes of death to be given a rank order). This suggests an interpretation of this factor as *emotional or affective meaning of suicide.*

The remaining two factors each explained considerably less than 5% of the total variance and are thus of minor importance.

Factor V: "The probability of suicide by people in general in case of physical and/or social impairment."

Factor VI: "Consequences of suicide." The highest loadings on this factor came from the subscales containing items regarding the consequences of suicide by the different referents for the different recipients.

The results of the principal component analysis were significant in a number of ways. First of all, they reconfirmed the fact that the attitude toward suicide is not a unitary phenomenon. Its instrumental, cognitive, and affective components are relatively independent of one another, the latter emerging as such in part as a consequence of reformation of subscales. Furthermore, the attitude toward the probability of suicide committed by oneself or one's most beloved is relatively independent from the attitude toward the probability of suicide committed by people in general. The results also suggest that this distinction may be important in the study of the attitude – behavior relationship in suicidology since it might very well be that only the attitude toward suicide as a behavioral alternative for oneself or one's most beloved is related to or predictive of actual suicidal behavior.

Differences in Attitudes Between Social Groups

Since that SUIATT was devised as an instrument to measure differences in attitudes toward suicide between social groups, we need to consider whether it does indeed reveal such differences in a meaningful way. To answer this question, the relationship between a number of demographic variables, gender, age (5 levels), marital status (3 categories), level of education (4 levels), religious affiliation (3 categories), political affiliation (5 categories), broadcasting network subscription (7 categories), and level of occupation (5 categories) on the one hand, and the scores on the 19 subscales, on the other hand, was investigated. Since we had to deal with (only) two data sets of which one contained variables measured at either a nominal (6) or ordinal (2) level and were essentially interested in computing the largest subspace contained in both sets of variables, nonlinear canonical correlation analysis seemed to be the most logical choice of procedure (Gifi 1981).
    The method of nonlinear canonical correlation analysis, used here, was developed by Gifi (1981) under the name of CANALS and has received international recognition since (Burg et al. 1983). CANALS differs from linear canonical correlation analysis (CCA) in the following way. CCA maximizes the correlation between a weighted sum of one set of variables and a weighted sum of another set of variables. These weighted sums of the variables are called canonical variates or the canonical scores and the correlation between the canonical variates is called the canonical correlation. However, if one had to interpret the measurement level of the variables as nominal or ordinal and not as numerical, the raw scores have the meaning of category numbers, possibly with an order relation between the categories of a variable. Category numbers may

then (have to) be rescaled into category quantifications, maintaining the original classifications and, if necessary, the order.

Combinations of rescaling the category numbers with CCA is a nonlinear CCA, such as the CANALS program performs. CANALS is an *Alternating Least Squares* program, which means that it solves for the different sets of parameters (canonical weights and category qualification) alternatingly using a least squares approximation, implying that the algorithm is interactive. The decrease of *stress* in the outout of the CANALS program shows the progress in the interaction process. The stress is one minus the mean of the squared canonical correlations.

According to Gifi (1981), it is preferable to interpret the canonical solution via the correlations (canonical loadings) between the variables and the canonical variates. To avoid unique patterns, the responses of only those subjects ($n = 479$) who did not fail to fill out any of the SUIATT items were used.

The stress turned out to be 0.76 and the canonical correlations 0.63 and 0.49, which can be considered satisfactory. Table 8 shows the correlations between the optimally rescaled 8 demographic variables and 19 SUIATT subscales and the canonical variates of the 19 SUIATT subscales. The data in Table 8 can be interpreted as follows (cf. Doob and McDonald 1979).

The first set of canonical variables (third column) suggests that those who consider suicide absolutely the worst thing they or others can do (SA 1, 2, 3), who think that one always has to be mentally ill or out of his mind to do such a thing (SA 4, 5, 6), who consider suicide always as an act with terrible consequences for others and society (SA 7, 8), who deny themselves and others always the right to commit such a crime (SA 9, 10), who seldom or never have contemplated suicide and estimate the chance of ending their life by their own hand equal to zero (SA 11), who reject any involvement or assistance with suicide by others (SA 12, 13), who consider it (very) improbable that they or their most beloved would commit suicide in situations of severe physical illness/suffering (SA 14, 15), and who consider it equally unprobable that they or others would commit suicide in severely adverse social situations (SA 17, 18, 19) are more often older persons (especially above 56 years of age), are less well-educated, more often religiously affiliated (especially Roman Catholic/Protestant), more often politically right wing, and have lower occupations.

The second set of canonical variables seems to indicate that individuals who consider suicide the worst thing to do by anybody or to happen to anybody (SA 1, 2, 3), who think they themselves never have the right to commit suicide (SA 9), indicate that they seldom or never have contemplated suicide and estimate their own chance to commit such a deed low or absent (SA 11), who think it is improbable that they or their most beloved would commit suicide because of severe physical or social adversities (SA 14, 15, 17) but who at the same time believe that others do not necessarily have to be mentally disturbed or impulsive to commit a suicidal act (SA 5, 6) and do not think it is improbable that other people might commit suicide under bad physical or social circumstances (SA 16, 19) are more often persons with higher (college) education.

While the first group (first canonical variable) seems to be characterized by an unequivocal negative or prohibitive attitude toward suicide, this group

Table 8. CANALS: correlations of variables with canonical variates of SUIATT subscales

Variables	High score indicates	Can. var. 1	Can. var. 2
Demographic			
D1 sex	Female	.162	.138
D2 age	Higher age	.377	.167
D3 marital status	Single/unmarried	−.049	−.125
D4 education	Higher education	.354	.327
D5 religious affiliation	Religiously affiliated	.363	.171
D6 political affiliation	Left wing	−.311	.080
D7 broadcasting corporation subscription	Left wing-humanistic	−.298	−.229
D8 level of occupation	Higler occupation	−.347	.038
SUIATT subscales	*Low score indicates*		
SA1 affective self	Suicide worst thing I can do	−.325	−.409
SA2 affective beloved	Suicide worst thing beloved can do	−.426	−.451
SA3 affective people	Suicide worst thing others can do	−.445	−.436
SA4 compos mentis self	Suicide by oneself always impulsive/insane	−.579	.015
SA5 compos mentis beloved	Suicide by beloved always impulsive/insane	−.418	−.392
SA6 compos mentis people	Suicide by others always impulsive/insane	−.522	.384
SA7 consequences self	Consequences of my suicide always terrible	−.347	−.188
SA8 consequences people	Consequences of suicide by others always terrible	−.215	−.113
SA9 right self	I never have the right to suicide	−.336	−.267
SA10 right people	Others never have the right to suicide	−.563	−.008
SA11 instrumental self	Never/seldom thought of suicide, future chance low/absent	−.127	−.278
SA12 instrumental beloved	Assisting with suicide of beloved one rejected (very) strongly	−.529	−.228
SA13 instrumental people	Assisting with suicide of others rejected (very) strongly	−.421	−.186
SA14 physical self	Suicide by me in situations of physical disruption (very) unprobable	−.585	.202
SA15 physical beloved	Suicide by beloved situations of physical disruption (very) unprobable	−.372	−.251
SA16 physical people	Suicide by others in situations of physical disruption (very) unprobable	−.119	.267
SA17 social self	Suicide by me in situations of social disruption (very) unprobable	−.208	−.264
SA18 social beloved	Suicide by beloved in situations of social disruption (very) unprobable	−.362	−.152
SA19 social people	Suicide by others in situations of social disruption (very) unprobable	−.257	.282

(second canonical variable) seems to entertain a double standard, one of prohibition and rejection as far as suicide as an option for themselves is concerned but one of understanding, perhaps even compassion as far as others, people in general are concerned.

Discussion and Conclusions

Attitude toward suicide appears to be a complex phenomenon. In the light of the results of this study, one should rather speak of attitudes toward suicides since individuals appear to have different feelings, cognitions, and action tendencies with regard to suicide as an act (to be) committed by themselves, the person most near and dear to them, and people in general. The attitude scale constructed in the present study, the SUIATT, seems to be an instrument that reliably measures these differences. Its internal structure as revealed by a principal component analysis indicates that an individual's perceived probability of committing suicide under conditions of serious physical or social disruption is relatively independent from his or her beliefs about how mentally or behaviorally disturbed one has to be to commit such an act or whether one has the right to do it or not. It is also relatively independent of how distressing or terrible an act like suicide is in the eyes of the individual. The latter three dimensions seem to be more abstract and presumably less action relevant than the first one. This might explain the fact that individuals at the same time can condemn suicide, consider it as the greatest "failure" in human life possible, and still go and kill themselves as suffering exceeds their level of tolerance.

For the sake of prediction and prevention, information on "the preceived probability of suicide" (as assessed by the SUIATT) seems to be of great importance in high-risk groups such as psychiatric outpatients as well as among individuals. Although further research into the relationship between the incidence of suicidal acts and this attitudinal aspect has to be carried out, inclusion of attitude measures in suicide prediction instruments as well as in clinical diagnostic interviews might be an important step toward improved detection of high-risk individuals in the near future.

This, however, will require the construction of a short form of the SUIATT since in its present form the scale is too time-consuming and complicated for clinical purposes.

Not surprisingly, attitudes toward suicide as measured by our scale vary with demographic characteristics such as age, religious and political affiliation, and level of education. What is surprising, however, is that the results of the nonlinear canonical correlation analyses suggest the existence of two groups of individuals with attitudes to suicide identical to those described by Bayet as far back as 1922. In that year this French scientist/philosopher and follower of Bayet (1922) published a monumental work in French entitled *Le Suicide et la Morale*, in which he described the development of Western attitudes toward suicide over more than 20 centuries. Bayet (1922) distinguished between two basic categories of "morale" toward suicide, a "morale simple" and a "morale nuancée." The first implies an absolute negative and prohibitive attitude whatever the circumstances of the act and the actor and is related to pagan-Christian dogmatism, lack or absence of intellectual education, and political feudalism or conservatism. The second category implies an attitude toward suicide that condemns it under certain circumstances and understands and accepts it, although does not approve of it, under others. According to Bayet, this attitude throughout the centuries has been characteristic of the better educated and the aristocracy. He described its essence as the recognition that although suicide cannot be considered as something right or as a right, it is at the same time a possibility that unavoidably for some people becomes a necessity and therefore can be deplored but not always prevented.

One of the educational applications of the SUIATT in the mental health professional curriculum might be to raise students' consciousness with regard to their own attitudes to this behavior.

References

Azjen I, Fishbein M (1980) Understanding attitudes and predicting social behavior. Prentice-Hall, Englewood Cliffs

Bayet A (1922) Le Suicide et la Morale. Felix Alcan, Paris

Diekstra RFW (1973) Crisis en Gedragskeuze: een theoretische bijdrage tot de studie van het zelfmoordprobleem. Swets and Zeitlinger, Amsterdam

Diekstra RFW (1974) A social learning approach to the prediction of suicidal behaviour Speijer N, Diekstra RFW, van de Loo KJM (eds) 7th Int conf suicide prevention. S and Zeitlinger, Amsterdam, pp 55–66

Diekstra RFW (1985) Suicide and suicide attempts in the European Economic Community: an analysis of trends with special emphasis upon trends among the young. Suicide Life Threat Behav 15:15–22

Diekstra RFW, Schippers GM, Ebskamp CA (1980) Ein additives Zweifaktoren-Modell suizidalen Verhaltens. In: Welz R, Pohlmeier H (eds) Selbstmordhandlungen: Suizid und Suizidversuch aus interdisziplinärer Sicht. Belz, Weinheim, pp 110–117

Domino G, Moore D, Westlake L, Gibson L (1982) Attitudes toward suicide: a factor analytic approach. J Clin Psychol 38:257–262

Doob AN, McDonald GE (1979) Television viewing and fear of victimization: is the relationship causal? J Pers Soc Psychol 37:170–179

Gifi A (1981) Non-linear multivariate analysis. Leiden University Press, p 53

Guttman L (1954) An outline of some new methodology for social research. Public Opinion Quarterly 18:395–404

Guttman L, Elisur D (1973) A facet theoretical analysis of behavior in organizations. Department of Economics and Research Committee, Bar-Ilan University, Ramat Gan, Paper no. 7309

Loevinger J (1956) Objective tests as instruments of psychological theory. Psychol Rep 3:635–694

Schuman H, Johnson MP (1976) Attitudes and behavior. Annu Rev Sociol 2:161–207

Secord PF, Backman CW (1974) Social psychology. McGraw Hill/Kokaguska, Tokyo

van der Burg E, de Leeuw J (1983) Non-linear canonical correlation. Br J Math Stat Psychol 36:54–80

Subject Index